Rethinking Schubert

Rethinking Schubert

EDITED BY
Lorraine Byrne Bodley and Julian Horton

OXFORD
UNIVERSITY PRESS

Oxford University Press is a department of the University of Oxford. It furthers
the University's objective of excellence in research, scholarship, and education
by publishing worldwide.Oxford is a registered trade mark of Oxford University
Press in the UK and certain other countries.

Published in the United States of America by Oxford University Press
198 Madison Avenue, New York, NY 10016, United States of America.

© Oxford University Press 2016

All rights reserved. No part of this publication may be reproduced, stored in
a retrieval system, or transmitted, in any form or by any means, without the
prior permission in writing of Oxford University Press, or as expressly permitted
by law, by license, or under terms agreed with the appropriate reproduction
rights organization. Inquiries concerning reproduction outside the scope of the
above should be sent to the Rights Department, Oxford University Press, at the
address above.

You must not circulate this work in any other form
and you must impose this same condition on any acquirer.

Library of Congress Cataloging-in-Publication Data
Rethinking Schubert / edited by Lorraine Byrne Bodley and Julian Horton.
pages cm
ISBN 978-0-19-020010-7 (alk. paper) — ISBN 978-0-19-020011-4 (alk. paper)—
ISBN 978-0-19-020012-1 — ISBN 978-0-19-020013-8
1. Schubert, Franz, 1797-1828—Criticism and interpretation.
I. Bodley, Lorraine Byrne, 1968- editor. II. Horton, Julian, editor.
ML410.S3R357 2016
780.92—dc23
2015031601

9 8 7 6 5 4 3 2 1
Paperback printed by WebCom, Inc., Canada
Hardback printed by Bridgeport National Bindery, Inc., United States of America

For Walther Dürr,
whose generous spirit, warm heart, and sterling
scholarship we treasure.

Contents

Acknowledgements   xi
Contributors   xv

Introduction: Rethinking Schubert: Contexts and Controversies   1
LORRAINE BYRNE BODLEY AND JULIAN HORTON

I Style

1 Is There a Late Style in Schubert's Oeuvre?   17
HANS-JOACHIM HINRICHSEN

2 Compositional Strategies in Schubert's Late Music   29
WALTHER DÜRR

3 Franz Schubert's 'New Style' and the Legacy of Beethoven   41
WILLIAM KINDERMAN

4 From Song to Instrumental Style: Some Schubert Fingerprints   61
SUSAN WOLLENBERG

5 The Sensuous as a Constructive Force in Schubert's Late Works   77
BRIAN BLACK

II Instrumental Music

6 The Myth of the 'Unfinished' and the Film *Das Dreimäderlhaus* (1958)   111
ANDREA LINDMAYR-BRANDL

7 Narrative Dislocations in the First Movement of Schubert's 'Unfinished' Symphony   127
XAVIER HASCHER

8 (Re-)Theorising Schubert's 'Reliquie': Precedents, the 'Great' Symphony, and Narrative   147
CAMERON GARDNER

9 Records of Inspiration: Schubert's Drafts for the Last Three
   Piano Sonatas Reappraised   173
   ANNE M. HYLAND AND WALBURGA LITSCHAUER

10 Musical Causality and Schubert's Piano Sonata in A Major,
   D 959, First Movement   207
   JULIAN CASKEL

11 Conspicuous 6-Phase Chords in the Closing Movement
   of Schubert's Piano Sonata in B♭ Major (D 960)   225
   DAVID DAMSCHRODER

12 Schubert, Social Music and Melancholy   237
   LEON PLANTINGA

III Music and Text

13 Axial Lyric Space in Two Late Songs: 'Im Freien'
   and 'Der Winterabend'   253
   MICHAEL SPITZER

14 Schubert through a Neo-Riemannian Lens   275
   SUZANNAH CLARK

15 Contextual Processes in Schubert's Late Sacred Music   295
   JAMES WILLIAM SOBASKIE

16 Elusive Intimacy in Schubert's Final Opera,
   Der Graf von Gleichen   333
   LISA FEURZEIG

17 The End of the Road in Schubert's *Winterreise*: The Contradiction
   of Coherence and Fragmentation   355
   DEBORAH STEIN

18 Dissociation and Declamation in Schubert's Heine Songs   383
   DAVID FERRIS

19 'The Messenger of a Faithful Heart': Reassessing the Role
   of 'Die Taubenpost' in Schubert's *Schwanengesang*   404
   RICHARD GIARUSSO

20 Disability, Self-Critique and Failure in Schubert's
   'Der Doppelgänger'   418
   BENJAMIN BINDER

Contents

21 Challenging the Context: Reception and Transformation
in Schubert's 'Der Musensohn', D 764, Op. 92 No. 1 437
LORRAINE BYRNE BODLEY

22 A Gauntlet Thrown: Schubert's 'Einsamkeit,' D 620,
and Beethoven's *An die ferne Geliebte* 456
SUSAN YOUENS

23 'Die Wegweiser'—Signposts on an Accompanist's Journey
to Scholarship: Homage to Walther Dürr 485
GRAHAM JOHNSON

Bibliography 497
Index 517

Acknowledgements

This book had its origins in a course I teach on late Schubert to students at the beginning of their academic career. My writing on this theme[1] and my love of Schubert's 'late' music inspired me to invite my dear friend, Julian Horton, to co-author a call for papers and co-organise the conference, *Thanatos as Muse? Schubert and Concepts of Late Style*, which took place at the Maynooth University Department of Music on 21–23 October 2011 in collaboration with the School of Music at University College Dublin. Following the success of this international gathering, scholars were invited to expand and develop their papers to become essays in *Rethinking Schubert*.[2] Seven new chapters were commissioned from leading Schubert scholars who were either unable to attend the conference or who were present but have written alternative chapters to fit the new remit. This book differs from many other volumes of essays on Schubert in two strategic ways. First, we have tried to integrate very detailed technical analyses with more general scholarly issues of Schubert reception. Secondly, the volume reflects our desire to include leading German-language and francophone Schubert research in an English-language volume of essays. In the interests of a wider English-speaking readership, Hans-Joachim Hinrichsen's stellar scholarship is made available in the opening chapter, which has been specially commissioned for this volume of essays. Early versions of previously published chapters appeared in Lorraine Byrne Bodley, 'Wandermotive in Schuberts Goethe Liedern', *Schubert Jahrbuch* (2014); Walther Dürr, 'Kompositionsstrategien des späten Schubert', in Klaus Aringer and Ann-Kathrin Zimmerman (eds), *Mozart im Zentrum: Festschrift für Manfred Hermann Schmid zum 60. Geburtstag* (Tutzing: Hans Schneider, 2010), pp. 367–79 and William Kinderman, 'Franz Schuberts "Neuer Stil" und das Erbe Beethovens', in *Schubert: Perspektiven* 9/1 (Stuttgart: Franz Steiner Verlag, 2009), pp. 60–79. A translation of Xavier Hascher's essay, 'Anti-parcours et non-narration dans le premier mouvement de la Symphonie inachevée de Schubert' will appear in Márta Grabócz (ed.), *Narratologie musicale: topiques et stratégies narratives en musique* (Paris: Éditions des Archives contemporaines, forthcoming). We would like gratefully to acknowledge permissions given by the publishers and the editors to include these essays.

Julian Horton and I have been fortunate in having particularly able advisors. For the production of this book we relied on the assistance of a number of people. Suzanne Ryan, the music editor at Oxford University Press, gave her unflinching encouragement and wise counsel from the very inception of this project. Damian Penfold and, in its early stages, Jessen O'Brien and Adam Cohen were superbly efficient in steering a complicated book into production. Likewise the reports of the anonymous readers consulted by Oxford University Press picked up on any shortcomings, asked some key questions and encouraged us in the final stage of our work. We thank them sincerely for their invaluable help.

Although we have worked together to bring this volume to completion, there are nevertheless thanks that are best offered separately; it is in this spirit that the following remarks are conceived.

Lorraine Byrne Bodley

I owe a special debt of gratitude to Walther Dürr, to whom this book is dedicated. Without his profound knowledge of Schubert and monumental contribution to Schubert scholarship, without his willingness to revise and rethink, without his example and inspiration, all our work would be very different. Walther chaired the first paper I gave at the International Schubert Conference at the University of Leeds, 29 June–1 July 2000, and took time from his busy life to travel to Dublin to read a paper on Schubert's sacred music at the first international conference I organized when I was a postdoctoral fellow in the Department of Germanic Studies in Trinity College, 4–5 April 2003.[3] I am deeply grateful to him for his encouragement on both occasions and at the international conference, 'Vom Wasser haben wir's gelernt', organized by the Deutsche Schubert-Gesellschaft, 27–29 September 2012, at which I read the German-language version of my chapter on 'Der Musensohn'. I am also profoundly grateful to him and his equally warm-hearted colleagues, Christine Martin and Rudolf Faber, for the generous welcome they gave me during my four months as visiting fellow at the Schubert-Archiv, University of Tübingen, which was made possible by Deutscher Akademischer Austausch Dienst and Gerda Henkel Foundation fellowships. Christine and Walther shared their office with me on many occasions as I worked on the final editorial points of this book. I warmly acknowledge the linguistic and scholarly acumen as well as the generosity of Jürgen Thym, who wanted to pay tribute to Walther by translating his chapter. I am deeply indebted to Graham Johnson, who in the midst of correcting the proofs for volume 3 of *Franz Schubert: The Complete Songs*, took time from his busy life to pay homage to Walther. I will always be immensely grateful.

Many colleagues and friends responded to inquiries for help and advice. Warm thanks are due to William Drabkin, whose professional know-how, optimistic spirit and generosity with his time were deeply appreciated in the early stages of conference planning. Nor will I easily forget colleagues and former students who worked so hard on the team to plan the conference, including Patrick Devine, Mark Fitzgerald, Paul Higgins, Kerry Houston, Wolfgang Marx and Barbara Strahan; I hope this book is proof that their time was well-spent. Profound thanks are due to the faculty, colleagues and students at the Department of

Music, Maynooth University, under the leadership of Christopher Morris, for their support and collegiality to me. They have provided not only unstinting support but the good-hearted cheer that is vital and appreciated.

I owe a deep debt of gratitude to Dan Farrelly, who gave my translations of William Kinderman's and Hans-Joachim Hinrichsen's chapters a painstakingly close reading that led to many improvements. As always, I found our discussions inspiring, especially where we sought for specific words that make all the difference to a sentence. When translating essays I am always aware how different even quite simple German academic discourse is from that in English, how the order of presentation and the logic of combining arguments are handled in entirely different ways. In some passages, therefore, the English-language text is a rewriting as well as a translation of the original German-language essays, though it tries faithfully to render the original meaning. I offer warm thanks to my gifted graduate student, the indefatigable Anja Bunzel, who graciously gave of her time to typeset some of the music examples, and to Chris Morris, at the University of Lethbridge in Alberta, who generously shared his expertise with colleagues across the Atlantic.

Harry White, of the UCD School of Music, deserves special recognition for his faith in this book and his unwavering encouragement of Julian and me. We should like to offer all contributors collectively our warmest thanks for their professional collaboration, which made this book a joy to edit. If I were permitted to single out one scholar who has been especially supportive of my work over the years, it would be Susan Youens, a guiding star in Schubert studies and a dearly loved friend, whose writing, like Schubert's music, bears testimony to the sovereignty of the human spirit. As ever, I must acknowledge the forbearance and inspiration of my beloved husband and companion, Seóirse Bodley, who endured my absences during many months of work; my gratitude to him has no limits. My best thanks go to him and to Bláthnaid, who is never far from my thoughts, and fills my days with a deep-seated joy.

Julian Horton

When Lorraine asked me to collaborate in bringing *Schubert and Concepts of Late Style* to fruition, I approached the project as an analyst with an interest in Schubert's music, rather than as a Schubert scholar, and therefore with a degree of trepidation. In the end, however, the tangible sense of overarching interdisciplinarity proved to be one of the conference's great strengths. This spirit of disciplinary collaboration has carried over into the preparation of *Rethinking Schubert*; the volume has merit not least because it reflects a kind of bifocal engagement, through which a range of disciplinary perspectives are brought to bear on Schubert's music, which then in turn serves as a means of refracting broader disciplinary debates. My first thanks therefore go to the community of Schubert scholars who have engaged with this project and tolerated my intervention. This encounter has greatly enriched not only my understanding of Schubert, but also my practice as an analyst.

The work for this project has been undertaken in the midst of a great many competing claims on my time, including the prosecution of my duties as Head of the School of Music at University College Dublin, and subsequently as Head of the Music Department at Durham University. The book's completion would not have been possible without the patience, support and understanding of colleagues in both institutions: at UCD, Majella Boland, Ciarán Crilly, Desmond Earley, Nicole Grimes, Jaime Jones, Frank Lawrence, Wolfgang Marx, Thérèse Smith, and Harry White; at Durham, Martin Allison, Martin Clayton, Nick Collins, Neil Combstock, Joyce Dent, Jeremy Dibble, Tuomas Eerola, Eric Egan, Alasdair Jamieson, Jess Lawrence, Laura Leante, Peter Manning, Simon Mills, Karen Nichol, Max Paddison, Richard Rijnvos, Faye Smith, John Snijders, Simone Tarsitani, Trevor Wishart, Bennett Zon and Patrick Zuk.

Profound thanks are due to my wife, Janet, and my children, Emma and Toby, for their selfless support, love and forbearance in the face of my ever-increasing workload. Above all, I would like to thank my co-editor and friend Lorraine, whose boundless intellectual energy has been the driving force behind this project, as with so many significant recent contributions to our understanding of Schubert, both as man and as musician. Working with her has been a very great privilege.

Notes

1. 'Late Style and the Paradoxical Poetics of the Schubert-Berio *Rendering*', in Barbara Reul and Lorraine Byrne Bodley (eds), *The Unknown Schubert* (Aldershot: Ashgate, 2008), pp. 233–50.

2. Further essays have been developed for Lorraine Byrne Bodley and Julian Horton (eds), *Schubert's Late Music: History, Theory, Style* (Cambridge: Cambridge University Press, 2016); a special edition of *Nineteenth-Century Music Review* guest-edited by Lorraine Byrne Bodley and James William Sobaskie (2016); and a special issue of *Music Analysis* devoted to Schubert's String Quintet (2014).

3. Goethe and Schubert in Perspective and Performance, Trinity College Dublin, 4–5 April 2003. Papers were published in *Goethe and Schubert: Across the Divide* (Dublin: Carysfort Press, 2003).

Contributors

Benjamin Binder is an associate professor of music at Duquesne University. As a musicologist, his research interests range widely within German Romanticism and lied studies. His publications include 'Kundry and the Jewish Voice: Anti-Semitism and Musical Transcendence in Wagner's *Parsifal*' (*Current Musicology*, 2009) and 'Robert, Clara and the Transformation of Poetic Irony in Schumann's Lieder' (*Nineteenth-Century Music Review*, 2013). His current research examines settings of Heine's poetry from throughout the nineteenth century through the lens of performance studies. He is also a collaborative pianist who serves as director of the Song Scholarship and Performance Program at the Vancouver International Song Institute.

Brian Black is an associate professor of musicology at the University of Lethbridge in Alberta. He received his PhD in musicology from McGill University, where his dissertation, 'Schubert's Apprenticeship in Sonata Form: The Early String Quartets,' was carried out under the supervision of William E. Caplin. He has published in *Schubert durch die Brille*; *Nineteenth-Century Music Review*; *Intersections*; and *Intégral*. He has presented papers at the annual meetings of the Society for Music Theory, the American Musicological Society and the Canadian University Music Society.

Lorraine Byrne Bodley is a senior lecturer in Musicology at Maynooth University. She is the first woman in Ireland to have had conferred on her a DMus in musicology, a higher doctorate awarded for published work (NUI, 2012). She also holds a PhD in music and in German from University College Dublin (2000). Recent awards include a Gerda-Henkel Foundation Scholarship (2014) and two DAAD Senior Academics Awards (2010 and 2014). In 2015 she was elected President of The Society for Musicology in Ireland and Member of the Royal Irish Academy. She has published thirteen books including *A Community of the Imagination: Seóirse Bodley's Goethe's Settings* (Carysfort Press, 2013); *Goethe and Zelter: Musical Dialogues* (Ashgate, 2009); *The Unknown Schubert* (Ashgate, 2008); *Proserpina: Goethe's Melodrama with Music by Carl Eberwein* (Carysfort Press, 2007) and *Schubert's Goethe Settings* (2003). Recent publications include *Schubert's Late Music: History, Theory and Style*, co-edited with Julian Horton (Cambridge University Press, 2016), and she will write a new biography on Schubert for Yale University Press.

Suzannah Clark is a professor of music at Harvard University. She previously taught at Oxford University. Her research interests include the music of Franz

Schubert, neo-Riemannian and Schenkerian theories, the history of tonal theory and medieval vernacular music. She has been awarded numerous fellowships, including, in the United Kingdom, from the AHRC and the British Academy; and in the United States, the National Humanities Center, Institute for Advanced Studies, in Princeton, New Jersey, and the ACLS. She contributed an essay on Schubert to *The Oxford Handbook of Neo-Riemannian Music Theories*, edited by Alexander Rehding and Edward Gollin, and her book *Analyzing Schubert* appeared with Cambridge University Press in 2011.

Julian Caskel studied musicology, philosophy and political sciences at the universities of Heidelberg and Cologne. He completed his PhD on scherzo movements in 2009. Afterwards he was employed at the University of Cologne in a research project on the aesthetics of musical rhythm in the twentieth century. Published and forthcoming articles cover topics ranging from Haydn, Mahler and Eisler to contemporary composition and film music. He is also the co-editor of the *Handbuch Dirigenten* that has been released by Bärenreiter.

David Damschroder, who teaches at the University of Minnesota, inaugurated his harmony project with *Thinking about Harmony: Historical Perspectives on Analysis* (Cambridge University Press, 2008), which is being complemented by monographs on individual composers, *Harmony in Schubert* (Cambridge University Press, 2010), *Harmony in Haydn and Mozart* (Cambridge University Press, 2012), *Harmony in Chopin* (Cambridge University Press, 2015), *Harmony in Beethoven* (Cambridge University Press, 2016), and *Harmony in Mendelssohn and Schumann* (in preparation). The project, intended to span the long nineteenth-century, will soon proceed to harmony after 1850 (Verdi to Debussy). In addition, Damschroder's *Tonal Analysis: A Schenkerian Perspective* is forthcoming from W. W. Norton.

Walther Dürr was born in 1932 in Berlin. He studied musicology with Walther Gerstenberg and German und Italian languages and literature at Tübingen University. In 1956 he received his PhD. From 1957 to 1962 he was a lecturer at Bologna Univerity, and from 1962 to 1965 he was a lecturer and assistant at the Akademisches Auslandsamt of Tübingen University. From 1965 to 1997 he was an executive member of the editorial board of the *Neue Schubert-Ausgabe* (editor especially of the songs). In 1977 he became an honorary professor at Tübingen University. He retired in May 1997, but he is still a member of the editorial board of the *Neue Schubert-Ausgabe*.

Lisa Feurzeig, a professor of music at Grand Valley State University in Michigan, is a musicologist and singer. Her research emphasizes German-language vocal music: lieder, opera and operetta. Her book *Schubert's Lieder and the Philosophy of Early German Romanticism* was published by Ashgate in 2014. She has also published articles on Wagner, Fauré and Schubert and two critical editions. Feurzeig is drawn to interdisciplinary connections and to traditions where the arts mingle, such as the Viennese Volkstheater and Bollywood films. As a singer, she has performed art song and chamber music ranging from the twelfth to the twentieth century.

David Ferris is an associate professor of musicology at Rice University in Houston, Texas. He is the author of *Schumann's Eichendorff Liederkreis and the Genre of the Romantic Cycle* (Oxford University Press, 2000), and his work has appeared in the *Journal of the American Musicological Society, Journal of Musicology, Music Theory Spectrum*, and *Music and Letters*. He is currently editing two volumes of keyboard sonatinas for the new complete edition of the music of Carl Philipp Emanuel Bach and a volume of songs for the *Neue Robert-Schumann-Gesamtausgabe*.

Cameron Gardner is an associate lecturer in music at Cardiff University and an academic lecturer in music at the Royal Welsh College of Music and Drama, where he teaches undergraduate and postgraduate modules. In 2006 he completed his PhD at Cardiff University, a hermeneutic analysis of Schubert's 1825 piano sonatas (a chapter of which appeared in 'The Unknown Schubert', Ashgate 2008). He contributes regularly at international conferences, writes for the journal *Eighteenth-Century Music*, is active as a pianist and has worked for the BBC. In 2005, as a committee member of the Schubert Institute (UK), he directed the conference, 'Schubert's Instrumental Music: Performance, Genre, Completion' at Cardiff University.

Richard Giarusso enjoys a rewarding career as a scholar, educator, conductor and singer. An award-winning teacher, he is chair of the Department of Musicology at the Peabody Conservatory of the Johns Hopkins University and appears frequently as a lecturer for some of the leading arts organizations in the Mid-Atlantic States. In addition to his academic work, he serves as the conductor of the Georgetown Chorale in Washington, DC, and the Voce Chamber Singers in northern Virginia and he is in high demand as a solo and ensemble singer throughout the northeastern United States. Giarusso holds degrees in music and English from Williams College and a PhD in historical musicology from Harvard University.

Xavier Hascher is a professor of music theory at the University of Strasbourg. He is the author of several publications on Schubert's music, among them *Schubert: la forme sonate et son évolution* (Peter Lang, 1996) and *Symbole et fantasme dans l'Adagio du Quintette à cordes de Schubert* (L'Harmattan, 2005). He has edited *Le style instrumental de Schubert* (Publications de la Sorbonne, 2007) as well as the journal *Cahiers Franz-Schubert* (1992–2000), and has also contributed to Christopher Gibbs (ed.), *The Cambridge Companion to Schubert* (Cambridge University Press, 1997), and Michael Kube, Werner Adelhold and

Walburga Litschauer (eds), *Schubert und das Biedermeier: Beiträge zur Musik des frühen 19. Jahrhundersts* (Bärenreiter, 2002).

Hans-Joachim Hinrichsen was born in1952 and studied germanistics, history and later musicology at the Freie Universität Berlin, where he completed his doctorate and habilitation. Since 1999 he has been a professor of musicology at the University of Zurich. He is the co-editor of *Archiv für Musikwissenschaft, Schubert: Perspektiven* and wagnerspectrum. He was elected a member of the Academia Europaea in 2008 and of the Österreichische Akademie der Wissenschaften in 2009. He has published widely on music history from the eighteenth to the twentieth centuries and music aesthetics, as well as interpretative and reception history. His recent publications include *Bruckner-Handbuch* (Metzler and Bärenreiter, 2010), *Franz Schubert* (C. H. Beck, 2011), *Beethoven: Die Klaviersonaten* (Bärenreiter, 2013) and *Bruckners Sinfonien: Ein musikalischer Werkführer* (C. H. Beck, 2016).

Anne M. Hyland is a lecturer in music at the University of Manchester, having taught previously at Royal Holloway, University of London and Trinity College, Dublin. Her research centres on nineteenth-century instrumental form, and particularly on the analysis of Schubert's music. Her paper 'Rhetorical Closure in the First Movement of Schubert's Quartet in C Major, D46: a Dialogue with Deformation' was awarded the *Music Analysis* Twenty-fifth Anniversary Prize and was published in vol. 28/1 (2009). Her work has also appeared in the *Encyclopaedia of Music in Ireland, Irish Musical Studies*, vol.11, and she has chapters in *Schubert's Late Music: History, Theory, Style* (Cambridge University Press 2016) and *The String Quartet from 1750 to 1870* (Brepols, 2016).

Graham Johnson is one of the world's most sought-after song accompanists. *The Songmakers' Almanac: Twenty Years of Recitals in London* (Thames Publishing, 1996) tells the story of the groundbreaking series of concerts which established his reputatuon. He is particularly noted for his commercial recordings of lieder, most notably for Hyperion, with whom his most renowned project was a series of thirty-seven CDs of the complete lieder of Franz Schubert. Johnson is the senior professor of accompaniment at the Guildhall School of Music and Drama and has led a biennial scheme for young songmakers since 1985. He is the author of several books, including *The French Song Companion* (Oxford University Press; 2000); *Britten, Voice & Piano: Lectures on the Vocal Music of Benjamin Britten* (Guildhall, 2003); *Gabriel Fauré – The Songs and Their Poets* (Guildhall, 2009) and *Franz Schubert: the Complete Songs*, 3 vols. (Yale University Press, 2014). His numerous honours include an Order of the British Empire (1994), Royal Philharmonic Society's Instrumentalist of the Year (1998), membership in the Royal Swedish Academy of Music (2000), Chevalier in the Ordre des Arts et des Lettres by the French government (2002), honorary membership in the Royal Philharmonic Society (2010), the Gramophone solo vocal award (1989, 1996, 1997 and 2001), a doctorates of music honoris causa awarded by Durham University (2013) and Boston's New England Conservatory (2013), the Jerusalem Music Centre Medal (2013) and the Wigmore Hall Medal (2013).

William Kinderman's many books include *Beethoven's Diabelli Variations* (Oxford University Press, 1989), *Artaria 195: Beethoven's Sketchbook for the 'Missa solemnis' and the Piano Sonata in E Major, Opus 109*, 3 vols. (University of Illinois Press, 2003), *The String Quartets of Beethoven* (University of Illinois Press, 2006), *Mozart's Piano Music* (Oxford University Press, 2006), *Genetic Criticism and the Creative Process*, co-edited with Joseph E. Jones (University of Rochester Press, 2009), *Beethoven*, 2nd edn (Oxford University Press, 2009), *The Creative Process in Music from Mozart to Kurtág* (University of Illinois Press, 2012), and *Wagner's 'Parsifal'* (Oxford University Press, 2013). As a pianist he has recorded Beethoven's Diabelli Variations and last sonatas. Since 2001 he has been a professor at the University of Illinois and taught as a DAAD guest professor at the University of Munich. In 2010 he received a research prize for lifetime achievement from the Humboldt Foundation.

Andrea Lindmayr-Brandl studied musicology and philosophy as well as mathematics and music at the Paris-Lodron University Salzburg and at the Mozarteum, Salzburg. After postgraduate studies at the Schola Cantorum Basiliensis in Switzerland, she graduated in 1988 with a dissertation on Ockeghem from the Paris-Lodron University Salzburg. She finished her habilitation (professorial dissertation) on Franz Schubert in 2001 and was appointed an associate professor the same year. After holding the Austrian Chair Professorship at Stanford University (2006–7) and a guest professorship at the University of Vienna, she was appointed a full professor at the Paris-Lodron University Salzburg in 2010. She directs several research projects and is an active member of many academic institutions and organizations, for example, on the board of the *Neue Schubert-Ausgabe*. Her fields of research are studies in Renaissance music, source studies, notation, editorial work, the historiography of early music and Franz Schubert and his time.

Walburga Litschauer completed studies in musicology, philosophy and theatre at the University of Vienna Sciences and in piano at the Vienna Conservatory. In 1980 she earned a PhD from the University of Vienna. She is a member of the editorial board of the *Neue Schubert-Ausgabe* and director of its Vienna office. She has edited volumes of Schubert's piano music for the NSA and has also worked on the Anton Bruckner edition. Her numerous publications include two volumes of *Neue Dokumente zum Schubert-Kreis* (Musikwissenschaftler Verlag Wien, 1986) and *Schubert und das Tanzvergnügen*, co-written with Walther Deutsch (Holzhausen, 1997), as well as articles on Schubert, Bruckner and the music history of Carinthia. In 1992 she was awarded the Grand Prix

Franz Schubert for special achievement in Schubert research. She is president of the Carinthischer Sommer festival.

Leon Plantinga graduated from Calvin College in Grand Rapids, Michigan, in 1957. He received his master of music degree in piano at Michigan State University in 1959 and his PhD in the history of music from Yale University in 1964. He has been a member of the faculty of the music department at Yale since 1964, chairman of the department for a dozen years, and director of the division of the humanities from 1991 to 1997. As Henry L. and Lucy G. Moses Professor of Music Emeritus, he currently teaches one or two courses a year. Plantinga has published widely in the history of European music of the later eighteenth and nineteenth centuries, including a book on Robert Schumann as a music critic, a life and works of Muzio Clementi, a history of nineteenth-century European music, a book on the concertos of Beethoven and a great many articles and reviews. He has given lectures at many institutions in North America, Europe and Asia.

James William Sobaskie teaches at Mississippi State University and is the book reviews editor of the *Nineteenth-Century Music Review*. His publications on Schubert include studies of three late chamber works and an essay that portrays two late piano pieces as self-elegies. He also is a member of the *comité scientifique* of *Œuvres Complétes de Gabriel Fauré,* and his critical edition of Fauré's last two works, the Trio pour piano, violon et violoncelle and the Quatuor à cordes, inaugurated the monument in 2010. With Lorraine Byrne Bodley he is guest-editing a second special issue of the *Nineteenth-Century Music Review* entitled 'Schubert Familiar and Unfamiliar: Continuing Conversations'.

Michael Spitzer is Professor of Music as the University of Liverpool. Author of *Metaphor and Musical Thought* (University of Chicago Press, 2004) and *Music as Philosophy: Adorno and Beethoven's Late Style* (Indiana University Press, 2006), his many writings explore the interfaces between music theory, aesthetics and psychology. He is presently writing a history of music and emotion.

Deborah Stein teaches at the New England Conservatory and the Vancouver International Song Institute. She has published on relations between text and music in the German lied, including *Hugo Wolf's Lieder and Extensions of Tonality* (UMI Research Press) and *Poetry into Song: Performance and Analysis of Lieder* (Oxford University Press), co-authored with the pianist Robert Spillman and with a foreword by Elly Ameling and Max Deen Larsen. She also edited a book of essays, *Engaging Music: Essays in Music Analysis* (Oxford University Press).

Susan Wollenberg is a professor of music at the University of Oxford and a fellow and tutor of Lady Margaret Hall, as well as a college lecturer in Music at Brasenose College. She has contributed on Schubert to various journals

Contributors   xxi

and edited collections, including the chapter 'Schubert's Transitions', in Brian Newbould (ed.), *Schubert Studies* (Ashgate, 1998). Her monograph *Schubert's Fingerprints: Studies in the Instrumental Works* was published by Ashgate in 2011.

Susan Youens, who received her PhD from Harvard University, is the J. W. Van Gorkom Professor of Music at the University of Notre Dame and the author of eight books from Cambridge University Press, Princeton University Press, and Cornell University Press on the lieder of Schubert, Schumann, Wolf and others, as well as over fifty scholarly articles. She is a recipient of fellowships from the Humboldt Foundation, the National Endowment for the Humanities, the Institute for Advanced Study at Princeton, the Guggenheim Foundation, and the National Humanities Center, and has taught at the Ravinia, Aldeburgh and Oxford lieder festivals.

Introduction

Rethinking Schubert: Contexts and Controversies

Lorraine Byrne Bodley and Julian Horton

The time is propitious for a re-evaluation of Schubert scholarship. The last decade has witnessed a decisive flowering of research notable for its sheer disciplinary diversity. Important contributions in the fields of textual scholarship, reception and cultural history have evolved alongside a flowering of theoretical and analytical engagement, which has placed Schubert at the centre of mainstream music theory. Scholars approaching Schubert's music consequently have available an unprecedented wealth of historical data, textual sources, theoretical tools and analytical perspectives.

Song has necessarily been critical to these developments. Our understanding of Schubert's text-setting habits has been substantially enhanced by Susan Youens' numerous monographs and articles, from *Retracing a Winter's Journey: Schubert's Winterreise* to *Heinrich Heine and the Lied*;[1] by Walther Dürr's editorship of the lieder volumes in the *Neue Schubert-Ausgabe*—including most recently volumes 8 and 9, which contain such gems as 'Klage des Ceres' (D 323)—and his articles on music and text as well as source studies for his recent *Lied Lexikon*;[2] and by Graham Johnson's *The Hyperion Schubert Edition* and *Franz Schubert: the Complete Songs*.[3]

In addition to the contributions of this triumvirate of Schubertian song scholars, our knowledge of Schubert reception and its historical circumstances has been greatly increased by Scott Messing's two-volume study *Schubert in the European Imagination*,[4] as well as by numerous articles which have appeared in the *Schubert-Jahrbuch*, edited by Christiane Schumann and others (1996–2013);[5] *Schubert durch die Brille*, edited by Ernst Hilmar (1998–2003);[6] *Schubert: Perspektiven* (2001–), edited by Hans-Joachim Hinrichsen and Till Gerrit Waidelich;[7] *Cahiers Franz Schubert: Revue de musique classique et romantique* (1992–2009), edited by Xavier Hascher;[8] and *The Schubertian* (1996–), edited by Crawford Howie. Studies appearing in these and other journals have developed our understanding of the political milieu in which Schubert lived,[9] his social circle,[10] close friends,[11] possible relationships[12] and commissions received.[13] Over the past decade new documentary sources have augmented our understanding of biographical issues.[14] Our knowledge of such neglected repertoire as Schubert's operas has been greatly enhanced by recent volumes of the *Neue Schubert-Ausgabe*,[15] the recent editions of Schubert's part-songs,[16] lesser-known liturgical works,[17] symphonic sketches and fragments[18] and sketches for Schubert's final piano sonatas and piano duets.[19] And many neglected areas of research have been addressed by the series *Schubert: Perspektiven—Studien*[20] and such books as Lorraine Byrne Bodley and Barbara Reul's *The Unknown Schubert*.[21]

No less encouraging is the centrality of Schubert's music to the burgeoning theoretical and analytical literature on nineteenth-century harmony and form. The 'heavenly length' of his instrumental forms has been the site of much recent activity, prompting Hans-Joachim Hinrichsen's *Untersuchungen zur Entwicklung der Sonatenform in der Instrumentalmusik Franz Schuberts* (1994), Xavier Hascher's *Schubert, la forme sonate et son évolution* (1996) and Hascher's edited volume *Le Style instrumental de Schubert: Sources, analyse, évolution*.[22] Subsequent research in this area has crystallised around the dichotomy between hypotactic and paratactic modes of formal planning, the former associated with the teleological processes of Beethoven's instrumental forms, the latter with Schubert's episodic alternatives. Drawing on Carl Dahlhaus's notion of the Schubertian 'lyric-epic' and the topographical metaphors marshalled by Theodor Adorno, Scott Burnham, Su-Yin Mak, Poundie Burstein, Charles Fisk, Anne Hyland and others have established a sophisticated analytical framework operating in fruitful dialogue with the principal threads of modern *Formenlehre*.[23]

Schubert's music has played an even more significant role in the recent evolution of harmonic theory. Appropriations of Hugo Riemann's ideas tracking back to the work of David Lewin have spawned a rich legacy of research, to which Schubert's harmonic practice has been central.[24] Richard Cohn, David Kopp and Suzannah Clark, amongst others, have sourced key elements of neo-Riemannian theory in Schubert, and David Damschroder's novel extensions of Schenkerian theory for nineteenth-century music have also taken Schubert as pivotal.[25] The root of this interest is of course the harmonic 'purple patches' noted by Donald Francis Tovey, and especially the new freedom with which Schubert treats chromatic thirds and semitonal relations.[26] The realisation that these practices access an alternative triadic universe, governed by the logic of parsimonious voice leading and traceable to hexatonic and octatonic pitch collections, has made possible major advances in the study of nineteenth-century tonality, which expose the systematic basis of practices that theory has struggled to encompass.

In all, Schubert's importance for the present condition of musical scholarship is hard to overstate. Consequently, although *Rethinking Schubert* certainly pursues the revisionist agenda implied by its title, it also looks to consolidate the gains of recent research. The volume brings together some of today's leading Schubertians, both established voices and leading younger scholars, who collectively speak to the themes of the composer's importance and our perennial fascination with him. The book's aim is to subject recurring issues in historical, biographical and analytical research to renewed scrutiny, paying special attention to matters of style, the analysis of harmony and instrumental form, and text setting. Each of these fields has received fresh stimulus in recent years through the development of new hermeneutic and theoretical approaches and the discovery of fresh source materials. Our objectives are both to affirm and to extend these developments through a thematic exploration of Schubert's compositional style (in Part I) and by addressing issues in tonal strategy and form in Schubert's instrumental and vocal music (in Parts II and III). Within this framework, implicit dialogues—engendered in the book's multiplicity of voices—are presented kaleidoscopically. Collectively, the chapters yield new insights into Schubert, his music, his influence and his legacy, and broaden the interpretative context for the music of his final years.

While the essays consider some of Schubert's most famous music (the 'Unfinished' Symphony, the final piano sonatas and impromptus, *Winterreise* and *Schwanengesang*), they also crucially adjust judgements of his later works by explaining their musical features not in terms of an inability to break free from Beethoven's towering influence, but as the work of a composer forging his own musical vision. The notion that Schubert's style both deviates from and challenges Beethoven's precedent is affirmed throughout this volume by Hinrichsen, Kinderman, Dürr, Black, Spitzer, Caskel and Youens. Concomitantly, the exploration of Schubert's late style as critique (Binder) and synthesis (Hinrichsen, Dürr, Black and Wollenberg) endorses the image of a composer who was consciously shaping his musical style and career. In contrast to the postmodern view, Schubert is revealed as a musician deeply engaged with and responsive to his surroundings.

This characterisation ranges across textual, historical and analytical contributions. *Rethinking Schubert* reviews Schubert's revision process (Litschauer and Hyland), his formal prolixity (Gardner), the connection between song and instrumental music (Wollenberg), issues of reception (Lindmayr-Brandl) and the traditional association of Schubert's 'late' or 'mature' style with impending death (Hinrichsen, Dürr, Giarusso and Stein). The volume explores the themes of memory (Ferris and Spitzer), narrativity (Hascher, Gardner and Caskel), sensory studies (Black and Feurzeig), the novel handling of sonata form (Hascher and Gardner) and issues in harmonic theory (Damschroder's imaginative rethinking of voice-leading techniques and Clark's engagement with neo-Riemannian theory). New contexts are offered for familiar literature in Hascher and Lindmayr-Brandl's readings of the 'Unfinished', Stein's intepretation of *Winterreise* as a Romantic fragment and Byrne Bodley's re-contextualisation of 'Der Musensohn' (D 764). Less familiar lieder—'Einsamkeit' (D 620), 'Schwanengesang' (D 744) 'Im Freien' (D 880) and 'Der Winterabend' (D 938)—Schubert's sacred music and operatic genres are also explored (Youens, Clark and Spitzer). Bringing together varied and fresh approaches to both Schubert's best-known and his neglected works, this book provides the reader with an enriched understanding of Schubert the man and musician, and of the cultural context in which his music was composed. The essays assemble a portrait of the artist that reflects the different ways in which Schubert has been misunderstood over the past two hundred years and provide a timely reassessment of Schubert's compositional legacy.

Part I broaches a central question in Schubert studies: can one speak of late style for a composer who died at the age of thirty-one? In the opening essay, Hans-Joachim Hinrichsen addresses the crux of this controversy, asking whether one should subject Schubert's last works to an aesthetic discussion of late style. For Hinrichsen, even more important than the adequate naming of this style is the recognition that Schubert took a different compositional path in 1824, engendering stylistic features that have increasingly influenced subsequent composers, interpreters and listeners. Hinrichsen concludes by appraising Schubert's 'mature' style as belonging, alongside Beethoven's last style, to the most historically powerful compositional paradigm shift of the nineteenth century. Following on from Hinrichsen, Walther Dürr posits that Schubert's late compositions, especially the works from 1827–28, indicate his search for new paths—a direction that is not necessarily linked with his impending death. This idea lies at the crux of the current debate on the composer's 'late' style. Dürr's consideration of the Piano Trio in E♭ major instead endorses the idea of late style as synthesis, whereby Schubert employs and expands a series of techniques to create something substantially new. Through a consideration of contrapuntal techniques, motivic and sub-motivic connections between movements and the composer's reappraisal of tonality—including non-modulatory harmonic 'swerves'—Dürr isolates key musical features of Schubert's last works.

Following on from Hinrichsen and Dürr, William Kinderman opens up the discussion of two of the central ideas explored in this volume: Schubert's 'new style' as a self-assured alternative to Beethoven's legacy; and the relationship between the instrumental music and the lied. The aesthetic framework of Schubert's mature instrumental works—from the *Quartettsatz* of 1820 to the String Quintet and the final three piano sonatas of 1828—reveals a highly distinctive, original approach that is indebted to Schubert's profound experience with lieder. Kinderman endorses Hinrichsen's belief that Schubert's relation to Beethoven displays a 'self-conscious alternative position' through a reading of Schubert's final sonata trilogy, which also responds to Charles Rosen's reading of the A major Sonata and Charles Fisk's identification of the wanderer in Schubert's Piano Sonata D 960. Kinderman explores Schubert's characteristic lyricism by tracing poetic residues of 'Der Atlas' in the C minor Sonata (D 958) and in 'Ihr Bild' (D 960), arguing that Schubert's identification with the wanderer figure imbues his later instrumental works with an impressive post-Beethovenian originality. Picking up on this notion of late style as synthesis, Susan Wollenberg establishes a typology in chamber works such as the *Quartettsatz* (D 703), the G major Quartet (D 887), the String Quintet (D 956) and keyboard literature including the 'Wanderer' Fantasy (D 760), the Impromptus for Piano (D 899 no. 2 and no. 4), the Piano Duet Fantasy (D 940), the Piano Sonata in G major (D 894), and the last three piano sonatas. In order to define 'late' style, Wollenberg examines Schubert's characteristic treatment of episodic forms, especially in his slow movements, the ramifications of his major-minor usage, the application of variation processes in his instrumental forms, and the music's 'heavenly lengths'.

For Brian Black, Schubert's sensitivity to the sensual quality of sound and its expressive potential is a unique feature of his music lying at the heart of his innovative use of harmony and his affecting modulations. Yet Schubert's handling of such elements has also been criticised as self-indulgence, which sacrifices structural rigour to a hedonistic gratification of the moment. Black argues that this misunderstanding still colours recent responses to his music. In contrast to this reception history, Black shows how carefully marked sonorities or striking harmonic events in Schubert's vocal and instrumental works emerge as important structural components that also lend a given work its particular expressive significance. His chapter links with Kinderman's essay through his identification of a highly original treatment of form that depends upon allusion, recall and sudden transformation rather than the type of developing variation traditionally associated with Beethoven. Black's comparative analysis of 'Ihr Bild' and the Impromptu Op. 90 No. 3 sheds new light on the mutual enrichment of lied and instrumental music, revealing that in both pieces the dramatic flow and expressive content is conveyed by the transformation of a single sonority. Like Dürr, Black argues that this aspect of Schubert's music, though present from the very beginning of his career, becomes a powerful force in the masterpieces of his last years.

Parts II and III partner the debate about Schubert's compositional style with analytical excursions into style, harmony and form, with the result that familiar works are freshly understood. Part II focuses on the instrumental music, moving through orchestral works to studies of the late sonatas; Part III deals with vocal works. These essays find common ground in various shared preoccupations, notably debates about Schubert's relation to Beethoven and Classical practice, and also the thorny question of how best to theorise Schubert's adventurous harmonic idiom.

The theoretical diversity that Schubert's harmony encourages is apparent from a comparison of three chapters: Suzannah Clark's and Michael Spitzer's contributions to Part III, and David Damschroder's chapter in Part II. The neo-Riemannian tendency in recent tonal theory is represented here by Clark's analysis of 'Schwanengesang' (D 744). Her reading pays close attention to the theoretical problems generated by Schubert's ambiguous treatment of modality, demonstrating that the music's vacillation between A♭ minor and A♭ major can be explained in transformational terms without recourse to an overarching concept of key, thereby carrying the Schubertian purview of neo-Riemannian theory beyond its home territory of third relationships. Clark's approach stands in constructive opposition to Michael Spitzer's readings of 'Im Freien' (D 880) and 'Der Winterabend' (D 938), which develop a corrective to the neo-Riemannian emphasis on tertial structures: Spitzer argues that diatonic tonal relations remain the norm for Schubert's practice and explores the concept of axial lyric space as a means of capturing its melodic specificity. In his identification of these two neglected masterpieces as consummate examples of the composer's late style, Spitzer asks how and why Schubert's late style differs from Beethoven's, which is traditionally viewed through an Adornian lens. He subsequently explores how Heidegger illuminates the ontology of Schubert's late songs, with their ethos of sonority, lyric temporality and memory, thereby building on a phenomenological tradition of music analysis, as suggested by David Lewin's famous Husserlian analysis of Schubert's 'Morgengrüss', whilst reflecting Black's approach to the aesthetic domain of *Spätstil*.

David Damschroder also focuses broadly on Schubert's diatonic strategies, examining the role that scale degree 6 plays as a pivot between tonic and supertonic regions in the finale of the Piano Sonata D 960, throwing new light on the innovative ways in which Schubert explores mediant relations. Whereas Schubert's use of tonic and dominant 6-phase chords gives the opening movement a sombre cast, by the finale a new ebullience has emerged, which is characteristic of the composer's perspective; the chapter thereby explores an insightful intersection of theory and biography.

Together, these essays expose the centrality of Schubert's music for the theory of post-Classical tonality. Poised between the asymmetries of diatonic tonality and the symmetrical structures that increasingly pervade nineteenth-century practice, Schubert has become a testing ground for theoretical models, which seek to reconcile the triad's symmetrical and asymmetrical 'natures', as Richard Cohn has termed them.[27]

The remaining essays in Part II represent a broad constituency of scholarly attitudes. Andrea Lindmayr-Brandl surveys the reception of Schubert's 'Unfinished' Symphony to reveal the circumstances that created its extraordinary fame. Rather than appraise or adduce explanations of its incompletion, she examines three myths surrounding this work, which greatly contributed to its reputation. First, there is the rumour of a 'hidden' symphony, which can be traced to Schubert's first biographer, Heinrich Kreissle von Hellborn, who believed Anselm Hüttenbrenner and his brother Josef held back the most precious 'pearls' of Schubert's *oeuvre*. Second, there is the mystical correlation whereby Schubert stops composing the symphony at the same time Beethoven becomes deaf. Finally, there is the misconception of the 'Unfinished' as a *Sterbefragment*, a work that is incomplete because the composer died while working on it. Lindmayr-Brandl's foray into reception history complements Hascher's exploration of narrativity in the 'Unfinished' which examines the extraordinary tensions between sonata norms and symphonic style in the first movement and relates them to narrative sonata archetypes. Referencing the vocabulary introduced in Freud's dream theory, Hascher distinguishes between a 'manifest' narration on the surface, which follows the narrative programme normally associated with sonata form, and a deeper, hidden, 'latent' one that is obsessional in nature and accounts for the spectacular, violent outbursts that periodically interrupt its course. Reflecting Sonata Theory's characterisation of formal individuality as a consequence of the composer's dialogue with convention, and recalling Hugh MacDonald's 'Schubert's Volcanic Temper', Hascher's chapter elucidates the music's tendency to stage the dilemmas of the composer's subjectivity.[28]

Cameron Gardner turns to another unfinished work, claiming fresh significance for the unfinished Piano Sonata in C major ('Reliquie', D 840), which has been neglected in musicological and analytical studies. Gardner's chapter picks up on Hascher's theme of narrativity and places a welcome gestural spin on the concepts of development design bequeathed by Caplin and by Hepokoski and Darcy, identifying proportional and harmonic correspondences between this sonata and the 'Great' C major Symphony (D 944).[29] The essay opens up questions of how to understand Schubert's piano sonatas, which the subsequent chapters in Part II variously elaborate. Walburga Litschauer and Anne Hyland offer a rare portrait of Schubert in the process of sketching and revising the Piano Sonata D 960. Schubert's drafts for this work represent some of the most important documents of their kind: they shed light on his working methods and challenge the perception of Schubert as an undisciplined, spontaneous composer who was disinclined to revise. Their essay charts the compositional evolution of the sketches and autographs before offering a more detailed study of the Piano Sonata in B♭ major (D 960) in which a number of key features of Schubert's customary revisions are analysed from the perspective of thematic construction, phrase structure, hypermetre and performance practice.

Returning to the theme of Schubert's style as a deviation from and challenge to Beethoven, Julian Caskel's analysis of the first movement of Piano Sonata

D 959 subverts recent scholarly tendencies by associating the work's contrasts between teleology and improvisation with a subversion of Beethovenian heroism. The first movement could be connected to the second movement of Beethoven's Sonata Op. 31, via Schubert's formal mediation of improvisatory structural moments and a genuine ordering of sonata-form events in sonata form. For Caskel, this parallelism provides a clue as to why Schubert's final sonatas can—on the grounds of stylistic typology—be received as works written in a 'late style'. The originality of Caskel's contribution reinforces a synergy with Hinrichsen's and Spitzer's chapters: these authors observe that the historical discussion of the parameters of 'late style' are derived from Beethovenian models and are conceptualised as a departure from his 'heroic' style. Caskel shows how, in the first movement of D 959, Schubert departed from that model. He also draws on Adorno's dichotomy between extensive and intensive types of musical time to define Schubert's specific modes of departure, where the metamorphosis of the intensive into the extensive type lends the movement a narrative dimension.

Leon Plantinga concludes this section by expanding the purview of its repertoire, repositioning the composer within the Viennese musical vanguard by offering a broad study of Schubert's mature instrumental music in the cultural and political circumstances of Metternich's Vienna. Plantinga addresses the composite portrait of Schubert's Vienna reflected in the dual images of the composer in reception history and in the antinomies of his musical style. Plantinga argues convincingly that the composer's music constantly echoes the sounds heard in Vienna's taverns and ballrooms—the close harmony of the *Männerchor* and the infectious rhythms of *Ländler* and écossaises—while in later works Schubert plumbed new depths of tragedy and despair. In his consideration of the first movement of Schubert's Fantasie in F minor, a processional march for piano duet, and the slow movements of the final two piano sonatas (D 959 and D 960), both of the *Ländler* type, Plantinga shows how these two tropes are mingled in Schubert's most impressive late music.

Part III takes up questions of text setting in Schubert's vocal literature but parallels Part II in its progression from public works through to studies of individual songs. These essays explore text setting in Schubert's lieder, stage and sacred works in the context of their development in his final years. By exploring a range of Schubert's late sacred music written during an extraordinarily productive period when Schubert's health may have prompted meditations on his own mortality—the 'Schlussgesang' and 'Das Gebet des Herrn' of Schubert's *Deutsche Messe* (D 948), the Sanctus and Agnus Dei of Schubert's uncommissioned Mass in E♭ major (D 950) and his final two sacred works, *Tantum ergo* (D 962) and *Offertorium: Intende voci* (D 963)—James Sobaskie broadens our vision of Schubert's spirituality and reveals a composer deeply engaged in the vicissitudes and possibilities of human temporality. Schubert's last opera *Der Graf von Gleichen* is Lisa Feurzeig's quarry in a provocative new interpretation addressing questions of text and meaning. In a comparative study of Eduard von Bauernfeld's libretto with its folk sources, Feurzeig shows how Schubert's last opera moves towards a bold exploration of the theme of sexual intimacy—a three-way marriage—in a plot that would never pass muster with Metternich's censors.

An exploration of text setting in *Winterreise* (D 911) and *Schwanengesang* (D 957) ensues in a sequence of essays employing diverse musicological and analytical methods. Firstly, Deborah Stein builds upon recent research on *Winterreise* by offering three approaches to interpreting the cycle's end, which respectively emphasise poetic progression, tonal design and chromaticism, the latter picking up again on the recent flowering of theoretical interest in Schubert's late harmony. In contrast to readings of *Winterreise* which locate the musical climax in the final song, 'Der Leiermann', Stein recognises the cycle's culmination in 'Der Wegweiser', arguing that the weary wanderer does not embrace death but arrives at a critical point in his troubled journey, and that the signpost points away from his torment and towards uncharted territory. Stein's provocative conclusions about the cycle's close leads her to link it with the German Romantic fragment through its championing of incompletion, irresolution and ambiguity. David Ferris, Richard Giarusso and Benjamin Binder offer contrasting perspectives on *Schwanengesang*, which, for Ferris, leads to a consideration of Schubert's settings of Heinrich Heine. Ferris shows how two of the six settings, 'Der Atlas' and 'Der Doppelgänger', are concerned, like many of the poems in Heine's *Buch der Lieder*, with themes of memory and loss. In an analysis of the interplay of tonality, voice leading, texture and hypermetre, he unveils Schubert's manipulation of the declamatory patterns in Heine's poems in order to express narrative and semantic levels musically, offering a new approach to the vexed question of how these songs cohere. Binder focuses on one of these settings in a reading that relates Schubert's 'Der Doppelgänger' both to Adorno's association of late style with self-critique and Joseph Straus's identification of it as inscribing physical or mental disability. Binder reads 'Der Doppelgänger' as a late work in *both* respects: Schubert's artistic response to his physical and psychological disabilities takes the form of a reflective self-critique. Finally, Giarusso's essay addresses the debate over the role 'Die Taubenpost' plays in *Schwanengesang*. In contrast to many performers and critics, who dismiss the song as a trifling successor to the weighty Heine settings, he argues that the tenor of Schubert's last lied—and the antinomy it creates with the Heine settings—embodies the quintessence of Schubert's late style. While recognising the physical and emotional struggle of Schubert's final years, Giarusso identifies the cautious yet resilient optimism at the heart of Schubert's 'swan song', arguing that its place at the end of the cycle is utterly appropriate.

Returning to the central trope of Schubert's *Winterreise*, Byrne Bodley contextualises the composer's lifelong preoccupation with the wanderer figure through her consideration of Schubert's Goethe settings of 1822, most notably 'Der Musensohn' (D 764). She re-evaluates Schubert's reception by his favourite poet and addresses the vexed question of how—or whether—pathways between life and art can be mapped. Byrne Bodley's exploration of the wanderer trope is answered by Susan Youens's consideration of antique and contemporaneous debates about the nature of solitude in relation to Schubert's setting of J. B. Mayrhofer's 'Einsamkeit' (D 620), which she reads as an acknowledgement of and a challenge to the Beethovenian model of *An die ferne Geliebte*. Youens's chapter unveils subterranean connections between the confluence of *Erlebnislyrik* (the poetry of personal experience) and an artistic credo in Alois Isidor Jeitteles's poems for Beethoven's cycle, and a similar confluence, very differently expressed, in 'Einsamkeit'. Finally, Youens's deliberations are aptly followed by Graham Johnson's Postlude, which explores intersections between the worlds of performance and musicology in a tribute to Walther Dürr, who has done so much to rethink Schubert, and to whom this volume is warmly dedicated.

Taken together, the articles gathered here go some way towards apostrophising the lasting fascination Schubert's music has for both musicologists and music theorists. The most readily explicable aspect of this appeal is undoubtedly our continuing engagement with the songs. Schubert will always be the first port of call for scholars interested in the relationship between music and the poetic text; the contributions to that area in *Rethinking Schubert* amply demonstrate why this should be so. Yet perhaps more striking is the depth of thought that attaches to the instrumental works in this volume. Their highly protracted dissemination has combined with a habitual critical hostility to produce a reception history that has proved uncongenial to musical analysis. Empowered by the new momentum behind theories of nineteenth-century harmony and form, the breadth and sophistication of approaches assembled here show decisively that it is no longer acceptable to dismiss Schubert's instrumental forms as flawed lyric alternatives to Beethoven.

What *Rethinking Schubert* provides, then, is not only a conspectus of current scholarship, but also a mandate for future research. There are, of course, neglected corners of Schubert's output which remain to be investigated in detail, and these may well provide areas of scholarly growth in future. Yet whether we pursue unknown repertoire or refresh canonical works, *Rethinking Schubert* reveals with particular clarity the extraordinary methodological variety that is now available to research. The contemporary Schubert, in short, is vibrant, plural, transnational and complex.

Notes

1. Susan Youens, *Retracing a Winter's Journey: Schubert's Winterreise* (Ithaca, New York: Cornell University Press, 1991), and *Heinrich Heine and the Lied* (Cambridge: Cambridge University Press, 2007).
2. See, for example, Franz Schubert, *Neue Ausgabe sämtlicher Werke*, ser. IV, *Lieder*, vols 1–14 (1970–2011), and *Kritische Berichte*, vols 1–14 (1972–2014); and Walther Dürr, Michael Kube, Uwe Schweikert and Stefanie Steiner (eds), *Schubert-Liedlexikon* (Kassel: Bärenreiter Verlag, 2012).
3. Graham Johnson, *Franz Schubert: the Complete Songs* (London and New Haven, CT: Yale University Press, 2014).
4. Scott Messing, *Schubert in the European Imagination*, 2 vols (Rochester, NY: University of Rochester Press, 2006–7).
5. Christiane Schumann et al. (eds), *Schubert-Jahrbuch* (Kassel: Bärenreiter Verlag, 1996–2013).
6. Ernst Hilmar, ed., *Schubert durch die Brille*, vols 1–3 (Vienna: Internationales Franz-Schubert-Institut, 1988–9), and vols 4–30 (Tutzing: Hans Schneider Verlag, 1990–2003).
7. Hans-Joachim Hinrichsen and Till Gerrit Waidelich (eds), *Schubert: Perspektiven* (Stuttgart: Franz Steiner Verlag, 2001–).
8. Xavier Hascher (ed.), *Cahiers Franz Schubert: revue de musique classique et romantique* 1–17 (1992–2009).
9. See, for example, Michael Aschauer, 'Drei Stationen einer Auseinandersetzung mit dem System Metternichs: Franz Schuberts politische und weltanschauliche Haltung, dargelegt anhand seiner Schriften, ausgewählter Liedtexte und dreier Freundesgestalten', *Studien zur Musikwissenschaft* 48 (2002), pp. 373–88.
10. See, for example, Ilija Dürhammer, 'Homoerotische Chiffren im Schubert-Kreis', *Kunstpunkt* 24 (2002), pp. 19–20; and Alice Hanson, 'The Significance of the Ludlamshöhle for Franz Schubert', in Barbara Haggh (ed.), *Essays on Music and Culture in Honor of Herbert Kellman* (Paris and Tours: Minerve, 2001), pp. 496–502.
11. See, for example, Andrea Gottdang, ' "Ich bin unsern Ideen nicht untreu geworden": Moritz von Schwind und der Schubert-Freundeskreis', *Schubert: Perspektiven* 4 (2004), pp. 1–48; Michael Ascher's recent reseach on Anselm Hüttenbrenner in Ulf Bästleine, Alice and Michael Aschauer (eds), *Lieder für eine Singstimme mit Klavierbegleitung*, 3 vols (Warngau: Accolage, 2008–10); and Till Gerrit Waidelich, ' "Torupson" und Franz von Schober: Leben und Wirken des von Frauen, Freunden und Biographen umworbenen Schubert- und Schwind-Freundes', *Schubert: Perspektiven* 6 (2006), pp. 1–237, and 7 (2007), pp. 107–20.
12. See, for example, Rita Steblin, 'Schubert's Love Affair with Marie von Spaun and the Role Played by Helene Schmith, the Wife of Mozart's First Violinist', *Schubert: Perspektiven* 8 (2008), pp. 49–87, and 'Schubert's Pepi: his Love Affair with the Chamber Maid Josepha Pöcklhofer and her Suprising Fate', *Musical Times* 149 (2008), pp. 47–69.

13. See e.g. Charles Jurgenmeiser, 'Salomon Sulzer and Franz Schubert: a Musical Collaboration', in Leonard J. Greenspoon (ed.), *I Will Sing and Make Music: Jewish Music and Musicians throughout the Ages*, Studies in Jewish Civilization 19 (Omaha, NE: Creighton University Press, 2008), pp. 27–41. See also Sabine Lichtenstein, 'Franz Schubert en Salomon Sulzer: Een joods-christelijke samenwerking in romantisch Wenen', *Nieuwsbrief Schubert Stichting* 13/1 (2008–9), pp. 3–12, and Rita Steblin, 'Who Commissioned Schubert's Oratorio *Lazarus*? A Solution to the Mystery: Salieri and the Tonkünstler-Societät', *Schubert-Perspektiven* 9/2 (2009), pp. 145–81.

14. See, for example, Till Gerrit Waidelich, *Franz Schubert: Dokumente 1817–1830*, vol. 1, *Texte: Programme, Rezensionen, Anzeigen, Nekrologe, Musikbeilagen und andere gedruckte Quellen*, ed. Till Gerrit Waidelich in collaboration with Renate Hilmar-Voit and Andreas Mayer, Publications of IFSI 10/1 (Tutzing: Hans Schneider Verlag, 1993); Till Gerrit Waidelich, 'Unbekannte Schubert-Dokument aus Breslau', *Schubert-Perspektiven* 8 (2008), pp. 17–48; and Rita Steblin and Frederick Stocken, 'Studying with Sechter: Newly Recovered Reminiscences about Schubert by his Forgotten Friend, the Composer Joseph Lanz', *Music & Letters* 88 (2007), pp. 226–65. See also Ernst Hilmar and Margret Jestremski (eds), *Schubert-Enzyklopädie* (Tützing: Schneider, 2004), which first appeared as *Schubert-Lexikon* (Graz: Akademische Druck- und Verlagsanstalt, 1997).

15. See, for example, the operatic editions and critical reports for Franz Schubert, *Neue Ausgabe sämtlicher Werke*, ser. II, *Bühnenwerke*, vols 1–18, especially vols 8a–c, *Fierrabras*, ed. Thomas Denny (vol. 8a) and Christine Martin (vols 8b and 8c) (Kassel: Bärenreiter, 2005, 2007 and 2009); vol. 12, *Adrast*, ed. Mario Aschauer (Kassel: Bärenreiter, 2010); vol. 14, *Claudine von Villa Bella*, ed. Christine Martin and Dieter Martin (Kassel: Bärenreiter, 2011); vol. 17, *Der Graf von Gleichen*, ed. Manuela Jahrmärker (Kassel: Bärenreiter, 2006); and vol. 18, *Operneinlagen* (*zu 'Hérolds Zauberglöckchen'*), ed. Christine Martin (Kassel: Bärenreiter, 2010).

16. See, for example, Franz Schubert, *Neue Ausgabe sämtlicher Werke*, ser. III, vol. 4, *Mehrstimmige Gesänge für gemischte Stimmen*, ed. Dietrich Berke (Kassel: Bärenreiter, 1996).

17. See, for example, Franz Schubert, *Neue Ausgabe sämtlicher Werke*, ser. I, vol. 9, *Kleinere kirchenmusikalische Werke II*, ed. Rudolf Faber (Kassel: Bärenreiter, 2014).

18. Franz Schubert, *Neue Ausgabe sämtlicher Werke*, ser. V, vol. 6, *Sinfonische Entwürfe und Fragmente*, ed. Michael Kube (Kassel: Bärenreiter, 2012).

19. See, for example, Schubert's sketches for his Sonata in G major, Op. 78, as well as for the last three piano sonatas—the Sonata in C minor, D 958; the Sonata in A major, D 959; and the Sonata in B♭ major, D 960—in Franz Schubert, *Neue Ausgabe sämtlicher Werke*, ser. VII, vol. 2, *Klaviersonaten III*, ed. Walburga Litschauer (Kassel: Bärenreiter, 1996); also see the sketches for Schubert's Fantasy in F minor, D 940, and Rondo in A major, D 951, in Franz Schubert, *Neue Ausgabe sämtlicher Werke*, ser. VII, vols 1–3, *Werke für Klavier zu vier Händen III*, ed. Walburga Litschauer (Kassel: Bärenreiter, 2011).

20. Christine Blanken, *Franz Schuberts 'Lazarus' und das Wiener Oratorium zu Beginn des 19. Jahrhunderts, Schubert: Perspektiven—Studien 1* (Stuttgart:

Steiner, 2002); Andrea Lindmayr-Brandl, *Franz Schubert: Das fragmentarische Werk, Schubert: Perspektiven—Studien 2* (Stuttgart: Steiner, 2003); and Ivana Rentsch and Klaus Pietschmann (eds), *Schubert: Interpretationen* and *Schubert: Perspektiven—Studien 3* (Stuttgart: Franz Steiner Verlag, 2014).

21. Lorraine Byrne Bodley and Barbara Reul, *The Unknown Schubert* (Aldershot: Ashgate, 2008).

22. Hans-Joachim Hinrichsen, *Untersuchungen zur Entwicklung der Sonatenform in der Instrumentalmusik Franz Schubert* (Tutzing: Hans Schneider Verlag, 1994); Xavier Hascher, *Schubert, la forme sonate et son évolution* (Bern: Peter Lang, 1996), and *Le Style instrumental de Schubert: Sources, analyse, évolution* (Paris: Publications de la Sorbonne, 2007).

23. Carl Dahlhaus, 'Die Sonatenform bei Schubert: Der erste Satz des G-dur-Quartetts D. 887', *Musica* 32 (1978), trans. Thilo Reinhard as 'Sonata Form in Schubert: the First Movement of the G major String Quartet, Op. 161 (D. 877)', in Walther Frisch (ed.), *Schubert: Critical and Analytical Studies* (Lincoln, NB: University of Nebraska Press, 1986), pp. 13–30; Theodor Adorno, 'Schubert' (1928), trans. Jonathan Dunsby and Beate Perrey, *19th-Century Music* 29/1 (2005), pp. 3–14; Scott Burnham, 'Landscape as Music, Landscape as Truth: Schubert and the Burden of Repetition', *19th-Century Music* 29/1 (2005), pp. 31–41; Su-Yin Mak, 'Schubert's Sonata Forms and the Poetics of the Lyric', *Journal of Musicology* 23/2 (2006), pp. 263–306, and *Schubert's Lyricism Reconsidered: Structure, Design and Rhetoric* (Saarbrücken: Lambert, 2010); Poundie Burstein, 'Lyricism, Structure and Gender in Schubert's G major String Quartet', *Musical Quarterly* 81/1 (1997), pp. 51–63; Charles Fisk, *Returning Cycles: Contexts for the Interpretation of Schubert's Impromptus and Last Sonatas* (Berkeley and Los Angeles: University of California Press, 2001); Janet Schmalfeldt, *In the Process of Becoming: Analytic and Philosophical Perspectives on Form in Early Nineteenth-Century Music* (New York and Oxford: Oxford University Press, 2011); Anne M. Hyland, 'The "Tightened Bow": Analysing the Juxtaposition of Drama and Lyricism in Schubert's Paratactic Sonata-Form Movements', in Gareth Cox and Julian Horton (eds), *Irish Musical Studies*, vol. 11, *Irish Musical Analysis* (Dublin: Four Courts Press, 2014), pp. 17–40. For a recent work-focused contribution which brings together form-functional, rhetorical and Schenkerian perspectives, see Nathan Martin and Steven Vande Moortele, 'Formal Functions and Retrospective Reinterpretation in the First Movement of Schubert's String Quintet', in 'Schubert's String Quintet in C major, D. 956: Papers Read at the Conference "Schubert and Concepts of Late Style", National University of Ireland, Maynooth, 21–23 October 2011', special issue, *Music Analysis* 33/2 (2014), pp. 130–55 and also Scott Burnham, 'Thresholds Between, Worlds Apart', in ibid., pp. 156–67; John Koslovsky, 'Timeless Reflections: Form, Cadence and Tonal Structure in the Scherzo and Finale of Schubert's String Quintet', in ibid., pp. 168–93; and Julian Horton, 'Stasis and Continuity in Schubert's String Quintet: Responses to Nathan Martin, Steven Vande Moortele, Scott Burnham and John Koslovsky', in ibid., pp. 194–213. The landmark texts in *Formenlehre* that we have in mind are William E. Caplin, *Classical Form: a Theory of Formal*

Functions for the Instrumental Music of Haydn, Mozart, and Beethoven (New York and Oxford: Oxford University Press, 1998), and James Hepokoski and Warren Darcy, *Elements of Sonata Theory: Norms, Types, and Deformations in the Late-Eighteenth-Century Sonata* (New York and Oxford: Oxford University Press, 2006).

24. David Lewin, '*Auf dem Flusse*: Image and Background in a Schubert Song', *19th-Century Music* 6/1 (1982), pp. 47–59.

25. Richard L. Cohn, 'As Wonderful as Star Clusters: Instruments for Gazing at Tonality in Schubert', *19th-Century Music* 22/3 (1999), pp. 9–40, and *Audacious Euphony: Chromaticism and the Triad's Second Nature* (New York and Oxford: Oxford University Press, 2012); David Kopp, *Chromatic Transformations in Nineteenth-Century Music* (Cambridge: Cambridge University Press, 2002); Suzannah Clark, *Analyzing Schubert* (Cambridge: Cambridge University Press, 2011); and David Damschroder, *Harmony in Schubert* (Cambridge: Cambridge University Press, 2010).

26. Donald Francis Tovey, 'Tonality', *Music and Letters* 9 (1928), pp. 341–63.

27. Cohn, *Audacious Euphony*.

28. Hugh McDonald, 'Schubert's Volcanic Temper', *The Musical Times* 119 (1978), pp. 949–52.

29. Caplin, *Classical Form*, pp. 139–59; and Hepokoski and Darcy, *Elements of Sonata Theory*, pp. 195–230.

I
STYLE

1

Is There a Late Style in Schubert's Oeuvre?

Hans-Joachim Hinrichsen

Late Works?

'All works by Schubert are early works.' This formulation is not my own invention; with it I paraphrase the beautiful bon mot from the art historian Herman Grimm's classic work, which is still worth reading, about the Renaissance artist Raffaelo Santi, who died young. Grimm introduces the chapter on Raphael's last works with the statement 'All works by Raphael are early works', brusquely casting aside the solemn concept of 'late work', with its entire spectrum of meaning: 'after the completion of the *Sistine Madonna*, he had still three years to live. For those who have not yet reached the age of forty, the greater part of human life lies in the future. During one's thirties experience still surprises and appears as an adventure. Raphael was thirty-seven and still full of high expectations when he died; he had more to give.'[1]

If, however, all works by Franz Schubert, who died even younger, are *per definitionem* 'youthful works' (this is the proper and far more charming meaning of Grimm's original German expression 'Jugendwerke'), then the question of a 'late work' appears emphatically to be obsolete. In music historiography, the concept, which can be applied to Bach or Schoenberg, first made an entrance in Beethoven research. With a glance at the late work of Goethe, literary history had supplied a model for it; art history proceeded analogously with Michelangelo and Titian (and it was directly against these two contemporaries that Grimm aligned his 'youthful' Raphael in 1872.) Since then the intractable 'late work' of Beethoven—which Carl Dahlhaus certified, as it were, as 'chronologically displaced'[2] on account of its special reception history—has remained a particular subject of analysis and reflection.[3]

It is curious that Beethoven's late work blossomed at the same time as the final works of Schubert, who died so young. How far Schubert was aware of this must, for the time being, remain open. In any case, from the beginning there is in the solid corpus of Beethoven interpretation the conviction that this late work was surrounded by an aura of mystery and enigma. Paul Bekker apostrophised it in 1911 in his large-scale Beethoven monograph as 'the purest metaphysics of music'[4]—a completely contradictory compliment, in which admiration for 'the highest and most profound, which the imagination of a creative artist could generally perceive and reveal',[5] is connected with criticism of a much more blatant meaning of the extrasensory—to be precise, with the supposed nonchalance of the composer towards manifest sensual beauty. This alleged indifference towards a physical melodiousness, which one wanted to perceive everywhere in Beethoven's late style, was often ascribed to the 'otherworldliness'[6] of the composer, arising from his increasing deafness. As early as 1936, however, the Beethoven biographer Walther Riezler rightly warned against the dangers of an absolute mystification of the late work, which receives its solemnity by dint of being removed from reality and close to death: 'Beethoven, unlike Goethe, Michelangelo and Titian, is not over eighty, has not glimpsed even in the distance the threshold of old age. At the age at which he died, Goethe still had his last Indian summer before him'.[7] This statement, with its laconic emphasis on simple biographical facts, is reminiscent of Grimm's pointed remarks on Raphael; in any case, the remark on the 'lateness' of Beethoven's last works—as distinct from those of Goethe, Michelangelo or Titian—is important, because it makes clear that in Beethoven's case, lateness does not refer to a ripe old age and a glimpse of the approaching end. As one observes on closer inspection, Riezler conspicuously avoided the concept of 'late work' by giving the relevant chapter of his book the bare title 'The Late Style'. This, too, is interesting when looking at Schubert.

Let us linger for a while with late Beethoven. While his late style had long met with great resistance, its particular difficulties first became apparent in the twentieth century. Theodor W. Adorno's essay *Spätstil Beethovens*, published in 1937—which had a great impact on many readers through its treatment in Thomas Mann's musician's novel *Doktor Faustus* (1947)—played a significant role in this gradual reorientation. For Adorno, as for earlier reception, Beethoven's late style is characterised by a polarisation of extremes, which he wants to understand, however, not as the expression of an individual recklessly breaking the rules (as was usual until then), but as the objective 'formal laws' of the late works, which can be technically analysed. Adorno does not seek the key to these laws, however, primarily in Beethoven's inclination towards sharp contrasts, extremes of tessitura and abrupt transitions—all of which are emphasised often enough—but rather in those seemingly indifferent 'formulae and expressions of convention', by which are loosely intended the chains of trills, cadential figurations, ornaments or accompanying figurations that 'the middle period would barely have tolerated',[8] and which now vehemently rejected the integration found in the former stylistic unity. For Adorno, Beethoven's late style is not just the deliberate heightening of creative subjectivity but, on the contrary, a disturbing withdrawal from the dominant aesthetic, giving the impression of fragmentation and the demolition of form: 'It explodes them, not in order to express itself, but to throw off inexpressively the appearance of art'.[9] In this outlandish interpretation, Beethoven's unwieldy late style becomes a compositional self-criticism of the synthesis of styles in Viennese Classicism and, with it, a paradigmatic, classic case of aesthetic modernity. Beethoven's late works are for Adorno no longer graphic symbols, but allegories, which are difficult to decipher.

If today one wants to avoid the concept of the 'late work', laden as it is with ideologies and mystification, by falling back, like Riezler or Adorno, on the terminological possibility of 'late style', one in a certain sense jumps from the frying pan into the fire. This is because the musicological concept of style—although represented so prominently in Guido Adler's programmatic standard work[10]—is regarded with suspicion and, at least in German-language musicology, considered an idealist construct. One can infer this justifiable suspicion immediately from a critical analysis of Adorno's Beethoven essay, because here Adorno manages to separate the 'late style' of Beethoven, in a critically emphatic sense, from a quite retrospectively affirmative 'late work'. Nothing better clarifies that Adorno's historically and philosophically ambitious concept 'late style' is an ideological construct.[11]

Biographical Caesura

At least with respect to the tradition of German aesthetics and music philosophy, these rather complicated reflections are unfortunately necessary in order to free what follows from the ideological connotations of the concepts 'late work' and 'late style', even if they might appear to the English-speaking reader a little like conceptual acrobatics. In any case, we can now say that when it comes to Schubert we are naturally also concerned with 'last works'. In a purely chronological sense, this is a question of the works from the final years, which certainly have many important features in common with each other, whilst also being distinctive; as a result, they reject the collective singular of 'the' late work. It is true that one could play off an emphatic internalised 'late style' in such works as the last three Piano Sonatas, the Piano Trios, the String Quintet and the *Winterreise* or the Heine lieder against the far less subtle and external impact of such cautious 'late works' as the Violin Fantasie (D 934), the Rondo in B minor (D 895) and the *Konzertlied* 'Der Hirt auf dem Felsen'. This, however, would in effect repeat Adorno's sophistic argumentative trick. Obviously this captures an aspect of Schubert's late oeuvre: meditative works for private reception coexist with compositions full of effects for a more public performance; inwardness and virtuosity do not preclude one another, and that appears to follow an exactly calculated plan.

This is seen very impressively in the great four-movement Fantasie for Violin and Piano in C Major, D 934. In it many of the above-named characteristics are indissolubly united. First of all, it presents one of the innovative experiments with cyclical form that Schubert was presciently to develop (seminally in the 'Wanderer' Fantasy and later again in the F minor Fantasy,

D 940). By way of example, here is the sonata form that was obligatory for the great cycles of works (also in the other fantasies) in the triple Hegelian sense of the words of *delere, elevare* and *conservare*—literally removed, enhanced and (paradoxically) preserved. The work thereby profits from the type of development for which Schubert had paved the way in all large-scale instrumental forms around this time. Secondly, the fantasie presents, in addition to this complex constructivism, a certain inclination towards open virtuosity and obvious effect-chasing, which are generally associated with the solo concerto and therefore intended for the concert podium, to which Schubert the universalist did not contribute, as is well-known. The violin part exhibits tremendous technical difficulties, which are not to be found in any of the remaining chamber music—apart from the Rondo in B minor, D 895, which is related in form. Thirdly, this virtuosity is however directly connected with the series of variations in the third movement. And, in an impressive paradox, its point of departure is built on one of the most inward, beautiful and rapturous of Schubert's lieder, the Rückert lied 'Sei mir gegrüßt' (D 741). This is exactly the practice that Alfred Einstein rebuked in 1952 in the virtuoso flute variations composed a few years earlier on the sorrowful lied 'Trockne Blumen' from *Die schöne Müllerin*: 'Es betrübt den Verehrer Schuberts, ein Lied so einziger Innigkeit und Verhaltenheit überhaupt einer virtuosen Behandlung ausgesetzt zu sehen und schließlich verwandelt in einen triumphalen Marsch—ein Sakrileg, das sich niemand anders gestatten durfte als Schubert selbst' (It is depressing for any lover of Schubert to see a song of such unique intensity and restraint subjected to a virtuoso treatment and transformed eventually into a triumphant march—a sacrilege which no one but Schubert could have been allowed to commit).[12] Technically speaking, however, the overstepping of the formal boundaries and, sociologically speaking, the mixture of audiences is precisely consistent with the objectives of the 'late' Schubert; in these strategies experiences are merged, which draw upon paths taken in previous years. A fine example of this is the lied 'Der Hirt auf dem Felsen', composed in the last year of Schubert's life for Anna Milder, through which the addition of the obbligato clarinet crosses the boundary between lied and concert aria (and, with regards to the commissioner, was also intended for concert performance).

It is altogether problematic to divide up into different phases and epochs the oeuvre of one who died so young; in fact, Schubert's compositional development was fluent in the last year of his life. A definite break, however, is noticeable, which launches the strategic new orientation mentioned above. In the spring of 1824, when the composer was twenty-seven years old and on his way to recovering after a long illness, Schubert wrote the famous letter to his painter friend Leopold Kupelwieser in Rome after the prospects of a breakthrough with music-theatrical works for the Kärntnertortheater had gone up in smoke, for decisive external reasons:

Die Oper von Deinem Bruder (der nicht sehr wohl that, daß er vom Theater wegging) wurde für unbrauchbar erklärt, u. mithin meine Musik nicht in Ansprache genommen. Die Oper von Castelli, *Die Verschwornen*, ist in Berlin von einem dortigen Compositeur componiert, mit Beyfall aufgenommen worden. Auf diese Art hätte ich also wieder zwey Opern umsonst komponirt. In Liedern habe ich wenig Neues gemacht, dagegen versuchte ich mich in mehreren Instrumental-Sachen, denn ich componirte 2 Quartetten für Violinen, Viola u. Violoncelle u. ein Octett, u. will noch ein Quartetto schreiben, überhaupt will ich mir auf diese Art den Weg zur großen Sinfonie bahnen.—Das Neueste in Wien ist, daß Beethoven ein Concert gibt, in welchem er seine neue Sinfonie, 3 Stücke aus der neuen Messe, u. eine neue Ouverture produciren läßt.—Wenn Gott will, so bin ich auch gesonnen, künftiges Jahr ein ähnliches Concert zu geben.[13]

[The opera by your brother (who did not do too well in leaving the theatre) has been declared unsuitable, and thus my music was not considered. Castelli's opera, *The Conspirators*, has been set by a local composer in Berlin and received with acclamation. In this way I seem once again to have composed two operas for nothing. With regards to songs, I have not written many new ones, but I have tried my hand at several instrumental works, for I wrote two quartets for violins, viola and cello, and an octet, and I want to write another quartet; I intend to pave the way towards a grand symphony.—The latest in Vienna is that Beethoven is to give a concert at which he is to produce his new symphony, three movements from the new mass and a new overture.—God willing, I too am thinking of giving a similar concert next year.]

Many points, all tightly interconnected, can be singled out as noteworthy in this passage:

1. After the final rejection of the 'heroic-romantic' opera *Fierrabras* by the directors of the Kärntnertortheater,[14] Schubert himself becomes aware of a marked, conscious shift of focus away from opera and song, and towards instrumental works.
2. These instrumental works—by which is meant the great chamber music of the spring of 1824 (among them, the Octet, D 803, and the String Quartet D 810, *Death and the Maiden*)—are to 'pave the way to a great symphony'.
3. Schubert mentions Beethoven's announcement of a concert (which took place two months later in May 1824), which was to include the premiere of the Ninth Symphony and some movements from the *Missa solemnis*.
4. In the foreseeable future, Schubert wants to mount a similar concert, at his own expense and with his own works (a plan he in fact carried out, but only many years later, in March 1828).

Apart from the fact that the concert plan copied from Beethoven demonstrates remarkable self-confidence, there has been much debate about

Schubert's aim of a paving a 'way to a great symphony'. This formulation has mostly been taken to indicate that the great chamber works of 1824 were preliminary compositional exercises for something greater, which a year and a half later would in fact be tackled in the form of the 'Great' C major Symphony. This interpretation, however, makes little sense. The great, late string quartets would thereby be completely and very unreliably reduced to simple compositional, technical finger exercises. Yet Schubert had not the slightest need of such exercises in any technical, formal or instrumental sense.

One of the instrumental works mentioned in this letter shows evidence of a systematic synthesis of forms that predates the Violin Fantasie. The second movement of the String Quartet in D minor, D 810, develops seminally the technique of using a lied—and, indeed, one of a most inward character—as the foundation of a series of variations. There is also a significant element taken from *Fierrabras*, which is very subtle and almost untraceably concealed for the non-expert: the coda of the opening movement integrates that idiosyncratic and unmistakeable Schubertian cadential formula found in the duet sung by Emma and Karl (D 796, No. 19), which was sufficiently important as a harmonic invention for Schubert that he also added it to the beginning of the *Fierrabras* overture.[15] Lied, opera, chamber music and 'the way towards a great symphony' form a complex mixture in this compositional strategy, indicating the extent to which Schubert very rationally calculated his next steps.

From this point of view, a clear consciousness of the sociological and aesthetic aspects of the concept of musical forms manifests itself in Schubert's famous formulation of the 'path towards a great symphony'.[16] The system is striking whereby Schubert successfully takes the path, in the chamber music of 1824, which will lead him to the public forum of the great symphony: to paying listeners at a concert of works composed with them in mind as the target audience. This was a project which he was finally able to realise in his 'private concert' of 26 March 1828 (although not as a symphonic concert like Beethoven, but 'only' as a chamber music concert). For Schubert, a composer of chamber music and also of symphonies, this was a new approach, a radical, sociological change of paradigm in Schubert's compositional direction—enabled not least through the string-quartet subscription concerts led by Ignaz Schuppanzigh, who had just returned to Vienna,[17] in the framework of which one of the string quartets (A minor, D 804) mentioned in the letter to Kupelwieser was performed on 14 March 1824. From this point of view, the pioneering of a path to the 'great symphony' via the composition of large-scale chamber music follows an exact and rational calculation. By contrast with everything found in earlier chamber music composed for friends or family, the works of the spring of 1824—as expressed so clearly in the letter to Kupelwieser— are now ever more consciously aimed at the general public. This sociologically orientated change in Schubert's mature works corresponds completely to aesthetic, structural characteristics, which are first recognisable in the interaction with generic norms. The musical genre—here, the genre of the 'symphony'—is just as much an aesthetic logical form as it is a social institution.

Among the aesthetic-structural characteristics, I must at least emphasise—although for reasons of space I cannot elaborate upon—Schubert's constructive and innovative handling of sonata form, which would undoubtedly be considered as belonging to the most influential characteristics of the 'late' (or, better, mature) personal style, and which affected the wider history of instrumental music.[18] There are various interactive harmonic and structural measures, all of which occur in the works composed after the 'break' of 1824 (which today, however, I would no longer simply unite without reservation under the concept of the 'late work', as I did twenty-five years ago):[19] modulations, sudden shifts and key relations through which the dramaturgical model of sonata form has historically been hugely altered[20] and which has led to a certain expansion of form, which Robert Schumann called 'heavenly length'[21] and Martin Chusid labelled with the unsurpassable expression 'spaciousness'.[22] For the first time in the 'last' works of Schubert those risky and (according to 'Classical' sonata principles) unacceptable modulations through enharmonic keys in the exposition can finally be found through which a clear destination of the process intentionally becomes blurred and which were later taken up by Liszt, Bruckner and Dvořák as technical enrichment[23]—well-known examples are found in first movement of the E♭ major Piano Trio, D 929 (bars 36–45) and the last Piano Sonata, D 960 (bars 43–48).

Last Maturity

I had already mentioned the curious coincidence whereby Beethoven's 'late style', which is generally accepted in research, overlaps with the 'last' works of Schubert. This suggests that we come back once more to the characteristics of late style that Adorno emphasised in Beethoven. In his Schubert essay of 1928 Adorno characterised the enchantment, the surprise, but also the disturbing element of the almost completely personal style of modulation which can be found, for example, in the first movement of the great C major Symphony or the String Quintet, which Adorno, at the same time, attempts to contextualise from a perspective of compositional history and in a historical-philosophical frame of reference:

> Schubert's forms are forms of invocation of what once appeared, not of the metamorphosis of the invented. This a priori foundation completely took hold of the sonata. In place of developed connecting movements, there were harmonic shifts as round-exposures that would lead to a new topological area that knows as little development in itself as what has gone before.... Not for nothing are Schubert's changes of mood ... connected to the harmonic

shifts, the handling of modulation, which, by the same token, causes light to fall out of changing depths. Those sudden, unmediated modulations, incapable of development, like photographic filters, distort the light from above.[24]

It is therefore the absence of history and development in an emphatic sense that Adorno heard in Schubert's handling of sonata form. This circumstance of being out of time and space—and the broad dimensions of form engendered by such means (which, as mentioned above, Chusid called 'spaciousness')—permitted him to have recourse to one of the main characteristic metaphors of his entire essay: the presentation of Schubert's music not as a process, but as a landscape—and indeed, one whose details develop not in chronological succession but according to the spatial aspect of passing through it. It is evident that here the figure of the wanderer is modelled on the protagonists of the two great Wilhelm Müller song cycles—*Die schöne Müllerin* and *Winterreise*. Much more important, however, is that Adorno also applied a different aspect of his peculiar metaphor to Beethoven a little later. Here for the first time in his review of Beethoven's late bagatelles there is talk of a landscape consisting of rubble, which would already contain the ingredients that Adorno will diagnose in Beethoven's late style as the disassociation and decay of classical forms. At this stage of his own musical-aesthetic development, the mature Schubert and the late Beethoven are, for Adorno, the two composers who have broken through the affirmative appearance of Viennese classicism: Schubert through a rejection of the formal principles of the Classical sonata; Beethoven through a criticism of the classical principles of form through the composition of his own late works. This, at the same time, is why Beethoven, and not Schubert—exploited journalistically much earlier by Adorno—should become the central theme of his main musical, philosophical work, bearing the succinct title 'Beethoven'. Beethoven is, for Adorno—and this is the really fascinating aspect of Beethoven's career—a dialectical composer, so to speak, who in the course of his own development not only brought classical principles of form to an unparalleled zenith, but had developed his work into a criticism of his very own principle.

As already indicated, Adorno's interpretation of Beethoven implied the separation of some late works from the realm of late style—an almost absurd consequence of the imposed conformism to which he subjugated his own interpretation of style, a consequence that I do not want to pursue any further here. Yet Adorno's interpretation has also had consequences for Schubert reception—especially since the reissuing of the 1964 Schubert essays in the *Moments musicaux* by the author, who had in the meantime become famous. Schubert's music is—as we can all agree today—anything but charming, leisurely or harmless; rather, it is truly profound in thought and, as Thomas Mann once said about Schubert's long-undervalued contemporary, Adalbert Stifter, full of 'quiet catastrophes'. And often enough the catastrophes are not even quiet: one thinks, for example, of the middle sections of the slow movements of the late Piano Sonata in A major or the String Quintet, as well as some songs from *Winterreise*. The perception of this deeply disturbing dimension has conspicuously increased in Schubert studies since the mid-twentieth century, a change that, as mentioned, has essentially to do with the delayed reception of Adorno's great Schubert essay. Schubert has today—as if the Biedermeier cliché in reception history needed to be restored—been projected onto a sceptical, distraught state of the world; the image of his wanderer from *Winterreise* has virtually become a symbol of existential homelessness, if I interpret correctly the journalistic, popularised and even academic literature since the last two centenary years. The composer himself has basically been cured of the Biedermeier cosiness of the 'Dreimäderlhaus'—quite fortunately, one could say, if it had not been replaced by an equally distorted reception cliché. For it is hardly possible to integrate into the complete works those from the final years of Schubert's life, which cannot be mediated through this concept of the negation of life and history: first and foremost, the great, extroverted, virtuosic works such as the Violin Fantasie, and furthermore all the song and dance compositions, relate to a sphere of bourgeois sociability which to this day one can hardly grasp any better than by using the concept of Biedermeier.[25]

The entire complex of Schubert's last works is, therefore, very difficult to bring under a uniform concept of 'late works'. But there are, in this body of work, overarching stylistic traits which are characteristic of Schubert in 1828 and which had been prepared in the works since 1824—even if these are not 'late style' in the presence of death, but rather mark a mature middle style corresponding to the personal consciousness of a composer, which only through the biographical chance of the sudden early death has been imbued with the aura of 'lateness'. Equally interesting is the attempt to make visible some of these stylistic features of the late Schubert in a kind of productive assimilation through compositional reception history. In a tonal realisation of the 1828 sketch for the Symphony in D major (D 936A), of which Schubert could sketch only three movements before death took the quill from his hand, the Italian composer Luciano Berio logically developed this aspect of the material further. His instrumental reconstruction, with the telling title *Rendering* (1989–90), does not claim to realise as exact and philologically valid a picture as possible of this symphonic bequest, but rather to comment upon and to interpret it. As Berio proceeded, he further fragmented Schubert's already fragmentary sketch and connected the bequeathed fragments with passages of his own to form a complete composition. These added passages, however, have as their material basis melodic and harmonic citations from other works by Schubert in his last compositional year—for example, from *Winterreise, Schwanengesang* and the last Piano Sonata. Admittedly, all of these citations are no longer audible as such; they are only revealed from a close reading of the score or, even better, by research on the sketches that Berio has left behind.[26] Through this one forms a picture of the criterion for Berio's selection of these quotation fragments—which are partly insignificant—as *tertium comparationis*: they circle around a melodic sound in a way that is typical of Schubert's late melodic language, as in the second subject in the first movement of the String Quintet, D 956 (bars 60–100), or which a glance at the first subject of the B♭ major Piano Sonata, D 960, could establish. Berio's compositional commentary on Schubert's late work implies, therefore, a very peculiar Schubert interpretation: a kind of generative transfomational grammar of Schubert's late melodic construction. The great appeal of this work lies not least in that.

This 'last' style of Schubert's is, along with the melodic qualities singled out by Berio (which, incidentally, Peter Gülke also pointed out very powerfully in his monograph[27]), are nevertheless characterised above all by structural features that are established in the harmony and lead to the 'spaciousness' identified by Chusid: experimention with mediant relations, derivation of formal key schemes from the structure of 'symmetrical' key chords, the increasing radicalism of the process of modulation leading to the consequent functionalisation of enharmonics and a new kind of concern with contrapuntal techniques (most perceptible in the E♭ major Mass, the F minor Fantasy and the third movement of the D major symphonic fragments), which definitely contributed to the late decision to take a course with Simon Sechter.[28] The 'break' of the spring of 1824, emphasised above, very obviously triggered a strategic reorientation and an enormous dynamic in Schubert's development. It is probably much more appropriate, therefore, to speak less of a 'late' style than of a 'new' style.[29] When Johnnes Brahms was the age at which Schubert died, he had just reached his 'first maturity'.[30] Biographical chance has seen to it that in the case of Schubert the 'first' (or perhaps also already the 'second') has, regrettably, remained the 'last maturity'. Whether, therefore, as Franz Grillparzer formulated in his fine epitaph, the buried 'hopes' were more beautiful than the 'rich possession',[31] Robert Schumann already doubted, and with good reason. Schubert's 'late style', in complete contrast to that of the late Beethoven, is characterised not by serene consolidation and critical balancing, but by a euphoric departure on a journey which was broken off in mid-flight.

Translated by Lorraine Byrne Bodley

Notes

1. Herman Grimm, *Das Leben Raphael's* (1872; Berlin: W. Hertz, rev. 1896), p. 148.

2. Carl Dahlhaus, *Ludwig van Beethoven und seine Zeit* (Laaber: Laaber-Verlag,1987), p. 263.

3. See Michael Spitzer, *Music as Philosophy: Adorno and Beethoven's Late Style* (Bloomington: Indiana University Press, 2006).

4. Paul Bekker, *Beethoven* (1911; Berlin: Schuster und Loeffler, rev. 1912), p. 195.

5. Ibid.

6. Ibid.

7. Walther Riezler, *Beethoven* (Berlin: Atlantis-Verlag, 1936), p. 233.

8. Theodor W. Adorno, *Spätstil Beethovens* (1937), in Theodor W. Adorno, *Gesammelte Schriften*, ed. Rolf Tiedemann (Frankfurt am Main: Suhrkamp, 1970–86), vol. 17, p. 14.

9. Ibid., p. 15.

10. Guido Adler, *Der Stil in der Musik* (1911; Leipzig: Breitkopf & Härtel, rev. 1929).

11. On Adorno's Beethoven reception as a whole see Hans-Joachim Hinrichsen, 'Modellfall der Philosophie der Musik: Beethoven', in Richard Klein, Johann Kreuzer and Stefan Müller-Doohm (eds), *Adorno-Handbuch* (Stuttgart: Metzler-Verlag, 2011), pp. 85–96.

12. Alfred Einstein, *Schubert: ein musikalisches Porträt* (Zurich: Pan-Verlag 1952), p. 282.

13. Franz Schubert, letter to Leopold Kupelwieser, 31 March 1824; quoted in Otto Erich Deutsch, *Franz Schubert: Die Dokumente seines Lebens* (Kassel: Bärenreiter-Verlag, 1964), p. 235.

14. See Thomas A. Denny, 'Schubert's "Fierrabras" and Barbaja's Opera Business', in *Schubert: Perspektiven* 5 (2005), 19–45, especially 44.

15. See Hans-Joachim Hinrichsen, '"Bergendes Gehäuse" und "Hang ins Unbegrenzte". Die Kammermusik', in Walther Dürr and Andreas Krause (eds), *Schubert-Handbuch* (Kassel: Bärenreiter-Verlag, 1997), pp. 491 ff.

16. Note that in the original German wording ('den Weg zur großen Sinfonie') Schubert deliberately uses the definite article ('zur' is the abbreviation of 'zu der'), not the indefinite article as is the case in the common English version of this famous quote. What Schubert is aiming at can best be described as the idea of compositional 'greatness' which may be epitomized not in 'a grand symphony', but in 'the' great symphony as an ideal of greatness and grandeur altogether.

17. On Schuppanzigh's return to Vienna in April 1823, see Salome Reiser, *Franz Schuberts frühe Streichquartette: Eine klassische Gattung am Beginn einer nachklassischen Zeit* (Kassel: Bärenreiter-Verlag, 1999), pp. 206–11.

18. Hans-Joachim Hinrichsen, *Untersuchungen zur Entwicklung der Sonatenform in der Instrumentalmusik Franz Schuberts*, Veröffentlichungen des Internationalen Franz Schubert Instituts 11 (Tutzing: C. H. Beck, 1994).

19. Hans-Joachim Hinrichsen, 'Die Sonatenform im Spätwerk Franz Schuberts', *Archiv für Musikwissenschaft* 45 (1988), pp. 16–49.

20. The standard reference for this viewpoint is formed in James Webster, 'Schubert's Sonata Form and Brahms' First Maturity', *19th-Century Music* 2 (1978), pp. 18–35, and 3 (1979), pp. 52–71.

21. In the course of German- and English-language reception history, Schumann's term 'himmlische Länge' (heavenly length) has suddenly become appropriated in the plural ('Längen'), which is, in reality, a snide remark. Whereas *Länge* signals praise (or, at the very least, can be read that way), *Längen* in music is always negative.

22. Martin Chusid, 'The Chamber Music of Schubert' (PhD diss., University of California, 1961), p. 245.

23. Hans-Joachim Hinrichsen, ' "Romantische" Harmonik u. "klassisches" Sonatenprinzip: zum Funktionswandel der Sonatenexposition im 19. Jahrhundert', *Archiv für Musikwissenschaft* 50 (1993), pp. 217–31.

24. Theodor W. Adorno, *Schubert* [1928], in *Gesammelte Schriften*, 20 vols. (Frankfurt: Suhrkamp/Insel, 1997) vol. 17, 27 and 29 f.

25. Compare contributions in Michael Kube, Werner Adelhold, and Walburga Litschauer (eds), *Schubert und das Biedermeier: Beiträge zur Musik des frühen 19. Jahrhunderts; Festschrift für Walther Dürr zum 70. Geburtstag* (Kassel: Bärenreiter-Verlag, 2002).

26. The sketches are held in the Paul Sacher Stiftung, Basel. For a close reading of Berio's composition see Hans-Joachim Hinrichsen, ' "Rendering per Orchestra": Luciano Berios komponierter Essay über Schuberts Spätwerk', *Schubert: Perspektiven* 2 (2002), 135–66.

27. Peter Gülke, *Franz Schubert und seine Zeit* (Laaber: Laaber-Verlag, 1991), p. 319: 'Umkreisung könnte geradehin als der Grundhabitus schubertscher Musik gelten' (Circling could be considered the habitual basis of Schubert's music).

28. Rita Steblin, 'Studying with Sechter: Newly Recovered Reminiscences about Schubert by His Forgotten Friend, the Composer Joseph Lanz', *Music & Letters* 88 (2007), pp. 226–65.

29. Compare with William Kinderman, 'Franz Schuberts "Neuer Stil" und das Erbe Beethovens', *Schubert: Perspektiven* 9 (2009), pp. 60–79; translated into as chapter 3 in this volume.

30. James Webster, "Schubert's Sonata Form and Brahms' First Maturity", *19th-Century Music* 2 (1978), pp. 18–35, and 3 (1979), pp. 52–71.

31. 'Die Tonkunst begrub hier einen reichen Besitz, / Aber noch viel schönere Hoffnungen' (The art of music here buried a rich possession / But far fairer hopes). Deutsch, *Franz Schubert: Die Dokumente seines Lebens*, 580).

2

Compositional Strategies in Schubert's Late Music

Walther Dürr

Schubert's late compositions—that is to say, those written between 1826 and 1828—are commonly connected with two rather contrasting interpretations. On the one hand, there is the view expressed by Franz Grillparzer, a poet close to Schubert, whose epitaph, formulated nine months after Schubert's death, is often cited (though also with considerable reservations): 'The art of music here entombed a rich possession, but even far fairer hopes'.[1] On the other hand, there is that adopted by Walther Vetter, who gave the fifth and last part of his monumental Schubert biography the title 'Vollendung des Klassikers' ('Fulfillment of the Classical Composer'), a title that alludes not only to Schubert's 'fulfilment', but to that of an entire era in music history.[2] Even Peter Gülke, who sees anticipations of Gustav Mahler in the symphonic fragment D 936A (which originated shortly before Schubert's death),[3] insists in his Schubert monograph, 'Schubert never moved beyond the positions taken in *Lazarus*, the Mass in A♭ major, and the Unfinished Symphony'.[4] True, there is no longer any talk about 'fulfilment'—at least not explicitly. It is, however, implied: if Schubert continued to compose new works after those just mentioned, it only can mean that he wanted to consolidate positions he had reached. In the following, I would like to show that Grillparzer's statement at least jibes with Schubert's own judgement about the works of his last years: far from being a 'fulfilment', the works open new avenues for the composer, rather than consolidate existing positions. I will focus on the Piano Trio in E♭ major (D 929), composed in November 1827 (one year before Schubert's death), a work that—to quote Gülke again[5]—must be considered, together with the Piano Trio in B♭ major (D 897) and the String Quartet in G major (D 887), as one of those compositions that lead from the crisis years and the breakthroughs of 1824 to the instrumental music of Schubert's last months. It is a work that reveals, in exemplary fashion, the directions the composer was taking in his last years.

Three areas in particular seem to indicate the new directions: first, Schubert shows an increased interest in contrapuntal techniques; secondly, he pays more attention to thematic, especially motivic and submotivic relationships; and thirdly, we encounter a new kind of sonority. These areas, of course, are not really new, but their emphasis amounts to a new assessment of their importance for compositional structure. And it may also have something to do with Schubert's more intensive orientation towards the Beethovenian model.[6] It seems as if the younger composer is turning more freely towards the older one, especially since, after Beethoven's death, he believes that he no longer needs to compete directly with the master.

Counterpoint

Contrapuntal techniques had played a role in Schubert's oeuvre since his youth, especially since his counterpoint studies with Antonio Salieri.[7] These techniques had a clear function: Schubert used them as he had learned to do in his youth, as a means of characterisation in a certain style of sacred music. Thus, we encounter fugues in the concluding culminations in the Gloria movements of his masses, or as sections highlighting a particular number of a sacred work, for example in the middle and end of the German *Stabat Mater* (D 383). Furthermore, he used counterpoint in secular works, either in playful occasional music (in this case, he simply wrote canons for his circle of friends in the style of Michael Haydn or Salieri)[8] or for important moments in his operas (thereby meeting the expectations of opera audiences for intricate vocal ensembles, the so-called *pezzi concertati*).[9] In both instances, contrapuntal techniques are used selectively, as it were. In his later works, however, they pervade the texture of entire movements.

At this point it is worth remembering that Schubert studied the late works of Beethoven and alluded to them in his own compositions.[10] He was also occupied with compositions of the old masters. He regularly attended the private concerts of Georg Kiesewetter[11] and had got to know Bach and Handel, in addition to Palestrina. Since 1824 he had engaged in an intensive study of Handel and asked that Bach's *Well-Tempered Clavier* be sent to him.[12] Numerous works of his last years show traces of these studies, for example the Mass in E♭ major (D 950), not only the great fugues but also the canon in the 'Incarnatus est' of the Credo as well as the fugato in the 'Dona nobis pacem' of the Agnus Dei. And then there is *Miriams Siegesgesang* (D 942), the Fantasy in F minor for piano duet (D 940), and the finale of an unfinished Symphony in D major (D 936A).[13]

How Schubert manages contrapuntal techniques and how they define entire musical structures can be seen in the Piano Trio in E♭ major. I will focus initially on the Scherzo movement. Schubert himself—in a letter to the publisher Probst[14]—called the movement's trio a minuet and in the official title avoided the term 'Scherzo', replacing it with 'Scherzando'. The tempo indication 'Allegro moderato' makes clear why: it is indeed a minuet rather than a scherzo. And this tempo not only legitimises contrapuntal procedures (here one thinks of the contrapuntal style in some minuets by Joseph Haydn, which

Example 2.1 Schubert, Trio in E♭ major for Piano, Violin and Violoncello, D 929, iii, Scherzo, bars 1–8[29]

may have been a model for Schubert), but also allows an increased audibility of the individual voices by way of imitation: it makes them more transparent. Schubert organises the main section of the movement initially as a canon (see Example 2.1; the trio, as will be discussed later, follows different principles).

The beginning of the movement (the first twenty-seven bars) is a canon between the right hand of the piano and the two strings. Then, separated from the preceding through a typically Schubertian harmonic switch from A♭ major (arrived at in bar 23) to E major, a new section follows, in which Schubert replaces the strict canon with free imitation. Strictly speaking, the section continues in a two-part texture, now assigned to the piano's right hand and the cello, while the violin adds accompaniment figures and the left hand provides the harmonic foundation. It is noteworthy here that Schubert does not follow intervallic guidelines (in the sense of a 'real' answer). In the reminiscences of Joseph Lanz mentioned earlier, this issue is addressed as follows:

> One day, I showed him a little double fugue I composed [this may have been the beginning of their acquaintance]. The theme leaped from the tonic to the dominant and, in turn, the answer from the dominant into the tonic. He asked: 'Why did you not make the answer the same?' When I told him that I had proceeded according to generally accepted conventions in order not to move away prematurely from the home key, he smiled.[15]

Indeed, Schubert until about 1825 retained the real answer in his fugues, which he valued higher than the tonal one, hardly paying attention to the attendant problems of key;[16] after that, tonal answers became the rule. Schubert's (probably) ironic smile may be explained by a comment of Gottfried von Preyer, who, like Schubert, studied with Salieri: 'Schubert despised dry and monotonous didactic examples and the mechanical observations of pre-conceived formulas. He always thought that the barren system of rules would only limit his flight of thoughts'.[17]

After the middle section, the movement modulates back to E♭ major and returns to the initial theme and thereby to the canon of the beginning, but this time reversing the succession: the strings begin, the piano answers. Schubert tries out several other canonic possibilities before the movement concludes with a free coda of sixteen bars.

Canonic constructions also play a role in the Finale of the Piano Trio. Repeated pulsing quavers characterise the movement's secondary theme. They seem to be derived from the secondary theme of the first movement and thus appear almost as an episode whose sole function is to establish cyclical links. The theme is, however, of significance for the entire movement, as the continuation of the Finale shows. At the end of the exposition, it returns transformed, developing out of a diminished seventh chord and suddenly assuming the attributes of a three-part canon,[18] in which, however, the answer of the strings appears partly shortened (as if they try to catch up with the hurriedly advancing piano). Finally all three instruments land on the diminished seventh chord that got everything started, although it does not quite fit the canon's key. After that, everything begins anew until finally all three instruments find their way out of the playful conundrum (see Example 2.2).

Example 2.2 Schubert, Trio in E♭ major, D 929, iv, Scherzo, bars 165–178[30]

Despite all the apparent motion, we encounter stasis—comparable to the surprising fermatas and discontinuations so characteristic for Schubert's late works. Something entirely new can nevertheless evolve from them. The same constellation returns in the development section of the Finale, expanded to fifty bars, and also in the recapitulation, thereby imbuing the entire movement with an unmistakable identity.

Motivic and Sub-motivic Connections

Schubert scholars have repeatedly pointed out that his compositions are characterised by subliminal links, as it were, which hold together the individual sections of a composition, even when they are not thematically related. Peter Gülke has shown this, for instance, in the String Quintet of 1828, Carl Dahlhaus in the Unfinished Symphony (composed as early as 1822) and others even in the early string quartets.[19] In other words, this seems to be a consistent factor in Schubert's creativity. Yet it is hardly possible, as a rule, to distinguish whether such sub-thematic connections are intentionally employed to structure the music or simply manifest themselves as a result of his musical thinking. When we encounter, for instance, the interval f'-e' over and over again in similar constellations in *Winterreise*—the cycle begins that way—regardless in which key a song is written, we may assume that Schubert uses this feature in a calculated way. The pitches, we should remember, implied for the singer at the time a characteristic change of register, namely the change from chest to head voice. Thus, the interval becomes also one of those elements that weld the entire cycle into a unity, which the listener may perceive aurally, but which can be described only with difficulty.

A fortunate circumstance, however, makes it possible to witness Schubert's compositional process in detail in the Piano Trio in E♭ major—not only to observe the connections, but also to prove that Schubert did not use them casually. In the reminiscences of Leopold Sonnleithner we can read the following:

> The famous singer Josef Siboni, then director of the conservatory in Copenhagen, had a student named [Isak Albert] Berg, who was a young tenor of outstanding talent.... Berg, who later became the first teacher of Jenny Lind, arrived in Vienna in the winter of 1827–28 with a recommendation to the Mademoiselles Fröhlich [close friends of Schubert], in whose small social circle he frequently performed. With extraordinary beauty he sang Swedish folk songs, and Schubert, who heard him on one such occasion, was delighted by these Swedish songs. He asked for a copy and used the most outstanding ones in his E♭ major Trio.[20]

It has been difficult to find the Swedish songs that Schubert used in his Trio. But thirty years ago Manfred Wilford[21] was able to prove that Schubert did indeed use a Swedish song in the piece, perhaps a song composed by Isak Albert Berg himself,[22] beginning with the words 'Se solen sjunker' (See the sun setting). It is in D minor,[23] but it has the same motion and the same tempo as the Andante movement of the Trio. Schubert, however, did not use the beginning of the song, as one might assume from Sonnleithner's report; and he did not use it as the theme of the movement, but only in individual elements (see Example 2.3).

Example 2.3 Isak. A. Berg, 'Se solen sjunker' (transposed into C minor) and Schubert, Trio in E♭ major, D 929

The first of these elements (Berg, bars 14ff.; Schubert, bars 17ff.) is a longer section. True, it is not a complete theme, only the conclusion of the principal theme. Important for Schubert here was the melodic eruption, consisting of a large leap of a minor tenth in a relatively exposed register; there are similar melodic eruptions in the movement, including some without the linkage to the principal theme. The second element (Berg, bars 19ff.; Schubert, bars 11ff.) leads into an appoggiatura with the characteristic dissonance of a seventh, d′–e♭′, that may have attracted Schubert. In Berg's song, the appoggiatura directly follows the first passage; in the case of Schubert, it far precedes it. The musical context of both elements has been abandoned; they are used as individual, independent particles. The third element is of greatest significance for the movement (Berg, bars 9ff.; Schubert, bars 15ff.). It is a simple interval, the leap of an octave, connected in Berg's song with the word 'ferväl' (farewell). This leap is for Schubert so important—perhaps even in terms of content—that it appears in the movement repeatedly in all kinds of combinations, not only as an octave, but also as an individual motive. It can be easily discerned from the notation when the octave becomes a motive: as a rule, it appears with accents and staccato markings, as is the case in our example, and always in form of an upbeat. What I have in mind can easily be shown at the end of the movement (see Example 2.4).

As can be seen, the motive has the last word; even in triple *piano* it retains its accents and staccato markings. Just a little earlier, we also find it in the strings (bars 187–189) and the piano (bars 191–193), then again at the concluding 'Un poco più lento' in the piano (bars 196–98). In a varied and diminished version—as a descending and ascending third—it dominates the concluding section (already in bars 178–184). Indeed, Schubert developed out of it the continuation of the secondary theme. The interval, originally understood melodically, is transformed here into a rhythmic motive.

Thus we can see how Schubert derives materials (not themes) from Berg's song and how he works with these materials. It may be an obvious conclusion that

Example 2.4 Schubert, Trio in E♭ major, D 929, ii, bars 205–212[31]

he treats his own themes and thoughts in a similar manner. As is well-known, Schubert quotes the theme of the slow movement three times in the finale, and he quotes all three elements just discussed. Again, the octave leap is of particular significance. In the first and second instances (bars 302–306 and bars500–504, respectively), the octave leap is part of the thematic quotation; but at the end it becomes obvious that the resistant upbeat figures in the piano are to be understood as having been derived from the octave leap (note the accents and staccato markings in the strings in bars 831ff. and compare them with the piano passages that accompanied the thematic quotation earlier). In other words, this rhythmic motive—not the interval—becomes a constituent part also of the Finale.

Striving for a New Sonority

During Schubert's lifetime, the concept of sonority as an independent parameter and characteristic of a composition was something modern and forward-looking that, in turn, became important for the entire nineteenth century. Sonority played only a minor role for Schubert's classical models, Haydn and Mozart, and even for Beethoven. Contemporary reviewers noticed Schubert's novel approach to sonority. Thus, in a review of Schubert's Piano Sonata in G major, Op. 78 (D 894) in the so-called *Mozeitschrift*—a sonata that could be considered a paradigm, as it were, of the composer's striving for intensified sound effects—we read: 'Both hands are fully occupied, and doubling the upper voice an octave lower and having thirds and sixths move in parallels, a manner introduced by Beethoven, seems to be favored also by Herr Schubert, because he proceeds that way quite frequently in his constructions'.[24] We encounter this special interest in sonority in Schubert's early works, but what is new in the late works is perhaps that sonority becomes significant for the structure of entire movements. Although the concept of sonority is commonly associated with timbre, this is too narrow an understanding for the present purposes. Sonority extends to specific characteristics of dynamics, for example to the dynamic range of sections [*Klangstärkeflächen*] (this is precisely is the characteristic feature of the G major Sonata just mentioned, but it also manifests itself at the beginning of the String Quintet, D 956). Sonority also implies the use of specific instruments in passages where one would least expect them. I am thinking, for instance, of Schubert's frequent use of trombones (they are even used thematically—and that was unusual at the time—as in the Great Symphony in C major).[25] The contemporary press objected to Schubert's penchant for the trombone, as can be seen in a review in Vienna's *Sammler* of the premiere of the melodrama *Die Zauberharfe*. The trombonists 'ought to have a basis that lends stability to their playing, but if they constantly have to perform pizzicato in a tempo that among the fast tempos is not the slowest—the composer indeed specifies *Allegro maestoso*—they really do not know how many crotchets they have to devour per bar'.[26] No doubt, Schubert expected too much of the trombonists of the orchestra at the Theater an der Wien in the summer of 1820. But the review also makes it clear what the composer really asked of them: they were not simply to perform the usual chorale-like movements, but to act as melody instruments. In effect, he expected the bass trombonist to have the same skills as a double bass player.

Sonority plays a role in the Trio in E♭ major,[27] although one that is perhaps not quite as pronounced as in the examples just mentioned, or as in other works that may come to mind, such as the slow movement of the String Quintet or the similarly structured Andante sostenuto of the Piano Sonata in B♭ major (D 960). But sonority puts its stamp here on an entire section of a movement, namely in the trio of the minuet discussed earlier. A strong contrast in the compositional structure is characteristic for the relation between minuet and trio in general, and more specifically for Schubert. While the main section of the movement is laid out contrapuntally, the trio is defined by sonority and rhythm (see Example 2.5).

The constituent reason for the sonority here is perhaps that Schubert does not 'develop' any melodies here, as is often the case in his trio sections. Nothing is really developed; instead, he over-accentuates the metre (*fz–p–p*), on the one hand, and dissolves the third crotchet of the violin part into a whirring tremolo. When the passage is repeated (bars 13ff.), the strings play, to the continuing accentuation of the piano (*fz–p–p*), a descending fanfare that probably is derived from the principal theme of the first movement. It appears here hardly

Example 2.5 Schubert, Trio in E♭ major, D 929, iii, Trio, bars 1–18[32]

as a theme in its own right, but rather as a quotation. In the middle section of the trio, Schubert, in turn, provides us with a reminiscence of the secondary theme of the first movement, but without turning it into an independent theme. In short, rhythmic scansion is again the essential element. Instead of the repetition of single bars from the beginning, however, Schubert now brings bars in groups of two: the stomping motion becomes more sweeping.

There can be no doubt that Schubert—as his late compositions show—is searching for new ways to expand certain techniques that had been important for him in part for quite some time. We recall a letter he wrote to Sonnleithner (Deutsch dates it to January 1823).[28] He insists to his friend, who probably asked him for additional vocal quartets for the musical evening entertainments of the Gesellschaft für Musikfreunde in Vienna, that he would only do it if he 'might succeed in inventing some new form', since his future fate was of great concern to him. In a way, Schubert in his last years (and in 1827–8 he was still very young) is still concerned with this 'new form', with avenues that are forward-looking; he was not concerned with 'fulfilment' or rounding off his career. Although his classical models were Haydn and Mozart (not Beethoven, who was important to him for finding new ways), he left them far behind. And thus Grillparzer may have been right, after all, with his gravestone inscription: 'The art of music here entombed a rich possession, but even far fairer hopes'. We have doubtless dealt here with rich possessions, but, by doing so, we have also shed light on aspirations, which the nineteenth century in its entirety was to fulfill.

Translated by Jürgen Thym

Notes

1. See Otto Erich Deutsch (ed.), *Schubert: Die Dokumente seines Lebens* (Kassel: Bärenreiter, 1964), pp. 580f.; trans. Eric Blom in Deutsch, *The Schubert Reader: a Life of Franz Schubert in Letters and Documents* (New York: W. W. Norton, 1947), p. 899.

2. Walther Vetter, *Der klassiker Schubert* (Leipzig: C. F. Peters, 1953), vol. 2, p. 177.

3. Peter Gülke, 'Neue Beiträge zur Kenntnis des Sinfonikers Schubert ...', in Heinz-Klaus Metzger and Rainer Riehm (eds), *Musik-Konzepte Sonderband Franz Schubert* (Munich: Edition Text + Kritik, 1979), pp. 187–220, especially p. 219.

4. Peter Gülke, *Schubert und seine Zeit* (Laaber: Laaber-Verlag, 1991), pp. 281 and 176.

5. Ibid., p. 281.

6. On which subject see, for instance, John Gingerich, *Schubert's Beethoven Project* (Cambridge: Cambridge University Press, 2004).

7. See Franz Schubert, *Neue Ausgabe sämtlicher Werke*, ser. VIII, vol. 2, *Schuberts Studien*, ed. Alfred Mann (Kassel: Bärenreiter, 1986). Joseph Lanz, who

together with Schubert took a counterpoint lesson with Simon Sechter on 4 November 1828, repeated in his autobiographical notes a view current in the Schubert circle, namely that lessons with Salieri consisted only of reading through scores (whereby he refers to Schubert as a source). This view may have something to do with the fact that Schubert, after 1824 (when he and Lanz met for the first time), sensed that his contrapuntal skills were no longer up to the demands he placed on himself. He justified his insufficiencies by blaming them on having been taught poorly, with 'reading through scores' having taken up the lion's share of the time. For the newly discovered documents, see Rita Steblin and Frederick Stocken, 'Studying with Sechter: Newly Recovered Reminiscences about Schubert by his Forgotten Friend, the Composer Joseph Lanz', *Music and Letters* 88 (2007), pp. 226–65, especially p. 260.

8. See Gerhard Croll, 'Kanons von Michael Haydn', in Heinrich Hüschen (ed.), *Musicae Scientiae Collectanea: Festschrift Karl Gustav Fellerer* (Cologne: 1973), pp. 64–9.

9. The great canon in the Finale to Act I of *Alfonso und Estrella* (D 732, bars 123ff.) comes to mind. See Walther Dürr, 'Schuberts romantisch-heroische Oper Alfonso und Estrella im Kontext französischer und italienischer Tradition', in Erich Wolfgang Partsch and Oskar Pausch (eds), *Der vergessene Schubert: Franz Schubert auf der Bühne* [exhibition catalogue] (Vienna, 1997), pp. 79–105, especially pp. 94f.

10. See Richard Kramer, 'Gradus ad Parnassum: Beethoven, Schubert, and the Romance of Counterpoint', *19th-Century Music* 11 (1987–8), pp. 107–20.

11. See Herfried Kier, *Raphael Georg Kiesewetter (1773–1850): Wegbereiter des musikalischen Historismus* (Regensburg: G. Bosse, 1968), pp. 178ff.

12. Letter from Ferdinand Schubert to his brother, 3 July 1824; Deutsch, *Schubert: Die Dokumente seines Lebens*, pp. 247–9. See also Walther Dürr, 'Über Schuberts Verhältnis zu Bach', in Ingrid Fuchs (ed.), *Johann Sebastian Bach: Beiträge zur Wirkungsgeschichte* (Vienna, 1992), pp. 69–79.

13. See Gülke, 'Neue Beiträge', pp. 206–8.

14. Schubert wrote to Probst on 16 May 1828: 'Be sure to have it performed for the first time by capable people, and most particularly see to a continual uniformity of tempo at the changes of the time-signature in the last movement. The minuet at a moderate pace and *piano* throughout, the trio, on the other hand, vigorous except where *p* and *pp* are marked'. Deutsch, *Schubert: Die Dokumente seines Lebens*, p. 516; Deutsch, *The Schubert Reader*, p. 774.

15. See Steblin and Stocken, 'Studying with Sechter', p. 269.

16. These are particularly noticeable in Schubert's early fugues, written for his teacher Salieri; see Mann, *Schuberts Studien*, pp. 49f.; later he avoided modulations.

17. Fritz Lange, 'Schuberts letzte Pläne: Bisher unbekannte Reminiszenzen von Schubert', *Neues Wiener Journal vom 22.5.1910*, p. 6; and see also Steblin and Stocken, 'Studying with Sechter', 266.

18. Indeed, this is a free canon: the distances between the entries are not the same (two and a half bars for piano and violoncello, two bars for violoncello and violin), the incipit of the theme changes (the four quavers on c4 in the piano become g1–g1–c2–c2 in the violoncello, in analogy to the violin) and the second bar of the theme is foreshortened by half a bar.

19. Peter Gülke, 'Zum Bilde des späten Schubert: Vorwiegend analytische Betrachtungen zum Streichquintett, Op.163', *Musik-Konzepte*, ed. Heinz-Klaus Metzger and Rainer Riehm (Munich: Text+Kritik, 1979) also *Deutsches Jahrbuch für Musikwissenschaft* 18 (1973–77), 5–58.; Carl Dahlhaus, 'Franz Schubert und das "Zeitalter Beethovens und Rossinis"', in *Franz Schubert—Jahre der Krise 1818–1823: Bericht über das Symposion, Kassel 30.9–1.10.1982; Arnold Feil zum 60. Geburtstag am 2.10.1985* (Kassel, 1985), pp. 22–8, especially p. 27; and Salome Reiser, *Franz Schuberts frühe Streichquartette: Eine klassische Gattung am Beginn einer nachklassischen Zeit* (Kassel, 1999), pp. 191ff.

20. See Otto Erich Deutsch (ed.), *Schubert: Die Erinnerungen seiner Freunde* (Leipzig, 1957), p. 97.

21. Manfred Willfort, 'Das Urbild des Andante aus Schuberts Klaviertrio Es-dur, D 929', *Österreichische Musikzeitschrift* 33 (1978), pp. 277–83; see also Cesare Fertonani, *La memoria del canto: Rielaborazioni liederistiche nella musica strumentale di Schubert* (Milan, 2005), pp. 307–11.

22. Michael Kube pointed out that it had been impossible to determine whether it was a folk song or a song composed in the style of a folk song: '"Nährstoff" nationaler Identifikation: Zur Bedeutung der Volksmusik in nordeuropäischer Kunstmusik', in Walther Salmen and Giselher Schubert (eds), *Verflechtungen im 20. Jahrhundert: Komponisten im Spannungsfeld elitär–popular* (Mainz: Schott, 2005), pp. 88–130, especially p. 100.

23. Fertonani published the song in the original key (Fertonani, *La memoria del canto*, p. 310); Manfred Willfort, for purposes of comparison, in C minor (Willfort, 'Das Urbild des Andante aus Schuberts Klaviertrio Es-dur, D 929', *Österreichische Musikzeitschrift* 33/6 (1978), 277–283, p. 280).

24. *Wiener Zeitschrift für Kunst, Literature, Theater und Mode*, 29 September 1827, pp. 969–70; cited in Till Gerrit Waidelich (ed.), *Franz Schubert: Dokumente 1817–1830*, vol. 1, *Printed Sources*, Veröffentlichungen des Internationalen Schubert Instituts 10/1 (Tutzing, 1993), p. 361.

25. See Klaus Aringer, 'Zur musikalischen Funktion der Posaunen in Franz Schuberts letzten Sinfonien', *Schubert-Jahrbuch* (1998), pp. 87–101.

26. *Der Sammler* (Vienna), 26 August 1820, p. 409; cited in Waidelich, *Franz Schubert: Dokumente 1817–1830*, p. 42.

27. Manfred Kube has pointed out that in the Trio the specific characteristics of the participating instruments are leveled out, a procedure that, with the same musical material being played by them, leads to different sonority effects. See '"... dass alle Spieler hinlänglich beschäftigt sind": Schuberts Klaviertrio Es-dur (D929) aus satztechnischer Perspektive', *Schubert-Jahrbuch* (1998), pp. 125–32.

28. Deutsch, *Schubert: Die Dokumente seines Lebens*, p. 182; Deutsch, *The Schubert Reader*, p. 344.

29. Franz Schubert, *Neue Ausgabe sämtlicher Werke*, ser. VI, vol. 7, *Werke für Klavier und mehrere Instrumente*, ed. Arnold Feil (Kassel: Bärenreiter, 1975), p. 52.

30. Ibid., p. 64.

31. Ibid., p. 51.

32. Ibid., 55.

3

Franz Schubert's 'New Style' and the Legacy of Beethoven

William Kinderman

Today, more than two centuries after his birth, Schubert's instrumental compositions have begun to assume their rightful place beside those of Beethoven as works of an almost unsurpassed wealth of expression. That much of this music went long neglected was due to various factors. For one, the majority of Schubert's works remained for a long time unpublished. Also, in Schubert's music expression assumes primacy over overt virtuosity. Important too was the strong influence of Beethoven, whose works set standards which did not apply to Schubert. Accusations of Schubert's inability to handle large-scale forms, according to such critics as Arnold Whittall, who thought he identified in his work a collapse of sonata form, have also played a role, but these rest on an inadequate understanding of the aesthetics of Schubert's instrumental works.[1]

Schubert's music is less deterministic than Beethoven's and can seem to present no compelling, logical sequence of musical ideas. As the music unfolds, there is often a sense that it could have taken another path. Theodor W. Adorno sensed differences in the characteristics of this music: 'With Schubert'—unlike in a shallow 'potpourri'—'the themes are piling up, without congealing in a medusian figure'; 'the dissociated points of the landscape are sought out in a circular movement.'[2] Such perspectival shifts in Schubert represent a structural element of the musical form, through which a latent psychological symbolism is recognisable. A key to this symbolism lies in Schubert's songs, in which the protagonist or wanderer figure in the role of a lyrical subject is often confronted with an indifferent or comfortless reality. As a means of realising this experiential dichotomy in music, Schubert employs a confrontation of contrasting themes with a concurrent change of major to minor and the resource of abrupt modulation. An inner world of imagination, memory or illusion is conveyed through lyrical thematic material in the major tonality; this idiom is set against more dramatic, restless, dissonant music in the minor tonality, which expresses a gloomier external reality. After 1820 analogous artistic devices appear in Schubert's instrumental music, which essentially contribute to a development of his style, culminating in the three profound posthumous Piano Sonatas in C minor, A major and B♭ major.

Alfred Brendel has compared Beethoven the architect to Schubert the sleepwalker, characterising Beethoven as deterministic and calculating, Schubert as dream-like and visionary.³ Beethoven's music also embodies inner lyricism and dream-like psychic states; in his music, as in Schubert's, an inner vision of beauty, trust and hope is counterbalanced with dramatic external challenges. One thinks of Florestan's aria in the dungeon or the transition from the Adagio to the Finale in the Ninth Symphony. Many of Beethoven's instrumental works, from the 'Pathétique' Sonata to the cavatina and the *Große Fuge* in the original version of the String Quartet in B♭ major, Op. 130, present this duality of experience.

Wherein lies then the essential difference between these two great composers? Beethoven's more directional, forward-driven aesthetic matches well to the ethically-inspired concept of the work of art promoted by the poet and philosopher Friedrich Schiller, whom the young Beethoven already admired from his youth in Bonn. According to Schiller, a successful work of art becomes the epitome of freedom, since it serves as a dynamic 'symbol of excellence' (*Symbol des Vortrefflichen*). In its narrative course the *status quo* is cancelled and the implicit meanings of the unfolding work are unveiled. In line with this Schillerian aesthetic, the tragic resignation which is characteristic of Mozart seldom appears in Beethoven. Typically his works of a tragic character show resistance to suffering: a resistance which inclines toward revolution in the Fifth Symphony or ultimately resolves the dramatic tension as in the last Piano Sonata. In these pieces there is a process of moving forwards and upwards, an eventful trajectory, which usually also embraces regressive moments or episodes. The episodes serve to protect the affirmative artwork from the risk of a lapse into ideology.[4]

There are some very distinct, forward-driven passages within the concluding movements of such Beethovenian works. The coda of the finale of the Fifth Symphony leads to an unsurpassable C major culmination: the rhythmic tension acts so forcefully that the harmonic-melodic syntax is flattened with no fewer than twenty-nine closing bars filled with C major chords without any harmonic alteration. By contrast, the Arietta movement closing the Piano Sonata in C minor, Op. 111, presents a transcendental sequence, a synthesis of Becoming and Being. In the final variations of the Arietta theme in C major, rhythmic and polyphonic elements are recalled from previous variations, with the original theme heard in an ethereal high register and combined with a prolonged trill on the dominant G. The symbolic dimension of this music is as unmistakable as the monolithic climax on the high sustained E♭ major chord in the choral finale of the Ninth Symphony, set to the final lines of Schiller's text, with the implication of the divinity beyond the heavens: 'Über Sternen muss er wohnen' [above the stars must he dwell]. In such passages the music reaches its most extreme limit and points further—as a signpost points to infinity.

Schubert is less idealistic in his symbolism. The character of his art is closer to Mozart than to Schiller. For all the beauty of its melodic invention, Schubert's tragic perspective has a bleaker effect than that of Beethoven, with a deeper sense of resignation and a more enduring impression of loss. If the transcendental search is abandoned here, dream-like visions are offered as compensation—by means of an artistic strategy, which Schubert himself codified in his allegorical tale, 'Mein Traum', dated 3 July 1822.[5] In this narrative, the composer himself appears in the role of an archetypal wanderer. The reason for and the outcome of this journey are rooted in a similar way in the experience of the duality of love and pain: '... and for the second time, I retraced my steps, and with a heart full of infinite love for those who scorned me, I wandered into far-off lands. I sang songs for many, many years. Whenever I wanted to sing of love, it turned to pain. And when I tried to sing of pain, it turned to love. So I was divided by love and pain.' At the conclusion of the story the conflicting emotions, love and pain, become reconciled—in a magic circle beside the grave of a girl, where Schubert is embraced by his father, who had earlier scorned him.

The importance of this duality of experience is particularly evident in Schubert's lieder. Among the earliest examples are the two masterful songs from 1814–15, 'Gretchen am Spinnrade' und 'Erlkönig'. In the first there is a realistic, outwardly orientated accompaniment, which evokes spinning but also points to Gretchen's troubled mood. At the climax, the repetitious motoric motion of the accompaniment is interrupted and only hesitantly set into motion again. In 'Erlkönig', by contrast, the internal perspective, which is only subtly alluded to in 'Gretchen am Spinnrade', becomes the central dramatic aspect of the lied. For Schubert, the seductive vision of the Erlking is the boy's, not the father's. The psychological depth of the setting is made possible by a sudden alteration of perspective in the music, whereby Schubert does justice to the visual dimension of the poem as well as the inner subjective experience of the boy.

In 'Erlkönig', for instance, playful, seductive major melodies represent the Erlking as experienced by the boy, whereby the outer surroundings are predominantly presented in the minor, with octave repeats and a brisk rhythmic figuration in the piano, indicating the horse's hooves and the sound of the wind. The Erlking addresses the boy with beautiful melodies; only here does the lied's agitated character yield to lyricism. The contrast between the inner perspective—the vision of the boy—and the outer perspective is intensified through unexpected modulations and through the dissonance of a minor ninth between voice and piano as an expression of the response of the frightened child. Schubert's tonal plan, with his favourite artistic device of abrupt modulation, supports the effect of the change in perspective. Schubert coordinates the same occurrence of dream-like lyricism in the major yielding to sinister reality in the minor with the setting of the final words of the dying child: the inner vision disappears, and with it the boy's life.

Little by little Schubert recognised how such strongly contrasting dramatic levels could be assimilated into his instrumental music, a realisation undoubtedly helped by his knowledge of Beethoven's greatness. On 16 June 1816, when he was still under the conservative influence of his teacher Antonio Salieri, Schubert in his diary had expressed a strong ambivalence towards Beethoven:

> It must be beautiful and refreshing for an artist to see, with all his students gathered around, how each one strives to give of his best for his [teacher's] jubilee, and to hear in all these compositions the expression of mere nature, free from the all the bizarre elements which are common among composers nowadays and owed almost entirely to one of our greatest German artists; [free from] that eccentricity which does not distinguish the tragic from the comic, the agreeable from the repulsive, the heroic with howlings and the holiest from harlequinades; that moves people to madness instead of dissolving them into love, that incites them to laughter instead of raising them to the divine. To see this eccentricity banished from his circle of students and instead to look upon pure, holy nature must be the greatest pleasure for an artist who, guided by such [a composer] as Gluck, learns to know nature and to preserve it despite the unnatural conditions of our age.[6]

Yet only a few years later, this devout, conservative rejection of Beethoven's eccentricities and 'bizarreries' was replaced with an enthusiastic reverence, as shown by Schubert's troubled question: 'Who can achieve anything after Beethoven?'[7] It is noteworthy that after 1820 Schubert, too, found highly original means of expanding the spheres of expression of his instrumental music through extreme contrasts—contrasts which correspond to the duality of love and pain in his story of 1822.

Critics have sometimes doubted Schubert's handling of large-scale classical genres, regarding the looseness of his musical forms as a deficit. It is important to recognise, however, that Schubert's use of abrupt contrasts and radically condensed transitions in no way indicates a technical incompetence in composing extended transition passages. The many classicising works which Schubert wrote up to 1820 contradict this supposition. On the contrary, Schubert found that he could deepen his instrumental works through the use of heightened contrasts, which were already present in his songs. Schubert's music thus acquired a source of dramatic energy comparable to Beethoven's, and the approach helped him to cultivate further a style of remarkable originality and richness.

A key work in this regard is the *Quartettsatz* in C minor, D 703, of 1820, the first of several fragmentary masterpieces of these years. The turbulent darkness and chromaticism of the *Quartettsatz* are somewhat indebted to Beethoven and Mozart, but the execution is Schubertian through and through. The *Quartettsatz* begins with four imitative entries of a dark theme full of chromaticism, building with intensity to the emphatic Neapolitan sixth chord in bar 9. A variation of the theme, which appears three bars later, leads to a contrasting lyrical subject in the submediant, A♭ major, which is marked 'dolce'. It develops as a twelve-bar section which is repeated and then extended through more cadential prolongations. In this passage, the expected cadence leading

Example 3.1 Schubert, *Quartettsatz* in C minor, D 703, bars 48–61

to the repetition of the phrase is avoided (in bars 49, 53 and 59) before being asserted with a structural *sforzato* (see Example 3.1).

The cadential close coincides with the sudden disappearance of the lyrical theme and the resumption of the minor tonality. It is marked by thematic material related to the opening of the movement. Schubert's characteristic use here of a tri-thematic, three-key exposition, whereby the contrasting second theme commences and closes abruptly, is the outcome of an amalgamation of dramatic and lyrical elements, an approach that evokes latent associations with the wanderer symbolism of his songs.

In some ways the exposition of the first movement of the 'Unfinished' Symphony, D 739, from 1822 is similar to the exposition of the *Quartettsatz*, D 703, although the former possesses only two thematic complexes and two main key centres. Above all, the opening passage (in semiquavers) is reminiscent, with regard to its rhythmic and harmonic design, of the beginning of the *Quartettsatz*, though it is more extensive and concludes with an emphatic cadence in B minor in bar 38. In a short five-bar transition passage the pitch D—the third of B minor—is given a new interpretation as the fifth of G major, the tonic of the second lyrical theme, a key relationship that corresponds to that in the *Quartettsatz*. The two works resemble each other with regard to the handling of the second subject: the ten-bar melodic phrase of the 'Unfinished' is repeated immediately, its continuation prematurely broken off at the point of an anticipated cadence in G major (see Example 3.2).

Here the lyrical theme sinks into silence, and a passage derived from the opening theme in the minor follows, whereby the contrast is reinforced through orchestration and dynamics.

Example 3.2 Schubert, Symphony No. 7 in B minor, D 759 ('Unfinished'), i, bars 56–62

The contrasting relationship of both themes is consistently exploited throughout the course of the movement. In the development, for example, a powerful four-bar phrase, which is related to the movement's opening, is extended through a further four bars wherein the lyrical theme is delicately evoked as its syncopated accompaniment is taken up. In this way an eight-bar unit emerges which juxtaposes both themes, diametrically opposed as these are in their character and expression; this passage is restated in turn as modulations lead to new tonalities on ascending pitch levels. Such a structural juxtaposition of two themes—which, in their character and expression, are opposed to one another—is a procedure found in many of Schubert's late instrumental works. In the Symphony as in the *Quartettsatz*, the lyrical theme assumes a quality of intimate warmth and beauty, even a utopian character. As an implicit personal expression of the individual subject, such Schubertian themes often reveal themselves to be fragile. In the exposition of the 'Unfinished', the second theme, in G major, is suddenly broken off and thereby opens an empty space— a void—which is filled through the return of the dramatic music in the minor.

The tragic aspects of Schubert's handling of the wanderer motive are, above all, illuminated in *Winterreise*, the second song cycle from 1827 to texts by Wilhelm Müller. In *Winterreise* the gulf between the subjective self and the external world appears complete and irreconcilable. As Peter Gülke writes in his monograph on Schubert, the wanderer figure of the first song cycle, *Die schöne Müllerin*, participates in concrete poetic imagery, which is largely withdrawn in *Winterreise*.[8] The Wanderer in the *Winterreise* is not described poetically but himself becomes a poet. His identity and history remain shadowy. Particularly important is the correlation between his subjective state of mind and objects in nature such as the frozen stream, the cold wind, the encircling crows and the howling dogs. As in paintings of Caspar David Friedrich, this wanderer never gazes at us, but rather peers into the unknown and the unfathomable.[9] The ultimate goal of the *Winterreise* is identified with 'der Straße, die noch keiner ging zurück' (the road from which no one returns), namely death.

This aesthetic context is relevant to Schubert's masterful late instrumental music, such as the Piano Sonatas, the Quartets and the great String Quintet in C major, and helps us to evaluate his artistic interpretation of Beethoven. For Schubert, Beethoven's works served as a landmark and often as a source of inspiration: one example of this influence is the affinity between the opening movement of Beethoven's Violin Concerto, Op. 61, and the subsidiary theme in the finale of Schubert's 'Great' C major Symphony, D 944, which displays a similar employment of a repeated-note motive. Reminiscences of Beethoven's Ninth Symphony can also be felt in Schubert's C major Symphony.[10] The walking movement of the Allegretto of Beethoven's Seventh Symphony also left traces in various movements by Schubert. Despite the anxiety about influence, which was reflected in his question 'Wer vermag nach Beethoven etwas zu machen?' (Who can achieve anything after Beethoven?), Schubert showed himself astonishingly receptive to Beethoven's influence during his final years. This openness to Beethoven's legacy was surely enabled by Schubert's growing independence, which revealed itself in the impressive originality of his style.

Schubert in 1828: the Quintet in C and Final Sonata Trilogy

We turn our attention now to works Schubert wrote in 1828, the year after Beethoven's death: the String Quintet in C major, D 956, and last three Piano Sonatas, D 958–960. Schubert's preoccupation with Beethoven's legacy was particularly intensive towards the end of his life. On his deathbed he wanted to listen to Beethoven's C♯ minor Quartet, Op. 131. Schubert's String Quintet in C major can be compared to some of Beethoven's greatest compositions—including the C♯ minor Quartet—in its handling of structural and expressive tensions in the work as a whole. At the start, Beethoven's fugal subject contains a characteristic dissonance and instability. His harmonic penchant for the Neapolitan and subdominant in the opening fugue not only contribute to the penetrating melancholic mood of the music, but also hold implications for the tonal structure of the entire Quartet, particularly the finale. In Schubert's

Quintet, the initial gesture of a crescendo to an accented dissonance on the second chord, a diminished seventh, takes on a similar meaning, connected as it is to many later musical events, from the utopian lyricism of the second theme in the cellos in the flattened mediant to the wide-ranging role of tonal and harmonic semitone relations in every movement. It is striking how Schubert emphasises the motivic semitone movement from D♭ to C as strongly as possible at the end of the finale before he allows the work to close with a unison gesture, D♭ to C, in all five instruments. The harmonic tension is so potent that the major tonality of the work is seriously called into question.

The Adagio of the Quintet has a remarkable breadth and commences with an almost static first subject of a peaceful nature. The melody dwells on several important closely aligned pitches, while the accompaniment consists of repeated suspended figurations. The middle section, on the other hand, presents a drastic contrast but no definite theme; Werner Thomas aptly describes this passage as 'organisierte[s] Chaos am Rande einer Katastrophe' (organised chaos bordering on catastrophe).[11] A model for Schubert's treatment of this radically contrasting passage is presumably Mozart;[12] but Schubert's Quintet can also be compared to the transition from the slow movement to the finale in Beethovens 'Appassionata' Sonata in F minor, Op. 57. The entire process of unfolding variations on a chorale-like andante theme in the slow movement of the *Appassionata* is immersed in a character of dream-like reflection such that the first collision with dramatic action must shatter it. That collision takes place at the moment of harmonic reinterpretation of the high D♭—which would have been expected to conclude the cadence and with it the entire movement—with the intrusion of an arpeggiated diminished seventh at the beginning of the Allegro ma non troppo. In the Adagio of the Schubert Quintet, the tonic is likewise also given a new interpretation and destabilised. The E, which is played triple-*piano* by the cellos at the end of the first section, is reinterpreted as the leading note of F minor while an upbeat unison *fortissimo* trill sounds in all the instruments (see Example 3.3). This breaking into the wild, syncopated music of the middle section after the 'transcendently sustained music' of the main section has an effect like the outburst of pandemonium.[13]

Works like the Quintet remind us of the limitations of Brendel's suggestive metaphor, whereby Schubert is characterised as a sleepwalker.[14] Despite his evocation of dream states and the duality of experience in his music, which can oscillate swiftly from one level to another without transition, Schubert was master of a new kind of musical architecture. The narrative course of his music is less linear than that of Beethoven, but this difference should not be exaggerated, since the mature Beethoven also employed strong contrasts, digressions and parenthetical structures, contrasts which were sometimes regarded as 'Bizarrerie'[15] and are analogous to those of Schubert. On the other hand, the unfolding of musical time in Schubert is often broader than in Beethoven.

Example 3.3 Schubert, String Quintet in C major, D 956, ii, bars 26–30

Since his musical forms unfold so differently, Schubert could compose passages or entire movements while adapting the model of Beethoven without sacrificing his own originality or endangering his artistic standards.

Important for Schubert's artistic development in his final year was his discovery of Heinrich Heine's poetic cycle *Die Heimkehr*, a cycle later incorporated into Heine's *Buch der Lieder*. Schubert set six Heine poems, among them 'Der Atlas', which is motivically connected to the main movement of the C minor Sonata, D 958. According to Susan Youens, Heine created a new version of the myth in the poem 'Ich unglücksel'ger Atlas!' (I, the unfortunate ill-fated Atlas), in which the heroic greatness of the past and a modern renunciation of such greatness are fused.[16] In his C minor Sonata Schubert achieved a comparable synthesis which unites Beethoven's C minor pathos with a psychological depth that has little to do with heroism.

According to Charles Rosen, 'Schubert's innovations in sonata forms are not so much extensions of classical style than completely new inventions, which create a genuinely new style'.[17] Schubert's originality at the beginning of the C minor Sonata lies in the fusion of different thematic elements. This yields a concrete reference to Beethoven and not just 'a certain parallel brusqueness', as Whittall maintains.[18] Arthur Godel has drawn attention to the theme of Beethoven's C minor Variations, WoO 80, as a model for Schubert's opening subject,[19] and the parallel was originally even stronger. Hans-Joachim Hinrichsen has pointed out that Schubert, in his sketch of the passage, altered his rather direct reference to Beethoven through the insertion of a measure, whereby the melodic climax of the theme is delayed by one bar.[20] Apart from that, we are concerned here not simply with a distinctive Beethovenian theme, but with a short theme for variations based on models from the Baroque period. Hinrichsen sees in this movement 'die entschiedene Markierung einer selbstbewußten Gegenposition' (the resolute articulation of a self-confident antithesis)—not a reflection of Schubert's dependency on Beethoven.[21] What Hinrichsen stresses is the proud independence of Schubert's artistic path as opposed to any passive assimilation of Beethoven's influence.

The key role of the Atlas motive is lodged above all in its rhythmic contour, with a double-dotted upbeat on repeated crotchets underscored by octaves in the left hand. The G minor tonality of the lied is not retained in the Sonata, whose general affinity to Beethoven's C minor idiom extends to Schubert's choice of A♭ major for the slow movement, a tonal relation very characteristic of Beethoven. On the other hand, the initial gradual ascent from the tonic C to the dominant and then the sixth degree is adopted from the Beethovenian model, but with a decisive change: Schubert's theme is substantially broader than Beethoven's, and the tonal destination, A♭, is stressed in bars 7 and 9 before it resounds *fortissimo* in the highest register simultaneously with the 'Atlas' motive in octaves in the bass (see Examples 3.4 and 3.5a).

Example 3.4 Schubert, Piano Sonata in C minor, D 958, i, bars 5–13

Example 3.5a Schubert, 'Der Atlas', D 957/8, bars 4–7

Example 3.5b Schubert, 'Der Atlas', D 957/8, bars 16–18

The A♭ is then composed out by means of the rapid descending scale through all registers. Noteworthy is the ensuing rhythmic motive of three quavers, which leads to a rhythmic punctuated figure at the beginning of the following bar. This rhythmic figure is present in bars 16–17 of the Heine song, where the word 'Unerträgliches' (the unbearable) is stressed (see Example 3.5b).

In Schubert's Sonata, this motive plays an important role as an element of connection between the first subject and the lyrical second subject in E♭ major. The upbeat figuration in three quavers often appears in the subsidiary section and is paired with softly flowing movement, whereby the tension-laden semitone movement G–A♭ from the beginning of the movement now sounds quietly in the brighter E♭ major tonal area. [22] This collection of motives remains potent in the entire first movement of the C minor Sonata, and the Allegro closes with an inversion of the sequence of notes, resolved on the sixth. The music reaches a final climax in bar 263 of the coda on the A♭ in the highest register before it is gradually led downwards with a decrescendo to the *pianissimo* close.

The dark, challenging opening theme of the C minor Sonata harbours broader implications. Brendel even describes it as the 'Steinbruch, der die meisten Bausteine der Trias enthält' (the quarry that contains the main components of the three works).[23] The recognition that Schubert's three last Sonatas are related pieces sharing many motivic and tonal characteristics has gained ground. Yet the Sonatas have even more in common, because each of these pieces—in C minor, A major and B♭ major—contains allusions to Beethoven, who died in March 1827 and whom Schubert would outlive by only twenty months. It is enlightening to regard these Sonatas as companion works reflecting Schubert's affinity with Beethoven while at the same time demonstrating his own artistic sovereignty. The second movement of the C minor Sonata contains, for example, a hymn-like theme in A♭ major, which returns varied after episodes in different keys, just as in the slow movement of Beethoven's 'Pathétique' Sonata, also in A♭ major. The final section of the Schubert Adagio is particularly imaginative, where the main subject, with a *pianissimo* pizzicato bass, appears transfigured before modulating phrases occur and the music breaks off into complete silence—aspects which do not exist in Beethoven. The ostinato tarantella rhythm of Schubert's finale recalls the final movement of Beethoven's Piano Sonata in E♭ major, Op. 31 No. 3, but the content in Schubert is nonetheless highly original. The poetic character has much less to do with dance than with a horseback ride: exciting yet ominous. The obsessive quality of the music gives way in the central episode to a cajoling vision in B major, which recalls 'Erlkönig'.

As documented in Schubert's surviving draft manuscripts, it appears that the compositional evolution of these last three Sonatas came about gradually: his commencement of work on the final Sonata in B♭ major overlapped that on the penultimate Sonata.[24] As we have seen, there are important correlations between the first movement of the C minor Sonata and the lied 'Der Atlas', the first of the series of Heine settings in the 1828 Schubert manuscript that became the basis for the posthumous publication *Schwanengesang*. The difficulties with the order of these posthumously published songs have often been discussed.[25] Particularly curious is the position in Schubert's manuscript of 'Der Atlas' as the first and 'Das Fischermädchen' as the third song in the series. Schubert himself did not live to oversee publication of the songs, and there is no compelling reason to equate the order in the manuscript with an intended final version. A convincing solution to the problem has been put forward by Elmar Budde, whereby 'Das Fischermädchen' is placed at the beginning and 'Der Atlas' at the end. As Budde explains, it makes sense when 'Die Stadt', 'Am Meer' und 'Der Doppelgänger' follow one another, since these songs are recorded in that way in the manuscript. Alternatively, 'Am Meer' can be placed effectively before 'Die Stadt', since the opening sonorities at the beginning of 'Am Meer' can then be heard as resolving the pitches of the A♭ tonic triad from 'Das Fischermädchen' to C major before the key shifts to C minor in the following song, 'Die Stadt'. 'Ihr Bild' and 'Der Atlas' then come at the conclusion, just as in the sequence of Heine's *Heimkehr*, while 'Das Fischermädchen' can be meaningully placed only at the beginning. As Budde observes, in their revised order 'the succession of the songs and their tonalities exhibit an astonishing logical consistency'.[26]

The fact that in the manuscript Schubert composed the final song of the series, 'Der Atlas', first is worth pondering. This is likely related to his parallel project, the C minor Sonata. The thematic springboard to the sonata trilogy consists of an inspired fusion of two models: Beethoven's C minor theme and Schubert's own Heine setting of 'Der Atlas'. On the basis of a letter which Schubert wrote to the Leipzig publisher on 2 October 1828, we can assume that he wanted the Heine settings to be published as an integral whole. In the same letter Schubert mentions the sonata trilogy: 'ich habe unter andern 3 Sonaten fürs Pianoforte allein componirt, welche ich Hummel dediciren möchte.... Die Sonaten habe ich an mehreren Orten mit viel Beyfall gespielt' (I have composed, among other things, three sonatas for piano solo, which I would like to dedicate to Hummel.... I have played the sonatas with much success in several places').[27] It appears very possible and even probable that the compositional genesis of these projects was closely connected.[28]

In an essay entitled 'Influence: Plagiarism and Inspiration', Charles Rosen concludes that 'whenever the study of sources is at its most interesting, it becomes indistinguishable from pure musical analysis'.[29] This applies well in the case of the A major Sonata, D 959, since Schubert's allusions to Beethoven's model are particularly extensive. Only at the beginning of the 1970s—and independently of each other—did Rosen and Edward T. Cone demonstrate that Schubert's finale had been modelled on the final movement of Beethoven's G major Piano Sonata, Op. 31 No. 1.[30] The parallels between these movements are too obvious to be coincidental. Rosen has pointed out that Schubert outstripped his model, a feat nowhere more evident than in the extraordinary coda, where the phrases of the first subject break off into silence and, newly harmonised in unexpected keys, then resume. Just as the thread appears to have been found again, we hear a highly agitated presto, which is interrupted in turn by a resumption of the reprise of the rondo theme before the work closes in its final bars with an allusion to the main theme of the *first* movement.

Another Schubertian extension of artistic resources used by Beethoven occurs at the climax of the central episode of the finale, which leads to the recapitulation. Here Schubert opens a window on the tragic slow movement in F♯ minor, the Andantino, in which a static, almost hypnotic first subject in the middle movement is confronted with an outbreak of chaotic power. Schubert's recollection of the slow movement in the middle of the finale is astonishing: this massive passage does not lie on the dominant of A major, but on C♯, the dominant of the F♯ major tonality heard at the outset of the recapitulation. The arpeggios in the middle register stress the same notes as the main theme of the Andantino, and Schubert then intensifies the allusion to the slow movement in an unforgettable manner. The softly gliding F♯ major passage at the beginning of the reprise is no mere 'false' recapitulation: it offers a transfigured vision of the tonality of the tragic slow movement glimpsed through the veil of the rondo theme.[31] Beethoven's works offered models for this procedure—such as, for example, in the E major episode in the finale of the Third Piano Concerto in C minor, Op. 37—but Schubert's execution of this artistic device displays a subtle and profound character, which belongs to him alone (see Example 3.6).

In an analysis of the A major Sonata published a generation after the studies by Rosen and Cone, Robert S. Hatten contributed something new in his recognition that Schubert had improved his sketch of the main subject in the first movement with reference to the opening theme of Beethoven's Op. 31 No. 1.[32] In the draft, Schubert's theme is chorale-like; the staccato gestures are lacking in the bass and were clearly added later. These characteristisic staccato gestures on the tonic A receive a renewed acoustical resonance through the full-voiced chords in the treble. Some passages in the second and third movements of the sonata produce a similar effect through overtone relationships. This device is particularly conspicuous in the A major Sonata, D 959, in the recitative passage in the slow movement in bars 132–135, and in the trio of the Scherzo, above all in bars 99–101. A crucial point and source of inspiration for Schubert was undoubtedly the very beginning of Beethoven's G major Sonata, in which the opening notes produce this kind of acoustic effect. The creative development of the Beethovenian model is inseparable from Schubert's cyclical master plan, and it should not surprise us that Schubert, like Beethoven, closes his finale with a reminiscence of the first movement.

Like the Sonatas in C minor and A major, the final Sonata in B♭ major engages with Beethoven's legacy with imagination and mastery. One feels here an affinity

Example 3.6 Schubert, Piano Sonata in A major, D 959, iv, bars 211–222

to the opening theme of Beethoven's 'Archduke' Trio, Op. 97, which is in the same key.³³ The peaceful character in 4/4 time, the broad phrases, the full-voiced piano texture over a tonic pedal point and even the pause on the dominant in bar 8 invite this comparison. On the other hand, the deep, darkening trill on G♭ in bar 8 of Schubert's Sonata finds a parallel in his Heine setting of 'Ihr Bild', at the text 'und starrt' ihr Bildnis an' (stared at her picture).³⁴ As at the beginning of the C minor Sonata, the presence of a Beethovenian model is enriched through an expressive reference to a lied. In the Heine setting, this gesture represents a psychological turning point, since the inner life of the imagination is then evoked with consonant major chords at the ensuing words 'und das geliebte Antlitz heimlich zu leben begann' (and that beloved face began mysteriously to come alive).³⁵

The development section of the first movement begins with a variation of the opening theme in C♯ minor. This narrative section is soon redirected to A major and to the third thematic complex of the exposition, whose dactylic metre (long–short–short) and melodic profile recall Schubert's lied 'Der Wanderer', D 489, in a striking way.³⁶ A lengthy modulating passage then leads to a powerful climax in D minor. In the ethereal, delicate passage which follows, the opening theme is heard again, this time softly and high in the treble register, and preceded by the trill (see Example 3.7).

As the dynamic level withdraws to a delicate triple-*pianissimo*, B♭ major has been reached, yet we have not thereby arrived at the actual recapitulation. As Tovey and others have remarked, this return of the opening theme is sensitively poised, not 'in' but 'on' the tonic, experienced, as it were, from a distance.³⁷ In this way the meaningful trill, full of mystery, points ahead to the forthcoming return of the theme. The trills in this passage are also possibly influenced by Beethoven's drumrolls, heard at the approach to the reprise of the main theme in the first movement of his Fourth Symphony in B♭ major, Op. 60. In Schubert's case these are newly conceived as low trills in the piano, in a context in which the musical model is not merely imitated but deepened.

Example 3.7 Schubert, Piano Sonata in B♭ Major, D 960, i, bars 183–192

A final example of this kind is Schubert's handling of the conspicuous octave 'horn call' gesture on G at the beginning of the Rondo theme in the finale of the B♭ major Sonata, D 960. This idea recalls the replacement finale of Beethoven's quartet in this key, Op. 130, though in Schubert's hands the device gains in harmonic subtlety, since his theme consistently begins in the 'wrong' tonality—that is, in C minor instead of B♭ major.[38] At the same time, this octave call takes part in a cyclical dimension reaching back to the beginning of the opening movement. Already in the fourth bar of the main theme of the first movement, a suspension appears on G–F, a figure which is subsequently darkened by the mysterious G♭ trill. The later reinterpretation of this trill opens new tonal perspectives with the turn towards G♭ major in bar 20, a premonition of the later modulation to F♯ minor in bar 48. The important G–F motive then undergoes further treatment in the final movement. This leading idea surfaces in the form of the octave motive on G, embedded as the opening gesture of the rondo theme, until a decisive moment arrives at last in the coda: the octave call note falls from G through G♭ to F (bar 502) before the brilliant presto coda fully resolves the tension, capping Schubert's very last composition for the piano.

As we have seen, not only Schubert's lieder and song cycles but also many of his instrumental works display a consummate realisation. The combination of a directness and inwardness of expression, poetic sensibility and structural control and grandeur is characteristic of Schubert's mature musical style, which embodies, as we have seen, a 'vulnerable maturity, a platform for alternative and unregimented modes of subjectivity'.[39] His departures from Beethoven's more directional aesthetic are not in themselves a shortcoming but are often inseparably bound up with his ambition to explore the qualities of human experience from a standpoint embracing both the external world and the inner powers of the imagination. A cyclical procedure, which is characteristic of Schubert's arrangement of songs,[40] is further developed in his later instrumental works and reaches its climax in the final piano and chamber music works.[41]

Let us close these observations with thoughts regarding the reception of Schubert's and Beethoven's works. Unlike Beethoven's, Schubert's path to instrumental music was through text setting; by 1817 he had already composed more than half of his songs. Through his engagement with the wanderer archetype and everything associated with it, Schubert moves close to the heart of the listener. In *Die schöne Müllerin*, for example, one thinks of wandering, of the water as a metaphor of life, the mill wheels, the wild hunter, the linden tree, the melancholy with which the singer lets the lute hang on the wall because his 'heart is too full', the longing for death. All that is contained in Schubert's lieder, as for instance in 'Wohin?' from *Die schöne Müllerin*: 'Ich hört ein Bächlein rauschen / wohl aus dem Felsenquell, / hinab zum Tale rauschen / so frisch und wunderhell. / Ich weiß nicht, wie mir wurde, / nicht, wer den Rat mir gab, / ich mußte auch hinunter/mit meinem Wanderstab' (I heard a little brook babbling / from its rocky source / babbling down to the valley / so bright, so wondrously clear. / I know not what came over me, / nor who prompted me / but I too had to go down / with my wanderer's staff).

Hand in hand with this shared intimacy of feeling was Schubert's deep respect for Beethoven. Thomas Mann described Beethoven in his novel *Doktor Faustus* as 'the solitary prince of a realm of spirits'.[42] In *Fidelio* the exalted feelings of married love, of unswerving human fidelity, of the longing for freedom, of the frisson of happiness with which the trumpet proclaims the arrival of the rescuing minister remain at a certain idealising distance to the individual characters of the opera, reflecting the distant genius of sublimity. No less do we honour Schubert, whose painful early death moves us as do as his heart-warming lieder. The importance of Schubert's instrumental compositions in this context should not be undervalued. From the beginning of the 1820s his setting of texts diminished as the number of his instrumental works increased. In the masterful instrumental works of his final years—such as the sonata trilogy from 1828—we can recognise Schubert's 'new style' as a self-assured alternative to Beethoven's legacy.

Notes

I am grateful to Werner Grünzweig and especially Rainer Waubke for their helpful advice.

1. Arnold Whittall, 'The Sonata Crisis: Schubert in 1828', *The Music Review* 30 (1969), p. 124.
2. Theodor W. Adorno, 'Schubert', in Adorno, *Moments musicaux*, in *Gesammelte Schriften*, ed. Rolf Tiedemann (Frankfurt am Main: Suhrkamp, 1970–86), vol. 17, pp. 22 and 25. This essay dates from 1928.
3. Alfred Brendel, 'Form and Psychology in Beethoven's Piano Sonatas', in *Alfred Brendel on Musik: Collected Essays* (Chicago: A Cappella, 2001), p. 45.
4. See also William Kinderman, 'Das Werturteil in der Kunst und die Ästhetik Hermann Brochs: Beispiele aus der Musik Beethovens', in Michael Benedikt, Reinhold Knoll and Cornelius Zehetner (eds), *Philosophie in Österreich*, vol. 6 (Vienna: Facultas, 2010), pp. 750–764.
5. Till Gerrit Waidelich offers a detailed investigation into this source, with a reproduction and transcription of the original manuscript: see Waidelich, 'Zur Überlieferung des Textes "Mein Traum"', *Schubert: Perspektiven* 5 (2005), pp. 138–61. The text also appeared in Otto Erik Deutsch (ed.), *Schubert: Die Dokumente seines Lebens*, 2nd edn (Wiesbaden: Breitkopf & Härtel, 1996), p. 159.
6. Deutsch, *Schubert: Die Dokumente seines Lebens*, p. 45. The identification of 'one of our greatest German artists' with Beethoven is obvious and generally accepted.
7. See Walther Dürr, '"Wer vermag nach Beethoven noch etwas zu machen?" Gedanken über die Beziehungen Schuberts zu Beethoven', *Beethoven-Jahrbuch* (1973-7), pp. 47–68; reprinted in K.-H. Metzger and R. Riehn (eds), *Musik-Konzepte: Sonderband Franz Schubert* (Munich: edition text + kritik, 1979),

pp. 17ff. Jos van der Zanden has correctly pointed out that Schubert's diary entry ought to be understood in the context of a discussion about the threat of Beethoven's originality; it offers here 'keinen Anlaß zu der Annahme, Schubert habe sich von Beethoven abgewandt' (no reason to suppose that Schubert turned away from Beethoven). van der Zanden, 'Franz Schuberts "Ausfälle gegen seinen Abgott"', in *Bonner Beethoven-Studien* 2, ed. Sieghard Brandenburg and Ernst Herttrich (Bonn: Beethoven-Haus, 2001), 201–209, esp. 208–209.

8. Peter Gülke, *Franz Schubert und seine Zeit* (Laaber: Laaber-Verlag, 1991), pp. 236–9.

9. The affinity between Schubert and Caspar David Friedrich has been examined in detail in several studies by Elmar Budde. See Budde, 'Franz Schubert—Caspar David Friedrich: Eine Studie', in *Von Dichtung und Musik 1797—1997 "Der Flug der Zeit": Franz Schubert; Ein Lesebuch* (Tutzing: H. Schneider, 1997), pp. 127–62; Budde, *Modulationsmanie und Perspektivenwechsel: Über Franz Schubert und Caspar David Friedrich*, in Otto Kolleritsch (ed.), *"Dialekt ohne Erde ...": Franz Schubert und das 20. Jahrhundert* (Graz: Universal Edition, 1998), pp. 121–38; and Budde, 'Tonalität und Perspektive: Anmerkungen zu Franz Schubert und Caspar David Friedrich', in Thomas Ertelt (ed.), *Werk und Geschichte: Musikalische Analyse und historischer Entwurf* (Mainz: Schott, 2005), pp. 115–24. See also Edward Michael Hafer, "The Wanderer Archetype in the Music of Franz Schubert and the Paintings of Caspar David Friedrich" (PhD diss., University of Illinois at Urbana-Champaign, 2006).

10. See Franz Wirth, 'Zur Diskussion Gestellt: Anklänge an Beethovens 9. Symphonie in Schuberts C-Dur Symphonie D 944', in *Bonner Beethoven-Studien* 5 (2006), pp. 183–96.

11. Werner Thomas, 'Die fast verlorene Zeit: Zum Adagio in Schuberts Streichquintett in C', in Thomas, *Schubert-Studien* (Frankfurt am Main: Peter Lang, 1990), p. 150.

12. In particular one thinks of the slow movement of Mozart's A minor Piano Sonata, K 310/300d, of 1778. Maynard Solomon writes about Mozart's 'almost Schubertian dissonances' in the contrasting middle section of the movement in Solomon, *Mozart: a Life* (New York: Harper Collins, 1995), pp. 187–90.

13. Gülke describes the main section as 'transzendierend enthobenen Musik' in his *Franz Schubert und seine Zeit*, p. 296.

14. In the essay on 'Schubert's Last Sonatas', Brendel writes that 'in his larger forms, Schubert is a wanderer' who displays the 'assurance of a sleepwalker.' *Alfred Brendel on Music: Collected Essays*, p. 95.

15. See van der Zanden, *Franz Schuberts 'Ausfälle gegen seinen Abgott'*, especially pp. 204–9.

16. Susan Youens, *Heinrich Heine and the Lied* (Cambridge: Cambridge University Press, 2007), p. 13.

17. Charles Rosen, *Sonata Forms* (New York: W. W. Norton, 1980), p. 360: 'Schubert's innovations in sonata forms are less extensions of classical style than completely new inventions, which lead to a genuinely new style'.

18. Whittall, 'The Sonata Crisis', p. 125: 'The C minor piano Sonata is invariably described as Schubert's most "Beethovenian" work, but this means little beyond a certain parallel brusqueness'.

19. Arthur Godel, *Schuberts letzte drei Klaviersonaten (D 958–960): Entstehungsgeschichte, Entwurf und Reinschrift, Werkanalyse* (Baden-Baden: Koerner, 1985), pp. 123f.

20. Hans-Joachim Hinrichsen, *Untersuchungen zur Entwicklung der Sonatenform in der Instrumentalmusik Franz Schuberts* (Tutzing: Hans Schneider, 1994), pp. 323–5.

21. Hinrichsen, *Untersuchungen zur Entwicklung der Sonatenform*, p. 323. Charles Fisk, *Returning Cycles: Contexts for the Interpretation of Schubert's Impromptus and Last Sonatas* (Berkeley and Los Angeles: University of California Press, 2001), describes 'a powerful, contravening Schubertian response' to Beethoven's music (p. 181).

22. Whittall overlooks the traits common to the main subject and second subject and only mentions 'the more relaxed mood and relative major tonality of the second subject group'. Whittall, 'The Sonata Crisis', p. 125.

23. See Alfred Brendel, 'Schuberts letzte Sonaten', in Brendel, *Musik beim Wort genommen* (Munich: Piper, 1992), p. 110. In the parallel passage of Brendel's essay in English, he writes that 'Like a large quarry, this rugged theme contains building material for future use', while referring to examples demonstrating the motivic coherence of the three sonatas. Brendel, *Alfred Brendel on Music*, p. 176.

24. See Ernst Hilmar's text accompanying the facsimile edition, *Franz Schubert: Drei große Sonaten für das Pianoforte D 958, D 959 und D 960 (Frühe Fassungen)* (Tutzing: Hans Schneider, 1987), p. 18.

25. In his BBC Music Guide *Schubert's Songs* (1967), Maurice J. E. Brown already questioned the order of the lieder, pp. 59–61 (American edn, *Schubert's Songs*, Seattle: University of Washington Press, 1969). See also Harry Goldschmidt, *Welches war die ursprüngliche Reihenfolge in Schuberts Heine-Liedern?, Deutsches Jahrbuch der Musikwissenschaft für 1972* (1974), pp. 52–62; Richard Kramer, *Distant Cycles: Schubert and the Conceiving of Song* (Chicago: University of Chicago Press, 1994), pp. 125–47; and Martin Chusid, *The Sequence of the Heine Songs and Cyclicism in 'Schwanengesang'*, in Chusid (ed.), *A Companion to Schubert's'Schwanengesang': History, Poets, Analysis, Performance* (New Haven, CT: Yale University Press, 2000), pp. 159–73.

26. 'Die Aufeinanderfolge der Lieder in ihren Tonarten [weist] eine erstaunliche Konsequenz und Logik auf'. See Elmar Budde, *Schuberts Liederzyklen* (Munich: C.H. Beck, 2003), pp. 106–8.

27. Deutsch, *Schubert: Die Dokumente seines Lebens*, p. 540.

28. In Hilmar's commentary to the facsimile edition of the final piano sonatas (*Franz Schubert: Drei große Klaviersonaten*) in the section 'Zu Schuberts letztem Schaffensjahr', he writes as follows: 'Die Chronologie ist nicht immer präzise festzulegen. . . . So wird es ein schwieriges und kaum zu lösendes Unterfangen, eine endgültige Chronologie . . . zu geben' (the chronology is not always precisely fixed . . . and so it is a difficult and scarcely achievable undertaking to give a definitive chronology) (p. 7). His suggestion in a chronological table that Schubert first began work on the

Sonata in C minor in May 1828 and on the Heine lieder (as part of *Schwanengesang* [D 957]) in August of the same year is speculative, especially where the C minor Sonata is concerned (p. 8).

29. Charles Rosen, 'Influence: Plagiarism and Inspiration', *19th-Century Music* 4 (1980), p. 100.

30. Charles Rosen, *The Classical Style* (New York: W. W. Norton, 1972), pp. 456–8; Edward T. Cone, 'Schubert's Beethoven', *Musical Quarterly* 56 (1970), pp. 779–93; and Paul Henry Lang (ed.), *The Creative World of Beethoven* (New York: W. W. Norton, 1971), pp. 277–91.

31. For more detailed discussion of this passage, see William Kinderman, 'Wandering Archetypes in Schubert's Instrumental Music', *19th-Century Music*, 21/2 (1997), pp. 219–22.

32. Robert S. Hatten, 'Schubert the Progressive: The Role of Resonance and Gesture in the Piano Sonata in A, 959', *Intégral* 7 (1993), pp. 38–81, especially pp. 53–9. Hatten considers Schubert's handing of overtone resonance in this sonata unsurpassed until Elliott Carter's piano sonatas from 1945–6.

33. As noted in Joseph Kerman, 'A Romantic Detail in Schubert's "Schwanengesang"', in Walther Frisch (ed.), *Schubert: Critical and Analytical Studies* (Lincoln: University of Nebraska Press, 1986), p. 59.

34. See Hans Költzsch, *Franz Schubert in seinen Klaviersonaten* (Leipzig: Breitkopf & Härtel, 1927), p. 131.

35. See William Kinderman, 'Schubert's Tragic Perspective', in Frisch, *Schubert: Critical and Analytical Studies*, pp. 71–5.

36. The tonality at the beginning of the development in the sonata, C♯ minor, is the original key of Schubert's song setting of the text by Schmidt von Lübeck, which opens with the words 'Ich komme aus dem Gebirge her'.

37. Francis Donald Tovey, 'Schubert', in Tovey, *Essays and Lectures on Music* (London: Oxford University Press, 1949), p. 119. Brendel describes this passage as 'eine unvergeßliche harmonische Projektion ... [wir] erleben es, als der d-Moll-Sphäre angehörend, wie aus äußerster Distanz' (an unforgettable harmonic projection ... [we] experience it as belonging to the D minor sphere, as stemming from an extreme distance); 'Schuberts letzte Sonaten', p. 81. Fisk considers this passage not only as a 'window of memory' but also as an 'epiphany'; Fisk, *Returning Cycles*, p. 253.

38. Ludwig Misch compares these themes in the chapter 'Two B Flat Major Themes', in Misch, *Beethoven Studies* (Norman: University of Oklahoma Press, 1953), pp. 19–31. Misch fails to grasp the presence of a 'principle of tonal unity' in Schubert's work.

39. This formulation stems from Edward W. Said, *On Late Style: Music and Literature Against the Grain* (New York: Pantheon, 2006), p. 114, and well applies to Schubert despite the brevity of his life.

40. See especially Budde, *Schuberts Liederzyklen*, pp. 18–22.

41. For a discussion of cyclical aspects of the Fantasie in F minor for four hands, Op. 103, see Kinderman, 'Schubert's Tragic Perspective', in *Schubert: Critical and Analytical Studies*, pp. 75–83.

42. Thomas Mann, *Doktor Faustus*, vol. 6 of *Gesammelte Werke in dreizehn Bänden* (Frankfurt am Main: S. Fischer, 1974), , p. 676.

4

From Song to Instrumental Style

Some Schubert Fingerprints

Susan Wollenberg

In this chapter, developed from my previously published work on Schubert, I examine some of the stylistic 'fingerprints' evident in the instrumental works of his last decade (1818–28), and especially those of the 1820s.[1] These features contribute significantly to what I now regard as Schubert's successful creation of music on a large scale, achieving, in Schumann's famous formulation, his 'heavenly length'.[2] Among the broader themes of the discussion that follows will be a reconsideration of aspects of the relationship between song and instrumental music in Schubert's oeuvre, while the detailed technical aspects include further study of Schubert's apparent penchant for symmetry at a variety of levels, an idea planted in my earlier work on this repertoire.

As the chapter proceeds, I will also foreground certain works of the last decade in which Schubert's fingerprints are particularly richly present, including the 'Wanderer' Fantasy, D 760, and the Fantasy in F minor for Piano Duet, D 940. These two works will provide a path to reflections on the presence of violent elements in Schubert's instrumental works—principally among the solo piano and chamber genres. These various themes will be linked with ideas of 'late style' in Schubert. Thus, by way of introduction I offer some reflections on 'lateness' in Schubert's music before opening up avenues of discussion beyond this concept. I touch briefly on these ideas here as background to the main considerations of the chapter; clearly they belong with a wider exploration of 'lateness' in the arts that is beyond the scope of the present inquiry.

The categorizing of works belonging to Schubert's last decade as a special corpus within his oeuvre is made here partly in response to Martin Cooper's study of Beethoven's late style.[3] Alan Tyson (in conversation with the present author) once expressed his view that a composer's 'last decade' was a potentially dangerous notion, presumably in view of Tyson's celebrated aptitude for source studies that led to the revision of work chronologies, most notably for Mozart.[4] But in other respects the pinning down of a composer's last works (secure chronology permitting) as expressing 'lateness' raises questions worth considering as to its implications in relation to our view of the composer's style. One notable feature is the accelerated development (together with a remarkable rate of production) that may be seen in those whose creative life was cut short in particularly untimely fashion (it is surely unnecessary yet would seem strange not to invoke here the names of Mozart and Schubert, and we might add Fanny Hensel and Felix Mendelssohn).[5]

Another element in concepts of lateness can be the sense that the composer stands on the brink of a new phase of his personal development, and perhaps that in doing so he anticipates music beyond his own time: thus, for instance, Schubert's Tenth Symphony has been perceived as Mahlerian.[6] The somewhat illusory nature of this latter formulation (and others like it) nevertheless should not be allowed to mask the impression of a composer finding profoundly new ways of expressing ideas, an impression that certainly emanates from the late works of Schubert. Yet another approach, one that does not necessarily run counter to this, is to recognise (as Cooper did in Beethoven) the seeds of the late style in the early works.[7] In this respect, a particular work may be seen retrospectively to represent a turning point towards the future. Among Schubert's earlier chamber music, the G minor String Quartet, D 173, of 1816 is such a case, while among the works of his last decade the C minor *Quartettsatz*, D 703, seems to form the gateway to the three last Quartets and the C major String Quintet, D 956.

Finally to be mentioned here among the elements of 'lateness' is the intensification or adoption of a compositional domain linked with purity of style, as if the composer were trying to achieve a more crystallized and refined mode of expression, or to create a more intensely powerful effect, or indeed perhaps both. The turn towards strict or 'learned' counterpoint seen in the late works of numerous composers, including Heinrich Schütz, J. S. Bach (intensifying his lifelong preoccupation with counterpoint in the monumental last works), Mozart and Beethoven, as well as Schubert, signals this process.[8] All of these considerations of lateness are relevant in the case of Schubert specifically, and more generally they raise the question of a composer's awareness of his own mortality at the time of writing.[9]

In this regard, a thoughtful approach is manifested by Erik Entwistle, writing on Dussek's Sonata Op. 77, 'L'Invocation', in relation to 'the mystique of the last work'. Critical reception of Op. 77 has granted this work a special status, and Entwistle is prepared to dub it Dussek's 'musical testament'.[10] But while Entwistle acknowledges the particular interest possessed by 'works written at the end of a composer's life', he signals the dangers inherent in interpreting 'the ways in which [the works] might reflect upon death or foreshadow the composer's own demise'.[11] His standpoint is informed by due caution rather than assumed certainties, as when he posits carefully that last works 'encourage us to examine and question the boundaries between a composer's daily life and his or her musical art'.[12] In the case of Dussek, Entwistle observes that the precise medical details of the composer's last illness are not clear (a circumstance that chimes with Schubert's), and that moreover 'it is not known ... where the composition of "*L'Invocation*" figures in terms of his illness'.[13] He concludes that 'we are left to imagine the specific circumstances under which this sonata was composed; determining what extra-musical meaning it might possess, if any, entails some speculation'.[14]

Strenuous efforts have been made in recent years to argue for Schubert's self-identification (linked to questions of his sexuality) with the figure of the wanderer, a figure, alienated from society,[15] whose implications are reflected in the mysterious protagonist of the *Winterreise* cycle ('Fremd bin ich eingezogen, fremd zieh' ich wieder aus'), evidently pushed out from his social milieu, who ultimately aligns himself in the closing song of the cycle with the equally mysterious hurdy-gurdy man whom nobody listens to or looks at.[16] My concern here is, rather, with Schubert's compositional persona as manifested in the late instrumental works. In these Schubert seems, at this stage of his accelerated development as a composer, to achieve a peak in the assured manipulation of his personal stylistic fingerprints, producing a remarkable series of large-scale symphonic, piano and chamber works.

In terms of the external world, Schubert's ambitions were focused during his last decade on achieving publication and public performances for his music. In his negotiations with publishers at this time he was emboldened to offer the larger-scale, more demanding instrumental works. Writing to the Leipzig publisher Heinrich Albert Probst in August 1826, Schubert specified songs with piano accompaniment, string quartets, piano sonatas and four-hand pieces as well as mentioning the Octet (D 803). Publishers typically wanted compositions that were 'agreeable' and 'easily comprehensible', as Probst put it in his response, welcoming Schubert's approach with the caution that 'the distinctive, often ingenious, but at times also rather unusual nature of your mind's creations is not yet sufficiently and generally understood by our public'.[17] When Schubert offered his new Piano Trio in E♭ major, D 929, in April 1828, Probst replied: 'I accept . . . the Trio . . . but I still hope that you will shortly accede to my request to send me very soon some selected trifles for the voice or for four hands, a trio being . . . rarely capable of bringing in any money'.[18]

With regard to his interior world as a composer, Schubert seems at this stage to challenge to greater extremes than previously the received ideas of formal and tonal norms, as in the first movement of the G major Quartet, D 887, with its aggressive opening and ending gestures questioning the whole modal nature of its tonal centre, or in the slow movement of the A major Piano Sonata, D 959, with its unprecedentedly frenzied central section throwing new light on concepts of episodic form. He subverts generic associations, as in the powerfully conceived late piano duet works, notably the F minor Fantasy, D 940, and the Grand Duo, D 812; and he shows himself a master of the enigmatic final statement, transforming the character of Haydn's playful treatment of this aspect into a profoundly disturbing phenomenon, as with the ending of the String Quintet, D 956. Such works as these belong in the sphere of his 'strivings after the highest in art', as expressed in his letter to the publisher Schott in February 1828. In his Beethoven study, Martin Cooper identified a number of shared attributes among the works of the last decade and across a variety of genres, including recurrent motives, formal characteristics, and stylistic features.[19] Applying such categories with regard to Schubert's last decade, and taking the first of them, we find that probably the most pervasive motive shared by numerous of his works is that of the neighbour-note (or 'returning-note') figure, traced (among other melodic motives) by Charles Fisk in the C minor Piano Sonata, D 958,[20] and also traceable with particular persistence in the *Quartettsatz* in C minor, D 703. In the latter work it appears as a sequential unit in the winding version of the chromatic fourth or 'lament bass' figure that forms Theme I of the movement and informs all subsequent themes (and that is itself a recurrent type or trope in Schubert's music).[21]

Here in D 703 we encounter a phenomenon that can be seen as an important characteristic of design in Schubert's instrumental works: that is, the reproduction in miniature of the larger-scale relationships within a work or movement. In D 703 this pervasive process operates on three levels (at least): its use at the motivic level is brought to our attention from the start by its sequential repetition, built so intensively into the opening theme. Once this is perceived as a motive (hereafter referred to as 'x'), its ramifications can be seen to extend in various directions in regard to the texture and construction of the themes that follow. Thus the turn figure linking the first two phrases of Theme II (in A♭ major)—themselves related sequentially and casting a look back at the subdominant, D♭, which, as the Neapolitan in C minor, formed such a vital element in the continuation of Theme I and then as an agent of transition—is an expansion of motive 'x'. (Thanks to these motivic features, the movement's kinship with D 958, also a C minor work, becomes strongly evident.)[22]

At the harmonic level, in D 703 the 'x' motive is strikingly reflected in the key relationships among three of the themes, crossing over the divide between the exposition and development sections (if a sonata-form interpretation may be accepted for this formally enigmatic movement): these are Themes II, III and IV, which create the palindromic scheme A♭–G–A♭.[23] (This in turn reminds us that the motive itself is palindromic.) And finally, in the long-range perspective of the movement's structure, the surprising appearance of the opening motive in the coda position (functioning simultaneously as the displaced recapitulatory 'double return' of Theme I that was so conspicuously missing from its 'proper place' earlier) gives the movement its framing mirror effect, with the truly cyclic return of the first theme (and indeed of the otherwise largely absent tonic C minor) at the end, as if the movement could continue to go round again, only stopped at the last moment by the emphatic perfect cadence.[24]

Other examples could be cited of this Schubertian cyclic device, both seen within individual movements such as the first movement of the G major Piano Sonata, D 894, which recalls its opening theme in valedictory fashion at its finish, and given wider application as in the A major Piano Sonata, D 959, where the whole Sonata famously features the mirroring of its intensely memorable opening chordal sequence at the end of the finale. The natural habitat of the device may be found in the fantasy genre: thus Schubert's 'Wanderer' Fantasy, D 760, and the Piano Duet Fantasy in F minor, D 940 (both falling notionally into four movements on the symphonic plan which he favoured also in his piano sonatas), exhibit the strong urge to return in apocalyptic fashion, and with extreme contrapuntal intensity, to their opening material in their finales.[25]

The neighbour-note motive ('x') discussed above is shared among not only the instrumental works (including the first movement of the 'Unfinished' Symphony, D 759),[26] but also the songs, such as the opening song of *Winterreise*, 'Gute Nacht', D 911/1, where it features in the vocabulary of the slow march (a genre or topos that is itself recurrent in Schubert's oeuvre).[27] An especially significant instance of the motive is found in 'Schöne Welt, wo bist du?' ('Die Götter Griechenlands', D 677), since the material of this song, including what I have termed motive 'x', was then shared with the A minor Quartet, D 804, to beautiful and haunting effect. Taken together with the poetic text of the song, the figure is linked to the nostalgic and regretful or mournful mood of Schiller's words: 'Ah, only in the enchanted realm of song does the legendary trace live on ... only the shadow of that once vibrant image remains'.[28] Leo Black (apropos categories of variation in Schubert) has suggested, in view of the fact that three of its four movements derive from the song, that the A minor Quartet, D 804, constitutes 'a subtle "variation" masterpiece'.[29]

In terms of shared formal characteristics among the works of Schubert's last decade, the role of variation forms part of the sense they convey that the composer is pursuing a determined project (and indeed Schubert, in an oft-quoted passage, expressed this idea explicitly in the 1820s).[30] The impression of a compendious project to redefine and construct anew the role of variation processes in instrumental forms is linked to every movement type that Schubert cultivated in the last decade, ranging from fully worked out first-movement forms to the miniature trio sections of his scherzos. Sonata forms grow in scale and expressive scope through this means, with the first movements of the G major Quartet and the String Quintet providing particularly expansive and richly developed examples of this process.[31] Schubert's concern for symmetry appears within the key scheme of the variations set constructed on Theme II in the exposition of the first movement of the G major String Quartet, D 887: the three variations here, on the tonal plan D–B♭–D, respond to the dual G major– G minor of the movement's overall key, a duality which is itself mirrored in the opening of the recapitulation.[32] The long-range tonal plan of the discrete set of variations on Theme I of this movement seesaws on a central axis, with major-minor implications formed by the variations in E♭ and E major in the development section, placed between G major on either side in the exposition and recapitulation.[33]

Tonal agendas of an interesting kind are among the shared features that characterise the works of Schubert's last decade, appearing not only in general types (as with his characteristic Neapolitan usage, in the minor form and extended as a key area), but also in specific terms. The interlinked scheme within the first movement of the B♭ Piano Sonata, D 960, whereby B♭–G♭–B♭ (the keys of the first theme's ABA format) link with the enharmonically reinterpreted F♯ minor of Theme II, develops further when this in turn becomes an enharmonic Neapolitan minor in relation to the exposition's third key area of the dominant, F major.[34] The F minor Piano Duet Fantasy, D 940, with its symmetrical plan of f–f♯–f♯–f for its four 'movements', and its turn to the parallel major in the outer sections (as well as the repeated emphasis on the Neapolitan major chord, G♭, in passages of these outer sections), plays with a similar palette of harmonic and tonal resources to D 960; these are important not only for their exotic effect but also in creating the tightly knit structure that typically underpins Schubert's most exploratory music of this period.

Beyond these detailed considerations, if we were to seek elements of an overarching artistic character linking the diverse instrumental productions of Schubert's last decade, this might take one of two forms: first, we might perceive the large-scale tension between, on the one hand, the intensely referential, tightly knit structures together with the material they contain, as seen in the examples commented on thus far, and on the other hand, the breaking or disruption of unity and continuity, at least at the surface level, represented in Schubert's much-discussed violent outbursts (as in the central section of the Andantino of D 959). On closer examination, these disruptions may prove to retain features that reflect Schubert's underlying concern with unifying his movement structures and textures.

If the *Quartettsatz*, D 703, may be seen as a turning point within Schubert's chamber music production, then among the solo piano works the 'Wanderer' Fantasy, D 760, marks a watershed in that sphere (as Elizabeth McKay has implied) in its expression of violence.[35] A remarkable aspect of this is the transformation of the song material, since the original lied 'Der Wanderer', D 489, contained none of the 'sinister exuberance' which McKay noted in the Fantasy's character.[36] Its contrast of, on the one hand, the wanderer's disillusionment with the world, conveyed in the text of the passage on which Schubert based the central variations of the Fantasy ('The sun seems so cold here, the flowers faded, life old, and what people say is nothing but empty sound') with, on the other hand, the vision of the 'land, so green with hope', is mild in comparison with the violent eruptions in the Fantasy. Also important to note is the dual nature of Schubert's contrapuntal language in D 760, expressed in the uncompromisingly stern counterpoint springing from the opening dactylic motive, as evidenced in the outer sections of the work, and, at the opposite extreme, in a passage such as that containing the gently applied contrapuntal texture of Theme II of the Fantasy's first Allegro (the lyrical E major theme introduced at bar 47), portraying the dactylic motive here in a very different light from its wilder surroundings.[37]

In the case of the song-derived A minor Quartet, D 804, the plangent falling triadic theme shared by the opening of 'Schöne Welt, wo bist du?', D 677, and the Quartet's first movement is transformed in the latter into a dramatic gesture, featuring in a developmental passage where in relation to the opening mood it acquires a noticeably explosive character by contrast (allied to a new contrapuntal agenda). The context as well as the local content of such episodes creates the violence in Schubert's instrumental writing: this is true also, for example, of the *Moments musicaux*, D 780, No. 2 in A♭, where at the close of the three-part (ABA) scheme enclosing the central episode in the exotic choice of F♯ minor, a series of unmistakably 'final' gestures creates a winding-down effect at a *pianissimo* dynamic level, all designed to signal the end. The abrupt *forte* eruption of the F♯ minor material in right-hand chords that evoke Brahms (the melody was originally heard at the lower octave and in a single line, *pianissimo*) is shattering.[38]

The second overarching characteristic we can identify resides in the ways in which song informs Schubert's instrumental writing more intensely in the late works than ever before. The connection between song and instrumental music appears as a complex phenomenon with many facets in the works of Schubert's last decade, going beyond the impression of 'sounds like' and the basic similarities of mood which John Reed observed in his catalogue of such resemblances.[39] Schubert's use of parallel major and minor, perhaps the most pervasive of his stylistic fingerprints, echoes from songs to instrumental works and back again. Thus 'Mut', D 911/22, from *Winterreise* seems to realise in miniature the major-minor 'plot' that earlier informed the events of the G major String Quartet, D 887, now allied to the images evoked by the song text ('If the snow flies in my face, I shake it off') and to the narrator's effort to brave the elements and his own despair. Working in the opposite direction, the miniature water scene painted in 'Auf dem Wasser zu singen', D 774, is later enlarged to the generous proportions of the A♭ Impromptu, D 899/4: their shared (and unusual) minor-major scheme, allied to motivic connections between the two works, suggests a direct kinship.[40]

Undoubtedly the most famous epithet applied to Schubert's fingerprints is that of 'heavenly length', coined by Robert Schumann.[41] A tradition of denigrating Schubert's ability to organize a movement (or whole work) on a large scale has persisted in recent reception of such lengths in his music. Thus Basil Smallman suggested that 'effective finales are notoriously difficult to write, and it is likely that Schubert may at times have found them particularly troublesome',[42] before describing the Finale of the E♭ Piano Trio, D 929, in comparison with that of the B♭ Trio, D 898, as 'more problematic'.[43] Smallman's view of the reasons for its alleged problematic status belongs with the views I have myself disowned (see n. 2): he goes on to assert that 'organized very sectionally, in loosely connected paragraphs, it is long and discursive, and relies heavily for its effect upon the character of its principal themes, which are not of the first order' (he does subsequently grant it a more successful effect 'when presented with authority and panache' in performance).[44]

An alternative approach to this is to consider Schubert's compositional strategies here as delivered with that 'authority and panache' which Smallman attaches to the performers' desired efforts. The Finale of D 929 combines in exhilarating fashion the various fingerprints that help give Schubert's instrumental writing its scope for expansion, including 'forms within forms', themes with tonally exploratory character, and topical variety (with a generous measure of the 'brilliant' or virtuoso topic), working together with the crux of the structure: that is, the return of material from a previous movement, a plan that in its realization here provides ample justification for a finale at greater length. In other instances even without this particular justification, the resolution of a

Example 4.1 Schubert, Fantasy in F minor, D 940, bars 561–570

From Song to Instrumental Style 69

Example 4.2 Schubert, Fantasy in F minor, D 940, bars 474–483

binding element traced through the whole work gives the finale's length, again, a strong sense of *raison d'être*: the C minor Piano Sonata, D 958, and the B♭ Sonata, D 960, are such cases.

Did Schubert have a 'late style'? Certainly we should have no difficulty acknowledging the works of the 1820s as involved in an ambitious project, in which Schubert set out to explore territory beyond received compositional frontiers, interpreting forms in new ways and creating new sounds. In works such as the F minor Duet Fantasy, D 940, the G major String Quartet, D 887, and the C major String Quintet, D 956, Schubert gathered his stylistic fingerprints into powerful and dramatic statements, preserving—however expansive their proportions—an integrity of purpose.[45] This integrity is seen even in the tiniest fragments of the music, a process that perhaps began with the intensity of the *Quartettsatz*, D 703, and culminates in, to give just one example, the deeply affecting ending of the F minor Fantasy. There, at the end of D 940, the harmonic minor scale that descends with such fateful effect in the Secondo part (bar 565: see Example 4.1), echoes the countersubject material introduced in the gargantuan fugue heard earlier in the finale (Example 4.2), which itself realized fully the project begun in the first movement (Example 4.3).

Example 4.3 Schubert, Fantasy in F minor, D 940, bars 47–58

Example 4.4 Schubert, Fantasy in F minor, D 940, bars 1–10

The fugue subject that is introduced there transforms the decorated appoggiatura motive from its original lyrical character at bar 8 (Example 4.4) into the explosive statement designed to shock on its first entry, (*subito*) *forte* at bar 48 after the preceding *pianissimo* (Example 4.3).[46]

And, also recalling its origins in the opening section of the work, the closing utterances of D 940 bring back the Neapolitan (G♭) colouring that featured in the original statement of the first, plaintive F minor theme of the work. Now, as the finale draws to a close, this harmony (poignantly extended) precipitates the perfect authentic cadence bringing closure at the penultimate stage (bars 561–563), before the valedictory final bars with their majestic cadential closure. In this last passage of the music, the rise from C to D♭ which marked the opening theme at the point where it left the F minor harmony for other harmonic choices, at bar 5 (and which has been heard again here with the return of the theme from bar 555 onwards), is resolved in reverse by the two final chords of the piece (the first of these surrounding the D♭ with the same chord as originally harmonized it in bar 5), conveying the sense of a grand and meaningful gesture in one of Schubert's most powerful mirror effects. Whatever we interpret those final bars of D 940 as representing—death, resignation, grandeur, or sorrow (Atlas with his unending misery)[47]—they, together with the closing passage as a whole, speak with a largeness of spirit and depth of experience which we could view as essentially the product, in instrumental terms, of a composer steeped in poetic expression throughout his creative life.

Notes

1. For an overview of this topic see Susan Wollenberg, *Schubert's Fingerprints: Studies in the Instrumental Works* (Farnham: Ashgate, 2011).

2. I take this opportunity to renounce my early criticisms of Schubert's finales as unjustifiably lengthy: time, and with it the further opportunity to study the late works, have helped me to see the error of these criticisms (for example, the unwarranted assertion made *en passant* apropos the finale of the G major Piano Sonata, D 894, in Susan Wollenberg, 'Schubert and the Dream', *Studi musicali* 9 [1980], p. 141, n. 13, a movement which I would now understand very differently and far more sympathetically). Such criticisms have persisted in recent analytical and critical literature, including for example the views of Basil Smallman, writing (in his survey of the piano trio repertoire) of the E♭ major Piano Trio, D 929, and Michael Talbot, in his study of the finale in Western instrumental music: see Smallman, *The Piano Trio: its History, Technique, and Repertoire* (Oxford: Clarendon Press, 1990); and Michael Talbot, *The Finale in Western Instrumental Music* (Oxford: Oxford University Press, 2001). For details see the discussion of 'heavenly length' (pp. 67–8).

3. Martin Cooper, *Beethoven: The Last Decade, 1817–1827* (Oxford: Oxford University Press, 1970; rev. edn, 1985).

4. Alan Tyson, *Mozart: Studies of the Autograph Scores* (Cambridge, MA, and London: Harvard University Press, 1987). For Schubert the best=known example of revised dating is that of the 'Great' C major Symphony, D 944, summarised in John Reed, *Schubert: the Final Years* (London: Faber, 1972).

5. For example, as I have written elsewhere, apropos discs 7–12 of the Hyperion *Complete Songs of Schubert* (CDS44201/40, issued 2005), in my contribution to a collaborative review of the collection: 'These six CDs contain a total of 133 lieder dating from the beginning of June 1815 to the end of February 1816, giving cause for contemplation of Schubert's sheer productivity as well as astonishment at his 18-year-old achievement in, frequently, the depth of his poetic interpretation' (*Nineteenth-Century Music Review* 6 [2009], p. 129).

6. Among comments along these lines, Robert Winter has expressed this perception of Schubert's Tenth with special reference to the B minor Largo: 'The remarkable slow movement ... has an uncanny foretaste of Mahler'. Winter, 'Schubert', in Stanley Sadie and John Tyrrell (eds), *The New Grove Dictionary of Music and Musicians*, 2nd rev. edn, (London: Macmillan, 2001), vol. 22, p. 689, and *Grove Music Online*.

7. Cooper, *Beethoven: the Last Decade*, pp. 415–16.

8. On Schubert's study of strict counterpoint with Simon Sechter in 1828 see Alfred Mann, 'Schubert's Lesson with Sechter', *19th-Century Music* 6 (1982–3), pp. 159–65; and Elizabeth Norman McKay, *Franz Schubert: a Biography* (Oxford: Oxford University Press, 1996), p. 302, quoting Schubert's words (inspired by his acquaintance with Handel's oratorios): 'Now for the first time I see what I lack: but I will study hard with Sechter so that I can make good the omission'.

9. How far such personal awareness can be read from the music itself is debatable, but certainly critical reception of Schubert's music has found that 'no composer delivers better the message of our mortality'; David Cairns, 'Unravelling this Mortal Coil', *The Sunday Times*, 5 January 1997, 10, p. 25.

10. Erik Entwistle, 'Dussek's *"L'Invocation"* Sonata and the Mystique of the Last Work', in Roberto Illiano and Rohan H. Stewart-MacDonald (eds), *Jan Ladislav Dussek (1760–1812): a Bohemian Composer "en voyage" through Europe*, Quaderni Clementiani 4 (Bologna: Ut Orpheus, 2012), p. 348.

11. Ibid., p. 347.

12. Ibid.

13. Ibid., p. 348.

14. Ibid.

15. See especially Charles Fisk, *Returning Cycles: Contexts for the Interpretation of Schubert's Impromptus and Last Sonatas* (Berkeley and Los Angeles: University of California Press, 2001).

16. Ian Bostridge has spoken eloquently of the enigmatic nature of these two figures (in his lecture as Humanitas Visiting Professor at the University of Oxford, 'Why Winterreise? Schubert's Song Cycle, Then and Now', St John's College, 18 November 2014). See also his *Schubert's Winter Journey: Anatomy of an Obsession* (London: Faber and Faber, 2015).

17. Peter Clive, *Schubert and His World: a Biographical Dictionary* (Oxford: Clarendon Press, 1997), p. 157.

18. Otto Erich Deutsch, *Schubert: A Documentary Biography* (London: J. M. Dent & Sons, 1946), p. 767.

19. See especially Chapter 20, 'Characteristics of the Late Style', pp. 415–38, on the stylistic features linking Beethoven's late works.

20. See Fisk, *Returning Cycles*, pp. 180 ff.

21. For more on D 703 see Wollenberg, *Schubert's Fingerprints*, pp. 128 and 130.

22. On its kinship with the motivic fabric of *Winterreise*, see p. 65.

23. The wrapping of such patterns in the key schemes of entire works is perhaps most familiar from the String Quintet, D 956, with its slow movement's central Neapolitan minor episode forming the tonal design E–f–E within the larger C/c–D♭–c/C of the whole (in the diagrammatic representation of keys, as here, capital letters indicate major keys and lowercase letters, minor keys). On a similar instance of 'wrapping' noted by Hinrichsen in the first movement of the B♭ major Piano Sonata, D 960, see Wollenberg, *Schubert's Fingerprints*, Chapter 7, 'Threefold Constructions', pp. 208–9, referring to Hans-Joachim Hinrichsen, *Untersuchungen zur Entwicklung der Sonatenform bei Schubert* (Tutzing: Hans Schneider, 1994).

24. Among examples of this process in Schubert's songs are the powerful evocations of a lingering mood in 'Gretchen am Spinnrade', D 118, and 'Der Atlas', D 957/8, where the opening lines of the text are recalled at the end of the setting.

25. These various examples overlap to some extent with what seems a rather different case, in which a more introductory function characterizes the opening bars of a movement, so that their return at the end is evocative of the song-related device whereby a piano prelude returns as the postlude to the song. Such a case is the F minor Impromptu, D 935/1, discussed in a compelling analysis by John Daverio, *Crossing Paths: Schubert, Schumann, and Brahms* (New York and Oxford: Oxford University Press, 2002), Part 1, Chapter 2, 'The Gestus of Remembering', pp. 47–62.

26. The treatment of the 'x' motive in Theme I of the first movement of D 759 (beginning with the two preparatory bars of accompaniment texture before the theme enters at bar 13) ingeniously incorporates it within the semiquaver *moto perpetuo* pattern of the accompaniment, as well as in the theme itself in augmented values, and with its first phrase repeated immediately, thus bringing it to the listener's attention all the more insistently. It then continues to be worked into both theme and accompaniment in a variety of ways, including melodic inversion and rhythmic mutation. The combination of an intensely expressive thematic statement with a high degree of technical ingenuity is characteristic of late Schubert.

27. See Wollenberg, *Schubert's Fingerprints*, pp. 208–9 and Examples 7.10 (a) and (b).

28. For an examination of the relationship between the song and the Quartet, see Nicholas Rast, '"Schöne Welt, wo bist du?" Motive and Form in Schubert's A Minor String Quartet', in Brian Newbould (ed.), *Schubert the Progressive: History, Performance Practice, Analysis* (Aldershot: Ashgate, 2003), pp. 81–8. On the role of memory in the A minor Quartet see Benedict Taylor, 'Schubert and the Construction of Memory: the String Quartet in A minor, D.804 ("Rosamunde")', *Journal of the Royal Musical Association* 139/1 (2014), pp. 41–88.

29. Review of Wollenberg, *Schubert's Fingerprints*, *Musical Times* (Winter 2012), p. 100. This creates a phenomenon comparable to the pervasive use of the song material throughout D 810 (the 'Death and the Maiden' Quartet), creating also in that case a variations piece 'writ large', beyond the formal variations of its slow movement.

30. See McKay, *Franz Schubert*, pp. 201–2, quoting, from Otto Erich Deutsch, Schubert's remark to Leopold Kupelweiser in March 1824 that he intended his efforts at instrumental forms to 'pave my way towards a grand symphony'.

31. For further discussion of the differing uses of variation processes in Schubert's instrumental forms see Wollenberg, *Schubert's Fingerprints*, Chapter 8, 'Schubert's Variations', pp. 214–43.

32. For more on these aspects see Wollenberg, *Schubert's Fingerprints*, especially pp. 59–61.

33. See ibid., pp. 235–40.

34. Suzannah Clark rehearses the debate about the value of elaborate descriptions of tonal phenomena in Schubert, particularly between Richard Cohn (against) and Charles Fisk (in favour), in *Analyzing Schubert* (Cambridge: Cambridge University Press, 2011), pp. 152–5; it could be argued, however, that such descriptions aptly convey the intricacy and inventiveness of Schubert's tonal imagination.

35. McKay, *Franz Schubert*, p. 148, refers to D 760 as standing out 'in the context of musical evidence of Schubert's disturbed moods and the aggression of which he was capable'; I would add that this is not necessarily to argue for his reflecting his own mood in a particular piece, but rather for his creation of the psychological character to his music that Robert Schumann identified.

36. Ibid., p. 149.

37. These kinds of transformations also inform the proceedings in the later F minor Duet Fantasy, D 940, discussed further below.

38. Of the performances I have heard, that of Mitsuko Uchida, *Schubert: Piano Sonata in E♭ Major, D568; 6 Moments musicaux, D780* (Philips CD 470 164-2, 2001) most intensely conveys the shock effect of this moment.

39. John Reed, 'Thematic and Stylistic Links between the Songs and the Instrumental Works', in *The Schubert Song Companion* (Manchester: Manchester University Press, 1985), pp. 494–8.

40. For more on this topic see Susan Wollenberg, 'Schubert's "Water Music": Case Studies in the Instrumental Works', *Schubert-Jahrbuch 2010-2013*, vol. 1 ('"Vom Wasser haben wir's gelernt": Wassermetaphorik und Wanderermotiv bei Franz Schubert', Internationaler Schubert-Kongreβ Duisburg 2012, ed. Christiane Schumann, Deutscher Schubert-Gesellschaft 2014), pp. 73–81.

41. A detailed exploration of this aspect is included in Wollenberg, *Schubert's Fingerprints*, chapter 9, 'Heavenly Length', pp. 245–86.

42. Smallman, *The Piano Trio*, p. 76.

43. Ibid., p. 79.

44. Ibid., pp. 80–1. A derogatory attitude to Schubert's organisational ability is shown in Talbot, *The Finale in Western Instrumental Music*, for example in his reference to Schubert's '"laissez faire" approach to modulation' (p. 97).

45. For a variety of analytical responses to these late works see particularly William Kinderman, 'Schubert's Tragic Perspective', in Walther Frisch (ed.), *Schubert: Critical and Analytical Studies* (Lincoln: University of Nebraska Press, 1986), pp. 65–83; Walther Frisch, '"You Must Remember This": Memory and Structure in Schubert's String Quartet in G Major, D 887', *Musical Quarterly* 84/4 (2000), pp. 582–603; and John Gingerich, 'Remembrance and Consciousness in Schubert's C-Major String Quintet, D956', *Musical Quarterly* 84/4 (2000), pp. 619–34.

46. Performers who add a crescendo in bar 47 defeat this effect. Schubert reserved the crescendo for the bar before the analogous fugal passage in A minor (bars 74–89), by which point the explosive mood has already been well established.

47. Among their multiple referents is the descending chromatic fourth traditionally associated with death and lamenting and (as mentioned earlier)

found throughout Schubert's oeuvre as a recurrent musical topos. For Schubert it may have resounded with echoes of Mozart's 'Dissonance' Quartet, K 465: see Susan Wollenberg, 'The C Major String Quintet D 956: Schubert's "Dissonance Quartet"', *Schubert durch die Brille* 28 (2002), pp. 45–54. In keeping with its profundity, the F minor Fantasy has elicited a variety of critical interpretations: besides Kinderman, 'Schubert's Tragic Perspective', see Nicholas Rast, 'Une déclaration d'amour en code? la Fantaisie en *fa* mineur D940 de Schubert et la comtesse Caroline Esterházy', *Cahiers Franz Schubert* 13 (October 1998), pp. 5–16; and Philip Brett, 'Piano Four-Hands: Schubert and the Performance of Gay Male Desire', *19th-Century Music* 21/2 (1997), pp. 149–76, for a highly personal contextualization of his 'too, too tragic version of the Fantasy' (p. 176). Leo Black offers a searching personal interpretation of Schubert's spiritual outlook; Black, *Franz Schubert: Music and Belief* (Woodbridge: Boydell Press, 2003).

5

The Sensuous as a Constructive Force in Schubert's Late Works

Brian Black

Schubert's acute sensitivity to the purely sensuous quality of sound and its expressive potential is a feature of his style that sets his music apart from that of virtually all of his contemporaries. It lies at the heart of his innovative use of harmony, his affecting modulations, and his intense lyricism. And out of this sensitivity flows a unique dramatic process that brings to his music a powerful concentration and unity, evident above all in the works of his last years.

The sensuous in Schubert's music might at first seem like a tantalisingly vague notion, yet it is possible to define it more concretely. By 'the sensuous', I mean those elements in his music that stand out as particularly vivid and affecting sonorities or events and as such imprint themselves on the memory of the listener. This involves parameters in music that are often considered secondary, such as register, chord configuration and voice leading, which contribute to the sonority's specific character. It also includes the means by which Schubert highlights that sonority and successively reveals its significance as the piece progresses. To be more precise musically, the sensuous in Schubert's music may be seen as a combination of three characteristic elements of his style. The first consists of the basic musical material he uses, specifically his interest in modal mixture and third relations, both harmonic and tonal. The second concerns the manner in which he handles this material, above all his cultivation of common-tone shifts and enharmonic reinterpretation coupled with a profound understanding of the special colouring of register and chord disposition. The third involves the way his music unfolds across a movement or a piece. Here we are dealing with an idiosyncratic developmental process, one which contrasts sharply with that of his Classical contemporaries, especially Beethoven.

Beethoven's style has long been considered the perfect embodiment of what Schoenberg referred to as 'developing variation'—the successive alteration of a motive across a movement.[1] What is particularly characteristic of Beethoven's developing variation is its emphasis on fragmentation,[2] in which increasingly shorter motivic units drive the music forward.[3] As has often been pointed out, Schubert's music has a less dynamic character.[4] His developmental processes depend more on cross-references, in which motivic events are recalled across longer stretches of music than those involved in the immediate generative transformations of developing variation.[5] Both the effect and the mechanics of Schubert's developmental processes are thus radically different from his predecessors'.[6] Owing to the absence of intensifying fragmentation, the recurring motivic event seems to intrude into the musical discourse, rather than to direct its unfolding, and the type of change that marks the music is one of sudden transformation—a moment of revelation—as opposed to goal-oriented striving. It is this aspect of Schubert's style that colours his music with the aura of memory, a topic of importance in recent Schubert scholarship.[7]

Such a developmental process depends heavily on the sensuous aspects of music for its intelligibility. Carefully established parallels involving the return of certain key sonorities are crucial in the projection of the different stages of the drama and their meaning. These sonorities often arise from a striking progression based on a common-tone chord shift, a harmonic third relation or enharmonic reinterpretation. Their returns are underlined by audible connections through the music's sounding surface involving register, timbre and chord configuration. And it is the resulting web of allusions and reminiscences that makes the dramatic process and the significance of its tonal relations audible to the listener.

The elements that I have isolated as the sensuous in Schubert's music—modal mixture and harmonic and tonal third relations, for instance—are usually considered non-functional in that they are often taken to be of only local significance, rather than serving the larger form. Furthermore, Schubert's sensuous handling of them stands outside the conventional norms of the Classical style, a style synonymous with solid, logical musical construction. (Indeed, his use of sudden common-tone modulations and enharmonic reinterpretation often produces effects that reflect the concerns and aesthetics of early Romanticism.) The association of the term 'sensuous' with the unconventional, apparently non-functional elements which are also deeply characteristic of his music—its quintessentially Schubertian qualities, so to speak—raises an important question. The adjective itself brings with it certain implications in modern usage, above all the privileging of the senses over the intellect, as if the enjoyment of the experience were an end in itself. Thus the effect of, say, a common-tone modulation can be looked on as a touching but isolated moment in the music where the immediate pleasure of the effect trumps the overall logic of the form. This is, in fact, how some of the sensuous aspects of Schubert's music have been viewed in the past, a topic that will be addressed in the next section. But there is no opposition between the senses and the intellect in Schubert's music. In fact, Schubert takes the sensuous elements of his style and, rather than endowing them with only a limited formal function, through great artistry and intellectual control transforms them into a constructive force that helps to define the musical structure and its tonal hierarchy while generating the music's great expressive power.

The Sensuous in the Reception History of Schubert's Music

Throughout the nineteenth century and well into the twentieth, the sensuous aspects of Schubert's music were viewed as indications of a *sensual*,[8] non-reflective approach to composition that sacrificed structural rigour to a hedonistic gratification of the moment. Schubert's interest in third relations, which were considered colouristic rather than functional, contributed to this view.[9] Furthermore, his use of repetition, his non-dynamic developmental process and his unusual methods of modulation led to accusations of formal weakness in the first detailed theoretical treatments of his music from the early twentieth century. Donald Francis Tovey, for instance, referred to even Schubert's 'maturest works in large instrumental forms' as 'diffuse and inconsistent',[10] while Felix Salzer condemned Schubert's sonata form as a self-indulgent expansion of the Classical model.[11] As late as 1978, James Webster still observed weaknesses in Schubert's handling of the form arising from the composer's putative inhibitions.[12]

What seems to have been the main stumbling block for Schubert's critics was essentially the unconventional characteristics of his music with respect to the preceding Classical style. Rather than a radical departure from that style, these unusual elements consist of subtle changes which were thus viewed as a misunderstanding or mishandling of what were considered the basic principles of sound musical construction. His approach to sonata form received the most criticism in this respect. Here, for example, Schubert's exploration of third relations was treated as merely the cultivation of local effects, which, as non-functional digressions, bloated the form while undermining the conventional tonal poles of tonic and dominant. This is essentially Salzer's objection to Schubert's three-key expositions.[13] Schubert's unconventional modulations, which often rely upon a sudden tonal shift rather than a careful dominant preparation for the new key, also drew some fire. Tovey referred to them as 'abrupt and sometimes primitive dramatic stroke[s]',[14] while Webster considered them to be indicative of Schubert's 'antipathy to the dominant', a supposed formal shortcoming in the composer's style.[15] We will return to these ideas later and deal with them in more detail.

The last two decades have seen a number of attempts to shine a more positive light on the unique characteristics of Schubert's music. Some writers embrace the music's sensuous aspects, simply reinterpreting as strengths what were once considered weaknesses. In her discussion of the second movement of the 'Unfinished' Symphony, D 759, for instance, Susan McClary proposes that Schubert has deliberately constructed a new subjectivity, which 'disdain[s] goal-oriented desire per se for a sustained image of pleasure and an open, flexible sense of self' by the way the main theme appears to 'drift freely through enharmonic and oblique modulations, rather than establishing a clear tonic and pursuing a dynamic sequence of modulations'.[16]

Other writers have attempted to establish an innovative logic in Schubert's harmonic practice. Richard L. Cohn, for instance, proposes that certain chromatic passages involving third relations, modal mixture, common-tone shifts and enharmonic reinterpretation reveal an alternative method of organisation in which functional harmony is replaced by progressions best understood through neo-Riemannian voice-leading efficiency.[17] Cohn's focus on defining harmonic relations through semitonal displacement, however, eliminates the sensuous aspect of such progressions—their expressive effect—which depends upon expectations arising in the listener from the underlying implications of functional tonality.

To understand Schubert's music, we need not view it as a process of free association ruled by the principle of sustained pleasure; nor must we ignore its sensuous qualities in order to establish its fundamental logic. Schubert's cultivation of the sensuous in his mature works is crucial to their success, both expressively and structurally. Not only is the dramatic process made audible to the listener through the music's sensuous aspects, but these aspects generate a new subtlety and emotional complexity in its key relations while maintaining a clear focus on the fundamental tonal underpinnings of the form. A good example of this is found in one of Schubert's late lieder, 'Ihr Bild' from *Schwanengesang*.

The Sensuous and the Projection of 'Ihr Bild''s Cycle of Loss

Heine's poem enacts the reawakening of grief for a lost love (Table 5.1). As the lover stares at the portrait of his beloved, her presence comes alive in his

Table 5.1 Heinrich Heine, 'Ihr Bild,' text and translation[a]

Ich stand in dunkeln Träumen	I stood darkly dreaming,
Und starrt' ihr Bildnis an,	staring at her picture
Und das geliebte Antlitz	and that beloved face
Heimlich zu leben began.	sprang mysteriously to life.
Um ihre Lippen zog sich	About her lips played
Ein Lächeln wunderbar.	a wondrous smile.
Und wie von Wehmutstränen	And as with sad tears
Erglänzte ihr Augenpaar.	gleamed her eyes.
Auch meine Tränen flossen	And my tears flowed
Mir von der Wangen herab.	upon my cheeks.
Und ach! Ich kann es nicht glauben,	And ah, I cannot believe
Daß ich dich verloren hab!	that I have lost you!

[a] Text and translation from Dietrich Fischer-Dieskau, *The Fischer-Dieskau Book of Lieder*, trans. George Bird and Richard Stokes (London: Victor Gollancz, 1976), p. 334.

imagination so vividly that he feels the pain of her loss as acutely as in the moment he first lost her. Schubert translates the poem's cycle of grief into an ABA′ structure in which sensuous harmonic relationships—the modal shift between tonic minor and major and the third relation between the tonic, B♭, and the submediant, G♭—carry the poem's narrative. These relationships and their expressive significance are conveyed by the different colourings of B♭, whose successive reinterpretation, as William Kinderman has pointed out,[18] marks each stage of the drama (Example 5.1 and the summary in Example 5.2).

The emergence of the first stanza from the bleak loneliness of the lover into the first stirrings of life he sees in the portrait is expressed by the move from the stark B♭s in the vocal part, doubled by the piano in its low register, to the transformation of the same melodic B♭ by the modal change from minor to major in bar 9 coupled with the change first to a full four- and then to a six-part homophonic texture in the piano. The comforting indications of recognition and sympathy that he projects onto the portrait's face in the second stanza are expressed in the new, warmer colouring of B♭ by the expanded submediant chord (G♭ major) in bars 18 and 22. However, the illusion fades under the low B♭s of bars 23–24 when the G♭ harmony turns back as a neighbouring augmented sixth to an empty B♭ chord. This transformation sets the stage for the return of the A section in which the lover's intense eruption of grief is accomplished by the same modal change as in the first stanza (bars 31ff.; see the summary in Example 5.2).[19] The finality of his loss is then hammered home by the concluding emphatic cadence in B♭ minor.

What is particularly striking in the poem is the immediacy of the beloved to the lover. Here we experience a yearning so intense that it wills the object of its longing into an active physical presence that recognises the lover and sympathises with him. Schubert conveys this aspect of the text by establishing an apparent solidity in those tonal regions that represent the beloved's presence, B♭ major and G♭ major, before undermining them in favour of B♭ minor. The tonal solidity of each region is accomplished through a strong affirmation of its tonic. In the B♭ major section (bars 9–14), the crucial D natural of the modal shift is actually the initial bass tone of a perfect-cadential progression (bars 9–12). The chromatic alteration and the less stable first inversion of the tonic triad give this progression a propulsive energy that suggests desire itself, while the firm cadential arrival in bar 12 paints the longed-for presence as something concrete. The actuality of this presence is reaffirmed by a second cadence closing the A section (bars 13–14).

B♭ major, though, is immediately undercut by the turn towards G♭ major (bars 15–16), a move that brings us back to the harmonic relationships of B♭ minor. In fact, the recall of the opening texture of the song—the B♭ octaves between piano and voice—and the line's downward unwinding through A♭ to G♭ suggest more a return to B♭ minor than an escape into G♭ major at this point. (The balance is tipped in favour of G♭ only with the arrival of its dominant

Example 5.1 Schubert, 'Ihr Bild', D 957/9, bars 1–36

The Sensual in Schubert's Late Works 83

Example 5.2 Schubert, 'Ihr Bild', D 957/9, Section A, D 957/9, bars 1–25

Example 5.3 Schubert, 'Ihr Bild', D 957/9, summary of inner voice descent from B♭ to F, bars 15–24

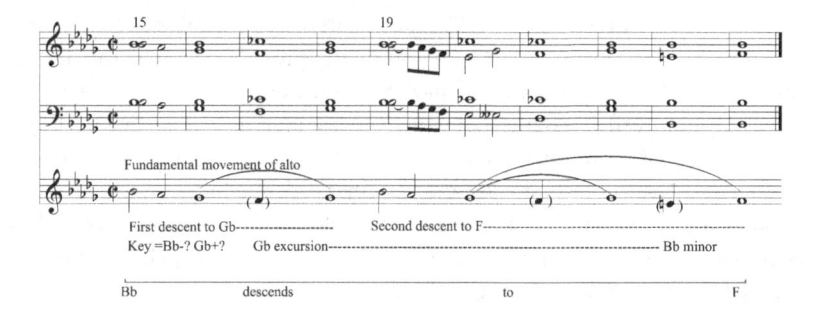

seventh in bar 17.) Thus the music moves immediately from certainty to uncertainty coloured by a reference to its first state of loneliness.

The two lines of the poem set in G♭ major represent the turning point in the narrative, for the portrait's loving smile acknowledging the lover constitutes the beloved's most palpable presence, while her tear brings the lover back to the realisation of his loss. Once again G♭ is given substance by the emphatic dominant–tonic gestures that close each of the two poetic lines (bars 17–18 and 22–23). The opening of each line, however, is tonally ambiguous, poised between B♭ minor and G♭ major. Furthermore the whole section is built upon an expansion of the cadential bass line of bars 12–13, now transferred to an inner voice and outlining a descent from tonic to dominant in B♭ minor (bars 15–17, repeated expanded and varied in bars 19–24), with the final arrival of F as the dominant degree delayed until bar 24 (see the summary in Example 5.3). G♭ major thus turns out to be only a momentary diversion along this path—a distraction from the line's ultimate goal of a return to B♭ minor.

The gesture that achieves this return in bars 23–24 is one of the most strikingly sensuous in the lied.[20] It brings together two motivic reminiscences that clarify the true significance of G♭ major: the framing B♭ octaves recall the piano's two opening B♭s, now further darkened by a lower octave;[21] and the inner motion from G♭ to F recalls the bass of the piano's interlude in bars 7–8, echoing the vocal line in bars 5–6. These parallels, which are made explicit by the same low registral colouring and which culminate in the stark sonority of the B♭ chord, make the actual lifelessness of the portrait immediately audible to the listener. And the descending-third motive ('x'), which suggested the playfulness of a living smile in bar 18, now anticipates the lover's first tears.

The G♭–F component of the gesture in bars 23–24 is itself motivic, linking crucial points in the song. Like the B♭, its reinterpretation constitutes an expressive component of each of the three tonal areas—tonic minor, tonic major and submediant. It first appears as the lover is lost in the 'dark dreams' of the opening stanza, outlining a 6–5 movement in B♭ minor (Example 5.1, bars 5–6, echoed in the piano's bass, bars 7–8). In bar 13 it reappears transformed as a G natural–F 6–5 motion underpinning the concluding cadence in B♭ major (bars 13–14). The motive then functions as a 1–7 motion in G♭ major at the point of diversion to the submediant (bar 17; repeated in bar 21). It subsequently marks the return to B♭ minor in bars 23–24 and finally provides the bass line for the concluding cadence in B♭ minor in bar 35. Three points in particular are connected through easily recognisable returns of the motive in the same rhythmic and melodic configuration: the concluding cadence of the B♭ major section, the subsequent diversion to G♭ major and the final cadence in B♭ minor. Thus the two keys that represent the illusion of the beloved's presence are denied by the emphatic closing gesture of the song, which explicitly dispels the previous parallel cadence in B♭ major—the springboard of the lover's hopes.

Viewing 'Ihr Bild' now from a broader perspective, we find an idiosyncratic yet highly effective developmental process. Much depends upon the new colorings of those elements common to all three keys—the recurring B♭ and the G♭–F gesture. Rather than forming the substance of a process of intensification through immediate fragmentation and motivic spinning out, these motives emerge as recurring sonorities, the transformation of which gives meaning to the various stages of the drama. And their web of cross-references, linked through common register and sonority, establish both the expressive and the structural significance of the keys involved in the song's tonal plan.

The Sensuous and Tonal Relationships in the Impromptu in G♭ Major, Op. 90, D 899, No. 3

A similar process of allusion and transformation is found in the Impromptu in G♭ major, D 899, Op. 90 No. 3. Here the piece's main tonal relationship—between the tonic, G♭ major, and its submediant, E♭ minor—is projected through the different harmonic colourings of, once again, a single note, B♭. Harmonic transformations of this note mark the principal stages of the music's unfolding drama (Example 5.4).[22] Three passages are crucial to this process: the shift from tonic to submediant at the beginning of the Impromptu

(Example 5.4a, bars 1–2), the turn to E♭ minor initiating the central B section (Example 5.4b, bar 25) and the modal change from E♭ minor to major towards the end of that section (Example 5.4c, bars 47–49). In all instances the B♭ appears in the same register with the same right-hand chordal configuration, yet each time it is animated by a new character.

Example 5.4a Schubert, Impromptu in G♭ major, D 899/3, opening shift from I to VI, bars 1–2

Example 5.4b Schubert, Impromptu in G♭ major, D 899/3, shift from G♭ major to E♭ minor, bars 24–25

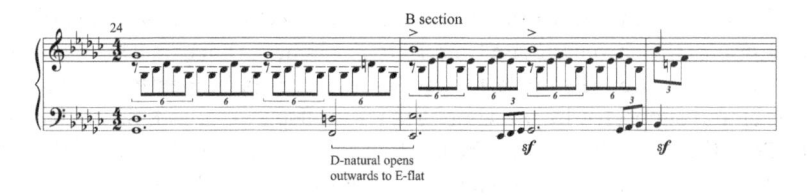

Example 5.4c Schubert, Impromptu in G♭ major, D 899/3, shift to E♭ major in interior of B section, bars 47–49

Example 5.4d Schubert, Impromptu in G♭ major, D 899/3, return to G♭ major and A′ section, bars 54–55

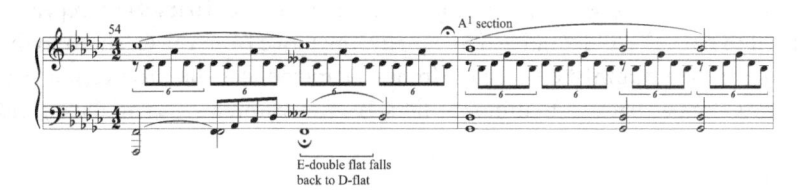

In the first instance, the submediant of the initial tonic–submediant progression is projected as something oracular and unsettling owing to the new colouring of the melodic B♭ by the E♭ minor chord (Example 5.4a). This effect is heightened by the move in the left hand from the G♭–D♭ fifth to the stern E♭ octave. In the turn to E♭ minor at the beginning of the B section (Example 5.4b), the bass's E♭ octave is once again preceded by the G♭–D♭ fifth in the same register, thereby reinforcing the parallel with the opening of the impromptu; but now the E♭ octave has become more forceful, launching the scalar figure in the bass that rises against the repeated B♭ in the treble. Thus, as the music erupts into the key its first harmonic gesture foreshadowed, it also releases the latent anguish of that gesture. In the third instance, this anguish is stilled by a sudden turn to E♭ major (Example 5.4c, bar 48). However, the E♭ chord is now in the less stable $^6_3$ position, and when it finally reaches stability at the cadence in bar 51, the music quickly darkens in a retransition that returns through a tonicisation of A♭ minor to the A section and G♭ major.

Both the entrance and exit points of the B section highlight a carefully established enharmonic link between G♭ major and E♭ minor—the D natural/ E double ♭. This pitch connects the E♭ octave of the submediant chord to the G♭–D♭ fifth of the tonic. At the entrance to the B section it opens outwards as D natural in the chromatic rise from D♭ to E♭ (Example 4b, bars 24–25). At the end of the B section (Example 4d, bar 54) it returns prominently in the same register and supported by the same bass F to collapse back as E double ♭ onto the D♭ of the home dominant—the last harmonic gesture in the preparation of the return to G♭ major. The double nature of this one pitch thus provides the doorway into and out of the emotional heart of the piece.

The Impromptu involves one more important key: C♭ major. That key and its relationships are essential in establishing the character and structure of the middle section. In the A section, C♭ has a conventionally functional role, in that it serves as the cadential pre-dominant in two of the section's cadences (bars 7–8 and 14–16). In the B section, C♭ takes on a sensuous role in that it does not contribute to the functional reinforcement of the second key, E♭ minor, but instead represents an escape from it, which undermines E♭'s stability and colours it with a sense of yearning. C♭'s appearances in the A section, however, already foreshadow its character and relationship with E♭ minor in the B section. As Charles Fisk points out, C♭'s first entrance in bar 7 blocks the immediately preceding dominant of E♭ minor.[23] Furthermore, the expansions of C♭ in the A section are each prepared by a sequential move from A♭ to C♭ that gives C♭ the yearning quality it projects in the B section (bars 9–12; repeated varied in bars 17–20, Example 5.5). Finally, the move from the C♭ chord to the common-tone diminished seventh in bar 21 introduces the progression that brings C♭ major back to E♭ minor in bars 39–40 (Examples 5.5a and 5.5b, and see Example 5.7).

Example 5.5a Schubert, Impromptu in G♭ major, D 899/3, A section, sequential move to C♭ chord, bars 17–21

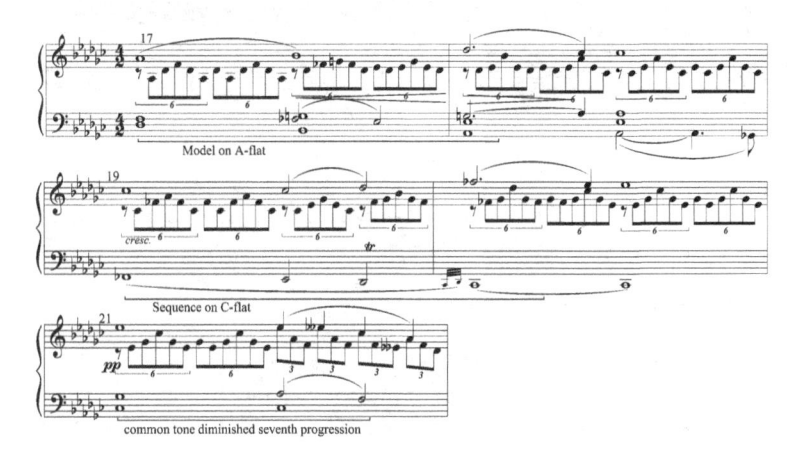

Example 5.5b Schubert, Impromptu in G♭ major, D 899/3, A section, basic progression, bar 21

The B section is built in two outwardly striving arcs—the first moving to C♭ major, the second to E♭ major. The modulation to C♭ suggests a sudden release. This effect is created by a cadential deflection in which a thrice-evaded cadence in E♭ minor is unexpectedly diverted to C♭ major (Example 5.6, bars 27, 30 and 31). The crucial hinge here is the F♭$_3^6$ chord, which, instead of acting as the Neapolitan sixth in E♭, becomes the IV$_3^6$ of C♭.[24] The unexpected shift to C♭ is thus endowed with a certain sensuous quality, a particular emotional colour that suggests both a longing for that key and the key's dream-like fragility.

Soon after its cadential arrival, C♭ dissipates through the common-tone diminished-seventh progression that shifts the music to the diminished seventh of E♭ minor (Example 5.7a and b, bars 39–40).

The shift to the diminished seventh of E♭ minor initiates the section's second arc, culminating in a perfect cadence in E♭ major (bar 51). Here the previous diversion to C♭ is corrected by a passage (Example 5.8, bars 46–51) that clearly

Example 5.6 Schubert, Impromptu in G♭ major, D 899/3, diversion to C♭ major in B section

Example 5.7a Schubert, Impromptu in G♭ major, D 899/3, return to E♭ minor in B section, bars 39–40

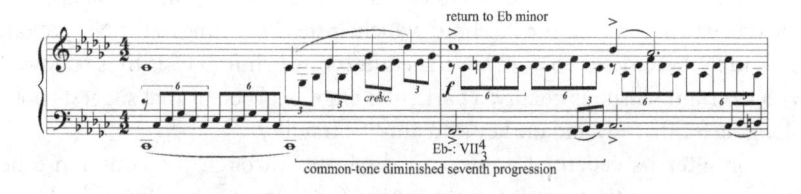

Example 5.7b Schubert, Impromptu in G♭ major, D 899/3, basic chord progression, bars 39–40

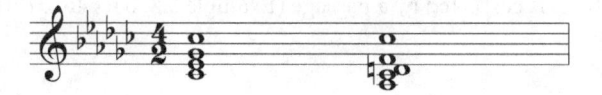

Example 5.8 Schubert, Impromptu in G♭ major, D 899/3, move to E♭ major, bars 46–51

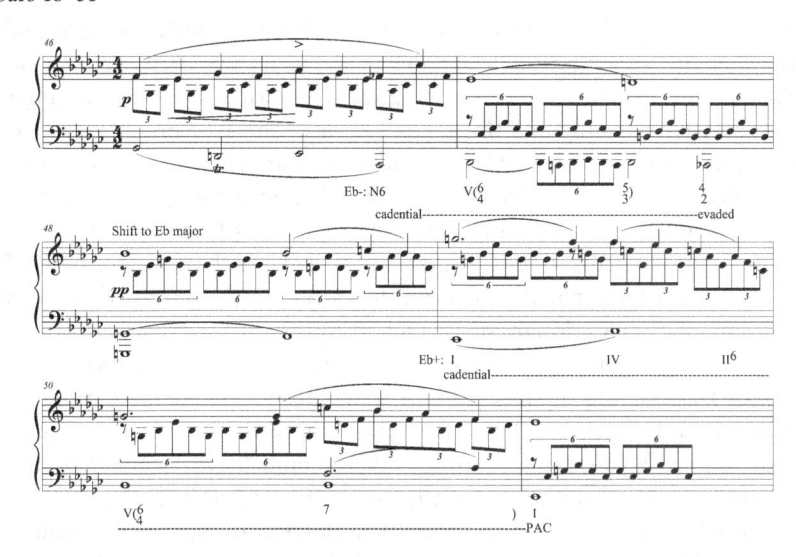

parallels the deflection to C♭ major in bars 31–35, once again employing the F♭$^6_3$ (bar 46). Now, however, the chord functions as a true Neapolitan sixth, maintaining the tonic focus of E♭.

The Impromptu's B section provides a good example of the tonal and e‑motional complexity of Schubert's second key regions. Such regions are not monochromatic, but are built up by contrasting tonal excursions.[25] In the present case, C♭ major becomes an expressive foil to E♭ minor, one that affects the latter's structural significance and emotional meaning. As in the G♭ passage in 'Ihr Bild', the unusual way C♭ is entered and the manner in which it is left create the aura of its insubstantiality. And its visionary intrusion in turn suggests the essential instability of E♭, which, with the cadential arrival of E♭ major, also darkens and subsides before the return of G♭ major. In fact, the point of this return (bar 54) is marked by the same diminished seventh chord in the same register as the evaporation of C♭ major before E♭ minor in bar 40. Thus C♭ is contained within E♭ as E♭ is eventually contained within the home key of G♭. The B section thus reveals what might best be called a sensuous handling of key relationships. Rather than a carefully prepared linear movement between successive keys, one key unexpectedly intrudes upon another and then disappears, overlaying the original key with a new emotional patina, much like the subtle transformation of colours through glazes in oil painting.[26]

The Sensuous in Schubert's Sonata Forms

So far in our treatment of the sensuous in Schubert's music we have dealt with what are usually considered secondary musical parameters: connections through common register, chord spacing and transformations in the harmonic and expressive meaning of a single note. All have involved progressions that themselves are usually treated as sensuous or colouristic in their significance, as opposed to the perceived structural role of fifth relations. Since both of the examples we have considered are intimate miniatures that represent simple ternary designs based exclusively upon keys related by a third, the sensuous elements we have highlighted also have a clear structural significance. But what about a more complex design, such as sonata form?

Schubert's cultivation of the sensuous has often been portrayed as the root cause of a distracting expansion of his sonata form—one that compromises the form's inherent logic. This is the chief complaint of Felix Salzer, two of whose charges have exerted a strong influence on Schubert scholarship over the twentieth century. The first is that Schubert's extended lyricism has no place in sonata form. According to Salzer, such lyricism supplants the improvisatory drive of motivic development by the over-repetition of a basic idea and thus runs counter to the form's basic principles.[27] The second charge is that Schubert's famous three-key expositions weaken the unity of the form by positing two competing keys as poles to the home key. To these charges must be added what Webster considers to be Schubert's failures in handling the form, expressed as the composer's supposed inhibitions 'against leaving the tonic, against establishing new keys by dominant preparation, at times against the dominant itself, and against placing an entire large section in a single key'.[28]

All of the features attacked by Schubert's critics are products of his cultivation of the sensuous. They come together in Schubert's treatment of third-related keys in his sonata forms. Here, once again, he differs from Beethoven.[29] When Beethoven turns to third relations in his sonata forms, as in the famous opening movement of the 'Waldstein' Sonata, these key regions usually supplant the dominant as the tonal pole to the tonic through their careful preparation by their own dominants, a procedure that is considered a formal orthodoxy.[30] Schubert's treatment of third-related keys is more complex and involves the type of overlaying already hinted at in 'Ihr Bild' and the G♭ Impromptu.

In the first place, the dominant is often maintained as the exposition's tonal pole, even in the minor mode, where such a role traditionally fell to the relative major key. The result is Schubert's three-key exposition, in which a middle key, often related to the tonic by a third, is interposed between the home key and its dominant. Thus the exposition not only must establish a tonal pole to the tonic, but in so doing must also clarify the relationship between the two subordinate keys. In such cases the middle key is subordinated to the exposition's concluding key. This is accomplished by projecting the middle key as a less stable entity than the concluding key, and at times by inflecting the former towards the latter. On the other hand, events in the middle key are often of expressive significance to the concluding key. Consequently, the relationship between the two keys is both structural, in that a hierarchy is established between them, and sensuous, in that one colours the other emotionally. The way this relationship is achieved and made audible depends upon Schubert's handling of the 'secondary' sensuous musical elements we have looked at in the previous examples. Here repetition, circular movement and parallelism become important vehicles for the listener's experience of the true structural and expressive significance of the keys involved. As an example, we turn briefly to the first movement of the String Quartet in D minor, D 810, 'Death and the Maiden'.[31]

The Sensuous and the Thematic and Tonal Relations in the First Movement of the String Quartet in D Minor, D 810, "Death and the Maiden"

This movement's exposition is one of the three-key types condemned by Salzer (Table 5.2).

Its two subordinate tonalities of F and A are both substantial regions that are cadentially grounded. Their apparent equality thus suggests a redundancy in which two keys are arrayed against the tonic.[32] In actual fact, F major is undermined and eventually subordinated to A minor. This is accomplished in a number of ways. First, the relative substance of the two keys is suggested by the manner in which they are approached. The first transition (from D minor to F major) quickly gains the dominant ninth of A minor (Example 5.9, bar 45); it immediately turns back towards D but then is suddenly deflected to F major (bar 51), a move that suspends on F the chromatic descent from A in the first violin.

Table 5.2 String Quartet in D minor, D. 810, "Death and the Maiden," I, Tonal plan of exposition

Exposition (1–140)					
	b. 45 ————	digression	————————	b. 97	
	A: V⁹		A:V⁹		
Main Theme	1st transition	1st Subordinate Theme	2nd transition		2nd Sub. Theme
bb. 1–4 1	41–60	61–83	83–101		102–40
D–	D F+	F+	F+ A–		A+ (102–113) A–
	{	Digressive key	}		

Example 5.9 Schubert, String Quartet in D minor, D 810, 'Death and the Maiden', i, first transition, bars 43–54

The shift itself has a sensuous, visionary quality to it which suggests that there is something insubstantial about the nature of the new key. The end of the second transition (from F to A minor) moves emphatically to the dominant ninth that began the first transition and fully grounds it in an imperfect cadence (Example 5.10, bar 97). Here the second transition seems to correct the first transition's diversion to F major by taking up the chromatic descent from A again in the first violin in the same register and continuing it a semitone lower to the new dominant, E (bars 90–93), then sweeping down again a full octave from A to the A–G♯ resolution of the transition's concluding imperfect cadence (bars 93–97). The transitional process thus follows a circular trajectory in which the F major region occupies the position of a momentary digression from the true tonal goal of the exposition.

The key of F is also undermined by its inflections towards A minor. Its principal cadences are all given a strange A minor colouring (a III $_3^6$ sonority) by their unusual voice leading (Example 5.11, bars 64–66; see also bars 69–70 and 82–83).

The pervasive chromaticisms of the melodic line, G♯ and B♮, also point towards A minor and are taken up in the second transition as components of the

Example 5.10 Schubert, String Quartet in D minor, D 810, 'Death and the Maiden', i, end of second transition, bars 80–102

VI–V progression that eventually accomplishes the modulation to the second subordinate key. Finally, F is revisited and highlighted in the concluding cadences of A minor as the expanded submediant chord (bars 114–132). Thus the first subordinate key is ultimately reduced to a cadential harmony that contributes to the confirmation of A minor.

The relationship of the subordinate keys is also expressed in the developmental process, which extends from the first subordinate theme through the second transition and into the second subordinate theme. These sections are all

Example 5.11 Schubert, String Quartet in D minor, D 810, 'Death and the Maiden, i, beginning of first subordinate theme, bars 61–66

dominated by a chromatic neighbour-note figure, doubled in thirds or sixths, which first emerges as the basic idea of the first subordinate theme (Example 5.11, bars 62–63). This brings us to another criticism Salzer levels at Schubert's sonata forms: their widespread repetition of the same motivic chain, often with minimal changes. Indeed, in the present case there is little development in the Beethovenian sense—the idea's rhythm and unit length remain intact, while its crucial neighbour-note figure continues to be highlighted as a characteristic element. Salzer considers such a process essentially static, blocking the dynamic drive of the form. But this is not the case: the process is rather one of successive transformation by projecting the same pitches (those in the neighbour-note figure) against different tonal backgrounds. The effect is analogous to that of the different colouring brought to a single common tone by an underlying chordal shift. This can be seen in following the first neighbour-note figure (on C) in the basic idea. What begins as a playful chromatic embellishment of the F major tonic in the first subordinate theme (Example 5.11, bar 62) becomes something sweet and vulnerable in the change of C to C♯ at the beginning of the second

The Sensual in Schubert's Late Works 95

subordinate theme in A major (Example 5.12a, second violin and cello, bars 102–103). It finally turns into a desperate cry in A minor at the end of the exposition (Example 5.12b, first and second violins, bars 134ff.).

There is thus a larger process than motivic development at work in the subordinate theme region of the exposition, one that involves both tonal and

Example 5.12a Schubert, String Quartet in D minor, D 810, 'Death and the Maiden, i, neighbour-note motive across latter half of the exposition, beginning of second subordinate theme in A major, bars 102–106

Example 5.12b Schubert, String Quartet in D minor, D 810, 'Death and the Maiden, i, second subordinate theme closing section, bars 134–140

motivic relationships between the two subordinate themes. Here the themes, although closed off cadentially, are in fact interdependent, for the second essentially reinterprets the first. Tonally, the key of the first subordinate theme is finally absorbed into the key of the second—an outcome already suggested by the tonal inflection of F towards A in the first theme. Thus, while F is coloured by the foreshadowing of A minor, A minor is coloured by the memory of F. Motivically, the main material of the first subordinate theme is transformed by its projection against different structural contexts and tonal backgrounds. Its final statement in the closing bars of the second theme thus brings with it all of the layers of meaning it has accumulated so far. It is this layering that brings such a rich emotional quality and significance to the second theme and creates such a compelling thematic process.

The Motivic Development of the Sensuous in the First Movement of the String Quintet in C Major, D 956

A similar, albeit broader, thematic process is found in the first movement of Schubert's last great masterpiece, the String Quintet in C major, D 956. Here the main motivic material, motive A in Example 5.13a, itself is best described as sensuous. It consists of the overshadowing of the tonic chord by its common-tone diminished seventh, which in turn brightens to the tonic again (Example 5.13a, bars 1–6). The darkening of the C in the first violin through the chromaticism of the inner voices constitutes the motive's most striking effect. As in the beginning of the G♭ major Impromptu, there is something oracular about the progression, and this characteristic is emphasised by the two-bar prolongation of each of the chords involved—thus allowing the progression's unsettling quality to impress itself on the ear of the listener.

Motive A pervades the movement, serving as the harmonic framework for crucial passages in the form. Its exact returns are varied by arpeggiations embellishing the sustained chords of the original, as in the outset of the transition (bars 34–38) and the beginning of the recapitulation (bars 267–272). In other returns, the sustained chords are filled out as harmonic prolongations. Thus, in the concluding cadential progression of the main theme, motive A prolongs the cadential dominant (Example 5.13a, bars 26–33, and the summary in Example 5.13b). It also serves as the progression that achieves the modulation to the dominant key at the end of the first subordinate theme (Example 5.14a, bars 92–97 and the summary in Example 5.14b). Here it is stated on C and prolongs IV in G major as the cadential pre-dominant.[33]

Motive A is also subject to a development process in which its principal voice-leading characteristic—the projection of chromatic inner lines against stable bass and treble pedal tones—is intensified. Thus the passage building from the

Example 5.13a Schubert, String Quintet in C major, D 956, i, main theme, bars 1–34

Example 5.13b Schubert, String Quintet in C major, D 956, i, final PAC of main theme, derivation of V^7 prolongation from motive A

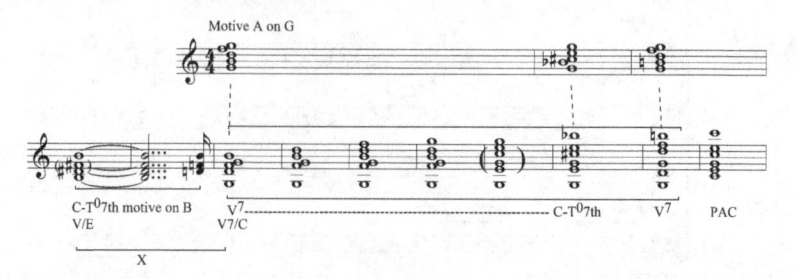

tonic chord to the powerful explosion on B in the main theme (Example 5.13a, bars 19–24) is a clear derivative of motive A in its interior chromatic ascent against the framing C and E pedals.[34] Likewise, the end of the transition (bars 49–59) echoes the dominant statement of the motive (bars 26–32) in its projection of a chromatic ascent against the G bass pedal.

A further derivation of the principal motive may be seen in the first subordinate theme, which begins on E♭ major and ends with a perfect cadence in G major (Example 5.14a). Here the new expressive shading of motive A's sustained tones through inner-voice chromaticism becomes the theme's main focus. The initial modulation to E♭ sets the stage.[35] It consists of a direct move from the G dominant chord to the E♭ tonic (bars 79–81). This chord progression by descending major third (motive 'x') is the same as that which brought the music back to C major after the explosion on B in the main theme (bars 24–26). Its effect, in which the sustained G is coloured by the underlying chord change, recalls the common-tone diminished-seventh component of motive A.[36] The G's change in colour and function projected by this initial move then becomes the predominant feature of the new theme, emphasised in bars 58–60 (repeated in bars 79–81), bars 65–66 (repeated in bars 86–87) and bars 68–71 (repeated in bars 89–92).[37]

There is also an important tonal implication in motive A which is pursued in the movement. This is contained in the expressive core of the motive, its common-tone diminished seventh on C, which has the potential of functioning in E minor. The movement of the bass from C to B under the diminished seventh yields the dominant seventh of E—and this is what essentially occurs in the unsettling outburst on B in bars 19–24, where the C chord resolves to the dominant of E minor as the latter's augmented sixth (Example 5.13a). Thus E minor threatens momentarily to intrude on C—a striking occurrence that suggests something disturbing under the music's surface, linked in some way with the initial gesture of the movement.[38] Yet this threat is immediately contained in bars 25–26, when the B dominant shifts to the home dominant seventh.[39]

Example 5.14a Schubert, String Quintet in C major, D 956, i, second statement of subordinate theme 1, bars 79–100

Example 5.14b Schubert, String Quintet in C major, D 956, i, motive A as framework for modulation to G, bars 92–100

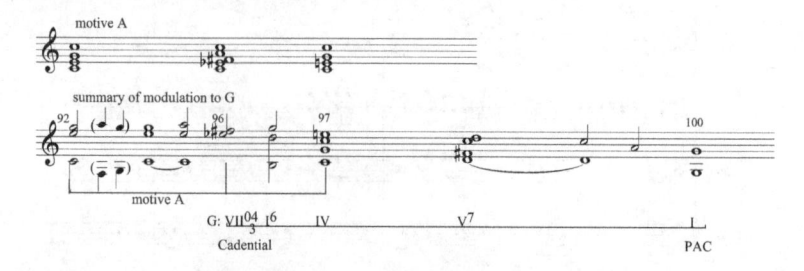

Example 5.14c Schubert, String Quintet in C major, D 956, i, derivation of move to E♭ from common-tone diminished-seventh gesture

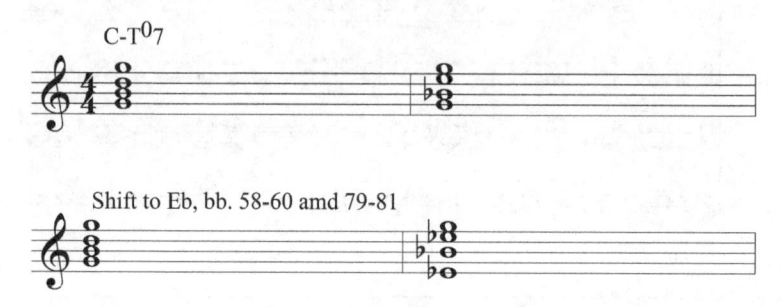

This last progression, motive 'x', becomes a characteristic feature of the second subordinate theme (Example 5.15, bars 100–112) which highlights the contrast in sonority between the B major and G major chords.

The theme's opening phrase (a compound basic idea) prolongs the G chord (bars 100–104), while the ensuing continuation prolongs the B major chord (bars 106–110).[40] The B major chord's resolution to E minor is blocked by the common-tone shift on B back to the G chord in bar 110, recalling the same move in the main theme, bars 25–26. This progression then dominates the theme's concluding cadences, with the G chord now functioning as an applied dominant seventh to C—the cadential pre-dominant (Example 5.16, bars 138–146).[41] Thus, as in the main theme, the second subordinate theme is haunted by the latent presence of E minor contained within the latter's dominant; this colouring gives the theme a particularly poignant and vulnerable character that emerges in its continuation phrase (bars 106–110).

As can be seen from this brief description, a major portion of the exposition, from the main theme to the end of the first subordinate theme, is taken up with the development of the movement's opening harmonic gesture. And this development is not concerned with the typical motivic manipulation usually associated with such a process, one that drives the music forward by

Example 5.15 Schubert, String Quintet in C major, D 956, i, second subordinate theme, antecedent, upbeat to bars 100–112

Example 5.16 Schubert, String Quintet in C major, D 956, i, second subordinate theme, concluding cadences, bars 138–146

progressively intensified fragmentation. In fact, such a fragmentation process is largely absent here, with statements of motive A maintaining roughly their original length in each statement.[42] The maintenance of motive A's length is due to its function as an underlying harmonic frame. Fragmentation does occur on the surface, as in bars 126–130, but when it begins to get under way (bar 130) it is immediately checked by dwelling on the arresting element of the progression, the common-tone diminished seventh and its return to the G major chord in bars 131–136.

Since it is the sonorous characteristics of motive A that are important, the focus falls on the motive's specific voice-leading procedures and their sensuous effects. These effects emerge at crucial junctures to form a chain of relationships. Thus the brightening of the G in the shift to E♭ major at the beginning of the first subordinate theme answers the darkening of the C in the movement's first gesture. Similarly the shadow of E minor cast by the intrusion of its dominant in the main theme also touches the subordinate key of G major. In this last instance we have the same type of key coloration we have seen in the G♭ Impromptu and the D minor String Quartet. The only difference lies in the fact that E minor does not emerge fully in either of the exposition's tonal regions;

this is reserved for the development section, which reaches a perfect cadence in E at its midpoint in bars 202–203.

The Sensuous and the Projection of Tonal Structure in Schubert's Late Music

In 1858 Schubert's close friend Joseph von Spaun prepared a memoir of his relationship with Schubert apparently for Ferdinand Luib, who was planning a biography of the composer. In this manuscript Spaun confronted the notion that Schubert was primarily a song composer by enumerating the great instrumental masterpieces that had been revealed since the composer's death. His one regret was that Schubert did not revise his compositions enough; yet he admitted that 'on the other hand they have something original and fresh about them, which very often would be lost with much polishing'.[43]

This assumption of the opposition of fine craftsmanship and spontaneous creation is perhaps the one attitude that has dogged the proper appreciation of Schubert's accomplishment for so long. What sounds so 'original and fresh' essentially constitutes the sensuous in Schubert's music—those moments that make it so unique and compelling. But such moments are not spontaneous inspirations; they arise from detailed planning. Nor are they merely local effects, for they form part of a logical, carefully worked out system that allows foreground details to project the deeper dramatic and expressive structure of the form through allusion, recall and transformation.

Thus it is precisely Schubert's handling of the sensuous aspects of his music that reveals his great craftsmanship. This can be seen above all in his idiosyncratic treatment of key relations. Here he draws meaning from, on one level, the sensuous colourings of a single note, as in 'Ihr Bild', and on another, the recurrences of the same key against different tonal backgrounds, as in the G♭ Impromptu, the 'Death and the Maiden' Quartet and the C major String Quintet. These colourings have an immediate expressive impact, contributing to the emotional complexity of both Schubert's home and subordinate key areas with passages of prophecy, yearning and reminiscence. They also have a structural significance, however, which is made palpable by the immediacy of their sensuous qualities. Such qualities become, in fact, a constructive force in the form, for they project something about the substance of the key they colour by the suggestion of impermanence or instability in the way a key emerges, or by the way one key is undermined by its inflection towards another. Thus the sensuous creates a tonal focus at specific junctures of the form that contributes to the delineation of an overarching hierarchy of keys. What is particularly beautiful in this is that here expression and structure have become one, and out of this union arise the great emotional force and concentration of Schubert's late works.

Notes

1. Arnold Schoenberg, *Fundamentals of Musical Composition* (London: Faber & Faber, 1967), p. 8.

2. For a definition and discussion of the term 'fragmentation', see William Caplin, *Classical Form: a Theory of Formal Functions for the Music of Haydn, Mozart, and Beethoven* (New York and Oxford: Oxford University Press, 1998), pp. 41 and 255 (glossary).

3. For an excellent discussion of the dynamic, teleological character of Beethoven's motivic process see Carl Dahlhaus, 'The Symphonic Style,' in *Ludwig van Beethoven: Approaches to His Music*, trans. Mary Whittall (Oxford: Clarendon Press, 1991), pp. 81–4. See also Scott Burnham, *Beethoven Hero* (Princeton, NJ: Princeton University Press, 1995), especially Chapter 2, 'Musical Values: Presence and Engagement in the Heroic Style,' pp. 29–65.

4. One of the finest comparisons of Beethoven's and Schubert's styles is found in Carl Dahlhaus, 'Sonata Form in Schubert: the First Movement of the G-Major String Quartet, op. 161 (D 887),' in Walther Frisch (ed.), *Schubert: Critical and Analytical Studies*, trans. Thilo Reinhardt (Lincoln: University of Nebraska Press, 1986), pp. 1–12, especially p. 7. Here Dahlhaus effectively separates the motivic complexity of Schubert's music from the purported necessity of a forward-driving dynamic.

5. The present chapter arises from the closing arguments of a previous article of mine on harmonic motives in Schubert. See 'The Functions of Harmonic Motives in Schubert's Sonata Forms,' *Intégral* 23 (2009), pp. 60–1.

6. L. Poundie Burstein has dealt with the lack of fragmentation and its relationship to the lyrical qualities of Schubert's music in 'Lyricism, Structure, and Gender in Schubert's G Major String Quartet,' *Musical Quarterly* 81/1 (Spring 1997), pp. 52–3.

7. For memory in Schubert see *Musical Quarterly* 84/4 (Winter 2000), which devotes a section to this topic with contributions by Walther Frisch, John Daverio, John Gingerich, Charles Fisk and Scott Burnham.

8. The word 'sensuous' is distinct from the word 'sensual': the 'sensuous' refers to someone alive to the senses, while 'sensual' refers to someone entirely governed by the senses and their pleasures. See *The Oxford English Dictionary*, 2nd edn, s.v. 'sensuous, 3', 'Readily affected by the senses; . . . *occas.* of a poet or artist, moved by, or appealing to the sensuous imagination'; and 'sensual, 4b', 'Absorbed in the life of the senses, indifferent to intellectual and moral interests'.

9. For a discussion of the difficulties third relations presented to music theory in the nineteenth and twentieth centuries, see the introduction in David Kopp, *Chromatic Transformations in Nineteenth-Century Music*, Cambridge Studies in Music Theory and Analysis 17 (Cambridge: Cambridge University Press, 2002), and the review of the theoretical treatment of chromatic third relations in Chapters 3–5.

10. Donald Francis Tovey, 'Franz Schubert', in Hubert J. Foss (ed.), *The Heritage of Music* (Oxford: Oxford University Press, 1927), vol. 1, p. 100.

11. Felix Salzer, 'Die Sonatenform bei Franz Schubert', *Studien zur Musikwissenschaft* 15 (1928), pp. 86–125.

12. James Webster, 'Schubert's Sonata Form and Brahms's First Maturity, I' *19th-Century Music* 2 (1978), p. 35.

13. Salzer argued that when the middle key is fully established, the resulting structure pits two competing subordinate tonalities (the second of which is usually the dominant) against the tonic. See 'Sonatenform bei Schubert', p. 102, and also n. 32.

14. Tovey, 'Franz Schubert', p. 105.

15. Webster, 'Schubert's Sonata Form, I', p. 24.

16. Susan McClary, 'Constructions of Subjectivity in Schubert's Music', in Philip Brett, Elizabeth Wood and Gary C. Thomas (eds), *Queering the Pitch* (New York: Routledge, 1994), p. 223. Susannah Clark has countered McClary's argument by pointing out that what McClary presents as a porous sense of tonic at the beginning of the movement in fact involves quite the opposite: a very careful delineation of the home key, upon which the theme's oblique harmonic shifts depend for their effectiveness. See Clark, *Analysing Schubert* (Cambridge: Cambridge University Press, 2012), pp. 189–93. The continuing relevance of the tonic-dominant axis of the Classical style in Schubert's music is also defended by Charles Fisk against McClary's characterisation of Schubert's harmonic practice as well as the arguments of scholars such as Hans-Joachim Hinrichsen and Arthur Godel, who see the composer's third-related modulations as an end in themselves rather than something that draws its character and meaning from its relationship to the underlying structural poles of tonic and dominant. See Fisk, *Returning Cycles: Contexts for the Interpretation of Schubert's Impromptus and Last Sonatas* (Berkeley and Los Angeles: University of California Press, 2001), pp. 17–19.

17. Richard L. Cohn, 'As Wonderful as Star Clusters: Instruments for Gazing at Tonality in Schubert', *19th-Century Music* 22 (1999), pp. 231–2. For a discussion of Cohn's proposed system based upon what he refers to as hexatonic cycles and Charles Fisk's critique of it, see Clark, *Analysing Schubert*, 146–51.

18. See William Kinderman, 'Schubert's Tragic Perspective', in Walther Frisch (ed.), *Schubert: Critical and Analytical Perspectives* (Lincoln, NB: University of Nebraska Press, 1986), p. 71.

19. At this point there is an apparent dissonance between the poem and its musical setting. The last stanza represents an intensification of the grief of the first, above all in its direct and desperate address of the lover to his beloved in the last two lines. Logically, a return to the same music of the first stanza should not be able to express this new intensity, yet Schubert's returning A section does just that, and so perfectly that the shift to B♭ major that painted the coming to life of the beloved earlier has now become the reawakened agony of the lover, but on a higher level. The effect here goes far beyond what a more literal reading of the text might suggest: the simple refusal to accept reality by clinging to a former happiness. Instead, we encounter a grief that, rather than collapsing in on itself, expands outwards in its rawness; this intensity seems to arise from the tonal colouring of the preceding B section and its vivid re-enactment of the loss of the beloved.

20. This sensuous quality is due to the unconventional embellishment of the tonic by the augmented sixth chord and the funereal colouring of the progression by the low register and static B♭ frame.

21. For a discussion of this passage linking it to the opening introduction, see Joseph Kerman, 'A Romantic Detail in Schubert's *Schwanengesang*', in Walther Frisch (ed.), *Schubert: Critical and Analytical Studies*, (Lincoln: University of Nebraska Press, 1986), pp. 57–8.

22. See also Fisk, *Returning Cycles*, for a discussion of the Impromptu's key relationships with a special emphasis on their cyclic nature within the Op. 90 group. Murray Dineen also discusses the chromatic alterations in the Impromptu as a Schoenbergian problem in 'Tonal Problem, Carpenter Narrative, and Carpenter Motive in Schubert's Impromptu, Op. 90, No. 3', *Theory and Practice* 30 (2005), pp. 97–120.

23. See Fisk, *Returning Cycles*, 117–18.

24. I have discussed the strategy and effect of such cadential diversions in 'Remembering a Dream: The Tragedy of Romantic Memory in the Transitional Process of Schubert's Sonata Forms', *Intersections* 25/1–2 (2005), pp. 207–9.

25. Among those who have dealt with tonal excursions and references in Schubert's primary and secondary key areas are Charles Fisk, 'Edward T. Cone's "The Composer's Voice": Questions about the Persona of Schubert's "Wanderer" Fantasy', *College Music Symposium* 29 (1989), pp. 19–30; Brian Black, 'Schubert's Apprenticeship in Sonata Form: The Early String Quartets' (McGill: doctoral dissertation, 1996), pp. 282–97; L. Poundie Burstein, 'Devil's Castles and Schubert's Strange Tonic Allusions', *Theory and Practice* 27 (2002), pp. 69–84; and Susan Wollenberg, *Schubert's Fingerprints: Studies in the Instrumental Works* (Wey Court East: Ashgate, 2011), especially Chapter 4, 'Schubert's Second Themes', pp. 99–131.

26. The dependence of this process on parallel passages that recall marked sonorities has an effect on the way the music unfolds. There is now a circular movement in that the music reaches a new stage of development only through revisiting and reinterpreting previous events.

27. See Salzer, 'Sonatenform bei Franz Schubert', pp. 88–9.

28. Webster, 'Schubert's Sonata Form, I', p. 35.

29. In other forms, however, the two composers can be similar in the handling of such relations. The Adagio molto e cantabile of Beethoven's Ninth Symphony, for instance, has modulations as sensuous and 'Schubertian' as anything in Schubert's oeuvre. The first outward modulation from D major to B♭ major (bars 19–24) also uses a type of cadential evasion similar to Schubert's deflection strategy and creates the same floating effect.

30. See Charles Rosen, *Sonata Forms*, rev. edn (New York: W. W. Norton, 1988), p. 354.

31. The following discussion summarises the main points of my analysis of the movement in a previous article, while adding a number of important details. See 'The Functions of Harmonic Motives', pp. 42–6.

32. See Salzer, 'Sonatenform bei Schubert', p. 102. In referring to this movement in particular, Salzer concludes that the equal breadth of the two subordinate keys results in 'a tonal equilibrium, and it is impossible, in comparison to the Beethoven examples, to speak of a main tonality of the subordinate theme. We are thus dealing here with three distinct keys in the exposition' (Die Folge davon ist, Dass wir ein Gleichgewicht der Tonarten vorfinden und es unmögligh ist, analog der Beethovenschen Beispielen von einer Hauptonart des Seitensatzes zu sprechen. Wir haben es also hier in der Exposition mit drei verschiedenen Tonarten zu tun).

33. In this case a 5–6 motion in the first violin anticipates the A of the common-tone diminished seventh, and the diminished seventh itself resolves to the G^6_3, which returns to the originating C chord. See Brian Black, 'The Functions of Harmonic Motives in Schubert's Sonata Forms', *Intégral*, 23 (2009), pp. 13–15, for a more detailed discussion of this progression as well as its function and derivation.

34. The parallelism between this passage and the preceding tonic (bars 1–6) and supertonic (bars 11–16) statements of motive A as well as the ensuing dominant statement (bars 26–32) are pointed out by the turn figure that marks each progression.

35. Rosen has discussed the fragility of E♭ at this juncture in *Sonata Forms*, pp. 256–7.

36. The approach to E♭, though is different, since the second cello slips down from G to E♭—a gesture that reverses the E♭–G chromatic ascent of the first cello in the transition (bars 53–6).

37. The significance of the changing functions of this one pitch has been discussed by John Gingerich, 'Remembrance and Consciousness in Schubert's C-major String Quintet, D 956', *Musical Quarterly* 84 (2000), pp. 619–20, and Clark, *Analyzing Schubert*, pp. 182–6.

38. Indeed, this event has ramifications that stretch into the recapitulation, where the augmented sixth is converted into the dominant seventh of F major (bars 288–95) to reroute the recapitulation towards the subdominant.

39. The progression involves an initial common-tone move from the B major chord to the B diminished chord, bar 25, which replays the common-tone diminished component of motive A on B.

40. For the terms 'compound basic idea' and 'continuation', see Caplin, *Classical Form*, pp. 61 and 10–11 respectively.

41. Similarly, at the end of the development section, the home dominant seventh is approached through the dominant of E minor (bars 249–251).

42. Lack of fragmentation also marks Schubert's use of large harmonic cells in the first movement of the Piano Sonata in A major, D 959, as identified in Ivan Waldbauer, 'Recurrent Harmonic Patterns in the First Movement of Schubert's Piano Sonata in A major, D 959', *19th-Century Music* 12 (1989), pp. 64–73. See also Burstein, 'Lyricism, Structure, and Gender', pp. 52–3.

43. 'Dagegen haben sie etwas Ursprungliches und Frisches an sich, das sich sehr oft durch vieles Feilen verliert'. Joseph von Spaun, 'Aufzeichnungen über meinen Verkehr mit Franz Schubert (1858)', in Otto Erich Deutsch, *Schubert: Die Erinnerungen seiner Freunde* (Leipzig: Breitkopf & Härtel, 1957), p. 163.

II

INSTRUMENTAL MUSIC

6

The Myth of the 'Unfinished' and the Film *Das Dreimäderlhaus* (1958)

Andrea Lindmayr-Brandl

In studying Schubert's late style, the Symphony in B minor, D 759, seems at first glance to be an unlikely candidate. When the work was composed, in 1822, Schubert was only twenty-five years old and had some fruitful years to come. But chronology and the concept of 'late', which are contextually dependent, can be tricky benchmarks. If one's perspective shifts from the music's production to its reception by the nineteenth-century Viennese musical public, then the Symphony figures as a late or even posthumous work of a great master.

The first performance of the 'Unfinished' took place in 1865, forty-three years after its origin, at a time when Schubert's œuvre was known only in extracts. Until the middle of the nineteenth century, most concert-goers knew primarily the songs, either in the original version with piano and voice, in a virtuoso piano arrangement by Franz Liszt, or in orchestrations by other composers of the time. Instrumental music by Schubert appeared only tentatively on programmes, and in particular his music for full orchestra had no tradition in the Viennese concert halls.[1] Thus the 'new' symphony that fascinated the audience from the beginning left them with the impression of being quite a recent work. Some imaginative people might have experienced it even as a reverberation from another world. In this spirit, the famous Viennese music critic Eduard Hanslick reported the impression made by the premiere:

> When after several introductory bars the clarinet and the oboe in unison intone their sweet song over the calm murmur of the violins, then every child knows the composer, and the half-suppressed exclamation 'Schubert' buzzes in whispers through the hall. He has hardly entered, but it is he, as one knew him from his step, from his way of opening the door handle.[2]

But let us go back to its time of origin. When Schubert sent the manuscript of his Symphony in B minor to the provincial town of Graz as a sign of gratitude for his honourable membership of the Steiermärkische Musikverein, he could not know or even expect that a hundred years later this uncompleted work would become one of his most successful compositions, and indeed one of the most often performed of all classical symphonies. The 'Unfinished'—as the composition is called in the vernacular—inspired the musical world not only with its beauty but also because of the exciting story of its rediscovery in the 1860s and the myths that have since entwined around its composition. In this chapter I will not investigate the still inconsistent historical documents concerning its transfer into the property of Anselm Hüttenbrenner in Graz, nor will I enter into discussion about the various opinions as to why the 'Unfinished' remained incomplete.[3] It is rather my intention to reveal the circumstances and arguments that created and built the extraordinary fame of the 'Unfinished' and to uncover the events that kept rumours alive for more than a century.

To begin with, one can discern three basic strands in the rumours that make up the complex and (to a certain extent) still influential story: the strange circumstances of the work's rediscovery, the presumed relationship to Schubert's biography and the apparent relation to Beethoven, the reception history of which culminates in the film *Das Dreimäderlhaus*.

The Myth of the 'Hidden Symphony's' Discovery

There is, first of all, the rumour of a 'hidden' symphony—an accusation that goes back to Heinrich Kreißle von Hellborn, the author of the first comprehensive biography of Schubert that was essential for his music's reception among music lovers.[4] In this book, published in 1865, Kreißle indirectly blamed the Hüttenbrenner brothers for holding back a completely unknown symphony that was considered to be of extraordinary beauty, thus nurturing an exaggerated expectation of what was actually hidden. The relevant passage reads as follows:

> One of the more important compositions of this year [1822] is a *symphony* for orchestra in B minor, which Schubert assigned in return for the certificate of honour of the music society of Graz to its director, *Anselm Hüttenbrenner* in its actual state, namely half finished. According to a communication from Mr. Josef Hüttenbrenner, [the first and second] movements were entirely finished and the third (Scherzo) only partially. The fragment in the ownership of Mr. Anselm Hüttenbrenner at Graz is supposed to be of great beauty, the first movement in particular. If this is the case, the intimate friend of Schubert perhaps should soon decide to release the completely unknown work of his highly respected master from under lock and key to introduce Schubert's admirers to it.[5]

The premiere of the Symphony in the Hofburg's Großer Redoutensaal at the Hofburg took place shortly after Kreißle's biography appeared and was a sensation in Viennese concert life. The manager and conductor of the Hofburg, Hofkapellmeister Johann Ritter von Herbeck (1831–1877), an ardent Schubert lover and a central personality in Viennese concert life, played an important role in bringing the Symphony to light. According to the posthumous biography written by his son, he had known of its existence five years earlier but maintained complete silence on the issue.⁶ Herbeck was worried that foreign Schubert lovers would hear something about the Symphony and premiere the music abroad, as in the case of the Symphony in C major, D 944, which was rediscovered by Robert Schumann and first performed in 1839 in Leipzig.⁷ In Herbeck's opinion, the premiere of the new Symphony should definitely take place in Schubert's native Vienna. The other reason was a far more personal one: Herbeck wanted to be the first to present the Symphony to the public. And indeed, the premiere was a triumph, not only for the work and for the composer, but also for the conductor. According to the memoirs, this event 'was one of the most joyful and glorious days' in Herbeck's life.⁸

The layout of the concert programme reveals that certain events must have influenced the preparations for the premiere. It is astonishing that this Sunday afternoon concert on 17 December did not open with the sensational new Schubert work but with an overture by Anselm Hüttenbrenner. Equally perplexing is the fact that the overture was announced as *neu* but not the Symphony. This eye-catching remark would have been more effective in connection with the following number, Schubert's 'Sinfonie in H-moll', which was 'completed' by the final movement of Schubert's Symphony in D major, D 200 (see Figure 6.1).⁹ A grateful acknowledgement to Hüttenbrenner explains indirectly the unusual nature of the programme planning: after years of effort, the only way Herbeck could get hold of the Schubert manuscript was by promoting the relatively minor music of its owner.

Reviews of the concert in the Viennese press mentioned the opening number only in passing while concentrating on Schubert's 'new' work. Not only did they report the enthusiastic reception of the Symphony and describe the music in glowing prose, but they also devoted a long section to the story of its rediscovery. These reports confirm the rumours that Herbeck himself must have spread in his circles and can be traced in his aforementioned biography. The journalists of the Viennese daily newspapers praised Herbeck for snatching the manuscript from the hands of an egoistic owner and blamed Hüttenbrenner for hiding the Symphony for such a long time.¹⁰ Thus, the early friend and former fellow student of Schubert appears as a somewhat nasty and bitter character, an old man weary of life, who was only interested in his own late fame.

Hanslick took the opportunity in his review of the concert to criticise the so-called Schubert friends in general by separating them into two groups: the 'careless' or 'centrifugals', those without responsibility, who give away their treasures for a small sum to American music collectors, or—even worse—as wrapping paper to a cheese-shop owner; and the 'stubborn' or 'centripetals', those who lock their pearls in a suitcase and go to bed with the key, unwilling to share them with the public. Although Hanslick explicitly excludes Anselm Hüttenbrenner

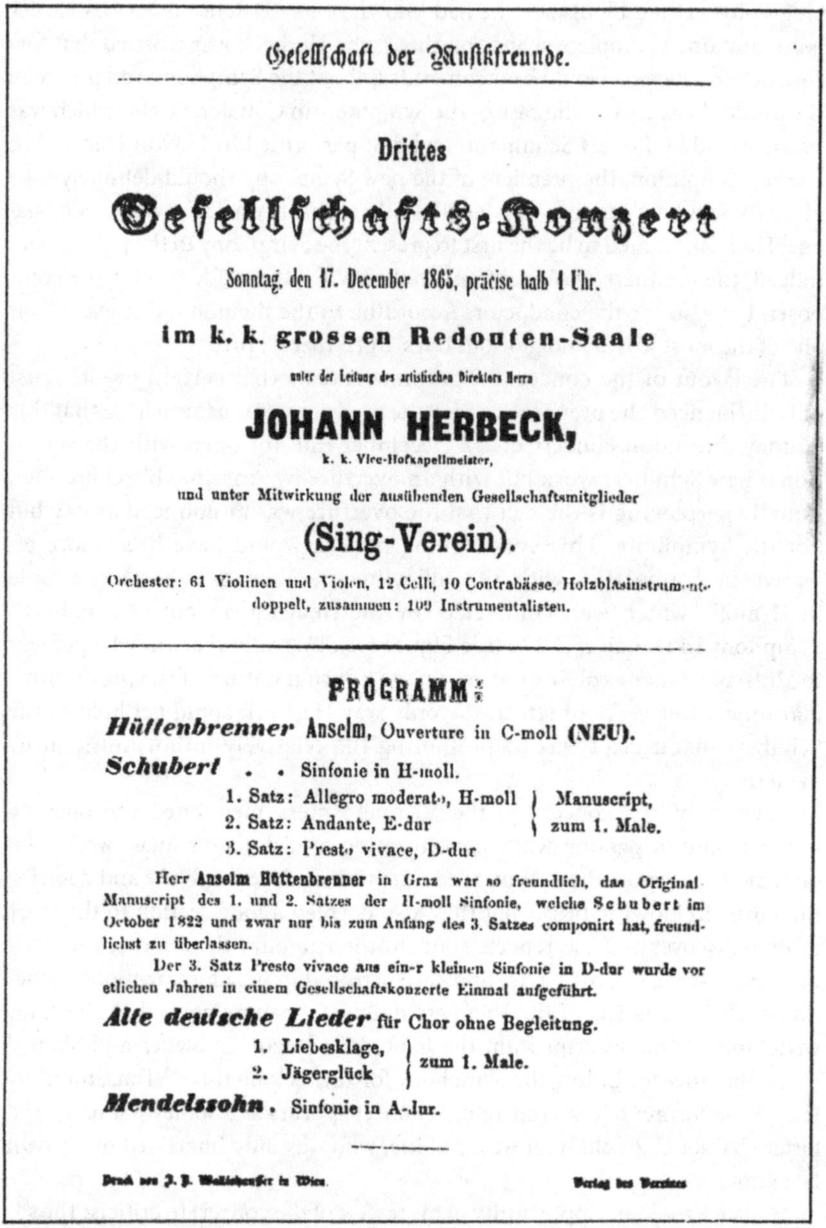

Gesellschaft der Musikfreunde.

Drittes

Gesellschafts-Konzert

Sonntag, den 17. December 1865, präcise halb 1 Uhr,

im k. k. grossen Redouten-Saale

unter der Leitung des artistischen Direktors Herrn

JOHANN HERBECK,

k. k. Vice-Hofkapellmeister,

und unter Mitwirkung der ausübenden Gesellschaftsmitglieder

(Sing-Verein).

Orchester: 61 Violinen und Violen, 12 Celli, 10 Contrabässe, Holzblasinstrumente doppelt, zusammen: 109 Instrumentalisten.

PROGRAMM:

Hüttenbrenner Anselm, Ouverture in C-moll **(NEU).**

Schubert . . Sinfonie in H-moll.

1. Satz: Allegro moderato, H-moll } Manuscript,
2. Satz: Andante, E-dur } zum 1. Male.
3. Satz: Presto vivace, D-dur

Herr **Anselm Hüttenbrenner** in Graz war so freundlich, das Original-Manuscript des 1. und 2. Satzes der H-moll Sinfonie, welche **Schubert** im October 1822 und zwar nur bis zum Anfang des 3. Satzes componirt hat, freundlichst zu überlassen.

Der 3. Satz Presto vivace aus einer kleinen Sinfonie in D-dur wurde vor etlichen Jahren in einem Gesellschaftskonzerte Einmal aufgeführt.

Alte deutsche Lieder für Chor ohne Begleitung.

1. Liebesklage, } zum 1. Male.
2. Jägerglück }

Mendelssohn . Sinfonie in A-Dur.

Druck von J. B. Wallishausser in Wien. Verlag des Vereines

Figure 6.1 Programme note of the premiere

from the latter group, he indirectly condemns him for failing to give access to the 'Unfinished' for so many years.[11]

All in all, the sensation surrounding the first performance was due not only to the music's discovery and its extraordinary beauty, but also to the story of wrong-headed friends, an egoistic antagonist, and a spirited champion who saved the music for posterity. People are perennially attracted by such stories, and authors of popular biographies on Schubert retell them again and again, embellishing them with more or less detail.

Biographical Relations

The second strand of the reception of the 'Unfinished' is based on the myth that the Symphony is closely related to Schubert's own biography, reflecting his whole life or at least aspects of it and his character. In the nineteenth century it was not unusual for music to be appraised as the most personal expression of a composer's inner life, but rarely has this approach been so concentrated on a single work. Several of the biographies that were published during the Schubert anniversary in 1928 address this idea. So does the booklet by Joseph Lux, who calls the chapter on the 'Unfinished' 'eine Seelenbeichte in Tönen' (a confession of the soul in tones).[12] Later publications with a strong popular impact have continued this theme by offering different interpretations on the relation between life and music. In Paul Stefan's Schubert biography the Symphony perfectly reflects the sweet Viennese sadness of the great melancholic composer who suffered so much in this world.[13] Fritz Hug regards the 'Unfinished' as 'der Inbegriff Schubertscher Seelenwärme und Empfindungstiefe' (the epitome of the warmth of Schubert's soul and the depth of his sentiments).[14] On the other hand, Heinrich Werlé is convinced that the Symphony is closely related to a particular incident in Schubert's experience, where he was affected by a hazy demon. This demon allegedly flashes up in the first movement's primary theme,[15] described in flowery language by Hanslick in the review quoted at the beginning of this chapter.

A more elaborate approach in this field originates with the German musicologist Arnold Schering. In his 1939 essay, which bore the meaningful title 'Franz Schuberts Symphonie in h-moll und ihr Geheimnis', Schering interprets the two movements of the Symphony based on Schubert's 'Traumerzählung'. These very personal notes were taken a few months before composing the 'Unfinished', and Schering tries to demonstrate in close detail how this text's subject matter—events in Schubert's parental home and the death of his mother, as well as supernatural consolation and transfiguration—served as a poetical programme for the Symphony.[16] Although scholarly Schubert research never fully accepted this strange pseudo-psychological interpretation with its questionable methodology, the same idea was taken up by several authors of popular Schubert biographies up until at least the 1950s.[17]

In addition to these attempts to forge a link between the Symphony and Schubert's life, the music's unfinished condition has been set in parallel with the 'unfinished' life of the composer who died so young. The most famous figure promoting this view was the composer and critic Hugo Wolf. In a review of a turn-of-the-century performance of the Symphony at the Birmingham Festival, he states: 'Schubert's B minor symphony, a true mirror of the artistic individuality of its creator, has unfortunately remained a fragment. In this sense it resembles also in its form the external course of the master's life, who was carried off by death in the flower of his life, in the full vigour of his creative power.'[18] The same idea, expressed more directly, can be found in the title of a book on Schubert's life by Helmuth Böttcher: *The Unfinished: Franz Schubert and his Circle*.[19]

The film industry also made use of this topos. In 1953 a movie entitled *Franz Schubert—Ein Leben in zwei Sätzen* (a life in two movements), written and produced by the Austrian director Walther Kolm-Velte, was released. This first colour film biography of Schubert was a great success in Austria and Germany and also won prizes in the United States.[20] The film's title was intended to be seen in two ways: it related both to Schubert's short lifespan and to his unrequited love of Therese Grob, transferring the idiom of an 'unfinished' life to an unhappy love story that goes back to a movie from the 1930s. In the first Wien-Film production *Leise flehen meine Lieder*, the debut of the famous Willi Forst, the beloved was Schubert's student Caroline Esterházy. With the title of its English-language version, *The Unfinished Symphony*, this part of the story comes full circle.[21]

The idea of a great but unfinished work acting as a symbol for an unfinished life has also been transplanted into the world of literature. The Austrian writer Hans Weigel (1908–1991) used the topos in his novel *Unvollendete Symphonie* when describing the intellectual life of Vienna during the early postwar years. The novel is a hidden autobiography written from the perspective of the young Ingeborg Bachmann. The Jewish Weigel compares his life as an emigrant, returning home after World War II, with an unfinished symphony—always saying goodbye to friends who are scattered all over the world, never experiencing a full life in the same place.[22]

The Relation to Beethoven—*Das Dreimäderlhaus* as Paradigm

The third and final strand is based on the problematic and still obscure personal relationship of Schubert to his great contemporary, Beethoven.[23] This topic was brought up again and again in popular literature, playing with the image of a soft, almost feminine composer who was overshadowed by the heroic and successful musical icon who dominated Vienna's concert life. Very often authors exalted the personal contact between the two composers by inventing stories lacking in any historical validity. One of the most influential books fostering the problematic relationship of the two composers working at the same time in the same city was Rudolf Bartsch's *Künstlerroman*, entitled *Schwammerl* (1912).[24]

The 'Unfinished' Symphony was related to Beethoven even before its official rediscovery. In a letter from Josef Hüttenbrenner to Herbeck, written on 3 May 1860, in which the music is mentioned for the first time, Beethoven's symphonies served as a benchmark: 'but with Schubert's *b-minor symphony* he [his brother Anselm] owns a treasure, which we equate *with every symphony by Beethoven*' (emphasis in original).[25]

Hanslick took the same line in his report on the inauguration of the Schubert Monument in the Stadtpark in 1872, the programme of which included the 'Unfinished'. The Symphony's first eight bars reminded the music critic of Beethoven's alleged words on his deathbed: 'Fürwahr, in diesem Schubert steckt ein göttlicher Funke' (Indeed, in Schubert a divine spark is contained). In Hanslick's opinion, no other composer is so closely related to the great master of the symphony, although the younger man could not surpass him in this genre.[26]

Several fictional biographies directly compare the 'Unfinished' with Beethoven's œuvre. Lux, to name just one example, writes in his 1922 book: 'In the eyes of his [Schubert's] contemporaries, the greatness of Beethoven still pushed him too much into the shadow, although he was already an accomplished composer. The B minor symphony represents the finished state.'[27]

The tendency to stress a mystical relationship to Beethoven culminates in the film *Das Dreimäderlhaus* (1958), directed by Ernst Marischka.[28] With Karl-Heinz Böhm playing Schubert, it was one of the most successful productions of the Wien-Film company. Böhm, an Austrian movie idol, had already appeared in the leading role of another very popular film by the same director, the Sissy Trilogy, which immediately preceded the Schubert film. *Das Dreimäderlhaus* takes a very similar kitschy and trivialising tone.

Its scenario also goes back to the very successful operetta of the same title by Heinrich Berté (1916), as well as the novel *Schwammerl*, and tells the story of the poor but brilliant composer who falls in love with one of the three girls of the 'Dreimäderlhaus'.[29] She finally marries his best friend, and Schubert comes away empty-handed. In this naive and sentimental film, the desire of the postwar German-speaking people for a happy, witty and easy-going world was perfectly satisfied by re-inventing the good old times of Old Vienna, an idealised retrospective cityscape before the construction of the Ringstraße.[30] Moreover, Schubert, as the principal character, was not only the embodiment of the Biedermeier period but also a symbol of Austrian cultural identity of which one could be proud. At the same time, the audience could sympathise with his soft and clumsy character, a mixture of genius and awkwardness. The great success of the movie even beyond the borders of Austria and Germany inspired a whole generation of music lovers. It is responsible for the popular perception of Schubert's character, one based on clichés and historical inaccuracies. Even those of later generations who have not seen the movie seem to be influenced by these ideas.

The plot of *Das Dreimäderlhaus* (see Table 6.1) is framed by another element of Schubert's biography, which gives the 'Unfinished' a more central role than in the earlier operetta and novels.[31] The new element is the composer's relationship to Beethoven and the connection of the heroic master's destiny with the incompleteness of Schubert's Symphony. Ernst Marischka, who was also responsible for the script, makes the lives of the two composers cross several times and stresses Schubert's high esteem of Beethoven. In the dramatic third scene Beethoven steps out of his house in an emotional mood, hearing the music of the 'Eroica' in his inner ear, while Schubert is present but unobserved. This suggests that the occurrence directly inspired Schubert to compose the first bars of the 'Unfinished'. When he indicates to his admiring friends that this work could be the way to a great symphony, a famous passage from a letter by Schubert is quoted—but with a twisted meaning since the original remark refers to another genre, namely the string quartet.[32] An alleged influence of Beethoven on the origin of the 'Unfinished' is also suggested when Nannerl listens to the piano sketch of the new Symphony and asks Schubert how musical ideas come into his mind. He responds that he normally does not know, but in the case of this Symphony, he does: 'It originates from a deep feeling of a burning adoration and humility towards the greatest among us: Beethoven'.[33]

The relationship between the admired master and the fate of the Symphony culminates in Scene 10. At the beginning of this scene, Schubert is still working on the music, surrounded by his friends, while Kupelwieser arrives in a deranged mood. The following dialogue is central and therefore is quoted fully in translation:[34]

> SCHUBERT: Kupelwieser, what do you look like? You are totally distressed!
> KUPELWIESER: I've come from the final rehearsal. Beethoven had to stop conducting.—He is completely deaf.—
> SCHUBERT: I feared this day for a long time.—How did he take it?
> KUPELWIESER: 'Enough', he said, 'this is the end'.
> MAYRHOFER: This is terrible. Go on playing, Franzl. Or no, it's better ... *(to the friends:)* Come on, let's go, let's leave him alone. *(To Schubert, gently patting his back:)* Continue [working], finish writing this wonderful symphony!
> SCHUBERT *(shaking his head)*: Enough. It's over. (Puts the music paper on the piano, turns around and resignedly leaves the room, with the first eight bars of the 'Unfinished' as background music.)

Table 6.1 *Das Dreimäderlhaus*, (Wien-Film 1958), 97 minutes; directed and written by Ernst Marischka[41]

Scene	Time	Scene
1	0:00	*Vorspann/Opening credits* Introduction of the main scenes of the movie; medley of Schubert melodies
2	4:30	*Das Vorbild/The model* Beethoven in concert—In Diabelli's music shop
3	13:54	*Warten auf Beethoven/Waiting for Beethoven* In front of the Beethoven house at Heiligenstadt—Schubert working at the 'Unfinished' in his home, visit of his friends
4	22:15	*Kleinholz/Chopped wood* Cooking and singing with friends—meeting with girls in front of the Karlskirche
5	30:03	*Beim Heurigen/At the inn with new wine on tap* At an outdoor inn—At the Dreimäderlhaus, preparing for an outing into the country
6	37:51	*Wo ist Puzzi?/Where is Puzzi [the dog]?* In the countryside around Vienna—At the Dreimäderlhaus, two fiancés waiting for their brides—Picnic under the lilac tree
7	44:01	*Eine große Bitte/A great favour* At the Tschoell shop—At Schubert's home, Schubert teaching Nannerl
8	52:50	*Wie ein Bruder/Like a brother* At the Belvedere garden, Nannerl meeting Schober—concert at the Eszterházy palace
9	1:00:40	*Hochzeitsvorbereitunge/Preparations for the wedding* At the Dreimäderlhaus—At Schubert's home, composing his first love song
10	1:09:35	*Verlust eines Genies/Loss of a genius* In the concert room, Beethoven's breakdown—At Schubert's home, Schubert's reaction—At the Dreimäderlhaus, two sisters leaving for Italy
11	1:21:51	*Die Einladung/The invitation* At Schubert's home—At the Dreimäderlhaus, Schober sings Schubert's love song to Nannerl—Wedding ceremony in church
12	1:32:34	*Auf die Musik!/To the music!* At the wedding party—On the way home—At Schubert's room, Schubert collapsing on his table

One could not highlight more emphatically the fictional coincidence of Beethoven's loss of his sense of hearing and Schubert's abrupt interruption of the composition process of the 'Unfinished'. Although there is absolutely no historical evidence for this specific relationship, it must have left a strong impression in the viewer's mind.

The 'Death Fragment'

The film addresses not only the topic of Beethoven (although it is central), but also two other elements that contribute to the myth of the 'Unfinished'. One is Schubert's failed relationship to a beloved expressed as an unfinished love story, as discussed above. The second element is the basis of the most stubborn rumour concerning the 'Unfinished', namely its reputation as a 'death fragment'—a work that remained unfinished because the composer died while working on it. Although there was a time span of six years between the autograph dating of the manuscript and Schubert's death (which was mentioned both in the programme notes of the premiere and in Hanslick's review), this rumour spread quite early among the musical public. And as typical of rumours, it is hard to track down its point of origin. Only a few hints are discernible that reveal what presumably was in the back of the minds of many music lovers.

One is a note in the catalogue of the Vienna Schubert exhibition of 1928. There the annotator of the manuscript of the 'Unfinished' felt the need to say that the Symphony did not remain unfinished because the composer died—'as it was often thought'.[35] Another document is a record of several fragments of piano music by Schubert, played by Alfons Kontarsky. In the CD booklet the pianist recalls that during his childhood he imagined Schubert as God, an old man with a white beard working on the 'Unfinished' until the pen slipped out of his hand and he faded away. This was the story that his uncle suggested to him when he asked why the final movements of the Symphony were missing.[36] Such childhood stories endure for a long time and are hard to extinguish, even when one subsequently learns otherwise.

Das Dreimäderlhaus addresses the topic of the death fragment at the very end. In the final scene, starting with the wedding feast, Nannerl and Schubert engage in an intimate dialogue. After she rejects him in favour of his best friend, Franz Schober, Schubert heroically wishes her all the best and stays behind with the words 'Ich habe ja meine Musik' (I have my music instead).[37] He then leaves the ballroom thoughtfully and walks home through the dark alleys of Vienna. Arriving at his room, he lights the lamp while one hears the theme of the second movement of the 'Unfinished' in the background. Schubert looks out the window, a heartfelt violin line interrupts, and dissonant sounds in the film score lead into the main theme of the first movement. Meanwhile Schubert sits at his piano, the manuscript of the 'Unfinished' in front of him, but he is not able to continue writing. Suddenly the passage of Nannerl's song 'Ungeduld' interrupts as a kind of leitmotif, indirectly quoting the words 'Dein ist mein Herz und will es ewig bleiben' (My heart is yours and wants to stay yours forever). At this moment Schubert collapses on the instrument, his head on the unfinished manuscript of the Symphony. Again the Symphony is heard, and the film ends in darkness.

It is interesting to note that most people only remember the superficial plot of the film—the unhappy love story between Schubert and his piano student Nannerl—and forget the integrated parallel story about Beethoven and the correlation of the 'Unfinished' with him and the girl's destiny. These observations, made in personal conversations by the author of this paper with friends and colleagues, can be verified by checking several film websites. Almost all of them— filmportal.de, kino.de, cinema.de, moviepilot.de, studiocanal.de, and amazon.de—give only a short summary of the love story and mention neither the appearance of Beethoven nor the Symphony.[38] Only film.at, a website maintained by the Austrian media company Telekurier, mentions the 'Unfinished' when comparing this movie with an older one that uses the same music. However, the site says nothing about the plot, but only states that *Das Dreimäderlhaus* offers an explanation of why Schubert did not finish the work.[39] An American database, Turner Classic Movies, provides the reason explicitly: Schubert left it unfinished out of respect for his 'friend' Beethoven.[40]

Even more one-sided than the synopsis are the reviews of individuals that have been uploaded to the site. They almost always retell the love story—some critically, others enthusiastically—but none mentions the central role of the 'Unfinished' in relation to Beethoven or to Nannerl. This astonishing oversight could be explained by the fact that the Symphony is never mentioned by name in the film, so that uninformed viewers would not recognise it. In my opinion, however, this strange reception is underpinned by a psychological issue. It seems that those passages that strongly provoke positive feelings in the audience overshadow and thus cover the negative parallel story, which is suppressed into the subconscious—a location where many myths are housed.

As the above considerations and observations have shown, the deconstruction of the myth of the symphony is not an easy task. Myths address not the intellect, but an intuitive, holistic and blurred emotional understanding. They are another form of truth that appears to be irrational and dark, but at the same time fascinating. The myth surrounding the 'Unfinished' operates as a driving force in its successful reception, and it will continue to do so even after the myth has been debunked.

Notes

1. Cf. Otto Brusatti, *Schubert im Wiener Vormärz: Dokumente 1829–1848* (Graz: Adeva, 1978), pp. 10f. A detailed reception history of Schubert's music in nineteenth-century Vienna still has to be written.

2. 'Wenn nach ein paar einleitenden Tacten Clarinette und Oboe einstimmig ihren süßen Gesang über dem ruhigen Gemurmel der Geigen anstimmen, da kennt auch jedes Kind den Componisten, und der halbunterdrückte Ausruf "Schubert!" summt flüsternd durch den Saal. Er ist noch kaum eingetreten, aber er ist es, als kennte man ihn am Tritt, an seiner Art, die Thürklinke zu öffnen.' Eduard Hanslick, *Aus dem Concert-Saal: Kritiken und Schilderungen aus 20 Jahren des Wiener Musiklebens, 1848–1868* (Vienna: W. Braumüller, 1897), vol.2, pp. 392–3.

3. On these questions see Andrea Lindmayr-Brandl, *Franz Schubert: Das fragmentarische Werk* (Stuttgart: Franz Steiner, 2003), pp. 242ff.; see also Rudolf Weber, 'Mythen und Legenden um die Entstehung von Schubert Unvollendeter', in Claudia Bullerjahn and Wolfgang Löffler (eds), *Musikermythen: Alltagstheorien, Legenden und Medieninszenierungen* (Hildesheim and New York: Georg Olms Verlag, 2004), pp. 191–221; and John M. Gingerich, 'Unfinished Considerations: Schubert's "Unfinished" Symphony in the Context of his Beethoven Project', *19th-Century Music* 31/2 (2007), pp. 99–112.

4. Christopher H. Gibbs, 'German Reception: Schubert's "Journey to Immortality"', in Gibbs (ed.), *The Cambridge Companion to Schubert*, (Cambridge: Cambridge University Press, 1997), pp. 241–53, stresses the role of Kreißle's biography as being central in the third period of Schubert's reception, which starts about 1860.

5. 'Von größeren Compositionen gehören diesem Jahr [1822] noch an: Eine Sinfonie für Orchester in H-Moll, welche Schubert zum Dank für das ihm von dem Gratzer Musikverein ausgestellte Diplom eines Ehrenmitgliedes desselben dem Vorstand der Gesellschaft, Anselm Hüttenbrenner, in dem Zustand, in welchem sie sich eben befand, nämlich halbvollendet, übergab. Nach einer Mittheilung Herrn Josef Hüttenbrenner's ist nämlich der erste und zweite Satz vollständig componirt und der dritte (Scherzo) zum Theil. Das Fragment, im Besitz des Herrn Anselm Hüttenbrenner in Gratz, soll—namentlich der erste Satz—von hoher Schönheit sein. Ist dies der Fall, so dürfte sich wohl der intime Freund Schubert's demnächst entschließen, das noch ganz unbekannte Werk des von ihm hochverehrten Meisters, von Schloß und Riegel zu befreien, und die Freunde der Schubert'schen Muse damit bekannt zu machen.' See Heinrich Kreißle von Hellborn, *Franz Schubert* (Vienna: Carl Gerold, 1865; repr., Hildesheim and New York: Georg Olms Verlag, 1978), pp. 255f.

6. Ludwig Herbeck, *Johann Herbeck: Ein Lebensbild* (Vienna: Albert J. Gutmann, 1885), pp. 164–9.

7. For a discussion of the first performance of the symphony see Werner Aderhold, foreword to Franz Schubert, *Neue Ausgabe sämtlicher Werke*, ser. V, vol. 4, *Sinfonie Nr. 8 in C D944*, ed. Aderhold (Kassel: Bärenreiter Verlag, 2003), pp. XIV–XX.

8. Herbeck, *Johann Herbeck: Ein Lebensbild*, p. 179.

9. In a second performance of the symphony on 4 November of the same year, Herbeck dared to omit the added music, performing only the original two movements.

10. 'Von den drei Schubertschen Fragment-Symphoniesätzen, welche Hrn. Herbeck vergönnt war, den Tiefen egoistischen Alleinbesitztums zu entreißen, an den Tag heraufzuholen und zum Gemeingute der Kulturwelt zu machen, sind der erste und der zweite Satz wahre Perlen.' *Wiener Blätter für Theater, Musik und Kunst*; cited in Otto Schneider, 'Vor 100 Jahren: Eine Schubert-Uraufführung im Jahre 1865', *Österreichische Musikzeitschrift* 20 (1965), p. 608.

11. Eduard Hanslick, *Aus dem Concert-Saal: Kritiken und Schilderungen aus 20 Jahren des Wiener Musiklebens, 1848–1868*, 2nd edn (Vienna: Braumüller, 1897), pp. 391–3.

12. Joseph August Lux, *Franz Schubert: Ein Lebensbild aus deutscher Vergangenheit* (Berlin: Fleming & Wiskot, 1922), p. 80.

13. Paul Stefan, *Franz Schubert* (Berlin: Wegweser Verlag, 1928; reprint, Vienna: Ullstein, 1947), p. 175.

14. Fritz Hug, *Franz Schubert: Tragik eines Begnadeten* (Munich: Wilhelm Heyne Verlag, 1976), p. 216.

15. Heinrich Werlé, *Franz Schubert: Der Mensch und sein Werk* (Bayreuth: Gauverlag Bayerische Ostmark, 1941), pp. 203–4.

16. Arnold Schering, *Franz Schuberts Symphonie in h-moll ('Unvollendete') und ihr Geheimnis* (Würzburg-Aumühle: Triltsch, 1939).

17. See, for example, Helmuth M. Böttcher, *Der Unvollendete: Franz Schubert und sein Kreis* (Rudolstadt: Greifenverlag, 1954), pp. 385ff.

18. 'Schuberts H-moll-Symphonie, ein treues Spiegelbild der künstlerischen Individualität ihres Schöpfers, ist leider Fragment geblieben. So gleicht sie auch in ihrer Form dem äußeren Lebensgang des Meisters, der ja in der Blüte seines Lebens, in der Vollkraft seines Schaffens, vom Tode hinweggerafft wurde.' Hugo Wolf, cited in Andrea Lindmayr-Brandl, *Franz Schubert: Das fragmentarische Werk* (Stuttgart: Franz Steiner, 2003), p. 11.

19. Helmuth M. Böttcher, *Der Unvollendete: Franz Schubert und sein Kreis* (Rudolstadt: Greifenverlag, 1954).

20. Friederike Jary-Janecka, *Franz Schubert am Theater und im Film* (Anif and Salzburg: Müller-Speiser, 2000), pp. 187f.

21. Friederike Jary-Janecka, *Franz Schubert am Theater und im Film* (Anif and Salzburg: Müller-Speiser 2000), p. 184f.; Gertraud Steiner Daviau, 'Opposing Views: Franz Schubert in the Films of Willi Forst (1933) and Fritz Lehner (1986)', in Robert Pichl and Clifford A. Bernd (eds), *The Other Vienna: the Culture of Biedermeier Austria/Österreichisches Biedermeier in Literatur, Musik, Kunst und Kulturgeschichte* (Vienna: Lehner, 2002), pp. 315–22. See also Cornelia Szabó-Knotik, 'Franz Schubert und die österreichische Identität im Tonfilm der 1930er Jahre', in Michael Kube, Walburga Litschauer and Gernot Gruber (eds), *Schubert und die Nachwelt, I. Internationale Arbeitstagung zur Schubert-Rezeption Wien 2003: Kongreßbericht* (Munich and Salzburg: Katzbichler, 2007), pp. 315ff.

22. Hans Weigel, *Unvollendete Symphonie: Roman* (Graz: Styria, 1992); see, for example, pp. 161f. Weigel discusses the topos of unfinished works in relation to Schubert's work in another book entitled *Flucht vor der Größe: Sechs Variationen über die Vollendung im Unvollendeten* (Salzburg: Residenz Verlag, 1907).

23. Walther Dürr, 'Wer vermag nach Beethoven noch etwas zu machen? Gedanken über die Beziehungen Schuberts zu Beethoven,' in Heinz-Klaus Metzger and Rainer Riehn (eds), *Franz Schubert* (Munich: Edition Text + Kritik, 1979), pp. 10–25.

24. Rudolf Hans Bartsch, *Schwammerl: Ein Schubertroman* (Leipzig: Staackmann, 1912); see also Alexander Stillmark, '"Es war alles gut und erfüllt": Rudolf Hans Bartsch's "Schwammerl" and the Making of the Schubert Myth', in Ian F. Roe and John Warren (eds), *The Biedermeier and Beyond* (Bern: Peter Lang, 1999), pp. 225–34, especially pp. 227f.

25. See Siegfried Mühlhäuser, *Die Handschriften und Varia der Schubertiana-Sammlung Taussig in der Universitätsbibliothek Lund*, Quellenkataloge zur Musikgeschichte 17 (Wilhelmshaven: Nötzel, 1981), pp. 126–7 (H 113) and Table XX: 'einen Schatz besitzt er aber in Schuberts "H-moll Synfonie", welche wir ... *jeder Beethoven'schen gleich stellen.*'

26. Eduard Hanslick, *Concerte, Componisten und Virtuosen der letzten fünfzehn Jahre, 1870–1885: Kritiken*, 2nd edn (Berlin: Allgemeiner Verein für Deutsche Literatur, 1886), p. 56.

27. 'Die Größe Beethovens drückt ihn in den Augen der Zeitgenossen noch zu sehr in den Schatten, obgleich er bereits ein Vollendeter ist. Die H-Moll-Sinfonie ist das Vollendete.' Joseph August Lux, *Franz Schubert. Ein Lebensbild aus deutscher Vergangenheit* (Berlin: Flemming und Wiskott, 1922), p. 82.

28. See Jary-Janecka, *Franz Schubert am Theater und im Film*, pp. 188f.; Jary-Janecka, 'Schubert—Zweifach Populär: Das Dreimäderlhaus—von der Operette zum Film', in Peter Csobádi, Gernot Gruber, Juergen Kuehel, Ulrich Mueller and Oswalk Panagl (eds), *Das Musiktheater in den audiovisuellen Medien* (Anif and Salzburg: Müller-Speiser, 2001), pp. 446–57; and Manfred Permoser, 'Der Schubert-Film nach 1950: Anmerkungen zur jüngeren Rezeptionsgeschichte', in Michael Kube, Walburga Litschauer and Gernot Gruber (eds), *Schubert und die Nachwelt, I. Internationale Arbeitstagung zur Schubert-Rezeption Wien 2003: Kongreßbericht*, (Munich and Salzburg: Katzbichler, 2007), pp. 321–8.

29. There were several movies on the *Dreimäderlhaus* plot. The earliest was a silent film with the same title from 1918, directed by Richard Oswald. See Helga Belach and Wolfgang Jacobsen (eds), *Richard Oswald: Regisseur und Produzent* (Munich: Edition Text + Kritik 1990), p. 149.

30. Cf. Wolfgang Kos and Christian Rapp (eds), *Alt-Wien: Die Stadt, die niemals war; Sonderausstellung des Wien Museums im Künstlerhaus, 25. November bis 28. März 2005* (Vienna: Czernin Verlag, 2004), especially two chapters by Ulrike Spring, 'Der Himmel über Wien: Franz Schubert, sein Körper und Alt-Wien', pp. 151–8, and 'Schwammerls Wien: Schubert als personifiziertes Biedermeier,' pp. 423–39.

31. In the operetta, the 'Unfinished' is only quoted once, in the finale of Act II; see Ernst Hilmar, 'Die musikalischen Vorlagen in Bertés "Dreimäderlhaus"', *Schubert durch die Brille* 13 (1994), pp. 129–32. And in the novel the symphony is only intimated when Schubert asked Schwind to leave the room and plays the guitar in B minor; see Bartsch, *Schwammerl*, p. 39.

32. Letter to Leopold Kupelwieser, 31 March 1824: 'In Liedern habe ich wenig Neues gemacht, dagegen versuche ich mich in mehreren Instrumental-Sachen, denn ich componirte 2 Quartetten für Violinen, Viola u. Violoncelle u. ein Octett u. will noch ein Quartetto schreiben, überhaupt will ich mir auf diese Art den Weg zur grossen Sinfonie bahnen.' Otto Erich Deutsch (ed.) *Schubert: Die Dokumente seines Lebens*, 2nd edn (Wiesbaden: Breitkopf & Härtel, 1996), p. 235.

33. Chapter 7, 47:50–48:38.

34. Schubert: 'Kupelwieser, wie schaust denn du aus, du bist ja ganz verstört!' / Kupelwieser: 'Ich komm' von der Generalprob'. Der Beethoven hat müssen aufhören zu dirigieren.—Er ist vollkommen taub.—' / Schubert: 'Diesen Tag hab ich schon lang gefürchtet.—Wie hat er's denn aufgenommen?' / Kupelwieser: 'Aus' hat er gesagt, "Es ist zu End." / Mayrhofer: 'Es ist grausam. Spiel weiter, Franzl. Oder nein, es ist besser ... *(zu den Freunden:)* Kommt's, wir gehn, lass man allein. (Zu Schubert, sanft auf den Rücken klopfend:) Arbeit weiter, schreib sie zu End' diese wunderbare Symphonie!' / Schubert *(kopfschüttelnd)*: 'Aus. Zu Ende.' *(Legt das Notenpapier aufs Klavier, dreht sich um und verlässt resigniert das Zimmer mit den Anfangstakten der 'Unvollendeten' im Hintergrund.) Das Dreimäderlhaus*, Kinowelt DVD 501618 (2009), 1:13: 02–1:14:32.

35. *Katalog der Schubert-Zentenarausstellung der Stadt Wien 1928 im Messepalast* (Vienna, 1928), p. 121, No. 573 ('Das Werk blieb nicht etwa—wie vielfach gemeint wird—unvollendet, weil "Schubert über der Komposition gestorben wäre, sondern aus irgendwelchen anderen Gründen".')

36. Alfons Kontarsky. *Franz Schubert: Fragmente*, Lotus Records CD 9724 (1997), booklet, p. 3.

37. Chapter 12, 1:34:15.

38. The description of the movie on amazon.de is in the same style but gives also a quite different synopsis of the musical *Das Dreimäderlhaus* without comments. This confusion seems to be based on the entry in the German Wikipedia that incorrectly claims that the plot of the movie is exactly the same as that of the musical. See http://de.wikipedia.org/wiki/Das_Dreimäderlhaus (1958) (accessed 4 January 2013).

39. See http://www.film.at/das_dreimaederlhaus/. 'Nach 'Leise flehen meine Lieder' bietet dieser Film eine weitere Erklärung, warum Schuberts 8. Symphonie unvollendet blieb' (accessed 4 January 2013).

40. 'Synopsis: Composer Franz Schubert falls in love with Hanner[l], one of three sisters, but he is too shy to express his feelings. He asks a young baron to sing her a lieder [*sic*] that he has written, but Hanner[l] falls in love with the baron. Resigned to the romance between the baron and Hanner[l], Schubert plays his "Ave Maria" at their wedding. Later, while composing his Eighth Symphony, Schubert hears that 'Beethoven has become deaf, and he leaves the symphony unfinished out

of respect for his friend.' http://www.tcm.com/tcmdb/title/510219/The-House-of-the-Three-Girls/ (accessed 4 January 2013).

41. *Das Dreimäderlhaus*, Kinowelt DVD 501618 (2009). See also YouTube: www.youtube.com/watch?v=0J1TrTAkjGo. The English-language adaptation of the movie was released in 1961 under the title *The House of the Three Girls*.

7

Narrative Dislocations in the First Movement of Schubert's 'Unfinished' Symphony

Xavier Hascher

Together with the *Quartettsatz*, D 703, of 1820, the 'Unfinished' Symphony, D 759, written in 1822, marks an essential turning point in Schubert's compositional evolution. Both works display a deliberate change in style and conception, which contrasts with everything that Schubert had achieved until then. In particular, the Classical-like turns of phrase and stock accompaniment figures that had abounded in his earlier instrumental works are abandoned in favour of entirely new and idiosyncratic material which Schubert is able to draw from his experience with the lied, and which matches the tonal adventurousness that has been a characteristic of his handling of Classical forms—and particularly first-movement sonata form—since the beginning. While biographical reasons may also have contributed to it, the slowing down of his production in that period attests to his awareness of his relationship to the Classical tradition and the realisation that the demand for originality was much greater than he had suspected if he wished to affirm himself in the wake of the masters whom he admired. With these works, therefore, Schubert—only twenty-five years old when he wrote the Symphony's two completed movements and the draft of the Scherzo—set higher goals for himself than ever before. Though it could be argued that they inaugurate Schubert's mature instrumental style, they are probably even more innovative in their design and demanding on the listener than anything he was to write later on.

In this chapter I will examine the first movement of the 'Unfinished' Symphony from the perspective of its narrative trajectory as a means of highlighting the novelty of Schubert's conception and the way it leaves behind its Classical models, transcending them in order to break an entirely new—and unique—path.

The Symphony as a Narrative Trajectory

Drawing on theories of semiotics and language, let us assume for the purpose of this essay that the narrative trajectory of a piece of music in sonata-allegro form is structured around a primary narrative programme (NP) which unfolds twice.[1] Based on the definitions of these terms given by Algirdas J. Greimas and Joseph Courtès,[2] this trajectory may be stated as follows:

Primary NP (1st occurrence):

- A presentation of subject 1, of dynamic character (the *subject of doing*);
- A 'journey-episode' that leaves the opening realm 1 behind with effort, as in an ascent;
- A presentation of subject 2, of static character (the *subject of state*), in its own realm (realm 2) in conjunction with associated attributes (values);
- A conclusion in the realm of subject 2.

Secondary NP(s), offering up various incidents (trials);

Primary NP (2nd occurrence):

- A new, victorious presentation of subject 1;
- A modified 'journey-episode' (for the sake of form);
- A new presentation of subject 2, brought back into the realm of subject 1;
- A conclusion in the realm of subject 1, where the attributes associated with subject 2 are also brought back.

This outline reveals that the overall narrative trajectory amounts to little more than an annexation, whereby subject 1 leaves its realm for that of subject 2, seizes the latter and brings it back, lock, stock and barrel, to realm 1. Subject 1 is the actor, the 'agent of action', in this trajectory, in which subject 2 plays a passive role. The central NPs help to delay the return of subject 1, which will come back as triumphant, as the trials have been many and difficult, in particular when they include passing through unknown regions (i.e. remote keys). Relating to these subjects, to the realms and attributes attached to them, as well as relating to the various events in the trajectory are topics, or, in Leonard Ratner's words, 'characteristic figures',[3] which the listener understands as referring more or less conventionally to the real world, notably through the social function of music.[4]

Although cast in sonata form, the first movement of the 'Unfinished' Symphony departs significantly from the customary template. The movement nevertheless pays lip service to the model in that it has the expected two subjects and the dual unfolding of the NP. In other words, the movement obeys a structural framework characterised by a two-theme exposition and recapitulation. Looking more closely at these themes, however, one is struck by the absence from the first theme of the dynamic character normally associated with subject 1. Moreover, the realm in which it evolves is unstable, or rather bi-stable, as it swings three times from B minor to D major (bars 17, 26 and 31). Each of these changes is followed by a rectification that brings back B minor, finally imposing it in a particularly assertive fashion in bar 38. The 'journey'

Example 7.1 Schubert, Symphony No. 7 in B minor, D 759 ('Unfinished'), i, tonal shifts from B minor to D major and dominant 'rectifications' in the first part of the exposition (bars 15–38).

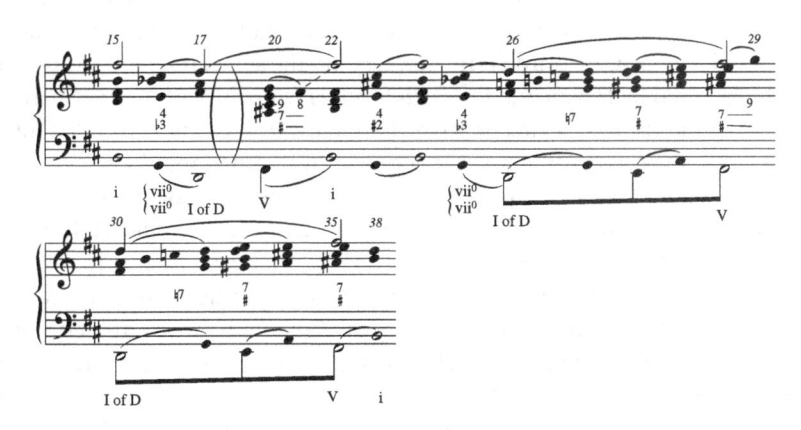

corresponding to the transition in sonata form is thus conjured away. In its place is a counterstatement of the first theme and the two crescendo returns of D major towards F♯, the dominant of B, via the sequence D–E–F♯ in both the bass and the upper part (bars 26–29 and 31–35). (See Example 7.1.)

Owing to the extraordinary way in which Schubert shapes the first half of the exposition, this 'counterstatement' does not resemble the usual beginning of a transition, in which it should follow a firm cadence in the main key. Schubert chooses instead to divert his theme into the relative major, where it cadences rather inconclusively (this becomes even more obvious if we try to transpose the cadence back into B minor). The counterstatement should then offer a dynamic contrast by beginning *forte*—an unimaginable solution here.[5] In a transition, new material would normally be introduced after the first four bars of the counterstatement, or these would be shortened to two bars only and then transposed to launch the modulation to the secondary key. Schubert's continuation follows neither possibility; it merely recombines elements from the second half of the theme and places them in the middle and low woodwinds, relaying the main melody of the first oboe and clarinet. The sequential repetition, leading back to the dominant, creates an effect of 'amplification', as Martin Chusid rightly describes it—but not that of a transition.[6]

Yet, on hearing the return to the soft dynamic at the beginning of bar 22, we do not know if Schubert is starting a new period or merely answering the first phrase of the theme, this time to cadence in the tonic. As it happens, he does both. Susan Wollenberg labels the passage a 'quasi-transition' to emphasise the fact that it stays in the main key,[7] but we need not refer to a transition at all. The exposition's first half follows a standard bipartite *dispositio*, with two main cadences in bars 20 and 38. This division is a consequence of the arrangement of the temporal framework into sections marked by a certain periodicity rather than the harmonic necessity of establishing the secondary key. For Heinrich Christoph Koch, writing in the last decades of the eighteenth century, it is customary for the ensuing third period to carry out the structural modulation—a model followed by Haydn and to which Schubert's practice of the modulating second theme, as in the C major String Quintet D 956, can be linked.[8] Whilst it should have been that the first cadence was in B minor and the second one in D major (preferably an imperfect cadence, but a perfect cadence directly introducing the subordinate theme could also be acceptable), Schubert disposes his cadences the other way around. It is perhaps the premature arrival of the cadence in D major that prompted Schubert to keep it unstressed, while the horns' and bassoons' rectification in bars 20–21 would have been ineffective had the cadence been too strong. Thus, from the outset, Schubert cancels the usual narrative that opposes the two relatives as distinct tonal 'realms' by associating them within one complex, ambiguous whole (where B minor is the main point of equilibrium) and closes the first group onto itself with a *fortissimo* perfect cadence in the tonic.

One does not leave, then, but escapes. There is no sense of departure as we simply slip away. This is what the often commented-upon held notes of the horns and bassoons in bars 38–41 render concrete by providing a magical entry into the realm of the second subject.[9] The feeling is one of effortlessness, and also of being outside of time. The held note, D, is the common element that by analogy enables the scene to be transformed, drawing attention to itself via its offbeat, which then proceeds to merge into the new scenery. What characterises the second realm, however, is that it is placed not above but below the first realm. G major, the exposition's secondary tonality, is in fact the relative of the subdominant of B minor, where we should take the term 'subdominant' to mean the dominant below, or the lower dominant. And, effectively, the path from B minor to G major need only let itself slide. Finally, a violent eruption (bars 63ff.) follows the presentation of the second subject, which is left dangling, without conclusion, the phrase broken off and followed by a bar of silence. This *abruptio* finds its justification in the unexpected outburst marked by the dramatic string tremolos and held winds that follow it.

The movement does have a development section, but it should not be interpreted as a collection of secondary incidents related to the primary NP. In fact, they are absent. The return of the first subject has nothing victorious about it—it is simply re-established with its own realm. The characteristic contrasts and rectifications of its first presentation seem at first softened, and its new entrance (bars 231ff.) in E minor reveals a mollifying turn that is quite usual at this stage. If G is the secondary tonality in the exposition and E the principal tonality of the development section, then we see that the

Example 7.2 Schubert, Symphony No. 7 in B minor, D 759 ('Unfinished'), i, tonal framework of the movement as a descending sequence.

recapitulation resumes this descent by taking it a step further, leading the new statement to the subdominant of the subdominant (i.e. A), approached as minor but finally revealing itself as major. However, this tonality is none other than the relative of the dominant minor, F♯, which Schubert reaches not via the effort and ascent mentioned above, but via a sequence of descents (see Example 7.2).

In this way, the recapitulation paradoxically accomplishes the journey evaded in the exposition. Thus, without formally deploying a transition, Schubert leads the new presentation of the first subject to the dominant in bar 251. A magical passage similar to the one heard previously opens out onto the second subject in D major, the tonality towards which the first subject tended to gravitate repeatedly in the exposition, and which we normally would have expected for the second subject in the same exposition. The second subject is thus reintroduced into the aspect of the first realm that marked the latter's ambivalence before combining with it by imbuing it with B major (rather than minor) colouring.

This can hardly be described as a conquest, whether amorous, military or personal. Entering only in bar 13, the first subject is more an evocation of a landscape than an individual: we do not detect a sense of 'I'. The topic to which it belongs could be of a sylvan and nocturnal nature, something mysterious or unreal. B minor is an uncommon tonality, particular for a symphony, where it is almost unprecedented. The first realm is not of this world; it is unearthly. A four-bar introduction of hushed shimmering strings stirred by a slight semitonal tremor, first between F♯ and E♯, then between G and F♯ (the figure itself shifting up a semitone from F♯ to G, whose importance we shall see later on) paints a pale moonlit scene, out of which appears the first subject. Its falling interval of a fifth is characteristic of the kind of *Naturthemen* found later in Bruckner, which also float above the persistent backdrop of the strings; yet it is the fact that the fifth is descending here that gives the theme its nocturnal atmosphere.

G major, on the other hand, is a more 'down-to-earth' tonality, which expresses 'everything that is *rural, idyllic* and *lyrical* ... all sweet and peaceful emotion'.[10] The topic of the second subject, as Hanslick noted when the Symphony was first performed in 1865, is a Ländler.[11] We pass then from a natural to a human context, possibly personal and emotional, and not one that is necessarily socialized, as the idea of the dance might suggest. The moment is one of quiet confidence and ease, something which the restlessness and instability of the first theme fail to provide.[12] Both Hanslick and Wollenberg have noted the singing, lied-like quality of the second theme's melody, though the real lied ambience lies with the first theme, because of the accompaniment.[13] The accompaniment to the second theme is a conventional syncopated orchestral formula, which nonetheless has thematic importance within the Symphony (in Schubert's mature works, an accompaniment always relates to the overall fabric of a piece) but does not match that of the first theme for originality or sheer strikingness.

How then—given the quiet ethos that defines it—can we explain the brusque interruption that severs the second subject from its conclusion, and the violent upsurge that follows? Is this flare-up simply gratuitous, or is something simmering beneath the surface, something that has not yet been identified? And how are we to interpret the choice of G major over that of D major as the tonality for the second subject in the exposition, and more generally the disparities observed with the narrative model of the sonata?

The answer to these questions requires consideration of the NP that we have analysed as being in reality dependent on another, more fundamental programme which is subjacent to it and at the same time influences it. Adopting for a moment the terminology that Freud used in his writings on the content of dreams, we may posit that there is a manifest NP with the two subjects already mentioned and a latent one that will turn out to be an anti-NP involving a non-trajectory.[14] I will term this obsessive and non-evolving NP '$\sim NP_0$'—where the tilde denotes its opposition to the notion of a trajectory being 'a linear and directed disposition of . . . elements . . . suggesting a progression from one point to another by way of intermediate domains'.[15] Consequently, I will term the manifest, primary NP 'NP_1'.

The 'O' Theme

The first movement of the Symphony begins, as we know, with a strange, deep rumble in the cellos and double basses; they play an eight-bar theme which then fades away and disappears altogether, not to reappear in the rest of the exposition. That alone is enough to make this theme enigmatic: for the sake of economy, Schubert could have started the work with the shimmering strings of bar 9, possibly preparing this with a two-bar statement based only on the basses' rhythm of a dotted crotchet and three quavers, or even via a simple chord in the woodwinds. For our analysis, we shall call this theme 'O', representing origin, opening or obsession. It has two features: it is entirely unharmonised, standing out against the rest of the exposition by virtue of its deep sound and low register; and it conveys a feeling of incompleteness when it comes to rest on the dominant, held for three bars, without being followed by a response leading to the tonic, as it thus contradicts the Classical rule of formal symmetry that governs the construction of themes. Instead of this response, the symphony seems to start *ex nihilo* without our being able to say whether there is any link between the opening bass-line theme and this new beginning. But the chain of events nevertheless establishes causality: even though the theme appears to go nowhere, it acts as if it were a catalyst—as if it had in fact prompted what follows. Although deprived of a formal consequent, it is not without consequence: and that is the exposition itself, and with it the start of the narrative.

However, we need to take a closer look at this theme to understand the role it plays in relation to what has been provoked. As shown in Example 7.3, the 'O' theme is built on a motive (M_0) of three notes spaced over an interval of a minor third divided into a whole tone and a semitone (whether ascending or descending). The semitone, whilst the least represented interval in the scale and with a variable position depending on the mode—the identification of which it therefore enables—is also the most noteworthy interval in that it conveys the most information. The two diatonic semitones belonging to the key of B minor, F♯–G and C♯–D, here stand out starkly. The harmony underlying the theme involves the same F♯–G semitonal movement in the succession from the tonic to the submediant, and the low G, the root of the implied chord, thus remains suspended at the end of bar 4 before resolving onto F♯ in bar 6.[16] The transformation of the motivic figure M_0 into M'_0 is essential for this effect, which would not exist if Schubert had thought it sufficient to give a simple descending linear presentation of the three notes A–G–F♯ in response to the initial B–C♯–D.[17] Interestingly, the beginning of the Scherzo sketch traces what

Example 7.3 Schubert, Symphony No. 7 in B minor, D 759 ('Unfinished'), i, analysis of the 'O' theme and comparison with the opening of the Scherzo.

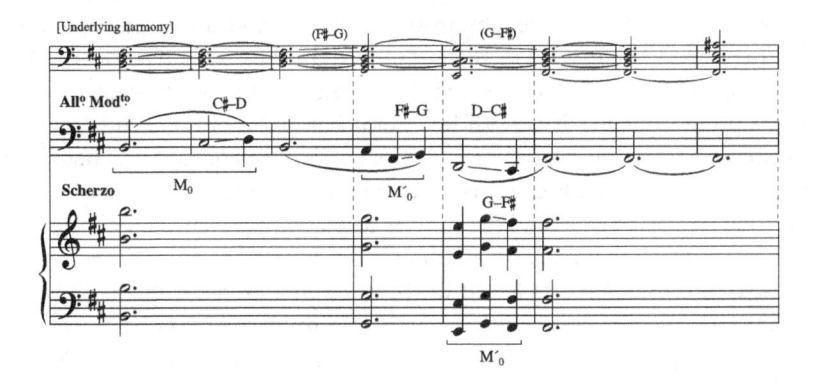

happens at the outset of the first movement and simplifies it.[18] And as with the exposition of the first movement, the first repeat moves to G and completes in G (bars 32ff.).[19]

In the Scherzo, the insistence on the pitch G, which is heard several times and which contrasts with the G♯ in the major-key version of the theme, confers on this modulation a character of obviousness, if not of necessity. There is a clear analogy between the structure of the theme, with its descending three-note arpeggio, B–G–E, that opens the movement—forming the subdominant chord rather than the tonic—and the main structural features of the Scherzo itself, the beginning of whose second repeat modulates in its turn to E minor as in the first movement's development section. Now, whilst the relationship between the theme and the overall organisation of the movement is explicit in the Scherzo, it remains implicit in the Allegro moderato.

Like a magic spell, the 'O' theme opens the doors to the dream world that forms the material of the first movement. The surface or manifest narration borrows some of its characteristic features from the theme as well as its most important event, that is, the modulation to G major. But this borrowing is done in a non-rhetorical, undemonstrative way via the presence of common traits that are set back and seem to establish a secondary level of listening, that of the ground (in terms of gestalt psychology), against which the figures in the foreground stand out. It is the background details that are perceived without being heard, yet if these were modified they would give us a very different sound image of the work. However, at times these elements cross the space separating the background from the foreground and therefore pass from one to the other.

We saw above how the shimmering string figurations that precede the entry of the first subject (which we might term a 'pre-subject') highlight two semitone embellishments on the pitches F♯ and then G; now we have a clearer understanding of the choice of these two pitches, which accompany a plagal shading of the harmony on the pedal B. The figure then moves up and articulates the pitch sequence A♯–B–C♯, again delineating the motive M_0. This motive stands out all the more from the texture in that it is separated from the preceding F♯–G movement by an augmented second, an unusual and thus striking melodic interval. For this reason I term the distinctive F♯–G–A♯–B that frames this augmented second 'M_1' (see Example 7.4). Is what we hear at this point a theme? It is both less than that and more than just accompaniment, first because such a figure has never been encountered before in the history of the symphony: this is far from the conventional formulae that precisely for this reason lend themselves to accompaniment, indicating that we need not pay them undue attention. The hierarchy is not, however, so transparent here. What is heard begins by being an accompaniment, but once the M_0 motive appears, doubt enters our minds: we know perfectly well that it is still part of the ground, but something is conveyed that is no longer neutral.

Example 7.4 Schubert, Symphony No. 7 in B minor, D 759 ('Unfinished'), i, entry of the first theme, bars 11–14.

There is a point here that needs underscoring: the M_0 motive is not recognised as such upon first hearing but is revealed only through analysis. A transformation event has taken place that we can describe with hindsight as being a transposition and diminution compared to the first presentation of the motive, an event of which the listener nevertheless remains unaware for the moment owing mainly to the association of this motive with a new context. When the same succession of A♯–B–C♯, placed identically on the last three quavers of the bar, is integrated in the first theme, it is still far from certain that the listener will connect it to what has gone before. The veiled presence of M_0 is extended further when, after reaching again the initial high F♯, the first subject changes in bar 17 to D and continues to rise through E and then F♮: what we hear from the A♯ in bar 16, the first subject's lowest note, is the first six notes of an octatonic scale (i.e. A♯–B–C♯–D–E–F♮), where each trichord of adjacent notes states a form of the M_0 motive.

It would perhaps be injudicious to analyse the use of the M_0 motive in a constructivist manner; nevertheless, it can be said to be omnipresent in the movement, whether hidden or explicit. The motive appears in the continuation of the counterstatement of the first theme (bar 26, then bars 31ff.). It is concealed and set to a dotted quaver–semiquaver rhythm in the second subject, where it spans a third over F♯–G–A, and then in the subsequent reproductions of what is now a motive in itself—henceforth termed 'M_2'—that we do not immediately associate with M_0 and 'O' (see Example 7.5). The M_2 motive takes up the entire end of the exposition. The development section, where both the first and second subjects are absent, focuses on the 'O' theme and consequently on M_0. This is thrust into the foreground at the end of the development, in bars 198 onward, where it is played inverted and *fortissimo* over four octaves, following on from its altered form C(♮)–B–A♯.[20]

In bars 14 and 16 the bass line of the first subject has a revealing detail that is already present in the harmony of the pre-subject (bars 10 and 12). This concerns the low G that alternates with the B at the end of the bar. (This G is circled and annotated with an exclamation mark in Example 7.4.) What is striking is

Example 7.5 Schubert, Symphony No. 7 in B minor, D 759 ('Unfinished'), i, entry of the second theme, bars 44–47.

that the actual dominant, F♯, is never played in the bass, the G acting as its substitute. The replacement of the actual dominant chord by a third inversion of the diminished seventh chord of the leading note in the main key of B minor (figured ♯4/2 where the seventh is the lower note) removes its marked character from the V–I progression and avoids movement in the bass by a tonally precise ascending fourth or descending fifth in favour of a far less determined leap of a third. The resolution of this G is deferred, however, as it was a little earlier in the 'O' theme. It is only in bar 20 that the basses finally give the low F♯. The other advantage of deploying the G is that it allows an immediate reinterpretation of the chord as a second inversion (figured ♭3/4) of the diminished seventh chord in D leading into that key, while the G–D movement in the bass gives the progression a paradoxical plagal feeling. The seeming anomaly of this G, which can of course be linked to the harmonic progression underpinning the 'O' theme, nonetheless helps explain the choice of tonality for the second subject.

We have seen that in our narrative programme 'realm 1' shifts three times from B minor to its relative major, D, each time involving a rectification. It is the first of these that coincides with the first statement of the V chord in root position in bar 20. This moment is noteworthy for at least two reasons: first, the horn's semitone oscillation between G and F♯ in the middle register, which picks out the rhythmic feature that we find at the end of the first subject; and secondly, the fact that it comes not at the beginning of the bar but on the offbeat, marked by a *forzato*. There is something analogous between the dissonant imbalance of the minor ninth which is detached from the octave—as if peeled off or excoriated—and the imbalance created by the metre.[21] The same 'peeling off' is projected in the higher notes of the entire orchestra in bars 28–29, where the dominant chord is anticipated on the last beat. The third time is none other than that 'magical' transition towards the second realm where the note D is played *fortepiano* and once again on the second beat. The F♯–G interval here is in the bass between the dominant leading to the cadence in bars 36–37, and the tonic of the second subject, bar 42. It is exactly the inverted figure that is produced at the end of the exposition when, after the cadence on G in bar 104, the note B is played emphatically by the whole orchestra, once again on the second beat. And whilst the horns and woodwind sustain the B, the lower strings descend symmetrically from G to F♯ and then state the other semitone, D–C♯, reaching back over the whole exposition to the 'O' theme to which this descent leads.

Moments of Crisis

Thus, the semitone F♯–G, the most elementary melodic movement caused by the harmonic progression from B minor to the submediant, G major, is recognisable both in the foreground material and at a deeper structural level, where the secondary tonality of G major appears as an upper embellishment of F♯.[22] Reflecting Freud's comment that *'a single dream-thought is represented by more than one dream-element'*,[23] each of the constitutive elements of the 'O' theme underpins practically every element of the exposition. It is in the back and forth between the levels, between the latent and the manifest, that we find the locus of the movement's distinctive character. Behind the apparent unfolding of the sonata's narrative trajectory is something permanent and immobile. If there is indeed a trajectory, we can only trace its outline on the surface, a surface beneath which lies a dark, subterranean and limitless expanse, like an underground lake that remains the same wherever one attempts to fathom its depth. Sometimes this layer is concealed, whilst at other times it rises to the surface and permeates it; and sometimes something uncontrollable gushes out from it forcefully: these are the moments of crisis. If these eruptions strike us as unexpected, that is because nothing in the foreground NP_1 has prepared us for it. Such eruptions are to be understood as the consequence of the compression to which $\sim NP_0$ has been submitted, and the way it thwarts its burial by letting traces drift to the surface to alter its features.

The whole first movement is punctuated by four such moments of crisis. The first has already been described with respect to bars 63ff., where, as the bass line sets out the motive M_0 on C–D–E♭, the violins surge upwards to a high B♭. This sundering of the register marks an extreme and demonstrative gesture that can be described as hysterical in nature. It strikes the ear as one of this movement's characteristic sonorities.

Such a sundering is also found in the development section, first where the violins reach their high *forte* G over the low F♯ pedal in the basses (bars 134ff.). This moment represents a tremendous amplification of the horns' modest rectification that in bar 20 brings us back from D to B. (Indeed, one of the features of the development section is the projection—in an already highly emotional register—of elements that when heard for the first time were devoid of any affect.) The sound of the minor ninth is combined here with the 'O' subject (or headmotive), the motive M_0, thus ' overdetermining' (in a Freudian sense) this episode. The high, almost shrill G passage that continues an upward motion to G♯ (bar 146) opens onto a critical episode. The descending two-octave arpeggio answers the ascending arpeggio over two octaves plus a fifth that occurred in bars 67–71. But the new presentation clearly makes reference to the 'O' theme, because it reproduces its rhythm, the same 'O' theme with which the development had started by dropping towards the lowest note of the movement, the C♮ of the cellos and double basses in bar 122 (with the violins rising progressively during this time, highlighting the interval of a semitone).

What is happening at this juncture is symptomatic. The causal order—that is, the temporal order in musical terms—is reversed. The first crisis is understood only when the development has been heard; the development explains this to us. It is, so to speak, a premonition, but it remains without justification up to that point.[24] It is derived from an event that has not yet occurred. In the same way, the minim rhythm (bars 134–138) and then crotchets (bars 139–41) in hemiolas initiate the syncopations that follow (bars 150–153). These are, however, the syncopations that framed the episode built on the third bar of the second subject during the first crisis, especially its culmination in bar 81 and after. First and foremost, they are the same syncopations that form the accompaniment to the second subject as well as, subsequently, the exposition's closing theme (bars 94ff.). To return finally to the crisis at the outset of the development section, when we consider the staccato notes played by the strings on the first beat of bars 150–153, we notice that they form a motive derived from M'_0 (G♯–A–F♯–G♯). (See Example 7.6.)

Example 7.6 Schubert, Symphony No. 7 in B minor, D 759 ('Unfinished'), i, registral tension and 'crisis' in the development, bars 142–154.

In the recapitulation, the third crisis forms the counterpart to the first.

The fourth occurs in the movement's coda. Its beginning presents a close similarity with that of the development section, and especially the build-up climaxing with a new sundering of the register marked by the violins' surge up to a high B. Whilst we might be tempted to hear the end of the recapitulation—richly bathed as it is in the magical colours of B major—as a sort of oneiric wish-fulfilment, the coda, in returning to the 'O' theme, seems to indicate nevertheless that this goal has not been reached.

The whole of the development section should in fact be considered as a huge central crisis. The repeat of the 'O' theme in E minor, played *fortissimo* by the entire orchestra at bar 170, participates in this emotional upheaval. In particular, it permeates the furious ornamental line of the violins in this repeat, which builds toward an extremely strained version of the F♯–G 'peeling off' and augmented second of the M_1 motive.[25] The same transformation, via an overload of affect, concerns the distinctive dotted rhythm of the second subject, here transformed into a persistent military hammering that accompanies the climax of the development section (bars 184ff.). Thus material from the exposition reappears in unrecognisable form in the development section, fragmented and enlarged, as if under the lens of a giant microscope.

Contrary to what we would expect in Classical sonata form, the F♯ dominant that precedes the recapitulation does not build up the tension that aims to lead us back—as a logical necessity—to the home key and the first subject. Against the somewhat theatrical and formal *forte* expected at this juncture, Schubert writes instead a *fortepiano* followed by a *decrescendo*. The V chord, just as in bar 20 of the exposition, presents itself as a rectification of the D chord to which it is juxtaposed. As we have already seen, this alternation projects the harmonic ambiguity of the first subject into the foreground and the ensuing climb from D to F♯ (bars 26–29 and 31–34). But while at that moment it is only perceived as a middleground phenomenon, Schubert turns it into a vehement conflict that is resolved only by the return of the original circumstances and dream-like state—namely the exposition and the first (pre-)subject. It falls to motive M_1, now somewhat dissipated, to reintroduce the latter by restoring the sonority of the minor ninth and its associated 'peeling-off', as well as the dotted-crotchet-plus-three-quavers rhythm. This rhythm acts as an association of ideas enabling the basses to resume it immediately in order to begin the recapitulation (see Example 7.7).

Just as in the exposition (bars 14 and 16, then bars 23 and 25), the alternation between the dominant of B and the tonic of the relative major, D, is introduced at the end of the development by a diminished seventh chord on G. In the exposition, this chord passes almost unnoticed (something that commentators have ignored even though it is somewhat unusual) but is later subjected to an intense magnification. First introduced as a $^6_4$ chord towards the endpoint of the development section's climax (bar 194), it then becomes an inverted augmented sixth

Example 7.7 Schubert, Symphony No. 7 in B minor, D 759 ('Unfinished'), i, the *decrescendo* dominant pedal and the start of the recapitulation, bars 208–218.

chord before transforming into a diminished seventh chord (bar 198).[26] The magnification is such that the chord is not recognised through its constitutive motivic relationships. It refers to something elusive, to something heard before in confusion. But it is indeed the same chord as the one present in the harmony of the exposition's theme and on the same pitches. (Schubert even goes so far as to resume the enharmonic spelling between A♯ and B♭, bars 199 and 201; see Example 7.8.) And not only that: this low G, introduced as a dissonance, goes down one semitone further towards F♯.

Plagal Harmony and Reversal of Logic

The last aspect that seems to me worthy of mention is the importance of plagal movement in the harmony. Reference has already been made to the beginning of the 'O' theme and the comparison with the opening of the Scherzo. If the melodic movement from F♯ to G originates in the descending progression from B minor to G major, then this movement is maintained when the descending progression is repeated to reach E minor from G major. This is no doubt the reason (other than allowing him to keep the bass immobile) that Schubert deployed plagal harmony to undergird the start of the first subject, where the falling F♯–B fifth of the oboe and clarinet would at first sight have implied a dominant-to-tonic progression. The theme is thus essentially based on a plagal balance; and as we have seen, the authentic movement of the bass is carefully avoided. The other striking moment is the retrograde progression of the dominant, D, to the subdominant, C minor, at the outset of the first

Example 7.8 Schubert, Symphony No. 7 in B minor, D 759 ('Unfinished'), i, end of the development section: diminished chord and motive M_0, bars 196–202.

crisis (bars 61ff.). There is no error of harmony, since the bass comes back to D on a minor $^6_4$ chord, but nevertheless the second subject remains broken off and deprived of its conclusion, which is reached only with the resolution of the crisis in bar 93. The effect produced is an extremely powerful one. The last moment occurs in the coda, when, after the authentic cadence (bars 350–352), the 'O' theme's opening figure is repeated in alternation with the winds and strings, whereas the harmony—over a pedal, as under the first subject—passes from the tonic to the subdominant, highlighting one last time the semitone F♯–G.[27]

The movement's apparent thematic diversity is deceptive: the material ultimately proves to be extremely minimal. This is the import of what I have tried to show in this essay. It is not, however, a question of thematic economy in the Classical sense. (Recall how Haydn was noted for his ability to extract enough material for a whole movement from a small sequence of notes—perhaps the most striking application of this principle being of course Beethoven's Fifth Symphony.) Indeed, the links and logical derivations are not designed to be perceived as such and followed as they unfold. It matters little whether or not this conception is intentional; it results from the particular way in which the material is actually put together and how we become aware of it. This is a crucial point: Schubert avoids giving the impression of logical continuity, of a formal 'teleology'. Motives are not modified incrementally so as to provide a deductive 'unfolding'. Under the seeming guise of progression, the dominant character is, rather, one of permanence and persistence. Despite their diversity, the themes articulate the same pitches and relationships that appear as an underlying thread throughout the fabric of the movement. The fact that distinct events do not refer to each other on the same level but pass instead from the foreground to middleground and background means that their identification is rendered more difficult and affects such events' linearity. Thereby the Classical elaboration of themes is replaced, where the different levels can be linked but where each one progresses according to its own perceptible logic. In this movement, the steps that normally allow us to follow the motivic transformations are skipped over, or certain elements are submitted to such extreme magnification as to render them unrecognisable. Instead of a fluid and regular continuity, the movement progresses (if it can be said that it does so at all in the usual teleological sense) by crises, stalling and reversals.

There is an essential point to be addressed here. The recurrence of specific sonorities refers back to their earlier occurrences via our memory and undermines the progression of the movement by unveiling a secret topology that short-circuits it. Mysterious subterranean levels link up with more or less distant events, and we realise that instead of advancing, as we thought, we are in fact in the same place. The 'O' theme, we have seen, does not progress. It is obsessive, and all elements emerging from it are devoid of a sense of 'becoming'. However, this theme is also the common denominator of the first and second subjects; each of these themes makes reference to 'O', and they refer to each other through it. Here the emphasis on the subdominant aspect considered above takes on an additional meaning. 'Action', in tonal music, corresponds to movement toward the dominant. But between the exposition and the recapitulation, Schubert opts for an inverted narrative model, an anti-narrative that is superimposed onto the non-narrative impulse of the 'O' theme. The harmonic progression from G to D major, the tonalities of the second subject between the two outer sections of the movement, has nothing to do with the authentic resolution of sonata form. It is still a plagal movement.[28] But as with the development section, where some elements from the exposition find their origins and justification via a logical reversal, the inversion of the harmonic order is also a temporal and logical reversal whereby the effect precedes the cause. There are, however, several other worlds where such a reversal might take place: the realms of dreams, or at least of the imagination.

Conclusion

The difficulty of the challenge that Schubert had set himself, as he was exploring entirely new directions, may account for the incompleteness of both the *Quartettsatz* and the 'Unfinished' Symphony, rather than any alleged impoverishment of his inspiration or tales about his lack of artistic ambition (which have luckily been swept away by recent musicology). The task of not merely assimilating musical classicism but going beyond it in a way that was recognisably individual and owed nothing to anyone but himself was enormous. What Schubert had to express musically was of an altogether different nature to what the theatricality of Classical forms could allow: the vocabulary of Classicism, as much as its syntax, had exhausted themselves, and Schubert could not carry on repeating the same things. It can be supposed that Schubert was confronted with the problem of bending what had now become the artificiality of the four-movement sonata cycle to his new aesthetic aim, which may have led him to the provisional but also forward-looking solution of a synthesis exemplified in the 'Wanderer' Fantasy, D 760, for which Schubert received the commission when he was working on the 'Unfinished'. In later works he would provide different but perhaps more conservative solutions to the question of the formal and stylistic renovation of the scherzo and the finale.

Notes

1. The original text of this essay, to be published as 'Anti-parcours et non-narration dans le premier mouvement de la Symphonie inachevée de Schubert', in Márta Grabócz (ed.), *Narratologies musicales: topiques et stratégies narratives en musique* (Paris: Éditions des Archives contemporaines, forthcoming), was translated by Philip Clarke thanks to a special grant from the GREAM Laboratory of excellence of the University of Strasbourg (ANR-10-LBX-27). It has been revised and slightly expanded for the purpose of the present publication. I am deeply grateful to Lorraine Byrne Bodley for offering to include it here.

2. Algirdas J. Greimas and Joseph Courtès, *Semiotics and Language: an Analytical Dictionary*, trans. Larry Crist, Daniel Patte, James Lee, Edward McMahon II, Gary Phillips and Michael Rengstorf (Bloomington: Indiana University Press, 1982). Although it refers in part to the terminology established by Greimas and Courtès, the sonata trajectory offered here is mine.

3. Leonard G. Ratner, *Classic Music: Expression, Form, and Style* (New York: Schirmer Books, 1980), p. 9; emphasis in original.

4. In what follows, I will be using the term 'narrative' in a more abstract sense than that defined by Márta Grabócz (see, for example, 'Classical Narratology and Narrative Analysis in Music', in Robert S. Hatten, Pirjo Kukkonen, Richard Littlefield, Harri Veivo and Irma Vierimaa (eds), *A Sounding of Signs: Modalities and Moments in Music, Culture, and Philosophy; Essays in Honor of Eero Tarasti on His 60th Anniversary*, Acta Semiotica Fennica 30 [Imatra: International Semiotics Institute, 2008], pp. 19–42). I am therefore adopting a viewpoint whereby a narrative sense—as distinct from a signification—emerges from the grammatical organisation of a musical structure. I nevertheless do not deny the importance of topics and share with Grabócz the opinion that they constitute one of the main semantic articulations of music; I also share with Kofi Agawu (*Playing with Signs: a Semiotic Interpretation of Classic Music* [Princeton, NJ: Princeton University Press, 1991]) the idea that a complete analysis should take this aspect into account. Unfortunately, a more detailed discussion of these points is beyond the scope of this essay.

5. The first part of Schubert's exposition violates the Classical principle of dynamic contrasts between *forte* and *piano* sections. No exposition before that had ever maintained a global *pianissimo* to *piano* dynamic range for so long, with the

exception of local outbursts, all of which connect with the restoration of the F♯ dominant.

6. Martin Chusid, 'Analysis', in Chusid (ed.) *Schubert: Symphony in B Minor ('Unfinished')* (New York and London: Norton, 1971), p. 72.

7. Susan Wollenberg, *Schubert's Fingerprints: Studies in the Instrumental Works* (Farnham: Ashgate, 2011), pp. 61–62.

8. Heinrich Christoph Koch, *Versuch einer Anleitung zur Composition* (Leipzig: Adam Friedrich Böhme, 1793), vol. 3, pp. 342ff.

9. No one has treated the subject of Schubert's transitions with more care or sensitivity than Susan Wollenberg, who has devoted several essays to it. I borrow the notion of magic from her idea of a 'magical' transition type, which she has developed in 'Schubert's Transitions', in Brian Newbould (ed.), *Schubert Studies* (Aldershot: Ashgate, 2003), pp. 16–61, and 'Schubert's Poetic Transitions', in Xavier Hascher (ed.), *Le Style instrumental de Schubert: sources, analyse, évolution* (Paris: Publications de la Sorbonne, 2007), pp. 261–77. See also her more recent chapter on the question, 'Poetic Transitions', in Wollenberg, *Schubert's Fingerprints*, pp. 47–97.

10. 'Alles *Ländliche, Idyllen-* und *Eklogenmäßige* ... jede sanfte und ruhige Bewegung des Herzens'. Christian Daniel Friedrich Schubart, *Ideen zu einer Ästhetik der Tonkunst* (Hildesheim: G. Olms, 1990), p. 380.

11. 'An enchanting passage of song of almost *Ländler*-like ease'. Eduard Hanslick, 'On The First Performance', in Martin Chusid (ed.), *Schubert: Symphony in B Minor ('Unfinished')* (New York and London: Norton, 1971), p. 114.

12. I am grateful to Professor Harry White of University College Dublin for underlining this aspect in conversation.

13. Wollenberg, *Schubert's Fingerprints*, p. 125.

14. 'We must make a contrast between the *manifest* and the *latent* content of dreams'. Sigmund Freud, 'The Interpretation of Dreams', in James Strachey (ed. and trans.), *The Standard Edition of the Complete Psychological Works of Sigmund Freud*, vol. 4 (London: Hogarth Press, 1953), p. 135; emphasis in original.

15. 'Trajectory', in Greimas and Courtès, *Semiotics and Language*, p. 347.

16. That A and F♯ act as a double appoggiatura to the harmonic note G is apparent from bar 189, in the development, where the motive is sounded against the rest of the chord, i.e. B and D, in a i–VI succession from the previous bar, as at the beginning of the movement.

17. This descending presentation of M_0 does occur in the movement's coda, in bar 339, in the very last presentation of the theme leading to the final cadence (bars 336–352), following on from an unmodified presentation (bars 328–336) where the sustained F♯ is harmonised as a 6 chord followed by a dominant seventh to cadence on the tonic. The melodic transformation may be due to the avoidance of the parallel fifths that would otherwise result between the bass and the upper part that enters in canon.

18. Unlike theme 'O', the beginning of the Scherzo gives an answer to the original phrase. Starting on G and ending on B, this answer in turn gives prominence

to the semitone C♯–D. (It will be recalled that the Scherzo exists only in sketch form, written out on one or two staves, of which Schubert managed to orchestrate the first twenty bars. See Chusid, *Schubert: Symphony in B Minor*, pp. 64–9.

19. Ibid., pp. 64–5.

20. This diminished third reflects the rising figure C♯–D–E♭ that occurs at the moment of crisis in bar 69, whereas the inversion (or retrograde) was already accompanying the entry of subject 1, bar 14.

21. This 'peeling off' enables the transformation of the dissonance on the interval of a second between E–F♯ into a minor third, which is itself dissonant against the rest of the chord. This alternation between second and third—or 'friction-detachment', as it may be called—constitutes one of the characteristic sounds of the movement.

22. For Schenker, one of the ways to understand the submediant is as a neighbour note to the dominant; he also assigns it (though incompatibly) the role of 'a third-divider within the descending fifth I–IV', indeed mentioning the 'Unfinished' Symphony's first movement as an example where the descending subdominant arpeggiation serves to prolong the I–V fundamental arc. See Heinrich Schenker, *Free Composition*, trans. and ed. Ernst Oster (New York: Longman, 1979), p. 140. Despite Schenker's exclusion, the two roles can be reconciled provided they do not concern the same structural level.

23. Sigmund Freud, 'On Dreams', in James Strachey (ed. and trans.), *The Standard Edition of the Complete Psychological Works of Sigmund Freud*, vol. 5 (London: Hogarth Press, 1953), p. 653; emphasis in original.

24. Michael Spitzer deals with similar issues of emotional state in this movement, albeit in different terms, in 'Mapping the Human Heart: a Holistic Analysis of Fear in Schubert', *Music Analysis* 29/1–3 (2010), pp. 149–213.

25. Another striking 'peeling off', involving the same pitches and the same key of B minor, happens in 'Der Doppelgänger' (D 957/13) at the moment when the poet recognises his own features ('meine eig'ne Gestalt') on the face of the stranger whom he encounters standing in front of his former beloved's house.

26. It is in this passage, as we have seen above, that we find motive M_0 in inverted form (see section 2).

27. The culminating point of the development section, in bars 184–193, is based on a sequence of three segments linked by falling fifths: F♯ minor, B minor and E minor (thus undoing the previous rising sequence of fifths from E to F♯ in bars 176–184). But the passage from one key to the other is done via a regression of the dominant to the subdominant, where the iv chord is then taken as i of the new stage of the sequence: this is exactly the progression that will lead to the recapitulation in the second movement of the same symphony, in bars 140–142 (second inversion of the dominant seventh chord on F♯, i.e. the dominant of the dominant or altered supertonic, resolving to the tonic of E major). Note that here again the bass moves by a leap of a third.

28. Schubert had already used a similar harmonic pattern in the first movement of his Symphony No. 4 in C minor, D 417 (1816), where the second theme

appears in A♭ major, the subdominant relative, in the exposition and is then recapitulated in the relative major, E♭, switching to the tonic major for the rest of the movement. There is an essential difference, though, in that the recapitulation begins in the dominant minor key of G.

8

(Re-)Theorising Schubert's 'Reliquie'

Precedents, the 'Great' Symphony, and Narrative

Cameron Gardner*

Introduction: Presenting Methodologies

In her Schubert biography, Elizabeth Norman McKay claims considerable significance for the unfinished Piano Sonata in C major, 'Reliquie', D 840. Her views are inspired by an expansive rise-and-fall trajectory in the first-movement development and central section of the Minuet: 'In each case, Schubert builds up the tension to a mighty climax, following it with a passage of almost identical length, as the tension subsides into a deathly calm'.[1] For McKay, these approaches to and retreats from a peak suggest a 'narrative content', in particular an 'epic character, of a kind not found in any of his music before 1825', the year of the Sonata.[2] Later in her biography, she reiterates her comments to highlight comparative moments in the 'Great' C major Symphony, D 944, a connection supported by the close chronology of the two works.[3] Although these descriptions are brief, they provide contexts for the 'Reliquie' that McKay and other scholars have left unexplored,[4] which, in turn, have implications for the reception of the Sonata and of Schubert's developments in general. McKay's observation of a corresponding gestural arc in the first movement and Minuet prompts consideration of the movements as artistically comparable; this contributes further to the shift away from the earlier reception history, which casts the unfinished Minuet as inferior.[5] Because the examples appear in a development, there is also an opportunity to concentrate on an aspect of Schubert's sonata and ternary forms which has received far less attention than his expositions and recapitulations. More locally, McKay's focus on expressive shape implies that register and dynamics are integral to the Sonata's artistic maturity and its embodiment of a new, more sophisticated narrative. Although specific musical illustrations are lacking, McKay's remarks suggest that register and dynamics are analytically fundamental.

This essay responds to McKay's reading of the 'Reliquie' by examining the processes of build-up and dispersion in the first and third movements and investigating generic precedents (especially Beethoven) and corresponding practices in Schubert's earlier instrumental works. Equivalent passages in the 'Great' Symphony elicit further assessment of the special status McKay assigns to the Sonata. In a more isolated context, analysis of the two examples in the 'Reliquie' will focus on a circle of thirds in the first movement and two 5–6 shifts in the third movement in order to understand the preparatory stage of the tonal design. The difference between these linear progressions and those analysed by David Damschroder in other Schubert compositions will clarify the work's harmonic and tonal particularities.[6] For the Minuet, another analytical tool applied by Damschroder, which he terms 'enharmonic equivalence', will illuminate a dual role for particular harmonies and offer a more structurally appropriate spelling.

For both movements, Thomas Denny's threefold characterisation of Schubertian developments and recapitulations supports the analysis's extension to the moment of recapitulatory return, which McKay does not consider.[7] Denny's design includes (1) a clear development section, (2) an elision during the initial stages of the recapitulation where developmental features also occur and (3) a later point of unequivocal reprise corresponding to equivalent parts of the exposition. While all three elements are present in the first movement of the 'Reliquie', the third is absent from the Minuet, since Schubert only sketched six bars of the recapitulation.

The later stages of this essay will contextualise salient details of each example via Emil Staiger's theory of poetics, in particular his correlation of temporal states of being as understood by Martin Heidegger with complementary poetic genres: past/lyric, present/epic, future/drama.[8] Further reinforcement of the compatibility of these correlations derives from the association of each component with narrative, a medium primarily concerned with conveying human content. Poetic genres contain either a narrative or a narration centred on different individuals' actions or the thoughts and feelings of a single speaker. Time may also be intimately linked with narrative, as Paul Ricoeur has argued, because narrative is 'the human relation to time'.[9] Further significance is found in the conclusion of each example, where, following a lowering of register and dynamics and a dissipation of texture, there is a return to a more lyrical version of the main theme in a non-tonic key at the beginning of the recapitulation.

To formulate a narrative interpretation for McKay's examples in the 'Reliquie' and for the reprises that follow, a process of sign translation and isomorphism is undertaken. Sign translation is a method for conveying meaning, whereby a sign in one system (such as a 'sound unit' or 'phoneme') acquires significance from a more explicit sign in another system (often a written language).[10] When translation occurs between two systems having parallel or similar rules or conventions, an isomorphic relationship results, as the semiotician Roman Jakobson was the first to recognise. This offers a more sophisticated and rigorous approach to musical meaning than a simplistic 'one-to-one mapping of definitions in the manner of "minor mode music equals sadness" or "the perfect authentic cadence equals resolution and finality"'.[11] In the 'Reliquie', elements that adhere to or depart from patterns in other sonata forms, whether by appearing concurrently or at different places in a movement, prompt an isomorphic process. This involves a translation of a particular feature of the Sonata into a unit of signification or 'morpheme' through a musical language that addresses texture, phrase structure, harmony, tonality and form. Tracing the effect of a compositional detail then leads to the possibility of further translation, through recognising situations that are similar to Staiger's merging of temporal existence with poetic genre.

Determining Precedents

Despite McKay's assertion that the intensification and abatement of musical energy in the first and third movements of the 'Reliquie' marks a new departure for Schubert, the composer would have been familiar with such passages from the developments of late Mozart and Haydn, and particularly middle-period Beethoven.[12] This knowledge is evident from the musical characteristics of each example: registral rise and fall, fragmentation, sequences, major-minor shifts, repetitive rhythmic ideas, a diminuendo and textural thinning.[13] The communicative power of this detail further reflects on earlier sonata-form developments, as *Sturm und Drang* qualities of 'restlessness' and 'instability' are conveyed.[14] Other features, including the sustaining of a *forte* dynamic level with vigorous antiphony in the climax of the first movement also suggest *Sturm und Drang*.

One striking precedent for the two extracts from the 'Reliquie' appears in the first movement of Beethoven's 'Eroica' Symphony, Op. 55. In the earlier work, a prolonged build-up (bars 338–361) to a brief peak (bars 362–366) mirrored by a withdrawal of similar length (bars 367–397) shapes the final stages of the development and leads to the beginning of the recapitulation (bar 398).[15] Although longer than both of Schubert's examples, this design would have provided the composer with a template of how to pace an expressive rise and fall to reach the reprise. He applies it not only to the first movement but also to the third, where there is no precedent in length in any Beethoven minuet or scherzo. If inspired by corresponding passages in the development of the first movement of the 'Eroica', Schubert's choice of harmony, tonality and thematic presentation nevertheless remains individual. In neither example of the Sonata is there, at any moment, an appearance of the home dominant. Without this preparation, there is no powerfully heroic, unambiguous recapitulatory downbeat where the tonic and main theme coincide. Instead, in both movements Schubert returns to a developmental version of his main theme in a key chromatically neighbouring the tonic, an elided non-tonic recapitulation.

To appreciate McKay's claim that the examples in the 'Reliquie' are unprecedented in Schubert, an examination of developments from the composer's earlier works is revealing, with certain genres either supporting or qualifying her view. There are no earlier piano-sonata first-movement developments with a comparable expressive design,[16] while several compositions on a grander scale (symphonies, overtures and larger chamber works) have varying degrees of intensification and dissipation of musical energy. No previous Schubert minuet or scherzo, in contrast, contains a trajectory analogous to the Minuet in the 'Reliquie': at most, either a build-up or a dispersion of considerable length appears, but neither shapes a central section. The presence of arch-shaped patterns in earlier first-movement developments seems initially to undermine the opinion that such passages are absent from Schubert's music before the 'Reliquie'. Yet closer inspection reveals differences of dimension and tonality. There is no match in terms of symmetry nor, in many cases, length

Example 8.1 Schubert, Sonata in C major, 'Reliquie', D 840, i, bars 126–150

Reappraising Schubert's 'Reliquie' 151

Example 8.1 Continued

to the eleven bars on either side of the peak in Example 8.1 (bars 127–137 and 138–149). In earlier developments, even when an approach to or retreat from a peak is longer, the two sides are more disproportionate, less balanced.[17] Tonal features reinforce the distinction: in earlier examples, a dispersion of energy usually leads to a conventional reprise in the tonic or, less often, in the dominant or subdominant; in Example 8.1 the withdrawal from the climax leads to a recapitulation in the subtonic, B major.

Example 8.2 Schubert, Sonata in C major, 'Reliquie', D 840, Minuet, bars 42–74

The 'Great' C Major Symphony

Turning to corresponding parts of the 'Great' Symphony reveals a closer relationship to the examples in the 'Reliquie' and further distances the Sonata from earlier compositions. At first glance it is possible to illustrate McKay's linkage of expressive design and harmonic sequence in the two works. The

Example 8.2 Continued

2

[musical score excerpt, mm. 67–80, with "RECAPITULATION" marked at m. 74 and "etc." at the end]

intensification to a peak and a subsidence of similar length are clearly defined in the development of the first movement of the 'Great', while a variety of sequences appear in both works, in the first- and third-movement developments. Other harmonic detail involves dominant prolongation and the suggestion of resolution to the minor mode at the recapitulation.[18]

Although this connection initially implies a potential pairing, a more in-depth comparison highlights variance. This applies to the examples in the first movements, where there is some similarity of contour and harmony, as well as to those in the third, where there is less. The expressive rise and fall in the developments of the first movements have the most symmetrical proportions: eleven bars fall on either side of the apex in the 'Reliquie', with thirty-six and thirty bars in the equivalent passage from the 'Great' (see Table 8.1). Although the tempo of the latter, an *alla breve* allegro ma non troppo, creates a 2:1 bar ratio with the moderato of the Sonata, it lasts longer and includes a culmination of ten bars. Placed in William Caplin's 'core' development structure, it commences from the first stage, with a model or initial phrase, whereas the Sonata example begins at the third stage with fragmentation.[19]

The examples in the third movements are less varied in size and more closely positioned in the core (see Table 8.2). The build-up in the Scherzo of the 'Great' starts at the development's second stage with model-sequence repetition, while

Table 8.1 Schubert, 'Reliquie', i, and the 'Great', i, comparison of bar duration and core placement of expressive designs

	Intensification	Peak	Dissipation
'Reliquie', i (moderato)			
Example 8.1	11 (bars 127–137)	beginning of bar 138	11 (bars 138–149)
Core	fragmentation (bars 127–149)	→	→
'Great', i (*alla breve* allegro ma non troppo)			
Example 8.4	36 (bars. 280–315)	10 (bars 316–325)	30 (bars 326–355)
Core	model (bars 280–287) sequences (bars 288–303) fragmentation (bars 304–355)	→	→

that of the Minuet of the 'Reliquie' starts with a combination of the second and third stages, employing sequences of fragmentation. The duration of these intensifications is differentiated, however, through a contrast of tempo overriding the disparity in bar length. With the Minuet in the 'Reliquie' governed by an allegretto tempo compared to the allegro vivace of the Symphony, the approach to a peak in the Sonata takes longer, despite the development being four bars shorter and affected by the early stages of an accelerando. From the brief climax there follows an eight-bar dissipation of energy and a nine-bar exit to the reprise. In contrast, there is no sustained winding down in the 'Great', only an immediate reduction of dynamic and instrumentation (bar 152) following a seven-bar peak (bars 145–151).[20] This quick change prior to the recapitulation does not proportionally balance with earlier passages of sustained energy. The symmetry present in the other examples is here lacking.

Together with register and dynamics, harmonic progressions and prolongations determine the contour of the expressive design of both works and further consolidate the distinctiveness of the 'Reliquie'. Local progressions in the Sonata and the Symphony (circle of thirds and fifths; other sequential patterns) help either to project towards or, in one case, away from a climax (bars 326–355 of the first movement of the 'Great'). Except for the latter, dominant harmony then appears at or close to the point of culmination, and, in the third movements, remains throughout the retreat through to the reprise. The longest

Table 8.2 Schubert, 'Reliquie', iii, and the 'Great', iii, comparison of bar duration and core placement of expressive designs

	Intensification	Peak	Dissipation
'Reliquie', iii (allegretto) Example 8.2	**14** (bars 42–56)	beginning of bar 57	**8** (bars 57–65) + **9** exit (bars 65–74)
Core	sequences of fragmentation		
'Great', iii (allegro vivace) Example 8.5	(bars 42–144) **18** (bars 127–144) sequences (bars 127–136) fragmentation (bars 137–152)	**7** (bars 145–151) →	bar 152, *p* echo →

prolongation occurs in the passage from the 'Reliquie' shown in Example 8.1. Here it spans the entire expressive design and is nuanced by the local appearance of the dominant just before the apex at the end of a thirds circle (bar 138; see Example 8.3). Another connection between the prolongations is the presence of pitches belonging to the tonic minor of each dominant (detailed in n. 18). With repetition, these pitches create the expectation of an arrival in the minor mode at the beginning of the recapitulation.

Of the sequences encountered, only the circle of thirds is common to both the 'Reliquie' and the 'Great'. This appears in the developments of the first movements and has little precedent in corresponding music by Haydn, Mozart or Beethoven; neither example is addressed in any discussion of sonata-form developments by Caplin or Hepokoski and Darcy. In this section of a Schubert movement, however, a circle of thirds is likely to occur, as Gordon Sly notes, and its presence elsewhere in the composer's music has elicited much analytical response, not least from David Damschroder.[21] Despite this attention, there has been no engagement with the example in the 'Reliquie' and, until recently, little with that in the 'Great'. Both provide an equal division of the octave, although the division in the 'Reliquie' into four ascending minor thirds (F♯–A^7–C^7–E♭^{7}–F♯; see Example 8.3) is less common in Schubert, who prefers major-third octave segmentation.[22] The progression in the Sonata also strongly defines the latter stages of the build-up, with a quickening of harmonic rhythm and fragmentation helping to complete the octave segmentation a bar before the apex.

The closest connection between the circles of thirds in the first movements of the 'Great' and the 'Reliquie' concerns placement within the developmental

Example 8.3 Beethoven, Symphony No. 3 in E♭ major, 'Eroica', Op. 55, i, bars 338–397

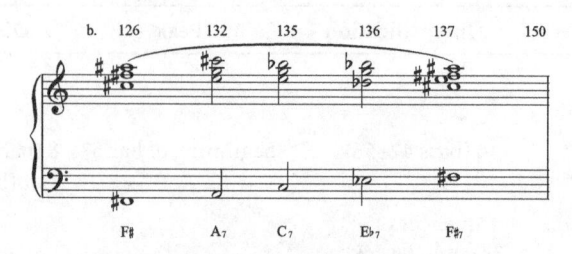

Example 8.4 Schubert, Symphony No. 8 in C major, D 944, iii, equal division of the octave with descending major thirds

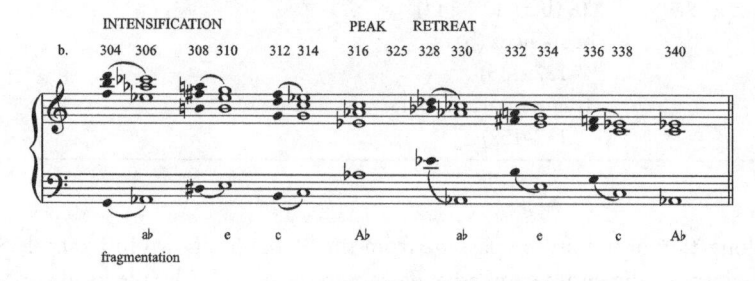

core and the expressive design: both appear at the fragmentary stage building towards a climax. While the Symphony has a more typical division of the octave, with three descending major thirds, it is characterised by an unusual change of mode: the circle begins in A♭ minor and ends in A♭ major (Example 8.4).[23] Although a comparative example appears in the Sanctus from the later Mass in E♭ major, D 950, the presence of a dominant for each third and the immediate return of the progression is not typical of Schubert's earlier works. Since the return occurs in the winding down towards the recapitulation, finishing with A♭ major at the beginning of the exit passage (bar 340), the thirds also participate in the expressive fall at the end of the development.[24] This far exceeds the scale of the minor thirds in the 'Reliquie' and therefore points up the more localised status of the progression in the Sonata.

With the build-ups in the central sections of the two works' third movements having less in common, a stronger degree of difference again reinforces the individuality of the 'Reliquie'. In the Symphony's Scherzo, the intensification builds upon sequential repetition of the model (based on the headmotives of the primary and secondary modules) and begins with the second sequence (from bar 127). The phrase then remains mostly unchanged throughout the registral and dynamic rise, with some fragmentation occurring near the peak (bars 137–144). In the Minuet of the 'Reliquie', however, there is a wider and more unusual range of progressions. This is apparent from the very beginning of the intensification, where a descending circle of fifths appears, which is different in content and size

Example 8.5 Schubert, Sonata in C major, 'Reliquie', D 840, iii, circle of fifths

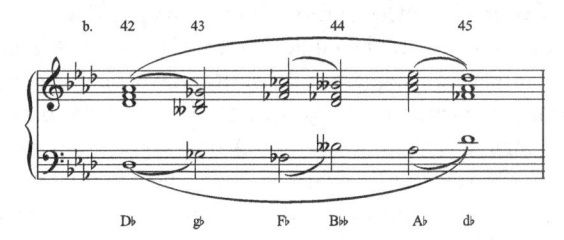

Example 8.6 Schubert, Sonata in C major, 'Reliquie', D 840, iii, 5–6 shifts

from most precedents (bars 42–45, Example 8.5). Instead of beginning with V–I in the home key, as a circle of fifths often does in earlier developments, the progression in the Minuet starts with IV (D♭ major) and ends with iv (D♭ minor). The sequence's distinctiveness also resides in the separation of each fifth relation by a third, forming a passage briefer than the first movement's circle of thirds.

Further motion away from D♭ major, the central section's initial key, helps to define the remainder of the build-up and confirm the movement as one of Schubert's most radical (Example 8.6). The progressions lead to the regions of D and A major and often involve harmony that embodies 'two separate syntactic events merged into the same moment in time'.[25] The labelling for much of this harmony, however, is derived retrospectively, especially when interpreted in A major, the key implied at the reprise following seventeen bars of dominant preparation.

The first progression after the circle of fifths, D♭ minor–A major–D major (bars 47–51, Example 8.6), suggests a I^{5-6} shift in D♭ minor moving to the flattened supertonic, enharmonically spelt as D major. As the outer harmonies have roots that form a second, the central A major essentially functions as an elaboration of the initial D♭ minor and prevents the potential problem of parallel fifths. In particular, while the root and the third of D♭ minor are retained, the A forms a passing note, a flattened sixth written as a sharpened fifth, to lead to D major. Although D♭ minor and A major are not in a 5–6 position, the labelling avoids interpreting the A as part of a new rather than pre-existing harmonic unit and reinforces Damschroder's need to clarify rather than increase 'local transformative processes within a governing key in Schubert'.[26] Although the same progression has appeared in the A section to facilitate modulation to A major (bars 15–16), further interpretation of the one in the central section derives from the harmony that follows. With the subsequent repeated alternations of A and D major (bars 51–52), dominant status is suggested for A major, a characteristic role for '6-phase' harmony.[27] Later, with the dominant of A reached at the peak and sustained through the retreat until the recapitulation (bars 57–74), the hierarchical relationship between A and D major reverses, so that the latter becomes, in hindsight, the subdominant to the former. This suggests a IV^6 role for the sequence of D major and D minor prior to the dominant arrival at the climax (bars 53–56). While a dominant following a IV^6 is common, the switch of mode just before and, in particular, the enharmonic relationship of these harmonies to the key of the flattened supertonic in a movement in A♭ major is not. Respelling A major as B major makes it possible to emphasise the tonality as distinctive without losing sight of its relation to the tonic, an event to which Schubert would have returned had he completed the movement.

Narrative, Temporality and Rotation

Since an unconventional tonal design appears with a compliant treatment of register, dynamics and texture balancing a build-up to a peak with dissipation, both examples in the 'Reliquie' would seem to confirm one of Byron Almén's prerequisites for constructing a musical narrative: a simultaneity of opposition. From a more immediate perspective, and one common to musical narratology, the examples' striking expressive shape also provides a default level for defining a narrative. Indeed, for Almén, 'when great excitement gives way to calm (or vice versa)' there is a strong prompt for the listener to 'infer a narrative, or devise one to fit, even in the absence of verbal cues'.[28] This parallels Emil Staiger's merging of psychological states in lyric poetry with Martin Heidegger's link between a dimension of time and a compatible way of being (see Table 8.3).

Table 8.3 Staiger's differentiation of poetic genres with Heidegger's understanding of temporal existence

Way of being +	Temporal mode =	Poetic genre
mood, state of mood	pastness, way of being	lyric
moment of vision or of bringing things into awareness	present-oriented, unconcealment	epic
resoluteness or care	futurity, unconcealment with attainment of future goal	drama

Heidegger found that the past is understandable through its relationship to certain types of existence; for him, being in a mood or state of mind is always a function of 'having-been' or 'pastness'. Furthermore, it is an 'attitude toward or a way of disclosing or viewing something' that makes description possible.[29] In response, Staiger recognised that as lyric poetry is predominantly concerned with conveying mood, it also connects with 'having-been' and noted that reflective moments often receive the most heightened level of description.

Before such contexts are considered for the recapitulations of the first and third movements, however, interpretation must be circumspect in dealing with the problematic presence of dominant preparation for a key chromatically neighbouring the tonic. Because each dominant at the end of the development projects, at some length, a particular tonal outcome, it is possible to form an isomorphic link to poetic drama, where 'existence is directed, is aimed at its goal'.[30] Functional characteristics of resoluteness and pragmatism, exemplified in the range and structural purpose of dominant harmony and in the protagonists and scenarios of dramatic narratives, also imply a forward-facing dimension. For Staiger, a future perspective distinguishes a dramatic from an epic style, with its focus on the present, and demonstrates how Heidegger's associations of a particular state of being with a particular temporal condition might link to another genre of poetry (see Table 8.3).[31] With both recapitulations beginning in the major following preparation that emphasises the minor, however, a less straightforward and more illusory drama for the dominants emerge retrospectively.[32] This interpretation subverts the potential to apply Staiger's unambiguous view of drama to the dominant harmony, of expectations eventually fulfilled.[33]

Faced with the recapitulatory arrival of keys adjacent to the tonic, an initial response might assume a crisis of tonality and view the prior prolongation as evoking a sense of imminence. Because a more lyrical version of primary material arrives at the reprise in both movements, however, there is a mollification of potential background tension. This process identifies a more elevated structural role for lyricism, with an emphasis on interaction, rather than conflict, with the tonal design.

Although the opening module of the first movement (hereafter P1.1) emerges from the dissipation with relative ease, retaining the same dynamic and dominant pitches, its return at the recapitulation suggests a less conventional status: rather than the original octave texture, a version from the development recurs. At the beginning of the movement, the module is unharmonised and placed within a somewhat indeterminate phrase structure; however, for the three later structural downbeats (the beginning of the development, recapitulation and coda) it appears in a melody and accompaniment texture and a clearly defined period (Examples 8.7a-d). This situation enacts an extensive reversal of Caplin's paradigm of an exposition opening with a tight-knit structure and a development with something looser.[34] It also qualifies the earlier claim that the reprise's lyricism is formulaic in opposition to the accompanying key of the subtonic.

When interpreting the post-expositional appearances of P1.1 and the non-return of its original guise, it is constructive to utilise Hepokoski and Darcy's idea of rotational form. For these theorists, rotation is not a tonal but a rhetorical principle, which prompts identification of the recurrence and recycling of thematic-modular elements.[35] Because a lyrical transformation of P1.1 at the development returns at the recapitulation and coda, and because there is no later reappearance of the module in its initial tentative presentation, a rotation has twice emphasised a preferred alternative. These three events create formal significance for what would clearly be more localised if only one had occurred. In addition, as each of the appearances is in a non-tonic key, including at the coda where the module returns for the final time, P1.1 also remains unresolved in its lyrical form.[36] This tonal context prevails up to a later point in the movement than the module's tonic presentation in the reprise (the local climax of the transition, bars 183–184, and the head of the closing theme, bars 248–255). Furthermore, this treatment contrasts with that of the three other primary units, all of which return to the home key and their original textural appearance in the coda.[37] Cast in a marked cantabile style and a tonality removed from more conventional sonata practice, P1.1 forms an isomorphic relationship with the existential concerns of an archetypal protagonist of a lyric poem, who is immersed in a realm distinct from external reality (see Table 8.4).

Further correspondence with temporal existence in lyric poetry extends to the ascending tonal circle of minor thirds from the beginning of the reprise: B, D and F major (bars 150–177). This progression is an example of a Schubertian developmental feature occurring in a relatively small part of the recapitulation, so the lyric qualities of brevity and transitoriness are evident. This interpretation is further underlined with the tonic's return after, at the transition's local climax (bar 184), the moment when Denny's final stage of elision, an unmistakable recapitulatory section, begins.

As no home key reappears in the unfinished Minuet, it is possible to identify a more profound transitory condition. With barely six bars of the reprise in sketched form, the suggestion of A major with a partially harmonised melody is analogous to the fragility that characterises the relationship of the lyric protagonist to the outside world (see Table 8.4). Relating the unfinished passage to the

Example 8.7 Schubert, Sonata in C major, 'Reliquie', D 840, i, comparison of primary modules: (a) initial presentation, bars 1–4; (b) period of beginning of development, bars 105–112; (c) beginning of recapitulation, bars 151–154, based on consequent of opening period of development; (d) beginning of coda, bars 276–279, based on antecedent of opening period of development.

Table 8.4 Summary of isomorphic translation of 'Reliquie', i and iii

Movements	Phonemes (sound units)	Morphemes (units of signification)
i and iii	dominant preparation for non-tonic recapitulation, suggestion of minor-mode resolution	extensiveness of dominant preparation for non-tonic recaps
		↓
		poetic drama: 'where existence is directed, is aimed at its goal?'
	major mode resolution at recaps	illusory drama, in retrospect, for dominants
i, beginning of development, recap and coda	P1.1 in non-tonic compared with P1.1 in tonic elsewhere in recap + with tonic and original textural return of other P modules in coda	P1.1 exists in preferred *rotational* alternative distinct from sonata-form norms
		↓
		poetic lyric: complete self-immersion and removal from external reality
i, beginning of recapitulation	circle of thirds (B–D–F major)	displacement of Schubertian developmental norm
		↓
		lyric qualities: brevity and transitoriness (tonic return follows)
iii	recapitulation (incomplete; only six sketched bars)	suggestion of A major (incomplete harmonisation)
		↓
		fragility of the lyric moment remains undisturbed from the potential intrusion of an external reality, as there is no later tonic return
		incompleteness of lyric moment also = impossibility of the lyric's ever being fully realised
		↓
		complementary epic or dramatic element required before and after: dramatic element only in previous passages of energy drive and dispersion

earlier part of the movement as a tentative rotation, where A major was clearly established and the main theme's quaver decoration was more sustained (A section, bars 18–30), further emphasises a fragile state. This relationship between the reprise and earlier passage also correlates to pastness, which, for Staiger, distinguishes the lyric genre, even though a poet often writes a lyric poem in the present tense. As a structural arrival, the recapitulation clearly suggests the present, yet as a recollection of an earlier variant of the main theme in the same non-tonic key, it also strongly evokes the past. Taking into consideration the absence of any further composition to the movement, however, distance from lyric verse arises. While this incompleteness reflects on the impossibility of the lyric concept's ever being fully realised in poetry, the presence of a dramatic or epic element on either side of a moment of lyricism to compensate for a lack of completion receives only partial correspondence in the preceding energy drive and dispersion. Without the imminent return of the home key, in particular, there is an absence of musical realism to break the mood of reflection at the reprise. Instead, and especially with the da capo repeat of the Minuet following the completed trio, the movement remains forever cast in an idealised tonal design, forever lost in the transience of a key that can only be implied.

The Significance of the Recapitulation in the Tonal Schemes of the First Movement and Minuet

Although each reprise implies a moment of 'intuition',[38] where the major mode emerges at the last minute and there is a return to an altered, rather than the initial, version of the main theme, neither arrival is arbitrary in the respective movement's tonal structure. This organisation emphasises each recapitulation, despite its unusual key and thematic presentation, as crucial to the movement in which it appears. On an isomorphic level and relevant to the earlier analytical considerations, the symmetry of the tonal design relates to the shape of the build-up, peak and retreat in the preceding passages of the development. When Brian Newbould considered the tonality of the Minuet alongside the palindrome in *Die Zauberharfe*, D 644, as the 'most daring technical experiments ever undertaken by Schubert', he inadvertently identified a feature of the opera applicable to the potential key scheme of the movement and the contour of its central section.[39] If the Minuet had been finished, there would have been a return to the tonic, A♭ major, at the end, resulting in a completely symmetrical or palindromic key plan (see Table 8.5). This pattern mirrors the treatment of register and dynamics throughout most of B, in particular the rise-and-fall trajectory.

Because the first movement is complete, its tonal balance is more strongly defined by the recapitulation, with B major marking the beginning of a key reversal: C major–B minor (first and second themes, exposition), B major–C major (beginning and end of the recapitulation). This moment, as Suzannah

Table 8.5 Tonal design of the 'Reliquie', iii.

A	B	A'
A♭ major–A major	E major (V/A major)	A major–*A-flat major*

Clark observes, also forms an important stepping stone to A minor, the second-theme reprise's key, so that the stepwise descent and reversal of mode between the expositional first and second themes is maintained: C major–B minor (exposition), B major–A minor (recapitulation).[40] Such juxtaposition counters the local implication, from the previous dominant, of a reappearance of B minor and thus negates the surprise effect of the parallel major.[41] Determining the significance of the recapitulation's key prompts further appreciation of the prior arch-shaped design. The impressiveness of sound generated by the intensification and dispersion of musical energy compels attention, so that there is considerable engagement with the listener by the time B major arrives, which elicits a degree of focus suitable to the arrival of a structurally pivotal tonality. For a similar connection between the tonal symmetry of the movement and the expressive rise and fall in the development, the reversal of keys from the exposition to the recapitulation, C–b → B–C, mirrors the reversal of register and dynamic after the peak at bar 138.

Rather than allowing his choice of an unorthodox key for the recapitulation in the first movement to inhibit him, Schubert makes B major critical to the tonal structure. Indeed, the arrival of the subtonic not only reveals a concern for large-scale organisation (in its relationship to earlier and later tonality) but also marks a structural downbeat of greater expressive interest than later ones in the tonic. From Heinrich Schenker to Hepokoski and Darcy, structural closure in the tonic is asserted as the *raison d'être* of sonata form. Schenker identified this goal with the full close in the home key before the coda, Hepokoski and Darcy with the perfect authentic cadence in the tonic at the end of the recapitulation's secondary space, prior to the closing section and coda. Although plausible candidates for each example can be located in Schubert's movement, neither is as captivating as the beginning of the reprise nor prepared as strikingly. For Schubert, recapitulatory structural closure appeared to have less expressive appeal.[42]

Conclusion: Relationship to Reception

This essay's approach, in which theoretical concepts help to illuminate the distinctiveness of a Schubert piano sonata with other works serving as a foil, marks another step away from the older practice of interpreting the composer against analytical norms. In keeping with the recent preference for reforming traditional methodologies, this analysis employs theoretical tools receptive to the 'Reliquie' that interconnect and enable discussion to move smoothly towards a subjective reading. Although the Sonata is seldom the basis of a case study, in the last twenty-five years it has enjoyed a more rigorous level of engagement, with scholars no longer deterred by aspects of the composition that earlier generations ignored or viewed negatively. Thomas Denny's 1988 article on the 'Reliquie' marks a crucial turning point in the work's reception.[43] Denny confronts the Sonata's flawed reputation, particularly issues of its incompletion, form and tonality, by using biographical and musical material to construct a more considered and less value-laden interpretation than hitherto. Although discussion centres on the finale, the comparison with other Schubert works helped the 'Reliquie' to emerge from its relative isolation. In another essay by Denny from the same year, the Sonata is included in an assessment of structural elision in Schubert, alongside a wide range of examples.[44] This breadth of reference helps to justify using Denny's model of elision and prompts further examination of the formal parameters of the first and third movements that he briefly identifies. As a notable Schubertian structural device, the fusion of developmental elements in a non-tonic recapitulation elicits further narrative interpretation, an area not explored by Denny. His preference for comparing musical works rather than relying on departures from theoretical paradigms is also invaluable, even if it leads him to illustrate a stylistic trend of Schubert's. In this discussion, comparison of examples of expressive rise and fall does not show a consistency of compositional habit, in contrast to the three-stage design Denny finds in the composer's non-tonic recapitulations elided with developmental features. Instead, for the developments and recapitulations of the first and third movements of the 'Reliquie', analysis reveals few precedents in formal symmetry and no equivalent in tonality in any earlier or later work. The latter distinction differentiates the Sonata from the 'Great' and moves beyond any quick assumption that two compositions from the mid-1820s are indicative of a later style.

Since Denny, the tonality of the 'Reliquie' has become the primary focus of scholarly engagement with the work: an area often regarded by earlier critics as eccentric and wayward, it now receives more considered analysis.[45] The response to the first movement's tonal design consolidates not only formal positioning, particularly for the recapitulation, but also the preparation of keys and the connections between them. Suzannah Clark's observation of B major working in tandem with other harmonic stations demonstrates the assimilation of a radical choice of tonality into a sonata form, a reconfiguration of tonal space away from conventional fifth relations.[46] By simply juxtaposing the expositional keys of the first and second theme with those in the recapitulation, she reveals a symmetry and logic to which traditional frameworks no longer apply. Her analysis encourages further exploration of tonal balance in the movement and its potential to relate to the contour of intensification and dispersion.

Despite the analytical reception of the first movement's subtonic usage, less attention has been given to the flattened supertonic in the Minuet and virtually none to its preparation in the central section. Even Richard Kramer, who engages more with the movement than other scholar, recognises only the Neapolitan key in the first section and reprise and the dominant preparation for the latter.[47] In light of this oversight, my analysis of the build-up to the recapitulation uses strategies pioneered by David Damschroder which address the pre-prolongational harmony and demystify, but do not detract from, the movement's tonal particularity. One device involves the 5–6 shift, a Schenkerian linear progression which is responsive to the impending tonal arrival and helpful for making the analysis of the development less cluttered. Alongside Clark's tonal pairings, the 5–6 shift is another example derived from a scholar who utilises and adapts an established analytical idea to construct a theory sympathetic to Schubert.

Although the beginning of the recapitulation of the first movement and the Minuet elicit a more sustained subjective reading than do earlier passages, differences of interpretation reflect differences of musical material. For the first-movement reprise, an integration of music, narrative and poetic theory suggests an existential withdrawal from the outside world. Hepokoski and Darcy's rotation idea highlights the preference for a lyrical, non-tonic version of the opening primary module, one that persists for the remainder of the movement. A further distinction of P 1.1's rotation comes from its opposition to Caplin's archetype of an exposition beginning with clarity of harmony and phrase structure and a development that is more loosely organised. Although this is a rare occasion of interpreting Schubert against a theoretical norm, it provides an opportunity to reassess lyrical presentation as more unconventional. This marks a shift away from the initial view of musical elements at the recapitulation that claimed the key of the subtonic as exceptional and the lyrical character, conveyed through texture and phrase structure, as orthodox. With the lyrical context of the module becoming less oppositional, it is possible to trace a more integrative relationship with tonality, offering a situation that Almén considers conducive to a narrative interpretation on a theoretical level.[48]

For the reprise in the Minuet, a sustained identification with musical detail, rather than theoretical contexts (the relative lack of rotation highlights the incompleteness of the movement), is vital to the isomorphic exchange with Staiger's poetic theory. Of the different states of being associated with a particular poetic genre, a condition of vulnerability connects Schubert's melodic sketch, with its unfinished harmonisation and suggestion of the Neapolitan key, to lyric poetry. Through tracing a relationship to an earlier version of the main theme, the brief reprise is also imbued with 'the past', a temporal dimension fundamental to Staiger's understanding of lyric existence. Despite additional correlation—with the previous build-up and dispersion suggestive of a dramatic or epic narrative that partly amends for the relative lack of reprise—the return of a more lyrically heightened unfinished theme has no equivalent in Staiger's theory. With the vulnerability of the Minuet's recapitulation remaining permanent, further subjectivity suggests a more intense version of the primary module's narrative interpretation in the first movement.

Although this reading engages more directly with compositional detail and leaves behind the multidisciplinary approaches used in this essay, the work itself has significantly shaped the interpretation. Whether mediated by music or literary theory, the analysis of different musical elements reappraises McKay's linkage of the 'Reliquie' and the 'Great' and her analogy between the Sonata and an epic narrative. The reprises themselves have yielded further understanding of Schubert's combination of lyricism and tonal chromaticism, a musical coincidence that is usually only examined in the composer's second themes.[49]

While the narrative interpretations of the first and third movements articulate a situation common to lyric literary genres, this is nuanced by each movement's particular musical context and its isomorphic relationship with Staiger's poetic theory. With the unfinished Minuet eliciting a narrative that is more independent of Staiger, the championing spirit of McKay's initial comments is sustained. Both movements receive recognition for their contribution to an emerging and varied late style. This distances my reading from the older reception history—which regarded the 'Reliquie' as regressing to the years of crisis (1818–23), when Schubert left many of his large-scale instrumental compositions incomplete—and further supports the last two decades' more sympathetic and comprehensive engagement with the work.

Notes

I would like to express my enormous gratitude to Maja Palser for all her work on the musical examples.

1. Elizabeth Norman McKay, *Franz Schubert: a Biography* (Oxford: Oxford University Press, 1996), p. 215.

2. Ibid., p. 214.

3. Ibid., pp. 260–1. The close proximity can be understood from the date on the autograph of the 'Reliquie', April 1825, and the probability that the 'Great' C major Symphony was begun shortly after Schubert's departure from Vienna, when the composer took an extended vacation in Upper Austria, around 19 May 1825. For a critique of the literature on the dating of the symphony to 1825–6 (extended to August 1827, when the orchestral parts were copied), see Paul Badura-Skoda, 'Possibilities and Limitations of Stylistic Criticism in the Dating of Schubert's 'Great' C major Symphony', in Eva Badura-Skoda and Peter Branscombe (eds), *Schubert Studies: Problems of Style and Chronology* (Cambridge: Cambridge University Press, 1982), pp. 187–8.

4. As part of a collection of essays by different scholars on the 'Reliquie', McKay has already highlighted the same musical examples in the Sonata as embodiments of a new epic narrative; it is curious, however, that, in a discussion which traces the evolution in form from the First Piano Sonata to the 'Reliquie', there is again no analytical comparison made with earlier developments. McKay, 'Schuberts

Klaviersonaten von 1815 bis 1825-dem Jahr der *"Reliquie"*', in *Franz Schubert, Reliquie Sonata, mit Betragen*, ed. Hans-Joachim Hinrichsen (Tutzing: Hans Schneider, 1992), pp. 43–66. As far as drawing parallels between the 'Reliquie' and the 'Great' Symphony are concerned, Andreas Krause is one of the few scholars to find any specific relationship: for him, each work begins with intervals characteristic of horn writing. See Walther Dürr and Andreas Krause, *Schubert-Handbuch* (Kassel: Bärenreiter, 1997), pp. 414 and 419.

5. Denny has neatly summarised the prevailing critical consensus, pre-1990, of each movement as evidence of an overall view of the 'Reliquie' as 'glaringly uneven in quality', with 'a masterful first movement, acceptable inner movements, but an execrable finale', in 'Schubert as Self-Critic: the Problematic Case of the Unfinished Sonata in C major, D 840,' *Journal of Musicological Research* 8/1–2 (1988), p. 91. For a representative of the earlier ambivalent value judgement, see Maurice J. Brown, *Schubert: a Critical Biography* (London: Macmillan, 1966), pp. 190–1. For the occasional more positive appraisal of the Minuet from the same generation of scholars, see Harold Truscott, 'Schubert's Unfinished Sonata in C major,' *Music Review* 18/2 (1957), p. 114; Howard Ferguson, editorial comments in *Schubert: Complete Pianoforte Sonatas*, vol. 2 (Southampton: Associated Board of the Royal Schools of Music, 1980), p. 133; and John Reed, *Schubert* (London: J. M. Dent, 1987), p. 135.

6. David Damschroder, *Harmony in Schubert* (Cambridge: Cambridge University Press, 2010).

7. This definition relies upon Denny's summary of elision from his study of Schubert's recapitulations, centred on the last movement of the late Piano Trio in B♭ major, D 898. See Thomas A. Denny, 'Articulation, Elision, and Ambiguity in Schubert's Mature Sonata Forms: the Op. 99 Trio Finale in its Context,' *Journal of Musicology* 6/3 (1988), p. 351. Further definition, for the second stage and actual moment of elision, is given in Denny, 'Schubert as Self-Critic', p. 98.

8. Emil Staiger, *Grundbegriffe der Poetik* (1946), trans. J. C. Hudson and L. T. Frank as *Basic Concepts of Poetics*, ed. M. Burkhard and L. T. Frank (University Park, PA: Penn State University Press, 1991). This essay has relied on a critique of Heidegger's *Sein und Zeit* (Being and Time), Staiger's primary inspiration, from Luanne Frank's introductory essay, pp. 5–7, 10–17 and 19–35, and from Staiger himself, in the final chapter, pp. 188–9.

9. Paul Cobley, *Narrative* (London: Routledge, 2001), 17.

10. 'Phoneme' is a linguistic term used in literary narrative theory that Almén has applied to his own musical narrative theory, often with his equivalent, 'sound unit'. Ibid., pp. 41–2 and 44.

11. Ibid., p. 44.

12. Schubert's comprehensive knowledge of Mozart, Haydn and Beethoven is well attested by his friends Joseph von Spaun, Leopold von Sonnleithner and Eduard von Bauernfeld. See Otto Erich Deutsch (ed.), *Schubert: Memoirs of his Friends*, trans. R. Ley and J. Nowell (London: Adam and Charles Black, 1958), pp. 10, 18, 26, 126 and 363.

13. The presence of these features in the Minuet reflects the general trend in the nineteenth century for dance movements to become more ambitious in scale and to adopti the processes of sonata forms.

14. William Caplin, *Classical Form: a Theory of Formal Functions for the Instrumental Music of Haydn, Mozart, and Beethoven* (New York: Oxford University Press, 1998), p. 142.

15. To accompany the highlighted passages of the first movement of the 'Eroica' (bars 338–398), see *Beethoven Symphonie Nr. 3 in Es-dur, "Eroica", op. 55*, ed. Jonathan Del Mar (Kassel: Bärenreiter, 2001), pp. 24–6.

16. However, a sustained lowering of register and dynamic to a hushed recapitulatory return distinguishes the occasional first movement and minuet/scherzo of earlier piano sonatas. A close registral parallel to the retreat in the first movement of the 'Reliquie' can be found in the equivalent place of the Sonata in A minor, D 784, bars 153–156, and a prolonged diminuendo with some drop in tessitura marks the end of the central section of the scherzo of the Sonata in B major, D 575, bars 43–52.

17. For example, the 'Grand Duo' Sonata for Piano Four Hands in C major, D 812 (written in 1824, a year before the 'Reliquie'), has a diminuendo and some registral descent in the recapitulation of its first movement (bars 156–175) more protracted than the intensification before (bars 147–151). Elsewhere, in the development, there are sustained passages of little expressive change. The first movement of the 'Unfinished' Symphony in B minor, D 759, is marked by a series of build-ups to peaks that become more heightened over the course of the development; these are always followed, however, with an immediate collapse of register, texture and dynamics. In the early String Quartet in C major, D 46, there is a central culmination seven times the size of the approach and retreat on either side. This disproportionate design covers the entire development (bars 84a–159).

18. In the dominant preparations for the recapitulations of the first and third movements of the 'Reliquie' and 'Great', there is a strong presence of pitches belonging to the minor key of the respective dominant. In Example 8.1 of the Sonata, there is a preponderance of D♮s to suggest resolution to B minor. This provides evidence of Richard Kramer's view that the dominant is 'decidedly in B minor', in 'The Hedgehog: of Fragments Finished and Unfinished,' *19th-Century Music* 21/2 (1997), p. 140. In the Minuet, Example 8.2, F♮s are similarly pervasive, marking the final stages of build-up (bars 55–56), most of the retreat (bars 57–63) and the exit passage (bars 66 and 70) to imply a tonal outcome of A minor. Both examples in the symphony borrow from the parallel minor of C major, the key of their reprises: the first movement has an exit passage built around a repetition of an extended cadential phrase on the flattened submediant and v_4^6 (bars 340–353), while the Scherzo has the flattened third, E♭, near the moment of climax (bars 139 and 141–144). To accompany analysis of bars 280–357 of the first movement of the 'Great', refer to Franz Schubert, *Neue Ausgabe Sämtlicher Werke*, , ser. V, vol. 4a, *Sinfonie Nr. 8 in C, D 944* ed. Werner Aderhold (Kassel: Bärenreiter, 2003), pp. 41–9.

19. For further discussion of the developmental core, see Caplin, *Classical Form*, pp. 141–59.

20. See Schubert, *Sinfonie Nr. 8 in C*, pp. 155–6.

21. Gordon Sly, 'Innovations in Sonata Form: Compositional Logic and Structural Interpretation,' *Journal of Music Theory* 45/1 (2001), pp. 130–4. For Damschroder's analysis of thirds circles in different parts of a sonata form,

instrumental works not in a sonata form and vocal compositions, see *Harmony in Schubert*, pp. 52–6, 70–1, 81, 86–8, 115, 176, 184, 250–2, 258, 276, 295 and 301–2.

22. This preference for complete circles of major rather than minor thirds is highlighted in Damschroder, *Harmony in Schubert*, p. 4. The added minor seventh to each of the thirds in between the F♯ octave is also rare and, for McKay, in her monograph on Schubert's piano music, creates 'a rather unsatisfactory and unsystematic series of modulations' (*Schubert: the Piano and Dark Keys* [Tutzing: Hans Schneider, 2009], p. 77). Since McKay overlooks the preceding F♯, the contribution of these inner harmonies to a complete circle of thirds is not recognised, and they appear more arbitrary. Her labels of D major (bars 132–134), F major (bar 134) and A♭ major (bar 137) also suggest dominant roles for A^7, C^7 and $E♭^7$ respectively, a potential she claims is left unresolved. All three of her tonal regions, however, appear later in the movement: D and F major are juxtaposed in the recapitulation following B major at the beginning of the section, and the coda starts in A♭. While resolution cannot be claimed for any of these, since none is the tonic, their presence helps define a long-range connection to the inner thirds and makes the latter seem less localised.

23. Gingerich does not describe this circle of thirds in the symphony as 'complete' but draws attention to the consummation of the sequence with A♭ major at the peak of the development (bars 316–325). For him, this also fulfils the sequence as it appears in the exposition, where G major is instead the goal following A♭ minor, E minor and C minor and marks the beginning of the closing section (bars 288ff.). For further discussion, see John Gingerich, *Schubert's Beethoven Project* (Cambridge: Cambridge University Press, 2014), pp. 222–5.

24. Although Gingerich recognises the expressive intensification and dispersion that accompanies the two thirds circles in the development, he does not consider the second sequence as complete because it is elided into the exit passage (bars 340ff.), even though he identifies the chain of A♭ minor, E minor and C minor before (bars 328–339). Ibid., p. 223. Mark de Voto briefly notes the repetition of the sequence in its entirety in *Schubert's Great C Major: Biography of a Symphony* (Hillsdale, NY: Pendragon Press, 2011), p. 50.

25. Damschroder's dual interpretation is first applied to his analysis of the finale of Schubert's Piano Sonata in A minor, D 537, bars 59–66. This movement serves to introduce his methods, terms and symbols. See *Harmony in Schubert*, p. 6.

26. Ibid., p. 3. The D♭ minor–A major–D major progression of bars 45–51 conforms to Damschroder's model 3 of a I^{5-6}–II, p. 6.

27. 'Phase' is the Damschroder employs to highlight the voice-leading and hierarchical relationship that enables what would otherwise be separate individual harmonies to be connected. Here, in bars 45–51 of the Minuet, the harmony of A major is linked both to the D♭ minor that comes before, a 'parent 5-phase' to its '6-phase', and to the D major that comes after, a tonic to its dominant. The latter interpretation of the A major as functioning as a dominant is also an example of what Damschroder has identified as 'assertion', where the '6-phase' chord 'may come to life, undergoing transformations'. Damschroder, *Harmony in Schubert*, p. 6.

28. Byron Almén, *A Theory of Musical Narrative* (Bloomington, IN: Indiana University Press, 2008), p. 29.

29. Staiger, *Basic Concepts*, p. 32.

30. Ibid., p. 188. In the first and third movements, the dominant preparation for the recapitulation is placed earlier and lasts longer in a development than many of those found in works of earlier composers. Each has been placed in Caplin's core, where the main structural processes of the development take place, rather than the briefer final section, the retransition, where Caplin usually identifies a dominant: see Caplin, *Classical Form*, pp. 157–9. This distinction also departs from Denny's view that all harmonic preparation for tonic and non-tonic reprises in Schubert appear in a retransition: see Denny, 'Articulation, Elision and Ambiguity', p. 360.

31. Staiger, *Basic Concepts*, p. 187.

32. The ambiguity of a dominant as relating to either the major or minor mode is presented more explicitly in the corresponding part of the first movement of the Piano Sonata in A major, D 959, with the dominant preparation for the recapitulation preceded by the tonic minor and then followed by the tonic major. For Rosen, this outcome represents a triumph of the major mode rather than that of the home key; see Charles Rosen, 'Schubert's Inflection of Classical form' in Christopher H. Gibbs (ed.), *The Cambridge Companion to Schubert* (Cambridge: Cambridge University Press, 1997), p. 91.

33. Staiger, *Basic Concepts*, p. 33.

34. Caplin, *Classical Form*, p. 139.

35. For a more comprehensive definition of the term, refer to 'Appendix 2' in *Elements of Sonata Theory*, pp. 610–11.

36. Although Su Yin Mak has highlighted the placement of Schubert's extended lyrical themes in remote tonal regions, she emphasises their separateness by noting the stability of the former and the instability of the latter. This differs from the interpretation of this essay, one that stresses interaction between lyrical themes and non- tonic keys so that any structural tension traditionally associated with the latter is modified and leads to further understanding with Staiger's theory of lyric existence. Mak, 'Schubert's Sonata Forms and the Poetics of the Lyric,' *Journal of Musicology* 23/2 (2006), pp. 288–9.

37. These returns in the coda occur in bars 314–317 (P1.2), 288–290 (P1.3) and 291–292 (P1.4).

38. This view draws upon the reception value that Suzannah Clark has distilled from earlier scholarship on Schubert's instrumental music. The composer's 'presentation of intuition' is addressed in Clark, 'Schubert, Theory and Analysis,' *Music Analysis* 21/2 (2002), p. 225; associated states of 'naturalness' or 'clairvoyance' are treated in Clark, *Analyzing Schubert* (New York: Cambridge University Press, 2011), pp. 6, 7, 8–10, 12, 26, 34, 55, 169, 186 and 268.

39. Brian Newbould, *Schubert: the Music and the Man* (London: Victor Gollancz, 1997), 322. For a fuller description of the palindrome in *Die Zauberharfe*, see Newbould, 'A Schubert Palindrome,' *19th-Century Music* 15/3 (1992), pp. 207–10.

40. This parallel movement between the exposition and recapitulation, between the keys of the first and second themes, is highlighted in Clark, *Analyzing Schubert*, pp. 257–8. For discussion by Clark on the problems balancing the seventh degree in a tonal design, see ibid., pp. 246–9.

41. Clark has explained the avoidance of B minor at the recapitulation by drawing upon a nineteenth-century handbook: 'since modulation to new keys is a powerful means of creating variety, a composer should not return to the same remote key in the same mode within a single movement ... [this] compositional advice did not exclude the possibility of returning to different modes of the same remote tonic, as Schubert does with B minor and major'. Ibid., p. 258. The principle of non-repeat of a distant key in a particular mode is taken from John Taylor, *The Student's Textbook of the Science of Music* (London: George Philip & Son, 1876), p. 290.

42. Schenker's final cadence in the tonic, before the coda, appears in bar 270 and is also identified in the analysis of the 'Reliquie' in Clark, *Analyzing Schubert*, p. 257. This arrival follows an extended and recomposed closing section, where Schubert's triad- and sequence-dominated melody is relatively uninspired (bars 264–270). Hepokoski and Darcy's 'essential structural closure' prior to the closing section can be found at bar 255, a full close in the home key that corresponds to the 'essential expositional closure' or full close in the subordinate key at the same point in the exposition, bar 97. This comes after the varied repeat of the second theme in the tonic that, as in the exposition, is a less interesting version of the theme. The presence of P1.1 in this repeat compared to its appearance at the beginning of the recapitulation further underlines the more enthralling experience for the listener of the latter.

43. Denny, 'Schubert as Self-Critic,' pp. 91–117.

44. Denny, 'Articulation, Elision, and Ambiguity', pp. 340–66.

45. For analysis of the tonal design of the first movement, see Kramer, 'The Hedgehog', pp. 134–49; Hans-Joachim Hinrichsen, 'Zur Bedeutung des Werks in Schuberts Sonatenschaffen', and Andreas Krause, ' "*Reliquie*", Beethovens VII. Sinfonie und der "Weg zur großen Sinfonie"', in *Franz Schubert: Reliquie Sonata, mit Betragen*, pp. 7–18 and 67–80 respectively. For analysis of the transition to the second theme in B minor, see Susan Wollenberg, 'Schubert's Transitions', in Brian Newbould (ed.), *Schubert Studies* (Aldershot: Ashgate, 1998), pp. 56–8.

46. Clark, *Analyzing Schubert*, pp. 253–9.

47. Kramer, 'The Hedgehog', pp. 138–40. This brevity of discussion contrasts with Kramer's more extended response to the first-movement development.

48. Although Almén emphasises 'interaction' rather than 'conflict' between different musical elements as essential for constructing a musical narrative, only 'conflict' regularly appears throughout his analytical interpretations. On the rare occasion when interaction is mentioned outside theoretical discussion, it serves only as a means to establish moments of conflict. See Almén, *Musical Narrative*, pp. 13, 74, 79, 227 and 229.

49. Several cantabile secondary themes in remote keys have been addressed in James Webster, 'Schubert's Sonata Forms and Brahms's First Maturity (1),' *19th-Century Music* 2/1 (1978), pp. 18–31; and Mak, 'Schubert's Sonata Forms', pp. 267, 273, 281–6 and 294–302.

9

Records of Inspiration

Schubert's Drafts for the Last Three Piano Sonatas Reappraised

Anne M. Hyland and Walburga Litschauer

'Zu solchen Korrekturen—wie sie vor uns lagen—habe [ich] keine Zeit'[1]

Introduction

No aspect of Schubert's life and work has been more grievously affected by Romantic myth making than that of his methods of composition. A young, spontaneous composer of the miniature, rich in lyric imagination, but lacking discipline, formal training, self-confidence, and a 'scientifically trained friend to enlighten him', Schubert had a reputation as a creative somnambulist, a view firmly established from the outset by utterances such as this from Josef von Spaun's memoirs:[2]

> It is true that Schubert did not revise his compositions, did not subsequently polish them, and that, because of this, tedious and faulty passages crept in, but on the other hand, they have a certain originality and freshness which too much polishing very often destroys.[3]

The apparent ease with which Schubert was reported to dash off his compositions—recounted in an array of anecdotes, primarily by Spaun and Johann Michael Vogl—added to this image of a 'natural' composer, writing as if under divine inspiration such that he might later fail to recognise his own work.[4] Schubert's was not a mind predisposed to serious labour or self-reflection, we were told; instead, the composer was portrayed, as in Herbert Antcliff's memorable estimation, as 'entirely a creature of impulse'.[5]

The tenacity of this view through the first half of the twentieth century is one of the many curiosities of Schubert's reception history, and was arguably a result of—among other things—the lack of accessibility to Schubert's modest body of sketches, continuity drafts and autograph scores. In a 1941 publication, for instance, Richard Aldrich echoed Spaun's 1858 sentiment very closely when he wrote that:

> Schubert never bothered to revise; he was an improviser with an improviser's wealth of ideas. He would never had been one of those 'best writers' shown us by Voltaire in his poem, 'The Temple of Fame', gathered in the Holy of Holies engaged in improving their own works—chiefly by making extensive 'cuts' in them.[6]

Lacking access to the manuscripts, writers such as Aldrich were influenced by the historical documentation, including early biographies and friends' memoirs, much of which was inevitably speculative (nay, misleading) with regard to Schubert's compositional practices.[7] The situation began to change with the publication of two articles in the 1940s by T. C. L. Pritchard which awakened interest in Schubert's compositional methods from the perspective of the autograph scores and sketches.[8] In his 1942 exploration of the manuscript of the 'Unfinished' Symphony, for instance, Pritchard identified two distinct categories of correction made by Schubert in revising the work: corrections arising from the modification of an initial idea (such as a change of harmony), and those caused by inattentiveness to clefs, errors in writing out repetitions and absent or superfluous accidentals. Pritchard also compared the manuscript to Schubert's sketches for the work, which were, he argued, 'a kind of shorthand. Often they were unrhythmical [sic] and ill-balanced and the necessary adjustments, continuation of figures, varied repetitions and harmonies were left to be implied.'[9] Through a process of revision, Pritchard argues, Schubert would eventually raise such preliminary sketching to the full splendour of the finished work—a view of the composer's working methods that fundamentally challenges the earlier stereotype.

Initially, many subsequent English-language examinations of Schubert's sketches and autographs followed Pritchard's lead in being largely concerned with the symphonic repertoire.[10] Two early contributions to this end come from John Reed (1975) and L. Michael Griffel (1977), whose work focuses on the 'Great' C major and 'Unfinished' Symphonies, respectively.[11] Both of these examinations identify a number of Schubert's compositional practices with evidence gleaned from the sketches for the symphonies, and begin to unveil a more logical and systematic process of revision on the composer's part. Similarly, Robert Winter's rigorous study of Schubert's music paper (1982) focuses to a large extent on the 'Great' C major Symphony, and the symphonies feature heavily in Reinhard Hoorickx's chronology of Schubert's sketches, in which he demonstrates that Schubert re-used sheets of manuscript paper for the purpose of revising, a practice which suggests that revision was continuous.[12] Finally, much of the work of Brian Newbould, which itself provides an invaluable source of primary material, has been dedicated to the sketches of both finished and incomplete symphonic works.[13]

While this tendency to focus on the symphonies is understandable given the historical neglect of Schubert's career as a symphonist (as well as the inherent interest of the sources themselves), it is nonetheless disquieting that comparable engagement with the continuity drafts and autographs of the late piano sonatas has not hitherto been advanced outside of critical commentaries attached to scholarly editions. That is not to say that these sources have been neglected; quite the contrary. Two key publications appeared in the 1980s, the first from Arthur Godel, whose comprehensive overview of the drafts and fair copies of Schubert's last three piano sonatas was accompanied by a detailed analysis of each movement of the sonatas.[14] Following this was the publication, in 1987, *Drei großen Sonaten für Pianoforte*, of the autograph scores, edited with commentary in German by Ernst Hilmar, a key resource which has significantly aided subsequent Schubert scholarship.[15] Within the sphere of English-language scholarship, the references to preliminary sketches in Charles Fisk's work on the Impromptus and last sonatas as well as Nicholas Marston's analytical work on the retransition of the first movement of D 960 (which takes into account the changes made by Schubert between the continuity draft and the final version) are just two instances of how sketch studies have been integrated into musicological scholarship on a more localised level. Despite these contributions, however, comprehensive engagement with the continuity drafts as a body of work, and the employment of this as a lens through which to scrutinise Schubert's compositional practices on a wider scale, remains to be undertaken. A substantial amount of groundwork has been set out by Godel's and Hilmar's research, but the addition of an interpretative framework is required if these sources are to be fully understood. Indeed, such a venture would not only address the current lacunae in Schubert sketch studies, it would also provide a means of bridging the gap between existing German and English scholarship.

To that end, the present chapter examines the continuity drafts and autograph scores for the Piano Sonatas D 958, D 959 and D 960. The publication in 1996 of the Bärenreiter *Neue Schubert Ausgabe* of the last four piano sonatas (D 894, D 958, D 959 and D 960), with accompanying transcriptions of the sketches for the works, as well as extensive critical commentary on the sources and their interpretation, opened up new possibilities for further research into these sources by making them readily available. These drafts, which Walburga Litschauer edited in the volume *Klaviersonaten III* of the *Neue Schubert-Ausgabe*, represent the most important documents of their kind and offer a means by which to reappraise Schubert's methods of composition for the piano sonata, particularly what are arguably his greatest contributions to the genre.

In what follows, we first chart the compositional evolution of the sketches and autographs, in terms of location and approximate time of composition, before giving an overview of the disparities between the continuity drafts and the final versions of the last three sonatas. This overview permits a more detailed study of the Piano Sonata in B♭, D 960, in which a number of key features of Schubert's revisions are examined from the perspective of thematic construction, phrase structure and performance practice, with particular attention afforded to the first movement's first-time bars and expositional repeat. We shall argue, *contra* Spaun and Aldrich, that not only did Schubert heavily revise these works for publication, but he 'improved' on them by expanding upon his initial ideas and adding to the original conception of the work, rather than by 'making ... "cuts"'; the drafts thereby reveal the indispensability of this music's ostensible redundancies.

Compositional Genesis of the Sonatas

Schubert's piano sonatas stem from different creative periods of his life, the first of which culminated in 1817. This was a year in which Schubert devoted himself to the composition of piano music, writing several piano pieces and no fewer than six piano sonatas. After having finished the last of these sonatas, his interest turned to composing in other genres. We then find a second point of culmination for Schubert's piano sonatas around 1825. The sonatas he wrote at this time, however, differ considerably in quality to the earlier examples in showing a marked maturity of style. This is evident in the fact that Schubert immediately sent them off for publication and referred to them as 'Grande' Sonatas. The Sonata in A minor, D 845, which was composed in the spring of 1825, appeared in print as *Prèmiere grande Sonate*, Op. 42; the Sonata in D major (D 850), which was completed in August 1825, became the *Seconde grande Sonate*, Op. 53; and the Sonata in E♭ major (D 568), which Schubert himself prepared for printing, became the *Troisième grande Sonate*, Op. post. 122, published posthumously in 1829.

Schubert originally intended his Sonata in G major, D 894—composed in October 1826—to be published as the fourth of these 'Grande' Sonatas. Although the composition is entitled 'IV Sonate' in the autograph, it appeared not as a sonata but as a series of piano pieces, namely 'Fantasie, Andante, Menuetto and Allegretto'. We do not know whether the idea for this publication stemmed from Schubert or from his publisher, Tobias Haslinger. After completing D 894, Schubert refrained from writing any more sonatas for almost two years, except for a fragment of a piano piece in C major (D 916B), presumably composed in the summer of 1827. During this time, Schubert devoted himself to the composition of piano pieces which he put together in several series entitled *Moments musicaux* (D 780) and of the Impromptus (D 899 and D 935). In their musical aspirations, these works seem clearly to be related to the 'Grande Piano Sonatas', which induced Robert Schumann to characterise them as 'movements of hidden sonatas'.[16]

Shortly before his death, Schubert's compositional interest turned once again to the piano sonata. His last three piano sonatas—completed in September 1828—very probably represent his last completed instrumental compositions, and certainly the pinnacle of his exploration of the genre. According to Walther Dürr, they 'represent, in some way, a summary of Schubert's lifelong battle with Beethoven'.[17] Andreas Krause argues, alternatively, that for Schubert this body of work was 'not the approximation of a great role model . . . but rather a gradual emancipation . . . through several quantitatively distinct stages of reflection . . . a certification of his own image of self-confidence as Beethoven's successor.'[18] All three pieces survive in a single fair copy in Schubert's hand—dated at the beginning 'September 1828' and at the end '26. September 1828'. This leads to the conclusion that the three works must have been handed down immediately, one after the other, and that they therefore form a kind of set or trilogy.

Although it is not known exactly when Schubert began work on the sonatas, several compositional drafts (all of which are undated) suggest that they occupied his attention for a relatively long while. This period can probably be assigned to the weeks or even months before Schubert moved into the apartment of his brother Ferdinand in the Kettenbrückengasse, on 1 September 1828; before this, Schubert had lived with his friend Franz von Schober in Tuchlauben, in the inner city. Since Schubert was not in the habit of saving sketches or drafts of compositions he had completed, we may assume, as Godel does, that in the case of these sonatas he still needed the drafts in order to prepare the fair copies and took them with him when he moved, leaving behind 'preliminary labours for his other works . . . in Schober's apartment.'[19]

There is, moreover, diverging opinion in the secondary literature concerning the date of composition of the drafts. Hilmar dates those of the Sonata in C minor, D 958, 'on [the basis of] writing style and paper', to 'late spring' 1828; a similar dating to that proposed by Winter: 'these drafts probably date from the spring of 1828'.[20] Hilmar further claims that the drafts for D 959 and D 960 originated 'side by side . . . in the months between June and August' of 1828.[21] In support of this theory, he points out that Schubert, using the verso of the first leaf of his first draft for D 959, 'inserted the ending of the B-flat major Sonata's opening movement in the remaining blank space' and adds that 'a comparison of the ink, the handwriting, and finally the paper used for the final two Sonatas shows that these early versions clearly arose in close temporal proximity'.[22] Winter's analysis of the paper reveals conversely that three of the six leaves employed for the drafts of D 960 stem from a brand of paper that Schubert had already used seven months before the early part of 1828. Winter concludes that 'the composition of the B-flat Sonata may have stretched out over a time period considerably longer than hitherto suspected.'[23] Still, it should be borne in mind that unrelated sketch paper can at best provide a *terminus ante quem non*, for Schubert resorted time and again to blank leaves in his manuscripts.

The Continuity Drafts

A comparison of the extant drafts with the finished versions of the last three sonatas offers a unique glimpse into Schubert's compositional 'workshop' and sheds light on the genesis of these towering masterpieces. Godel characterised the drafts of these three Sonatas as 'records of inspiration, in which everything follows just as it occurred in the act of composition'.[24] According to him, Schubert thought in terms of 'firmly defined musical processes' and started immediately to work in 'continuity drafts', omitting 'only the recapitulation in the sonata-form movements' because it could be 'transferred directly from the draft into the fair copy, being a transposed and merely modified repeat of the exposition'.[25] Because Schubert used loose leaves and bifolia for his drafts, it is possible that some sections of the manuscripts have been lost. In the case of the fourth movement of D 960, this probably applies to a leaf containing the music from the opening to bar 147, since the remaining draft begins at bar 148.[26]

Generally, one can say that Schubert's changes in his fair copy concern mainly the expansion of single parts, the elaboration of transitional phrases and a different arrangement of repeated passages. A preliminary comparison of bar numbers in the draft and final version of D 958, provided in Table 9.1, shows how Schubert added to the earlier version of the work such that, in almost every section of the four movements, the final version is longer.

The continuity drafts for D 959 reveal a similar process of expansion. The draft for the first movement is a particularly interesting case in point, since two different versions of the movement exist, as well as the autograph score. The second version is by far the more extensive, and its first page, with its neat handwriting and smaller script, has the appearance of a fair copy, most likely having been copied from the first version. This first sheet contains bars 1–144 of the first movement, followed by the coda of the first movement of D 960, bars 342–357, as mentioned earlier. The second and third sheets of this second version are quite different, however, returning to the character of a sketch, with a number of 'missing' bars and written in a more fluid, sketch-like hand.[27]

Table 9.2a shows a comparison of the two versions of this first movement of D 959 against the final version. As the table illustrates, both drafts are significantly shorter than the corresponding sections in the final version. The exposition of the second version is shorter than the earlier draft only because Schubert did not copy out all of the draft in the second version, but the implication is that the material is to be included. The recapitulation is represented by one bar, followed by the indication 'etc.', perhaps adding fuel to the already fiery debate that Schubert's recapitulations are a mere formality. Only the development section works in the opposite way, the draft of which is seventy bars long, in contrast to sixty-nine bars in the final version. This is due to the omission of two repeated bars and the addition of a single bar in the final draft (see Examples 9.1a and b).[28]

Table 9.1 Sonata in C minor, D 958

Movement	Continuity draft (bars)	Final version (bars)	Difference (bars)	Description of additional bars
1st mvt (incomplete)				
Exposition	96	98 *(1—98)*	2	Bars 12–13 (single bar in draft) & bar 83
2nd mvt (complete)				
A	14	18 *(1–18)*	4	Bars 14, 15, 16 & 17 (octave repeat)
B	21	24 *(19–42)*	3	Bars 38, 39 & 40 (bar 41 is different)
A	14	19 *(43–61)*	5	Bars 54^3–55^3 & 57^2–61^2
B	30	31 *(62—93)*	2	Bars 88–91 are two bars (bar 92 is different)
A	22	22 *(94—115)*	—	—
3rd mvt (complete)				
Minuet				
Theme	12	12 *(1–12a & 12b)*	—	—
	27	29 *(13–41a & 41b)*	2	Bars 33 (silent bar) & 36 (silent bar)
Trio				
A	9	10 *(1–10a & 10b)*	1	Bar 1 (silent bar)
B	22	26 *(11–36)*	4	Bars 15–18 (octave repeat)
4th mvt (incomplete)				
A	69	90 *(1–90)*	21	Difficult to categorise: material is so different in many respects
B major section	65	67 *(243–309)*	2	Bars 244–245 (repetition of Alberti bass)
	79	79 *(310–88)*	—	—

This is one of the rare occasions where Schubert revised by cutting bars to render the work more concise, although the one-bar difference is negligible. Similarly, in the fourth movement, shown in Table 9.2b, the transition (TR) at bar 200 is two bars longer in the draft.[29]

Table 9.2a Sonata in A major, D 959

Movement	Continuity draft (bars)	Final version (bars)	Difference (bars)	Description of additional bars
1st mvt (incomplete)				
1ST VERSION				
Exposition	114*	132 *(1–132a)*	18	Bars 53–54, 60–64, 67–68, 77, 86–91, 112 (silent bar) & 121–122 (plus 1 additional silent bar)
2ND VERSION				
Exposition	65	132 *(1–132a)*		Bars 66–132 are not in this 2nd version
Development	70	69 *(129b–197)*	1	Bar 160; two-bar addition between bars 196-197 in the draft which is absent from the final version
Recapitulation	1	160 *(198–357)*	159	One bar written out, then marked 'etc.'

* The final staves of this folio contain bars 342–357 of D 960/i.

Example 9.1a Schubert, Piano Sonata in A major, D 959/i, second version continuity draft, bars 195–198

Example 9.1b Schubert, Piano Sonata in A major, D 959/i, final version, bars 196–197

These, however, are isolated instances of Schubert's cutting bars from the draft in the final version; even a cursory glance at Tables 9.1 and 9.2 demonstrates more or less unequivocally that Schubert's more usual revision process involved the expansion, via repetition or sequence, of an initial idea. Indeed, this tendency was recognised by Godel when he wrote that:

> By far, the most frequent changes in the fair copy are extensions: repetitions of single bars, phrases and whole periods, partly connected with changes of sound space, newly added pauses, extended and articulating breaks, additional variants of thematic motives, extended *Fortspinnung* or development.[30]

Schubert's revisions may be classified into four categories: the addition of literal and varied repeats; the repetition and registral displacement, up or down, of a phrase or bar (i.e. octave repeats); the writing in of sequences; and the addition of silent bars. An example of the first kind of revision can be seen in the second movement of D 959. Here, bars 124–125 and 130–131 (both repetitions) do not appear in the draft but are a later addition. Examples 9.2 a and b place a transcription of the continuity draft alongside the final version, highlighting the additional bars.

The second characteristic revision—the repetition of a phrase at an octave's displacement—is one of the most familiar of Schubert's 'fingerprints'.[31] It is also one of his most consistent additions to the drafts in the final version, suggesting that it was more often than not a later addendum rather than part of his original conception of the phrase in question. By far the most striking instance of the addition of material at a higher registral plane occurs, again, in the slow movement of D 959, where the A theme (bars 1–32) is repeated an octave higher in bars 33–64 in the final version but not in the drafts, which move directly from bar 32 into a statement of the B theme (bar 65).

The same practice can be observed on a more localised level in the A theme of D 958's second movement. Here the repetition of a four-bar phrase at a higher octave is absent from the drafts but realised in the autograph at bars 14–16 in the statement of A, as shown in Example 9.3, and again at bars 57^2–61. The insertion of these bars affects the balance of the phrase, which is fourteen bars long in the draft (4 + 4 + 4 + 2) and eighteen (4 + 4 + 4+ 6) in the final version.

A similar addition is evident in the work's third movement, as shown in Examples 9.4a and 9.4b. At first blush, this four-bar insertion seems to be a repetition at a lower octave in the right hand of bars 11–14. As is characteristic of Schubert, however, this is no mere repeat: in fact, bars 15–18 articulate the phrase in E♭ minor, the parallel mode to its initial appearance in both versions, at bars 11–14 (9–12 in the drafts). This has the effect of introducing the parallel minor mode much sooner than was the case in the draft.

Table 9.2b Sonata in A major, D 959

Movement	Continuity draft (bars)	Final version (bars)	Difference (bars)	Description of additional bars
2nd mvt (complete)				
A	32	64 *(1–64)*	32	No repeat of A at the higher octave
B	53	82 *(65–146)*	29	'Missing': bars 78, 80, 82, 84, 87, 89, 91, 93, 96, 98, 100, 102, 104, 124–125 (repetition), 130–131 (repetition), 138–141 & 143. The following bars are written as single bars in the draft: bars 114–115, 116–117, 118–119, 120–121, 126–127 & 144–146
RT	12	12 *(147–158)*	—	—
A	44	44 *(159–202)*	—	—
4th mvt (incomplete)				
A	32	32 *(1–32a)*	—	—
TR	14	14 *(32b–45)*	—	Bars 41–45 written separately in the draft
B* & RT	79	79 *(46–125)*	—	—
A & A' (dev.)	71	74 *(126–199)*	3	bars 163 & 164
TR	23	21 *(200–220)*	2	Draft is 4th below the final version
A => TR	22	37 *(221–257)*	15	One additional bar. Draft breaks off at bar 241, followed by the indication 'etc.'
B => RT	2	70 *(258–327)*	68	No sketch material for bars 258–326
A (fragmentary)	21	21 *(328–348)*	—	
Presto	32	34 *(349–382)*	2	Bars 354–355 and 358–359 are one single bar each in the draft

*B enters much later in the drafts than in the final version.

Example 9.2a Schubert, Piano Sonata in A major, D 959/ii, continuity draft, bars 73–78

Example 9.2b Schubert, Piano Sonata in A major, D 959/ii, final version, bars 122–133

Example 9.3 Schubert, Piano Sonata in C minor, D 958/ii, final version, bars 9–18

Example 9.4a Schubert, Piano Sonata in C minor, D 958/iii, Trio, continuity draft, bars 9–14

Example 9.4b Schubert, Piano Sonata in C minor, D 958/iii, Trio, final version, bars 11–19

not in draft

Sequences are a vital feature of Schubert's developments generally, not only on a large scale, whereby a development section is structured around a large section of material which is repeated in sequence (recall, for instance, the development of the first movement of the G major String Quartet, D 887), but also locally, on the level of the individual bar. The latter part of the development section of D 960's first movement, where the music modulates from A major to D♭ major, offers a case in point: bars 133–135 and 142–144, two three-bar phrases, do not appear in the continuity draft for the movement but are a later addition to the material, as Examples 9.5a and 9.b illustrate.

The ramifications of these additions for the hypermetre of the phrase merit some consideration. In Schubert's original conception of the section, the fourteen bars of music consisted of a series of equal three-bar phrases (3 + 3 + 3), followed by a five-bar phrase (bars 146–150). This grouping is replaced in the final twenty-bar version with a nine-bar phrase (4 + 5), followed by a further

Drafts for the Last Three Piano Sonatas

Example 9.5a Schubert, Piano Sonata in B♭ major, D 960/i, continuity draft, bars 112–125

eleven-bar phrase (4 + 7) leading into the next section. Interestingly, in this case the one-bar repetitions (bars 132, 138 and 147) are all included in the draft; it is only the inner parts of the phrases, constituting the sequence, that are added later.

The addition of silent bars in the final version of a work is demonstrated by the third movement of D 958, wherein bars 32 and 37 of the Minuet and bar 1 of the Trio—all silent bars—are later additions (see Examples 9.6 and 9.7).

There are also occasions, of course, where substantial rewriting of the draft in the final version is masked by the fact that the number of bars is identical. As shown in Table 9.3, although there are four additional bars in the A section of the first movement (occurring between bars 39 and 40 of the final version), they do not affect the proportion of the group, since Schubert cuts four other bars in the final version. Otherwise, Table 9.3 illustrates that the general tendency in this work is clearly towards Schubert's characteristic expansion of material in the final version.

Moreover, Schubert did not just emend single parts, but also on occasion changed them substantially by re-composing them for the final

Example 9.5b Schubert, Piano Sonata in B♭ major, D 960/i, final version, bars 131–150

version—something that a raw comparison of bar numbers or a description in the tables obscures. Such remodelling can be found in the middle section of the second movement, the two versions of which do differ in the number of bars: the draft comprises thirty-four bars and seems to be rather aimless in the melody as well as in the harmony, while the final version—extended by an insertion of thirteen bars—could be said to be more organically unified

Example 9.6 Schubert, Piano Sonata D 958/iii, Scherzo, final version, bars 31–38

Example 9.7 Schubert, Piano Sonata D 958/iii, Trio, final version, bars 1–3

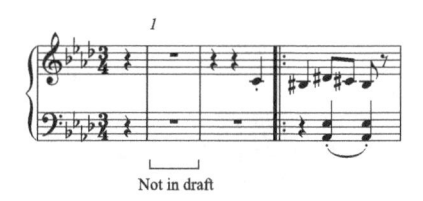

Table 9.3 D 960

Movement	Continuity draft (bars)	Final version (bars)	Difference (bars)	Description of additional bars
1st MVT (incomplete)				
Exposition				
A	48	48 *(1–48)*	—	Bars 9, 32, 35 & 41. Insertion of 4 bars between bars 39 and 40
TR	17	31 *(49–79)*	14	Bars 53, 57, 59–66, 73 & 77–79
B	33	46 *(80–125a)*	13	Bars 108, 111–116; 118a–121a & 117b. Bars 124a–125a are a single bar in the draft
Development	48	56 *(118b –73)*	8	Bars 133–135, 142–144 & 171–172
RT*	34	42 *(174–215)*	8	Bars 186 (trill), 206–209 & 214 (lower-octave trill). Bars 185 & 187 and bars 213 & 215 are each single bars in the draft

* The draft of the final bars of RT (beginning at bar 198) appear on a different folio, after the end of D 960/iv.

(continued)

Table 9.3 Continued

Movement	Continuity draft (bars)	Final version (bars)	Difference (bars)	Description of additional bars
2nd MVT (complete)				
A	44	42 *(1–42)*	2	Two additional bars between bars 42 & 43
B	34	47 *(43–89)*	13	Circa bars 79–89
A	45	49 *(90–138)*	4	Bars 128–131
3rd mvt (complete)				
Scherzo:				
A	16	16 *(1–16)*	—	—
B	42	52 *(17–68)*	10	Bars 34, 39–40, 45–46 and 62–66
A	22	22 *(69–90a)*	—	—
Trio:				
A	10	10 *(1–10)*	—	—
B	18	18 *(11–28a & 27/28b)*	—	—
Coda	0	4 *(29–32)*	4	No coda in the draft
4th mvt (incomplete)*				
B (section of)	74	78 *(148–225)*	4	Bars 217–218 and 223. Bars 183–184 are one single bar
A	52	87 *(226–312)*	35	Bars 230–253 ('wie oben' after bar 229), 274–281 and 302–303
Final section	48	52 *(489–540)*	4	Bars 496, 502, 532 and 540 (silent bar)†

*The surviving draft for this movement begins at bar 148.
† The final two staves on this folio comprise twelve bars from the end of the RT of D 960/i, corresponding to bars 198–215 (eighteen bars) in the final version.

and self-consistent. Of greater significance, however, is that Schubert also changes the focal points of melody and harmony, as Examples 9.8a and 9.8b show: by repeating the first chord of the theme, he expands the melody for another crotchet beat, which results in a shift in metric emphasis. This is augmented by the change in position concerning melody and accompaniment in the two versions: typical for the draft is the light accompaniment in

Example 9.8a Schubert, Piano Sonata in B♭ major, D 960/ii, continuity draft, bars 45–53

Example 9.8b Schubert, Piano Sonata in B♭ major, D 960/ii, final version, bars 43–50

the right hand, while in the final version the accompaniment drops to the bass, creating a darker sound.

In the next section, we draw upon a number of specific practices in the first movement which arise from the expansion of parts in order to analyse them more closely: thematic construction, phrasing and hypermetre in the first theme; modulation in the second theme; the use of repetition as thematic elaboration, and finally the first-time bars and expositional repeat. In so doing, it is hoped that a more comprehensive picture can be drawn of the implications of these changes to the form of the movement.

Case Study: D 960

The first issue to consider in comparing the continuity draft and final versions of D 960, particularly in relation to the addition of extra material, is thematic construction. Although Godel remarked that 'These extensions are usually the formal balance, the tectonic balance within individual parts, the "correction" of asymmetric periods and sentences', careful attention to the main theme of the sonata's first movement suggests otherwise.[32] What one might call the 'germ cell' of the theme can be seen in the sketch, where it is notated only in the upper voice, as shown in Example 9.9a.

Out of this comes the well-known phrase of the final version, reproduced in Example 9.9b.

As well as filling in the full chords in the right hand and outlining the harmony in the bass line, Schubert's revision of this opening phrase is significant on two accounts: first, the G♭–F trill (Tovey's 'distant thunder') is placed at the lower octave in the final version, thereby heightening its ominous effect, and secondly, it is prolonged for one more bar than in the draft, making the first phrase a rather asymmetrical nine bars. The effect of this asymmetry creates a discernible gap between the first and second phrases, drawing attention to the trill as a disruptive moment in the texture. The dynamic level is also altered: Schubert's original conception of the phrase was at a *piano* dynamic rising to a sudden and short-lived *fortepiano* marking in bar 5, whereas in the final version a more subdued atmosphere is created by the *pianissimo* marking of both the first bar and the trill.

Example 9.9a Schubert, Piano Sonata in B♭ major, D 960/i, continuity draft, bars 1–8

Example 9.9b Schubert, Piano Sonata in B♭ major, D 960/i, final version, bars 1–9

Example 9.10a Schubert, Piano Sonata in B♭ major, D 960/i, continuity draft, bars 8–17

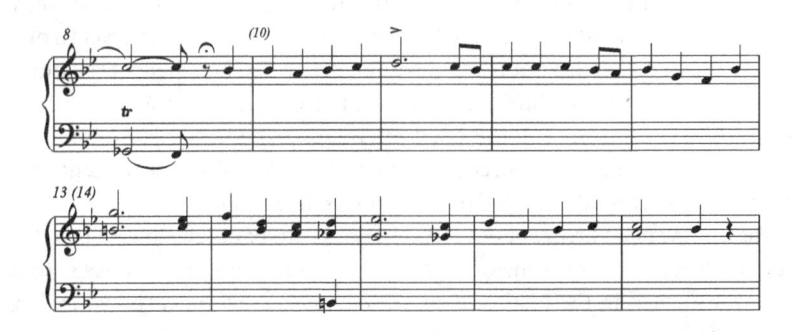

Even more alterations are visible in the varied repetition of the opening phrase, shown in Examples 9.10a and 9.10b.

Here, Schubert changed the melodic line in the second phrase at bars 12^4–15 in the draft, corresponding to bars 13^4–16 in the final version. The melody line of this phrase, as Schubert first conceived of it, originally began on $b\flat^1$ and jumped a sixth to g^2 in bar 13—a fourth higher than the final version. It continued at a tone higher in bar 14 (15) and a third higher in bar 15 (16). The harmonic trajectory of the phrase in the final version, which progresses (in B♭) VI–ii–ii°–V–V$_4^6$–$_3^5$—I, is suggested as VI–V–IV–V$_4^6$–$_3^5$–I in the draft. Elsewhere in the drafts, we can see a similar practice of revising the sketched material upwards or downwards by a particular interval. The first movement of D 959, in both versions, offers a further example of this practice from bar 27 onwards.

Example 9.10b Schubert, Piano Sonata in B♭ major, D 960/i, final version, bars 9–18

The second theme of D 960/i presents a particularly interesting case for the examination of phrase structure and elaboration. It begins in the draft and final version at bar 48, in F♯ minor, with the theme being outlined by the left-hand part beginning on the dominant. In the draft, the theme consists of two four-bar symmetrical phrases, the first ending on the dominant seventh of the relative major (A major) but reverting to F♯ minor for the repeat of the phrase, which ends the second time with a V–I cadence in A major, although maintaining $\hat{5}$ in the top voice. It therefore resembles an eight-bar period structure consisting of a four-bar antecedent followed by a four-bar consequent which provides slightly weakened cadential function in A major.

The final version brings about a number of significant revisions of this draft. First, the suggestion of A major leading into the repeat of the phrase is somewhat diminished in the final version, which, upon arriving at the same dominant seventh of A major at the fourth bar of the phrase (bar 52), sustains it for two more beats (bar 53) before transforming it, through a semitonal voice-leading shift inwards in the left hand, to the dominant seventh of the local tonic, F♯ minor, in bar 53[3] (Example 9.11b). The antecedent phrase therefore ends with a smooth return to F♯ minor for the beginning of the consequent, which now ends with a more convincing perfect authentic cadence (PAC) in A major at bar 58. The return to F♯ minor's dominant seventh at the end of the antecedent results in a rather irregular five-bar phrase, and the entire theme therefore consists of a ten-bar period phrase: the space required for the harmonic transformation from one dominant seventh to another has here resulted in a two-bar expansion of the draft. Thus, although the large-scale modulation to F♯ minor for this theme is part of Schubert's original conception, the manner in which the harmony leads from this key to its relative major is afforded more space in the final version.

Example 9.11a Schubert, Piano Sonata in B♭ major, D 960/i, continuity draft, bars 48–56

Of course, the final version also differs substantially in aesthetic effect from the original draft. The decision to alter the accompaniment from repeated quavers to triplets results in a less languorous passage, and the intermittent triplet-quaver rests heighten the passage's energetic effect in the final version. They also allow the new countermelody in the upper voice to ring out clearly above the accompaniment, and the changes in dynamics introduce a sense of growth to the latter half of the five-bar phrases each time, which were comparably static in the earlier version.

Although the transformation of this passage in the final version is quite remarkable, even more interesting is the ensuing elaboration of the theme, which spans just ten bars in the draft and twenty-two bars in the final version. Example 9.12a takes up precisely where Example 9.11a left off, with bar 57 of the draft.

As Example 9.12a shows, the elaboration of the theme begins with the repetition of a two-bar fragment (bars 57–58), which is extended on second hearing via a descending melodic line to B♮, supported by a G major seventh chord in last inversion (bar 62). This is followed by a four-bar phrase, the final cadence of which (a PAC in F major) is elided with the beginning of the next theme, a genuine secondary theme in the dominant.

The final version's expansion of this passage illuminates the ways by which Schubert develops his original material by repetition at the level both of the phrase and of the individual bar. Again, almost all of the material for this section as seen in the final version is present in the draft, and the final version serves to bring about a fuller realisation of its potential via the use of repetition and variation. The most obvious disparity between the two versions is that the final version begins with a double repetition of the original four-bar phrase of the theme, as can be seen by comparing Examples 9.11a (bars 49–56) and 9.12b.

Example 9.11b Schubert, Piano Sonata in B♭ major, D 960/i, final version, bars 48–58

Example 9.12a Schubert, Piano Sonata in B♭ major, D 960/i, continuity draft, bars 57–66

Drafts for the Last Three Piano Sonatas 195

Example 9.12b Schubert, Piano Sonata in B♭ major, D 960/i, final version, bars 59–66

These two four-bar phrases stabilise A major and act as a kind of re-presentation of the model about to be developed, before the more modulatory passage at bar 67 commences. From bar 67 the hypermetre shortens, and we are given the same two-bar fragment as in the draft at bars 57–58. The repetition of this fragment is, however, expanded from four bars in the draft to five bars in the final version in a manner not wholly dissimilar to the expansion of the dominant seventh chord in bar 53, discussed above. The b^1 which was held for the duration of a single bar in the draft is here rendered in octaves and prolonged over two full bars (bars 72–73), the first of which is supported by diminished harmony, thus heightening the tension in the music. Further expansion is created via the repetition of the material original heard only at bars 63–64 in the draft, now encompassing bars 74–77 (as Example 9.13 demonstrates).

This transformation of material points to the central role played by repetition in thematic development on a local level. In the next section, we explore the use of the large-scale formal repeat in the movement.

D 960: First-Time Bars and the Expositional Repeat

The generous proportions of Schubert's expositions, particularly in the last three piano sonatas, raise the question of whether to observe the expositional repeats, which are marked by the composer in each case. Perhaps no single piece in Schubert's oeuvre has generated more debate on this issue than the

Example 9.13 Schubert, Piano Sonata in B♭ major, D 960/i, final version, bars 67–80

first movement of D 960. Alfred Brendel (who routinely performs the last three sonatas in a single evening) makes a firm case for the omission of this expositional repeat, arguing that it exists only because Schubert, unlike Beethoven, was unable to 'resist the pressures of convention'.[33] Brendel holds that the first-time bars add nothing of interest to the work, and indeed that the exposition ends in such a way as to make a return to the opening material sound awkward. Among Brendel's specific criticisms of the first-time bars are that they are unannounced and thus foreign to the surrounding material, that they are not taken up later in the Sonata and therefore upset the 'magnificent coherence' of the movement and finally that they rob the development section of its 'grand dramatic climax'.[34] His main objection to performing the formal repeat, however, lies in how one might 'justify' the explosive nature of the first-time bars in the context of the movement, in particular the *fortissmo* articulation of the trill figure which elsewhere is rendered as *pianissimo*: 'Most painful to me, however, is the presentation of the trill in *fortissimo*: an event which elsewhere remains remote and mysterious is here noisily exposed.'[35] For Brendel, the magnitude of this disruption not only renders the motive obvious and obtuse, but also—and we concur—has the potential to disrupt the overall aesthetic of the movement.

Brendel's arguments have been most directly disputed by Walther Frisch, whose response to the article 'Schubert's Last Sonatas' in *The New York Review of Books* (16 March 1989), focused on Brendel's reading of these first-time bars. Frisch counters that because these nine bars were 'specifically written out by the composer' and are heard nowhere else in the movement, they ought to be realised in performance, despite the considerable challenge repeating the exposition presents to the performer's stamina.[36] Without the expositional repeat, in other words, these bars would be entirely lost for the listener.

Before turning to the draft, the (in)dispensability of these bars can be assessed through analysis of their relationship to the exposition *in toto*, and in particular the role of the trill figure at bars 124–125a. The quietly ominous trill in bar 8 of this movement, which introduces the chromatic pitch G♭ into the harmonic realm of F major, is both expressively and structurally significant for the remainder of the movement, despite its ostensibly innocuous initial presentation.[37] The tumultuous tonal path of the exposition (during which B♭ vies with G♭ [F♯] as the tonal centre) eventually leads to the expected secondary dominant (a C pedal, at bar 74), and the bright F major theme which follows (beginning at bar 80) affirms this key and cadences on the downbeat of bar 99 with a PAC in F major. The subsequent closing theme, shown in Example 9.14, is, however, harmonically restless. Despite the repeated cadential arrivals on the dominant at bars 109–110 and 115–116, the lack of melodic closure (the final F-major chord

Example 9.14 Schubert, Piano Sonata in B♭ major, D 960/i, final version, bars 109–116

each time has $\hat{5}$ in the top voice) retrospectively weakens the resolution apparently afforded by bar 99, and creates a sense of irresolution.

The first-time ending which follows this (Example 9.15), as Fisk has elsewhere argued, 'only makes this questioning more radical—even astonishingly so' by its reintroduction of the G♭ trill.[38] The reiterated attempts to assert F major are once again contrapuntally frustrated, remaining each time on $\hat{5}$, thus mimicking those chords which ended the exposition. This initiates a violent *fortissimo* affirmation of F major via a series of hammer blows in bar 123a, which is destabilised once again by a return to the G♭ trill—now also *fortissimo*—in bar 124a.

These bars ultimately lead back to the exposition repeat in B♭, and as such the reassertion of F major here acts as dominant preparation, albeit one that is complicated by the persistence of G♭. The second-time bar, 117b (as can be seen in Example 9.15) hardly redresses this issue, instead bringing the music from the F major of bar 116 straight into C♯ minor, thus mirroring the fall from B♭ to F♯ minor at bars 44–48 while employing the same dactylic motive from bars 118a and 120a. The indispensability of these first-time bars therefore becomes clear: they reveal the potential of the trill to act as a powerful disruptive force in the music. In so doing, they permit a reinterpretation of the opening trill figure, and of its destructive path through the exposition, upon second hearing. This potential is only fully realised later in the movement, when the retransition, hailed by James Webster as one of Schubert's finest, ends in a similar way, heralding the recapitulation with the G♭ trill.[39] Thus these bars significantly, and meaningfully, re-contextualise the exposition's material.

Example 9.15 Schubert, Piano Sonata in B♭ major, D 960/i, final version, bars 117a–117b

Part of Brendel's discomfort with the first-time bars is that their clearly intrusive nature is reminiscent of the dramatic, uncontrolled extremes of the Sonatas in A major and C minor—we think particularly of the middle section of D 959/ii—which have, he argues, no place in the more serene and balanced aesthetic of the B♭ Sonata:

> Only those transitional bars in the first movement ignore the newly acquired countenance—an intrusion from the feverish regions of the two other sonatas carried over from an earlier phase of conception that seems to me no less ill-advised than the execution of the repeat which these bars instigate.[40]

Looking more closely at the continuity draft of these bars in Example 9.16a, however, revels that the drama of the transitional bars was in fact born of a later rather than an earlier phase of conception, and a number of aspects of Schubert's revisions suggest a *heightening* of the passage's dramatic effect in the final version instead of an attempt to subdue it.

Example 9.16a Schubert, Piano Sonata in B♭ major, D 960/i, continuity draft, bars 87–98

* indicates a rhythmic error: the left-hand part is not notated as triplets, although that is the clear intention.

First, as Brendel rightly notes, the trill is indicated as *pianissimo* in the draft and is altered to *fortissimo* in the final version—the only place in the entire movement where it is heard at this dynamic. That Schubert reviewed his earlier draft in this way seems to suggest that the 'irate dynamic outburst' of the trill, as Brendel memorably called it, was both a considered decision on his part, possibly arising from dissatisfaction with the earlier version, and something which is integral to the compositional dynamic of the movement, as he eventually wrote it.[41] In making this alteration, Schubert lays bare the potential of the trill, which elsewhere in the movement is only evoked.

A number of other alterations made to this transitional passage support this reading. Schubert's dramatic use of silence is here in plain view in his treatment of bars 87–90 of the draft, which correspond to bars 102–105 in the final version shown in Example 9.16b. In the earlier version, the phrase progresses uninterrupted in a series of crotchet beats from bar 103, giving the effect of a single four-bar phrase that ends with a minim rest. In the final version, however, the phrase has a 2 + 1 + 1 hypermetre, with the final two bars broken up by the introduction of crotchet rests in bars 104 and 105. The dynamics and accents added to these bars in the final version reinforce this new paratactic construction by placing an emphasis on the third beats of bars 103, 104 and 105, thus emphasising their independence. Moreover, the final version re-imagines the four-bar phrase that follows in the draft (bars 91–94) as an asymmetrical five-bar construct by the insertion of a single bar (bar 108) between two closely related two-bar phrases, revising the 2 + 2 phrasing of the draft to 2 + 3 in the final version. This five-bar phrase is then heard as an expanded six-bar phrase (2 + 4) in the final version with a number of variations, such as the rendering of the B♭ major chord (bar 107) as an arpeggiated figure spanning two octaves (bar 112) and the dramaticisation of the dynamics in bars 113–116, changing the *piano* marking in bar 108 to a forceful *fortepiano* and juxtaposing that with newly accented notes and an eventual lowering of the dynamic marking to *pianissimo* at bar 115.

Taking all of these changes into account, and regardless of whether these bars are heard in performance, it is clear that Schubert's process of revision brought to fuller realisation the inherent drama in his original compositional idea. When this is accomplished through the addition of single bars, the dramatic effect on the hypermeter—and on the attendant asymmetrical phrases—is heightened by the dynamics and accents added to the final version.

Conclusion: Into the Light of Day

The designation of '3. Sonate' at the head of the first page of drafts for D 960/i has suggested to many that, with these compositions, Schubert intended to

Example 9.16b Schubert, Piano Sonata in B♭ major, D 960/i, final version, bars 102–125a

write a cycle of three related sonatas. Further evidence that he regarded these three works as a self-contained cycle is found in the finished manuscript of September 1828, where the sonatas are referred to as 'Sonate I, Sonate II and Sonate III'. It was in this form, too, that Schubert offered the works to the Leipzig publisher Heinrich Probst in a letter of 2 October 1828:

> Among other things I have written three Sonatas for solo pianoforte solo, which I should like to dedicate to Hummel ... the Sonatas I have played with much success in several places.[42]

It is not known, however, when and where Schubert played his last Piano Sonatas, if at all; the sceptical mind might infer that this was merely a ruse to stimulate the publisher's interest.

Of course, Schubert died before the works appeared in print, and after his death the fair copies passed to his brother Ferdinand, who sold them to the Viennese publisher Tobias Haslinger in December 1828. Shortly thereafter Haslinger, in the *Wiener Zeitung*, announced the publication, soon to appear, of a 'more detailed advertisement on the publication of [Schubert's] three new piano sonatas'; this, however, was indefinitely postponed, as Haslinger became increasingly busy publishing *Schwanengesang* and the second part of *Winterreise* instead.

We do not know when and under what circumstances the manuscript for the sonatas came into the possession of the publisher Anton Diabelli, who had bought all of Schubert's sonatas and some instrumental works in the composer's estate from Ferdinand in November, 1829. It is possible that on that occasion he also took possession of the still unpublished piano sonatas. Whatever the case may be, it can be said with some certainty—inferred from the chronology of Diabelli's plate numbers—that the sonatas were already engraved as early as 1831, although they were not published until 1839. Schumann must have seen this still unpublished print of D 960 early in 1838, for he mentioned it on 5 June of that year in a by now well-known article in the *Neue Zeitschrift für Musik*:

> The sonatas, being Franz Schubert's final work, are distinguished and remarkable enough. . . . As if it [D 960] could never find an end, never be at a loss for continuation, it ripples along from page to page, always musical and full of song, interrupted now and then by violent outbursts which quickly calm down again.[43]

Schumann, however, was mistaken in believing that the three sonatas had already been published. Yet, his interest in and praise of the works might have been the reason why Diabelli finally decided, in April 1939, to publish them with the dedication to 'Herrn Robert Schumann in Leipzig'.

The final sonata of this set, and Schubert's last, ends with a Rondo which no one would guess is his last piece of piano music. Its unrelenting energy and buoyant, even triumphant ending make it one of his strongest articulations in the genre. Schumann, in the 1838 article mentioned above, wrote of the movement that Schubert 'closes with a light heart, gently and amiably, as if he could start afresh the next day', thus acknowledging the creative strength displayed in the work.[44] In 1989, Brendel echoes these remarks:

> Schubert's last three sonatas should not be taken as a final message . . . it seems to me that Schubert had no intimation that his own death was imminent when he finished his last sonatas, and most probably also his C-major Quintet, in the autumn of 1828.[45]

Our examination of the continuity drafts for these works leads to the same conclusion: the fluency with which they were written, and the remarkable heights to which they were raised via a process of systematic revision, are suggestive of an incredibly engaged and enduring artistic mind at the pinnacle of its powers. In breathing new life into these extraordinary sources, it has been possible to revive an image of the composer's working methods that had been distorted through lack of engagement. Schubert's practices of revision and rewriting, as displayed here, are informed by a willingness to repeat, to expand, and to augment his early musical ideas. It is this process which attests to his ability to handle large-scale form, and, indeed, logically to work through the potentialities of his initial inspiration.

Notes

1. Schubert, quoted in Otto Erich Deutsch, *Die Erinnerungen seiner Freunde* (Leipzig: Breitkopf & Härtel, 1966), p. 272.

2. Johann Friedrich Rochlitz, letter to Ignaz von Mosel, 1826; translated in Otto Erich Deutsch, *Schubert: a Documentary Biography*, trans. Eric Blom (London: J. M. Dent, 1946), p. 523. An even more direct statement regarding Schubert's circle of friends comes from Leopold von Sonnleithner: 'It is much to be regretted that, especially in his earlier days, Schubert chose scarcely a single musical artist for his closest and most intimate relationship, but for the most part only artistic practitioners. . . .. An excellent, experienced composer would probably have guided Schubert towards even more works of the larger kind and stood by him as adviser in matters of outward form, well-planned disposition and large-scale effect.' Deutsch, *Schubert: a Documentary Biography*, p. 856.

3. Josef von Spaun, quoted in Otto Erich Deutsch, *Schubert: Memoirs by his Friends*, trans. Rosamund Ley and John Nowell (London: A & C Black, 1958), p. 140.

4. Recall, for instance, Spaun's anecdote regarding 'Der Erlkönig', which, he says, was finished on paper 'in no time at all (just as quickly as one can write)'. Ibid., p. 131.

5. Herbert Antcliffe, *Schubert* (London: George Bell & Son, 1910), p. 36.

6. Richard Aldrich, 'The Heavenly Lengths in Schubert', *The New York Times*, (9 November 1919), section 8, p. 3.

7. Clarification of the historical documents has been afforded by the work of Christopher H. Gibbs, 'Poor Schubert', in Gibbs (ed.), *The Cambridge Companion to Schubert* (Cambridge: Cambridge University Press, 1997), pp. 36–55; Gibbs, *The Life of Schubert* (Cambridge: Cambridge University Press, 2000); and Suzannah Clark, *Analyzing Schubert* (Cambridge: Cambridge University Press, 2011), especially pp. 6–55. Clark, for instance, debunks a number of myths by calling attention to the fact that Schubert often retired to compose in isolation, rather than producing new music on the spot.

8. We refer here to T. C. L. Pritchard, 'The Unfinished Symphony', *Music Review* 3 (1942), pp. 10–32; and Pritchard, 'The Schubert Idiom', in Gerald Abraham (ed.), *The Music of Schubert* (New York: W. W. Norton, 1947), pp. 234–53.

9. Pritchard, 'The Unfinished Symphony', p. 18.

10. Flothius is an exception. He attends instead to ten lieder which were revised for different settings. His systematic report on the categories of alterations made by Schubert to these songs remains a valuable source, alongside Pritchard's, for revealing that Schubert did indeed adopt a critical attitude to his work. See Marius Flothius, 'Schubert Revises Schubert', in Eva Badura-Skoda and Peter Branscombe (eds), *Schubert Studies: Problems of Style and Chronology* (Cambridge: Cambridge University Press, 1982), pp. 61–84.

11. John Reed, 'How the Great C Major was Written', *Music and Letters* 56/1 (1975), pp. 18–25; and L. Michael Griffel, 'Reappraisal of Schubert's Methods of Composition', *Musical Quarterly* 63/2 (1977), pp. 186–210.

12. See Robert Winter, 'Paper Studies and the Future of Schubert Research', in Eva-Badura-Skoda and Peter Branscombe (eds), *Schubert Studies: Problems of Style and Chronology* (Cambridge: Cambridge University Press, 1982), pp. 209–76; and Reinhard van Hoorickx, 'The Chronology of Schubert's Fragments and Sketches', in ibid., pp. 297–326.

13. See Brian Newbould, 'Schubert's Last Symphony', *Musical Times* 126/1707 (1985), pp. 272–5, and his discussion of the Tenth Symphony in *Schubert and the Symphony: a New Perspective* (Surbiton: Toccata Press, 1992).

14. Arthur Godel, *Schuberts letzte drei Klaviersonaten (D958–960): Entstehungsgeschichte, Entwurf und Reinschrift, Werkanalyse* (Baden-Baden: Valentin Koerner, 1985). All translations are our own unless otherwise indicated.

15. Ernst Hilmar, *Franz Schubert: Drei große Sonaten für das Pianoforte, D 958, D 959 und D 960 (frühe Fassungen): Faksimile nach den Autographen in der Wiener Stadt- und Landesbibliothek* (Tutzing: Hans Schneider, 1987).

16. On this, see Robert Schumann, *Gesammelte Schriften über Musik und Musiker*, ed. M. Kreisig, 2 vols (Leipzig: Breitkopf & Härtel, 1914), vol. 1, p. 372.

17. 'In gewisser Weise als Resümee einer lebenslangen Auseinandersetzung Schuberts mit Beethoven gelten'. Walther Dürr, 'Klaviermusik', in *Reclams Musikführer: Franz Schubert* (Stuttgart: Reclam, 1991), p. 289.

18. 'Nicht die Annäherung an das im Vorjahr (März 1827) gestorbene große Vorbild, sondern die schrittweise Emanzipation scheint das Ziel dieser über mehrere qualitative unterscheidbare Stufen durchgeführten Reflexion zu sein—ein Zeugnis des Selbstvertrauens wie des Selbstverständnisses in der Beethoven-Nachfolge.' Krause, *Die Klaviersonaten Franz Schuberts: Form, Gattung, Ästhetik* (Bärenreiter: Kassel, 1991), p. 217.

19. 'Vorarbeiten zu anderen Werken liess er in der Wohnung von Schober zurück.' Godel, *Schuberts letzte drei Klaviersonaten (D 958–960)*, p. 34.

20. Winter, 'Paper Studies', p. 252.

21. 'Hand in Hand ... in der Zeit von Juni-August'. Ernst Hilmar, *Verzeichnis der Schubert-Handschriften in der Musiksammlung der Wiener Stadt- und Landesbibliothek*, Catalogus Musicus 8 (Kassel: Metzler Verlag, 1978) p. 99.

22. Ibid.

23. Winter, 'Paper Studies', p. 253.

24. 'Die Entwürfe sind Erfindungsprotokolle, in denen alles so aufeinander folgt, wie es im Kompisitionsakt entstand.' Godel, *Schuberts letzte drei Klaviersonaten*, p. 41.

25. 'Die Entwürfe enthalten (soweit erhalten) die vollständigen Werke. Weggelassen wurde jeweils nur die Reprise in den Sonatenhauptsätzen und in den Sonatenrondo; als transponierte und höchstens leicht modifizierte Wiederholung der Exposition konnte sie bei der Reinschrift direct aus dem Entwurf übernommen werden.' Godel, *Schuberts letzte drei Klaviersonaten*, p. 107.

26. On this see Hilmar, 'Zu den Manuskripten' in *Franz Schubert: Drei große Sonaten*, p. 24.

27. On this see 'Quellen und Lesarten', in Franz Schubert, *Neue Ausgabe sämtlicher Werke*, ser. VII, *Klaviermusik*, part 2, *Werke für Klavier zu zwei Händen*, vol. 3, *Klaviersonaten III*, ed. Walburga Litschauer (Kassel: Bärenreiter, 1996), pp. 235–45.

28. In all musical examples, the numbers in parentheses correspond to the bar numbers in the final version, as given in Franz Schubert, *Neue Ausgabe sämtlicher Werke*, ser. VII, part 2, vol. 3, *Klaviersonaten III*, ed. Walburga Litschauer (Kassel: Bärenreiter, 1996).

29. The third movement is not included here because the entire movement is present in the continuity draft.

30. 'Weitaus die häufigsten Veränderungen bei der Reinschrift sind Erweiterungen: Wiederholungen von Einzeltakten, Phrasen und ganzen Perioden, teilweise verbunden mit Klangraumwechsel, ferner neu hinzukommende Fermaten, verlängerte und gliedernde Pausen, hinzugefügte Varianten thematischer Motive, erweiterte Fortspinnung oder Entwicklung.' Godel, *Schuberts letzte drei Klaviersonaten*, p. 107.

31. See Susan Wollenberg, *Schubert's Fingerprints: Studies in the Instrumental Works* (Farnham: Ashgate, 2011).

32. 'Diese Erweiterungen dienen meist dem formalen Ausgleich, dem tektonischen Gleichgewicht innerhalb einzelner Ausschnitte, der "Korrektur" asymmetrischer Perioden und Sätze.' Godel, *Schuberts letzte drei Klaviersonaten*, p. 107.

33. Alfred Brendel, *Music Sounded Out: Essays, Lectures, Interviews, Afterthoughts* (London: Robson Books, 1990), p. 83.

34. Ibid.

35. Ibid., p. 84.

36. Walther Frisch, ' "Schubert's Last Sonatas": an Exchange', *New York Review of Books* (16 March 1989), p. 42.

37. For a sensitive and persuasive reading of this, see Charles Fisk, 'What Schubert's Last Sonata Might Hold', in Jenefer Robinson (ed.), *Music and Meaning* (Ithaca, NY: Cornell University Press, 1997), pp. 179–200.

38. Charles Fisk, *Returning Cycles: Contexts for the Interpretation of Schubert's Impromptus and Last Sonatas* (Berkeley: University of California Press, 2001), p. 246.

39. See James Webster, 'Sonata Form,' in Stanley Sadie and John Tyrrell (eds), *The New Grove Dictionary of Music and Musicians*, 2nd edn (London: Macmillan, 2001), vol. 23, p. 696. This retransition is interesting from the perspective of paper ‚studies since its first part is contained within one sheet of manuscript while the material from bar 198 to the end of the section is found on a separate manuscript sheet, tagged on to the end of the Finale.

40. Alfred Brendel, 'Schubert's Last Three Piano Sonatas', *RSA Journal* 137/5395 (June 1989), p. 409.

41. Indeed, if one takes into account the similar changes made at the point of recapitulation, where the low-register trill is a later addition to the final version and absent from the draft, a similar conclusion may be reached. On this see Nicholas Marston, 'Schubert's Homecoming', *Journal of the Royal Musical Association* 125/2 (2000), pp. 248–70, especially pp. 253–4.

42. Deutsch, *Schubert: a Documentary Biography*, pp. 810–11.

43. 'Die Sonaten sind als das letzte Werk Schubert's bezeichnet und merkwürdig [*sic*] genug. . . . Ale könnte es gar kein Ende haben, nie verlegen um die Folge, immer musikalisch und gesangreich rieselt es von Seite zu Seite weiter, hier und da durch einzelne heftigere Regungen unterbrochen, die sich aber schnell wieder beruhigen.' Schumann, 'Aus Franz Schubert's Nachlaß', *Neue Zeitschrift für Musik* 8/45 (5 June 1838), p. 179.

44. Ibid.

45. Brendel, 'Schubert's Last Three Piano Sonatas', p. 401.

10

Musical Causality and Schubert's Piano Sonata in A Major, D 959, First Movement

Julian Caskel

A Typology of Musical Causality

Wer A sagt, muss auch B sagen. This German saying suggests that causality is not just a concept of the natural sciences but also implies an inherent moral obligation. The aesthetic idea of musical causality refers to this aspect as well. Logical consistency is attributed to works that evoke an impression of inevitability despite the absence of clear-cut causal chains of propositional logic. The name associated hermeneutically with this aesthetic idea is that of Beethoven; Adorno's critique of its limits takes as one of its starting points the verse 'muss ein lieber Vater wohnen', from Beethoven's setting of Schiller's text, since the word 'must' is merely suggesting but in no way proving causality.[1]

Franz Schubert, in turn, composes at the very end of the first movement of his Piano Sonata in A major, D 959, an ancillary 'coda of the coda', which is in fact saying B once again (through an unexpected arpeggio in B♭ major) after having said A (through the prior tonic cadence in A major). Those last bars have received little attention in previous analyses[2]—maybe because of their felt lack of causal necessity. This essay argues, on the one hand, that this ending is the movement's proper logical ending; and on the other, that the coda's 'transfigurative'[3] character shall be respected by exploring alternative types of musical causality.

The final bars of the first movement in fact are the surprisingly soft ending of a formal narrative that starts with a perhaps equally surprising harsh thematic idea. The following essay in a way mirrors this design, since it proceeds from a quite condensed typology of musical causality but subsequently delves into a wide-ranging analysis of Schubert's first movement. The outline of three types of musical causality is necessary because the analysis will focus less on long-range formal processes and more on the syntactic causal consequences generated by the manipulation (i.e. unusual handling) of a small musical formula containing a relatively fixed semantic meaning.

A base level of first-order causality is generated by musical norms that, for instance, allow the perception of a stepwise descent after a larger melodic step as a normal case (the actual physical, anthropological or cultural reasons notwithstanding). Ultimately, however, even such cases seem subordinated to the intentional fallacy *post hoc, ergo propter hoc*, which Roland Barthes claimed to be a basic condition of any narrative logic. Second-order musical causality, then, could be defined—marginally informed by Leonard B. Meyer's work on information theory—as the generation of expressive sense through deviations from this proto-discursive layer of succession.[4] The thickness of a musical texture can be increased by taking away redundancy or reduced by adding redundancy. (Addition of redundancy here and in subsequent instances means presenting more material than would be necessary in a concise statement.) This simple model implies contrasting modifications of the quasi-inevitability within a chain of musical events. The reduction of redundancy can give rise to the impression that an inner inevitability is maintained, even though its deduction from the directly previous musical event is no longer possible. The result is music that gives the impression of *propter hoc, ergo non post hoc*. The addition of redundancy, however, encourages an auditory impression in which a lack of causal necessity is perceived even though musical events still generate each other smoothly and directly. The result is music that gives the impression of *post hoc, ergo non propter hoc*.

This dichotomy can be related to Theodor Adorno's distinction between intensive and extensive types of musical time and its inner dialectics.[5] The extensive type is the critical corrective of the intensive type (as the latter's pretence of causal coherence is overturned). The extensive type is not however immune to its own ideologies and inferiorities, since its lack of causality is of positive dialectical value only as a negating critique of causality. In other words, the intensive type is also intensive in its critical potential, pointing inwardly to itself; meanwhile, the extensive type is also extensive in its critical potential (pointing outwardly again to the intensive type).[6]

Third-order causality, then, could basically comprise meta-references to music's own causal premises (including the premise of causality).[7] This sketched typology allows us to predict one solid configuration for such moments (that likewise tend to be suggested but not proven) since they often involve a direct confrontation of heightened and reduced redundancy. The addition of redundancy should not, however, simply coincide with the normative model of extensive time, and the reduction should not coincide with the normative model of intensive time. The beginning of Schubert's Sonata presents a particularly succinct illustration of an isolated musical event that can be described as a central agent of the movement's unfolding if it is interpreted within the foregoing theoretical framework.

The Exposition: Exposure of a Cadential Formula

Schubert's penultimate sonata begins with declamatory gestures that emphasise prototypical signals of intensive musical time (see Example 10.1). The *Atlas-Motiv*, taken from the Sonata D 958, the rhythmically accelerating chords

Example 10.1 Schubert, Piano Sonata D 959, i, bars 1–8

and the prominent bass leaps of a ninth and a tenth in bars 2f. all expose that the sonata begins *in medias res*. The cadential formula introduced in bar 6 is, however, a major instance of redundancy, since the cadence's harmonic goal is taken as the melodic starting point of a delaying turn figure. Paul Badura-Skoda has noticed in this old-fashioned cadential formula and its links to rural church music a possible attribute of Schubert's late style (and Adorno's famous dictum of re-emerging musical conventions is indeed suggestive here). Yet in the other examples cited by Badura-Skoda, the formula appears only as an ornamentation of relatively weak inner cadences.[8]

Thus the semantic potential of the cadential formula can be activated by a syntactically exposed entrance, and it can be levelled by a syntactically more integrated entrance. An integrative interpretation maintains a basic stabilisation of this cadence but does not single it out as a narrative event in itself. An instance can be found in the first movement of the 'Unfinished' near the end of both the exposition and the recapitulation (first in bars 98 and 103). In three songs of *Winterreise*, however, Schubert uses the cadential formula in a more exposed way, so that a subtle meta-reference to the immanent act of musical closure is felt. The cadential formula is connected in No. 14, 'Der greise Kopf', and in No. 17, 'Im Dorfe', with the final phrase of the vocal part; in No. 20, 'Der Wegweiser', it is employed in the cadence of the introduction. Except for an incomplete anticipation in bar 39 of 'Im Dorfe', the formula is used only once in each song, and its entrance is marked in all three instances by phrase elisions or elongated periods as a syntactic 'outsider' (see Examples 10.2 a–c).

The emphasis on musical closure seems to be particularly distinct in 'Der Wegweiser'. As in the Sonata D 959, the cadential formula is more exposed because the textual context forces the listener to perceive an integrating cyclic return (here of the walking rhythm of 'Gute Nacht'). Therefore in both works the first cadence—which conventionally implies a change into more neutral textures—advances into a more individual textual shape.[9] Richard Kramer has

Example 10.2a Schubert, *Winterreise*, D 911/14, 'Der greise Kopf', bars 40–45

Example 10.2b Schubert, *Winterreise*, D 911/17, 'Im Dorfe', bars 43–46

Example 10.2c Schubert, *Winterreise*, D 911/20, 'Der Wegweiser', bars 1–5

described 'Der Wegweiser' as the structural finale of the cycle. This function is mirrored in the song's first five bars, which establish a prematurely strong ending *en miniature*. 'Der Wegweiser' also has been described as a teleological course that can by no means return to its piano prelude.[10] This irreversibility is again effectively mirrored by the cadential formula, since it was previously heard as part of the termination of two songs (the prelude already includes its own little 'false recapitulation'). This song, then, is from its beginning about the end.

In the Sonata in A major, two pivotal points in the application of the cadential formula are modified. It is restated consistently in the first movement (therefore becoming more strongly integrated) and it is denied its proper tonic resolution at its first occurrence (therefore becoming more strongly exposed). No longer is a cadence exposed by the cadential formula; rather, the cadential formula itself is exposed by the absence of a cadence. Hence the term 'musical formula' feels appropriate, since semantic content is fixed in a concise syntactical entity. The melodic turn figure in bar 6 is too gesturally isolated to be a musical topic, but it is also too topically fixed to be labelled as an individual musical gesture.[11]

The impact of these departures can be shown through a comparison with the single appearance of the formula in Weber's *Der Freischütz* (Example 10.3). There are some similarities to Schubert's sonata, since the formulaic fixation of the cadence is slightly subverted by the abrupt entrance of arpeggiated triplets. Such a sudden exchange of semantic reference fields—sacral prayer giving way to hunting music—can be legitimised easily on the operatic stage. In instrumental music, Schubert's analogous moment can be heard either as an ingredient of a conventional formal plan (thereby reducing its semantic exposure) or as a short-lived but nearly existential threat to this formal plan (thereby damaging syntactic integration). For a start, in D 959 the textual break of the triplets could be called a complementary reduction of redundancy. This status is, however, attributable only to bars 7ff. in a 'synchronic' analysis that takes the cadential formula's semantic quality and unusual handling as its point of reference. An analysis referring basically to the diachronic process could claim those bars to be a redundant addition, since the dominant-seventh prolongation also represents the extensive type of musical time. This interpretation seems to be indicated particularly by the fact that the cadential formula is properly resolved at its second appearance in bars 21f. But this passage also confirms the synchronic interpretation. In bars 6f. a musical causal connection misfires, and the contiguous succession of *Credo* and *Capriccio*[12] briefly challenges causal processuality in such a blatant way that the ensuing music has in essence to act

Example 10.3 Weber, *Der Freischütz*, Act I, No. 2, bars 129–138 innocently. The formal unfolding in bars 21ff. has to clarify something which is uncertain from the outset (which should be transparent). The dominant-to-tonic progression is repeated three times (in the sound shape of the chordal texture and contrasting arpeggio taken from bars 6f.) in the same way one might repeat a technical procedure, such as turning a key again after it failed to work. This 'compulsive repetition' might also open up some links to the aesthetics of the uncanny, not least since the cadential formula, with its traces of something known from earlier times but not fully exposed, might be a part of this experience as well.[13]

The modifications of the main theme in bars 16ff. all seem to serve the purpose of casting additional musical safety nets, so to speak. The triplets are embedded into the theme in bar 18, and the rhythmic model of the cadential formula is anticipated in bar 19. Finally, in bar 21 the cadential formula itself is relegated to a middle voice; meanwhile, the dominant chord is modified and also less stable. The repetition of the main theme is rather its meticulous modification, which—and this is the paradox at work—basically ensures the success of the most simple cadence.

The diachronic analysis could still value the elaboration of the cadence as a consequence of Schubert's predilection for building his main theme as a small ternary form (again in line with the extensive type of musical time). This ternary design is, however, constructed of unstable materials and therefore has to be consolidated by extended and more artificial cadences. Yet the textual break established in bar 6 is also—viewed as an augmentation of a compulsive repetition—the starting point of the first movement's formal peculiarities. The caesura within the main theme's small ternary form initiates a modification of the exposition that is transformed into a paratactic succession of thematic and parenthetic sections; not only the main and subordinate themes but also their combined succession and even interruption by a developmental passage starting in bar 82 can be connected to the model of the small ternary. At the same time, not only the two themes but also some of the parenthetic sections are tied to specific harmonic models.[14] The movement is in a way repeatedly bouncing back to its springboard: the dichotomy of bars 1ff. and bars 7f. Those two textures, however, share a bass succession in parallel thirds, which is—initially in bar 8 and then concatenated to a specific rhythmic model[15]—chromatically tightened in the parenthetic sections.[16] The upward movement of the parallel thirds is resumed at exactly the point where it broke off in bar 3, so that subliminally this detail marks the emergence of the cadential formula as a first parenthesis. Within the ensuing thematic course, Schubert is for once outwardly conforming to the sonata scheme's harmonic polarity. Yet, this threatens to change the parentheses into pathetic sections that are formally dispensable, since their usual Schubertian *raison d'être*, the exploration of remote harmonic regions, is missing. Hence they transform into middle sections of song-like ternary forms, which establish a competing instance of formal wholeness (especially since the parenthetic sections often exhibit circular harmonic layouts as in bars 27ff.).[17]

The exposition comes into existence through this antagonism between a linear sonata design and a stacked hierarchy of ternary forms. Closure of the thematic sections therefore has to be safeguarded against the fact that everything else is formally closed as well. Timbral expansions of the cadences occur not only in bars 22ff. but, for example, again in bars 78ff., and often lead into multiple repetitions of arpeggiated motives. Instead of firm cadential steps, this sonata permanently exhibits an ethereal cadential space. The movement's agenda could therefore be summarised as an attempt to overcome and overhaul the motivic break of bars 6f. by establishing a synthesis of textual opponents. The coda of the coda can be heard as the final accomplishment of this task, but it succeeds only by excluding both the cadential formula and the harmonic polarity in favour of a further extreme within the sonata's exchange of linear logic for sound sublimity.

The coda of the coda is motivically bound to the triplet motion that materialises in bar 7, which is unambiguously allocated the role of parenthetic intrusion, but by bar 22 its inclusion in the thematic sections has already been achieved. The triplet quavers are hence the single element that is capable of interchanging at will between the separated spheres (another possible feature of uncanniness). A concise narrative of the formal plan could therefore read like this: the parenthetic sections try to pull the triplet motion back into their sphere but while doing so gain more and more thematic stability.

The basic conflict is fortified in the development section precisely because of its radical departures from the exposition. It can be perceived as an unwarranted thematic section, which brings the whole sonata movement dangerously close to a song-like ternary design.[18] And the mechanical recapitulation could be heard as inferior both to the transformative coda and to the development that is transformed into a character piece. The recapitulation is almost presented by Schubert as a phase of heightened redundancy and a pause within the narrative. The coda in fact should be analyzed not as the direct outcome of the recapitulation, but as a synthesis of the two junctions of the exposition's ending: the return to the main theme of the exposition repeat and the change into an estranged *pianissimo* of the development are combined. Thus the coda of the coda could feel like a last superfluous parenthetic segment, especially since its material is partly taken from the codetta of the exposition (bars 123ff.), which is heard again just before the coda (bars 324ff.). The exposition's codetta in fact has some importance in the formal narrative sketched here, since it attaches together one basic element of the thematic sections (the pendulum in parallel thirds) and one basic element of the parenthetic sections (the chromatic step E–F). This very conjunction still grounds the coda of the coda, the enhanced 'enigma' of which can therefore be explained in part if not entirely by the analytical tool of unification by reduction.[19] What follows explores some analytical options that try to explain those last bars both in their enigmatic exit from and their emergence out of the movement's previous causality.

The Coda: Exposure of Post-Cadential Space

The alternation of two keys a semitone apart constitutes in itself a combination of heightened and reduced redundancy. The alternating motion reduces the texture's density; the appearance of an unexpected key area enlarges it. The coda of the coda (Example 10.4) pushes this duality to its extremes.

When the Neapolitan key and its variant German sixth appear in bars 351f., the syntactic superfluity of the expanded triads is confronted by the semantic suggestiveness of an alienating harmonic effect. The cadential formula—a first moment of extensive time within an 'intensive environment'—is answered by a last moment of intensive time within an 'extensive environment'. Four analytical proposals shall address the hermeneutics of those final bars. In this section, the cyclicity of signposts of hearing and the structuring created by details of functional harmony will be examined. In the final section two

Example 10.4 Schubert, Piano Sonata D 959, i, bars 343–357

further interpretations of the coda as hidden recitative and as *mise en abyme* will be discussed.

The cyclical return of hearing signposts is illustrated by the motive of a semitone switch, which connects three surface surprises in the first two movements. In the first movement's development, the interchange of C major and B major can be perceived mainly as an addition of redundancy; meanwhile, in the slow movement its reduction is emphasised in the sudden change from C♯ minor to D major. The coda of the coda thus acts as a negotiator between the all too stable development and the all too unstable middle section of the following Andantino; in fact, the coda combines the plateau-like expansion and the effect of perforation of the two other sections. So the middle parts of the first two movements could be heard as outer parts of another ternary design built from these related syntactical signposts. Taken together, the pitches used in these three 'hot spots' are an extract from the chromatic scale whose initiating dyad, C–B, would then be expanded chromatically downwards and upwards (the C♯–D is also anticipated in the melody of the theme of the second movement in bars 5f.). The cyclical derivation of B♭ major's emergence in the coda gains further justification, since this key (and the pitch representing it) is not given much prominence within the first movement. Another instance of cyclic integration could also be considered, since B♭ major obviously is the main key of Schubert's last sonata—the first movement's pathway would thus lead from a citation of the theme of the earlier sonata to an anticipation of the key of the later one.[20]

The coda could also be heard as an allusion to the alienation effect of the trill on G♭ in the Sonata D 960. Thus sounding B♭ major makes reference to a feature of D 960 that is there necessarily deviating from its home tonic. Two details could support such an indirect intertextual reading: first, the most concrete analogue to the trill in D 959 is probably the low-register trill occurring in bar 152 of the second movement.[21] This moment, however, refers in the same indirect manner to D 959's tonic and (within the context of C♯ minor) to the submediant relation of the trill motive in D 960. Secondly, the beginnings of Schubert's last two sonatas share a significant structural parallel, despite their strongly differing gestural shapes: in both themes the dominant is reached early on so that a free space is created, which in both sonatas allows the establishment of the flattened submediant in the eighth bar (an unusual spot; a possible model might be Beethoven's 'Les Adieux').

Any analytical explanation for the momentary turn to B♭ major would also have to take into account the fact that the subdominant is avoided in the first movement in the main thematic areas.[22] However, Charles Fisk has pointed out (quite in line with the previous considerations of cadential spatialisation) that the traditional harmonic elements in the movement do not following their habitual rules: 'Instead of opposing dominant to tonic, this first movement might be viewed as establishing a tonal opposition between tonic and dominant together, taken as one pole, and the tonalities and tonal procedures that arise from the chromatic wedge, taken as the other'.[23]

The re-conquest of the subdominant area is a goal of the first movement and the entire sonata. D major is touched in the main theme, C major centres the development and F major is briefly tonicised in the altered section of the recapitulation (bar 225) and the coda (bar 344). B♭ major constitutes the 'utopian goal' or at least an unstable outer limit of these subdominant expansions—especially since the Scherzo and Finale show similar plans. In the Scherzo, F major is the second in a series of sudden harmonic shifts within the theme, C major is established as the contextual tonic of its middle section and F major appears again in the middle section of the Trio. In the Finale, C major (in the exposition) and F major (in the recapitulation) are secondary keys of the couplet-like theme. B♭ major, however, is only utilised once more, at the beginning of the Finale's coda, starting in bar 353 (a strange numerical echo of the B♭ major in bar 352 of the first movement). In a sense, the coda of the finale both ends with the beginning and begins with the ending of the first movement. Traces of this ending, though, are to be found within the very last bars of the sonata as well, since both outer movements do not really end with a proper cadence. In the Finale (Example 10.5), the return of the main theme of the first movement (but not of its original ending with the cadential formula) interrupts a soft alternation of dominant and tonic chords so that the arpeggiated triplets regain their original intrusion effect.

After a short hint at the subdominant by the usual turn of the tonic into V of IV, the dominant is only represented in bar 380 by its fifth and seventh. This

Example 10.5 Schubert, Piano Sonata D 959, i, bars 370–382

penultima, which is not very regular, is of course the diatonic variant of the first movement's closing material (including the parallel thirds.) In the final bars of the first movement, however, the symbolic conflict of harmonic areas is more or less suspended, since cadential harmony as a whole evaporates into the echo space of pure sound. The Neapolitan key is usually a stand-in for the minor subdominant. The addition of a German sixth, however, re-introduces the leading note, and the spacing of the chord in bar 352 is designed so that the right hand will play 'dominant' tones while in the left hand a more 'subdominant' chord prevails.

As a result, the coda of the coda also relativises the triumph of the subdominant that has taken place in the coda proper. To call this a triumph is not an overstatement, for several reasons. First, the dominant seventh, which in a sense compromised the theme in bar 7, is now dismantled by being placed before the theme's entrance in bar 329.[24] Second, a climactic moment of the development (bars 164f.) is cited in bars 337 and 346 and is combined with the aforementioned subdominant harmonic extension. Third, the theme's modifications allow a premature entry of the cadential formula, whose narrative agency is quite obvious here since it is resolved immediately into the expected chord, which turns out to be the subdominant. Fourthly, phrase elisions allow the cadential formula to precede the theme.

The signifying quality of the cadential formula might be further substantiated by another short look at one of the songs of *Winterreise*. 'Der greise Kopf' is characterised by the dominant's weakened formal significance.[25] A dominant seventh chord is exposed 'too early' in the second bar and is then replaced by a diminished chord. The first four bars make up, *pars pro toto*, an image of the song's four formal sections (excluding a recitative-like transition and the coda).[26] The difference between bar 2 and bar 3 (the explicit A♭ instead of the implicit A♮ of G major) becomes a reference point for the middle sections: an enlarged deceptive cadence from G major to A minor is the foundation of the second section comprising bars 11–16, and the third section does include a cadence in A♭ major in bar 20. At the same time, the song's coda can be heard as an attempted but ultimately failed reversal of the basic model. The A♭ is re-positioned on the second bar of a four-bar period (as part of the minor subdominant in bar 40) whose third bar now does include an A♮ (as a part of the cadential formula that is another sign of this attempted reversal). The song's central image—the illusory wish of old age that is deceptively fulfilled by the whitened hair of the protagonist—could therefore be linked to the dominant G major and the song's cadences that also seem 'deceptively aged'.

Such a use of syntactic details as narrative markers can also be found within the Sonata D 959. The extra-diegetic development is announced by the semiquavers appearing as an erratic element late within the exposition in bars 121f. Only at the outset of the development is the proleptic function of those semiquavers revealed. At the end of the recapitulation, however, the same motive displays an unconcealed analeptic function. This conspicuous and conspicuously isolated detail hides the fact that the development itself transfers the previous chord alternation upwards another fifth (the initiating semitone of which again refers back to bar 8). The 'magic' of this transition partly results from the unexpected interchange of the reference tone within a neighbouring motion, which is in itself not interchanged.[27] The coda on the other side further separates the contrasting motivic agencies of bars 6f.—the cadential formula and the triplets— into two individual formal sections. Thus the coda can be heard as magnifying once again this important single moment from the movement's exposition. Therefore the parenthetic final bars are on the one hand a recitative-like commentary placed outside the movement's formal course, and, on the other hand, a perfect mirror image of this formal course. In the final part of this essay, these meta-referential interpretations will be related to a consideration of Schubert's late style and its departure from Beethovenian models of musical causality.

The Historic Moment of Late Style

The term 'songfulness' encompasses two semantic levels that are not necessarily congruent. The aspects of melodic singability and of periodic syntax are often but not always combined. Wariness about song-like musical structures can remain valid even if the melodic design is as unsingable as the main theme of the Sonata D 959.[28] Such an autonomy of one aspect of songfulness (the formal parataxis) from the other (the presence of singable melodies) can be justified in a particularly easy manner within the rhetoric of instrumental recitative. A first feature of recitative transferable onto purely instrumental music is the attitude of vocal declamation. The impossibility of combining vocal gestures with verbal content is of central importance in many meta-referential moments of instrumental music (consider, for instance, Schumann's 'Der Dichter spricht' or the recitatives in Beethoven's Ninth Symphony). Yet recitative can also be evoked by purely instrumental means through the continuo's punctuations. The beginning of Beethoven's Sonata Op. 31 No. 2 is perhaps the prime example of recitative-like implementations that originate not from quasi-vocal declamation, but from punctuating chords. There are, however, some indications that this Sonata and its idea of taking recitative as a legitimating means of modifying standards of musical form might be a kind of photographic negative of Schubert's late sonatas. Different points could substantiate such an intertextual reading.

To begin with, a Beethovenian model—the finale of Opus 31 No. 1 and in particular its strongly segmented coda—has been extensively discussed with respect to the Finale of D 959.[29] Motivic allusions connecting Beethoven's Op. 31 No. 2 and Schubert's D 960 have also been mentioned by Arthur Godel.[30] But these allusions occur in material that has a counterpart in the rushing triplets starting in bar 95 of the first movement of D 959. This passage hints at the formal function that will be established by its motivic variant in the later sonata. The third thematic area so typical of Schubert's sonata expositions only gains its usual stability in D 960. In the Sonata in A major the triplets instead expand the minor dominant into the contrasting middle of an incomplete ternary form.

Furthermore, Schubert interrupted the sketching of the first movement of D 959, returning to the first draft of its exposition only after having worked intermittently on the Sonata in B♭. This first draft does not yet include narrative markers such as the cadential formula and the prolepsis of the development. Thus the strengthened narrativity and the evolving references to Beethoven's Op. 31 No. 2 might be the joint result of a strengthened cyclical planning.[31]

Gestures connecting Schubert's D 959 and Beethoven's Op. 31 No. 2 do exist, but their exploration certainly needs qualifying. The passage following the recitative in bars 159ff. of Op. 31 No. 2 could be related to bars 82ff. of Schubert's Sonata (not least because both textures are grounding a transition into instability). The harmonic shift of the coda of the coda—a repeated arpeggio encompassing a succession from consonance to dissonance and back to consonance—finds its possible parallel in the passage bridging exposition and development in Beethoven's Sonata. Finally, in bars 55ff. of the first movement of Op. 31 No. 2 there is a chord alternation of B♭ major and A minor. In Beethoven's Sonata this is an allusion to the key of its middle movement; but it is worth mentioning that in Op. 31 No. 2 the first two movements start with an arpeggio, in A major and B♭ major respectively.

Finally, Schubert's exposition could be called a textbook example of the theory of enhanced formal dynamism that Janet Schmalfeldt has developed out of the work of Carl Dahlhaus on Beethoven's Op. 31 No. 2. Schubert's initial shape is in a sense a theme 'not yet' and the following shape in bars 7ff. is a theme 'no more'.[32] Nevertheless, the convergences with Op. 31 No. 2 should be called contingent rather than concrete. The similar strategy of dispersing a whole formal section is softened from a quite unusual model (the recapitulation of Beethoven's 'Tempest' giving way to a recitative) into a more usual variant (development as a character piece), but the altered causal logic of *post hoc, ergo propter hoc* might reverberate a little within the formal experiment of Schubert's Sonata. This interpretation has to accept as its premise that the intrusion of the arpeggiated triplets in bar 7 is assumed to be a punctuating recitative-like gesture, so that the parenthetic sections originate from a declamatory musical attitude. The 'speaking' quality of the cadential formula is followed by a gesture of idealised speech; after that, the rhythmic gesture of bar 8 is consoling by virtue of its relative neutrality. The connection of recitative-like freedom with an old-fashioned cadential figure also creates another link to bar 6 of Beethoven's Op. 31 No. 2.

The actual attraction of such an interpretation is that the coda of the coda would then in a sense be a commentary on a commentary: the augmented sixth chord in bar 352 again can be heard as a punctuation mark that demarcates itself from the previous musical event. However, this chord would then be the symbolic double of this previous event, since it had been the commenting intruder itself. The augmented chord refers to a formal unfolding that increasingly integrates the triplets and reduces their initial effect of alienation—but it does so within a final effect of alienation that on the one hand uses the triplets no longer as the emerging figure but as the established ground; on the other hand, the triplets here also reprise their initial role as a kind of post-cadential reverberation.[33]

The last chords of the coda are also variants of the rhythmic gesture established in bar 8. Thus the element that supplied the solution to the elliptical first cadence is here treated elliptically itself, since the fermatas on the rests implicitly highlight the missing chords.[34] This shift provides a narrative frame for the movement: the recitative-like punctuation is in a way just pushed one bar to the right so that the cadential formula will be excluded from it and can instead be a firm part of the main theme thus completed and changed into songfulness.

The liquidation of songful structure into pure sound is of course nothing unnatural within a coda. Less usual is the amount of commentary in a texture of such heightened redundancy (this might allow the idea that heightened redundancy is also one of the subjects of the commenting voices). Even more unusual still, the liquidating final bars might also be taken as a last repetition of the Sonata's formal course in the manner of a *mise en abyme*. Schubert comments on a formal plan that permanently admits itself to parenthetic expansions by means of a last expansion which also includes a reference to a basic causal law of musical form—that one has to say A again after having said B. The formal array of exposition, unexpected middle and echo-like recapitulation of the coda of the coda is—even in fitting musical ciphers—just another ternary ABA design. This horizon of meta-referentiality can be used to sketch, as an afterword to the analysis, a short comparison of the types of musical causality used in the first movement of Schubert's D 959 and those implicated by style typologies considering late style.

Schubert's final works do not put the extremes of extensive and intensive time even further apart (as could be said of Beethoven's late quartets); rather, they allow the approximation and transformation of this polarity. To hear those works as being written in a late style could thus be the result of a simple logical fallacy: the premises that any late style is partly defined by the model of Beethoven's departure from his 'heroic style', and that Schubert has composed just such a departure, do not logically enforce the conclusion that Schubert's late works are also written in a 'late style'. As an aesthetic conclusion, this would obscure the extent to which Schubert relies on stylistic ingredients that are not so much features of an individual personal style or an esoteric late style but, more profanely, signs of a certain historic moment. The music of the *Restaurationszeit* not least yields the important insight that the 'Romantic' character piece is not just a less-developed and non-dialectical version of the 'Classical' sonata but can be used as a critical (and dialectical) counter-instance within new designs of sonata works.[35] To bring the character piece into the sonata results in a certain inevitability of moments of musical self-reflection: the implemented songfulness and the act of implementation will always separate a little, but this separation can be taken not as a deviation from but as an alternative fulfilment of sonata dialectics. In other words, sonata form will incessantly recognise in intruding song-like ternary forms its own mirror image. This process could be explored in the late quartets of Beethoven (probably as an outcome of the equally late Bagatelles), in the early Quartets of Mendelssohn modelled on those late Quartets, in Chopin's Sonata in B♭ minor, which replaces the crowning finale with a short étude, or of course in the early piano works of Robert Schumann. The model of *Beiwerk* ascending to *Hauptwerk* that John Daverio has discussed for Schumann's Fantasy, Op. 17, could be transferred seamlessly onto the development section of D 959.[36]

This interpretation of the first movement of D 959 as a network of allusions created by short but characteristic irritations appearing early on and very late within the sonata movement is also an attempt to transfer more firmly onto Schubert's work the results of a research project on musical self-reflection undertaken at the University of Cologne.[37] In these terms, the Schubert of 1828 could be seen not as a messenger from another world, but as a messenger of his own (musical) world drawing, in certain respects, conclusions from the Schubert of 1827.[38] At the end of that year Schubert had refined in the Impromptus and *Moments musicaux* the technique of building paratactic forms by intermixing small motivic variants and big harmonic surprises within hybrids of sonata and simpler ternary designs; he had also composed in *Winterreise* middle sections that emerge into full-blown alternatives of their outer frame. The A major Sonata, however, is this middle section in the cyclical plan of the late-sonata trilogy, and its first movement might be called one of the most serious undertakings within Schubert's project of establishing the formal strategies of his songs and character pieces in four-movement forms (which thereby could keep the outer model intact). Self-reflection is basically inherent in this through the idea that the missing implicitness of something formerly taken for granted is not denoted by something new suppressing the old, but by something old (the cadential formula) oppressing the new. Thus Schubert's Sonata shares one fundamental virtue with Beethoven's late style: the impression of being early witness to an emerging musical modernism.

Notes

1. See Theodor W. Adorno, *Musikalische Schriften I–III* (Frankfurt am Main: Suhrkamp, 1978), p. 271.
2. Three important previous analyses of the complete first movement will be found in Charles Fisk, *Returning Cycles: Contexts for the Interpretation of Schubert's*

Impromptus and Last Sonatas (Berkeley and Los Angeles: University of California Press, 2001); Robert S. Hatten, 'Schubert the Progressive: the Role of Resonance and Gesture in the Piano Sonata in A, D 959' *Intégral* 7 (1993), pp. 38–81; and Arthur Godel, *Schuberts letzte drei Klaviersonaten (D958–960): Entstehungsgeschichte; Entwurf und Reinschrift; Werkanalyse* (Baden-Baden: Koerner, 1985). The most important analytical discussion of the final bars of this movement, however, is Edward T. Cone, 'Schubert's Unfinished Business', *19th-Century Music* 7/3 (1984), pp. 222–32.

3. Cone, 'Schubert's Unfinished Business', p. 231.

4. See Leonard B. Meyer, *Music, the Arts, and Ideas: Patterns and Predictions in Twentieth-Century Culture* (Chicago: University of Chicago Press, 1994), pp. 81f. (considering music's diachronic primary layer).

5. See Theodor W. Adorno, *Beethoven: Philosophie der Musik; Fragmente und Texte*, ed. Rolf Tiedemann (Frankfurt am Main: Suhrkamp, 1993), pp. 134ff.

6. For Adorno's typology of time, see Nikolaus Urbanek, *Auf der Suche nach einer zeitgemäßen Musikästhetik: Adornos "Philosophie der Musik" und die Beethoven-Fragmente* (Bielefeld: Transcript, 2010), pp. 202ff.

7. For the terminology see Werner Wolf, 'Metareference across Media: the Concept, its Transmedial Potentials and Problems, Main Forms and Functions', in Wolf (ed.), *Metareference across Media: Theory and Case Studies*, (Amsterdam: Rodopi, 2009), pp. 7ff.

8. Paul Badura-Skoda, 'Possibilities and Limitations of Stylistic Criticism in the Dating of Schubert's "Great" C major Symphony', in Eva Badura-Skoda and Peter Branscombe (eds), *Schubert Studies: Problems of Style and Chronology* (Cambridge: Cambridge University Press, 1982), pp. 196f.

9. For this formal strategy see Wilhelm Seidel, 'Die Kadenz als Figur ihrer selbst', in Bert Siegmund (ed.), *Gestik und Affekt in der Musik des 17. und 18. Jahrhunderts* (Dößel: Stekoics, 2003), pp. 169–84.

10. See Richard Kramer, *Distant Cycles: Schubert and the Conceiving of Song* (Chicago: University of Chicago Press, 1994), p. 180; and Susan Youens, *Retracing a Winter's Journey: Schubert's 'Winterreise'* (Ithaca, NY: Cornell University Press, 1991), p. 106.

11. See the theory of gesture developed in Robert S. Hatten, *Interpreting Musical Gestures, Topics, and Tropes: Mozart, Beethoven, Schubert* (Bloomington: Indiana University Press, 2004), pp. 93ff.

12. See Alfred Brendel, *Musik beim Wort genommen* (Munich: Piper, 1992), p. 146. The difference of bars 1ff. und bars 7ff. is also highlighted in Fisk, *Returning Cycles*, p. 207.

13. This repetition of something well-known is linked to Freud's theory in Federico Celestini, *Die Unordnung der Dinge: Das musikalische Groteske in der Wiener Moderne (1885–1914)* (Stuttgart: Steiner, 2006), p. 80.

14. See Ivan F. Waldbauer, 'Recurrent Harmonic Patterns in the First Movement of Schubert's Sonata in A Major, D 959', *19th-Century Music* 12/1 (1988), pp. 64–73.

15. Hatten, 'Schubert the Progressive', pp. 44ff., explores the importance of this motive.

16. This is discussed in Martin Chusid, 'Cyclicism in Schubert's Piano Sonata in A Major (D 959)', *Piano Quarterly* 104 (1978), p. 39; and Godel, *Schuberts letzte drei Klaviersonatenen*, pp. 126f.

17. See Hans-Joachim Hinrichsen, *Untersuchungen zur Entwicklung der Sonatenform in der Instrumentalmusik Franz Schuberts* (Tutzing: Schneider, 1994), p. 61.

18. The model might be Schubert's earlier Sonata in A major. See Wolfram Steinbeck, 'Lied und Sonatensatzform bei Schubert: Zum Kopfsatz der Klaviersonate A-Dur D 644', in Wolfgang Horschmann (ed.), *Aria:Eine Festschrift für Wolfgang Ruf* (Hildesheim: Olms, 2011), pp. 601f.

19. See the analytical deductions in Cone, 'Schubert's Unfinished Business', p. 231; Hatten, 'Schubert the Progressive', p. 67; and Jerrold Levinson, *Music in the Moment* (Ithaca, NY: Cornell University Press, 1997), p. 142.

20. See also Andreas Krause, *Die Klaviersonaten Franz Schuberts: Form, Gattung, Ästhetik* (Kassel: Bärenreiter, 1996), p. 218.

21. See Nina Noeske, 'Schubert, das Erhabene und die letzte Sonate D 960 — oder: Die Frage nach dem Subjekt', *Schubert: Perspektiven* 7 (2007), p. 28.

22. See Cone, 'Schubert's Unfinished Business', p. 230.

23. Fisk, *Returning Cycles*, p. 210.

24. See David Lidov, *Is Language a Music? Writings on Musical Form and Signification* (Bloomington: Indiana University Press, 2005), pp. 139ff. Lidov's interpretation is based on this elliptical quality of the harmonic course.

25. Hans-Joachim Hinrichsen, 'Die Sonatenform im Spätwerk Franz Schuberts', *Archiv für Musikwissenschaft* 45 (1988), p. 32, is discussing the same effect in the Piano Trio D 898.

26. There are significant parallels to the interpretation of this song in Youens, *Retracing a Winter's Journey*, pp. 237f.

27. For the preparation of the development's central pitches see Charles Rosen, 'Schubert's Inflections of Classical Form', in Christopher H. Gibbs (ed.), *The Cambridge Companion to Schubert* (Cambridge: Cambridge University Press, 1997), p. 90; and also Richard Cohn, *Audacious Euphony: Chromaticism and the Triad's Second Nature* (Oxford: Oxford University Press, 2012), pp. 48ff.

28. Fisk, *Returning Cycles*, p. 235, is calling this theme "surely one of the most unsingable opening themes ever composed within the Viennese Classical tradition".

29. Edward T. Cone, 'Schubert's Beethoven', *Musical Quarterly* 56 (1970), pp. 789ff.

30. See Godel, *Klaviersonaten*, p. 149, for these connections.

31. See a commentary of the non-narrative quality of those early drafts in Godel, *Klaviersonaten*, p. 41. Schubert's sketches are also discussed in Hinrichsen, *Sonatenform*, pp. 329ff.

32. Janet Schmalfeldt, *In the Process of Becoming: Analytic and Philosophical Perspectives on Form in Early Nineteenth-Century Music* (Oxford: Oxford University Press, 2011), pp. 9ff.

33. See also Godel, *Klaviersonaten*, p. 153.

34. I am indebted to Ulrich Wilker for pointing out this fact to me.

35. This duality of classical and romantic textures is also discussed in Hatten, *Schubert the Progressive*, p. 64.

36. John Daverio, *Nineteenth-Century Music and the German Romantic Ideology* (New York: Schirmer, 1993), p. 26.

37. See Florian Kraemer, *Entzauberung der Musik: Beethoven, Schumann und die romantische Ironie* (Paderborn: Fink, 2014); and René Michaelsen, *Der komponierte Zweifel: Robert Schumann und die Selbstreflexion in der Musik* (Paderborn: Fink, 2013).

38. The analysis given here is indebted to similar premises and conclusions in Fisk, *Returning Cycles*, pp. 3ff.

11

Conspicuous 6-Phase Chords in the Closing Movement of Schubert's Piano Sonata in B♭ Major (D 960)

David Damschroder

The bold G that inaugurates the Finale of Schubert's final Piano Sonata is an unusual herald of a movement in B♭ Major. Yet it is closely affiliated with the tonic, for it corresponds to the 6 of what may be referred to as the tonic's 6-phase chord. Example 11.1 shows how 5-phase B♭–D–F may shift to 6-phase B♭–D–G. (Following the conventions of figured bass, the number 6 indicates a chord in ⁶₃ position.) Whereas in some cases such a 6 will revert to 5, resulting in an F<G>F neighbouring motion that expands the tonic harmony, often it serves instead to initiate a harmonic progression that will proceed to the supertonic and beyond. In that context the 6-phase chord plays an important voice-leading role: since tonic B♭–D–F and supertonic C–E♭–G share no chord members, B♭–D–G offers local connections with one or more common tones to facilitate the transition between those two more foundational harmonies.

In my recent book *Harmony in Schubert*, which contains numerous analytical examples demonstrating the shift from a chord's 5 to its 6 phase (especially in the connection between I and II and between IV and V), I explore how Schubert extends this notion by also deploying all three of the tonic 6-phase chord's consonant chromatic variants (displayed alongside the diatonic version in Example 11.1) in the Sonata's first movement: forward-driving B♮–D–G as well as mellow B♭–D♭–G♭ and forlorn B♭♭–D♭–G♭.[1] Playing in turn the tonic 5-phase chord followed by each of these four 6-phase chords offers a vivid demonstration of how chromaticism may impact the affect of a simple voice-leading device. Schubert conveys a sense of torment in the first movement by emphasising both the tonic's and the dominant's chromatically lowered 6-phase chords (variants nos. 2 and 3). In the Finale he steers clear of such eerie domains for the most part. Instead, he pointedly and repeatedly deploys the buoyant chromatically raised variant (no. 1). Given that I read the first movement as an evocation of the anguish brought on by his disease, this emphasis on the sharp side suggests that Schubert intended to convey a positive conviction about his own life's continuation, despite his health concerns.[2]

Example 11.2 shows how the movement's structure corresponds to the form traditionally referred to as sonata-rondo, which James Hepokoski and Warren

Example 11.1 A 5–6 shift applied to the tonic and the 6-phase chord's consonant chromatic variants

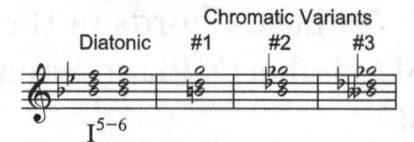

Example 11.2 Structural/formal analysis of the movement

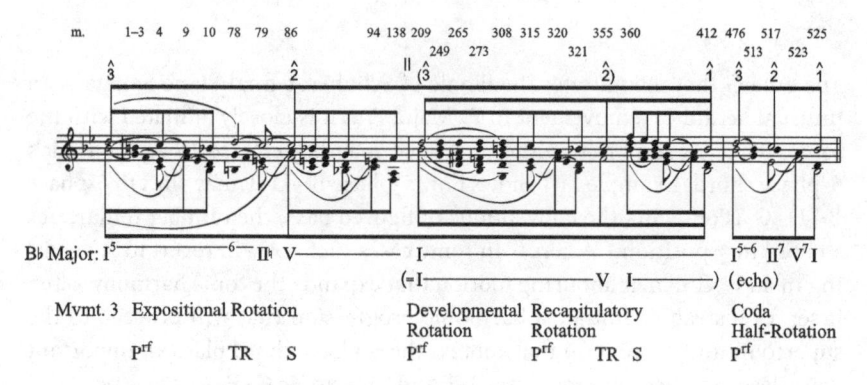

Darcy recently have renamed the Type 4 sonata.³ Expositional, developmental and recapitulatory rotations are followed by a half-rotation corresponding to the coda. Each begins with the refrain. In keeping with conventional sonata-form practice, the expositional and recapitulatory rotations' primary-theme and secondary-theme zones (P and S, respectively) are separated by a transition (TR). Because this movement's P performs the role of a rondo refrain, it is here labeled as P^{rf}. This graph's details will be fleshed out section by section over the course of this essay.

The Expositional Rotation's P^{rf} and TR Regions

In Hepokoski and Darcy's conception of sonata form, most expositions divide into two parts. The first part consists of P (P^{rf} in the Type 4 sonata) followed by TR. Given this movement's unusual start on G, the coda of the preceding movement comes into play as well, since the tonic root B♭ and the *Kopfton* D that ground P^{rf} are stated there.

P^{rf}'s internal form may be conveyed as follows:

	bars	1	20	32
		10	42	64
		|: a_1 :|	b	a_2 :|

Except for the fact that its initiating chord sounds before the movement commences, the structure of a_1 is straightforward. Example 11.3 shows how the third-progression D > C > B♭ is traversed in the melody, while harmonically the initiating tonic proceeds through its 6 phase (here unfurled into $\frac{5}{3}$ position: B♭–D–G is presented as G–B♭–D) to II and then V before the perfect authentic cadence on I.

The roman numerals deployed in Example 11.3 contrast the conventional practice of harmonic analysis in several ways. Note that the symbol I^{5-6} appears in the principal row of analysis. The essential connection between I and II is thereby emphasised, while the 6-phase chord's assertion as VI is relegated to a subordinate row below the principal one. Whereas usually the unfurling of the 6-phase chord into $\frac{5}{3}$ position would serve to highlight the fifth relationship between the submediant root, G, and the supertonic root, C, in this case Schubert retains G as bass for the II harmony, a choice that both weakens the sense of stability during the onset of a_1 and offers a suitable starting point for chromatic linear activity in the bass beginning in bar 6 (G > G♭ > F > . . .).

The manner of accounting for chromaticism on display in Example 11.3 likewise contrasts the conventional practice of harmonic analysis. Whereas most analysts would juxtapose two contrasting symbols for bars 1–3—namely, vi followed by V⁷/ii—here the two successive chords rooted on G are interpreted as phases of a single harmonic initiative.[4] Such chordal evolution generally works in the direction of increasing chromaticism and increasing dissonance as the succession to the next harmony (rooted a perfect fifth lower) draws near. Most analysts seek to find diatonic contexts for chromatic events (here interpreting the second G chord within C Minor, incorporating the common borrowing of the leading note from C Major); but in the style of analysis advocated here, such chords retain their status as chromatic entities within the principal key. A single roman numeral (in this case a quality-neutral capital VI) is retained for both chords, while arabic numerals and accidentals to the right indicate the evolving pitch content.[5] A similar evolution transforms the diatonic supertonic of

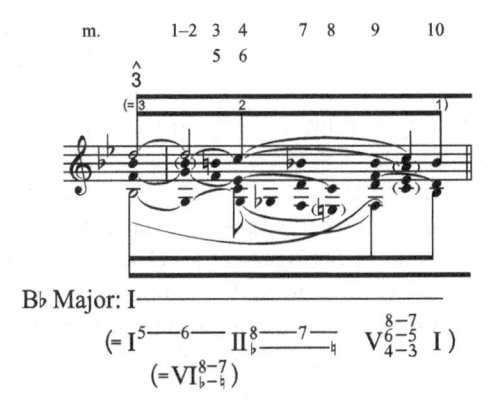

Example 11.3 Analysis of the expositional rotation P^{rf}'s a_1 region

bars 4 and 6 into a surging C–E♮–G–B♭ chord in bar 8. Although many analysts would juxtapose ii and V⁷/V numerals, here II is retained for both supertonic formulations, again in the context of the root succession of a descending perfect fifth: C leading to F. (In this case the seventh chord sounds in its second inversion, the $^4_3$ position. The parenthetical E♮ in Example 11.3 will be discussed presently.) Although many analysts would argue that the chord with E♮ and B♭ *is* a dominant (in the context of the key of F Major), I propose that it instead functions as an evolved supertonic whose structure *emulates* that of a dominant. The supertonic prolongation incorporates a passing chord—F–D–B♭—during bar 7. Indeed, analysis often requires subtle judgements regarding hierarchical relationships among chords. In this case, I propose that the supertonic function extends through bar 8, thereby allowing for the full flowering of its surging state. That interpretation contradicts the alternative view that the bass F in bar 7 initiates a dominant prolongation. As Example 11.3 shows, this F instead may be interpreted as a passing note between the supertonic harmony's G and E♮, even if the concluding F > E♮ segment of that line transpires in the tenor register. (In Example 11.3, an E♮ has been placed within parentheses in the lower register to display the normative structure that Schubert here modifies.) As a result, within the movement's first ten bars the pitch G is emphasised in the bass in three unconventional ways: during the initial chord (instead of the tonic root, B♭), at the arrival of II (instead of root C) and during the expansion of II (instead of E♮). Just after the cadence another G emerges—at beat 2 of bar 10—to initiate the written-out repeat of a_1.

The b region of P^{rf}'s |: a_1 :|: b a_2 :| form overtly expands the very B♭-to-G motion that transpired at the juncture between the Sonata's third and fourth movements. Here a zigzag soprano line that might have been supported by a circle of fifths within B♭ Major accommodates a lower-third shift of chordal root during bar 20, from which point the circle proceeds unimpeded to a G minor goal, as shown in Example 11.4. (Consequently the alternation between outer-voice 3 and 10 that appears to be established at the outset is transformed into an alternation between 5 and 12, starting with the C–G twelfth in bar 20.) As a result, the onset of the a_2 region in bar 32 lacks the startling impact of bar 1's unexpected G. Yet Schubert has more in store. During the b region's written-out repeat, the lower-third shift occurs once again, in bar 42. Yet this time the circle of fifths comes to a standstill before achieving its goal. Comparing the bass in Examples 11.4 and 11.5, note that the diatonic diminished fifth E♭–A in bars 23 and 24 is replaced by E♭–A♭ in bars 45 and 46 through the obstinate pursuit of perfect fifths. Though a continuation from A♭ to D and then G would be feasible, Schubert stalls on the A♭ chord and then wondrously hoists it upwards chromatically in three stages, arriving at a chord rooted on C in bar 60, as shown in Example 11.5. (I refer to such a hoist as a seismic shift: the tendency for continuation—additional descending-fifth moves—is retained by the chord as it is chromatically hoisted up three notches, so that the expected

Example 11.4 Analysis of the initial presentation of the expositional rotation P^{rf}'s b region

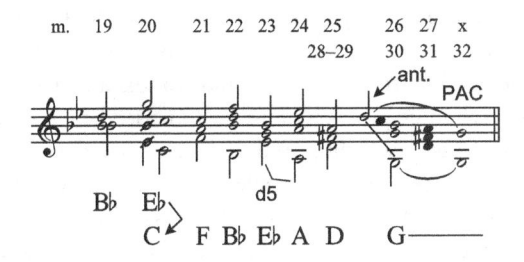

m. 19 20 21 22 23 24 25 26 27 x
                  28–29   30 31 32
                            ant.
                               PAC

B♭ E♭↘   d5
   C↙ F B♭ E♭ A D   G———

Example 11.5 Analysis of the modified written-out repeat of the expositional rotation P^{rf}'s b region

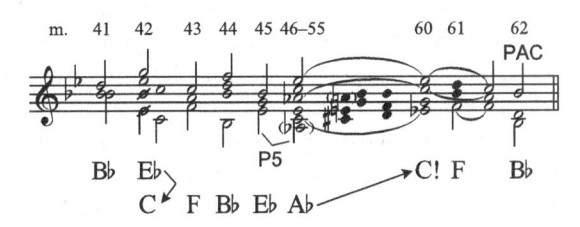

m. 41 42 43 44 45 46–55   60 61 62
                                   PAC

B♭ E♭↘   P5   →C! F   B♭
   C↙ F B♭ E♭ A♭—

continuation with D to G is realised as F to B♭.[6]) Thus the phrase concludes with a perfect authentic cadence in B♭ Major after all, in bar 62. Schubert then inserts a two-bar transition that pursues a B♭-to-G trajectory before embarking upon the concluding a$_2$ region in bar 64. The P^{rf} region closes with a perfect authentic cadence on the tonic, B♭, in bar 73.

Though the ensuing TR reiterates motivic elements from P^{rf}, a contrasting harmonic course is pursued. The most common trajectories for an exposition's TR would be either a connection between tonic B♭ and a medial caesura (MC) on an F major chord, anticipating the F Major tonicisation during S; or a connection to an MC on a C major chord, whose dominant-emulating tendency targets the impending F Major region. Though an F chord occurs in bars 75 and 77, Schubert does not allow it to take hold as the transition's goal. He instead extends the transitional progression to a C major chord in bar 79, as shown in Example 11.2. The MC occurs at the downbeat of bar 81. This II♮ harmony is extended via several bars of caesura-fill (CF), a descending melodic line that leads inexorably to the upcoming V harmony's root. As Example 11.2 shows, this II♮ serves as the fulcrum between the expositional rotation's tonic and dominant regions. (The dominant key, F Major, will be tonicised throughout S.) Comparing Examples 11.2 and 11.3, note how the local I$^{5-6}$–II♮–V–I progression of a$_1$ serves also as the foundation for the broad progression that extends through the entire movement.[7]

The Expositional Rotation's S and C Regions

Schubert's TR ably prepares the F major chord that initiates the secondary-theme zone (S), which transpires during bars 86–185. Its structure is guided by a descending fifth-progression from C (background $\hat{2}$, as displayed in Example 11.2) to F, supported by a harmonic progression in the tonicised key of F Major. Example 11.6 shows how the line descending from C is interrupted at G during the first phrase. The consequent phrase that complements that antecedent does not commence until bar 130. Displayed in Example 11.8, it is in fact a second try at achieving the expected perfect authentic cadence. Example 11.7 reveals how the phrase beginning in bar 96 appears at first to be proceeding along the expected path in F Major, but—in an extraordinary construction—Schubert allows the tonic's 6-phase chord of bar 100 to assert itself as an alternative to the F Major tonal center. This D minor upstart soon evolves into a D major chord, more fully mimicking the F major tonic that it usurps. Observe not only that a perfect authentic cadence in D Major occurs in bar 104 (supporting the endpoint of an A-to-D descending-fifth-progression, rather than the expected C-to-F fifth-progression), but also that, as the score reveals, an extended passage, to bar 116, celebrates this cadence on D, after which a reversion to D Minor and further disintegration occur. Schubert's focus on the third relationship between the keys of F Major and D Major, which in the recapitulatory rotation will sound as B♭ Major and G Major, corresponds to the harmonic succession that initiates P^{rf}. Schubert daringly invites listeners to accept the lower-third chord (the F tonic's 6-phase chord) as a replacement for the F major chord. Potentially the expositional rotation could conclude in D Major rather than in F Major, corresponding to the G substitute for B♭ at the onset.

Yet Schubert ultimately neutralises the D chord. From the broader perspective displayed in Example 11.9, we come to understand that the D chord's F♯ is a temporary wobble and that the sojourn on D ultimately resides within an expansive descending trajectory that connects the F tonic and its mediant (bar 128); after that, a dominant restores the state of affairs that prevailed in bar 95, before this wayward consequent began.

Example 11.6 Analysis of the antecedent phrase of the expositional rotation's S

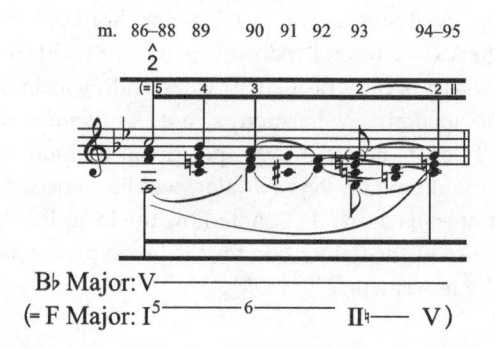

Example 11.7 Analysis of the first attempt at the consequent phrase of the expositional rotation's S

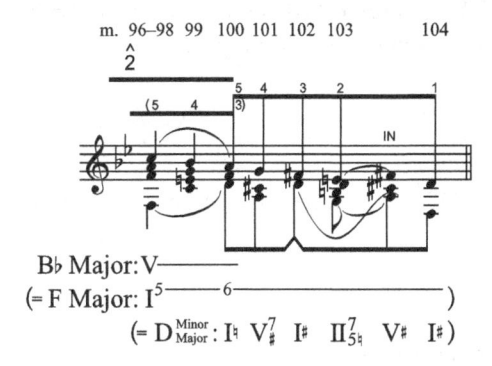

$$\text{B}\flat \text{ Major: V} \text{———}$$
$$(= \text{F Major: } \text{I}^5 \text{———} ^6 \text{—————————})$$
$$(= \text{D}^{\text{Minor}}_{\text{Major}}: \text{I}\natural \ \text{V}^7_\sharp \ \text{I}\natural \ \text{II}^7_{5\natural} \ \text{V}\sharp \ \text{I}\sharp \ )$$

Example 11.8 Analysis of the second attempt at the consequent phrase of the expositional rotation's S

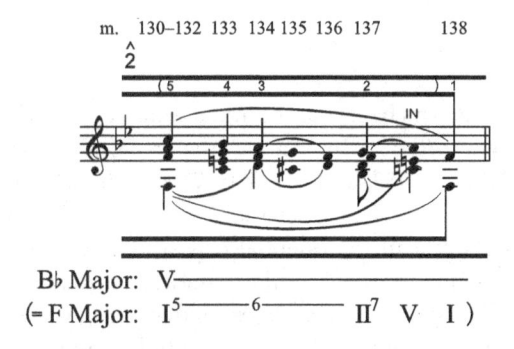

$$\text{B}\flat \text{ Major: V} \text{——————————————}$$
$$(= \text{F Major: } \text{I}^5 \text{———} ^6 \text{————} \ \text{II}^7 \ \text{V} \ \text{I} \ )$$

Example 11.9 Re-contextualisation of the material presented in Example 11.7

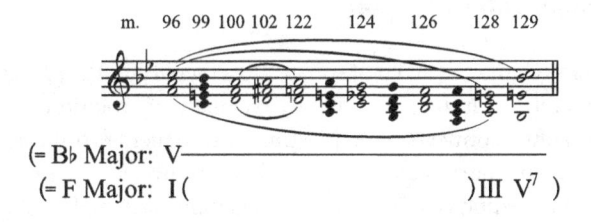

$$(= \text{B}\flat \text{ Major: V} \text{——————————}$$
$$(= \text{F Major: I} (\qquad\qquad\qquad) \text{III} \ \text{V}^7 \ )$$

We now can more fully appreciate the normalcy of Example 11.8. The D Minor prolongation in bars 134–136 does not expand into a more substantial region, and the distinctive cadential gesture that Schubert employed earlier in D Major now plays a cadential role in F Major, again followed by celebratory material (in bars 138–153).

Schubert is not ready to conclude the expositional rotation even at this point. Following the precedent of the D Major celebratory material shifting to

D Minor starting in bar 117, its F Major iteration begins a shift to F Minor in bar 151. That turn of events leads to a further extension of S, where the implications of this modal shift are worked out in the context of a vigorous theme in F Minor, which develops the harmonic progression

F Major: I   IV♭   V^7

from bars 152 and 153. The first transformation, in bars 156–167, is into

F Minor: I   ♭II   V$^7_{\flat}$

Next, the minor tonic is subjected to chordal evolution (resulting in a contrasting means of achieving the ♭II chord), in the progression

F Minor: I$^{8-7}_{\flat-\flat}$ IV$^{5-6}$ V$^7_{\flat}$ I

(=♭II)

during bars 168–175, which serve as the initial component of a broader progression that continues to the F Minor tonic's diatonic 6-phase chord in bar 180, to IV$^{5-6}$ in bars 181 and 182, and finally to V$^7_{\flat}$ resolving to I♭ in bars 183–185. F Major's tonic chord is restored at this cadence, which functions as what Hepokoski and Darcy call the essential expositional closure (EEC). A brief closing zone (C) follows, extending the exposition through to bar 201. Note how a I$^{5-6}$–II$^7_{\flat}$–V–I progression reminiscent of that which served as the foundation for P^{rf}'s a$_1$ region transpires during bars 190–193 (and 198–201).

The Developmental Rotation

Given its rondo character, a Type 4 sonata movement typically presents P^{rf} in the tonic key as a refrain at the outset of the developmental rotation. Consequently, a retransition often connects the exposition closing theme's tonicised dominant and the restated primary theme's tonic at this juncture. Because of P^{rf}'s uncharacteristic 6-phase emphasis, Schubert's retransition (sketched in Example 11.10) here overshoots the tonic goal, descending three (rather than two) thirds from the dominant root, F: through D and B♭ to G. No significant markers alert the listener that the B♭ chord of bar 209 serves as the tonic restoration, as my roman numeral in Example 11.10 proposes. Yet because the P^{rf} theme cadences decisively on B♭ in bar 233 (and again in bar 242), we may retrospectively interpret the B♭ chord within the retransition as the onset of the tonic. It provides grounding for P^{rf} during the developmental rotation, just as the B♭ chord at the end of the third movement grounds P^{rf} during the expositional rotation.

Example 11.10 Analysis of the passage from the expositional rotation's C through the onset of the developmental rotation's P^{rf}

m.   201 204 205 208 209   212 213 224–226

B♭ Major: V (   ) I^5 ———— 6 ————
                              (= VI♮)
End of C   Retransition   Beginning
                                     of P^{rf}

It seems at first that Schubert intends to reprise the entire P^{rf} theme to inaugurate the developmental rotation. Its a_1 component is stated and then repeated (bars 224–242), followed by a statement of b (bars 242–255). Yet b's cadence is followed not by a_2, but by extended developmental material that draws upon motivic content from the a_1 region, initially in a G Minor context. Example 11.11 shows how a harmonic progression from tonicised G through its subdominant, C, to the dominant, D, transpires through to bar 265.

During the expositional rotation the large-scale tonal motion proceeds from the tonic, B♭, to the dominant, F. Here the D dominant (bar 265) gives added weight to the G Minor tonal center within the developmental rotation, another instance of a 6-phase chord seizing the limelight from its 5-phase predecessor. Yet from that point onward the trajectories of the two rotations coincide. Recall from Example 11.10 that D Major played a connective role during the retransition. That moment corresponds to bar 265, while the B♭ of bar 209 corresponds to bar 273. Whereas in the retransition the continuing downward motion in thirds to the 6-phase G chord is immediate, in the developmental rotation the B♭ tonic is given a fuller presentation before the descent to G at bar 308, as Example 11.11 displays.

This progression is of great interest harmonically. Note how the B♭ major tonic is embellished in bar 283 by the second chromatic variant of its 6-phase chord: B♭–D♭–G♭ (see Example 11.11). This chromatic chord in B♭ Major is, of course, the tonic's diatonic 6-phase chord in B♭ Minor. Schubert acknowledges that relationship by incorporating further elements from B♭ Minor as the progression continues. Note especially the minor subdominant in bar 291, the subdominant's "Neapolitan" 6 phase, and the minor ninth G♭ within the dominant. Also note Schubert's more robust chordal activity between regions. Whereas little connective tissue comes between roots D and B♭ or between roots B♭ and G in Example 11.10, segments of the circle of fifths are employed at those junctures during the developmental rotation, marked by letter names between the staves in Example 11.11.[8]

Example 11.11 Analysis of the developmental rotation's P^{rf}

The Recapitulatory Rotation and the Coda Half-Rotation

Except for the elimination of the repeats during P^{rf} (bars 312–353), the recapitulatory rotation offers no surprises. As is typical within a recapitulatory context, S is presented in the tonic key (see Example 11.2). Consequently, the preceding TR is adjusted so that the MC occurs on V rather than on II♮: the dominant that was passed through in bars 75 and 77 takes on the role of medial caesura in bar 357. The fifth-progression of S transpires as F > E♭ > D > C > B♭ in B♭ Major. The concluding B♭ brings the background third-progression—here spanning more than four hundred bars—to a close, as shown in Example 11.2. That cadence is reinforced both during the remainder of S, with the essential structural closure (ESC) occurring in bar 459, and during C, whose final cadence occurs in bar 475.

In the coda half-rotation, which begins in bar 490, P^{rf} takes on a more expansive aspect, as Example 11.12 shows. The initial I–II–V–I progression expands to fill fifty bars—476 (the outset of the transition between rotations) to 525. Example 11.13 reveals that an earlier wrap-up would have been feasible had the potential F dominant of bar 502 resolved directly to the tonic. Recall, though, that a B♭/G dichotomy has been emphasised throughout the movement. Schubert further develops that relationship here via the inherent ambiguity of the diminished seventh chord in bars 496–501. Interpreted as F♯–A–C–E♭, it is an evolved state of the D^7 chord displayed in Example 11.12. Interpreted instead as G♭–A–C–E♭, it would resolve to the B♭ tonic. The G♭-to-F motion at bar 502 makes it appear that Schubert has elected to pursue the latter course. The astonishing F♯ in bar 512 is a down-to-the-wire switch back to the G-tending alternative, allowing the progression displayed in Example 11.12 to be traversed after all.

Conclusion

What is most striking about Schubert's intertwining of tonic B♭ major with G minor and G major chords and of tonicised dominant F major with D minor and D major

Example 11.12 Analysis of the coda half-rotation

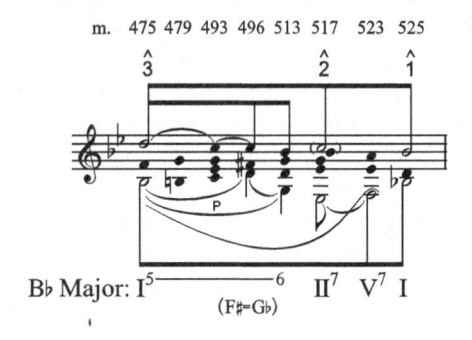

B♭ Major: I$^{5\text{———}6}$ II^7 V^7 I
(F♯=G♭)

Example 11.13 Exploration of alternative trajectories available during the coda half-rotation

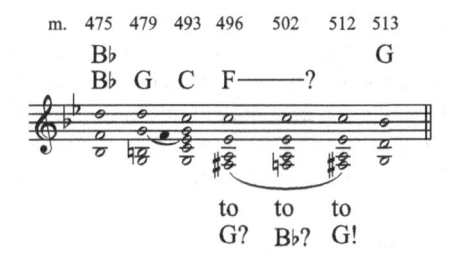

chords is his emphasis on the positive. These chords sometimes lead dynamically to the next chord of their progression, while at other times they vie for structural parity with the 5-phase chords from which they are derived. The pathos of the first movement, which stems in part from Schubert's emphasis on the 6-phase chords' more intense flat chromatic variants, is to a large extent avoided in the Finale. In my reading, the first movement stems from Schubert's willingness to take an unflinching look at his predicament, skilfully translated into tones. The Finale suggests that he was capable of mustering a positive outlook despite the grim facts concerning to his health and of crafting a movement that deploys devices shared with the first movement in a buoyant, life-embracing manner.[9]

Notes

1. David Damschroder, *Harmony in Schubert* (Cambridge: Cambridge University Press, 2010), Chapter 12, pp. 245–63.
2. Charles Fisk, 'Schubert's Last Finales', *The TASI Journal: a Publication of the American Schubert Institute* 1 (1997), pp. 3–17, offers insightful comments regarding the relationship between the B♭ Major Sonata's first and final movements,

corroborating the perspective presented here, as in the following: 'The joyous emotion of this second theme [beginning in bar 86] is apparent from its own character: the upward leap that begins it, its absolutely smooth stepwise descent, accompanied by ebullient right-hand arpeggiation and playful left-hand syncopation. But its tacit recollection, through motivic reference, of the unrest of the first movement's developmental journey and of the epiphanic release from the Andante's sadness only deepen this emotion, making it an affirmative response to its situation near the end of the sonata' (p. 6).

3. James Hepokoski and Warren Darcy have transformed the analysis of form in their monumental *Elements of Sonata Theory: Norms, Types, and Deformations in the Late-Eighteenth-Century Sonata* (New York and Oxford: Oxford University Press, 2006). Chapter 18 (pp. 388–429) is devoted to the rondo and the Type 4 sonata.

4. Given the context, listeners should imaginatively integrate the sounding G of bars 1 and 2 with a retained B♭ and D from the third movement's concluding chord to form a G–B♭–D submediant harmony of minor quality. That notion pertains to bars 10–11 and 32–33 as well. In contrast, the transition of bars 62–64 concludes with a G chord containing a B♮, thereby eliding the submediant's diatonic state.

5. The two styles of scale-step harmonic analysis in favour today deploy capital roman numerals in contrasting ways. Whereas in one style a capital roman numeral indicates that a chord is of major quality, in the style that is employed here a capital roman numeral with no accompanying symbols indicates that the chord is diatonic. Thus VI in B♭ major is a minor chord, G–B♭–D, whereas VI♮ is a major one, G–B♮–D.

6. The notion of seismic shift was introduced in my *Thinking about Harmony: Historical Perspectives on Analysis* (Cambridge: Cambridge University Press, 2008), pp. 230–7, and recurs in both my *Harmony in Schubert* and *Harmony in Haydn and Mozart* (Cambridge: Cambridge University Press, 2012). Observe in Example 11.5 how one of the internal chords during the hoist mutates: instead of a succession of four $^6_3$ chords in an upward chromatic trajectory, C♯–E♮–A is realised as C♯–E–G–B♭.

7. This observation would be lost if one interprets the C major MC instead as V within the emerging F Major dominant tonicisation (as would Hepokoski and Darcy). In Example 11.2 it is displayed at the same hierarchical level as the I of P[rf] and the V of S.

8. These letter names reveal how roots may be determined in a manner that is at variance with conventional modern analytical practice. For example, I propose that an unsounded G serves as the root of bar 268's B♮–D–F–A♭ chord. For a discussion of this notion drawing upon writings by theorists from the eighteenth and nineteenth centuries (including Johann Philipp Kirnberger), see my *Thinking about Harmony*, pp. 17–24.

9. Similar extramusical associations are assessed by Robert S. Hatten and by me in our analyses of a work composed soon after Schubert's illness struck: the second movement from his Piano Sonata in A Minor (D 784). See Hatten, *Interpreting Musical Gestures, Topics, and Tropes: Mozart, Beethoven, Schubert* (Bloomington: Indiana University Press, 2004), pp. 194–8, and my *Harmony in Schubert*, pp. 179–90.

12

Schubert, Social Music and Melancholy

Leon Plantinga

What was life like in Schubert's Vienna? Something of a composite portrait has come down to us. There was Alt-Wien, a place of comfortable, orderly middle-class life with sensible domestic architecture and decoration that has acquired the unlikely name 'Biedermeier' (named after a foolish middle-class character in a series of satirical poems). In this society traditional, conservative standards of morality reigned, and home was the center of social life—a welcome refuge now that Napoleon and his threat of chaos were safely deposited on the island of Elba, in the middle of the Atlantic. Entertainment, too, centred in the home. Reading, innocent play-acting, charades and music around the piano in the parlour were agreeable ways to spend long winter evenings. Even that most-loved entertainment the waltz—domesticated from its purported north Austrian and Tyrolean origins, and danced endlessly at the Congress of Vienna—came under suspicion as maybe too licentious for the decent, peace-loving citizens of Vienna.

But if there was a Biedermeier Vienna, there was also Metternich's Vienna. Prince Klemmens von Metternich (1773–1859), the Austrian Minister of Foreign Affairs and principal architect of the Congress and of the German Confederation that followed, remained a central force in European polity until the revolutions of 1848–9. Under his regime Austria became a place of iron-fisted social control designed to squelch any lingering liberal and egalitarian views that had arisen during the French Revolution and been nourished in some quarters throughout the Napoleonic years. Young people and students came under special scrutiny. When in 1819 a disturbed student murdered the arch-conservative historian and playwright August Kotzebue, the Diet of the German Confederation responded with the draconian Carlsbad Decrees, which muzzled the press, dissolved student organisations and assured that persons suspected of various sorts of non-conformity—say, religious or moral—could be prosecuted as dangerous to the state. Punishments ranged from flogging to imprisonment or exile. The physical conditions of life in Vienna, too, were rather dismal. Back in the 1780s Joseph II had undertaken efforts to improve sanitation in the city, including the washing down of the main streets with water during the summer months. But with the stirrings of the Industrial Revolution and the concomitant rapid rise in population in the first decades of the new century, no new measures were undertaken, and several observers testified to the possible dangers of breathing the air and drinking the water.[1]

If we have inherited distinctly competing visions of Old Vienna, the same seems to be true of her native son Franz Schubert—the only one of those renowned Viennese composers from the decades around 1800 who was actually from that city. The Schubert rediscovered in the late nineteenth century and portrayed in biography and operetta was a very sympathetic figure: Schubert the guileless composer of lilting songs and ingenuous instrumental music whose rhythms and textures echoed the sounds of comfortable and carefree Old Vienna. Occasional patches of melancholy in this music probably reflected the disappointment of an early unrequited love. This Schubert was one of a rather ethereal group of good-natured friends who met to sing and play in gatherings that came to be called Schubertiades. Carl Schorske described Gustav Klimt's painting of the composer at the century's end as 'a lovely dream, glowing but insubstantial, of an innocent, comforting art that served a comfortable society . . . for Klimt and his bourgeois contemporaries, the once-hated age of Metternich was recalled now as the gracious, simple age of Schubert—a Biedermeier Paradise lost.'[2]

More recently, of course, that other Schubert has emerged, fittingly situated in that other Vienna. Schubert was there as a turbulent chapter of the city's history unfolded. It was in the year of his birth that Napoleon first conquered Vienna, and during his childhood, in 1805 and 1809, he witnessed two more invasions and occupations. The second of these must have made a particularly resounding impression on the boy: a shell from Napoleon's cannons burst through the roof of the Kaiserlich-Königliches Stadtkonvikt, where he lived and studied. And the adult Schubert was very much caught up in the repressive period that followed. In March of 1820, not long after the enactment of the Carlsbad Decrees, he and two of those amiable friends were arrested for participation in suspicious meetings; one, the poet Johann Senn, was jailed, then exiled. Another central focus of the newer portrait of Schubert is his desperate illness, which began towards the end of 1822: this was a man who evidently suffered from a venereal disease, probably syphilis, and despaired of ever recovering. During the summer of 1823 he spent time in hospital and wore a wig to conceal his lack of hair—shorn, as his friend the painter Moritz von Schwind explained, because of a severe rash—and for long periods he kept to himself. A poem he sketched in May of that year includes this stanza: 'Look, destroyed lies in the dust / Prey to unheard-of sorrow, / My life's martyred course / Nearing final oblivion.'[3]

The song texts Schubert chose to set may serve to reinforce our polarised vision of the composer's mental state. There are the utterly simple settings of the magisterial Goethe in his folk-like guise ('Heidenröslein', 'Trost in Thränen') and ingenuous celebrations of innocent pleasures out-of-doors, such as 'Auf dem Wasser zu singen' by one Friedrich Leopold, Graf zu Stolberg. But from the first there was also a notable concentration of poems on the melancholy or even tragic side. Sometimes they were the stuff of nightmares: a son wrenched from his father's arms by a demon only the son can see in 'Erlkönig', the wounded Romantic wanderer who moves inexorably towards physical or psychological destruction in the Müller cycles and the rejected lover tormented by harrowing visions of his former life in 'Der Doppelgänger'. A composer's choice of texts for musical setting in itself hardly constitutes reliable evidence of his frame of mind. But together with the other indicators we have, Schubert's song texts, especially in the later years, are suggestive of an increasingly pessimistic outlook.[4]

Our view of the music itself tends to be similarly bifurcated. Schubert alone among the greatest Viennese composers grew up listening to the musical sounds of Vienna: the close harmonies of the Männerchor, the duple rhythms of the écossaise, the lilt of the dances in triple time known variously as Deutscher, Ländler, and waltzes. Such music could be heard—can sometimes still be heard—in those ubiquitous taverns and coffee bars of the city. (These were favourite gathering places for various social groups: for artistic and intellectual types such as Schubert and Beethoven and their friends; and, contrary to the Biedermeier stereotype of the home-bound bourgeois, respectable, middle-class residents of the city could be seen in the taverns as well, because their typically small apartments weren't very good for socialising.)We hear these sounds of Vienna in many of Schubert's compositions, most clearly in what we may call his 'domestic' or 'social' music: pieces he wrote (and to a considerable extent published) in great profusion, especially in the earlier part of his career—songs, part-songs and dance music for piano that gained him increasing admiration in Viennese social circles.

Schubert earned this local reputation while his fellow resident of Vienna, Beethoven, was achieving European-wide renown, mainly with big instrumental pieces: symphonies, sonatas and large works for chamber ensembles. In the formulation of another citizen of Vienna of that time, the music historian Raphael Kiesewetter, the current musical culture could be summed up as an 'Era of Beethoven and Rossini.' Schubert's Viennese reputation, in Kiesewetter's formulation—or, particularly, in that of his explicator Carl Dahlhaus—would pretty clearly have been on the 'Rossini side.' Schubert's overtly 'social' music was work whose full worth lay in the entertainment value of its performance. The notion of a composition as a single inviolable 'text' which could lay claim to the status of 'art' and to which the performer owed dutiful adherence was foreign to this repertoire.[5]

But Schubert's image has of course changed radically, particularly as the full range of his instrumental music has come to be known. In the last half-dozen years or so of his life, and particularly from 1824 on, Schubert himself, it seems, consciously worked to effect such a change. Probably against the advice of his publishers, and surely contrary to his own financial interests, he devoted a huge share of his energies to big, ambitious instrumental pieces, compositions he was now willing to publish and to let stand as his legacy. Thus we have that breathtaking series of late works: the 'Unfinished' and 'Great' C major Symphonies; the String Quintet D 956; the String Quartets beginning as early as the *Quartettsatz*, D 703 (1820), followed by the Quartets D 804, 810 and 887; the two late Piano

Trios D 898 and 929; and the final three massive and marvelous Piano Sonatas, D 958, 959 and 960 from the last year of the composer's life. Schubert's motives for this drastic change in the course of his career, for devoting himself to the creation of a body of big works for which he had scant hope of either performance or publication, is not immediately clear.[6] But John Gingerich argues persuasively that Schubert took this radical course of action in a desperate attempt to measure up, in some way, to Beethoven—to share, to some degree, in the particular veneration accorded Beethoven as an artist. Feeling he had not long to live, and acutely aware of the disparity between his profile as a composer and that of Beethoven, he plunged into this vast project of composing Beethoven's sort of music.[7]

For many of us, these late works explore a uniquely broad landscape of musical expression. On one hand there is the verve and infectious lilt of, say, the Scherzo of the String Quartet in G, D 887, or of the Piano Trio in B♭, D 898. But, particularly in some slow movements of the sonatas and chamber works (as well as in, say, the late Heine songs) listeners feel that Schubert has also plumbed new depths of pessimism and melancholy in musical utterance. Just one example among many, but one unsurpassed in its effect, is the Adagio movement of the String Quintet. In its outer sections, in E major, the midrange voices move quietly at a measured pace suggestive of grave resignation, while the first violin in its fitful and disjointed commentary leaves an impression of something like suppressed hysteria.

Lately we have become better aware that the dividing line between Schubert's overtly 'social' music and his 'serious' compositions is often an indistinct one. If there was a musical type explicitly associated with amateur music making in a social setting, it is music for piano four-hands. But in Schubert's late work four-hand keyboard music sometimes achieves a convincing 'upward mobility' (Margaret Notley's term[8]); this is particularly striking in two compositions from his last year, the Rondo in A, D 951, and the hauntingly impressive F minor Fantasy, D 940. And characteristic textures from four-hand music often show up in the more 'elevated' genres. In perhaps the most usual of these textures, the *primo* plays the melody in octaves while the *secondo* supplies a chordal accompaniment.[9] Schubert freely imports this sort of sound directly into his chamber music for piano and strings. One example is the engaging subsidiary theme of the first movement of the E♭ Trio, D 929, composed at the end of 1827 (Example 12.1).[10]

Another sort of social music that Schubert produced in great profusion was the dance for solo piano. His friend Leopold Sonnleithner reported that he sometimes improvised such pieces at balls to accompany the dancing, and 'those he liked he repeated in order to remember them and write them out afterwards.'[11] Publishers such as Diabelli and Cappi were only too happy to print them for other Viennese dance enthusiasts. But if Schubert's Ländler may be thought of as 'written-out improvisations,' his contemporaries probably also heard them as, in a sense, transcriptions, or reductions. For in the dance halls

Schubert, Social Music and Melancholy 241

Example 12.1 Schubert, Trio in E♭, D 929, i, bars 48ff.

and taverns of Vienna, the Ländler and allied types of social music were most often played, we are told, by small string ensembles, usually two violins and string bass, sometimes augmented with a clarinet and percussion.[12] Schubert surely listened a good bit to such ensembles during the many hours he spent in Viennese *Kneipen*. And in at least one case, in a manuscript evidently from early 1816, he wrote a series of Ländler for violin (D 374), some of which he later transcribed for piano (D 378).[13]

In some of his Ländler for piano we can hear pretty clearly their conceptual origins in string ensembles—particularly in an incessant pizzicato of the double bass. Example 12.2 shows two instances of this, the beginnings of the fifth and eighth numbers from D 734 (1826).

And as is true of Schubert's four-hand music, his dances, especially the later ones, are sometimes ambitious and artful. Their harmony is at points highly sophisticated, with off-tonic beginnings and abstruse modulations after the double bar. Maurice J. E. Browne showed us quite a few years ago that in the D minor Quartet ('Death and the Maiden') of 1824, the Scherzo is largely a revision of No. 6 of the Twelve Deutsche for Piano, D 790, composed the previous year.[14] But perhaps we might more properly see the Scherzo as something of a simplification of that dance. The Ländler, in G♯ minor, begins rather at sea harmonically; in the first eight-bar period there is but one fleeting reference to the tonic harmony, in bar 6. The Scherzo begins much more conventionally, solidly on the tonic, delaying its imitation of the Ländler's harmonic divagations until its second phrase (see Examples 12.3 a and b).

An impressive and characteristic achievement of Schubert's late big pieces is the mingling of those seemingly divergent themes: the social, celebratory sounds of the tavern and dance hall juxtaposed with—or, indeed, mingled

Example 12.2 Schubert, Sechzehn Ländler und zwei Ecossaisen, D 734, No. 5 and No. 8

Example 12.3a Schubert, Twelve Deutsche for Piano, D 790/6, bars 1–8.

Example 12.3b Schubert, String Quartet in D minor, D 810, 'Death and the Maiden', Scherzo, bars 1–12.

within—movements of solemn, even tragic import. Tragedy unfolds in the midst of celebration, as if, outwardly, carefree life in Vienna goes on in the face of private disillusionment or despair. This seems particularly noticeable in the late piano sonatas. An example is the B minor movement of the Piano Sonata in G, D 984, which Andras Schiff calls a 'sinister minuet.'[15] And in the final Sonata in B♭, D 960, the excruciatingly despondent—but at least distantly dance-like— Andante sostenuto in C♯ minor is followed by a deliciously ebullient Scherzo, which itself is interrupted by a Trio of dark, maybe menacing exoticism.

Perhaps the *locus classicus* for Schubert's success in mixing stylised dance with elements of lament or despair in his big instrumental pieces is the Andantino movement of the Sonata in A, D 959. This movement could be described as a stylised Ländler. Its triple meter and marking of andantino suggest a moderate tempo, which concurs with contemporary descriptions of that dance. And the incessant staccatos in the accompanying left-hand figure in its outer sections seem to imitate the pizzicato of the bass instrument that typically participated in this dance (see Example 12.4).

A couple of points regarding performance practice are probably relevant here. Many pianists play this movement in ways that tend to obscure its affiliations with the dance. To begin with, I believe we generally hear it played too slowly. It is not immediately clear just what Schubert meant by andantino: does the diminutive ending make it faster or slower than andante? Beethoven asked this very question in a letter (written in uncertain French) to his publisher George Thompson of Edinburgh in February 1813. Among the pieces he agreed to arrange for Thompson was an Andantino; Beethoven asked, 'I pray you, tell me if this Andantino is understood to be slower or faster than an Andante, since the meaning of this term (like many others in music) is so uncertain that often andantino approaches allegro, and many other times is played almost like an Adagio.'[16]

Beethoven's puzzlement about this term was well founded: some writers from the time say that andantino is faster than andante, while others it is say

Example 12.4 Schubert, Sonata in A major, D 959, ii, bars 1–16

slower.[17] But there is good reason to agree with Clive Brown that 'Schubert, who, unlike Beethoven, frequently used the tempo direction "Andantino", undoubtedly intended it to indicate a tempo considerably faster than that indicated by "Andante"'; Brown cites a series of examples to show that Schubert apparently considered andantino to fall somewhere between andante and allegretto.[18] But that of course merely shifts the question to the meaning of andante.

It seems fairly clear that for Beethoven, at least, the tempos at the lower end of the scale were rather faster than we tend to think of them.[19] For three movements of his, roughly comparable in metre and motion to the outer sections of the Schubert movement at hand, Beethoven later supplied metronome markings. These are the Andante cantabile of the String Quartet Op. 18 No. 5 (♪. = 100), the Andante scherzoso quasi Allegretto of Op. 18 No. 4 (♩. = 56), and the Andante cantabile con moto of the First Symphony (♪. = 120).[20] A few, almost randomly selected recordings of the outer sections of the Schubert movement, on the other hand, show remarkable unanimity, and much slower tempos (see Table 12.1).

At such tempos (with the possible exception of Schiff's) this movement's invocation of the dance is undermined. Playing the outer sections that slowly also spoils any chance for consistency of tempo with the radically contrasting middle section, which—all these performers seem to agree—needs to go very much faster, but for which Schubert gave no new tempo indication.

Schubert's articulation of the left-hand accompaniment figure in the first section is a staccato quaver followed by two slurred quavers; he doesn't bother to write these details consistently, but their fairly consistent presence at new beginnings of the theme surely suggests that this articulation is meant to apply throughout. Most pianists, including all of those cited above, obscure any association of this figure with the sound of plucked strings by pedaling through Schubert's dots and slurs.[21] This issue may be elucidated (or perhaps complicated) by comparison with a somewhat similar accompanying figure in the corresponding movement of the following sonata, D 960 in B♭, composed virtually at the same time, in September 1828. In this morose but magical movement in C♯ minor, marked Andante sostenuto, and also in triple meter, the

Table 12.1 Tempos of select recordings of Schubert, Sonata in A major, ii

Pianist/recording	Tempo
Artur Schnabel (EMI)	♪. = 76
Rudolph Serkin (Sony)	♪. = 80
Andreas Staier (Teldek)	♪. = 76–80 (fortepiano ca. 1825)
Maurizio Pollini (DGG)	♪. = 76–80
Alfred Brendel (Philips)	♪. = 80
Andras Schiff (London)	♪. = 88

basic pulse presumably goes a little slower than that of the Andantino of D 959. Example 12.5 shows its beginning.

Here Schubert indicates nearly the same articulation for the accompanying figure in the left hand, except that the dot over the initial bass tone of the pattern has been transferred to the offbeat crossover soprano pitches (in this movement Schubert is even less consistent about writing in those dots). At the beginning of this movement, under the bass, he writes 'col pedale'. But what does he mean by this? Is he instructing us to hold the pedal down for the entire duration of each harmony, as most pianists (including all of those mentioned above) seem to do? Surely it is reasonable to think he may have meant something less drastic, such as using the pedal simply to add some resonance to the first chord of the pattern, still allowing us to observe the articulation Schubert indicated.

Another example of this sort of accompanimental figure occurs in the Ländler D 790/7. Here Schubert marks all the bass notes staccato. And once more he writes 'col pedale'. Because of the wide range of these accompanimental figures in both the sonata and the Ländler, if the staccato notes are played very short, we might imagine hearing staccato articulations and imitations of pizzicato strings even with the pedal held straight through (see Example 12.6). But this exercise requires a rather less active imagination if we play these examples on the less resonant Viennese pianos of Schubert's time. To a degree this seems to be the case in the Staier recording mentioned above, and the result was similar when I tried these two passages on a Bösendorfer piano built in about 1828, the birth year of these two sonatas.[22] But in the case of the F♯ minor movement from the Sonata D 959, at least, where there is no pedal indication, presumably we are free to take Schubert's instructions literally: to imitate those pizzicatos with a clear conscience and much less pedal.

In both of these slow movements of his final two sonatas, Schubert alternates the dolorous dance in minor with a more sanguine version of it

Example 12.5 Schubert, Sonata in B♭ major, D 960, ii, bars 1–8

Example 12.6 Schubert, Twelve Deutsche for Piano, D 790/7, bars 1–16

Example 12.7 Schubert, Sonata in A major, D 959, ii, bars 19–26

in the relative major. In both cases the major version is played *pianissimo*, making these passages seem insubstantial, dream-like. In the F♯ minor movement, these sections are very fleeting, their tenuousness underscored by tonic sounds only in second inversion; and as early as the consequent phrase even this disappears—the melancholy minor-key dance reasserts itself (see Example 12.7).

After two rounds of this minor-major alternation and an unemphatic close, the middle section of this movement comes on with no further thought of the dance, or even of any sort of identifiable thematic matter or melody. Restless arpeggio and scale figures over a bass motion from G♯ to G gradually lead to the very distant key of C minor in bar 85. From this point the music becomes increasingly agitated as even this key center evaporates. A huge climax on a careening downward C♯ minor scale in bar 107 plunges without relief into another anguished build-up and an even greater climax, still in C♯ minor, in bar 122. If music is capable of expressing something like frenzy or hysteria, surely it does so here (see Example 12.8).

Things finally calm down, and the movement finds its way back to the opening dance. The string-bass staccatos return, and the slurred-note figure above reappears slightly elaborated. But Schubert also adds an obsessive four-note rhythmic figure in the treble that sounds faintly ominous—as if the newly regained grasp on reality is still tenuous (see Example 12.9).

Example 12.8 Schubert, Sonata in A major, D 959, ii, bars 105–122

Example 12.9 Schubert, Sonata in A major, D 959, ii, bars 159–166

[musical score]

The major version of the theme then returns, *pianissimo*, now with the original string-like accompaniment, but sounding more insubstantial than ever. The minor key reasserts itself as the dance comes to a somber close.

As he so often does, Schubert puts all that angst and despair behind him for a sparkling and distinctly cheerful Scherzo in A major. Then, after the double bar, a rollicking extension of the theme wends its way to C major, where a sudden and wholly unexpected flashback to the previous movement intrudes: in a clear reminiscence of the turbulent middle section a quite irrelevant C♯ minor scale plummets downwards from a high A. But the troubled vision is fleeting; a diminuendo on the way down suggests immediate second thoughts about such a feverish outburst. As the movement regains its bearings, we seem to be abandoned in the rather distant key of C♯ minor. Then, as Schubert pulls things back together, A major reappears via a typically Schubertian sleight of hand (a Neapolitan sixth in C♯ minor is reinterpreted as a subdominant in A), and we are safely back in the proper key for the ebullient recapitulation.[23] Private despair has for the moment been suppressed; life in outwardly carefree Vienna goes on.

In most ways, the final years of Schubert's life seemed to trace a downward spiral. Plagued by illness, now without his important friends of earlier years, and periodically in financial need, he moved restlessly from one dwelling to another in and around Vienna, living mainly in places where he did not even have direct access to a piano. But in this period his productivity as a composer, if anything, went in the opposite direction. His persistent effort at this time culminated in a stunning series of major compositions completed in the final two and a half months before his death in November 1828: *Schwanengesang*, those final three spacious Piano Sonatas, and the String Quintet. Melancholy and lament certainly play a central role in this remarkable music, yet each of these compositions also has moments evocative of dance or high-spirited celebration. Schubert's mental state, like life in his city, remained a multi-faceted thing.

Notes

1. See Leon Botstein, 'Realism Transformed: Franz Schubert and Vienna', in Christopher H. Gibbs (ed.), *The Cambridge Companion to Schubert* (Cambridge: Cambridge University Press, 1997), pp. 15–17.

2. Carl Schorske, *Fin-de-Siècle Vienna* (New York: Alfred A. Knopf, 1980), p. 221. See also Alice M. Hanson, *Musical Life in Biedermeier Vienna* (Cambridge: Cambridge University Press, 1985).

3. 'Sieh, vernichtet liegt im Staube, / Unerhörtem Gram zum Raube, / Meines Lebens Martergang / Nahend ew'gen Untergang'. See Otto Erich Deutsch (ed.), *Schubert: Die Dokumente seines Lebens* (Kassel: Bärenreiter, 1964), p. 185.

4. Since the late 1980s discussion of Schubert's life and personality has been dominated by a flood of talk about his sexual orientation that began with Maynard Solomon, 'Franz Schubert and the Peacocks of Benvenuto Cellini', *19th-Century Music* 12/3 (1988–9), pp. 114–25. This was followed with an entire issue of *19th-Century Music* (17/1 [1993–4]) devoted to this subject, with contributions from Rita Steblin, Kristina Muxfeldt and, again, Maynard Solomon. While it appears to me likely that Schubert was mainly homosexual, I have seen no convincing argument that this in itself contributes much to our understanding of the man and his music.

5. See R. G. Kiesewetter, *Geschichte der Euopaisch-Abendländischen oder unser heutigen Musik* (Leipzig: Breitkopf & Härtel, 1846), pp. 98–101; and Carl Dahlhaus, *Die Musik des 19. Jahrhunderts* (Wiesbaden: Akademische Verlagsgesellschaft Athenaion, 1980), pp. 7–13. These starkly contrasting views of the nature and status of musical composition later hardened among German-speakers into a polarity between *Unterhaltungsmusik* (entertainment music) and *Kunstmusik* (art music). Dahlhaus here claims, surely with a bit of exaggeration, that Beethoven single-handedly won for music the status and dignity of 'art'. But English attitudes towards the oratorios of Handel, beginning in the 1780s, and even the canonisation of the works of Palestrina after the Council of Trent (1546–63) suggest kindred attitudes.

6. Of the twelve compositions mentioned in this paragraph, only two (the String Quartet in A minor, D 804, and the Piano Trio in E♭, D 929) were printed and performed in public during the composer's lifetime.

7. John Gingerich, *Schubert's Beethoven Project* (Cambridge: Cambridge University Press, 2014). Gingerich presents parts of his argument in 'Unfinished Considerations: Schubert's "Unfinished" Symphony in the Context of his Beethoven Project,' *19th-Century Music* 31/2 (2007), pp. 99–112. Martin Chusid had touched on this subject in 'Schubert's Chamber Music: Before and After Beethoven', in Christopher H. Gibbs (ed.), *The Cambridge Companion to Schubert* (Cambridge: Cambridge University Press, 1997), pp. 174–92.

8. Margaret Notley, 'Schubert's Social Music: the "Forgotten Genres"', in Christopher H. Gibbs (ed.), *The Cambridge Companion to Schubert* (Cambridge: Cambridge University Press, 1997), p. 149.

9. This arrangement also made its way into the solo piano repertoire of a more popular cast. A well-known example is the signature theme of Schumann's *Papillons*, Op. 2 (1830–1).

10. Some other examples of the texture in this repertoire: in the same Trio, second movement, bars 23ff.; in the Piano Trio in B♭, D 898, first movement, bars 26 and 212, and fourth movement, bars 27 and 68; in the Piano Quintet, 'Die Forelle,' D 667, first movement, bar 162, and second movement, bar 26; and the Adagio and Rondo Concertant for Piano Quartet, D 487, Rondo, bar 117.

11. See Otto Erich Deutsch, *Schubert die Erinnerungen seiner Freunde* (Leipzig: Breitkopf & Härtel, 1957), p. 141. See also Otto Erich Deutsch, *Schubert: Memoires by his Friends* (London: A. & C. Black, 1958), p. 121. Like many of Schubert's acquaintances who provided reminiscences about the composer, Sonnleithner recorded his many years after the fact, in 1857. They were ultimately incorporated into the first substantial biography of Schubert, published in 1865 by Kreißle von Holborn.

12. See Karl Horak, 'Ländler', in Walther Deutsch, Harald Dreo, Gerlinde Haid and Karl Horak (eds), *Volksmusik in Oesterreich* (Vienna: Oesterreichischer Bundesverlag Gesellschaft), pp. 59 and 65; and Mosco Carner, 'Ländler', in Stanley Sadie and John Tyrrell (eds), *The New Grove Dictionary of Music and Musicians*, 2nd edn (London: Macmillan, 2001), vol. 14, p. 223. Mozart greatly augmented the usual scoring of such pieces in his Sechs Ländlerische Tänze, K. 606, of 1791. They survive, however, only in a later transcription for the usual ensemble of two violins and string bass.

13. See Otto Erich Deutsch, *Franz Schubert: Thematisches Verzeichnis seiner Werke in chronologischer Folge* (Kassel: Bärenreiter, 1978), p. 224.

14. Maurice J. E. Brown, *Schubert: a Critical Biography* (London: St. Martin's Press, 1961), p. 230.

15. Andras Schiff, 'Schubert and the Ungers', in Brian Newbould (ed.), *Schubert Studies* (Aldershot: Ashgate, 1998), p. 203.

16. Ludwig van Beethoven, *Briefwechsel Gesamtausgabe*, ed. Sieghard Brandenburg (Munich: G. Henle Verlag, 1996), vol. 2, p. 321.

17. See Clive Brown, *Classical and Romantic Performing Practice, 1750–1900* (Oxford: Oxford University Press, 1999), pp. 351–7.

18. Ibid., pp. 355–6.

19. See my *Beethoven's Concertos: History, Style, Performance* (New York: W. W. Norton, 1999), pp. 298–304.

20. See Brown, *Classical and Romantic Performing Practice*, p. 359.

21. Serkin comes closest to suggesting something like pizzicato on certain notes by playing them extremely softly while holding the pedal through; but this occurs consistently on the third note of each group—which Schubert did not mark staccato.

22. This piano is in the Yale Collection of Musical Instruments.

23. The Rondo finale of the Sonata borrows its main theme from the slow movement of Schubert's Sonata in A minor, D 537, of 1817. Because this, like so many of Schubert's bigger instrumental works, remained unpublished, he apparently felt free to borrow from it. In the earlier version of the theme its left-hand accompaniment is of the 'pizzicato' type so prominent in the slow movement of D 959; perhaps this similarity reminded Schubert of his much earlier sonata as he contemplated a finale for his A major Sonata.

III

MUSIC AND TEXT

13

Axial Lyric Space in Two Late Songs
'Im Freien' and 'Der Winterabend'

Michael Spitzer

One of the many delights of the Hyperion Schubert Edition of the complete songs, aside from the unprecedented quality of the programme booklets written by Graham Johnson, the project's curator, is that it brought to attention a treasure trove of gems seldom captured by the routine compilations.[1] Schubert's 'Im Freien' (March 1826) and 'Der Winterabend' (January 1828) are two late masterpieces easily the match of anything in *Winterreise* or *Schwanengesang*, and arguably more ambitious because of their sheer length, six and eight minutes respectively. These songs have suffered almost total analytical and critical neglect; if this chapter does nothing else but introduce them to new listeners, then that will be enough. But I also have other fish to fry. In recent years Schubert has become an arena for neo-Riemannian theory because of his harmonic experimentation, particularly his penchant for third-related chords. Whilst providing new tools for understanding chromatic progressions which seemed to defy diatonic logic, neo-Riemannian mania has distorted as much as it has illuminated. The analytical fashion for seizing upon Schubert's mediant-based harmonies has tended to foreground obscure or outlier songs—that is, songs whose theoretical interest potentially outweighs their aesthetic quality.[2] Tertial harmonies are present in much of Schubert's instrumental and vocal music. It bears stressing, however, that *most of his music is diatonic for most of the time*. The problem is not just music theory's hyperbolic magnification of the harmonic minority; it is also the reductionism of picking out brute chords at the expense of the melodic, rhythmic and formal treatment which surely constitutes the essential fabric of Schubert's musical language.[3]

One suggestive product of the neo-Riemannian engagement with Schubert is Suzannah Clark's conception of Schubert's 'axial' tonal choices.[4] According to Clark, a tonic for Schubert is not a pole but an axis or a centre, around which tonal space gradually expands, with harmonic range typically increasing first in one direction, and then in another, bound by a fifth. For instance, the first movement of the 'Unfinished' Symphony modulates to the submediant (G major), balanced a fifth below by the mediant (D major) in the recapitulation. In the 'Trout' Quintet, a pair of rising fifths in the first movement (exposition: A–E; recapitulation: D–A) is complemented by a pair of falling fifths in the finale (exposition: A–D; recapitulation: E–A). The 'Trout' is pertinent because it reminds us that axial symmetry of dominant and subdominant (upper and lower fifths) around the tonic is intrinsic to diatonic pitch space and its circle of fifths, and thus is distinct from the tertial symmetries of the *Tonnetz*.[5] Why, then, is Schubert's diatonic pitch space any different in essentials from the sensibility for tonal balance at the heart of Charles Rosen's vision of the Classical style, as epitomised by Mozart's poised sonata forms?

Clark tentatively relates this axial tonal expansion to two other aspects of Schubert's practice: his use of common tones and his spiralling melodic contours.[6] An example of the former is the successive keys of the roving tonality of 'Trost'—G♯ minor, B major, B minor, G major and E major, all of which share the common tone B. According to Clark, the song's tonal architecture makes better sense in relation to a focal pitch, B, rather than to any central tonic. Famous examples of Schubert's spiralling melodic contour include the opening themes of the 'Great' C major Symphony and of his Piano Sonata in B♭. These melodies creep around an axial pitch, in these cases (but not always) the tonic, with gradually widening oscillations. Axial melodies were first theorised by Leonard Meyer, and it is important to stress that he believed that they were intrinsically non-implicative: he foregrounded their static symmetry, as prolongations of a central tone through their upper and lower neighbours, rather than their drive for growth.[7] As well as focusing on axial melodies' tendency to expand, I will depart from Meyer's theory in another important respect: the axial progressions in 'Im Freien' and 'Der Winterabend' are asymmetrical. Overall, the melodies in these two songs tend to drift upwards, the drive towards ascent interacting with the circularity of axial progressions. Asymmetry also pertains to axial harmony. The very highest note in 'Im Freien' is the c^4 of bars 83 and 87, carried by celestial piano octaves, yet this melodic highpoint occurs in the subdominant key, A♭ major. Harmonic climax on the subdominant side—including representation by the submediant, the 'agent' of the subdominant—is of course very typical of Romantic character pieces and lieder.[8] In 'Der Winterabend', the third below the B♭ tonic (G major) is given much more prominence than the third above (D major). The song's expansive middle section begins and ends in G major.

I shall argue that axial lyric space is both more basic and more general than 'axial tonal' space, if only because it engages Schubert's melodic, rhythmic and formal fabric, and because it is present even when the music is absolutely diatonic. In one of the two songs I consider, 'Im Freien', chromatically speaking, 'nothing happens': the music keeps to simple diatonic chords and never travels beyond dominant and subdominant keys. The later song, 'Der Winterabend', would satisfy neo-Riemannians' interest in tertial harmony because of the striking descending-thirds key progressions in its middle section (B♭–G– E♭–C minor). However, it is more revealing to approach the harmonically adventurous song from the perspective of the diatonic one; invoking dogs and tails,

'Im Freien' wags 'Der Winterabend', rather than the other way round, as seems to be increasingly the case in current music theory.

'Im Freien' and 'Der Winterabend' are particularly fine instances of Schubert's landscape trope. Both are moonlit nocturnal journeys across landscapes of nature and memory, the moon singling out a succession of musical objects for attention and seemingly the source of the songs' ecstatic radiance. Although Schubert's late songs do not lack for acute psychological portraits, the impersonal qualities of 'Im Freiein' and 'Der Winterabend' comport with notions that late styles are abstract.[9]

'Im Freien'

The text of 'Im Freien' is by Johann Gabriel Seidel, who contributed a number of poems for Schubert's late songs. It begins: 'Now once more I stand outside in the vast night; its bright starry splendour gives my heart no peace'. A song 'floating enticingly through the air' draws the poet through the landscape, the moonlight 'lingering' on a cottage, a house by the brook, a tree glittering with 'silver flakes'. 'Wherever a moonbeam falls, cherished treasure entices'. Because the song is so dominated by its piano accompaniment, Johnson calls it a kind of impromptu, with the vocal line an afterthought. The repeated chords of the introduction never relent, although they are subject to subtle and constant changes so that practically no phrase is exactly the same (Example 13.1). This *mélange* of through-composition and repetition unfolds at the formal level in a seamless blend of strophic variation, rondo and da capo return.

The opening part of the song, in which the vocal melody mostly cleves to the material of the piano introduction and the tonality remains in the tonic of E♭ major, consists of verses 1 and 2 (bars 1–30). The second, central, part, which sets the majority of the text, verses 3–6, introduces a new thematic idea based on rising skips of thirds and fourths, in contrast to the circling and linear contour of the main theme. Tonally, it roves to the dominant (verse 3, bars 31–47), back to the tonic (verse 4, bars 48–61), to the dominant again (verse 5, bars 62–73) and then to the subdominant (verse 6, bars 77–91), climaxing with verse 7 (bars 92–101)—a 'standing-on-the-dominant' lead-back to the tonic da capo of verse 8 (bars 102–132).

Cutting to the chase, one of the many miracles of this song is how its architecture is predicted by a piano introduction which outwardly seems—texture aside—melodically and harmonically unremarkable. The song as a whole traverses an arc of intensification, a *Steigerung*.[10] After beginning with G, the mediant degree, successive high points project the pitches B♭, E♭ and G an octave above, and the step A♭–B♭ is featured as an important event. These elements are indeed implicit within the introduction, which demonstrates that 'promissory notes', *pace* Edward T. Cone, don't necessarily need to be chromatic.[11] There is far more to bars 1–8 than first meets the eye.

Example 13.1 Schubert, 'Im Freien', D 880, bars 1–30

[Musical score: Mässig, mit Innigkeit; bars 1–12, with vocal entry at bar 9: "Drau-ssen in der wei-ten Nacht steh' ich wie-der"]

The piano melody starts by tracing an axial progression around G at two levels, bars 1–2, as well as across bars 1–4 (G–F, a step below; A♭ –G, a step above). The melody then rises to circle B♭ (B♭–C–B♭, bars 5–7), climaxing with an axial turn around E♭ (D–E♭–F–E♭, bars 7–8) (Example 13.2).

The axial lyric trajectory in 'Im Freien' is made up of three modules: (1) an initial circling of a focal pitch, G; (2) an ascent to the dominant, B♭; and (3) a further ascent to a high point, E♭. The ascent is also associated with melodic expansion, a move from compression (neighbour-note motion around G) to a more expansive idiom (the rising scale C–D–E♭–F at bar 7), as well as a sense of circular return.

Example 13.1 Continued

Example 13.1 Continued

[musical score: mm. 27ff, voice and piano, text "grüss' dich, Trau-ter, du, grüss' dich, Trau-ter, du!"]

Example 13.2 (a–c) (a) Axial progression on G at two levels; (b) Axial progression on B♭; (c) Axial progression around E♭

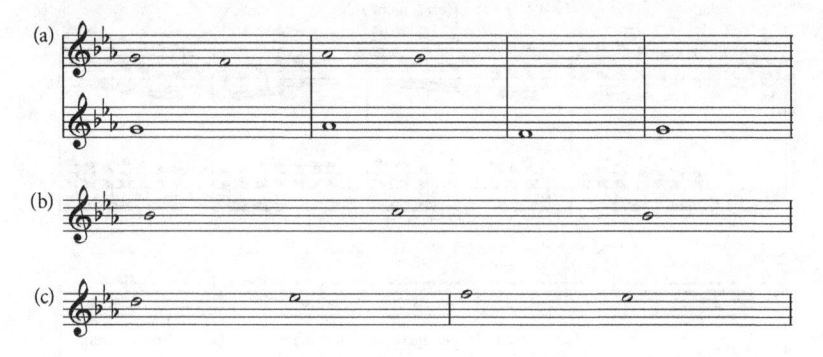

[musical examples (a), (b), (c)]

The climax of the phrase, the repeated tonic chords at bar 8, essentially repeats bar 1, but covered by higher pitches of the tonic triad (E♭s and B♭s).

In the first module, much of the interest in the G–F–A♭–G axial progression turns on the preparation and resolution of its main note of dissonance, the A flat, the song's Conian 'promissory note'. Its metrical placement is oddly syncopated, a dissonant passing note from the octave B♭s on the first beat, suspended for two whole bars to resolve to the G at bar 4 (the local resolution to the G at the very end of bar 2 is a feint, what Schenker would call a 'consonant passing note' within a V^7 harmony). The story of the A♭ in 'Im Freien' tells of its literal 'freeing' from the gravitational downward pull of the dominant harmony, particularly the underlying tritone A♭–D, which initially compels the note to descend to the G. Its eventual freedom is expressed by its capacity to rise to the B♭, transcending the pull of tonal forces.

B♭ is the midpoint of the *Steigerung* and occupies more than two bars (including the C neighbours which elaborate it), twice as long as the single bars dedicated to the $\hat{3}$–$\hat{4}$–$\hat{4}$–$\hat{3}$ steps. B♭ is thus the phrase's formal centre of gravity; it is extraordinary how many melodic snippets in the song are anacrusic steps or leaps to a strong B♭, beginning with the skip from G to B♭ across bars 1–2, which turns out to be seminal for later strains. A hypermetrical perspective on A♭ as spanning bars 2–4 (i.e. the A♭ set up at bar 2 arcing over bar 3 to resolve at bar 4) makes the note durationally almost equivalent to the B♭, suggesting that, at this middleground level, the A♭ actually rises, not falls. Certainly, A♭'s ambiguity (does it fall to G or rise to B♭?) compounds its problematic character, and it is one of the first things the voice takes up and explores. A hypermetrical reduction of bars 1–4 as an amphibrach (a prolongation of the short–long–short pattern of bar 2) reveals bars 5–6 to be a kind of metrical liquidation: the B♭–C–B figures project amphibrachs four times as fast, that is, condensing the four-bar pattern into single bars (Example 13.3).

Hence the phrase is capped and tailed by one-bar versions of the short–long–short pattern, with the four-bar expansion in the middle. If the one-bar amphibrachs are dubbed 'tonic' versions, and the fourfold expansion 'dominant', then the phrase's metre is axial by analogy to the melodic structure—a departure from and return to a metrical quasi-tonic.[12]

The apex of the introduction on the E♭ of bar 8 is fitting, as the melody attains the octave. Although the E♭s consign the original Gs of bar 1 to an inner voice, they will re-emerge at the true high points of the song on high G♮s (bars 54 and 97). The deeper question, however, is why, as is so common in Schubert's lieder, the melody drifts upwards, against the descending gravitational flow standard in theories of instrumental music. One can speculate that lyric song follows the propensity of conversational speech to rise, or that lieder instantiate Goethe's theory of poetic *Steigerung*.[13] The facts are, however, that the phrase is nudged upwards with lots of little implicative rising gestures: the left hand's initial octave leap is not innocent but implies future ascents to B♭ and E♭; the melody even breaks up into miniature $\hat{6}-\hat{5}-\hat{1}$ cadential figures articulating B♭ (G–F–B♭, bars 1–2), A♭ (F–E♭–A♭, bars 3–4), and E♭ (C–B♭–E♭, bars 5–7). Another explanation for *Steigerung* is that Schubert's ethos of repetition is committed to progressive intensification as the only possible way of keeping interest alive in the face of information redundancy.[14]

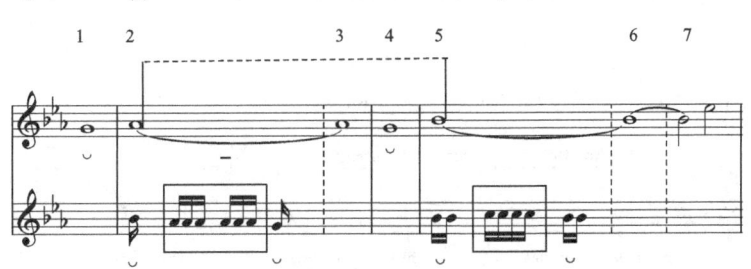

Example 13.3 Hypermetrical reduction of bars 1–7, amphibrachs at various levels

The piano introduction circumscribes the axial lyric space of the entire song. The architectural proportions of 'Im Freien' trace an almost perfect amphibrach. Thirty bars head and tail (bars 1–30, verses 1 and 2; bars 102–132, verse 8), framing a central sixty-two-bar episode (bars 31–101, verses 3–7) of virtually double their length: thirty bars (weak)–sixty-two bars (strong)–thirty bars (weak). The process of expansion begins with verse 1, which starts by mapping the introduction quite faithfully (bars 1–4 onto bars 9–12) before being derailed, as might be expected, by the recalcitrant A♭ of bar 13. This pitch instigates a different species of musical logic, independent of harmony, voice leading or phrase structure. A♭s fall on the first beats of bars 13, 15 and 17 at two-bar intervals, the last not resolving to a G (the melody rises to the E♭ at bar 18) but connecting across the cadence to the B♭ at bar 21, verse 3, which continues this pattern through the C of bar 23 and the D of bar 24 up to the E♭ of bar 25. The G–E♭ *Steigerung* of bars 1–8 is thus doubled in length to sixteen bars (bars 9–25) and staked out more forcefully in rising scale steps. In particular, the duration of the A♭ is quadrupled to eight bars (bars 13–20), creating a meta-amphibrach of 4–8–4: four bars of G, eight bars of A♭ and four bars squeezing in the rest of the scale.

The mini-scale F–G–A♭, unnoticed at the start (bars 2–3 and bar 11) gradually comes to the fore as a seed of the dominant tonicisation. Its expansion is similarly geometric: one bar's dominant seventh chord in verse 1 (bar 11), four bars' rise to a dominant half-close in verse 2 (bars 21–24) and sixteen bars' tonicising B♭ major in verse 3 (bars 31–47). This quadratic expansion ushers in a sea change towards countervailing compression, coinciding with the arrival of the new theme, which itself encapsulates the *Steigerung* as a disarmingly simple tune (bars 56–59). The liquidation of the G–A♭–B♭ ascent (bars 56–57), each step a crotchet apart, into semiquavers at the end of the tune (bars 57–58) nails down its derivation from the innocent-seeming F–G–B♭ skip of the song's incipit (bars 1–2) (Example 13.4).

Note that the liquidation of crotchets into semiquavers takes the quadratic progression into reverse gear. The arpeggiated expansiveness of this tune, however, measures the distance travelled from the song's opening along the *Steigerung*'s ascent from crabbed axial motion to melodic freedom. The tune is reiterated in the keys of B♭ and A♭.

Part of the song's beguiling subtlety is that it distributes its climax across three separate high points. Technically, the very highest notes in the song are

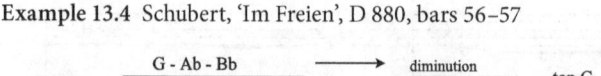

Example 13.4 Schubert, 'Im Freien', D 880, bars 56–57

the piano octaves at the end of the middle-section, which touch 'c⁴ Heaven' at bars 83 and 87 (Example 13.5).

This climax occurs in the subdominant and is the apotheosis of A♭ in 'Im Freien'. It upstages the top E♭s (e♭²) of the song's da capo, which themselves add nothing new to the *Steigerung*, having been anticipated at many earlier points, including the end of part 1 (bar 25), and indeed the cadential $\hat{3}-\hat{2}-\hat{1}$ descents from the G (g⁴) above at bars 54–55 (the tonic episode of the middle section). The song's major climax, and arguably its affective high point, is the retransition on the dominant pedal, bars 92–101 (verse 7). Its force is due to the

Example 13.5 Schubert, 'Im Freien', D 880, climax

Example 13.5 Continued

wrench from A♭ major to V of E♭, pivoting on the tritone A♭–D♮ at bar 91, the crux of a vertiginous descent of nearly two octaves from the top C (c⁴). The D rudely transforms the tonicised A♭ at bar 92 into a seventh of B♭ and is itself pushed up by the expressively marked A♭–D tritone, a final step to its E♭ home.

The subdominant–dominant wrench dramatises the central tonal issue of 'Im Freien', the rising step from A♭ to B♭. Moreover, the $\hat{6}-\hat{7}-\hat{8}$ scale-step progression across bars 81–102 (supported by the A♭–B♭–E♭ harmonic progression) massively expands the C–D–E♭ climax of the song's opening section, bars 23–25, on which it is modelled (i.e. from two bars to twenty-two). Comparing the D steps of bar 24 with its expansion across bars 93–101 reveals the exquisitely subtle changes which transform the retransition into a variant of the song's opening bar. Schubert doubles the length of the suspension to a crotchet (an extra semiquaver E♭ either side of the bar line), gives the piano Gs rather than parallel octave E♭s, approaches the suspension via a tonic rather than a secondary dominant and re-introduces the leap between the left hand's bass and repeated-chords filler, a constant throughout the song yet conspicuously neutralised at bar 24. The whole of 'Im Freien' is enveloped in a web of similarly microscopic nuance, wherein the genius of Schubert's deceptive simplicity runs its seamless and analytically elusive course. In this particular instance, its object is to disclose an aspect of the opening bar which had remained hidden in full sight: turned against the moonlight, as it were, 'wohin ein Strahl nur sinkt', the repeated tonic chords of bar 1 can be heard as suspensions against the penultimate dominant chord (with the final semiquaver taken as a consonant passing chord rather than a tonic resolution). The poet-composer revisits his home to find it 'unheimlich', uncanny, as has been shown of Schubert's other late returns, although more softly so in 'Im Freien' than, say, in the B♭ Piano Sonata.[15]

In the context of 'Im Freien''s axial lyric journey, the lovingly repeated E♭–D gestures, elaborated into a full turn figure, D–E♮–F–D–E♭, at bars 94–95 and with a climactic leap to high G at bar 97, serve to project the octave goal of its *Steigerung* ascent. We have seen this octave rise at hierarchically ascending levels of the song: those of the piano introduction, the song's first part (bars 1–25), and finally the architecture.

Before we turn to 'Der Winterabend', we should draw some interim conclusions about what is meant by 'axial'. The song is not axial in the sense of melodic patterns circling its axis G equally in both directions because, as we have seen, it is dominated by progressions in a single direction: ascents from the G, arpeggiating the tonic towards an apex on a top E♭. Rather, 'Im Freien' is axial in the following three respects. (1) The musical materials circle each scale-step staging post of the arpeggio ascent in turn—G, B♭ and E♭. 'Im Freien' actually extends a third higher, to a G an octave above its starting point (g^2). The reason for interpreting the goal of the *Steigerung* as $e♭^2$ rather than g^2 is because these Gs (bars 54, 58 and 97) are no longer axial centres, being redirected downwards to E♭ as $\hat{3}-\hat{2}-\hat{1}$ cadential resolutions. (2) The song's overall trajectory is to *escape* the axial constraints of its opening, both by rising (as opposed to circling) and by unfurling its melodic wings into more expansive gestures. Escape is also harmonic, as in A♭'s freeing from the original gravitational pull down to G, effected by the (implied) tritone D♮ component of the

V⁷ chord. (3) The song's dominant and subdominant harmonies circle the tonic, a mild, quasi-diatonic equivalent of the tertial polarities elsewhere in Schubert's music. The counterpoise of fifths either side of E♭ (B♭ major up, A♭ major down) is grandest at the song's sixty-two-bar middle section, with its key progression B♭–E♭–B♭–A♭ (with a short tonic return at bars 77–80 mediating between dominant and subdominant). The subdominant key is particularly prominent, and indeed is given the song's registral climax, the top Cs of verse 6. One doesn't wish to use the word 'problematising' for such an emollient song. Nevertheless, those top Cs shadow the 'proper' E♭ vocal apex at the end of the song like a lunar penumbra, just as there is something uncanny about the melodic A♭ rise to B♭, in defiance of the gravitational pull of V⁷. The greatest mystery of all, so strangely almost ignored in the literature, is why the lyric voice (in song and instrumental music alike) should want to rise at all. Voice and piano levitate, as it were, *in Freiheit*.

'Der Winterabend'

'Der Winterabend' sets a poem by Karl Gottfried von Leitner. The sun has set, and an old man sits silently in his darkening house by the window. All is quiet and secluded, and then the moonlight steps softly into his room and 'takes up his work, the spindle, the gold, and spins and weeps silently, smiling sweetly'. The man turns to gaze out of his window at the clouds and stars, 'thinking back to long, long ago, to a beautiful vanished past'. He 'thinks of her, of love's happiness and sigh[s] softly and muse[s]'. The piano introduction sets up a texture of relentless chord repetitions similar to 'Im Freien', except that over it Schubert lays a real melody, characterised by note repetitions at a slower metrical stream (Example 13.6).

Youens hears its dotted rhythms as reminiscent of 'Das Zügenglocklein', where the repeated notes evoke the tolling of a funerary bell.[16] 'Der Winterabend' is celebrated, when it is discussed at all, for the luminous tonal changes the moon effects at its entrance, particularly the enchanting common-tone modulation from G major to E♭ major (Example 13.7).

Pivoting on a shared G♮ and contrary-motion semitone slides from B♮ to B♭ and from D to E♭, the neo-Riemannian transformation is par for the course in current theory, as is the song's tonal architecture. 'Der Winterabend' tilts towards keys a third above and below its B♭ tonic: D major and G major. The song breathes the same air as the B♭ Piano Sonata, whose first movement explores *flat* versions of those keys, G♭ major/F♯ minor and D♭ major/C♯ minor. The middle section of 'Der Winterabend' intercalates the keys of G and D within a descending-third cycle of B♭ major–G major–E♭ major–C minor, with D integrated as V of G (Example 13.8).

Axial Lyric Space in Two Late Songs

Example 13.6 Schubert, 'Der Winterabend', D 938, bars 1–9

A tonal chart of this middle section shows that the song is actually far more invested in G than in D. Unlike the G and E♭ major episodes, D major is never tonicised via a V–I cadence (C minor is even weaker, only passing). On the contrary, the D major passage itself (bars 56–60) serves as a dominant to the middle section's G major conclusion, making good on how the interlude had originally slipped from B♭ to G *without* a dominant pivot (at bar 31 Schubert slides directly from a B♭ triad to a G major triad via repeated D♮ common tones). There is a sense, then, that G major is progressively established throughout the song along its lyric trajectory.

Example 13.6 Continued

Thus the chief interest lies not in these—for Schubert—routine key progressions in themselves, but in the role they play within the song's axial lyric space. Unlike that of 'Im Freien', the melodic axis of 'Der Winterabend' is the tonic rather than the mediant. Another difference to the earlier song is that its melody meanders more below this axis than above it, the axial motion encapsulated in two complementary falling and rising third progressions in the piano introduction, $\hat{3}-\hat{2}-\hat{1}$ and $\hat{6}-\hat{7}-\hat{8}$, with the latter gradually eclipsing the former. These differences are in part a function of sheer vocal range, consequent on key. 'Der Winterabend' is placed a fifth above E♭, the tonic of 'Im Freien', putting its top B♭ octave (and certainly the D above that) out of range. The falling and rising axial progressions are both remarkable, and I shall consider each in turn.

'Im Winterabend' takes its impetus from the jarring B♮ quaver in its opening bar, a textbook instance of a Conian promissory note. It is easy to hear it pulling towards C minor, a harmony which is realised in passing at bar 4 and more fully at bars 16–17. However, in the first instance the B leapfrogs over the expected C to a D which forms a pungent dissonance against the V^7 harmony. Because of its placement between the D and the B♭, the C at bar 2 makes equal

Example 13.7 Schubert, 'Der Winterabend', D 938, bars 37–43

Example 13.8 Schubert, 'Der Winterabend', D 938, tonal architecture

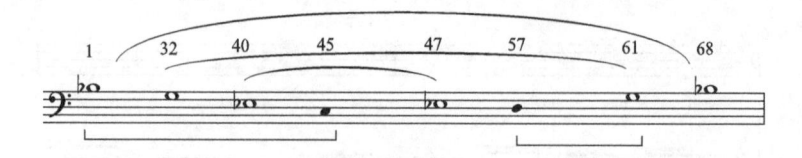

sense as a delayed resolution of the B♮ and as a passing note between D and B♭, its tonic third progression out of kilter with the left hand's dominant harmony. The B♮ thus discharges both up (to C) and down (to B♭). Discharging a semitone down to B♭, it mirrors the leading-note A–B♭ resolution in a focal B–B♭–A–B♭ progression.

In the face of this generative chromatic event, the melody makes three attempts to descend from D to the tonic. The first attempt, at bar 1, as we have seen, is stymied because both the D and the B♭ jar against the V⁷ harmony. The second attempt at bar 4 goes further awry, the D subsumed as a passing note within a descending third from the neighbour note E♭ and the B♭ naturalised. The third time being a charm, bar 5 supplies a consonant $\hat{3}-\hat{2}-\hat{1}$ as part of the cadence (the consonance of the D compromised by the I⁶₄ harmony).

Countervailing the descent from $\hat{3}$ is a rising progression initiated by the G at bar 3 and continued two beats later by the A. Its B♭ resolution is delayed until bar 5 by the C minor parenthesis of bar 4, and interrupted in particular by the B♮. These three pitches, A, B♮ and B♭, are placed at four-crotchet intervals, creating a striking hypermetrical cross-rhythm to the phrase—indeed, a hypermetrical expansion of the 'focal' A–B–B♭ axial progression of bars 1–2 (Example 13.9).

The two axial progressions reveal their secrets over the course of the song, 'above' and 'below' the B♭ axis. 'Above' the axis, the melody is initially capped at E♭. At the climactic phrase of the da capo (bar 85), the B♭ repetitions are replaced by an ecstatic descent from a high F, the song's high point (Example 13.10).

That this high point is only one note above the original limit, the E♭, may be thought to be disappointing, compared, say, with the much more expansive ascent in 'Im Freien'. But that tells us something important about 'Der Winterabend'—that most of its progress occurs 'from below', in the unfurling of the third-below cadence, $\hat{6}-\hat{7}-\hat{8}$. Only hinted at in the introduction (frustrated by the B of bar 4), it comes to the fore in the voice's first cadence (bar 9) and is elaborated at many later points, including the singer's last major cadence (bars 90–91), sometimes with octave displacement (bars 13, 38, 64 and 71). These $\hat{6}-\hat{7}-\hat{8}$ ascents emerge most forcefully in the song's central episode in G and E♭ major (bars 37–38, 42–43 and 47–50) in the context of a distinctive

Example 13.9 Hypermetrical axial progression, bars 3–5

Example 13.10 Schubert, 'Der Winterabend', D 938, bars 85–96

Example 13.10 Continued

new idea based on upwardly striding scales, climbing from scale step 4 to 8 (see again Example 13.7). It is in the nature of the song's tonal design that rising to a high tonic is impossible in its home key but achievable in its central keys of G and E♭—or, more specifically, in E♭ major alone. The ascent to a top G at bar 38 turns back at the last moment, after the high E♮, to an octave-displaced 7–8. By contrast, the rise to the top E♭ five bars later (bar 43) is attained quite comfortably.

The tonal correlatives of the two axial progressions are the triads of D and G major. The harmonies and keys of D and G figure powerfully later in the song, displacing the C minor shadows of its opening: the Cohnian *Tonnetz* displaces the Conian promissory note, as it were. It is fascinating to see how this development is already suggested within the piano introduction. The diminished seventh chord formed by the B♮ of bar 1 is functionally a G⁷; the D at bar 2 briefly, yet tellingly, makes a D minor chord with the left hand's F and A, a fraction of a beat before the E♭ semiquaver comes in. Hence the G and D chords, the 'destiny' of the song, are implicit at its outset. The sublation of one harmonic logic by another is encapsulated by directly comparing the voice's first line (bars 5–9), a subtly 'squarer' version of the introduction, with its transfigured version at the song's climax (bars 85ff.). Stretched from four bars to seven (with a five-bar appendix taking it to twelve bars), the expansion pivots on cancelling the passing B♮, transforming the V⁷ into an F♯ diminished seventh chord (a functional analogue of a D major chord) and leading into a transmutation of the B♭ tonic triad into a triad of G major. In short, mapping between the two phrases, it is transparently clear that G is a substitution for B♭.

The eclipse of C minor by the axial keys of G and D major reflects back on our understanding of the refractory B♮. The 'story' of 'Der Winterabend' partly tells of the cancelling of B's obligation to resolve up to C, commuting the logic of the song from tonal pitch space to (presumably) a neo-Riemannian *Tonnetz*, from the sublunary to the transcendental. From an axial perspective, this shift involves a reorientation of the B♮'s obligations downwards, where the B♮–B♭ motion complements the leading-note-to-tonic resolution (B–B♭–A–B♭). The latter part of the song becomes increasingly permeated with harmonic excuses for direct B♮–B♭ motions: for example, from a G major triad, as V of C minor, to a G minor chord (bars 45–46, repeated at bars 52–53 and bars 54–55, Schubert making a point of it); the retransition itself pivots on a G major–G minor progression (bar 66). To appreciate fully the dramatic force of this reorientation, let us consider the climax of the song in all its hermeneutic glory.

Like 'Im Freien', 'Der Winterabend' constantly revisits its opening material from shifting angles and in changing light, culminating in one of the most breathtaking revelations in all of Schubert. The poem's final couplet, to which the song dedicates nearly thirty bars (bars 78–96), discloses the prime mover of the entire cycle of reflections to be the old man's lost love: 'Denk an Sie, and das Glück der Minne, seufze still und sinne'. Setting these words, Schubert reconstitutes the original melody as a two-part counterpoint, one strand of which is the *Rosamunde* motive (shared by the B♭ Impromptu, D 935 No. 7, in the same key). This 'secret melody' is so simple, so intrinsic to the basics of the B♭ harmony, that it seems to have been there all along, requiring only reflection—*sinnen*—to bring it out. The object, as well as the medium, of this reflection is the extraordinarily protracted B♮s over a G major harmony in bars 80–81 (repeated in bars 88–89). These chords shine brightly and are as much marked for our consciousness as they are representations of the man's. Eventually, they do discharge diatonically; but to focus on the B♭'s conventional resolution up to C at bar 82 (recruiting D and G major into a routine III–VI–II–V–I circle-of-fifths return home) is to miss the force by which the G and D chords are momentarily coaxed out of time and inspected as objects in themselves. The parallel, even more radical moment of reflection comes in the voiceless postlude, with its stark juxtaposition of D and B♭ triads. F♯ is shorn of any obligation to resolve upwards to G. The tonal emancipation of these mediant and submediant triads is analogous to what we saw in 'Im Freien', when A♭ was freed from the pull of musical gravity. And as in the earlier song, their emancipation is transitive with respect to axial preoccupations within the piano introduction.

Conclusion

Two interesting aspects of Schubert's style get lost amidst the furore over his tertial harmony: the axial tendencies of his music and its proclivity to rise. These facets are under-explored, and it is hoped that the present chapter brings more attention to them. 'Im Freien' and 'Der Winterabend' indicate that, melodically and tonally, Schubert's axial progressions can be asymmetrical in these songs' respective emphasis on ascending line and subdominant harmony (the fifth below the tonic) and on $\hat{6}-\hat{7}-\hat{8}$ progressions and the submediant key (the third below the tonic). It is vital to integrate these melodic and tonal dimensions within the same analysis, because too often Schubert's harmonic practice is uprooted from the fabric of his style. Broadening the purview yet further, the songs show that melodic and tonal axial processes are themselves symptoms of Schubert's general sensibility to balance. Thus the ebb and flow between geometrically expanding and contracting metrical transformations in 'Im Freien', as well as the 30–62–30 dimensions of its architecture, are axial in the broadest sense. Similarly, the interlude in 'Der Winterabend', where rising scales are finally given free rein, is framed 'axially' by the tonic sections of the song where the melody is reined back around B♭. It is 'para-axial', so to speak. 'Der Winterabend' is also fascinating because its profiled $\hat{6}-\hat{7}-\hat{8}$ cadences traverse a notorious seam in music theory. That is, music theorists have never convincingly demonstrated that scale step $\hat{6}$ is permitted to resolve upwards to $\hat{7}$, against its more normative tendency to discharge down to 5.[17] Schubert loves $\hat{6}-\hat{7}-\hat{8}$ cadences (see 'An die Musik', for instance), and their very underdetermination could be heard as the gravity-defying booster rocket of lyrical *Steigerung*.

The deepest arbiters of Schubert's axial lyric space are tonal choice, consequent on register and text hermeneutics. The 'fate' of the song depends on the selection of tonic or mediant (or even dominant, in songs such as 'Trockne Blumen')[18] as axis, and on its key relative to the singer's vocal range. 'Im Freien' is centrifugal, rising away from the initial axis, because it is set out-of-doors. 'Der Winterabend' is centripetal, its *Steigerung* rising from the depths below, because it is placed inside a house and expresses profound interiority, akin to Rembrandt's famous painting *The Philosopher*.

Notes

1. Hyperion released the set of forty CDs in 1995. Featuring a galaxy of singers, the two constants are Johnson's piano accompaniment and scholarship.

2. See, for instance, 'Orest auf Tauris', which features in Suzannah Clark's recent *Analyzing Schubert* (Cambridge: Cambridge University Press, 2012). In devoting thirty pages to 'Ganymed', partly as a response to Lawrence Kramer, Clark perpetuates what could be called an 'analysis tradition' of this song.

3. Clark makes the metaphorical comparison between lenses and analytical and ideological systems of reception. See my review-article, 'Of Telescopes and Lenses, Blindness and Insight', *Journal of the Royal Musical Association* 138/2 (2013), pp. 415–29. A celebrated article which has emerged as a classic exposition of the neo-Riemannian case for Schubert is Richard Cohn, 'As Wonderful as Star Clusters: Instruments for Gazing at Tonality in Schubert', *19th-Century Music* 22/3 (1999), pp. 213–32.

4. Clark, *Analyzing Schubert*, pp. 226–8.

5. See Fred Lerdahl, *Tonal Pitch Space* (New York: Oxford University Press, 2004).

6. Clark, *Analyzing Schubert*, pp. 100–5.

7. Leonard B. Meyer, *Explaining Music: Essays and Explorations* (Chicago: University of Chicago Press, 1973), pp. 183–91.

8. See Daniel Harrison, *Harmonic Function in Chromatic Music* (Chicago: University of Chicago Press, 1994).

9. See my 'Notes on Beethoven's Late Style', in Gordon McMullan (ed.), *Late Style and its Discontents* (New York: Oxford University Press, 2016). The essays in McMullan's collection give a useful overview of 'lateness' in many of the arts, including music.

10. Goethe's immensely influential concept of *Steigerung*, derived as much from his colour theory as his poetics, blends notions of intensification and ascent with cyclical return (revisiting and transforming the starting point from a 'higher' perspective). See my *Metaphor and Musical Thought* (Chicago: University of Chicago Press, 2004), pp. 294–5. For *Steigerung* in Schubert's 'Trockne Blumen', see my 'Sad Flowers: Affective Trajectories in Schubert's "Trockne Blumen"', in Tom Cochrane, Bernardino Fantini, and Klaus R. Scherer (eds), *The Emotional Power of Music: Multidisciplinary Perspectives on Musical Arousal, Expression, and Social Control* (Oxford: Oxford University Press), pp. 7–22.

11. For the notion of 'promissory note', a salient or troublesome pitch introduced early on which gradually increases in significance, see Edward T. Cone,

'Schubert's Promissory Note: an Exercise in Musical Hermeneutics', in Walther Frisch (ed.), *Schubert: Critical and Analytical Studies* (Lincoln: University of Nebraska Press, 1986), pp. 13–30.

12. For quasi-tonic/dominant analogies between pitch and metre building on David Lewin's and Richard Cohn's theories, see Scott Murphy, 'On Metre in the Rondo of Brahms's Op. 25', *Music Analysis* 26/3 (October 2007), pp. 323–53.

13. Spitzer, *Metaphor and Musical Thought*, p. 295.

14. Spitzer, 'Of Telescopes and Lenses'. For a fresh exploration of related issues, see Elizabeth Hellmuth Margulis, *On Repeat: How Music Plays the Mind* (New York: Oxford University Press). See, for instance, Margulis's waveform visualisations of performances of the main theme on each of its recurrences during Sokolov's performance of Chopin's Polonaise in A major, Op. 40 No. 1, showing how the pianist endows the repetitions of the theme with a sense of progression.

15. See Nicholas Marston, 'Schubert's Homecoming', *Journal of the Royal Musical Association* 125 (2000), p. 248; and Spitzer, *Metaphor and Musical Thought*, p. 70.

16. Susan Youens, *Schubert's Late Lieder: Beyond the Song-Cycles* (Cambridge: Cambridge University Press, 2006), p. 294.

17. See Harrison, *Harmonic Function in Chromatic Music*, pp. 93–96. According to him, 'music theorists in the function-theory tradition have always felt some roughness in the melodic connection of these two scale degrees [$\hat{6}$ and $\hat{7}$] even when separated by a whole tone' (p. 93).

18. See Spitzer, 'Of Telescopes and Lenses'.

14

Schubert through a Neo-Riemannian Lens

Suzannah Clark[1]

On 24 June 1824, an anonymous review of four books of Schubert's songs appeared in the Leipzig *Allgemeine musikalische Zeitung*. The reviewer, thought to be Gottfried Wilhelm Fink, explained that 'with the fresh courage of youth, [Schubert] disdains the old, well-trodden ways and clears a new path'. He accused Schubert of being uninterested in writing songs (*Lieder*) 'properly speaking' and of preferring instead to compose 'free vocal pieces [*Gesänge*], some so free that they might possibly be called caprices or fantasies'.[2] Yet, in an aside, Fink identified no fewer than six out of the eleven of the songs he was reviewing as coming 'more or less near' to being 'songs, properly speaking'. Schubert's 'Schwanengesang' ('Wie klag' ich's aus'), D 744, was amongst them.

In this essay, I will focus on 'Schwanengesang' in order to illustrate what neo-Riemannian theory brings to the analytical table. To choose a song that falls into Fink's category of conventional song may seem like an unpromising starting point for an essay on a novel analytical system that purports to elucidate those passages that elude conventional diatonic theory. Yet, as I shall argue, it was certain diatonic signposts in this song, coupled with obvious structural points of repetition, which undoubtedly drew Fink's attention to its strophic quality—signposts that belie the striking harmonic and formal metamorphosis that the apparent strophic repetitions go through. Indeed Fink, who was no fan of novelty, was perhaps all too eager to see conventional traits in Schubert's work. The conventional aspects of 'Schwanengesang' are, I will contend, best highlighted through a Schenkerian lens. Yet looked at another way—with the aid of a neo-Riemannian lens—Schubert's rich harmonic tapestry reveals the 'fresh courage of youth' and the 'new paths' that he clears through tonal space.[3]

The text of 'Schwanengesang' is by Johann Chrysostomus Senn (1795-1857), who was a school friend of Schubert's. He, Schubert and two others in the Schubertian circle were arrested on 20 January 1820 on suspicion of political activities against the State. Senn spent fourteen months in jail awaiting trial and was eventually exiled from Vienna, although he was never actually charged with a crime.[4] Franz von Bruchmann (1798-1867), one of the four arrested on that fateful night, visited Senn in Innsbruck in September 1822 and is thought to have returned with at least two poems written by Senn for Schubert. In 1823 Schubert published his settings of 'Selige Welt' (D 743) and 'Schwanengesang' as Op. 23.[5] 'Selige Welt' was also listed by Fink in the category of 'songs, properly speaking'. Its form is the familiar ABA', with striking modulations that Fink nonetheless deemed 'mild and therefore praiseworthy'.[6] Intriguingly, 'Selige Welt' and 'Schwanengesang' share many of the same modulations, although Fink made no specific comments on the harmony of the latter. While I would not necessarily wish to attribute to Schubert political cunning in the shaping of these particular musical settings, if the censors possessed anything like the musical sensibilities of Gottfried Fink, it would have been advantageous if they too saw the old, rather than the boldly new, in 'Selige Welt' and 'Schwanengesang'.

Table 14.1 reproduces the layout of 'Schwanengesang', as published in Senn's *Gedichte*.[7] Clearly he imagined it to be a strophic song of three stanzas and a one-line envoy. Senn's strophic conception is further underscored by the fact that the poem is entitled 'Schwanen*lied*' in his *Gedichte*, despite the envoy's declaring that 'Das ist des Schwanen *Gesang*!' It is generally agreed that in the early nineteenth century *Lied* meant strophic song and *Gesang* meant non-strophic song, a distinction that Fink made in his review. As Marie-Agnes Dittrich explains: 'During [Schubert's] day, the word "Lied" invariably implied a strophic song in which deliberate simplicity—both textual and musical—guaranteed tuneful primacy. In support of this, the text's regular meter is matched by the music's symmetrical form, almost always major-key harmonies, and, if accompanied at all, is done so with a minimum of fuss'.[8] More elaborate settings were called 'Gesänge', 'Balladen' or 'Kantaten'. At first glance, both Senn and Schubert seem to adhere to this aesthetic of the lied in 'Schwanengesang', but on closer inspection they each undermine it in subtly

Table 14.1 Text of 'Schwanengesang' as it appeared in Senn's *Gedichte*

	Schwanenlied		
1	'Wie klag' ich's aus	a	4
2	Das Sterbegefühl,	b	5
3	Das auflösend	c	4
4	Durch die Glieder rinnt?	d	5
5	Wie sing' ich aus	a	4
6	Das Werdegefühl,	b	5
7	Das erlösend	c	4
8	Dich, o Geist, anweht?'	d'	5
9	Es klagt', es sang	e	4
10	Vernichtungsbang,	e	4
11	Verklärungsfroh,	f	4
12	Bis das Leben floh.	f	5
13	Das ist des Schwanen Gesang!	e	7

different ways. In particular, the differences in their treatment of strophic form has profound implications for their contrasting hermeneutics of song.

If Senn's quatrains give off an air of strophic simplicity, the internal structure of each stanza reveals a more complex construction. First, the presence of a song within a song separates out the first two stanzas from the rest. Secondly, the word repetitions and syntactical parallelisms between the first two stanzas are not present in the narrator's commentary. Observe that the swan's song comprises two questions, each with a similar syntax and syllable count, and plenty of word repetition. In particular, each question opens with the same clause, albeit contrasting 'klagen' and 'singen', which is followed by a noun ending in '-gefühl'. Only the last line of each stanza breaks any sense of a pattern, although there is alliteration in 'durch' and 'dich' and 'Glieder' and 'Geist'. The swan's song itself is beautifully structured to be strophic.

The narrator's commentary begins at line 9; observe the shift from 'ich' to 'es' and the shift from the present to the past tense ('wie klag', 'wie sing' to 'er klagt', er sang').[9] The juxtaposition of 'Vernichtungsbang' (fearful of extinction) and 'Verklärungsfroh' (joyously awaiting transfiguration) in lines 10 and 11 turns the narrator's stanza inwards to a more palindromic structure. Again, the alliteration compounds the effect. Additionally, both words are four syllables; this may seem like a small detail, but the arrival of the four-syllable 'Vernichtungsbang' in line 10 breaks the alternating syllable count, 4–5–4–5, established in the first two stanzas, producing instead a 4–4–4–5 pattern (see Table 14.1). In many ways, then, Senn's third stanza breaks the strophic model set up in the first two stanzas. As we shall see, Schubert exploits this seemingly insignificant detail—and the moment will be suitably neo-Riemannian.

What about the envoy? Senn's seven-syllable line is awkward. Its irregular length and meter do not ensure 'deliberate simplicity'; furthermore, they make it difficult for the composer to fit them to music of the earlier stanzas. Perhaps this is why Schubert's setting has another textual variant here: instead of Senn's 'Das ist des Schwanen Gesang!' Schubert has 'Das bedeutet des Schwanen Gesang!' The adjustment is deft.[10] Significantly, now that the line is nine syllables long, it could be sung to the same music as, say, the first two lines of the first stanza, thus providing a shortened reprise to round off the song. Curiously, Schubert does not exploit this potential. Nor, for that matter, does he exploit much else of the strophic potential offered by Senn's poem in Table 14.1. Why?

Schubert ignores both the series of quatrains and Senn's ready-made strophic pairing of lines 1 and 5, 2 and 6, 3 and 7, and 4 and 8 of the swan's song. He does nonetheless craft a strophic song out of another configuration of Senn's text, one which emphasises the shift from the swan's song to the narrator's voice. A visual representation of the text according to Schubert's modified strophic form is given in Table 14.2: the whole of the swan's song is one stanza,

Table 14.2 Layout of text of 'Schwanengesang' according to Schubert's musical form; translation adapted from Wigmore (2005).

1	'Wie klag' ich's aus, das Sterbegefühl,	a	9		'How shall I lament the presentiment of death,
2	Das auflösend durch die Glieder rinnt?	b	9		The dissolution that flows through my limbs?
3	Wie sing' ich aus, das Werdegefühl,	a	9		How shall I sing of the feeling of new life
4	Das erlösend dich, o Geist, anweht?'	c	9		That redeems you with its breath, O spirit?'
5	Er klagt', er sang,	d	4		He lamented, he sang,
6	Vernichtungsbang,	d	4		Fearful of extinction,
7	Verklärungsfroh,	e	4		Joyously awaiting transfiguration,
8	Bis das Leben floh.	e	5		Until life fled.
9	Das bedeutet des Schwanen Gesang!	d	9		That is the meaning of the swan's song!

and the commentary on it is a highly compressed second stanza. The final line is a separate musical and textual envoy.[11]

How, then, does Schubert cloak this text in music? The song begins with a four-bar prelude, divided into 1 + 1 + 2 bars. As shown in Example 14.1, each of the opening two bars articulates tonic-to-dominant harmony in A♭ minor and A♭ major respectively—a surprising order of the modes given that the key signature is major. The final prelude ends an inconclusive imperfect authentic cadence (IAC) in A♭ major; that is, with $\hat{3}$ (E♭) over the tonic in the upper voice.[12] The prelude is also characterised by an ominous long–short–short–long–long rhythm that Schubert tends to use to represent death.[13] Modal mixture, the IAC cadence and the $\hat{E}$♭ it highlights, as well as the ominous rhythm, will permeate this song.

The voice enters with the $\hat{E}$♭ just heard in the IAC cadence, but the harmony reverts to A♭ minor. The first stanza occupies eight bars, divided into 2 + 2 + 2 + 2, each of which tonicises a different harmonic station: A♭ minor, C♭ major, A♭ major and E♭ major respectively. The differences in detail of both the openings and cadences in each phrase are important. The first two bars of the vocal line open with a clear A♭ minor arpeggio that seemingly overextends itself by breaking the steady 1 + 1 + 2 phrase structure of the prelude. This phrase concludes with an IAC in A♭ minor, with $\hat{C}$♭ in the upper voice (bar 6). The next phrase is in C♭ major. While the key changes, the voice maintains a common tone over the boundary of the phrase. The

Schubert through a Neo-Riemannian Lens 279

Example 14.1 Annotated score of Schubert's 'Schwanengesang', D 744

[musical score]

C♭ that was just heard as $\hat{3}$ of A♭ minor becomes $\hat{1}$ of C♭ major. It is accompanied by a I⁶ harmony, which yields a voice exchange between the outer voices when the IAC arrives with E♭ ($\hat{3}$ of C♭ major) in the vocal line at the end of bar 8. Once again the vocal line holds on to the E♭ common tone in bar 9, but the accompaniment provides a vertical sonority comprising only the interval

Example 14.1 Continued

C♮–E♭. Is the interval part of a C minor or an A♭ major harmony? As we shall see, neo-Riemannian theory is especially well equipped to help us digest this moment, as well as the two other times this interval features in this song (bars 11 and 17). For now, I shall presume it belongs to an A♭ major triad, an assumption that is confirmed when this phrase concludes with an IAC cadence in A♭ major. However, throughout this phrase an $\hat{E}♭$ is stubbornly repeated in the bass, denying A♭ major a proper tonic function; the tonic of the IAC in bar 10 appears in the unusual $^6_4$ position with $\hat{C}$ ($\hat{3}$) in the upper voice. The fourth and final phrase of the first stanza repeats the interval $\hat{C}$-$\hat{E}♭$, this time dropping the $\hat{E}♭$ in the bass. This is the first time a common tone is not held over the bar line to begin a new phrase; instead, the outer voices engage in voice exchange. Again one may wonder whether the interval implies a C minor or an A♭ major harmony. Although the latter provides no harmonic movement across the bar line, it seems the logical choice in the context of the final phrase, which leads to a large-scale half cadence (HC) in A♭.

The HC feels like a Schenkerian interruption yearning for a reprise, and for an answer to the swan's question. The reprise ensues, but it holds no answers, for it is nothing more than the narrator's ear- and eyewitness account of the dying swan. The shift in the text from 'ich' to 'er' and from the present to the past tense is reflected in the music. Observe the temporal shift of the entrance of the vocal line, which now enters on the up- rather than the downbeat—it is like a shift in perspective. The ominous death rhythm is now left to the piano in bar 14. There are additional variations in the vocal line of this phrase: it ends on $\hat{1}$, simulating a PAC, while leaving the piano to effect the IAC. The real recomposition of the first stanza begins with the next phrase (bar 15^4). Responding no doubt to the juxtaposition of the words 'Vernichtungsbang' and 'Verklärungsfroh', Schubert transposes a fragment of the first phrase up a minor third (see the material in the two boxes in Example 14.1). This transposition also takes advantage of the errant syllable count mentioned above. 'Vernichtungsbang', which in order to continue the alternating 5–4 syllable pattern established in lines 1–8 ought to have been five syllables, can be musically matched by the expected four-syllable 'Verklärungsfroh'.

Indeed, the material within the two boxes stands out as the only music in the song that is repeated exactly, albeit in transposition. As a direct transposition, it breaks the pattern of harmonic unfolding established by the swan's song, even though the parallel passage in the first stanza (bars 5–8) also goes from A♭ minor to C♭ major. It is fitting that this moment involves a neo-Riemannian transformation unlike any of the others in the song. Although the transformation from the A♭ minor of 'Vernichtungs*bang*' to the C♭ major of '*Ver*klärungsfroh' involves R, the whole of the boxed material exhibits what Julian Hook coined a 'signature transformation'. As a diatonic transposition operating in a mod-7 environment, it is labelled t_3.[14] The break in the strophic repetition portrays a narrator who, unable to replicate the swan's song, is revealed to be an unreliable earwitness. Perhaps, however, the direct transposition from minor (the sadness of the lament) to major (the joy of transfiguration) marks the moment the narrator is eyewitness to the swan's transfiguration. To hear how this might be the case, we must attend to additional details in bar 12.

Although globally it is an HC to A♭ major, locally the cadence is a perfect authentic cadence (PAC) in E♭ major, with $\hat{E}♭$ in the upper voice. This interruption does not attain the quintessential $\hat{2}/V$ with $\hat{B}♭$ in the upper voice. Schenker has a provision for the salient $\hat{E}♭$, however. As explained in *Free Composition* and shown in Example 14.2, which is modelled on his concept, the *Urlinie* still descends to $\hat{2}$, but the outer-voice $\hat{5}$ is an 'upward register transfer of the octave at $\hat{2}/V$'.[15] The Schenkerian slur extends from the end of the swan's song to the retaking of the primary tone $\hat{5}$ in bar 17. With the swan's final note continuing to haunt the atmosphere, the narrator begins his narration, only to witness (in bars 15–16) the swan's death. Jolted by the realisation of what he is seeing, the narrator takes up the $\hat{E}♭$ that has hung in the air since the swan's final note and brings the *Urlinie* to a close on $\hat{1}/I$ with the words 'until life departed'.

The PAC into bar 18 brings about the strongest sense of closure in the whole song. However, the material immediately following it seems less the start of a coda than an echo of the cadence that sets up yet another structural dominant. With its quintessential voice leading $\hat{2}/V$, it has all the hallmarks of an

Example 14.2 A Schenkerian reading of 'Schwanengesang'

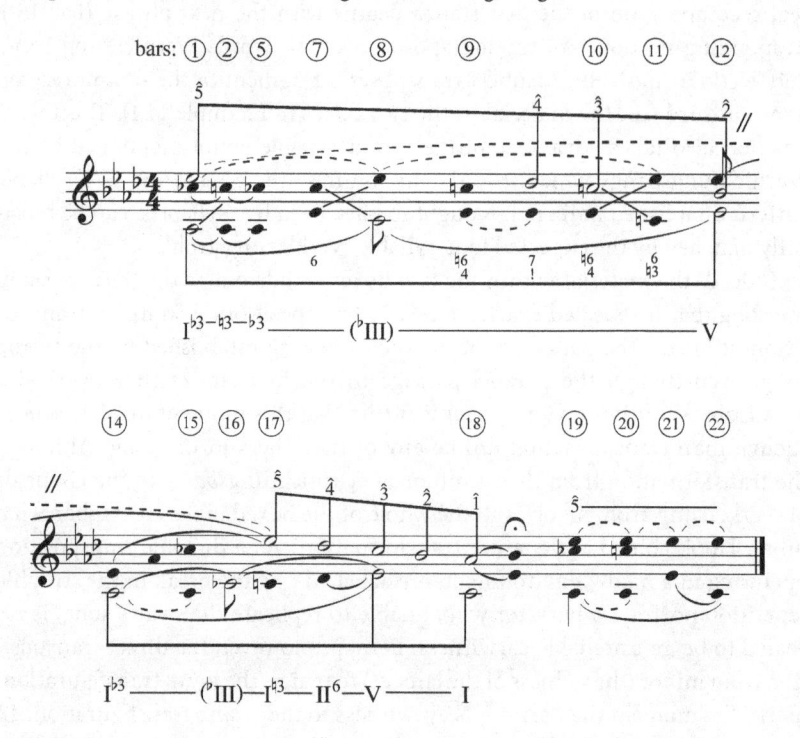

interruption. Even Schubert's fermata produces the typical cliffhanger effect of an interruption and obviates any sense of a cadence eliding with the reprise of the prelude in bar 19. By appearing *after* the structural closure, the interruption highlights how Schubert invokes powerful diatonic signposts demarcating musical form but dislodges them from their usual positions. Moreover, from a Schenkerian perspective, the postlude makes an unsatisfactory reprise—not because the surplus interruption prompts the narrator to sing out his surplus poetic line, but rather because there is no *Urlinie* descent to $\hat{1}$/I. Both the piano and the vocal line remain haunted by the swan's $\hat{E}\flat$. The IACs in bars 22 and 23 leave the vocal line and the piano's final echo poignantly open-ended with $\hat{5}$ ($\hat{E}\flat$) in the upper voice.[16]

$\hat{E}\flat$ is a conspicuous pitch in 'Schwanengesang'. Significantly, neo-Riemannian theory suggests a radically different interpretation of this pitch than does my Schenkerian reading in Example 14.2. In essence, Schenker argues that the background *Kopfton* $\hat{E}\flat$ must be mentally retained as a $\hat{5}$, no matter what the middle- and foreground harmonic elaborations hold. By contrast, neo-Riemannian theory, which attends to triadic transformations, invites a hearing of $\hat{E}\flat$ as a pitch that transforms its identity in each new harmonic context. This song certainly also challenges the most basic principles of monotonality. Riemannian theory famously relieves us of the duty of deciding the key of a piece. We need only observe how the harmony unfolds through some tonal space or other. In other words, while a Schenkerian must ask, What is the prevailing key of this song, A♭ major or A♭ minor?, a neo-Riemannian must perhaps ask, Which *Tonnetz* is best suited to illustrating this song's tonal path? As we shall see, it is also necessary to decide which aspects of Schubert's song continue to invite a functional-harmonic analysis and which invite neo-Riemannian interpretation. To illustrate these points, I shall revisit the observations I have already made about 'Schwanengesang' and reinterpret them through a neo-Riemannian lens.

The song's first transformation may be said actually to be silent. 'Schwanengesang' is one of a number of pieces by Schubert that are notated in A♭ major but begin in A♭ minor. Other examples are 'Auf dem Wasser zu singen', D 774, and the Impromptu Op. 90 No. 4. In each case, only the key signature suggests the surprising opening of A♭ minor—a notation that implies a P transformation before the work has even begun. In 'Schwanengesang', it is as if the A♭ major signature represents the swan's life prior to the beginning of his final lament. Riemann might have liked the effect. This poignant moment is visual, rather than oral; gnostic, rather than drastic. As Riemann explained in his seminal essay 'On the Imagination of Tone', key signatures are important to performers and score readers who must anticipate in their minds the next tone(s) and look ahead in the notation to measure their expectations against the realised tone(s). This silent P calls into our imagination the happy prior existence of the swan (A♭ major) and the realisation in the notation that we are about to experience the swan's final, most beautiful sounding moment.[17]

The actual sounds in the first two bars of the prelude raise a thorny issue for neo-Riemannian theorists. In roman-numeral terms, the first two bars may be identified as A♭ minor: i–V and A♭ major: I–V (see Example 14.3a). Between the two tonics is a P transformation, which is all that neo-Riemannian theorists are likely to agree on about these two bars (Example 14.3b). What transformations—if any—should be used for the two statements of tonic to dominant? There are many competing nomenclatures, especially for fifths. A purist would regard L, P and R as the only necessary transformations because any imaginable transformation can be derived through their compounds. Under these conditions, bar 1 is either PLR or LRP and bar 2 is LP (Example 14.3c). However, critics of such an analysis question the effect compounds may have on our perception of a transformation. The fact that the placement of P and the order of L and R change within the PLR or RLP compound indicates a fundamental conceptual problem with compounds. Although advocates of the system argue that the analyst is not meant to imagine compounds as containing an implied route from one harmony to the next, the decision to label bar 1 as either PLR or RLP does at least suggest a choice between whether one assumes the mode change applies to the A♭ minor or the E♭ major triad.

Technically, a neo-Riemannian theorist should be agnostic about the choice, but the choice is critical in diatonic theory. Ever since the eighteenth century, a leading question for diatonic theorists was whether v or V is the inherent diatonic

Example 14.3 The range of existing nomenclatures for the transformations in 'Schwanengesang', bars 1–2

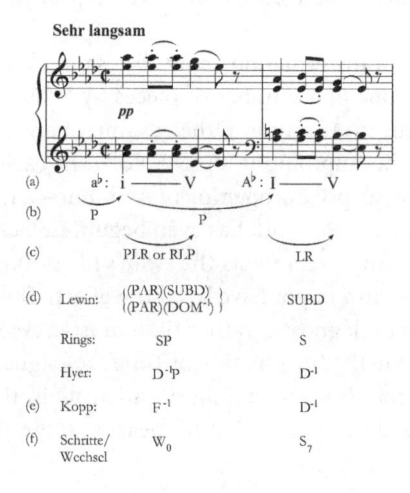

(a)		a♭: i —— V	A♭: I —— V
(b)		P P	
(c)		PLR or RLP	LR
(d)	Lewin:	(PAR)(SUBD) / (PAR)(DOM⁻¹)	SUBD
	Rings:	SP	S
	Hyer:	D⁻¹p	D⁻¹
(e)	Kopp:	F⁻¹	D⁻¹
(f)	Schritte/ Wechsel	W_0	S_7

dominant of the minor key. Schubert's contemporary Gottfried Weber was adamant that it was V, and in so believing he overturned the views of his teacher Abbé Vogler. A. B. Marx followed Weber's cue. More recently, Schoenberg allowed for either, while Schenker—and Donald Tovey, should we need names who weighed in specifically on Schubert's tonality—advocated for v.[18] RLP would satisfy Vogler, Schenker and Tovey: accordingly, the diatonic fifth is obtained first (A♭ minor to E♭ minor), then the dominant is transformed into major. For Weber and Marx, PLR would serve as a means to retreat from this view.

Even amongst those who advocate unary labels, few have come up with a solution that distinguishes fifths that preserve mode from those that do not. David Lewin proposed DOM and SUBD to denote falling and rising fifths respectively, Brian Hyer, D and D^{-1} and Steven Rings, D and S.[19] Under these proposals, both bars 1 and 2 are SUBD, D^{-1} or S (Example 14.3d), but bar 1 additionally requires an indication of P either before or after the fifth transformation, which once again produces a compound. David Kopp, who is arguably the strongest advocate for unary transformations, champions a common-tone theory with no fewer than thirteen unique transformations.[20] As shown in Example 14.3e, he would label bar 1 F^{-1} and bar 2 D^{-1}. Another solution that caters to unary labels and accounts for mode change and preservation involves the 'Wechsel' and 'Schritte' transformations.[21] Depending on the set or cycle under reference, these are labeled W_n and S_n, where n refers to the distance travelled in a set or cycle. If, for example, the cycle were the mod-12 chromatic scale, then bar 1 would yield W_0 (assuming a dualistic treatment of the common tone) and bar 2 would yield S_7 (Example 14.3f).

In order to proceed with the rest of my neo-Riemannian analysis, I need to make three critical theoretical choices. First, I will confine myself as much as possible to the PLR transformations. This will align my reading of 'Schwanengesang' most closely to neo-Riemannian theory, as opposed to transformation theory more broadly. Secondly, apart from relying almost exclusively on PLR, neo-Riemannian theory is also a system rooted in cycles of alternating major and minor triads. I shall therefore consider cycles in my analysis. Thirdly, I will retain a diatonic reading of the harmonies internal to each phrase. I do so because each phrase so clearly unfolds with T–Pd–D–T (or some fragment thereof), which transformation theory would obscure rather than illuminate. Moreover, neo-Riemannian theory is not well equipped to analyze dissonances or non-major or non-minor triads.[22] With the cadences and clear functional harmony settling in our ear, we can begin to listen for those moments best described in neo-Riemannian terms. Significantly, these appear at the junctures between phrases. I shall argue, therefore, that diatonicism or functional harmony governs the harmonic unfolding within the phrase level, and phrases in turn are governed by neo-Riemannian operations. To be sure, one could, on an even larger level, impose a Schenkerian background over the neo-Riemannian operations, especially as many of them produce arpeggiations. The result would be *Schichten* that emerge from diatonicism at the background to neo-Riemannian transformations at the middleground to diatonicism again at the foreground. This would conform to the role often assigned to neo-Riemannian cycles. They are typically understood to spin off from diatonic structural pillars.[23] But such a background would undo the story I wish to tell about the $\hat{E}\flat$ in this song. My background structure will instead be a cycle, taken from the so-called chicken-wire *Tonnetz* (see Example 14.4a).[24] The story will be about how $\hat{E}\flat$—the egg, as it were—hatched into a hexagon on the chicken-wire *Tonnetz*.

Example 14.1 exposes the transformations in 'Schwanengesang'. Some have already been discussed: the piano prelude plays with the P transformation, from the key signature and back again. Another P takes place as the voice first enters. R occurs between phrases 1 and 2. Depending on which triad one assumes the $\hat{C}$–$\hat{E}\flat$ belongs to, either R or SLIDE obtains between phrases 2 and 3, and IDENTITY or L obtains between phrases 3 and 4. In the second stanza, R appears again between phrases 1 and 2, and either RP or SLIDE between phrases 2 and 3. The arrival of A♭ major in bar 18 brings about P again for the return of the piano prelude—this time a heard transformation, not a silent one imagined from the key signature. The same transformations obtain within the postlude as in the prelude. Each of these transformations invites comment, especially for the manner in which Schubert voices the pitches within the triadic fabric, an important detail all too rarely brought out in neo-Riemannian analyses. Voicings may be tailored to emphasise either the common or displaced tone(s), a compositional choice that influences the perceived degree of smoothness or displacement of a transformation.[25]

It is no accident that the prelude prepares both the upper and lower register in which the $\hat{E}\flat$ will sound. When in bar 5 the voice enters with yet another

Example 14.4 PLR cycle from the chicken-wire *Tonnetz* oriented as in (a) Douthett and Steinbach (1998) and (b) Tymozcko (2012)

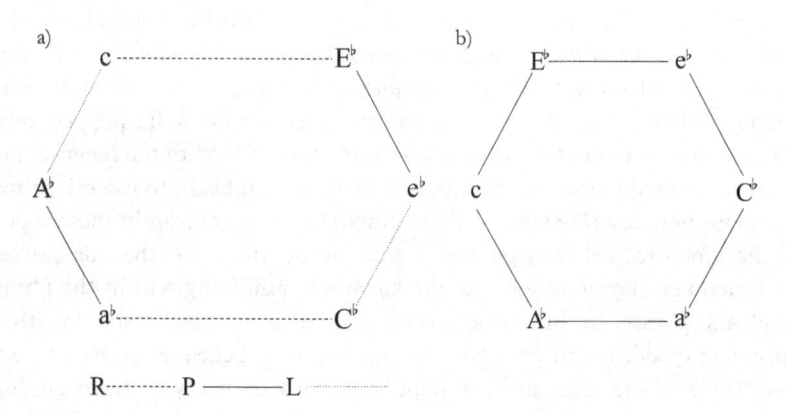

P transformation, the same chord arrangement as that of the fermata chord is struck. The common tone is emphasised. At the end of the next phrase, the voice repeats the $\hat{C}\flat$ over the bar line, transforming it from $\hat{3}$ of A♭ minor ($\hat{3}$, -) to $\hat{1}$ of C♭ major ($\hat{1}$, +).²⁶ Underneath this common tone, an R transformation takes place. This key is tonicised in the following bar through another cadential progression. This time the vocal line ends on $\hat{E}\flat$ ($\hat{3}$, +), which again is held over as the music shifts to a new sonority. We hear only two pitches: the $\hat{E}\flat$ common tone and the $\hat{C}$, which indeed constitutes a single semitone displacement from the $\hat{C}\flat$ of the C♭ major triad in the previous bar. But the rest of the triad is missing. If we fill it out with a $\hat{G}$ to produce C minor, we obtain a SLIDE transformation, and $\hat{E}\flat$ is ($\hat{3}$, -). If we fill out the harmony with an $\hat{A}\flat$, we obtain an R transformation, and $\hat{E}\flat$ is ($\hat{5}$, +). As the phrase unfolds it comes clear—in retrospect—that the interval was part of A♭ major.

The perception of this interval is different the second time around (bar 11) and not because the $\hat{E}\flat$ changes from being either ($\hat{3}$, -) or ($\hat{5}$, +) or indeed that its companion $\hat{C}$ would be either ($\hat{1}$, -) or ($\hat{3}$, +) of C minor or A♭ major respectively, but because of the transformation that brings it about. The immediate context of the interval—the A♭ major sonority preceding it at the end of bar 10—means that there are no displaced tones over the bar line. Even without filling in an implied full triad, the interval is IDENTITY (IDENT) because there are no displaced tones. Some recordings play up the static smoothness of this moment.²⁷ Others aim to recapture the sense of surprise the interval generated a few bars back. In so doing, they manage a rather extraordinary feat, a trick played on the ear: they feign the quality of non-IDENT in an IDENT, even though we can anticipate from having already heard the interval that it also belongs to A♭ major on the repeat.²⁸ This is possible because of the memory of the effect of the interval on its first hearing. The choice is up to the performers, but the effect is far more powerful than if Schubert had provided the full C minor harmony, making the SLIDE into bar 9 and the L into bar 11 unequivocal.²⁹ With the upper-octave $\hat{E}\flat$ ringing in the ear at the start of bar 11, the melody descends as if the swan's lungs were beginning to collapse, until he strains to reach back up to the $\hat{E}\flat$ ($\hat{1}$, +).

It has already been stated that in the second stanza of Schubert's song the piano provides a better memory of the swan's song than the narrator does. The voice disrupts the common tones that threaded the swan's phrases together. Instead, as shown in Example 14.1, the piano holds on to the common tones. How apt, too, that the actual moment of the swan's transfiguration is marked by the only time in the song that Schubert breaks the pattern of PLR transformations, only to introduce another, t_3.

Cycles lie at the heart of neo-Riemannian theory. Thus, if this song in some way exhibits classic neo-Riemannian principles, its harmonic profile ought to fit onto a cycle of some kind. The main harmonic stations are A♭ minor,

Ab major, Cb major, Eb major—with potentially C minor, if the implied SLIDE is included. This list may seem remarkably diatonic insofar as it contains the diatonic mediant and the cadential (major) dominant of both the major and minor tonics. The list makes up nearly all of the components of the PLR cycle in Example 14.4a. The song is missing only Eb minor, although given that Eb major appears only at cadential points, this absence is unsurprising. Indeed, perhaps the theoretical backdrop of this PLR cycle might persuade us to take the implied SLIDE more seriously. However, as can be seen by comparing Examples 14.1 and 14.4a, the music does not unfold through the PLR cycle systematically. It is important to tread carefully after making such an observation, especially as it is a common habit to draw hermeneutic conclusions in the face of music that resists theoretical models.

The fact that the order of harmonies of this song might initially strike the analyst as belonging more to a tonal system than to a neo-Riemannian system, which is normally associated with chromatic harmony, says something profound about the nature of PLR. If a piece explores all elements in the PLR cycle, there is only one arrangement of its triads that yields an essentially tonal feel. As shown in Example 14.5, only if the overall tonic of a passage or piece contains the common tone as ($\hat{5}$, + or -) will harmonies in the cycle yield I–iii–V and i–III–V of their respective major or minor tonic. If the common tone belongs to the overall tonic as either ($\hat{3}$, + or -) or ($\hat{1}$, + or -), then the harmonic landscape will lack a dominant, as illustrated in Example 14.5.

In this respect, a comparison of 'Schwanengesang' with 'Selige Welt' and 'Auf der Donau' is instructive (both of these songs appeared alongside 'Schwanengesang' in the Op. 23 publication). On the surface, 'Selige Welt' is strikingly similar to 'Schwanengesang'. Its A section explores Ab major, Ab minor and Cb major, and its shorter A' section remains in the tonic, Ab major, throughout. The harmonic stations of the B section, which perhaps were the ones

Example 14.5 Roman-numeral analysis of triads of the PLR cycle when each of the six major and minor triads in the cycle is treated as a tonic

	P	R	L	P	R	L
Ab:	I	i	bIII	v	V	iii
ab:	I	i	III	v	V	#iii
Cb:	VI	iv	I	iii	III	#i
eb:	IV	iv	VI	i	I	#vi
Eb:	IV	iv	bVI	i	I	vi
c:	VI	vi	bI	iii	III	i

Fink referred to when he said that 'even the most remote modulations are mild and therefore praiseworthy', are encased between C♭ major and C minor, which form a SLIDE. Nonetheless, each of these two appears near its diatonic tonic: C♭ major emerges after A♭ minor and C minor morphs into A♭ major through an L transformation, although the $\hat{3}$ of C minor becomes the $\hat{5}$ of the A♭, which serves as its brief single-pitch dominant preparation. Although $\hat{E♭}$ is not a salient pitch in the melody in 'Selige Welt', the order of the appearance of the harmonies clearly satisfy the condition of the roman-numeral analysis most suited to a tonic-dominant framework shown in Example 14.5.

By contrast, $\hat{E♭}$ is salient in the vocal line of 'Auf der Donau'. Its A section covers much of the same tonal space as 'Schwanengesang' and 'Selige Welt'. As Fink remarked in the review cited at the outset of this chapter, it goes from E♭ major to C minor, A♭ major, A♭ minor and C♭ major.[30] These yield the transformations R, L, P and R—an order that dutifully follows the cycle in Example 14.4a. My roman-numeral analysis of the members of the PLR cycle predicts that because the common tone $\hat{E♭}$ sets out as ($\hat{1}$, +) in 'Auf der Donau', the ensuing harmonies that belong to the cycle feel more adventurous. Some sense of this is captured in the different look of the two *Tonnetze* in Example 14.4. Both are PLR cycles and therefore represent the same tonal space, but the one on the left corresponds to Douthett and Steinbach's original orientation and the other (Example 14.4b) is modelled on Tymozcko's, which more clearly highlights the relationship between the fifths, specifically with the dominants above the tonics.[31]

The common-tone technique suggests that the unfolding of harmony is, for Schubert, more driven by melodic thinking than bass-line or harmonic-progression thinking. This may explain why it features prominently in his songs and lyric moments in the instrumental music. Indeed, he may have gotten the idea from Italian opera.[32] It will be recalled from my consideration of Senn's text that the swan's song could have mimicked a miniature strophic song—marking the moment as a song within a song. But, as my analysis showed, Schubert did not take up what was on offer in Senn's text. Instead of dividing the eight bars of the swan's song into a paired repetition—say, a period structure—to make a strophic form aa or aa', he divided them into 2 + 2 + 2 + 2 to produce an internal form abcc' of constant transformations. Schubert seems to have rejected the kind of aesthetic of the lied described by Dittrich or by one of Schubert's predecessors, Johann Friedrich Reichardt, who wrote:

> Song melodies with which everyone who has no more than ears and a throat will be able to join in must so exactly strike the tone [*Weise*] of the [poetic] lied—as *Herder* more aptly terms what one otherwise just calls its melody—in the simplest progression of tones, in the most certain motion, in the most precise agreement of divisions and sections, that once one knows the melody,

one will no longer be able to think of it without the words, nor the words without the melody; that the melody will be everything for the words and nothing for itself.

Such a melody—to say it to the artist in a single word—will always have the character of unison, and thus require no accompanying harmony or else allow it only as a concession.

This is the way all lieder were created in the times when our German *Volk* was still rich in song.[33]

Senn may have anticipated that Schubert would cloak the swan's words in music of the *Volkslied* aesthetic, forever binding the words and music together in everyone's memory.

Schubert had other things in mind. In his aural imagination, the swan sings phrases that metamorphose before our very ears: no two are exactly alike. Schubert crafted a *Gesang* rather than a *Lied* for the swan's song. When the narrator recounts the swan's final moments, he picks up on the swan's musical thread, but Schubert designs a modified strophic repetition, as if to portray the swan's song as not particularly memorable. Or perhaps the narrator does not wish to replicate it—who might dare to? Singing such a song induces death. He manages only a faint echo of the lament; the pianist manages a better memory of it. The song, like the swan, is gone forever.

As I have argued elsewhere, such passages or even whole songs by Schubert seem to be more 'around a pitch' than 'in a key'. Given that he has a penchant for exploiting common tones in his melodies, it is perhaps unsurprising that Schubert ended up 'discovering' all of the components of the PLR cycle. The cycle, after all, comprises all of the possible major and minor triads around a single pitch. Schubert seems to have intuited the contents of this cycle because of his fondness for colouring repeated pitches with different harmonic hues. This technique aptly symbolises the swan's metamorphosis. It equally has a profound effect on the aesthetics of song, for the metamorphosis of pitch comes about because the accompaniment changes the harmony while the voice maintains the common tone. Unlike the song aesthetic advocated by Reichardt, where the 'melody . . . require[s] no accompanying harmony or else allow[s] it only as a concession', Schubert's pitch metamorphosis necessitates the accompaniment. In short, it serves as a means through which Schubert could eschew 'old, well-trodden ways and clear a new path'—Schubert was rethinking tonal space and rethinking the aesthetics of song. How apt it was for him to explore these novelties in a swan song. Since, as legend has it, the swan, which is mute throughout life, sings just before death a song that he has never sung before, it would not do to invoke strophic song, nor commonplace tonal structures, to depict such a moment. Rather, Schubert is tasked with imagining a musical song that can only happen once, that can have no precedent and that knows no rehearsal.

Notes

1. I am grateful to William O'Hara for setting the musical examples and for stimulating conversations during the preparation of this essay.
2. A translation of the review appears in Otto Erich Deutsch (ed.), *Schubert: a Documentary Biography*, trans. Eric Bloom (London: J. M. Dent, 1946), pp. 352–5. Deutsch proposed Fink as the likely author of the review.
3. The metaphor of a lens comes from Richard Cohn, 'As Wonderful as Star Clusters: Instruments for Gazing at Tonality in Schubert', *19th-Century Music* 22/3 (1999), pp. 213–32. For more on how music theory serves as a lens through which music is interpreted and meanings are constructed, see my *Analyzing Schubert* (Cambridge: Cambridge University Press, 2011), pp. 4–5.
4. For a detailed account of this event, see Alice Marie Hanson, *Musical Life in Biedermeier Vienna* (Cambridge: Cambridge University Press, 1985), pp. 55–6.
5. Schubert, *Die Liebe hat gelogen, Die selige Welt, Schwanengesang, Schatzgräbers Begehr: Vier Gedichte in Musick gesetzt für eine Singstimme mit Begleitung des Piano Forte* (Vienna: Sauer & Leidesdorf, 1823). Ernst Hilmar incorrectly states in *Franz Schubert in his Time* (Portland, OR: Amadeus Press, 1988), p. 22, that Senn's name is not mentioned in the first edition; in fact, his name appears in the upper right-hand corner of the title page of each song. From this it is clear that Schubert did not have to hide the authorship of the poem.
6. I have elsewhere analyzed 'Selige Welt' with a view to understanding why Fink thought that the modulations were 'mild and therefore praiseworthy' when they appeared in this song, given that he disdained identical modulations in other songs. I argue that the difference lies in how Schubert modulates, not which keys he visits. See my *Analyzing Schubert*, pp. 67–73.
7. Johann Senn, *Gedichte* (Innsbruck: Wagner, 1838), p. 15.
8. Marie-Agnes Dittrich, 'The Lieder of Schubert', in James Parsons (ed.), *The Cambridge Companion to the Lied* (Cambridge: Cambridge University Press, 2004), p. 91. See also Susan Youens, 'Schubert: the Lied Transformed', in Rufus Hallmark (ed.), *German Lieder in the Nineteenth Century*, 2nd edn (New York: Routledge, 2010), p. 63.
9. There is a variant in Schubert's text here: the shift is from 'ich' to 'er', not 'es'. The translation in Table 14.2 is adapted from Richard Wigmore (trans.) and Graham Johnson (ed.), *Schubert: the Complete Song Texts* (London: Hyperion, 2005), p. 249. Wigmore translated line 5 as 'It lamented, it sang', which I have modified to 'He lamented, he sang' to match Schubert's text. I therefore refer to the swan as 'he', rather than 'it', throughout this chapter, recognising of course that the gesture is allegorical.
10. Without a copy of the manuscript that Bruchmann brought to Schubert, it is impossible to trace whether Schubert himself made the textual adjustment or the version in the *Gedichte* is a variant of what Senn gave to Schubert.
11. Again, without the original manuscript, we cannot know for certain whether the layout in Senn's *Gedichte* is what Schubert received. Not all modern

editors lay out the text as I have in Table 14.2. Wigmore and Johnson, *Schubert: the Complete Song Texts*, p. 249 and Michael Hall, *Schubert's Song Sets* (Farnham: Ashgate, 2003), p. 103 show the poem as a quatrain followed by a quintain. Roman Roček, *Dämonie des Biedermeier: Nikolaus Lenaus Lebenstragödie* (Vienna: Böhlau, 2005), p. 78, does not separate out the nine lines of my Table 14.2. It is generally clear that their layouts are an attempt to extract the form of Senn's poem from Schubert's setting, but for an exception, see Christine Blanken, *Franz Schuberts 'Lazarus' und das Wiener Oratorium zu Beginn des 19. Jahrhunderts*, Schubert: Perspektiven—Studien 1 (Stuttgart: Franz Steiner Verlag, 2002), p. 186, which has seven continuous lines with a 9-9-9-9-8-9-9 syllable pattern.

12. Throughout this study, I employ the Schenkerian caret above letters to denote pitches.

13. John Reed, *The Schubert Song Companion* (Manchester: Manchester University Press, 1997), p. 376; Brian Newbould, *Schubert: the Music and the Man* (Berkeley and Los Angeles: University of California Press, 1997), pp. 160–1; and Marjorie Wing Hirsch, *Schubert's Dramatic Lieder* (Cambridge: Cambridge University Press, 1993), pp. 40–1.

14. 'A diatonic transposition operator t_n transposes notes of a form up n steps within a diatonic scale, leaving the key signature unchanged'. Julian Hook, 'Signature Transformations', in Jack Douthett, Martha M. Hyde and Charles J. Smith (eds), *Music Theory and Mathematics: Chords, Collections, and Transformations* (Rochester, NY: University of Rochester Press, 2008), p. 142. The lowercase 't' is deliberate.

15. Schenker, *Free Composition*, translated and edited by Ernst Oster (New York: Longman, 1979), p. 39. My treatment of the $\hat{B}\flat$ and slur to the primary tone in bar 17 is modelled on Schenker's Figure 25.

16. Neither pianist in the recordings by Robert Holl and Konrad Richter, *Lieder von Franz Schubert*, Preiser Records CD 93356, and Rainer Trost and Ulrich Eisenlohr, *Schubert's Friends*, vol. 3, Naxos CD 8.557567, plays the final $\hat{B}\flat$ in bar 23, which destroys the open-ended effect of the song.

17. Hugo Riemann, 'Ideen zu einer "Lehre von den Tonvorstellungen"', trans. Robert W. Wason and Elizabeth West Marvin, *Journal of Music Theory* 36 (1992), pp. 81–117.

18. Gottfried Weber, *Versuch einer geordneten Theorie der Tonsetzkunst*, 3 vols (Mainz, 1817–21); Abbé Georg Joseph Vogler, *Handbuch zur Harmonielehre und für den Generalbaß* (Prague: K. Brath, 1802); A. B. Marx, *Die Lehre von der musikalischen Komposition*, 4 vols (Leipzig: Breitkopf & Härtel, 1837, 1838, 1845 and 1847); Arnold Schoenberg, *Theory of Harmony*, trans. Roy E. Carter (London: Faber & Faber, 1978); Schenker, *Free Composition*; and Donald Francis Tovey, 'Tonality in Schubert', in Hubert J. Foss (ed.), *The Mainstream of Music and Other Essays* (Oxford: Oxford University Press, 1949), 134–159.

19. DOM or D for all of these theorists is the transformation down a fifth, following the direction of the cadence. See David Lewin, *Generalized Musical Intervals and Transformations* (New Haven, CT: Yale University Press, 1987);

Brian Hyer, 'Reimag(in)ing Riemann', *Journal of Music Theory* 39 (1995), pp. 101–38, and Steven Rings, *Tonality and Transformation* (New York: Oxford University Press, 2011).

20. David Kopp, *Chromatic Transformations in Nineteenth-Century Music* (Cambridge: Cambridge University Press, 2002), pp. 2 and 170.

21. For a lucid explanation of how 'Wechsel' and 'Schritte' work in a neo-Riemannian context, see especially John Clough, 'Flip-Flop Circles and Their Groups', in Jack Douthett, Martha M. Hyde and Charles J. Smith (eds), *Music Theory and Mathematics: Chords, Collections, and Transformations* (Rochester, NY: University of Rochester Press, 2008), pp. 23–48.

22. As Ernest G. Porter astutely put it before the advent of neo-Riemannian theory: 'The key [of 'Schwanengesang'] fluctuates between A flat minor and major as representing death and resurrection, and makes use of the swinging triad in which the change is carried out with unusual discords and the use of first inversions'. Neo-Riemannian theory may have made headway on the 'swinging triad' but it has yet to deal convincingly with discords—or even showing sensitivity to inversions. Porter, *Schubert's Song Technique* (London: Dennis Dobson, 1961), p. 108.

23. For an elegant series of analyses demonstrating this perspective, see Matthew Bribitzer-Stull, 'The A flat–C–E Complex: the Origin and Function of Chromatic Major Third Collections in Nineteenth-Century Music', *Music Theory Spectrum* 28 (2006), pp. 167–90.

24. Jack Douthett and Peter Steinbach, 'Parsimonious Graphs: a Study in Parsimony, Contextual Transformations, and Modes of Limited Transposition', *Journal of Music Theory* 42 (1998), pp. 241–63.

25. Kopp, *Chromatic Transformations in Nineteenth-Century Music*; Michael Siciliano, 'Neo-Riemannian Transformations and the Harmony of Franz Schubert' (PhD diss., University of Chicago, 2002); Siciliano, 'Two Neo-Riemannian Analyses', *College Music Symposium* 45 (2005), pp. 81–107; and William Rothstein, 'Common-Tone Tonality in Italian Opera: an Introduction', *Music Theory Online* 14 (2008), para. 12.

26. I developed this notation in my essay 'On the Imagination of Tone in Schubert's *Liedesend* (D473), *Trost* (D523), and *Gretchens Bitte* (D564)', in Edward Gollin and Alexander Rehding (eds), *The Oxford Handbook of Neo-Riemannian Theories* (New York: Oxford University Press, 2011), pp. 294–321, and *Analyzing Schubert*. $(\hat{1},+)(\hat{3},+)(\hat{5},+)$ and $(\hat{1},-)(\hat{3},-)(\hat{5},-)$ refer to the tonic, mediant and fifth of major and minor triads respectively. This notation could be extended to harmonies other than major or minor triads, with symbols such as ø7 after the comma denoting half-diminished seventh chords, for example. This idea was inspired by Hugo Riemann's explanation of the shifting meaning of common tones within different harmonic contexts in 'Ideen zu einer "Lehre von den Tonvorstellungen"'. Here, I retain only the six possibilities listed above since neo-Riemannian theory generally deals only with major and minor triads. The power of this notation is that it can be used to define the unfolding of harmony around a common tone.

Concurrently, Rings, *Tonality and Transformation*, pp. 41–9, developed a similar idea, dubbed 'scale-degree qualia', whose conceptual lineage he traces to David Huron, *Sweet Anticipation: Music and the Psychology of Expectation* (Cambridge, MA: MIT Press, 2006), especially pp. 144–7. Huron was interested in how experimental subjects characterise the 'qualia' or 'different psychological flavor[s] or feeling[s]' (p. 144) of each degree of the major and minor scales (p. 145) and chromatic mediants (pp. 271–5). In contrast, my purpose is to explore how a common tone changes quality, as it shifts location within a major or minor triad in the course of neo-Riemannian transformations.

27. See n. 16 for recordings that emphasise the smoothness of IDENT.

28. A recording that recaptures the non-IDENT effect is Brigitte Fassbaender and Graham Johnson, *Schubert: the Hyperion Schubert Edition*, vol. 11, Hyperion CDJ33011.

29. Examples where Schubert showcases SLIDE include between the first and second themes of 'Lebensstürme' (D 947), the outer harmonies of the B section in 'Selige Welt' and the first two sections of 'Gretchens Bitte' (D 564). Local-level examples include 'An Schwager Kronos' (D 369), bars 37–43; 'Willkommen und Abschied' (D 767), bar 32; and Grand Duo (D 812), bars 33–34.

30. Deutsch, *Schubert: a Documentary Biography*, p. 354.

31. For an expanded view of both tonal spaces, see Douthett and Steinbach, 'Parsimonious Graphs', p. 248; and Dmitri Tymoczko, 'The Generalized Tonnetz', *Journal of Music Theory* 56 (2012), p. 2.

32. Rothstein, 'Common-Tone Tonality in Italian Opera'.

33. Cited in David Gramit, *Cultivating Music: the Aspirations, Interests, and Musical Limits of German Musical Cuture, 1770–1848* (Berkeley and Los Angeles: University of California Press, 2002), p. 74.

15

Contextual Processes in Schubert's Late Sacred Music

James William Sobaskie

Contextual Processes in Schubert's Instrumental Music

Among the more intriguing innovations in Franz Schubert's music are the contextual processes that animate some of his works. Edward T. Cone's classic essay on the 'promissory note' of Schubert's *Moment musical* in A♭ major (D 780, Op 94 No. 6; 1824) revealed how persistent expectations of resolution elicited by a prominent chromatic pitch heard early in this beloved piece were sustained until satisfied by a decisive semitonal rise near the end.[1] Cone's discovery prompted accounts of other unique event sequences in Schubert's oeuvre that engage attention, elicit anticipation and evoke expectations, complementing familiar tonal and thematic processes and demonstrating new sources of coherence and drama.[2] Some of these suggestive successions shape single movements, while others span several, yet all contribute to impressions of momentum and unity in Schubert's music.

For instance, I have shown that comprehensive contextual processes unfold across three of Schubert's greatest chamber works, conferring impressions of teleology and coherence.[3] In his Quartet in A minor (D 804, Op. 29; 1824), an ongoing dialectic between a thetic melodic motive and its more expansive motivic antithesis leads to a pivotal reconciliation and persuasive synthesis near the end. Within the Piano Trio in E♭ major (D 929, Op. 100; 1827), an emerging narrative involving a musical gesture from the first movement and a more extended theme from the second movement produces a triumphant transformation in the Finale's coda. Finally, in Schubert's String Quintet in C major (D 956, Op. posth.; 1828), pursuit of a musical problem proceeds through all four movements, furthered by transformations that represent hypotheses, until a contextually satisfactory solution arises near the end.[4] Each of these projects its own distinctive effects of striving towards success, portraying its composer as optimistic and determined even as he faced increasingly daunting personal challenges.

Certain contextual processes in Schubert's late piano music betray other intentions and bear very different expressive messages. For instance, I have demonstrated that Schubert's Impromptu in G♭ major (D 899, Op 90 No. 3; 1827) and the Adagio from his B♭ major Sonata (D 960, Op. posth.; 1828) also simulate the expression and resolution of musical problems.[5] In these pieces, however, distinctive details within carefully constructed contexts communicate lamentation. Each essay imparts impressions of grief and reconciliation through its pursuit of a unique musical problem that is not surmounted until near the composition's end, and each carries clues that point to Schubert himself. In turn, these forward-focused works may be understood as instances of a novel genre, the musical self-elegy, analogous to the then recently emerged Romantic poetic form that mourns its author's own impending death. Uttering his 'posthumous voice' in these two threnodies—one formal and public, the other frank and private—Schubert may have gained some measure of satisfaction and control over his future by pre-empting what would befall him one day.[6] Nevertheless, the acquiescent and adaptive resolutions in these works also offer the barest of hints that the composer may have begun to contemplate transcendence, even as their introversion intimates despair and distance from its comfort.

One might expect that any contextual processes appearing within Schubert's late sacred music also are likely to communicate similarly sad sentiments, since debilitating illness and professional insecurity dominated what would become Schubert's last year.[7] Alternatively, one could assume that these church compositions conveyed pleas for respite or even release from these desperate circumstances. And, on behalf of those who may harbour doubt about Schubert's religious faith, perhaps it may be allowed that whatever internal processes are found within these late vocal works actually reveal nothing personal about their composer, save for a fascinating side of his genius. Indeed, is there anything special in the contextual processes within Schubert's late music that sets them apart from earlier works we know and love? There may be.

Towards the end of his life, Schubert seems to have sought refuge within his creative mind, where triumph and tragedy could be experienced and controlled, and where other outcomes and opportunities could be envisaged.[8] An astounding list of masterpieces—including the Piano Trio in E♭ and String Quintet in C, the Piano Sonatas in C, A, and B♭, *Winterreise* and *Schwanengesang*—all emerged during Schubert's final months. If one hesitates to call this output 'miraculous' or is reluctant to claim it was divinely inspired, then the prospect that this musical legacy arose as the product of contemplative self-therapy may appear plausible. And if so, perhaps other artistic expressions of imaginative transport served him as beneficial diversion.

Most remarkably, several of Schubert's late sacred works seem to confide aspirations for spiritual redemption, exhibiting contextual processes that suggest ascension, reconciliation, transformation and transition, all within settings that explicitly yearn for or address God.[9] While the contextual processes in these pieces surely underscore the religious sentiments of their texts, their ingenuity also would seem to reflect simultaneously the composer's own interiority. Let us survey seven of Schubert's late sacred works for traces of his hope.

Ingenuous Praise and Inspirited Prayer within Schubert's *Deutsche Messe*

'Schlussgesang', the recessional hymn of Schubert's *Deutsche Messe* (D 872, Op. posth.; 1827), projects simple, joyful praise.[10] Scored for oboes, clarinets, bassoons, horns, trombones and organ, its homophonic texture enables the four-part mixed choir to sound like a single, rich, vibrant voice. Table 15.1 presents its text, written by Johann Philipp Neumann[11], with a translation.

With deferential reverence, every two-bar phrase of 'Schlussgesang' save the last ends tentatively. Most conclude with two separate or elided descending melodic seconds whose oft-accented first tone sounds within an unstable sonority, as dotted brackets show in the following excerpt of the choral parts. Interrupted and imperfect cadences terminate several phrases, as Example 15.1 shows, while perfect cadences, save for the last, sound provisional because of voicing and registral factors that qualify their closure. All of this contributes to an earnest and mounting fervor corresponding to the pious text.

Coordinated with these devotional entreaties is a broad and gradual melodic ascent in the sopranos' melody, identified by the circled tones linked by broken slurs, whose structural pitches are heralded by the pitch hints identified by asterisks. As Example 15.1 reveals, the registral 'ceiling' of the uppermost part climbs slowly but steadily upwards towards a foreshadowed goal, buoyed by supplicative phrases, reaching a climactic high F5 in the penultimate bar that seems to summon the most satisfying cadence yet to conclude the hymn's contextual process. This ineluctable ascent of the soprano within the musical fabric gradually intensifies the text's expression while subtly illustrating the

Table 15.1 Schubert, *Deutsche Messe*, D 872: 'Schlussgesang' text and translation

Herr, Du hast mein Fleh'n vernommen,	Lord, you have heard my pleas,
Selig pocht's in meiner Brust,	Blissfully beats my breast,
in die Welt hinaus, in's Leben	Out into the world, into life
folgt mir nun des Himmelslust.	Heaven's joy now follows me.
Dort auch bist ja Du mir nahe,	There are You also near me,
überall und jederzeit,	everywhere and always,
allerorten ist Dein Tempel,	Your temple is everywhere
wo das Herz sich fromm Dir weiht.	Wherever the heart piously devotes itself to you.
Segne, Herr, mich und die Meinen,	Bless Lord, me and mine,
segne unsern Lebensgang,	Bless our lives' course,
Alles, unser Thun und Wirken	May all of our deeds and works
sei ein frommer Lobgesang.	Be a pious hymn of praise.

Example 15.1 Schubert, *Deutsche Messe*, D 872: choral parts of 'Schlussgesang', with analysis

Schubert's Late Church Music

Example 15.1 Continued

[Musical notation with lyrics:]

Seg - ne, Herr, mich und die Mei - nen, seg - ne un - sern Le - bens - gang!
V — vi   V — I

Al - les un - ser Thun und Wir - ken, sei ein from - mer Lob - ge
V — vi   V —

sang, sei ein from - mer Lob - ge - sang.
— vi   V — I

image of praise rising to its object. Surely this gentle tone painting, heard within the sincere and solicitous passage within which it unfolds, suggests Schubert's personal investment in the devotional message of 'Schlussgesang'.

In contrast, 'Das Gebet des Herrn', appended to the *Deutsche Messe* to serve as an optional insertion when the work is sung in a liturgical setting, elicits expectation in different ways. Founded on a gloss of the Lord's Prayer by Johann Philipp Neumann, its four stanzas appear in Table 15.2.

As the text and translation of Table 15.2 suggest, the familiar sentiments of the Lord's Prayer are introduced in the first stanza by a prologue similar to

Table 15.2 Schubert, *Deutsche Messe*, D 872: 'Das Gebet des Herrn', text and translation

Anbetend Deine Macht und Grösse versinkt in Nichts mein bebend Ich. Mit welchem Namen, Deiner würdig, Du Unnennbarer, preis ich Dich? Wohl mir! ich darf Dich Vater nennen,	Worshipping your power and greatness I tremble and sink into nothingness. With what name that is worthy of you, You ineffable one, shall I praise you? How blessed I am that I may call you Father,
nach Deines Sohnes Unterricht; so sprech' ich denn zu Dir, mein Schöpfer mit kindlich froher Zuversicht.	According to the teaching of your Son, Thus I speak to You, my Creator with childlike, joyful confidence.
O Vater, der Du bist im Himmel und überall zu jeder Zeit, zu preisen Deinen Vaternamen sei jedem Herzen Seligkeit! O lass durch Deine Huld und Liebe, erscheinen uns Dein Gnadenreich, und treues Tun nach Deinem Willen	O Father, You who are in Heaven and everywhere at all times, may all hearts rejoice in praising Your Name! O by your mercy and love let your kingdom of mercy appear to us, and let good deeds done according to Your will
mach' auch die Erde himmelgleich!	Make the Earth like heaven.
Herr, der Du nährst die jungen Raben, Du kennst auch Deiner Kinder Not. Nicht ist vergebens unser Flehen: Gib uns auch täglich unser Brod! Vergib uns, was wir irrend fehlten, wenn wir die Schuld vor Dir bereu'n, wie wir, auf Dein Gebot, den Brüdern,	Lord, You feed the young ravens, You also know your children's needs. Not in vain is our cry: Give us our daily bread! Forgive us our trespasses, when we set our misdeeds before you, as we are, at your command, all brothers,
wie wir den Feinden auch verzeih'n.	so we also forgive our enemies.
Will die Versuchung uns verlocken, gib Kraft, o Herr, zum Widerstand! So vor der Seele höchstem Übel, vor Sünde schütz uns Deine Hand!	Should temptation entice us, give us strength, O Lord, to resist it! Before the highest Evil, protecting our souls from sin by your hand.
Send' uns Geduld und Trost in Leiden!	Send us patience and consolation in our suffering,
Und kann's zu unser'm Heil gescheh'n, so lass durch Deine Vatergüte, den bittern Kelch vorübergeh'n!	By your fatherly goodness, enable our salvation, and let the bitter cup pass us by!

that traditionally recited by the priest; they are then extended via embellishment and interpolation that gradually unfolds over the following three stanzas. When experiencing a trope on a familiar text, listeners anticipate the arrival of familiar words or ideas within the expanded expression, engaged by memory of the traditional version and stimulated by its reinterpretation. Here that happens over a span of nearly eight minutes, given the length of the text and the moderate tempo of the hymn, so a progressive and absorbing musical setting is required.

Scored like those in Schubert's 'Schlussgesang', the wind parts of 'Das Gebet des Herrn' mainly double the voices, some instruments occasionally dropping out in softer passages while others split into two strands to produce differing types of audible thinness in their accompaniment. This irregular timbral and textual fluctuation establishes continual change in the instrumental tissue. Similarly, the choral parts alternate between chant-like phrases doubled at the unison and octave with chordal spans. Example 15.2 gives just the vocal lines of the hymn's first two strophes.

The cycling between thin and thick vocal sonorities seen in Example 15.2, complemented by the changes in orchestration, produces a foundation of aural flux to support a contextual process involving tonality.

As the first strophe unfolds, tonality seems to oscillate, with the keys of E minor and G major simulating an animated dialectical relationship marked by contrast and competition. Resolution occurs in the final phrase, when E major emerges to provide satisfying synthesis. Although E minor had priority, it never received confirmation via a perfect cadence. And although G major was twice tonicised by authentic cadences, it twice gave way to E. In retrospect, the empty octaves in the first, third and seventh phrases focus forwards and away from E minor, which sounds lacking and thin, making the full-textured E major sonority at the strophe's close most satisfying when it arrives. The transformation of the composition's tonality from E minor to E major, with the intervention of G major as catalyst, would seem to portray a process of becoming, perhaps similar to one that Schubert may well have wished for himself.[12] Of course, this reconciliatory sequence is apt to elicit somewhat less anticipation upon repetition in subsequent strophes, since its tonal outcome becomes known after the first. However, the expectation it generates still animates Schubert's trope on the Lord's Prayer, underscoring its petitional character and drawing attention ahead.

Schubert's *Deutsche Messe*, written in the late autumn of 1827, may seem modest in scope and complexity, but its sentiments appear heartfelt and its contextual processes persuasive. Indeed, the experience of creating such an unselfconsciously spiritual work may have prompted the composer to return to church music in the following year, when a range of sacred compositions proceeded from his pen. Let us now turn to a most evocative work.

Example 15.2 Schubert, *Deutsche Messe*, D 872: choral parts of 'Das Gebet des Herrn' (text by Johann Philipp Neumann), with analysis

Example 15.2 Continued

[musical score excerpt with lyrics:
"sprech' ich denn zu Dir___, mein Schöp-fer! mit kind - lich fro - her
treu - es Thun nach Dei - nem Will - len mach' auch___ die Er - de"
(E minor ?)   (E major ?)

"Zu - ver - sicht.
him - mel - gleich!"
E major !]

Tonal Peregrination and the Flight of Invocation in *Hymnus an den heiligen Geist*

Schubert's *Hymnus an den heiligen Geist* (D 948), composed in May 1828, employs an unaccompanied four-part male choir as well as four soloists.[13] Its text and a translation appear in Table 15.3, accompanied by a coordinated itinerary of its tonal scheme.

Inspired, no doubt, by the ancient hymn *Veni creator Spiritus, Hymnus an den heiligen Geist* belongs to the long-standing Roman Catholic tradition of beseeching the third person of the Trinity for comfort.[14]

Tonality plays a crucial role in the contextual process that animates Schubert's *Hymnus an den heiligen Geist*, and no fewer than eight keys participate, as the central column of Table 15.3 suggests. Example 15.3 offers a corresponding representation of the hymn's fluctuating tonality in which stemmed notes identify the locations of all tonicising cadences, while un-stemmed notes illustrate where new keys arise without cadentially confirmed modulation via subtle assumption, or, upon occasion, even abrupt assertion.

As Example 15.3 shows, the first third of the hymn explores keys on the flat side of C major, while what follows visits keys on the sharp side. This fluctuating tonality suggests a quest, for after having twice stopped at the major key of two

Table 15.3 Schubert, *Hymnus an den heiligen Geist*, D 948: text (Anton Schmidl), with tonalities and translation

Komm heil'ger Geist, erhöre unser Flehen,	(C)	Come Holy Spirit, hear our prayers,
die sehnend auf zu dir, zu dir, Verheiss'nem sehen;		that we send to you, to you, beheld Promised One;
herab auf uns komm Tröster du,	(d)	Come down upon us you Comforter,
herab auf uns komm Tröster du,	(F)	Come down upon us you Comforter,
in unser Herz leg' Himmelsruh!	(B♭)	Instill within our hearts heavenly peace,
in unser Herz leg' Himmelsruh!	(C)	Instill within our hearts heavenly peace.
Komm heil'ger Geist, erhöre unser Flehen,	(C)	Come Holy Spirit, hear our prayers,
die sehnend auf zu dir, zu dir, Verheiss'nem sehen;		that we send to you, to you, beheld Promised One;
herab auf uns komm Tröster du,	(d)	Come down upon us you Comforter,
herab auf uns komm Tröster du,	(F)	Come down upon us you Comforter,
in unser Herz leg' Himmelsruh!	(B♭)	Instill within our hearts heavenly peace,
in unser Herz leg' Himmelsruh!	(C)	Instill within our hearts heavenly peace.
O komm zu stärken unsern Glaubensmuth,	(a)	Come to strengthen our courage in faith,
O komm zu stärken unsern Glaubensmuth,		Come to strengthen our courage in faith,
Verlass', verlass' auf unserm Pfad uns nicht,	(e)	Leave, leave us not on our path,
Verlass', verlass' auf unserm Pfad uns nicht!		Leave, leave us not on our path,
Du Bote aus dem Himmelslicht	(b)	You, messenger from the heavenly lights
verlass auf unserm Pfad uns nicht		leave us not on our path,
und leite uns zu dem was recht und gut.		and lead us to what is right and good.
Du Bote aus dem Himmelslicht		You, messenger from the heavenly lights
verlass auf unserm Pfad uns nicht		leave us not on our path,
und leite uns zu dem was recht und gut.		and lead us to what is right and good.
O komm zu stärken unsern Glaubensmuth,		Come to strengthen our courage in faith,
Verlass' uns nicht auf unserm Pfad,		Leave us not on our path,

Table 15.3 Continued

O komm zu stärken unsern Glaubensmuth,		Come to strengthen our courage in faith,
Verlass' uns nicht auf unserm Pfad,		Leave us not on our path,
O komm heiliger Geist, erhöre unser Flehen, (*silence*)	(C)	Come Holy Spirit, hear our prayers, (*silence*)
Komm heiliger Geist, erhöre unser Flehen, (*silence*)	(A)	Come Holy Spirit, hear our prayers, (*silence*)
die sehnend auf zu dir, zu dir, Verheiss'nem sehen; (*silence*)	(C)	that we send to you, to you, beheld Promised One; (*silence*)
die sehnend auf zu dir, zu dir, Verheiss'nem sehen; (*silence*)	(A)	that we send to you, to you, beheld Promised One; (*silence*)
herab auf uns komm Tröster du,	(B♭)	Come down upon us you Comforter,
herab auf uns komm Tröster du,		Come down upon us you Comforter,
in unser Herz leg' Himmelsruh!	(C)	Instill within our hearts heavenly peace,
in unser Herz leg' Himmelsruh!		Instill within our hearts heavenly peace.

Example 15.3 Schubert, *Hymnus an den heiligen Geist*, D 948: tonal fluctuation

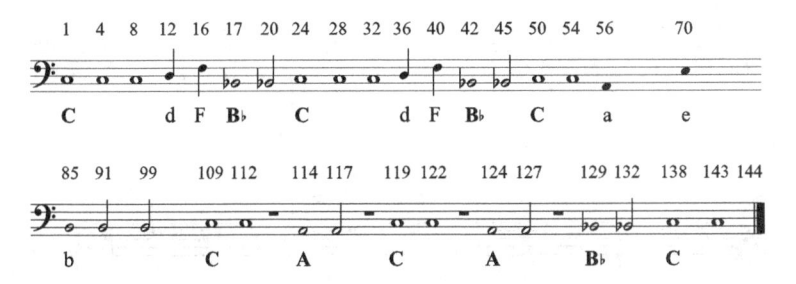

flats (B♭ major), Schubert's hymn abruptly turns towards 'sharp' keys, reaching the minor key of two sharps (B minor) before falling back to C. Ultimately, the even more tonally distant major key of three sharps (A major) asserts itself in bar 114 via abrupt tonal shift. Regained in bar 124 and framed by silences of five, three, four and four beats, respectively, as indicated by the rests, the determined attainment of A seems to symbolise success. And the subsequent return to C via B♭ revisits an earlier step of the process while serving as a quick route 'home'.

Yet Schubert's use of his performing forces personalises the hymn's message, increasing its persuasion. Soloists sing in just two passages within the work, first during the immediate reprise of opening material that occurs in bars 25–56, and later in bars 114–144. Example 15.4 gives the beginning of the first of these passages.

While the choir repeats its opening material, the soloists intone the same sentiments, their thinner-textured echoes simulating effects of distance, dimensionality and transformation. Hardly heard at first, they project more and more, gaining in independence and energy as the passage unfolds. Prompted

Example 15.4 Schubert, *Hymnus an den heiligen Geist*, D 948: bars 25–32

Schubert's Late Church Music

by the choir's rising tessituras, the tenor I soloist reaches the highest pitch of the work in bar 45, a B♭4 sung *pianissimo*, just as B♭ major is tonicised, portraying, perhaps, the aspirations of the choir's text arriving near their intended destination—heaven.

Later, the soloists' contribution becomes more dramatic, as Example 15.5 suggests.

Rectangles in the example highlight expressively significant silences. The soloists' echoes begin five bars later in bar 113, following a five-beat interval of silence, sung more softly and transposed to A major, via direct shift without modulation, as if the choir's petition had traveled to and resonated within a different dimension. The ethereal sequence repeats, following a short silence, again simulating the sound of a plea reverberating in a distant plane. This subtle effect of tone painting, so carefully and effectively wrought via the hymn's

Example 15.5 Schubert, *Hymnus an den heiligen Geist*, D 948: bars 108–13

Example 15.5 Continued

contextual process, offers a testament to Schubert's creativity, yet it also seems to reveal identification with the text's plea. One senses that Schubert may have taken some comfort in designing this delicate aural scenario of an earthly petition reaching the heavenly realm. And by entrusting it to male voices, he seems to have wished to personalise its message.

In *Hymnus an den heiligen Geist*, perhaps more so than in the 'Schlussgesang' and 'Das Gebet des Herrn' of the *Deutsche Messe*, Schubert seems to imply the notions of gaining peace through prayer and transcendence through the Holy Spirit. If so, we may witness here a glimpse of his spirituality. Schubert's next major sacred work may be even more self-revealing.

Example 15.5 Continued

Harmonic Transformation in the Sanctus and Agnus Dei of Schubert's Last Mass

Schubert's Mass in E♭ major (D 950, Op. posth.; 1828), his sixth contribution to the venerable genre, appears to have been written in June of his final year, less than six months before his death.[15] It was not performed during his lifetime, and we are not sure what motivated its composition.[16] Unlike his Fifth Mass in A♭ major (D 670; 1819–22, revised 1826), however, it is more introspective than ceremonial, an indiosyncratic statement of faith.[17] But like Mozart's last three symphonies, Schubert's Mass in E♭ seems to have been composed from inner necessity, conceived and created in mere months, arising as if it simply needed to be. In this light, the size and complexity of Schubert's last Mass, as well as its liturgical nature, invite us to consider it as a sacred offering. Scored for choir, soloists and full orchestra, including two horns, three trombones and timpani, though without flutes, its Sanctus features a contextual process that involves the systematic transformation by the movement's end of a distinctive harmonic element first heard near the start. Its Agnus Dei exhibits a tonal conflict whose instigator undergoes reconciliatory change as well. Both feature a fascination with musical transformation that may have implications beyond the music itself.

The Sanctus of Schubert's last Mass opens with great mystery and tremendous power. Example 15.6 presents just the vocal parts of bars 1–17.

A melodic sequence in the bass, E♭–B♮–G–E♭—which may be conceptualised as a series of descending major thirds framed first by tonic major and then by tonic minor harmonies—serves as the structural foundation of the remarkable opening passage.[18]

Surely the most impressive part of this imposing passage appears in bars 3 and 4 of Example 15.6, where the strikingly chromatic B minor sonority (♯v) sounds, sung *fortissimo* and supported by most of the orchestra. Enharmonically equivalent to the lowered submediant minor (♭vi), C♭ minor, this chromatic sonority (♯v) seems quite foreign and out of place with respect to the prevailing E♭ major tonality. In effect, this alien chord represents an unstable constituent at the very start of the Sanctus, one that holds thematic and dramatic implications. In effect, it represents 'a troubling element of which one expects to hear more', to borrow Cone's words.[19]

Three bars later, a harmony based on the lowered submediant major (♭VI), the enharmonic equivalent of the raised dominant, sounds again, articulated briefly on the third quaver of bar 7 on the first syllable of 'Deus'. But this time the quality of the C♭ chord is major, a transformation of the earlier B minor chord to C♭ major that brings the alien element a little closer to the realm of E♭ major, though still not purely diatonic.[20] And after a brief contrapuntal interlude in bars 9 and 10, the C♭ major (♭VI) harmony resounds again for all of bar 11, this time homophonically, sung to the text 'gloria tua', as if to reinforce the perception of changeability in that submediant chord a semitone above the diatonic dominant and to reveal that its quality may fluctuate from minor to major.

When the opening material returns in bar 13, the striking B minor sonority appears again, albeit for a shorter time, sounding just one bar instead of two. In this way, the chord on B♮ demonstrates that it remains an unresolved disturbance within the tonal environment. Yet the harmonic element has less impact than its initial appearance in bars 3 and 4, thus foretelling its own fate. So in the space of just a few bars, we experience a breathtakingly dramatic sonority and witness the tentative and gradual beginning of its metamorphosis.

Example 15.6 Schubert, Mass in E♭, D 950, Sanctus: bars 1–17 (voices only)

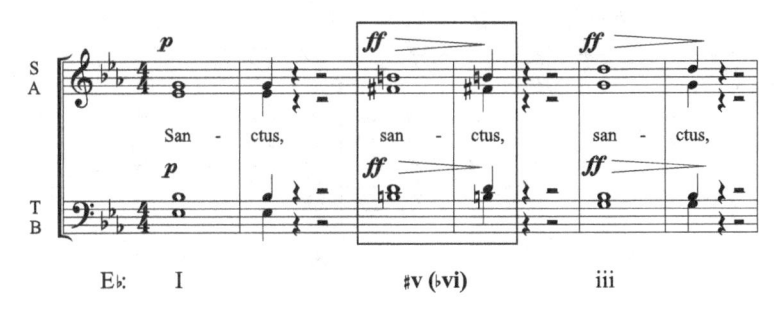

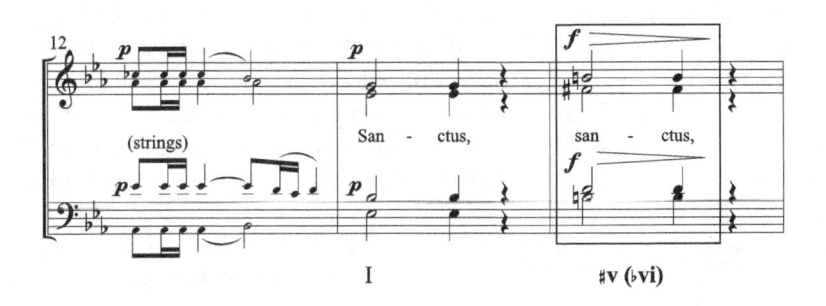

Example 15.6 Continued

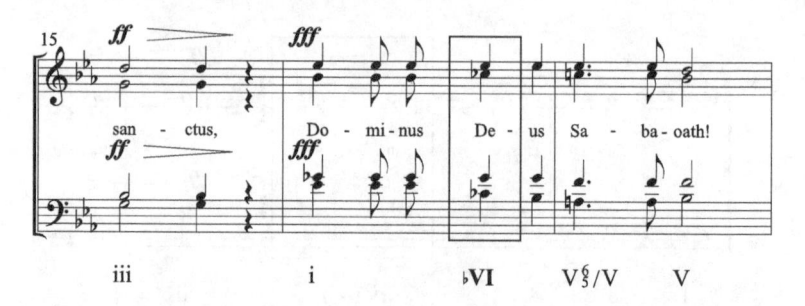

[musical notation: "san - ctus, Do - mi - nus De - us Sa - ba - oath!" with chord labels: iii, i, ♭VI, V⁶₅/V, V]

As just this much of the Sanctus hints, the contextual process here consists in the conversion of a conspicuous and persistent sonority, the B minor chord sounding a minor second above the dominant, which demonstrates an inherent potential for shifting from minor to major. A process of transformation, it reflects the notions of reconciliation and transcendence as the identity of this exceptional element evolves. Indeed, it would appear to have repercussions, for its flux seems to be echoed in reverse with respect to tonic, which alternates between E♭ major (bars 1, 9 and 13) and E♭ minor (bars 7, 10 and 16) in this brief excerpt at the start of the Sanctus.

The notation of this seemingly obstinate harmonic unit within the Sanctus is significant: in its first appearance, it is expressed as a minor sonority on the raised dominant, built on B♮, a semitone above the dominant of E♭. And while under conventional circumstances such an inflected degree would tend to resolve upwards, here its ultimate contextual resolution is to relax and relinquish its aspirations, first transforming into its enharmonic equivalent, C♭, before subsequently deferring to the diatonic dominant, B♭. In effect, this defiant B♮ degree, unlike the somewhat similar promissory note Cone observed in Schubert's *Moment musical*—also an inflected dominant degree—is destined not to rise here, but to fall, to relax, to submit, becoming its enharmonic equivalent to complete the contextual process of the Sanctus.

The conceptual and contextual conversion of this degree continues in the faster and fugal 'Osanna' section of the Sanctus (Allegro, ma non troppo, bars 24–87). Example 15.7 reveals a greatly extended octave progression in the structural bass voice, unfolding within a grand span that composes out the structural dominant of the movement (B♭), in which C♭—the enharmonic equivalent of B♮—is prominent (see the circled pitches in bars 37, 55, 66 and 72–73). Yet here that transformation of B♮ always yields to the dominant.

While the striking sonority of the opening bars does not appear upon these passing C♭ basses, and neither does the B♮, the sonority's link with these instances of the lowered submediant lingers. The expanded octave progression

Example 15.7 Schubert, Mass in E♭, D 950, Sanctus ('Osanna' section): expanded octave progression in bars 26–67

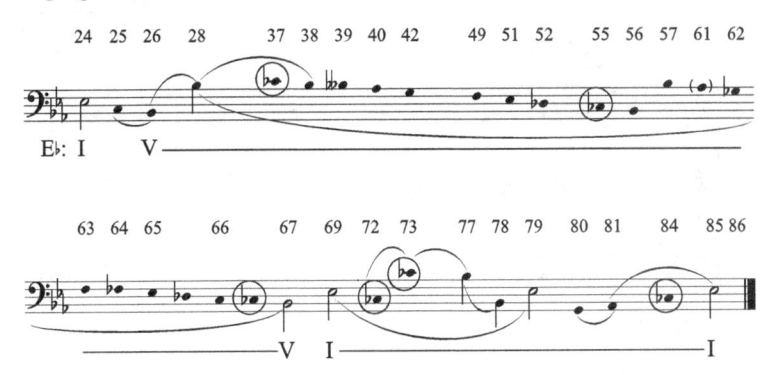

represented in Example 15.7, however, effectively diminishes it through subordination to the dominant, a procedure that continues to movement's end.[21] The chromatic degree B♮/C♭ loses the prominence it usurped at the start of the Sanctus and assumes its conventional function as a subordinate of the submediant and dominant.

The conclusion of the final 'Osanna' at the end of the Sanctus appears in Example 15.8.

C♭ still arises in the bass of the closing passage, though not associated with a root-position minor triad. In the closing bars, shown in Example 15.8, the lowered sixth scale degree, C♭, sounding in the bass is associated with no fewer than three different harmonies and even appears just before the closing sonority; but none of these is B minor, C♭ minor or C♭ major. While the lowered sixth scale degree itself remains a distinctive presence within the tonality of E♭ major, the original harmony with which it was associated—B minor—has been left behind, and indeed, no one sonority takes its place. The degree's previous identity has been shed, leaving just its essence, and that essence submits to the dominant, which, in turn, defers to the tonic of E♭. The musical idea represented by B♮/C♭ plays no role in the subsequent Benedictus section of the Mass, which is set in A♭ major, and indeed, when the 'Osanna' returns after the Benedictus section to provide closure to the Sanctus movement as a whole, the conversion-and-subordination process leaves the striking B minor harmony of bars 3–4 just a fleeting memory. Our perceptions of apprehension and anxiety at the outset of the Sanctus are thus transformed to a calmer, more stable state.

Schubert's interest in the sixth scale degree—the location of a major key's relative minor—continues within the Agnus Dei and leads to its exploitation in its contextual process that seems to bring satisfactory closure to the entire work. Indeed, C♭ serves here as a momentum-generating factor within an entirely new context. The movement also communicates transformation.

Example 15.8 Schubert, Mass in E♭, D 950, Sanctus ('Osanna' section): bars 67–86

Example 15.9 presents its opening bars, illustrating the surprisingly forceful way with which the image of the Lamb of God is portrayed.

This unexpected vehemence eventually subsides, pacified by gentler strains in the subsequent 'Dona nobis pacem' sections, but the initial impression remains vivid. As it happens, the pitches heard in the bass's first four bars—C, B, E♭ and

Example 15.9 Schubert, Mass in E♭, D 950, Agnus Dei: bars 1–23

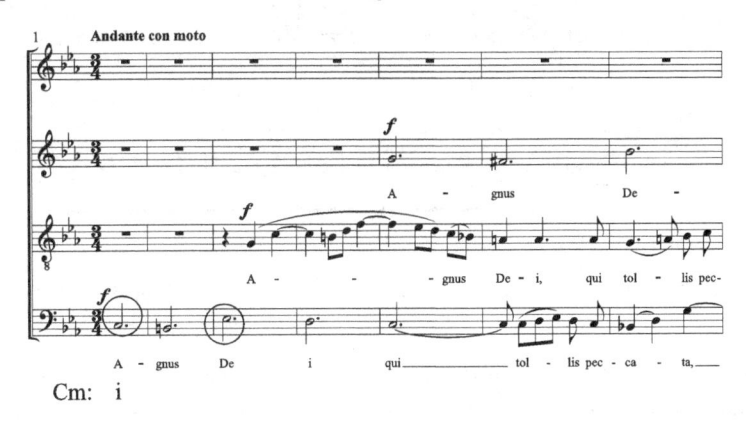

Cm: i

Example 15.10 Schubert, Mass in E♭, D 950, Agnus Dei: sectional and tonal structure

D—both initiate and summarise the contextual process the unfolds within the Agnus Dei. Emblematic of a minor key (C minor) and its relative major (E♭), each followed by its own leading note, this four-pitch motto summarises at the musical surface the dramatic contextual process about to unfold on a high structural level.[22]

A comprehensive sketch of the sectional and tonal structure of the Agnus Dei appears in Example 15.10.

As Example 15.10 suggests, the opening Agnus Dei section of the movement (bars 1–98) strongly and unambiguously asserts C minor. At the broadest structural level this passage represents an extended prefix to the main body of the movement, an instance of what I have called a *precursive prolongation*.[23] Its initial displacement of the primary tonic of the Agnus Dei and the Mass as a whole—E♭—with the local and temporary tonic of C is the foundation of the movement's contextual process, and the regaining of rightful priority by E♭ is the basis of the movement's dramatic conflict. Indeed, the imperfect cadence with which the C minor section ends in bar 98 opens the door to change, for it initiates a vacuum of expectancy whose space will be filled by the Mass's primary tonic.

In the subsequent 'Dona nobis' section, a tonally closed passage in E♭ that extends from bar 99 to bar 190, C does not rise and challenge E♭ in any way; indeed, it is undermined by the degree of C♭, most notably in the final bars. The demotive transformation of C continues in the following span, when the opening material, originally heard in C minor in bars 1–98, effectively is appropriated by the tonality of E♭ minor. Expressed in the tonic minor in bars 191–213, this passage of familiar material sustains the movement's contextual process by sowing some tonal uncertainty, for the expected E♭ major *still* has yet to arrive. Indeed, at the start of the final section, especially in bars 214–227, the key of C would seem to be reasserting itself, as if to suggest that the transformation of C from upstart and would-be usurper to assertive tonic had begun again. However, soon it is subordinated once and for all by E♭. This submission of the submediant degree of C to its tonic of E♭ completes the movement's contextual process, returning that once ambitious degree to its subordinate status within the grander tonal system.

Example 15.11 Schubert, Mass in E♭, D 950, Agnus Dei: bars 245–256 (voices only)

The closing bars of the choral parts of Schubert's Agnus Dei appear in Example 15.11.

E♭, firmly fixed at last, further marginalises its diatonic sixth scale step, C, by effectively banning it from the last nine bars of the work, allowing only C♭ to sound there. Schubert, having introduced pitch equivalents of each of these degrees at the very start of the movement in the first two notes sung by the basses—C and B (the enharmonic equivalent of C♭) thus foreshadows its process of functional transformation, which is concluded here with the close on E♭. The pitch C, which initially appeared to be tonic, ultimately assumes the submediant function, while B♮, which seemed at first to function as a leading tone, now emerges as a chromatic passing note between two diatonic degrees. In effect, their identities change as the movement's contextual process unfolds, fueling forward momentum.

There seem to be no obvious details in the Sanctus or Agnus Dei of Schubert's last Mass to suggest any specific personal reference to the composer or to encourage any particular metaphysical analogy. For instance, it would be unwise to envisage the musical transformations of the seemingly out-of-place B minor harmony of the Sanctus, or the initial local tonal centre of C in the Agnus Dei, as somehow symbolic of Schubert himself, or even as just generally representative of an errant soul gradually aligning itself with divine will. Yet what seems evident here is a preoccupation with the resolution of contextual conflict, initiated by a problematic element, via a persuasive transformation that allows it to transcend its original circumstances for another, more stable situation.[24] If Schubert was able to vicariously experience the pursuit and ultimately successful solution of a rewarding musical problem again and again as he developed and refined his String Quintet, enjoying triumph in the virtual reality of his imagination, it seems equally possible that he might benefit from repeatedly immersing himself in the mystery and revelation of his Mass's Sanctus, and quite plausible that he could lose himself in the wonder and anticipation of his Agnus Dei during the process of composition. And it appears that such therapeutic escape may well have served Schubert to his last days.

Harmonic Evolution in Schubert's Last *Tantum ergo*

In October 1828 Schubert completed his String Quintet and 'Der Hirt auf dem Felsen' (D 965, Op. posth.; 1828), for voice, clarinet and piano. In that same month before his death, however, he also finished two sacred works, his sixth *Tantum ergo* (D 962, Op. posth.; 1828) and the *Offertorium: Intende voci*, both of which feature contextual processes that underscore the aspirational impulses of their texts.[25] Each poses a harmonic problem in its opening bars: a memorable dissonance, contextually satisfactory resolution of which is persistently pursued and finally found by work's end.

The traditional text of the *Tantum ergo*, attributed to Thomas Aquinas, appears in Table 15.4.

In E♭ major, Schubert's hymn is strophically structured and syllabically set. Scored for mixed choir and four soloists, as well as a large orchestra that includes horns, trumpets, timpani and alto, tenor and bass trombones, though no flutes, the *Tantum ergo* begins with a remarkable blend of power and profundity that communicates supreme confidence and joy. Example 15.12 presents its opening bars, which are sung by solo quartet.

As the example shows, a dissonant half-diminished seventh sonority consisting of the notes C, E♭, G♭, and B♭ enclosed by the rectangle—rooted on the submediant degree C, stacked on the tone E♭ and sounding on the downbeat of the second bar—immediately injects instability even as it hints of mystery and potential.[26] A dramatic harmonic event in and of itself, the chord is brief

Table 15.4 Schubert, *Tantum ergo*, D 962: text (Thomas Aquinas), with translation

Tantum ergo Sacramentum,	So great a Sacrament therefore
Veneremur cernui,	Let us venerate with bowed heads,
Et antiquum documentum	And let the ancient document
novo cedat ritui.	Give way to the new rite.
Praestet fides supplementum	May faith avail a supplement
Sensuum defectui	For defective senses.
Genitori, Genitoque,	To the Begetter and the Begotten
Laus et jubilatio,	Be praise and joy,
Salus, honor, virtus quoque,	salvation, honor, and virtue also
Sit et benedictio.	may there be and blessing
Procedenti ab utroque	To the One proceeding from both
Compar sit laudatio. Amen.	May there be equal praise. Amen.

yet memorable, made prominent by metric stress, and it draws attention to the accented third syllable of the word 'sacramentum'. Instead of a conventional resolution that would immediately introduce the dominant harmony in E♭, two fully diminished sevenths follow, identified in the example by ovals, which, paradoxically, seem to sustain the engaging effect of the half-diminished seventh sonority. As the excerpt shows, that harmony soon returns in bar 6, again identified by the rectangle, where it now is associated with the third syllable of the word 'documentum'. Here it is followed by just one fully diminished seventh, as the excerpt shows, yet again, the half-diminished seventh sonority stands out as a distinctive harmonic event, emerging because of its dissonance, its metric stress and now its repetition. As a result, this persistent harmonic element enters our consciousness as a structural instability, the local 'resolutions' of which fail satisfactorily to settle.

The opening passage returns immediately, as Example 15.13 shows, now sung by the full choir at an elevated dynamic level.

The distinctive half-diminished seventh sonority correspondingly recurs in bars 11 and 15, sustaining our memory of its initial impacts. Slightly rescored, its soprano voice sounds C rather than B♭ in these instances, communicating additional urgency. More insistent, the chord remains a characteristic conflict within the context of the *Tantum ergo* that demands attention and resolution.

The centre of each strophe of Schubert's *Tantum ergo* briefly slips into the relatively distant key of G♭ major, introducing a higher tessitura as well as a fresh tonal plane. As one might expect, given the sequence of the opening section, the soloists venture there first, as Example 15.14 shows.

Example 15.12 Schubert, *Tantum ergo*, D 962: bars 1–8

Example 15.13 Schubert, *Tantum ergo*, D 962: bars 9–18

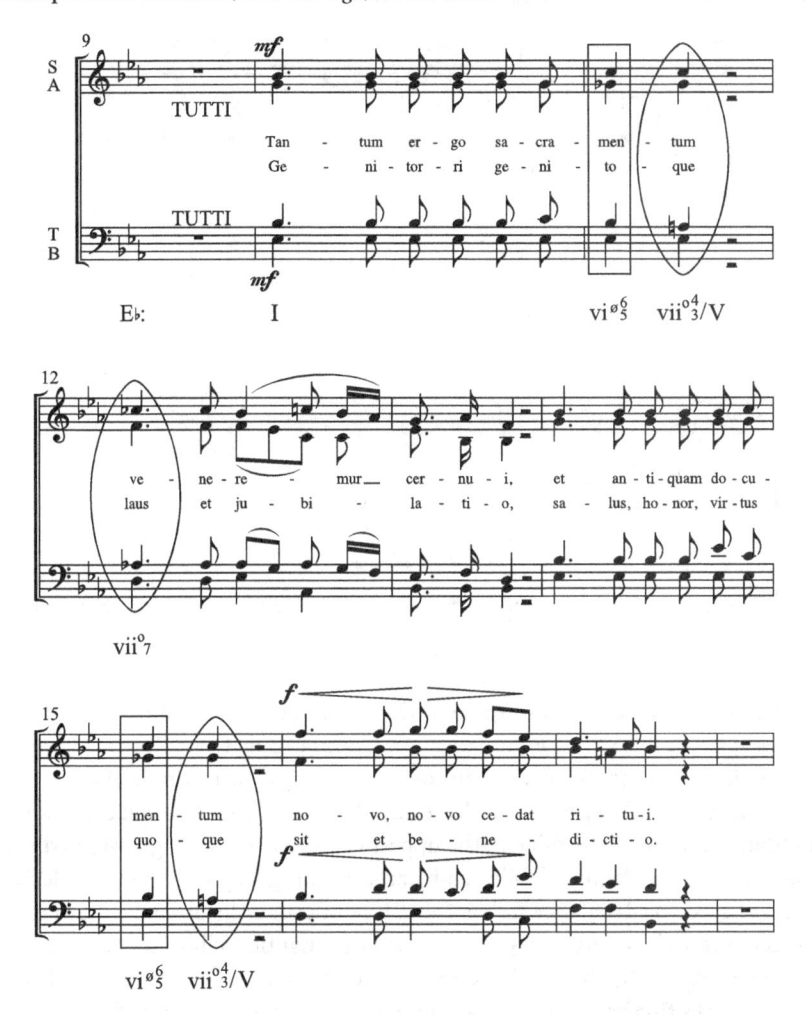

In Example 15.14, the circles reveal that G♭'s fourth scale step, C♭, gains a small degree of prominence as a contextually stabilised degree, the major third above the local tonic of G♭. Even so, its significance is not revealed until the end of the hymn, whose remaining vocal lines appear in Example 15.15.

As this suggests, the climax and structural cadence of Schubert's *Tantum ergo* occur in bars 27 and 28, respectively, after which a brief intoning passage brings a calm end. Curiously, however, the climax and cadence do not address the long-standing contextual conflict represented by the insistent half-diminished seventh that captivated us in bars 2, 6, 11 and 15. Yet the coda somehow brings more satisfying closure. Why?

Example 15.14 Schubert, *Tantum ergo*, D 962: bars 19–22

Two harmonic processes unfold in the *Tantum ergo*. One of these is a tonal unfolding—in the Schenkerian sense—of a minor tonic triad. A broad bass arpeggiation from I to ♭III to V to I unfolds in bars 1–28, as Examples 15.12–15.15 have suggested, all in support of the tonic. There is no conventional descending fundamental line discernible in the uppermost voice, but a long-sustained primary tone, scale degree 5, followed by an ascending leap from to scale degree 1 at the structural cadence in bar 28. While unusual, the absence of a typical descending *Urlinie* certainly contributes to the qualities of humility and anticipation expressed by the text.[27] Example 15.16 offers an extremely simple sketch that captures this broad structural counterpoint in bars 1, 19 and 28.

At the musical surface, the striking half-diminished chords in bars 2, 6, 11 and 15 participate in the composing out of the tonic triad and are readily explained in Schenkerian terms. Yet strict adherence to that perspective minimises their contribution to the hymn's drama. An alternative proposition accounts for their prominence.

A contextual harmonic progression involving those distinctive sonorities also unfolds in the *Tantum ergo*, proceeding from the sonority in bar 15 to the one in bar 30, as Example 15.15 implies. In the second bar of the final phrase (bar 30), a German augmented sixth consisting of the pitches C♭, E♭, F♯ (= G♭) and A♮ quietly resonates (C♭ is articulated by the bassoons, cellos and bass trombone), built above the tonic bass of E♭. A transformation of the distinctive

Example 15.15 Schubert, *Tantum ergo*, D 962: bars 23–33

Example 15.16 Schubert, *Tantum ergo*, D 962: sketch

sonority introduced in the movement's second bar (which contains the pitches A♮, C, E♭ and G♭), it is an intervallic inverse of that harmony that shares two of its pitches, E♭ and F♯/G♭. Remarkably, the German sixth does not resolve to the dominant, as one might expect, but embellishes the tonic harmony of E♭, which sounds at the end of the bar. Repeated in the following bar, this dominant seventh homonym continues on to a simpler ♭VI chord, shedding one of its pitches, which, in turn, becomes a iv with the change of one pitch, before the tonic triad arrives in the final bar to offer long-sought stability and peace. In the *Tantum ergo*, the distinctive dissonant sonority of bar 2 continues its evolution after the work's structural cadence, reaching resolution in the final bar.

Harmonic Metamorphosis in the *Offertorium: Intende voci*

One more choral composition issued from Schubert's pen in October 1828, just weeks before the composer's death, and like its predecessor, the *Offertorium: Intende voci* (D 963 Op. posth.; 1828) exploits expectations arising from a single provocative harmony. Table 15.5 offers the complete text of Schubert's *Offertorium*, which consists of just two verses from Psalm 5.

Scored for mixed choir, tenor solo and a large orchestra that includes solo oboe, horns and alto, tenor and bass trombones, though no flutes, the *Offertorium*'s dominant expressive impression in performance may be devotion. However, upon reflection, what may be most moving about this work is its concentration: ten minutes of music proceed from just three phrases from the psalmist. Anyone who might have been sceptical about Schubert's faith or his regard for the next life is apt to be rendered speechless in the face of this almost-three-hundred-bar essay, composed without commission or hope of performance. And anyone unsure about his innovative genius need look no further than the contextual process that contributes to its fervent focus as well as its continuity.

Table 15.5 Schubert, *Offertorium: Intende voci*, D 963: text (Psalm 5:3–4) and translation

Intende voci orationis meae,	Listen to the voice of my prayer,
Rex meus et Deus meus.	My King and my God.
Quoniam ad te orabo Domine	For to you I will pray, Lord.

Example 15.17 Schubert, *Offertorium: Intende voci*, D 963: bars 1–5

Example 15.17 presents just the opening bars of the *Offertorium*'s introduction, a purely instrumental introduction, which establishes the tonality of B♭ major.

In the third bar of Example 15.17, a D major sonority sounds, eliciting our curiosity. Will it prove to be a chromatic mediant, or perhaps a dominant prefix of the relative minor? In this current context, the former is true, and its distinctiveness enables it to serve as an anchor within a thematic harmonic progression whose variations continue throughout the *Offertorium*. By not resolving as we might expect within the home key of B♭ major, this engaging chord prompts us to anticipate an occasion in the future when it does.

Example 15.18 presents the essential voice leading of this passage, identified here as progression 'a)':

Instead of resolving to a G minor harmony, as we might expect, the third chord in the sequence is succeeded by the tonic harmony, its expectations

Example 15.18 Schubert, *Offertorium: Intende voci*, D 963: thematic progression variants

momentarily stifled. Like the other implicative elements we have observed in Schubert's music thus far, this would-be secondary dominant in B♭ major calls for a continuation yet to come.

Six other variants of the ritornello-like progression appear during the composition, as Example 15.17 reveals. The first two passages, represented by progressions b) and c) in the example, are set in the home key of B♭ and in context form the foundations of passages sung by the choir. In each, the D major chord in second inversion does not resolve up by perfect fourth to G minor, as expected, but proceeds elsewhere, leaving fulfilment of this harmonic hint for the future.

The next two variants of the thematic progression, both of which appear in instrumental interludes that serve transitional purposes, introduce aspects of progress. Progression d) of Example 15.17 effects a modulation to G minor, and in it, the chord in third position (bar 139) is repeated before resolving up a perfect fourth, as we might expect. A similar situation occurs in the modulatory progression e), which temporarily tonicises D minor. There, the G major chord of bars 157–158 resolves as a secondary dominant of C minor. In effect, these two instances may be interpreted as trials and breakthroughs, for the crucial sonorities do resolve in the same fashion as secondary dominants. Yet because these occur outside the tonic key, the implication and obligation of the original instance of bar 3 have yet to be realised.

The next instance of the thematic passage, represented by progression f) in Example 15.17, is in B♭ and forms the foundation of a span sung by the choir. The D major sonority, heard in bar 190 and repeated in bar 191, again fails to resolve as expected. Only in the final interlude before the close, represented by progression g), does the original D major sonority finally itself resolve as a dominant prefix of G minor in bars 271–272, as we have long anticipated. In effect, the identity of this D major harmony finally has been converted from an anomaly whose implications arouse wonder to an element that eventually meets its elicited expectations, its potential fulfilled.

Schubert's Aspirations

The contextual processes described here represent a testament to Schubert's creative imagination and musical innovation. Given the difficult circumstances of his final year, however, the progressive natures of these structures, and their settings within sacred music, they also may reveal Schubert himself. Naturally, we hesitate to speculate about a composer's personal intentions and internal motivation, but the coincidence of these three factors offers an opportunity to sketch a portion of Schubert's portrait that has heretofore remained rather obscure—the role of spirituality in his final years.

Surely the remarkable outpouring of sacred music from Schubert's pen during the short span from May to October 1828, which includes the last four works examined here, plus his settings of the Ninety-second Psalm (D 953; 1828), which appear in both Hebrew- and German-language versions, as well as a new 'Benedictus' (D 961; 1828) for the Mass in C major (D 452; 1816), composed a dozen years earlier, and a hymn (D 954; 1828) whose title, *Glaube, Hoffnung, und Liebe*, translates as 'Belief, Hope, and Love', all suggest a composer increasingly inspired by spirituality. However, the contextual processes illuminated in the seven works examined here, which engage attention, elicit anticipation and answer expectations to create impressions of flow and futurity, intimate neither lamentation nor abnegation, but yearning and fulfilment. Using musical means such as key relations, harmonic functions and voice leading, Schubert initiates a logical progression or introduces a musical 'problem' within these works in order to portray its pursuit and solution. The attainment of anticipated goals, often expressed by transformation, provides resolution, and the cumulative impression is one not of triumph, but of transcendence.

If Schubert recognised that his time was running short, then from the contextual processes evident within these seven sacred works we may surmise that he had begun to desire and expect what his Catholic faith had promised— release from earthly distress through corporeal death and heavenly redemption of his soul by his God.[28] And if he was looking forward to what lay ahead, I suspect he looked backwards as well, realising that the musical fountain he had become was nothing less than miraculous—more evidence of his God's love. We know that in the late autumn of 1828 Schubert prepared to study fugal composition with Simon Sechter, then the leading master of music theory in Vienna.[29] And about the same time, Schubert began his Tenth Symphony, whose three surviving sketches include the beginning of a rather contrapuntal Scherzo.[30] So perhaps Schubert simply sought to prolong his creative flow as long as he could. And perhaps he had finally found a measure of peace.

Notes

1. Edward T. Cone, 'Schubert's Promissory Note: an Exercise in Musical Hermeneutics', *19th-Century Music* 5/3 (1982), pp. 233–41. The initial statement of the 'promissory' note E♮5 occurs in bar 12, and its long-anticipated resolution to F5 occurs in bar 47. (This essay adopts the Acoustical Society of America's system for specifying pitches, in which 'middle C' is C4.)

2. For a discussion of a contextual process that involves meter, see Richard Kurth, 'On the Subject of Schubert's "Unfinished" Symphony: *Was bedeutet die Bewegung?*', *19th-Century Music* 23/1 (1999), pp. 3–32.

3. James William Sobaskie, 'Tonal Implication and the Gestural Dialectic in Schubert's A Minor Quartet', in Brian Newbould (ed.), *Schubert the Progressive: History, Performance Practice, Analysis* (Aldershot: Ashgate, 2003), pp. 53–80; Sobaskie, 'The "Problem" of Schubert's String Quintet', *Nineteenth-Century Music Review* 2/1 (2005), pp. 57–92; and Sobaskie, 'A Balance Struck: Gesture, Form, and Drama in Schubert's E flat Major Piano Trio', in Xavier Hascher (ed.), *Le Style instrumental de Schubert: sources, analyse, contexte, évolution* (Paris: Publications de la Sorbonne, 2007), pp. 115–46.

4. The concept of 'musical problem' originates with Arnold Schoenberg; for more on this notion, see Arnold Schoenberg, *Fundamentals of Musical Composition*, ed. Gerald Strang and Leonard Stein (New York: Faber, 1967), p. 102; and Schoenberg, *The Musical Idea, and the Logic, Art, and Technique of its Presentation*, ed. Patricia Carpenter and Severine Neff (New York: Columbia University Press, 1995), pp. 226–7 and 395–6. For another analytical application of the concept, see James William Sobaskie, 'Contextual Drama in Bach', in *Music Theory Online* 12/3 (2006), http://mto.societymusictheory.org/issues/mto.06.12.3/toc.12.3.html.

5. James William Sobaskie, 'Schubert's Self-Elegies', in *Schubert Familiar and Unfamiliar: New Perspectives*, special issue, *Nineteenth-Century Music Review* 5/2 (2008), pp. 71–105.

6. For more on the concept of 'posthumous voice', see Claire Raymond, *The Posthumous Voice in Women's Writing from Mary Shelley to Sylvia Plath* (Aldershot: Ashgate, 2006).

7. Schubert's close involvement with sacred music began with his appointment to the choir of the Stadtkonvict, the Imperial Seminary in Vienna, in October 1808, a tenure that lasted until November 1813; see Otto Erich Deutsch, *Schubert: a Documentary Biography*, trans. Eric Blom (London: J. M. Dent, 1946), pp. 10–11 and 41. During this time, Schubert studied counterpoint and composition with Antonio Salieri, Kappellmeister of the Imperial Chapel; see ibid., p. 24. The first of Schubert's works to be performed publicly was his Mass in F major (D 105; 1814), written when he was just seventeen. It was premièred under the composer's direction and in the presence of Salieri on 16 October 1814, with Therese Grob singing the soprano solo; see ibid., p. 44.

8. See my 'Schubert's Self-Elegies', pp. 102–5, where I suggest that Schubert's creativity may have served as a coping mechanism.

9. Schubert's sacred choral music in 1827 and 1828 included the *Deutsche Messe* (D 872); the *Hymnus an den heiligen Geist* (D 948); the Mass in E♭ (D 950); German and Hebrew versions of a setting of the Ninety-second Psalm (D 953), *Glaube, Hoffnung und Liebe* (D 954), a Benedictus in A minor (D961, intended as an alternative for use in the early Mass in C [D 452; 1816]); a *Tantum ergo* (D 962); and his last choral work, the *Offertorium: Intende voci* (D 963).

10. Schubert's *Deutsche Messe*, formally known as the *Gesänge zur Feier des heiligen Opfers des Messe*, belongs to the *Singmesse* tradition of vernacular Catholic worship that arose in Germany and Austria during the Enlightenment, perhaps best represented by the widely known examples by Michael Haydn (1737–1806). A series of songs intended to be sung while the priest quietly intoned the parts of the Mass, Schubert's *Deutsche Messe* included the following: 'Zum Eingang' (For the Procession), 'Zum Gloria' (For the Gloria), 'Zum Evangelium' (For the Gospel), 'Zum Offertorium' (For the Offertory), 'Zum Sanctus' 'For the Sanctus), 'Nach der Elevation' (After the Elevation), 'Zum Agnus Dei' (For the Agnus Dei), and 'Schlussgesang' (Recessional), plus an appended optional hymn, 'Das Gebet des Herrn' (The Lord's Prayer). The text of these songs echoed the sentiments of the corresponding parts of the Mass but elaborated their messages in language and manner typical of the age.

11. According to Deutsch, Neumann (1774–1849) was a professor of physics at the Polytechnischen Institut in Vienna and a poet who had written the libretto for Schubert's unfinished Orientalist opera *Sakuntala* (D701; 1820); see Deutsch, *Schubert: a Documentary Biography*, p. 681. The *Deutsche Messe* had been commissioned on behalf of an amateur choir at the institution where Neumann had taught since 1815. In a letter dated 16 October 1827, Schubert wrote: 'Most honoured Professor, I duly received the 100 florins, V.C., which you sent me for the composition of the vocal pieces for Mass, and only hope that the said compositions may be commensurate with your expectations. With all respect, Your most devoted Frz. Schubert'; see ibid., p. 681. Deutsch suggests that Schubert probably did not hear the work performed during his lifetime, however, and notes that the text was submitted to the censor's office of the Diocese of the Archbishop of Vienna in 1827,

where it was admitted but not sanctioned for official church use, a judgement not changed until the second half of the nineteenth century; see ibid., pp. 682–3. It is likely that Neumann's liberal theology and his use of the vernacular in this work did not please the conservative Catholic clergy of day, who may have sensed the unwanted influence of Protestantism. This may explain why the names of Neumann and Schubert did not appear on published copies until 1870, forty-three years after the piece first appeared. However, the work's chordal texture and limited vocal demands, coupled with its unaffected expression and tuneful melodies, won many admirers over the years; Maurice J. E. Brown relates that the *Deutsche Messe* 'became immediately, and has remained to this day in Vienna, very popular and greatly loved by the people. There are several arrangements to be had besides Schubert's own, and the first "number", which begins *Wohin sol lich mich wenden?*[,] is known and sung by many Viennese who have not the least idea it is by Schubert, but who know it in numerous versions as a popular piece of Church music.' Brown, *Schubert: a Critical Biography* (London: Macmillan, 1958), p. 251.

12. See the first chapter of Janet Schmalfeldt, *In the Process of Becoming: Analytic and Philosophical Perspectives on Form in Early Nineteenth-Century Music* (Oxford: Oxford University Press, 2011).

13. An earlier version of Schubert's *Hymnus an den heiligen Geist* has been lost, and a later arrangement, created in October 1828 and subsequently published with woodwind and brass accompaniment as Schubert's Op. 154, featured an altered text that removed references to the Holy Spirit ('Komm heiliger Geist' became 'Herr, unser Gott').

14. *Veni creator Spiritus*, a ninth-century hymn attributed to Rabanus Maurus, may be one of the most famous of chants of the early Christian church.

15. See Deutsch, *Schubert: a Documentary Biography*, pp. 742 and 790.

16. The Mass in E♭ was not heard until almost a year after the composer's death on 4 October 1829, performed at the Lichtental Parish Church in Vienna's Alsergrund district to honour posthumously the composer's request; see ibid., p. 804. Today this parish, near the University of Vienna, prides itself as the 'Schubertkirche'.

17. Schubert omitted certain lines of text from the traditional Latin Mass, as Brian Newbould relates: 'As usual, the reference to "unam sanctam catholicam Ecclesiam" in the Credo is gone. So is "Patrem omnipotentem", "genitum, non factum", and "consubstantialem Patri". These deviations—whether the result of religious conviction, oversight, or artistic strategy—have caused more problems for ecclesiastical posterity than they probably did in the liberal atmosphere known to Schubert in Biedermeier Vienna. At any rate, they did not stand in the way of a church performance at Holy Trinity in the Viennese suburb of Alsergrund within the year after Schubert's death.' Newbould, *Schubert: the Music and the Man* (Berkeley and Los Angeles: University of California Press, 1997), 285. For additional context, see John Gingerich, '"To How Many Shameful Deeds Must You Lend Your Image": Schubert's Pattern of Telescoping and Excision in the Texts of his Latin Masses', *Current Musicology* 70 (2000), pp. 61–99.

18. Richard Cohn describes this as a 'hexatonic cycle' and discusses this passage in his book *Audacious Euphony: Chromaticism and the Triad's Second Nature* (Oxford: Oxford University Press, 2012), pp. 30–2.

19. Cone, 'Schubert's Promissory Note,' p. 236.

20. Thus it is equivalent to a modal borrowing from E♭ minor.

21. For a discussion of a greatly expanded descending sixth, see my analysis of Bach's G♯ minor Prelude from the *Well-Tempered Clavier*, vol. 1, in James William Sobaskie, 'Contextual Drama in Bach', *Music Theory Online* 12/3 (2006), http://mto.societymusictheory.org/issues/mto.06.12.3/mto.06.12.3.sobaskie_frames.html.

22. Here, Schubert draws inspiration from a venerable source, as Newbould explains: 'Arrestingly, but unconventionally, the *Agnus Dei* begins with a fugal treatment of another Bach subject (the tortuous, claustrophobic one from the C♯ minor Fugue in Book 1 of the "Forty-eight")'. Newbould, *Schubert: the Music and the Man*, p. 288.

23. For more on precursive prolongation, see my 'Precursive Prolongation in the *Préludes* of Chopin', *Journal of the Society for Musicology in Ireland* 3 (2007–8), http://www.music.ucc.ie/JSMI/index.php/jsmi/issue/view/5, 25–61.

24. In a private communication, Lorraine Byrne Bodley captured the impact of the uniquely conceived large-scale harmonic conflict of the 'Agnus Dei' in a most eloquent way: 'I have always felt that Schubert's resumption of the *Dona Nobis* after the eventual dark return of the *Agnus Dei* enables him to conclude the work with the two moods—hope and fear—intermingled to the end'.

25. Newbould suggests that the *Offertorium: Intende voci* and the *Tantum ergo*, as well as the Mass in E♭, all may have been written for the Church of the Holy Trinity at Alsergrund, where Beethoven's funeral took place. See Newbould, *Schubert: the Music and the Man*, p. 284.

26. Of course, this sonority corresponds to what would become known as the '*Tristan* chord'.

27. See Sobaskie, 'Precursive Prolongation in the *Préludes* of Chopin', pp. 50–60, for a discussion of sustained primary tones.

28. One might question Schubert's religious convictions, especially in light of textual omissions in his Masses, passing comments in his letters and reports of conversations. However, it may be presumptuous to do so nearly two centuries later, given the character of this evidence and the impossibility of fully grasping the nature of his Catholic faith at that time and in that place, for we cannot help but bring twenty-first-century attitudes and preconceptions to such an interpretation. However, it seems to me that by composing large, imaginative and at times quite passionate sacred works, most without commission or even formally planned performances, Schubert made an indisputable statement of faith.

29. Schubert had his first lesson at Sechter's home on 4 November but did not keep his next appointment on 10 November. Deutsch speculates that Schubert's desire to study with Sechter came from the impression that Handel's music had

made on him; see Deutsch, *Schubert: a Documentary Biography*, p. 819. Schubert died of typhus, complicated by chronic syphilis, on 19 November 1828.

    30. Schubert's unfinished Tenth Symphony in D major was realised from surviving sketches by Brian Newbould; see Franz Schubert, *Symphony No. 10 in D major, D 936a* (London: Faber Music, 1995).

16

Elusive Intimacy in Schubert's Final Opera, *Der Graf von Gleichen*

Lisa Feurzeig

The legend of the Graf von Gleichen and his two wives can be traced back to the twelfth or thirteenth century, and it was told and retold in chronicles and literary works beginning in the sixteenth century.[1] The essential elements of the story are as follows: While crusading in the Middle East, the count of Gleichen is taken prisoner, becomes a slave to the sultan of Egypt and works in his garden, where he meets the sultan's daughter. She falls in love with him and helps him to escape, fleeing with him and converting to Christianity. When they return to Europe, the count receives permission, both from the pope and from his wife, to marry the Saracen princess who has rescued him from slavery. It is central to the story that in special circumstances, bigamy is appropriate and may even be sanctioned by the Church.

When Schubert and his friend Eduard von Bauernfeld began to discuss possible libretto material in 1825, Bauernfeld brought this story to Schubert's attention, and a libretto was completed in May 1826.[2] While other versions of the story may have been available to them, it is quite clear from plot similarities and from Bauernfeld's memoirs that one important source was the tale 'Melechsala', by Johann Karl August Musäus. Musäus's *Volksmärchen* (published 1782–6) are quite different from other fairy tales. Their mix of humour and rationalism clearly reflects attitudes of the late eighteenth century, as we can see from the comments of literary scholars.

> Musäus's position was from the first suspect: how is it possible for a proponent of rational thought to make use of such popular material and stay true to his enlightened ideas? His style is very far from the simple narratives of peasants or of the less-educated bourgeoisie: he is witty and clever; his diction is creative and whimsical; he makes constant references to topical events by means of humorous comparisons and metaphors.... Although marvels are never explained away by enlightened rational science, a rational attitude is just as likely to prove the correct one in a tale by Musäus as is the simple unquestioning acceptance of the magic of the world.[3]

The tales of the Brothers Grimm, published about three decades later, created a very different set of norms for *Märchen*, so that Musäus's approach must have seemed idiosyncratic by the 1820s.

If we approach Musäus's *Volksmärchen* with the measure of the Grimms' tales ... it would be just as if we desired that Fragonard and Boucher had painted like Moritz von Schwind ... or if we were disappointed by Mozart's *Così fan tutte* because this opera sounds so different from Humperdinck's *Hänsel und Gretel*.

The noble figures he writes about think and feel like Musäus and his friends of both sexes. How the folk expressed itself left him completely indifferent. ... The Middle Ages in which most of his tales play out is the 18th century.[4]

When Schubert and Bauernfeld took this story as their opera subject, they may have expected difficulties with the imperial censors, who did indeed forbid the performance of the work in October 1826. The ban shows the tightened standards in Vienna after the Carlsbad Decrees of 1818, for even in 1815 *Ernst, Graf von Gleichen*, a Volkstheater play (unfortunately no longer extant) with a text by Josef Alois Gleich and music by Franz Volkert, had been performed at the Leopoldstadttheater in Vienna. Despite the censors' decision, Schubert proceeded with his work on the opera, since he and Bauernfeld hoped that it would eventually be produced elsewhere. Bauernfeld states in his memoirs that Franz Grillparzer had offered to help arrange a performance in Berlin.[5]

In choosing a tale by Musäus as the source for his opera libretto, Bauernfeld had to move it from its ambiguous position within the genre of *Märchen* or legend into the genre of opera—at a time when opera was also at a turning point and the features of Romantic opera were being determined. My objective here is to compare and contrast the tale by Musäus with the libretto by Bauernfeld as Schubert set it to music, paying particular attention to what opportunities the characters have in each version to express their ideas and feelings about their unusual situation. I will argue that as a combined result of the change in genre and Bauernfeld's authorial decisions, some of the key information in Musäus's story was lost in the opera without any effective substitution's being made. The absence of that information became a flaw in the libretto that may help explain why Schubert never completed his sketches for the final act.

Genre Characteristics: Fairy Tale, Novella, Drama and Opera

Musäus included 'Melechsala' in his collection *Volksmärchen der Deutschen* (German Folk Tales).[6] As mentioned above, the Grimm brothers' fairy tales eventually came to define the *Märchen* genre, and Musäus's stories were then found wanting by comparison. Though the Melechsala tale is a legend with a long history that was most likely passed down through the oral tradition, it lacks some of the characteristics usually associated with fairy tales: most important, there is no magical element. For these reasons, the story does not easily match the characteristics of most *Märchen*—but it does match descriptions of the novella genre exceptionally well.

The novella is defined in a German handbook of genres as 'a literary narrative of medium length, which normally depicts an exemplary story with one central occurrence'. The emphasis on this central event is linked with the goal of 'educational and entertaining illumination of human relationships'.[7] The word *novella* is etymologically derived from the Latin word *novus* (new). While the genre is only loosely defined, there is broad agreement 'that the event that stands at the centre of a novella should have the character of newness, that is must be "unerhört" (Goethe), "außerordentlich" (A. Schlegel), "wunderbar" (Tieck), "eigenartig" (Heyse), or "außergewöhnlich" (Ernst)'.[8] This litany of German adjectives for what is remarkable, strange and extraordinary applies particularly well to the circumstances faced by the count of Gleichen and to his eventual double marriage. Furthermore, the novella took shape in the latter part of the eighteenth century.[9] With all these features in mind, it appears that novella is a better designation for 'Melechsala' than fairy tale.

A novella has a narrator, frequently third-person and omniscient, who is able to convey all sorts of information. This feature of the prose narration enables an author to tell readers in detail what the characters are thinking. As will become clear in the examples discussed below, Musäus makes ample use of this capability in 'Melechsala'.

Since opera is a genre within the broad category of drama, the story, rather than being told by a narrator, is enacted on stage. The audience can observe the characters' actions and hear their words directly, without an intermediary. While this brings the advantage of immediacy, it also takes away some of the complex kinds of information that may be difficult to convey through spoken dialogue. Furthermore, opera's historical development makes certain kinds of information more difficult to express than in spoken drama. For example, a narrator can explain a character's thought process in prose, and a playwright might convey these same ideas through a soliloquy—but opera tends to privilege the expression of emotion over that of discursive thought. Thus, within the conventions of opera, it is customary to portray characters' actions as motivated more by emotion than by thought. There is nothing inherent in sung drama that prevents characters from sharing their thoughts and ideas along with their feelings; but this is not a strong element in a traditional opera libretto, and the young Bauernfeld was rather conventional in his first attempt at one. As a result, he either had to omit some of the information found in Musäus or else find very different strategies for conveying it.

Meanings of a Flower, Differently Revealed

While my emphasis is on the later part of the story, when the count and his new beloved return to Germany, I begin with one significant earlier moment. This event is important because its presence in the Bauernfeld version establishes that he must have known the Musäus version. Also, this part of the story shows us much about how characterisations, actions and revelations are presented differently in the shift from the narrative genre of novella to the dramatic genre of opera.

In the novella, Musäus goes to considerable lengths to establish an important fact about Princess Melechsala: not only does she love flowers, but she is highly trained in the symbolic language of flowers as it is understood in the Middle East. We read, for example, of her habit of making bouquets that convey messages of appreciation or disapproval to her slaves. The sultan demands a European-style garden in order to please his indulged daughter, who loves flowers and is fascinated by stories of Europe—and thus the count is drawn into the situation as her head gardener. The key event that transforms the relationship between the princess and the gardener occurs when he offers her a new type of flower he has been growing in secret—unaware that it carries a special meaning in the flower language that she knows.[10]

A portion of this passage serves to convey the tumultuous situation, along with Musäus's ability to reveal his characters' emotions through a detailed description of their actions.

> Just at that time a spice-scented plant had come into bloom, which the Arabs call *muschirumi*, and which had never been found in the garden before. The count thought he would give innocent pleasure to the lovely flower lover who awaited him; he served up the flower, under which, instead of a platter, he had placed a broad fig leaf—on his knees, with a humble expression that nevertheless expressed his sense that he had served her well—and hoped to receive some small praise for it. But with utmost dismay, he realised that the princess turned away her face, dropped her eyes in shame (so far as he could observe under her thin veil) and looked ahead without saying a word. She hesitated and seemed embarrassed to take the flower, which she did not dignify with a glance and laid beside her on the grassy bank. Her cheerful mood had disappeared; she adopted a majestic attitude that conveyed proud seriousness, and after a few moments she left the grove without taking further notice of her favourite—but as she left, she did not forget the *muschirumi*, which she carefully hid under her veil.[11]

Musäus utilises considerable time and verbiage to go into the precise details of this scene; his descriptions of the characters' attitudes, positions and facial expressions all provide indirect insight into their thoughts. This technique is difficult to replicate in a staged work. Some of this descriptive language could be converted to stage directions, but they are rarely so specific. It is challenging to express the characters' attitudes and thoughts without the luxury of Musäus's remarkably complex sentences.

In the opera, Bauernfeld chooses a different narrative strategy: the information about the significant flower is not fully prepared in advance, but unfolds gradually in a dramatic way. We first meet the count when he sings a grief-filled recitative and cavatina (No. 2 in the *Neue Schubert-Ausgabe* edition) about his unfortunate situation as a slave, separated from homeland and family. In the brief speech that follows, he begins mournfully, but then remembers that it is Suleika's birthday: 'Just today must I be sorrowful, on the birthday of the sweet child who is so sisterly-minded towards me! I will go to see the lovely flower that I have tended for her—she will be happy. Perhaps her innocent chatter will banish my melancholy mood'.[12]

The next mention of Suleika and flowers comes when the count's squire, Kurt (who has also been enslaved), teases him about the princess's liking for him and claims that she has made great 'progress in botany' (*Fortschritte in der Botanik*) ever since he became her gardener.[13] This offhand, joking remark conceals a major alteration of Musäus's version, in which, as we have seen, the princess is first drawn to the gardener because of her love of gardens, not vice versa.

Suleika enters and sings an aria (No. 5a) about her attraction to the count. He enters and sings a recitative and duet with her (Nos. 5b–5c) in which the fatherly nature of his affection offends her. At the end of the duet, he offers her the flower, and we see her response only in the following stage direction: 'She stops suddenly in the melody that she has begun; the music is silent. Suleika glances alternately at the flower and the count, without taking the former. Meanwhile, a festive march sounds from afar, and at the first sounds Suleika is startled, takes the flower almost unwillingly and exits'. In the recitative that follows, the count is left to marvel at her strange attitude.[14]

In the stage direction, we can see the vestiges of Musäus's description of the princess's actions. The two princesses act somewhat differently—Melechsala turns away from both the count and the flower, while Suleika shifts her gaze between them—but they convey a similar state of mind. A reader of the novella is aware of why Suleika has responded in this way, while the opera audience has no information yet to explain her odd behaviour.

Bauernfeld begins to reveal the flower's meaning during the quintet that follows soon after. Three princes have come to court Suleika, and her father asks her to choose one of them; but she sings, in an aside, 'How my soul trembles in anguish and pain. O purple rose, do not doubt, my heart, he loves thee'. She then begs her father for more time to make her choice, adding in an aside, 'Beloved, I am consecrated to you'.[15] She has also obtained her father's agreement to free the Christian slaves as a birthday gift to her, but then is distressed as she realises that this means that she will be left behind to marry one of the princes while her beloved count sails home. This prepares the intense argument of the Act I finale. While realising that he will deeply miss Suleika, the count explains to her that he must return to his wife and child—upon which she confronts him with her accusation that he has deceived her by giving her the highly significant flower: 'for you knew well, whoever gives the purple flower to a maiden, he says to her: I love you—and you said it.' He replies: 'O Heavens! What have I done? You sweet girl, how I have deluded you without knowing it! This meaning is foreign to me'.[16] Now the opera audience finally has the knowledge that a reader of Musäus's novella would have possessed much earlier. This difference in how information is presented or withheld reflects genre characteristics: in a novella, narrative builds detailed knowledge of the characters that helps readers understand why they do what they do, whereas suspense and the sudden unveiling of motives make a drama more exciting.

Attitudes towards Emotion in the Eighteenth and Nineteenth Centuries

Musäus's writing provides an interesting case of a phenomenon that has been much discussed in recent scholarship on eighteenth-century attitudes. The era known as the Age of Reason has often been described as one in which rational thought was elevated above feeling. According to this view, the Romantic era then reversed those priorities, placing a premium on feeling and embracing irrationality in reaction against what the Romantics perceived as an overvaluation of reason.

Later scholars have modified this view, seeing much more continuity between eighteenth and nineteenth centuries. Ideas and artistic movements such as *Sturm und Drang*, sensibility (*Empfindsamkeit* in Germany) and the idealisation of the 'noble savage' all exemplify the new attention to emotional states that became important in the eighteenth century. In *The Navigation of Feeling*, the cultural anthropologist William M. Reddy observes that several new phenomena and institutions of the eighteenth century became 'emotional refuges' from the strict hierarchical practices of broader European life:

> It is only against this backdrop [of rigid hierarchy] that the salon, the literary correspondence, the Masonic lodge, friendship, and affectionate marriage can be understood as forms of emotional refuge. These freely chosen connections between persons were based not on family, office, or rank, but on merit or personal inclination. The rigidity of etiquette was ostentatiously set aside in favor of a more open, more egalitarian manner, which, as the eighteenth century wore on, became increasingly sentimental.[17]

Similarly, the literary historian Alastair Fowler observes that

> it was only in the eighteenth century that literature made a sustained attempt to express the individual feelings of those with the leisure to discover themselves. Paradoxically, this attempt often had the appearance of taking part in the Enlightenment's pursuit of general ideas.[18]

Musäus carefully prepares and explicates the grounds for his characters' emotional responses. At times—and this will be particularly clear in the examples that follow—he mixes reason and emotion in ironically comical ways. This blending of the two reflects the time in which he lived and wrote. In Bauernfeld's libretto, we see less reasoning and more emotional response from characters. This difference likely has two sources: his nineteenth-century perspective, which is more purely emotion based, and the shift in genre from narrative prose to opera.

Characters' Thoughts in the Denouement of 'Melechsala'

Musäus knew how the folk tale had to end; his task, then, was to bring this about in a way that suited his representation of the characters. If, as Berger states in the passage quoted earlier, we should understand those characters as typical of the German educated class of his own time and place, then we might expect them to blend rationalism with emotion. Indeed, this is just what Musäus depicts—with a pinch of cultural relativism thrown in for spice. After the shocking discovery that he has unknowingly made a declaration of love to Melechsala, the count tries to explain to her that he is bound by his marriage vows, but the princess is not persuaded.

> The young lady could not persuade herself that the count, as a young flourishing man, would not have eyes for her; she knew that she was worthy of love; and his frank confession of his heart's situation made no impression on her. Following the custom of her fatherland, she did not expect to have sole possession [of his heart], and she viewed the tenderness of men as a divisible property: for in the meaningful games of the seraglio, she had often heard that male tenderness was like a length of silk that can be divided and separated so that every part remains whole in itself.[19]

The count does not accept Melechsala's view, but he soon encounters a fortune-teller whose cryptic remarks lead him to believe that his wife has died during his absence. Now the way seems open to a marriage with Melechsala, so the count teaches her the Christian faith. They plan their escape, with the understanding that they will marry once they arrive in Europe; but when they land in Venice, the count meets an old retainer who has been sent out by the countess to find him, so he realises that his wife is still alive. It is at this moment that the count comes to the idea of having two wives simultaneously, and he sends the messenger back with a letter explaining that plan, hoping that the countess will consent. At first, the countess is quite unwilling to consider the idea, but a significant dream leads her to change her mind.

In the dream, she welcomes two pilgrims to her home who have just returned from the Holy Land. The first is her husband; the second is the angel Raphael, who explains to her that he is the companion of lovers (*Geleitsmann der Liebenden*) who is returning her husband to her from distant lands. When she wakes up,

> lacking an Egyptian sibyl, she interpreted the dream herself as best she could—and found so much similarity between the angel Raphael and the Princess Melechsala that she had no doubt that the second had been represented in her dream in the shape of the first. At the same time, she took into consideration that without the support of the same [person], her spouse would most likely never have escaped from slavery. Because it is seemly for the owner of a lost property to make an arrangement with the honourable one who returns it when he could have kept it entirely for himself, the countess saw no objection to the willing transfer of half her marital rights and privileges. The ship's captain was immediately sent back to Italy with the formal consent of the countess for her husband to make this clover-leaf marriage.[20]

The countess, as described here, combines a medieval belief in the power of metaphorical dreams with eighteenth-century logic, both portrayed in Musäus's ironic, tongue-in-cheek style. Finally—confirming the notion that eighteenth-century subjects linked rationality and feeling—she feels ashamed of her first unwelcoming thoughts towards Melechsala and secretly commissions the making of a new bed, wide enough for three, that is canopied 'in the color of hope'. After the marriage, Musäus explains, the countess, relieved of her loneliness, is able to fall modestly asleep beside her husband, so that he can fully enjoy his nights with his new bride.[21]

With all the advantages of prose narration at his command, Musäus is able to tell his readers how his characters approach situations, draw conclusions and act upon them, and finally how they respond emotionally. By discussing the construction and use of the extra-wide bed, he also directly addresses the issue of how one aspect of this three-way marriage will work in practical terms. By comparison, we have seen that the opera puts less emphasis on thought processes and more on feeling. One might expect, then, that Bauernfeld would show us even more of the characters' emotional responses to their remarkable three-way marriage—but instead, as we shall see, the opera seems to evade this revelation as it approaches its conclusion.

Der Graf von Gleichen: Design of Act II

The opera is divided into two acts, the first set in the East and the second in Germany. While the countess is introduced quite early in the novella, in the opera we do not encounter her until Act II. The chief dramatic purpose of this act is to show what transpires upon the count's return: the establishing of the three-person relationship, leading up to a celebration of the three-way marriage at the very end.

One might expect that the atmosphere of Act II, as the count, countess and princess move towards their marriage, would become progressively more intimate and tender. Instead, the Schubert-Bauernfeld version of the story seems to shy further and further away from intimacy as the opera approaches its end. The most musically expressive moments in Act II are two solo arias, one for each of the central women, and a quintet—numbers that feature either fewer or more characters than the three at the centre of the drama.

Bauernfeld wrote the end of the opera as a public scene. The count announces his marriage plans to his people, enters the church with the two women and emerges with them to general acclaim after the wedding ceremony. As a writer of discursive prose, Musäus was better able to end his work with a discussion of the marriage bed than was Bauernfeld. Nonetheless, ending the opera with the public wedding rather than the private wedding night means that it leaves open some of the most essential questions it raises. Perhaps this helps to explain why Schubert, though he wrote drafts for almost every number, did not write any music for the finale.

In Act II there are seven main characters: three nobles and four servants. The noble characters are Count Ernst von Gleichen; his wife, Countess Ottilie; and the eastern princess Suleika. (Though Suleika changes her name to Angelika between acts, when she converts to Christianity, I will refer to her by her original name.) The servant characters are Kurt, the count's squire; Susanne, the countess's maid; Fatime, Suleika's companion; and the *Burgvogt* or palace steward. The fact that there is an even number of servants is significant, as their romantic plot is set up as a direct contrast to that of the noble trio: the practical-minded servants reject the idea of a three-way arrangement and divide neatly and happily into couples.[22]

Even from a brief glance, one can see how the structure of Act II enables the unfolding of the drama. The act is divisible into four main sections, as shown in Table 16.1. In section 1, Ottilie is essentially alone. In section 2, Ernst returns, and husband and wife are reunited as a couple. In section 3, the three other travellers—Kurt, Suleika and Fatime—arrive and sing a trio. The count and countess then join them for a quintet. One dramatic function of this large ensemble is to transfer Suleika dramatically from her association with the servants to the more appropriate one with the aristocrats. The continuation of this process is left suspended for some comic relief, though, as the remainder

Table 16.1 Schubert, *Der Graf von* Gleichen, D 918: structure of Act II

1. The Gleichen estate without the count
   12 Chorus—Harvesters
   13 Aria (lament): Ottilie (cf. *Wonne der Wehmuth*, D 260)
2. The count's return
   14 Chorus—Pilgrims
   15 Recitative and aria—Ernst
   16 Recitative and duet—Ernst, Ottilie; arrival of their son, chorus
3. Arrival of the other travellers
   17a Trio—Suleika, Fatime, Kurt
   17b Recitative and quintet—same, with Ernst, Ottilie
   18 Song and chorus—Kurt (on Middle Eastern customs)
   19 Quartet—Susanne, Fatime, Kurt, Vogt squabble, divide into couples
4. Marriage arrangements
   20a Recitative—Ernst, Ottilie; Aria—Ottilie
   20b Duet—Ernst, Ottilie
   20c Aria (prayer)—Suleika
   20d Recitative and duet—Suleika, Ottilie
   20e Trio—Suleika, Ottilie, Ernst
   20f Quintet—same, with Fatime, Kurt
   [21 Duet—Kurt, Fatime]
   [22 Finale—all]

Note: Numbers refer to the numbering in the *Neue Schubert-Ausgabe*.

of section 3 depicts the castle servants and their adjustment to Kurt's return with a new girlfriend.

Section 4 brings us back to the love triangle, which we see in various configurations. First the husband and wife come to agreement on the situation and sing of their mutual appreciation. Next, Ernst leaves the stage so that Ottilie can probe Suleika and ascertain to her own satisfaction that Suleika truly loves Ernst. Suleika, believing herself to be alone, sings a prayer, but she then discovers that Ottilie has been listening, and the two women sing a duet in which the depth of Suleika's love and suffering becomes clear to Ottilie. Ernst enters to find the situation apparently unresolved, though actually Ottilie has made the decision to enter into the three-way marriage. But before these three characters reach a resolution, Kurt and Fatime enter. In the ensuing quintet, Ernst teasingly remarks on their fondness for each other and declares that they should marry, and Suleika resolves to be happy for her friends despite her own misery. Schubert did not compose the music from this point on, but the items in brackets in Table 16.1 show the planned ending. First there was to be a comic love duet for Kurt and Fatime. Then the finale: knights and ladies would enter a great hall, followed by Ernst, Ottilie, Suleika, Kurt and Fatime. The count would then announce to all that he was about to marry Suleika as a second wife, and all would process to the chapel. The marriage itself would take place offstage, followed by a chorus of celebration.

The act is designed so that the final resolution comes as a marvelous surprise for Suleika. By choosing to arrange it in this way, Bauernfeld clearly made the Arab princess the junior partner in the three-way marriage; she is still treated very much like a child. He also sacrificed the opportunity to show a moment of reflection and harmony for the count, the countess and Suleika. It seems safe to assume that no theatre in 1826 would have put a marriage bed wide enough for three on an operatic stage. To replace the information that bed had given in the novella, some type of verbal and musical affirmation was needed to portray the three-way love arrangement. To put it simply, Schubert needed a text for a love trio, and Bauernfeld did not provide one. [23]

Music of Emotions: Tension and Resolution

While we cannot know why Schubert stopped his sketches for the opera where he did, I suspect that the lack of resolution among the three main characters troubled him and made it difficult to compose the finale. The libretto sets up a joyful resolution without providing the psychological preparation to make it believable.

Two musical passages from the scene approaching the finale show how Schubert developed musical tension among his characters. In No. 20d, Ottilie questions Suleika after overhearing her prayer. The prayer is in A major, and the recitative begins with a harmonically unstable passage that reflects Suleika's chagrin when she realises that Ottilie has been listening to her private outcry. After quick cadences on G minor and A♭ major, the passage shown here settles into B major, setting up the duet that follows immediately in E major.

In Example 16.1, we see the countess pressing Suleika to admit that she loves Ernst. Suleika is unwilling to speak of her feelings and remains silent. The orchestra steps in as if to answer the questions in her stead—but even so, the instrumental passages end on implied dominant chords over a tonic pedal, resolution to the tonic coming each time only with Ottilie's next question.

The two women continue their emotional wrestling match in the following duet. They are interrupted when Ernst enters, eager to learn whether they have come to an understanding. Two of the three singers in the trio are still confused and anxious. Suleika knows nothing of the possible marriage; distraught

Example 16.1 *Der Graf von* Gleichen, D 918: the orchestra answers for Suleika, No. 20d, bars 14–25[24]

at having been asked to admit her love for Ernst, she does not see a resolution to her pain. Ernst, though he knows that the three-way marriage may resolve the situation, is unsure what has happened between the two women. Only Ottilie is in full command of the situation, as she has now tested Suleika and is resolved to move forward with the plan. Thus, we hear music not of tenderness and union, but of agitation and confusion. The trio opens with a harmonically volatile discussion among the three characters that eventually leads to the D major chord that we see at the end of Example 16.2.

In this passage,[25] the agitated soprano line in the orchestra (it is marked in semiquaver tremolo at first, and one would guess that Schubert intended to continue that throughout), along with a bass line that creeps up and down by semitones, creates a mood of distress. The countess does nothing to resolve the situation for the other two. Indeed, the stage direction 'schalkhaft' (roguishly) suggests that she is relishing her position of superior knowledge. Although the second part of the trio, finally in G major, is sung homophonically by all three characters, the ongoing quick rhythms nevertheless create a nervous atmosphere that belies the text: 'Nur ruhig, bald endet Angst und Beben' (Just be calm, soon fear and trembling shall end).

Thus, the only time that we hear the three characters who will enter into this marriage singing together and without anyone else, the music hardly foreshadows a good outcome. Interestingly, however, Schubert did write a piece in which the same characters sing in poignantly beautiful concord: the quintet, No. 17b, which takes place the first time that Suleika and the countess meet.

Example 16.2 Schubert, *Der Graf von* Gleichen, D 918: agitation and confusion in the trio, No. 20e, bars 11–26

The Quintet as a Symbol of Multivalent Love

Bauernfeld's text for the quintet offered Schubert an opportunity to show the potential in the dramatic situation for deep and multivalent love, of which he took full advantage in two ways. First, he gave dramatic weight to this moment: he extended it through textual repetitions and composed melodies and counterpoint that are both florid and stately, giving an air of solemnity and dignity to this moment. Secondly, Schubert's musical design carries implications about the relations among the singers, not only prefiguring deep love among the three central figures in the drama, but also showing their trusted servants to be involved and taking part in the significant event.

Table 16.2 shows the formal arrangement of the quintet. There are three sections, labelled by Schubert as recitative, quintet and Andante (which continues the quintet); these are in the top rows of the table. The bottom rows show bar numbers, and the middle rows formal structure and voicing, with formal divisions in boldface type and characters' initials in regular type.

Even apart from the musical content, which is discussed below, the singers and the order in which they sing convey strong messages here. In the first

Table 16.2 Schubert, *Der Graf von* Gleichen, D 918: structure of No. 17b (Recitative and Quintet)

Recitative	Quintet			
E	A—O	A—S	B—all/O, S/all	
	R—E, K, F	R—E, K, F		
1–22	23–47	47–72	73–103	
Andante				
I/v1—E	v2—O. E	v3—S, O, E	v4—F, S, O, E, K	C—all
104–117	118–127	128–137	138–47	148–160

E = Ernst, O = Ottilie, S = Suleika, K = Kurt, F = Fatime
A, B = formal sections of Quintet; **R** = refrain; **I** = introduction; **v1, v2**, etc. = verses of Andante; **C** = coda

part of the number, Ernst introduces Suleika to his wife; Ottilie welcomes her graciously, and the three onlookers (Ernst, Kurt and Fatime) sing a refrain praising the countess's goodness. Suleika then takes up the countess's melody, which is likewise followed by the refrain, the words this time expressing admiration of Suleika's innocence and grace. Finally, there is a B section in which all five sing together, with a middle part in which the two central women sing a duet. Through this structure, we are shown that Ottilie and Suleika are similar—vocally close enough that they can sing the same florid soprano melody—that Suleika is capable of viewing Ottilie as a model rather than a rival, and that the other three find the accord between these two women beautiful and admirable.

The Andante section consists of four verses, designed so that the number of voices increases in each one, from one to two to three to five, followed by a coda for all five characters. In each verse, the first character listed sings the main theme, while those that follow introduce and take up countermelodies. The three central characters are thus heard in order of age, and also in the order in which they came into each other's lives; finally the two trusted servants enter to create a five-voice texture. This musical design shows the potential for an ever growing community to live harmoniously in mutual love. The flexible interchanges among the characters imply mutuality and equality. The music goes beyond the drama in this dimension: while some aspects of the story imply hierarchy and inequality, Schubert's compositional choices portray a utopian society whose members can exchange roles and ideas.

The three people who will live together in marriage are included in this society, along with their servant-companions. While the presence of Kurt and

Fatime may seem awkward, in Act I these two were witnesses to the growing love between Ernst and Suleika. They are the only characters who can imagine, and perhaps sympathise with, what is about to transpire, so in some important way they do indeed belong in this intimate and private scene.

In a fascinating parallel, Rossini wrote a very similar ensemble in 1829, very soon after Schubert composed this quintet: the trio 'Je rends à votre amour un fils digne de vous' from Act IV of *Guillaume Tell*.[26] This trio features three female voices: those of the Princess Mathilde; Tell's wife, Hedwige; and his son, Jemmy (a trousers role). As in the Schubert Andante, we first hear a single melody sung by Mathilde; it is then repeated by Jemmy as Mathilde sings a second line opposite, and finally by Hedwige, with Jemmy on Mathilde's second line and Mathilde introducing a second countermelody. The last verse is followed by a coda for the full ensemble, just as in Schubert's quintet. Also similar to the Schubert, the central melody uses a good deal of arpeggiation (which makes it easier for it to accompany other melodies), and more ornamentation and chromaticism enter the piece as it progresses and more voices are added. In the Rossini example, just as in the Schubert, we witness the union of three people, one of whom would normally oppose the others. This parallel is all the more intriguing because neither composer had any opportunity to know of what the other did; Schubert's work was not disseminated at all for many years, and Rossini's opera had its premiere the year after Schubert's death.

Along with the musical structure, the specific musical material makes Schubert's quintet particularly lovely and affecting. Schubert uses dissonance sparingly and effectively, creating some poignant moments. One such moment comes in the final phrase of the solo line sung first by Ottilie and then by Suleika. Example 16.3 shows Suleika's version, chosen simply because her added leap to the high A enhances the melody. More important, though, is the striking use of expressive intervals, which create emotional depth while also suggesting the Middle East, Suleika's original home. In the first half of the phrase, a perfect fourth is followed by a diminished fourth, while in the second, which imitates it, the order of the intervals is reversed. The augmented second between F♯ and E♭ is masked by the G that intervenes, but its presence is felt.[27]

Example 16.3 Schubert, *Der Graf von* Gleichen, D 918: emotional poignancy in the quintet, No. 17b, bars 58–63

To illustrate the atmosphere of the Andante, Example 16.4 shows the beginning of verse 4, in which all five characters are singing.[28] Fatime's line is the main theme, which has already been sung successively by Ernst, Ottilie and Suleika; Suleika sings the first countermelody and Kurt the second, while both the count and countess sing new and very florid lines whose semiquaver passages interlock perfectly, symbolising their long-practiced marital accord. Note in particular the augmented triad that is sustained on the words 'und mil(de)'; this is present in all the verses, and the tritone, emphasised by placement and length, provides a hint of the intense emotions that are somewhat suppressed in this quintet by its stately pace and formal organisation.

Conflict of Public and Private Spheres?

Nicholas Cook and Nicola Dibben discuss a transition from music representing public to private experience, which they link to both time period and genre.

> As presented in baroque and classical opera, emotion belongs to the public sphere; to put it another way, it is conceived dramatically. The paradigm of nineteenth-century literature, by comparison, is the novel, where emotion subsists in private, subjective experience, to which the various characteristic devices of the novel give the reader access.[29]

While these observations do not fully match the two works examined here, they do intersect with my points in this essay by adding the categories of public and private spheres to the consideration of genre. Cook and Dibben point out that in the seventeenth and eighteenth centuries, opera had an inherently public quality, while the Romantic genre of the novel began to privilege the private world of individual subjectivity. Although Bauernfeld would eventually be known for his drawing-room comedies representing private life, his concept of opera when he first approached it—bear in mind that he was only twenty-four years old when he wrote this libretto—may have been strongly influenced by that model of public expression. This might help explain his decision to complete *Der Graf von Gleichen* with the grand public announcement of the marriage.

The public and private spheres are both present in the original folk tale. While love is a private emotion, its formalisation through marriage—particularly a marriage between aristocrats, and even more when the express permission of the Church is required—makes for a very public exposure of private experience. Wagner's *Lohengrin* raises similar issues, as Elsa and Lohengrin are hardly permitted to spend any time alone: their first meeting is witnessed by the whole community, and their wedding night is first interrupted by

Example 16.4 Schubert, *Der Graf von* Gleichen, D 918: shared ecstasy in the quintet, No. 17b, bars 138–146

assassins and then completely broken off as Lohengrin answers Elsa's private question about his origins in public, so that everyone can hear. Given the high rank of Ernst, the count of Gleichen, it is in some ways fitting that the final scene of the opera should be a grand public celebration. Yet something is lost in the process. The exploration of the characters' inner thoughts, included so naturally by Musäus, has been transferred by Bauernfeld into a portrayal of their emotional states, as is more common in opera. Yet at the key moment when that emotional aspect of the story could be brought to fullness, he is seduced by the opportunity to create excitement and suspense. Rather than resolve the turmoil of the trio, he moves quickly to the comic subplot, then to the count's dramatic announcement. Suleika is whisked from a state of renunciation and sorrow to one of sudden joy and fulfillment. The count and countess—behaving more like her parents than her new partners—graciously bestow her new status upon her. We, the audience–like Suleika herself–are deprived of a necessary emotional transition. Before the grand final chorus that Schubert never composed, we need that unwritten love trio to make us believe in this new configuration of three people in an institution usually designed for two. Schubert gave us a wonderful prefiguration in his exquisite quintet; we can only imagine what that trio might have been.

Notes

I would like to thank some colleagues from other disciplines who helped me in my work by listening to my ideas and pointing me towards helpful literature on genre and the history of emotion: from literature, Leigh Eicke and Ben Lockerd; from history, Marc Lerner and Jason Crouthamel.

1. Manuela Jahrmärker, who edited the *Neue Schubert-Ausgabe*'s edition of the opera, discusses many of the sources in the introduction to the volume: Franz Schubert, *Der Graf von Gleichen*, ed. Manuela Jahrmärker, *Neue Ausgabe sämtlicher Werke*, ser. 2, vol. 17 (Kassel: Bärenreiter, 2006), pp. xii–xix. See also the chapter on the opera in Kristina Muxfeldt, *Vanishing Sensibilities: Schubert, Beethoven, Schumann* (New York: Oxford University Press, 2012), pp. 43–83, especially pp. 43–52. Muxfeldt examines the relation of the Graf von Gleichen story to literature of Schubert's time, particularly Goethe's play *Stella*.

2. See Jahrmärker, introduction to Schubert, *Der Graf von Gleichen*, p. ix.

3. Laura Martin, review of Malgorzata Kubisiak, *Märchen und Meta-Märchen: Zur Poetik der 'Volksmärchen der Deutschen' von Johann Karl August Musäus*, *Marvels and Tales* 18/1 (2004), pp. 113–14.

4. 'Wenn man mit dem Maßstab der Grimmschen Märchen an die Volksmärchen von Musäus herantritt ... wäre aber gerade so, als wollte man von Fragonard und Boucher verlangen, daß sie wie Moritz von Schwind hätten malen ... sollen, oder wie man von Mozarts *Cosi fan tutte* enttäuscht wäre, weil diese Oper

so anders klingt als Humperdincks *Hänsel und Gretel*. Die erdichteten adligen Gestalten fühlen und denken wie Musäus, seine Freunde und Freundinnen. Wie das Volk dichtete, war ihm völlig gleichgültig. . . . Das Mittelalter, in dem die meisten Erzählungen des Schriftstellers Musäus spielen, ist 18. Jahrhundert.' Dorothea Berger, 'Die Volksmärchen der Deutschen von Musäus: Ein Meisterwerk der Deutschen Rokokodichtung,' *PMLA* 69/5 (December 1954), pp. 1205–6.

    5. See Eduard von Bauernfeld, *Bilder und Persönlichkeiten aus Alt-Wien*, ed. Wilhelm Zentner (Altötting: Verlag 'Bücher der Heimat', 1948), p. 37.

    6. J. K. A. Musäus, 'Melechsala', in *Volksmärchen der Deutschen*, complete edn following the text of the 1st edn (1782–6), with the 1841 illustrations (Munich: Winkler, 1961), pp. 657–744.

    7. 'Eine "Novelle" ist ein literarischer Erzähltext mittlerer Länge, der in der Regel eine musterhafte Geschichte mit einem zentralen Geschehensmoment schildert. . . . novellistischer Erzählen zielt in oft symbolhafter Zuspitzung auf die belehrend-unterhaltende Ausleuchtung menschlicher Verhaltensweisen.' Tom Kindt, 'Novelle,' in Dieter Lamping (ed.), *Handbuch der literarischen Gattungen* (Stuttgart: Alfred Kröner Verlag, 2009), 540.

    8. Ibid., pp. 542–3.

    9. Ibid., p. 541.

    10. Musäus, 'Melechsala', pp. 692–4.

    11. 'Es war gerade damals eine gewürzhafte Pflanze zur Blüte gelangt, welche von den Arabern Muschirumi genannt wird, und die vorher noch nicht im Garten anzutreffen war. Mit dieser Neuigkeit dachte der Graf der schönen Blumenfreundin, die sein harrete, ein unschuldiges Vergnügen zu machen, er servierte ihr die Blume, worunter er, anstatt des Präsentiertellers, ein breites Feigenblatt geschoben hatte, auf den Knieen, mit einer demütigen doch einiges Verdienst sich zueignenden Miene, und hoffte ein kleines Lob dafür einzuernten. Aber mit äußerster Bestürzung wurde er gewahr, daß die Prinzessin das Gesicht abwendete, die Augen, sofiel der dünne Schleier ihm zu beobachten gestattete, beschämt niederschlug, und vor sich hinsah, ohne ein Wort zu sprechen. Sie zögerte und schien verlegen die Blume in Empfang zu nehmen, die sie keines Anblicks würdigte, und neben sich auf die Rasenbank legte. Ihre muntere Laune war verschwunden, sie nahm eine majestätische Stellung an, die stolzen Ernst verkündete, und nach wenig Augenblicken verließ sie die Laube, ohne von ihrem Günstling weitere Notiz zu nehmen; doch vergaß sie beim Weggehen die Muschirumi nicht, welche sie aber sorgfältig under den Schleier verbarg.' Ibid., p. 703.

    12. 'Gerade heute muß ich trauern, an dem Geburtstag des zarten Kindes, das mir so schwesterlich zugetan ist! Ich will nach der schönen Blume sehen, die ich für sie gepflegt—sie wird sich freuen. Vielleicht vermag ihr unschuldiges Geschwätz, diesen Geist der Schwermuth zu bannen.' Schubert, *Der Graf von Gleichen*, p. 16.

    13. Ibid., 28.

14. 'Sie stockt plözlich in der angefangenen Melodie; die Musik schweigt. SULEIKA blickt abwechselnd die Blume und den Grafen an, ohne die erstere zu nehmen. Indeß ertönt ein Festmarsch aus der Ferne, bei dessen ersten Klängen SULEIKA erschrickt, die Blume fast unwillkürlich nimmt und abgeht.' Ibid., p. 45.

15. 'Wie bebt von Angst und Schmerz die Seele, O Purpurrose zweifle nicht mein Herz, er liebt dich ... Geliebter dir bin ich geweiht.' Ibid., pp. 53–5.

16. 'Denn du wußtest wohl, wer diese Purpurblume einem Mädchen gibt, der sagt zum Mädchen: Ich liebe dich,—und du, und du hast es gesagt.' GRAF: 'O Himmel! Was hab' ich gethan? Du süßes Mädchen, wie hab ich dich bethört, ohne zu wissen! die Deutung ist mir fremd.' Ibid., pp. 75–6.

17. William Reddy, *The Navigation of Feeling: a Framework for the History of Emotions* (Cambridge: Cambridge University Press, 2001), p. 149.

18. Alastair Fowler, *A History of English Literature: Forms and Kinds from the Middle Ages to the Present* (Oxford: Basil Blackwell, 1987), p. 184.

19. 'Das Fräulein konnte sich nicht bereden, daß der Graf, als ein junger blühender Mann, keine Augen für sie haben sollte, sie wußte, daß sie liebenswürdig war; und das freimütige Bekenntnis, von der Lage seines Herzens, machte gerade auf sie gar keinen Eindruck. Sie dachte, nach der Sitte ihres Vaterlandes, nicht daran, den alleinigen Besitz sich davon zuzueignen, und betrachtete die Zärtlichkeit der Männer, als ein teilbares Gut: denn in den sinnreichen Spielen des Serails, hatte sie oft gehört, daß die männliche Zärtlichkeit mit einem Faden Seide war verglichen worden, der sich trennen und teilen läßt, so daß jeder Teil dennoch, für sich, ein Ganzes bleibt.' Musäus, 'Melechsala', p. 714.

20. 'Und in Ermangelung einer ägyptischen Sibylle erklärte sie sich selbst den Traum so gut sie konnte, fand so viel Ähnlichkeit zwischen dem Engel Raphael und der Prinzessin Melechsala, daß sie nicht zweifelte, die letztere sei unter der Gestalt des erstern ihr im Traum vorgebildet worden; zugleich zog sie in Erwägung, daß ohne den Beistand derselben, ihr Gemahl schwerlich jemals der Sklaverei würde entronnen sein. Weil nun dem Eigentümer eines verlornen Gutes ziemet, mit dem ehrlichen Wiederbringer sich abzufinden, der es ganz für sich hätte behalten können: so fand sie keinen Anstand, zu williger Abtretung der Halbscheid ihrer ehelichen Gerechtsame sich zu entschließen. Unverzüglich wurde der, wegen seiner Wachsamkeit reichlich belohnte Hafenkapitän nach Welschland zurückbeordert, mit dem förmlichen Konsens der Gräfin für ihren Gemahl, das Kleeblatt seiner Ehe vollständig zu machen.' Ibid., p. 732.

21. The passage about the bed, 'mit der Farbe der Hoffnung überzogen', is on p. 737, and the description of the nights spent there on p. 739. At the end of the story it is further mentioned that a chip of the wood from the bed, worn in a woman's corset, is said to prevent jealousy in the female heart: 'Die berühmte dreischläfrige Sponde wird noch im alten Schlosse ... als eine Reliquie aufbewahrt, und ein Span davon, statt des Blankscheits in dem Schnürleib getragen,

soll die Kraft haben, alle Regungen von Eifersucht in dem weiblichen Herzen zu zerstören' (p. 745).

22. In the live recording made in 1997 of a performance in Bregenz, Austria, the servant parts are completely omitted. This decision is apparently linked to the use of only three singers for this recording, but whatever the explanation, it gives a skewed impression of the work as being solemn and emotionally fraught throughout. Bauernfeld and Schubert deliberately use the servant characters and subplot to create balance and comic relief. See Franz Schubert and Richard Dünser, *Der Graf von Gleichen*, Symphonieorchester Vorarlberg and Kornmarktchor Bregenz, cond. Christoph Eberle, live recording from the Festspielhaus Bregenz, Oehms OC 903 (2004).

23. Some might argue that I am making an assumption by stating that the three-way marriage should be affirmed as a good thing. When Dünser completed the work, he chose a deliberately mixed style for the Act II finale: 'In the course of the intensifying and ever stranger plot, this world is confronted by the "strange", the "contemporary"—which superimposes itself on the "old" and shows it in a completely different light. . . . Schubert uses this allusion [to the song 'Die Nebensonnen'] to relegate the opera's completely unexpected solution of bigamy into the realm of mad visions, a utopia, "unfinished". Is it only chance that he made no more sketches at the end? Or are there secondary wives where there are secondary suns?' Ibid., booklet notes, trans. Elizabeth Gahbler, p. 46. While I have little space here to explore the relevance of the 'Nebensonnen' quote, it is significant that Musäus actually uses the word 'Nebensonne' as a description for Melechsala in the very sentence that leads to the bed wide enough for three (p. 737). Dünser seems to regard the work's conclusion as an impossible fantasy and to assume that Schubert would agree. I find it hard to understand why Schubert and Bauernfeld would choose this story and Schubert would continue to champion it, by working on the opera even after it was forbidden by censors, if they did not think there was something valuable about its central idea. Rare and improbable, yes, but not necessarily a mad vision.

24. All music examples are based on the *Neue Schubert-Ausgabe* edition cited earlier, with a few changes. Clefs for singing parts have been changed to treble and bass clefs; voices have been separated onto their own staves rather than sharing staves with instrumental parts; and editorial brackets around cautionary accidentals and added text underlay have been removed. Any further changes are mentioned in footnotes to the examples.

25. For Example 16.2, the rhythm in the bass line was notated strangely by Schubert, so that measures appear to add up to four and a half beats. What I have notated on each third beat as a set of quaver triplets appears in Schubert's score as a dotted crotchet with a line across the stem to indicate that it is divided into quavers. I have added the natural sign on the first F in bar 15 (the score has one on the second F).

26. See Gioacchino Rossini, *Guillaume Tell*, vocal score, arr. Louis Niedermeyer (Mainz: B. Schott's Söhnen, 1829), pp. 379–85.

27. In bar 61, the beam linking the first two quavers has been removed to show syllable division.

28. In bar 146, the words 'hüllt uns ein' have been added in the four lower voices. In bars 142–143, Kurt's text underlay has been changed to what the Count sang on these notes in the previous verse: the word 'alte' has been removed and the other words shifted earlier in the phrase.

29. See 'Emotion in Culture and History: Perspectives from Musicology', in Patrik N. Justin and John A. Sloboda (eds), *Handbook of Music and Emotion: Theory, Research, Applications* (New York: Oxford University Press, 2010), pp. 49–50.

17

The End of the Road in Schubert's *Winterreise*
The Contradiction of Coherence and Fragmentation

Deborah Stein

Of the many fascinating issues that have challenged scholars and performers of Schubert's *Winterreise*, one of the most critical but elusive is how to understand the cycle's conclusion.[1] What happens to our beleaguered wanderer? Is the cycle's climax the final song, No. 24, 'Der Leiermann', where the wanderer succumbs to madness? Or is the climax song 20, 'Der Wegweiser', where the wanderer chooses the path from which no one returns? And what is this path of no return? Is it death? Madness? Or might it be something else?

While earlier studies by Richard Capell (1973) and John Reed (1985), among others, focus upon 'Der Leiermann' as the cycle's goal, I concur with the more recent view that 'Der Wegweiser' is both the cycle's climax and its goal. Susan Youens states: 'the image of the signposts is the key to unlock the mystery of [the wanderer's] self-exile and alienation'.[2] Charles Fisk calls the song 'a station of culminating revelation ... [with] the signpost pointing to the protagonist's death, whether actual or psychological'.[3] And Richard Kramer notes that in song No. 20 'a measure of time and distance ends.... Wegweiser is a signal of the end—of complete exhaustion.... The remaining songs are so many afterbeats, reflections on this condition of being without a future. The road does not end; it disappears into a void'.[4] I agree with Kramer that the final four songs serve as the denouement to 'Der Wegweiser', but I will offer an alternative to his void.

The role of 'Der Wegweiser' as the cycle's apogee turns on a nesting of contradictions within both that song itself and the cycle as a whole. As an individual song, 'Der Wegweiser' is formally ambiguous, functioning as both a clear climax and an unclear conclusion within the cycle. The cycle itself, meanwhile, embodies a contradiction of linearity versus disruption that continues beyond the putative end of No. 24, 'Der Leiermann'. On the one hand, there seems to be at least some sort of trajectory towards the climactic No. 20, making that song a critical, if ambiguous, point of arrival. This drive to 'Der Wegweiser' occurs within the poetry, of course, and is traced through a systematic chromatic preparation of the striking chromaticism in No. 20. On the other hand, however, the cycle does not end with No. 20, and indeed the last song, 'Der Leiermann', doesn't offer a convincing conclusion either. In addition, the cohesion leading up to No. 20 is undermined by a disruptive tonal scheme throughout the cycle where there is no governing tonic and Schubert opposes the flat side and the sharp side without any form of resolution.

'Der Wegweiser' is thus part of a cycle that involves two dichotomous processes: (1) a systematic trajectory towards the cycle's climax (detailed in the first part of this essay); and (2) a constant disruption of coherence that creates ambiguity and conflict, neither of which resolves (explored in the second part). To best understand *Winterreise*, then, I adopt the German Romantic concept of the 'fragment', that formal design that celebrates ambiguity, irresolution, and incompletion.[5]

The Linear Journey towards 'Der Wegweiser'

Müller's Poetic Journey

Since the cycle's opposing elements occur within the poetry, we begin as Schubert did: with examining Müller's poetry.[6] Table 17.1 traces the poem's psychological journey through a series of recurring poetic issues, many involving dichotomies such as fire versus ice, life versus death and nature in its nurturing versus menacing guise.[7]

The pacing of the psychological journey is facilitated by several poems that articulate important transformations within the wanderer's travels. In Part I, the protagonist begins with the well-known theme of loss and grief (No. 1) and anger (No. 2). These emotions will recur throughout the cycle, and Table 17.1 highlights the repetition of grief with arrows through No. 7. As is well-known, the poetic metaphor for grief in *Winterreise* is the opposition of burning tears and frozen ice; the tears expressing grief are frozen by the ice and snow of the wanderer's hostile world.[8] This dichotomy begins in No. 3, recurs in Nos. 4 and 6 and recurs again, for the last time, in No. 8, 'Rückblick,' the first of the transformational songs that denote a shift in the journey.

Two other recurring poetic ideas that recur in Part I are the lure of death and the wanderer's increasing alienation. The suggestion of death as a possible goal for this journey first occurs in two early songs: 'Der Lindenbaum' (No. 5) and 'Auf dem Flueße' (No. 7).[9] Both songs refer to the rejecting lover: the wanderer responds to rustling leaves as a possible end to his suffering in No. 5 and carves names and dates in the ice in what Youens suggests as a 'tombstone' in No. 7.[10] Song No. 7 also begins what will become the growing theme of alienation. The only other reference to the yearning for death and the alienation in Part I occurs in No. 9, 'Irrlicht,' where the wanderer recognises his need to 'stray' and that death is a means of escape.[11]

In German Romanticism, nature is a powerful vehicle for poetic expressivity, often a metaphor for the relation of the poet to his or her world. The wanderer's journey is a constant shifting from the external world of nature

Table 17.1 Schubert, *Winterreise*, D 911: The poetic and psychological journey

PART I:	#1 Gute Nacht	#2 Die Wetterfahne	#3 Gefror'ne Tränen	#4 Erstarrung	#5 Der Lindenbaum	#6 Wasserflut
Journey	farewell to **her**	fugitive from **her** anger	interior 1st weeping	panic search for remembering **her**	memory (**her**)/ departure	lament/defiance
	grief →		→ grief →	→ frozen heart →		▲ sorrow
			→ fire/ice →			▲ fire/ice
Death					lure to death?	
	#7 Auf dem Flusse	**#8 Rückblick**	**#9 Irrlicht**	**#10 Rast**	**#11 Frühlingstraum**	**#12 Einsamkeit**
Journey	interior	looks back in frenzy	interior/isolation must stray (cf #19 & 24)	interior cannot rest	dreams/reality escape	loneliness sluggish walking good vs bad nature
	mourning for **her**	→ fire/ice (last)			(cf #13 & 17)	
Death	tombstone?		yearns for death			
PART II:	**#13 Die Post**	**#14 Der griese Kopf**	**#15 Die Krähe**	**#16 Letzt Hoffnung**	**#17 Im Dorfe**	**#18 Der Stür Mor**
Journey	mail from her? (cf #9) posthorn=longing	interior life vs death	leaves town with crow	wants escape last weeping	reflections on village	energized by storm/defiance escape good nature
Death		yearns for death	crow= death?	death of hope?		
	#19 Täuschung	**#20 Der Wegweiser**	**#21 Das Wirtshaus**	**#22 Mut!**	**#23 Nebensonnen**	**#24 Der Leiermann**
Journey	delusion (cf #9) edge of sanity (cf #24) stasis	signpost to way of no return	seeks death	strides ahead in defiance	accepts loss	meets beggar vision of madness (cf #9 & 19)
Death		death at end?	death denied			

to the interior world of the psyche. In this way, the poet relates to nature in a profound dance of projection and empathy, where the poet can project difficult emotions onto, say, the tree (No. 5) or frozen river (No. 7) in order to experience his emotions through identifying with or feeling empathy for the natural element.[12] Thus the linden tree and the frozen river prompt emotions that otherwise would be extremely painful. As the cycle continues, the play of light in 'Irrlicht' (No. 9) expresses the wanderer's alienation with his need to 'stray'. Part I then closes with a poetic opposition of nature: the painful dream of nurturing nature (spring, green meadows) that opens No. 11, 'Frühlingstraum,' continues on to describe alienating nature (frozen leaves in winter); this dichotomy recurs in No. 12 as the wanderer seeks a storm rather than endure clear skies and gentle breezes.

Part II of the cycle begins curiously with 'Die Post,' where for the last time the wanderer thinks about his lost love.[13] There is a renewed energy as the wanderer senses that he must escape the town in which his pain began. The changing relationship between the wanderer and his town occurs within a series of actions and ruminations, all underscored by the promise of death's escape and his ongoing alienation. In No. 14, 'Der greise Kopf', he contemplates his desire to be old and thus closer to death, and in No. 15, 'Die Krähe', he leaves town accompanied by a crow, which had thrown snowballs at him in No. 8 but is now both a companion and a possible agent of death. In No. 16, 'Letzte Hoffnung', nature once again prompts thoughts of death, including, this time, the death of hope. In No. 17, 'Im Dorfe,' the wanderer reflects on the village he has left behind. This nocturnal moment is a great contrast to the first 'night' song, No. 1, where his journey began. In both songs dogs growl at him, but whereas in No. 1 he felt pain and loss, in No. 17 he feels disillusioned with the townsfolk and indeed all of humankind. In No. 18, 'Der stürmische Morgen', the wanderer experiences his escape from gentle but painful nature through a wild storm as, again, a dichotomy of nature depicts his tortured state. This stormy weather replaces the town as the wanderer's world.

As we approach the climax and denouement of the cycle, the wanderer has progressed from a hurt and angry rejected lover to an alienated, tormented man who has escaped the scene of his hurt but is as yet uncertain of where to go. The extent of his wounds is vividly portrayed in No. 19, 'Täuschung', where his deluded state leads to what Youens calls 'dancing on the edge of sanity'.[14] His long journey of ruminations, deliberations, actions and reactions has left him in a desperate and fragile psychological state of utter despondency. The delusion recalls song No. 9, 'Irrlicht' and adumbrates song No. 24, 'Der Leiermann'.

The fragility of song No. 19 thus sets up the need for a powerful change in the wanderer's journey. And so the decision of 'taking the road from which no one returns' is born. Song No. 20, 'Der Wegweiser', is thus the most powerful transformation of the cycle, and most of the primary poetic imagery mentioned above does not recur except for the notion of death: 'suche Ruh' (seek rest).

No. 21 then famously denies death to the wanderer, and the remaining songs create a summary of where he has been. Death is no longer mentioned after song No. 21, and the world of nature plays a minimal role in these final songs. In No. 22, 'Mut', the wanderer once again embraces the wind and storm in a defiant attempt at courage, and in No. 23, 'Die Nebensonnen', the three suns are at best abstract symbols of lost love. The wanderer is now resigned to this loss, just as he is to a life of wind and snow.

The final song, No. 24, 'Der Leiermann', relates back to earlier references to madness, especially 'Täuschung' (No. 19). This extraordinary poem and setting offer another alternative to the fate of the wanderer: he can join the hurdy-gurdy man in madness.[15]

As mentioned, the two transformational songs that lead to 'Der Wegweiser' are 'Rückblick' (No. 8) and 'Letzt Hoffnung' (No. 16). Both songs contribute, through shifts in the wanderer's psychological state, to the linearity of the poetic progression. In the context of the poetic progression, No. 8 combines several recurring dichotomies: recollecting the past even as the wanderer lurches ahead; the fire-versus-ice metaphor recalling the pain of loss; and snowballs thrown by crows as an emblem of his hostile world, which prepares for the recurrence of the crow as symbol of death in No. 15. Finally, for the critical moment in No. 8, the painful remembrance, Müller uses apostrophe at the end of Stanza 4: 'Da war's geschehn um dich, Gesell!' (then, my friend, you were done for!).[16] This is the last backward glance in the cycle, an important shift in the poetic progression.

Song No. 16, with its incomparable despair and hopelessness, marks another dramatic moment of change within the journey.[17] Through identification with the single leaf that falls, the wanderer continues on—but without hope. The rejection of the past in No. 8 thus is joined by a rejection of hope in No. 16; the wanderer trudges on towards the poetic climax in the dichotomous state of hopeless resignation mixed with a determination to move ahead.

Chromaticism as a Formal Agent

The climactic 'Der Wegweiser' is well-known for its stunning chromaticism (see Example 17.1). Two distinct forms of chromaticism recur throughout the cycle and thus adumbrate that of No. 20: the ascending and descending lines through chromatic passing tones or Ps, and the combinations of these lines into chromatic wedges. A third powerful chromatic element, the descending semitone progression, which occurs twice but is not prepared earlier in the cycle, will be examined below; this third form of chromaticism also has profound meaning for the cycle's climax.

Table 17.2 presents the six P forms in *Winterreise*, along with the number of recurrences. Table 17.3 charts this recurring chromaticism, showing both Ps and wedges.

Example 17.1 Schubert, 'Der Wegweiser', D 911/20: chromaticism, bars 69–81

Table 17.2 Schubert, *Winterreise*, D 911: Six forms of P motives

P1 = C–B–B♭–A (13)	P4 = G–G♯–A (8)
P2 = C–C♯–D (8)	P5 = E–E♯–F♯
P3 = F–E–E♭ (10)	P6 = F–F♯–G

Table 17.3 Schubert, *Winterreise*, D 911: P forms

P1 = C–B–B♭–A
P2 = C–C#–D
P3 = F–E–E♭
P4 = G–G#–A
P5 = E–E#–F#
P6 = F–F#–G

1. Gute Nacht—d	2. Wetterfahne—a	3. Gefror'ne Tränen—f	4. Erstarrung—c	5. Lindenbaum—E	6. Wasserfluth—e
P3	P2	P1	P1	P1	
P5		P3	⌐P2⌐	P3	
		Wedge: P1/P3	⌐P3⌐	P4	
			P6		P5
7. Auf Flusse—e	**8. Rückblick—g**	**9. Irrlicht—b**	**10. Rast—c**	**11. Frühlings—A**	**12. Einsamkeit—b**
P1	P1	P1	P1		P1
	⌐P2⌐		⌐P3⌐		
	⌐P3⌐		P4		P4
	P4	P5		P5	P5
P6	P6				Wedge: P1/P4
	Wedge: P2/P3		Wedge: P3/P4		
13. Post—E♭	**14. Kopf—c**	**15. Krähe—c**	**16. Letzte—E♭**	**17. Im Dorfe—D**	**18. Stürm Mor—d**
P1		⌐P1⌐	P1		
P2	⌐P2⌐	⌐P2⌐			
	⌐P3⌐	⌐P3⌐			
	P4	⌐P4⌐		P4	
	P5			P5	
P6		P6	P6		
19. Täuschg—A	**20. Wegweiser—g**	**21. Wirthaus—F**	**22. Muth—a**	**23. Nebensonn—A**	**24. Leiermann—b**
P1	P1	P1			
	⌐P2⌐	⌐P2⌐		P2	
	⌐P3⌐	⌐P3⌐		P3	
	⌐P4⌐	P4			
P5	P5	P5		P5	
		P6			
	Wedge: P2/P3/P4				

The chromatic Ps recur in all but three songs, either singly or in groups. Of the six distinct P forms, the first four are the most prominent and crystallise in 'Der Wegweiser'. Five songs have four P forms, four songs have three and nine of twenty-four songs have two P forms. Only five songs (6, 11, 22, 23 and 24) are either devoid of any P chromaticism or include only one of the rarer forms. No. 20, meanwhile, has five P forms.

The cycle begins with a frequent use of P1 (C–B–B♭) and P3 (F–E–E♭), see Example 17.2, where P1 and P3 are bracketed.

P3 occurs by itself right in No. 1, setting 'the maiden speaks of love' and thus beginning the wanderer's central psychological conundrum.. The two Ps (P1 and P3) depict the metaphors of hot tears and frozen ice in Nos. 3 and 4, convey restlessness in No. 10, and depict the struggle around death in No. 14.[18] In No. 20, then, P1 and P3 recur together in the song's G major middle section, bars 22–33, where the wanderer asks what foolish craving drives him into the wilderness.[19]

P2 (C–C♯–D) is initially heard in No. 8, along with P1 and P3, and recurs especially in Part II (Nos. 14 and 15), where the wanderer reflects upon death, as shown in Example 17.3. P2 supports various images of the wanderer's journey[20] and contributes to the build-up to No. 20, where P2 and P3 recur in invertible counterpoint within the wedges of 'Der Wegweiser'.

P4 (G–G♯–A), shown in Example 17.4, first appears in No. 5, 'Der Lindenbaum,' with the attempt to escape the present through memory of the past. P4 then recurs with greater frequency at the end of Part I and through the first half of Part II.[21] P4 then joins the chromatic Ps in the climactic No. 20.[22]

Table 17.4 shows the wedges that foreshadow those of 'Der Wegweiser'. The four songs (3, 10, 12 and 14) are all in minor keys, and they all depict the wanderer's interior ruminations. Table 17.4 also indicates critical textual issues being depicted; there is a dichotomous progression from hot tears versus winter's ice to the external versus the internal storm to the ambivalence of life versus death. As Example 17.5 demonstrates, the first two wedges occur within piano introductions, where the subconscious is at work before the wanderer begins to speak, and the latter two occur with intensely rising vocal lines expressing either the storm in No. 12 or yearning for death in No. 14. Within the wedges of these four songs, P2 recurs once while P1, P3 and P4 each recur three times.[23]

The P forms and wedges leading up to 'Der Wegweiser' intensify within the song's climax. As is well-known, the wedges in No. 20 prolong a diminished seventh chord: C♯–E–G–B♭. Diminished seventh chords generally are ubiquitous in Schubert's music, and all but two songs in this cycle include them in the different forms.[24] Thus the chromatic wedges accompany the wanderer even as he goes beyond his world of struggle. Indeed, the intense chromaticism—above which the wanderer strikingly sings a pedal G—may represent an internalising of the pain as a prelude to the refocused journey ahead.

While the recurring chromaticism functions as a form of coherence, the brevity and the variability of Ps and wedges create a sense of fragmentation

Example 17.2 Schubert, *Winterreise*, D 911: early P1s and P3s. a. No. 1, 'Gute Nacht', bars 19–21; b. No. 3, 'Gefror'ne Tränen', bars 3–5; c. No. 4, 'Erstarrung', bars 27–31

Example 17.3 Schubert, *Winterreise*, D 911: P2s. a. No. 8, 'Rückblick', bars 1–6; b. No. 14, 'Der greise Kopf', bars 21–22; c. No. 15, 'Die Krähe', bars 22–23

Example 17.4 Schubert, *Winterreise*, D 911: P4s. a. No. 5, 'Der Lindenbaum', bars 50–55; b. No. 10, 'Rast', bars 17–24; c. No. 12, 'Einsamkeit', bars 37–41; d. No. 14 'Der greise Kopf', bars 35–37

Example 17.4 Continued

(c) Ach, dass die Luft so ruhig! Ach, dass die Welt so licht!

(d) Wer glaubt's? und meiner ward es nicht

Table 17.4 Schubert, *Winterreise*, D 911: wedges

3. Gefror'ne Tränen—f	10. Rast—c	12. Einsamkeit—b
P1	P1	P1
		P2
P3	P3	
	P4	P4
Wedge: P1/P3	quasi Wedge: P3/P4	Wedge: P1/P4
weeps hot tears on winter's ice	cannot rest/ storm in heart	rejects bright & calm world for storm
14. Der greise Kopf—c	20. Wegweiser—g	
	P1	P1 = C–B–B♭–A
P2	P2	
P3	P3	P2 = C–C♯–D
P4	P4	
	P5	P3 = F–E–E♭
Wedge: P2/P3	Wedge: P2/P3/P4	P4 = G–G♯–A
yearns for death	accepts journey "never to return"	

Example 17.5 Schubert, *Winterreise*, D 911: chromatic wedges. a. No. 3, 'Gefror'ne Tränen', bars 3–5; b. No. 10, 'Rast', bars 1–5; c. No. 12, 'Einsamkeit', bars 28–29; d. No. 14, 'Der greise Kopf', bars 21–22

along with the continuity. As Table 17.2d shows, these small chromatic cells make up a tiny portion of each song (indicated as number of bars), fragmentary threads that start and quickly break off.

Nevertheless, Schubert does create an acceleration of chromaticism towards the cycle's climax. All instances over ten bars long are highlighted: beginning in No. 10, with a great increase in No. 13, and another long chromatic span in No. 17. These all prepare for the extensive chromaticism in No. 20.

The Journey that Never Ends

Winterreise as a Romantic Fragment Despite the steady crescendo to 'Der Wegweiser', the song and the rest of the cycle feature fragmentation and discontinuity. The early nineteenth-century concept of the fragment has been discussed in great detail by John Daverio, Richard Kramer, Charles Rosen, David Ferris, Beate Julia Perrey (2002) and Berthold Hoeckner (2006), among others.[25] The idea began with the Schlegel brothers, Friedrich and August Wilhelm,[26] who proposed a new literary aesthetic wherein the novel became, through interruptions, ambiguities, irresolution and incompletion, a more fluid form. As Daverio says, 'The fragment calls up a host of negatives: it is incomplete, detached, unfinished, isolated; it presupposes a perfectly shaped, but now broken or destroyed whole'.[27] Of Romantic poetry, Friedrich Schlegel states: 'Romantic poetry is constantly developing ... it can forever only become, it can never achieve definite form.... It alone is infinite'.[28] This profound literary movement then found its voice in music, when lied composers such as Schubert and Schumann could convey poetic progressions in dramatically new ways. Schumann's cycle *Dichterliebe* (1840) and his miniature piano works such as *Papillons*, Op. 2 (1829–31), and *Carnaval*, Op. 9 (1834), celebrated these principles,[29] as did some of Schubert's earlier songs, such as 'Erster Verlust' and 'Nähe des Geliebten' (both 1815).[30]

I propose that when Schubert composed *Winterreise* he returned to the fragment concept to convey the complex, often opposing emotions and conflicts of his wanderer, including the protagonist's ambivalence towards death.[31] Indeed, the poetry set by each song is but a moment in a lengthy, rambling journey, every song a vignette in which the wanderer attempts to cope with his chaotic and conflicting emotions.[32] The twists and turns of Müller's poetic journey have several transformational moments (Nos. 8, 16 and 20), but beyond the signpost of No. 20 there is no further poetic or musical goal. Thus the inherent, unfocused wandering and the open-ended nature of the cycle exemplify the chaos and incompletion of the fragment. The wanderer wants to escape his pain and approaches the signposts with resignation. The moment of truth finally arrives when he makes a decision to follow the road 'from which no one returns'. We will return to this fateful decision presently.

Table 17.5 Schubert, *Winterreise*, D 911: P forms as fragments

1. Gute Nacht—d	2. Wetterfahne—a	3. Gefror'ne Tränen—f	4. Erstarrung—c	5. Lindenbaum—E	6. Wasserfluth—e
105 bars	51 bars	55 bars	109 bars	82 bars	32 bars
		P1—6.5 bars	P1—5 bars	P1—4.5 bars	
P3—2.5 bars	P2—3 bars	P3—9 bars	P2—1 bar	P3—3 bars	P5—1 bar
P5—1.5 bars			P3—5 bars	P4—1.5 bars	
		Wedge: P1/P3	P6—1		

7. Auf Fluße—e	8. Rückblick—g	9. Irrlicht—b	10. Rast—c	11. Frühlings—A	12. Einsamkeit—b
74 bars	69 bars	43 bars	67 bars	88 bars	48 bars
P1—4 bars	P1—2 bars	P1—2 bars	P1—7 bars		P1—4 bars
P3—4 bars	P2—3 bars		P3—8.5 bars		P4—6 bars
P6—1.5 bars	P3—1 bar	P5—2 bars	**P4—13 bars**	P5—3 bars	P5—4 bars
	P6—1 bar		Wedge: P3/P4		Wedge: P1/P4

P1 = C–B–B♭–A
P2 = C–C#–D
P3 = F–E–E♭
P4 = G–G#–A
P5 = E–E#–F#
P6 = F–F#–G

(continued)

Table 17.5 Continued

13. Post—E♭	14. Kopf—c	15. Krähe—c	16. Letzte—E♭	17. Im Dorfe—D	18. Stürm Mor—d
94 bars	44 bars	43 bars	47 bars	50 bars	19 bars
P1—14 bars	P2—1 bar	P1—4 bars	P1—6 bars		P1—1 bar
P2—10	P3—2 bars	P2—1 bar		**P4—11 bars**	P4—1 bar
P6—12 bars	P4—6 bars	P3—2 bars	P6—4 bars	P5—4 bars	P6—1 bar
	Wedge:P2/P3	P4—1 bar			

19. Täuschg—A	20. Wegweiser—g	21. Wirthaus—F	22. Muth—g	23. Nebensonn—A	24. Leiermann—b
19 bars	83 bars	31 bars	46 bars	32 bars	61 bars
	P1—10				
P1—5 bars	**P2—21**	P2—4 bars			
	P3—11 bars	P3—5 bars			
P5—8 bars	P4—3 bars	P5—1 bar		P5—2 bars	
	P5—3	P6—3 bars			
	Wedge:P2/P3/P4				

The Tonal Design of Winterreise

Table 17.6 places the wanderer's emotional and psychological journey within Schubert's tonal design.[33]

To highlight dramatic tonal discontinuities, I distinguish the flat side from the sharp side of the minor tonalities used. The five major-mode keys, meanwhile, are indicated by dotted borders. Schubert's tonal scheme reflects the poetic progression thus: the wounded wanderer leaves the rejecting maiden's house in No. 1, in D minor, and No. 2, in A minor.[34] No. 3, in F minor, presents his first look inward at the depth of his pain and the first time he weeps. The ensuing songs present various psychological states as they combine or alternate with one another. The pain and brooding of No. 3 recur in Nos. 7, in E minor; 9, in B minor; 10 and 14, both in C minor; 16, in E♭ major; and 21, in F major. The memories and fantasies of the lost love occur in the major mode: No. 5, in E major, and Nos. 11, 19 and 23, all in A major. Occasional bursts of defiance occur in Nos. 6, in E minor; 18, in D minor; and 22, in G minor. And emotional frenzy is heard in Nos. 4, in C minor, and 8, in G minor. Meanwhile, the states of emotional stasis or near collapse occur in Nos. 12, in B minor, and, again, 19, in A major. The remaining songs continue the psychological portrait: major-mode song No. 13, in E♭, depicts his last yearning for his lost love from Nos. 1 and 2, and No. 17, in D major, continues the brooding over the wanderer's alienation from the world he is leaving. No. 15, in C minor, intensifies the idea of death from Nos. 5, in E major; 9, in B minor; and 14, in C minor, that accelerated throughout Part II. And No. 24, in B minor, offers the wanderer a vision—and possibly expresses his fear—of madness.

The number of different tonalities and the juxtaposition and/or alternation of distant keys in Winterreise have caused much consternation. Suurpää summarises four different approaches to this vexing issue:[35] (1) tonal coherence with prolongation,[36] (2) tonal coherence without prolongation,[37] (3) the absence of any tonal unity[38] and (4) Suurpää's own approach, where he states that 'it is not plausible to infer either a large-scale prolongational structure or a governing single background tonic'.[39] Suurpää then offers a twofold approach of Schenkerian analysis for individual songs and neo-Riemannian analysis for the cycle as a whole, particularly Part II. These diverse views of tonal design result in part from key considerations (manuscript versus publication keys), tonal center (D minor as tonic or not) and concepts of coherence versus discontinuity.

I offer an alternative approach that focuses upon two different issues: the dichotomy of flat versus sharp keys or tonal discontinuity, and, once again, the concept of the fragment.

Table 17.7 shows the keys of each song, with the number of flats indicated below and the number of sharps noted above the staff.[40] Most keys in the cycle recur at least once and usually more frequently.[41] Thirteen songs are in flat keys and eleven (including A minor) in sharp keys. Of

Table 17.6 Schubert, *Winterreise*, D 911: tonal plot

1. Gute Nacht	2. Die Wetterfahne	3. Gefror'n Tränen	4. Erstarrung	5. Der Lindenbaum	6. Wasserflut
d	a	f	c	E	e
7. Auf dem Fluße	8. Rückblick	9. Irrlicht	10. Rast	11. Frühlingstraum	12. Einsamkeit
e	g	b	c	A	b
13. Die Post	14. Der greise Kopf	15. Die Krähe	16. Letzte Hoffnung	17. Im Dorfe	18. Der stürmische Morgen
E♭	c	c	E♭	D	d
19. Täuschung	20. Der Wegweiser	21. Das Wirthaus	22. Mut	23. Die Nebensonnen	24. Der Leiermann
A	g	F	g	A	b

= flat side   = sharp side   = major-mode sharp

Chromaticism in *Winterreise*

the six major-mode keys, four are sharp-sided (E, A—twice—and D) and three are flat-sided (E♭—twice—and F). The number of flats and sharps also shows a pattern of proportion: keys with three flats occur six times, and keys with three sharps occur four times; keys with two flats occur three times, and those with two sharps occur four times. The four flats of F minor in No. 3 is balanced by the four sharps of No. 5, and the three songs with a single flat—D minor (twice) and F major—are balanced by two songs with one sharp. This balance of flats and sharps is indicated by the brackets in Table 17.7.

While the number of keys in sharps and flats seems close, I argue that the flat side proves more stable and significant. Both songs that begin Parts I and II are flat-sided (D minor and E♭ major, respectively), as are the critical songs along the journey: No. 3 in F minor, No. 8 in G minor, No. 16 in E♭ major and No. 20 in G minor. This suggests that the sharp-sided songs constantly disrupt the ongoing flat-sided world as an expression of the wanderer's ambivalence, confusion, disorientation and alienation. Significantly, however, while both parts of the cycle begin with flat keys, both end with sharp keys. The endings thus reflect a profound lack of closure: in Part I, Schubert changed the original

Table 17.7 Balance of flat side and sharp side

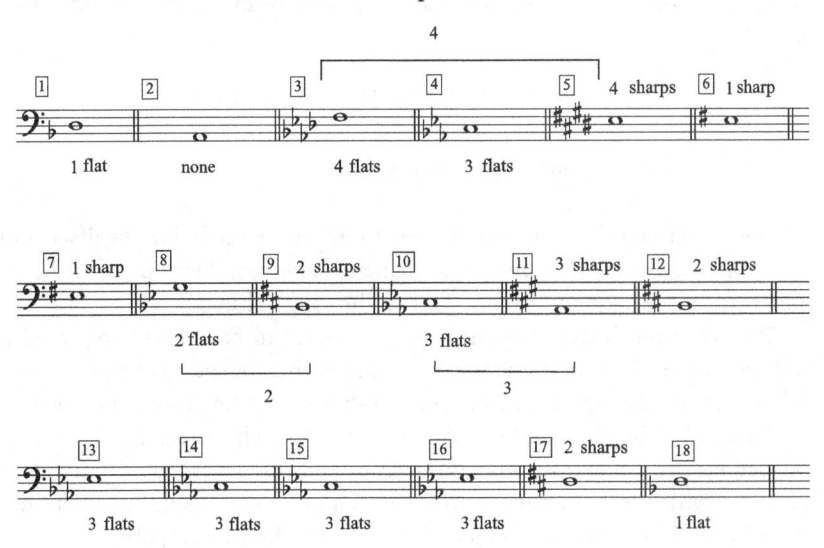

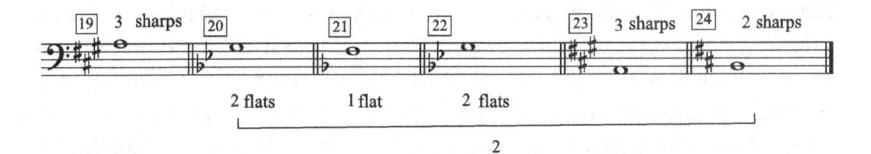

cycle concept which ended in D minor, to end in B minor; and at the end of Part II, the ending, again in B minor, contributes to the incompleteness of the cycle.

While the opposition of flat and sharp keys within Schubert's tonal design is continuous, many have noted that Schubert also groups certain keys, most notably the E major/E minor grouping of Nos. 5–7 and the C minor/E♭ major grouping of Nos. 13–16. However, the keys that are part of a tonal grouping are always offset by remotely related keys. For example, the three songs in E major/E minor (5, 6 and 7) are surrounded by minor flat keys:

  4 = C minor [5 = E major 6 = E minor 7 = E minor] 8 = G minor

And the grouping around C minor and its relative (Nos. 13–16) are approached by and followed by remote sharp keys:

12 = B minor [13 = E♭ major 14 = C minor 15 = C minor 16 = E♭ major]

    17 = D major

Meanwhile, though the keys of transformational Nos. 8 in G minor and 16 in E♭ major are closely related to each other and to 'Der Wegweiser', No. 8 is surrounded by remote sharp keys, and No. 16 is followed by a remote sharp key:[42]

    7 = E minor [8 = G minor] 9 = B minor

    15 = C minor [16 = E♭ major] 17 = D major

One final tonal element warrants attention. As mentioned in the discussion of chromaticism, a third chromatic element—one that does *not* occur before song No. 20—has a significant impact on the song's climax.

The powerful descending chromatic sequence in bars 11–14 (repeated in bars 46–49) depicts the wanderer reflecting on his journey as he prepares to follow a particular signpost. Example 17.6 shows how the progression includes P2 (denoted by bracket) and P3 (alto voice, bar 16), which recalls that pair described earlier.[43] But this poignant descent takes us to powerful tonal complexities, which in turn refer us to earlier songs, a remarkable recollection of the winter's journey at the moment the wanderer chooses his path.

The tonal meaning of the chromatic sequence itself is ambiguous. While the falling bass line summons up the descending lament progression from I to V, the sequence neither begins on i nor ends on V of G minor. And while the progression occurs within a tonic prolongation, it leads us to a cadence in F minor—on the deep flat side—which has no function in G minor. So the meaning of this descending sequence turns on why Schubert alludes to F minor here. The key of F minor sets only 'Gefror'ne Tränen', in which the wanderer first felt intense pain and then wept. Recollection of this first experience of despair is a requisite for

Chromaticism in *Winterreise* 375

Example 17.6 Schubert, 'Der Wegweiser', D 911/20: chromatic progression, bars 10–20

[musical notation]

moving beyond that pain, and thus Schubert returns to F minor twice in order to do so, albeit fleetingly, as F minor yields immediately to a return to G minor.

The recall of F minor is one of two such tonal recollections in No. 20. A similar tonal allusion to earlier songs occurs within the song's parallel mode, G major. The key of E minor—the sharp side—is prolonged in bars 27–34. This of course refers to a group of songs early in Part I, where the wanderer struggles to understand his torment: in the E minor section of 'Der Lindenbaum,' where leaves beckon him towards death; in the E minor of 'Wasserfluth', where he asks the snow what path it will take when spring comes; and in 'Auf dem Flusse', where the dichotomy of burning tears falling on frozen ice recalls song No. 3, in F minor. These songs, too, are introspective, and the prominent dotted rhythms in the bass in bars 16, 19, 51 and 54 (and in the vocal line in bars 17–18) recall song No. 7 as well.[44]

These are not real keys, of course, not even tonicisations. Yet F minor moments are expressed in perfect cadences, and E minor arrives with imperfect cadences. So why, at this critical moment in the cycle, do we summon up these would-be keys? I would argue that these tonal references are best understood as implied keys, keys suggested but not fully realised.[45] Such implied keys are often unacknowledged in analysis, but they have tremendous import in conveying the textual drama. Implied keys often suggest departure from, or motion to, a given key that either destabilises the tonality in which it occurs or creates tonal motion that, even in incomplete form, is felt as a tonal departure. In 'Der Wegweiser', such tonal references are powerful reminders of the journey that brought us to this climactic moment. Indeed, such implied keys are tonal images similar to nature images in poetry: they have literal surface meaning, but also a deeper interior meaning for our protagonist. The key of F minor symbolises pain, and the E minor allusion represents the twists and turns of the wanderer's grief in the snowy landscape.[46]

All the approaches to *Winterreise's* tonal designs reflect different interpretations of the poetic progression or narrative. In my reading, Schubert's ever-changing tonal focus portrays the poetic conflicts and oppositions, the stumbles and falls of the wounded wanderer, especially with regard to the option of death. And since I propose a chaotic poetic and psychological progression, I thus submit that the cycle's tonal design is also discontinuous and eschews any form of coherence; the ending of the cycle is inconclusive, as is the wanderer's fate.[47]

Ultimately, *Winterreise* is a cycle of fragments that is, as a whole and in the irony of the form, fragmentary. The notion of the song cycle as a fragment has been examined in considerable detail, and most of the authors already noted focus on Schumann's *Dichterliebe* as just such a group of individual fragments that make up an incomplete whole.[48] My premise of *Winterreise* as a cycle of fragments derives from both the tonal plot—so full of interruptions and discontinuity—and the cycle's ambiguous ending. Song No. 1 is not in a governing tonic, but rather is in a key that recurs only once (No. 18), and is never heard again. Indeed, if there is a tonic, I argue that it is G minor, the key of so much significance throughout the cycle: first heard in the epiphany song, No. 8; recurring in the climactic song, No. 20, which has such strong closure; and recurring as well in song No. 22, as the wanderer tries to gather courage for his new journey.[49] It is as if the wanderer had begun his journey in a D minor world that he must leave, after which a new tonal world of G minor emerges as the focus of the critical turning points along his path. Rosen's description of the opening of *Dichterliebe* is apt: 'The form is not fixed but is torn apart or exploded by paradox, by ambiguity . . . a close[d] circular form in which beginning and end are unstable—implying a past before the song begins and a future after its final chord'.[50] In *Winterreise*, although the individual songs may seem self-contained, their roles within the cycle are disrupted by tonal shifts as well as by their vastly different characters. This separation is also enhanced by the lengthy piano introductions and postludes, where the persona of these solos is the emotional or psychological state of the wanderer *before* he speaks: each introduction disrupts the previous song's ending.[51]

The twin issues of irresolution and incompletion within the fragment thus evolve through poetic struggles and through sharp-sided keys that continually interrupt the opening flat side and that close both Parts I and II. When the cycle closes in B minor, then, it is not over; there is neither tonal closure nor resolution of the conflict between flat versus sharp keys.[52]

In order to fully understand the impact of 'Der Wegweiser', let us look briefly at the songs that follow, which, like the implied keys of song No. 20, reflect the past even as the wanderer moves ahead. No. 21 is the last consideration of escape through death, which ceases to be an option; the song marks the end of the intense chromaticism and takes us to a new tonal plane of F major, which had depicted love and marriage in the opening song of D minor. No. 22 is a defiant attempt to be courageous, as the wanderer must continue; the key of G minor returns us to the frenzy of No. 8, 'Rückblick', as well as to the climactic acceptance in 'Der Wegweiser'. No. 23 is one more escape into fantasy and recollection (recalling the sharp keys A and E major), which leads to accepting the loss of love. The final song, then, provides the wanderer with an image of madness that some say represent his final state. I argue that addressing 'Der Leiermann's' numb torment propels the wanderer forward, but to another state yet to be understood.

The concluding four songs are thus in diverse keys and are fragmentary meditations, as if the journey's arrival at No. 20 has paused the ongoing motion. Each song is a different piece or fragment of the wanderer's consciousness, one preoccupation followed by another. In addition, the change in keys reflects the flat-versus-sharp progression: Nos. 21 and 22, from the flat side (F major and G minor), are followed by Nos. 23 and 24, from the sharp side (A major and B minor).[53]

The pivotal role of 'Der Wegweiser' thus embodies the ambiguity, oppositions and irresolution of the fragment. As a climax, No. 20 fulfills the poetic and chromatic trajectories from the opening of the cycle; a *part* of the journey has been completed and the song itself ends conclusively. But the cycle is incomplete, and thus song No. 20 is contextually a fragment.

Conclusion

Songs Nos. 21–24 thus show the wanderer coming to terms with the past in order to follow his future. What remains is to understand where he is in fact going. Both Youens and Kramer offer nuanced understandings of the wanderer's destiny. Youens acknowledges the ambiguity and paradox of the cycle's ending: 'When the quest culminates in partial understanding, the seeker wants only to reject what he finds, and the self is rent asunder all the more. . . . neither an alternative self nor death is within his grasp'.[54] Kramer's view is close to my own.[55] He believes that 'the narrative of *Winterreise* is effectively without end. The songs following "Der Wegweiser" neither confirm nor reinforce the sense of "Der Wegweiser" as a structural close, but rather dissolve from it'. Kramer believes that the cycle continues, but he calls this continuation a 'void'. For me, the cycle does not conclude so much as it ceases, like an incomplete fragment. The wanderer neither dies nor succumbs to madness. Rather, we have traveled with the wanderer on a journey that continues on *after* our engagement ends.

Like Müller and Schubert, I believe that the essence of *romantische Sehnsucht* (Romantic longing) is an insatiable quest to go beyond what is known.[56] But we readers and listeners need to know the wanderer's ultimate goal and to understand the road from which no one returns. The lack of tonal coherence and of a conclusive ending in the cycle leaves us puzzled and wanting. Schubert's last cycle is thus a stunning example of the Romantic fragment: a grouping of at times seemingly unrelated elements that remains unresolved and incomplete.

And what is this road from which no one returns? I submit that the wanderer will not go back to the locus of his loss and despair, but rather will move forward to a place as yet unknown, his fate extending beyond what we can know. Rather than call this a 'void', I suggest we think of the next steps of the journey as an imminent continuation. The wanderer knows he must go on. He will not return on this new path, because he is leaving his world and his sorrows behind. Just as Schubert continues to compose masterpieces in the face of his impending death, so the wanderer continues in his search for a new life in the future. According to Ferris, A. W. Schlegel 'offers a compelling metaphor for Schumann's songs when he argues that a Romantic work of art should be like a sketch.... The sketch is more a stimulus that we must continue to develop with our imaginations'.[57] In *Winterreise*, then, we are left with our pathos and our yearning to understand, but any conclusion must occur within our 'imagination', in our projection into an elusive future.

Notes

1. While many have studied *Winterreise*, this analysis is particularly indebted to the work of Susan Youens, *Retracing a Winter's Journey: Schubert's 'Winterreise'* (Ithaca, NY: Cornell University Press, 1991), and Richard Kramer, *Distant Cycles: Schubert and the Conceiving of Song* (Chicago: University of Chicago Press, 1994). All text translations come from Youens's monograph.

2. Youens, *Retracing a Winter's Journey*, p. 220.

3. Charles Fisk, *Returning Cycles: Contexts for the Interpretation of Schubert's Impromptus and Late Sonatas* (Berkeley and Los Angeles: University of California Press, 2001), p. 28.

4. Kramer, *Distant Cycles*, pp. 180–6.

5. I will not consider two other valuable approaches, Schenkerian analysis and motivic analysis, which have already received considerable attention. Schenkerian studies of *Winterreise* include V. Kofi Agawu, 'On Schubert's "Der greise Kopf"', *In Theory Only* 8/1 (1984), pp. 3–21; Walther Everett, 'Grief in *Winterreise*: a Schenkerian Perspective', *Music Analysis* 9/2 (1990), pp. 157–75; Kramer, *Distant Cycle* pp. 94–96 and 153ff.; David B. Lewin, *Studies in Music with Text* (New York: Oxford University Press, 2006) pp. 135–47; Edward D. Latham, 'Drei Nebensonnen: Forte's Linear-Motivic Analysis, Korngold's *Die tote Stadt*, and Schubert's *Winterreise* as Visions of Closure', *Gamut* 2/1 (2009), pp. 299–346, http://dlc.lib.utk.edu/web/ojs/index.php/first/issue/current; and Lauri Suurpää, *Death in Winterreise: Musico-Poetic Associations in Schubert's Song Cycle* (Bloomington: Indiana University Press), 2014, pp. 48ff. Both Lewin and Kramer discuss Schenker's sketch of 'Auf dem Flusse' (Heinrich Schenker, *Der Freie Satz*, 1979, fig. 40/2). Rhythmic motivic analysis includes Arnold Feil, *Franz Schubert: Die schöne Müllerin; Die Wintrerreise*

(Stuttgart: Reclam, 1975), pp. 29-44 and 87-129, and Susan Youens, "Wegweiser in Winterreise," *Journal of Musicology* 5/3 (1987), pp. 357-79, and *Retracing a Winter's Journey*, pp. 73-306. The studies by Everett, Lewin and Suurpää offer both Schenkerian and motivic analysis in great detail.

6. For a detailed account of how Schubert developed his cycle in two stages see Youens, *Retracing a Winter's Journey*, 24-45, and Kramer, *Distant Cycles*, 151-87.

7. Youens describes many poetic oppositions, pp. 126ff. and my co-author Robert Spillman and I discuss poetic dichotomy in *Poetry into Song* (Oxford: Oxford University Press, 1996), pp. 5ff.

8. Most authors discuss 'melting or thawing ice' imagery: for example, V. Kofi Agawu, 'On Schubert's "Der greise Kopf"', pp. 3-21; Youens, *Retracing a Winter's Journey*, pp. 139ff.; Kramer, *Distant Cycles*, pp. 153-159; and Suurpää, *Death in Winterreise*.

9. Suurpää, *Death in Winterreise*, believes the lure of death does not begin until songs 14 and 15, pp. 63-84.

10. Youens, *Retracing a Winter's Journey*, p. 177; and David B. Lewin, *Studies in Music with Text* (Oxford: Oxford University Press, 2009), pp. 111-25.

11. Youens, *Retracing a Winter's Journey*, p. 197, notes another kind of death: emotional death, where the wanderer fears he will lose his ability to remember and mourn his lost love.

12. Barbara Barry discusses a similar cycle of projection and empathy as a 'reflective' element of emotion in '"Sehnsucht" and Melancholy: Explorations of Time and Structure in Schubert's *Winterreise*', in *The Philosopher's Stone: Essays in the Transformation of Musical Structure* (Hillsdale, NY: Pendragon Press, 2000), pp. 181-202, especially p. 182.

13. Several have commented on the unexpected nature of No. 13. See Richard Capell, *Schubert's Songs*, 3rd edn (Old Woking, Surrey: The Gresham Press, 1928), p. 236; and John Reed, *The Schubert Song Companion* (New York: Universe Books, 1985), p. 451.

14. Youens, *Retracing a Winter's Journey*, p. 267.

15. Capell, *Schubert's Songs*, p. 239; and Brian Newbould, *Schubert: the Music and the Man* (Berkeley and Los Angeles: University of California Press, 1997), pp. 306-7.

16. 'The difference between past and present is heightened all the more by the third-person address. . . .. To mitigate the pain of remembrance, [the wanderer] divides himself into observer and observed, the one commenting ironically on the other'. Youens, *Retracing a Winter's Journey*, pp. 187-95. Both Kramer, *Distant Cycles*, p. 155, and Rufus Hallmark, 'The Literary and Musical Rhetoric of Apostrophe in *Winterreise*', *19th Century Music* 35/1 (2011), pp. 3-33, comment on apostrophe in *Winterriese*.

17. 'The musical introspection . . . is extreme. . . . *Letzte Hoffnung* is something of a watershed. What follows is the music of resignation'. Kramer, *Distant Cycles*, pp. 174-9.

18. No. 14 is shown in Example 17.2.

19. Suurpää believes the shifting to the parallel major as depicting 'joy'; *Death in Winterreise*, p. 66.

20. His alienation in No. 2, his frozen heart in No. 4, the symbol of the maiden's gleaming eyes in No. 8, lost love in No. 13, his youth's regret in No. 14 and his vulnerable body beneath the crow in No. 15.

21. Wanting to be old and closer to death in No. 14; the crow, again as agent of death, in No. 15; the wanderer's alienation from townsfolk in No. 17; and the relief of a stormy morning in No. 18.

22. Note two important P pairings in the cycle. P1 and P3 pair seven times (again denoted by brackets) and P2 and P3 pair four times (shown in boxes). These pairings then combine in No. 20.

23. Most, but not all, of these P forms are shown in Example 17.5.

24. The invariant C♯–E–G–B♭ recurs extensively: ten songs prior to No. 20 include this sonority, mostly as a vii^{o7} but twice as a CTo seventh chord. The songs prior to 'Der Wegweiser' set expressive words such as 'Thränen' (tears), 'Das heisse Weh'(my burning grief), 'Treue bis zum Grabe' (faithfulness unto the grave) and 'die hinter Eis und Nacht' (beyond ice, night). The sonority then is prolonged in 'Der Wegweiser' on the critical text: 'Einen Weiser seh' ich stehen/ unverrückt vor meinem Blick; / eine Straße muß ich gehen; / Die noch keiner ging züruck' (I see a signpost standing immovably before my eyes: I must travel a road from which no one has returned).

25. John Daverio, 'Schumann's "Im Legendenton" and Friedrich Schlegel's *Arabeske*', *19th Century Music* 11/2 (1987), pp. 150–63); Daverio, *Nineteenth-Century Music and the German Romantic Ideology* (New York: Schirmer Books, 1993); Daverio, 'The Song Cycle: Journeys through a Romantic Landscape', in Rufus Hallmark (ed.), *German Lieder in the Nineteenth Century* (New York: Schirmer Books, 1996), pp. 279–312; Kramer, *Distant Cycles*; Richard Kramer "The Hedgehog: of Fragments Finished and Unfinished," *19th-Century Music* 21 (1997), pp. 134–48; Kramer, *Unfinished Music* (Oxford: Oxford University Press, 2008), pp. 311–44; Charles Rosen, *The Romantic Generation* (Cambridge, MA: Harvard University Press, 1995); David Ferris, *Schumann's Eichendorff 'Liederkreis' and the Genre of the Romantic Cycle* (New York: Oxford University Press, 2000); Beate Julia Perrey, *Schumann's 'Dichterliebe' and Early Romantic Poetics: Fragmentation of Desire* (Cambridge: Cambridge University Press, 2002); and Berthold Hoeckner, 'Paths through *Dichterliebe*', *19th-Century Music* 30/1 (2006), pp. 65–80. Ferris and Perrey discuss the fragment in terms of Schumann song cycles. Their studies comprise an excellent explication of the Romantic fragment. Yonatan Malin's 2006 review of Perrey (*Music Theory Spectrum* 28 [2006], pp. 299–310) offers much insight into both Perrey's and Ferris's books.

26. The writings of Friedrich Schlegel (1772–1829) and August Wilhelm Schlegel (1767–1845) were published in their journal *Athenäum*, known today as *Athenäum Fragmente*, in Berlin, 1798–1800. The *Fragmente* are collected in *Kritische Friedrich Schlegel Ausgabe*; another good collection of Schlegel's writings is *Friedrich Schlegel: Dialogue on Poetry and Literary Aphorisms*, 1968.

27. Daverio, *Nineteenth-Century Music and the German Romantic Ideology*, p. 87.

28. Cited in Leonard G. Meyer, "Romanticism—the Ideology of Elite Egalitarians," in *Style and Music: Theory, History, and Ideology* (Chicago: University of Chicago Press, 1989), p. 197. This resonates with Janet Schmalfeldt's concept of the 'process of becoming;' see Schmalfeldt, *In the Process of Becoming: Analytical and Philosophical Perspectives* (New York: Oxford University Press, 2011), pp. 8–12.

29. Peter Kaminsky, "Principles of Formal Structure in Schumann's Early Piano Cycles," *Music Theory Spectrum* 11/2 (1989), pp. 207–25; Rosen, *The Romantic*

Generation, pp. 116–236 and 646–702; and Daverio, *Robert Schumann: Herald of a "New Poetic Age"* (Oxford: Oxford University Press, 1997), pp. 131–42.

30. I first discuss 'Erster Verlust' in Stein and Spillman, *Poetry into Song*, pp. 122–3. The song has also been analyzed in Newbould, *Schubert: the Music and the Man*, pp. 51–2; Lawrence Kramer, 'Performance and Social Meaning in the Lied: Schubert's "Erster Verlust"', *Current Musicology* 45 (1994), pp. 5–23; Kramer, 'Interpretive Dramaturgy and Social Drama: Schubert's "Erster Verlust"', in *Franz Schubert: Sexuality, Subjectivity, Song* (Cambridge: Cambridge University Press, 1998), pp. 9–26); Jonathan Dunsby, *Making Words Sing: Nineteenth- and Twentieth-Century Song* (Cambridge: Cambridge University Press: 2004), pp. 125–32; Walther Frisch, Schubert's '"Nähe des Geliebten" (D 162): Transformation of the Volkston', in Walther Frisch (ed.), *Schubert: Critical and Analytical Studies* (Lincoln: University of Nebraska Press, 1986), pp. 175–99; and Richard Kramer, *Distant Cycles*, pp. 13–16. Kramer also discusses it in *Unfinished Music*, pp. 346–9.

31. Barry discusses Schubert's own psychological struggles with his illness at the time he composed *Winterreise* in '"Sehnsucht" and Melancholy', pp. 185–8.

32. In his detailed description of the categories of musical fragments in Schumann, Daverio notes what Schumannn called 'Selbstvernichtung' or self-annihilation. For example, 'each successive *Papillon* effectively cancels out its predecessor'; *Nineteenth-Century Music and the German Romantic Ideology*, pp. 62–63.

33. While most of the keys of the cycle are straightforward, several were changed for various reasons. For these variances, I have chosen the later keys from the cycle's publication: in Part I, 'Wasserflut' is in E minor, 'Rast' in C minor and 'Einsamkeit' in B minor; in Part II, 'Mut' is in G minor and 'Der Leiermann' is in B minor.

34. In the tables, I use uppercase for major and lowercase for minor in both key names and roman numerals.

35. Suurpää, *Death in Winterreise*, p. xxxvii.

36. Kramer, *Distant Cycles*, Barry, '"Sehnsucht" and Melancholy', and Latham, 'Drei Nebensonnen'.

37. Christopher Lewis, 'Text, Time, and Tonic: Aspects of Patterning in the Romantic Cycle', *Intégral* 2 (1988), pp. 37–73.

38. Barbara Turchin, 'The Nineteenth-Century *Wanderlieder* Cycle', *Journal of Musicology* 5/4 (1987), pp. 498–525; Everett, 'Grief in *Winterreise*', pp. 157–75; Youens, *Retracing a Winter's Journey*, pp. 95–104; and Rosen, *The Romantic Generation*, pp. 203–4.

39. Suurpää, *Death in Winterreise*, pp. 173–4.

40. I will not discuss the interesting issue of 'key characteristics' in Schubert's music, which is amply discussed in Reed, *The Schubert Song Companion*; Youens, *Retracing a Winter's Journey*; Kramer, *Distant Cycles*; and Rita Steblin, *A History of Key Characteristics in the 18th and Early 19th Centuries*, 2nd edn, 2005.

41. Three songs, however, occur in unique keys. No. 2 is in A minor, relating closely to the D minor of No. 1 but remotely to No. 3. The pain and weeping of No. 3 is in the deepest flat key, removed from the opening two songs but then close to the C minor that follows. The key does not recur, possibly because that depth of pain never recurs in the same direct, innocent way. In addition, the four flats of F minor do anticipate important leading notes of keys to come: B♭ = A♯ to B minor (Nos. 9, 12 and 24),

E♭ = D♯ to E major (No. 5) and E minor (Nos. 6 and 7), A♭ = G♯ to A major (Nos. 11, 19 and 23) and D♭ = C♯ to D major (No. 17) and D minor (Nos. 1 and 18). Finally, the key of F major in No. 21 is anomalous; I believe it occurs not in relation to its parallel minor (No. 3), but rather as the relative to D minor songs. In No. 1, motion towards F major depicted images of love and hope for marriage, and in No. 18 F major is V/B♭, where the wanderer appreciates the lightning: 'Und rote Feuerflammen / Ziehn zwischen ihnen hin. / Das nenn' ich einen Morgen / So recht nach meinem Sinn!' (And red flames flash between [clouds]—this is what I call a morning after my own heart!).

42. The connection between Nos. 15 and 16 is, of course, the closest of relationships, which makes the succeeding key even more disruptive. To some, the tonal progression of E♭ to D major is significant in the context of the 'governing key' of D minor.

43. The chromatic descent recalls two of Schubert's earliest songs: 'Lied eines Schiffers an die Dioskuren' (1816) and 'Der Jüngling und der Tod' (1817), both of which depict moments of deep introspection.

44. No. 7, which features the dotted rhythm, includes a transposed version of the rising dotted-rhythm line in G minor, bar 64.

45. Robert Bailey (ed.), *Wagner, Prelude and Transfiguration from 'Tristan und Isolde'* (New York: Norton, 1985), pp. 125–6.

46. Note, too, that the song in F minor presents the first wedge of the cycle, and Nos. 5 and 7 include P1 and P3.

47. Both Barry and Latham consider the beginning in D minor and the ending in A minor to be 'permanent interruption' of I to V♭, a structure based on a back-relating dominant. Barry also suggests that other keys in the cycle create not a trajectory but a spiral around D minor. Barry, '"Sehnsucht" and Melancholy', pp. 191–7; and Latham, 'Drei Nebensonnen', pp. 330–7.

48. See note 25.

49. Kramer states that bars 55 to the end of 'Der Wegweiser' 'have a finality to them that is of a certain significance to the cycle. None of the remaining songs is about closure in any similar sense, nor do their tonalities point away from . . . G minor . . . along some teleological track.' Kramer, *Distant Cycles*, p. 182.

50. Rosen, *The Romantic Generation*, p. 51.

51. This is another form of 'Selbstvernichtung' or self-annihilation. Of the twenty-four songs, all but one have an introduction of from four to eight bars. All songs have postludes as well; many are from four to seven bars long, but eight (Nos. 8, 11, 12, 14, 18, 20, 21 and 23) are under four bars. In each of these eight, the brief postlude is followed by a lengthy introduction in the next song.

52. Youens notes that 'the tonal plan of *Winterreise* seems, in places, singularly *un*planned, "used to straying" [as the wanderer states in 'Irrlicht'] and haphazard, like the journey itself'; *Retracing a Winter's Journey*, p. 95.

53. Curiously, the original key for 'Mut' was A minor, which would have recalled that key in No. 2.

54. Youens, *Retracing a Winter's Journey*, pp. 311–12.

55. Kramer, *Distant Cycles*, p. 187.

56. Stein and Spillman, *Poetry into Song*, p. 5.

57. Ferris, *Schumann's Eichendorff 'Liederkreis'*, pp. 22–23. Ferris also describes the famous hedgehog and silhouette metaphors on pp. 63–6.

18

Dissociation and Declamation in Schubert's Heine Songs

David Ferris

The term 'doppelgänger' was first coined by Jean Paul in his 1796 novel *Siebenkäs*. He defines it in a footnote as a person 'in whom one sees oneself'.[1] This idea went on to become one of the central themes of German Romantic literature, but, as Otto Rank observes, the Romantics were in fact calling upon a long mythological tradition that originated in superstitions about the magical powers of shadows and reflections.[2] One of the earliest recorded versions that Rank cites is the Greek myth of Narcissus, the beautiful youth who fell in love with his own reflection. As Robert Graves tells the story, Narcissus left behind a trail of rejected suitors, one of whom, Ameinius, called upon the gods to avenge him and then committed suicide. The goddess Artemis punished Narcissus by making him 'fall in love, though denying him love's consummation':

> He came upon a spring, clear as silver ... and as he cast himself down, exhausted, on the grassy verge to slake his thirst, he fell in love with his reflection. At first he tried to embrace and kiss the beautiful boy who confronted him, but presently recognized himself, and lay gazing enraptured into the pool, hour after hour. How could he endure both to possess and yet not to possess? Grief was destroying him, yet he rejoiced in his torments; knowing at least that his other self would remain true to him, whatever happened.[3]

Rank claims that the frequent appearance of the doppelgänger in nineteenth-century literature is closely associated with the psychological disorder that is named after Narcissus—narcissism. The literary characters who are confronted by their doubles are often suffering from an overwhelming self-love, which prevents them from forming an attachment to someone else. Rank argues that the vision of one's double, and the fear and revulsion that it inspires, becomes a form of defense against narcissism by allowing the discharge of the love that one feels for oneself, transformed into the hate and fear of one's image.[4]

In an essay written a few years after Rank's study, Sigmund Freud associates the doppelgänger with another psychoanalytic concept. He describes it as an example of *das Unheimliche*, or the uncanny, which arouses fear because it seems at one and the same time unfamiliar but also eerily familiar. Freud defines the uncanny in psychoanalytic terms as something that has been repressed by the unconscious and then returns to consciousness in an altered form.[5] Both of these concepts—narcissism and the uncanny—are relevant to poem No. 20 of Heine's cycle *Die Heimkehr*, which Schubert set as 'Der Doppelgänger.'

The ostensible subject matter of *Die Heimkehr* is the protagonist's lost love, and yet the beloved herself is oddly absent from the cycle. In fact, Heine's poems focus exclusively on the inner emotional world of his protagonist, to the extent that the loss of the beloved is merely a catalyst that sets off his feelings of grief, bitterness and anger. In one poem after another he bemoans his present state, thinks back wistfully to happier times and rails against his faithless beloved. In the process, he leaves the reader wondering whether it is his obsession with himself that is the primary cause of his loneliness.

Michael Perraudin argues that poem No. 20 is the climax of a small 'sub-cycle of lyrics' within the larger cycle of *Die Heimkehr* that begins with poem No. 16, which Schubert also set, as 'Die Stadt', continues through No. 20, and also includes poem No. 26. Four of these poems—Nos. 16, 17, 18 and 20—were originally published separately in a literary journal in 1824, two years before the rest of the cycle appeared.[6] Perraudin describes them as 'Heine's original and essential "Heimkehr" sequence', as 'the "inner" *Heimkehr*', in which Heine narrates 'a homecoming to the urban site of past pains'.[7] It is a rather peculiar homecoming, however, since the protagonist is returning not to his own home, but to the home of his beloved—to the town that she had long since left, and to the house in which she used to live.

Heine's description of the town is suffused with the uncanny. It first appears, at the beginning of poem No. 16, in the distance, like a shadow in the dusk ('Am fernen Horizonte / Erscheint, wie ein Nebelbild, / Die Stadt mit ihren Türmen, / In Abenddämmerung gehüllt'). When the protagonist actually enters the town, it is apparently devoid of people, and the towers and gates themselves seem to come to life. In poem No. 17 he asks them where his beloved, whom he had entrusted to them, has gone ('Sagt an, ihr Türme und Tore, / Wo ist die Liebste mein? / Euch hab ich sie anvertrauet'). He wanders the familiar streets in poem No. 18 ('So wandl ich wieder den alten Weg, / Die wohlbekannten Gassen'), but they are transformed into a claustrophobic ghost town ('Die Straßen sind doch gar zu eng! / Das Pflaster ist unerträglich! / Die Häuser fallen mir auf den Kopf! / Ich eile so viel als möglich!'). When, in poem No. 20, the protagonist finally describes seeing a person, it turns out to be his own figure ('Der Mond zeigt mir meine eigne Gestalt'), who reenacts the gestures of the 'Liebesleid' that he himself had painfully acted out on the very same spot in the past ('Was äffst du nach mein Liebesleid, / Das mich gequält auf dieser Stelle, / So manche Nacht, in alter Zeit?').[8]

In one sense, we can interpret the homecoming as the protagonist's attempt to come to terms with his past—or, as Freud might see it, as his neurotic compulsion to return and relive a traumatic experience that he had repressed. When he sees his doppelgänger, then, he is seeing his past self, but he has split that self off from his present self in an attempt to distance himself both from the trauma and from his reaction to it. He now observes his anguished gestures—staring upwards and wringing his hands—as if they were performed by someone else, someone for whom he can feel pity ('You pale fellow!'), fear ('I shudder when I see his face') and contempt ('why do you ape my love's pain?').

S. S. Prawer has suggested that we can also understand the dividing and doubling of the self in this poem from another perspective. As the protagonist watches his doppelgänger act out the gestures of his sorrow, 'these gestures become ridiculous, a mockery of grief that may have been spontaneously real but has now become self-conscious and hollow'. As with so many of Heine's poems, we can simultaneously read the Romantic image of the doppelgänger as tragically sincere, but also as ironically self-conscious. For Prawer, 'the ultimate subject of this magnificent poem is not so much grief over lost love as grief over the lost simplicity of grief'.[9]

The self-reflexive irony that Prawer describes in poem No. 20 is even more prominent in poem No. 24, which Schubert set as 'Der Atlas'. In this poem, the protagonist explicitly turns himself into a Greek god, Atlas, who carries a world of suffering on his shoulders ('Die ganze Welt der Schmerzen, muß ich tragen'). As Susan Youens puts it, 'a Byronic Titan makes melodramatic mock of immense misery'.[10] Although the theme of the doppelgänger is less explicit in poem No. 24 than it is in poem No. 20, the protagonist again sees his past self as another, now in the form of his heart, who enables him to distance himself from his past trauma. In keeping with the mythological theme with which the poem begins, he accuses his heart of hubris for desiring eternal happiness. Ironically, his heart has managed to attain a divine state, but, like the god whom the protagonist has chosen for his namesake, the heart faces an eternity not of happiness, but of misery ('Du stolzes Herz, du hast es gewollt! / Du wolltest glücklich sein, unendlich glücklich / Oder unendlich elend, stolzes Herz, / Und jetzo bist du elend').

One of the most striking techniques that Heine uses to render the theme of the doppelgänger in both of these poems is an unexpected shift in narrative perspective, as the protagonist directly addresses his past self. In poem No. 20 Heine leads up to this moment in the melodramatic fashion of a horror movie, but in No. 24 the shift is completely unprepared. In the first stanza the protagonist describes his unhappy state in the first person; in the second he addresses his heart and blames it for causing his misery. In contrast to the carefully constructed dramatic narrative of poem No. 20, which in itself is the dramatic climax of a sub-cycle of poems, No. 24 is fragmentary, with very little transition from one stanza to the next, and no explanation of the story behind the poem. But in each of the poems the narrative shift plays a similar role: it depicts a process of psychological dissociation in which the narrator no longer simply remembers the past, but feels as if he is observing his past self in the present moment.

The links between these two poems are subtle enough that a reader might not be conscious of them, despite their proximity within Heine's published cycle. When Schubert set them as the first and last of his six Heine songs, however, he responded to their shared theme, and to Heine's unusual narrative technique, through a variety of musical elements, which not only create a connection between the two songs, but also set them apart from the rest of *Schwanengesang*. The pairing relationship between the two songs might not be perceptible to the listener, either, but in analysing the unusual aspects that the two songs share, we can learn something about how Schubert responded in musical terms to a particular poetic theme.

Voice-Leading Structure

One of the most striking and unusual characteristics of both 'Der Doppelgänger' and 'Der Atlas' is Schubert's treatment of musical texture. In the former song, he uses open fifths and thirds, with octave doublings, to create an eerily hollow sonority. In the latter song, continuous tremolos in the right hand, accompanied by doubled octaves in the left, create a powerful effect that is more orchestral than pianistic, and that captures perfectly the poem's mock-heroic tone. The vocal line at the beginning of each song has no independent melody, but simply doubles a voice of the accompaniment. In 'Der Atlas' it is the bass line, the only melodic line in the texture. In 'Der Doppelgänger' it is the alto voice, which consists of a dominant pedal. In each case a true vocal melody emerges at the moment in the text when the narrator's self divides: at his address to his heart in bar 23 of the former song, and at his first sight of the doppelgänger in bar 25 of the latter. The tonal structures of the two songs also share an unusual element: both are in minor keys, and in both Schubert tonicises the raised mediant, rather than the relative major. Although these tonicisations are heavily emphasised in each case through a variety of parameters—including dynamics, range, texture and harmonic progression—they actually play very different structural roles in the two songs.

In 'Der Atlas,' which is in G minor, the raised mediant acts as a divider harmony that substitutes for the relative major. The song has an apparent ternary form, in which the A section ends with an unexpected perfect cadence in B minor, and the B section, which sets the second stanza of the poem, begins in bar 22 in the key of B major. Schubert creates a further irregularity in the form by returning to G minor within the B section, which ends with the final structural cadence of the song, in bar 39. Although B♭ appears in the bass in bar 36, near the beginning of the phrase that leads up to this cadence, it is part of a i^6 chord. On the middleground level, the prolongation of B major leads directly to the structural dominant in bar 38 (see Example 18.1).

Example 18.1 Schubert, *Schwanengesang*, D 957/8, 'Der Atlas': voice-leading sketch

Because Schubert cadences in G minor at the end of the B section, the final section has an ambiguous role in the song. We hear a varied version of the opening vocal phrase—which sets a varied version of the first two lines of text—and therefore we understand this section as a reprise, and the form of the whole as a typical ternary ABA'. But since the final cadence comes at the beginning of the section rather than the end, the final section actually functions, in terms of the song's tonal structure, as a coda. David Bretherton has coined the term 'dimensional counterpoint' to refer to this type of discrepancy between form and structure. He observes that the third section of the song ends with a rhetorical gesture that is identical, in terms of rhythm and overall melodic shape, to the cadences at the ends of the A and B sections (compare bars 50–52 with bars 18–20 and 37–39). But because there is no V–I motion in bars 51–52, only a register transfer above a tonic harmony, Bretherton refers to this gesture as a 'mock' cadence.[11] It becomes another unusual element that Schubert uses to respond to the ironic grandiosity of Heine's poem.

If 'Der Atlas' is unusual because the relative major never appears, in 'Der Doppelgänger' this harmony is unusually prominent, actually displacing the dominant for most of the song (see Example 18.2). 'Der Doppelgänger' has a modified strophic form in which the first two stanzas are split, so that the first four strophes of the song each set half of a poetic stanza. Each strophe is further divided into two phrases, both based on a four-note passacaglia-style bass. Lawrence Kramer describes the bass pattern as 'an extended half cadence', and it is true that, at least in the first two strophes, both of the phrases end with some form of dominant harmony, and in the second phrase the vocal line implies a cadence by ornamenting its dominant pedal with a typical cadential melodic pattern (bars 11–12 and 21–22). This implication is further strengthened by the echo in the right hand.[12]

This impression of a half cadence is illusory, however, since no root-position dominant chord ever appears, and in the first two strophes the incomplete harmony at the end of the first phrase does not even have a leading note. The harmony that recurs in the fourth bar of each phrase functions not as a dominant, but as a passing chord. The first phrase is a prolongation of i, which moves to its first inversion in the third bar. In the second phrase, and thus in the strophe as a whole, i moves to III, which functions as a divider harmony. The final chord in each phrase leads back to the root-position tonic with which the bass pattern begins. There is thus a lack of correspondence between the recurrence of the pattern and the harmonic progression, as Richard Kurth observes. Although the pattern is apparently four notes long, 'with regard to tonal closure' it is actually five notes, but the 'fifth note is consistently elided, either to signal the beginning of another (four-note) repetition or some variant'.[13] There is also a lack of correspondence between the harmonic progression and the melodic phrase rhythm, since the melody cadences in the fourth bar, while the harmony continues on to the beginning of the next phrase.

Example 18.2 Schubert, *Schwanengesang*, D 957/13, 'Der Doppelgänger': voice-leading sketch

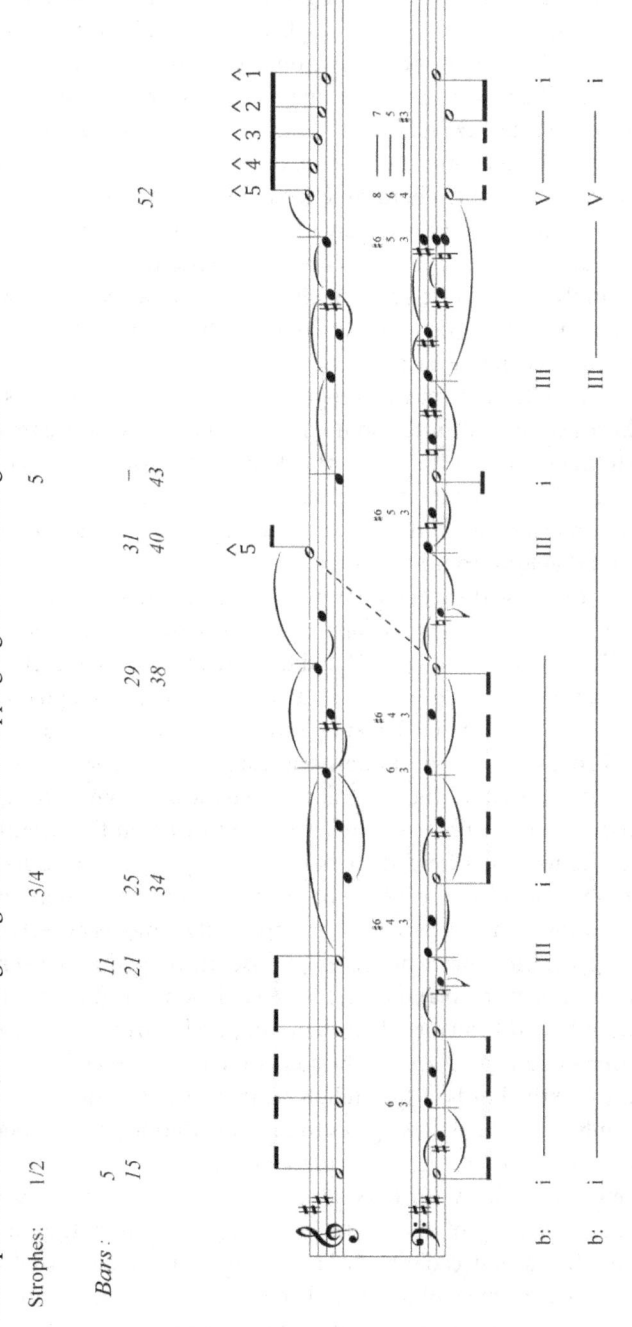

As the vocal melody begins to become more active and independent in the third and fourth strophes of the song, the harmonic progression remains the same. It is only at the end of each strophe, as the vocal line twice reaches a climactic high point—f♯′ in the third strophe (bar 31) and then g′ in the fourth (bar 41)—that Schubert varies the final harmony, by lowering the bass from C♯ to C♮. David Schwarz analyses the harmonies that result from this alteration as augmented sixth chords, one French and the other German, within the key of E minor.[14] But neither chord functions in this way. The interval of the augmented sixth does resolve normally to an octave B, but this B is the root of a minor triad that is clearly a tonic chord. Lawrence Kramer describes the first one as 'simply a dominant seventh with its fifth flattened from C♯ to C♮', and David Loberg Code argues that both of them 'function harmonically as dominant substitutes and physically replace the dominant seventh chord heard in the previous statements of this progression'.[15] One could perhaps argue that these chords substitute for the dominant in that they are dissonant chords that resolve to the tonic, but this sense of a dominant is so general as to be almost meaningless. They do, however, substitute for the specific dominant that they 'physically replace' in another, more meaningful sense: they too are passing harmonies that lead from III back to i.

Schubert sets the third and final stanza of the poem—the lines in which the narrator directly addresses his doppelgänger—with a single expanded strophe that finally moves beyond III to V and ultimately resolves to i. This is the only strophe that does not begin with a statement of the passacaglia bass pattern. Schubert retains the basic elements of the pattern, the motion from B to D and the chromatic semitone motion, but rearranges them such that the pattern itself is unrecognisable. The bass rises chromatically from B to D, arriving in the fourth bar of the phrase rather than the third, and then continues on to D♯, which is tonicised for four bars through a progression to its dominant. Because we have not yet heard a root-position dominant in B minor, the clear and straightforward tonicisation of an apparently remote key feels uncomfortably strong, a feeling that Schubert emphasises through the *fortissimo* dynamic and the accents in the piano part. Lawrence Kramer argues that D♯ minor is 'a far more forceful tonality than the tonic', and Kurth even suggests that it 'exerts tremendous pressure on the song's tonal coherence'.[16] But as with the augmented sixth chords at the end of the third and fourth strophes, the dramatic emphasis that Schubert gives to the tonicisation of D♯ minor belies the modest structural role that it plays in the song.[17]

The eight-bar phrase in bars 43–50 is analogous to the ten-bar phrase that comprises each of the first two strophes, in that the vocal melody clearly implies a half cadence in bar 50, now in the key of D♯ minor; but the harmony continues onward, and the entire tonicisation turns out to be a chromatic passing harmony that takes us from the III chord in bar 46 to the German sixth chord in bar 51, which in turn resolves to V. In terms of

Example 18.3 Schubert, *Schwanengesang*, D 957/13, 'Der Doppelgänger, bars 46–51: D♯ minor passing harmony

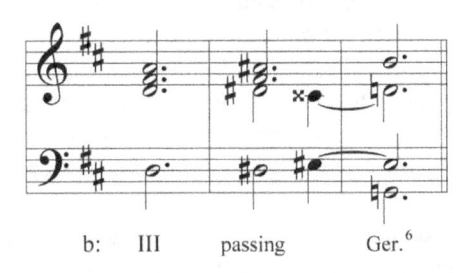

b: III   passing   Ger.^{6}

the voice leading, the pitch d♯ fills in the motion from d♮ to e♯, thus avoiding an augmented second. The V of D♯ minor results from an anticipation of two pitches of the German sixth chord—d′ (spelled enharmonically as c×′) and e♯ (see Example 18.3). Unlike the B major harmony in 'Der Atlas', then, which is clearly a substitute for the relative major, the D♯ minor harmony in 'Der Doppelgänger' has no structural role on the middleground level, but simply fills in the progression from the divider III, which has been reiterated four times within the strophic structure of the song, to the first and only root-position V.[18]

Declamation and Phrase Rhythm in 'Der Doppelgänger'

Another exceptional aspect of these two songs that makes them stand out within *Schwanengesang* is Schubert's free approach to rhythm, and in particular to the relationships between the hypermetre, the phrase rhythm and the declamation of the poetic text. In each of his other Heine settings, Schubert adopts one of the conventional 'declamatory schemas' that Yonatan Malin has identified and uses it, with occasional shifts and substitutions, for the entire song. Malin uses the term 'declamatory schema' to describe the basic patterns that nineteenth-century German composers use to fit poetic declamation to musical metre. In setting trimeter poems, the most common schema is [1, 2 / 1 -]. Tetrameter settings tend to be more varied, as Malin explains, but he identifies a handful of schemas that are commonly used.[19]

The texts of 'Der Doppelgänger' and 'Der Atlas' are both unique among the Heine poems that Schubert set. 'Der Doppelgänger' is the only one that consists entirely of tetrameter lines, and 'Der Atlas' is even more exceptional— each quatrain consists of three lines of blank verse in iambic pentameter followed by a single line of iambic trimeter.

This is unique not only among the texts of *Schwanengesang*, but among the poems of Heine's *Heimkehr*. In each of these songs, Schubert begins with a recognisable schema, but he uses it so irregularly that the declamation ultimately becomes free. In each case the most dramatic change in declamation corresponds to the most unusual moment in the tonal form, the arrival of the raised mediant, and thus to the moment of psychological dissociation depicted in the poem.

In 'Der Doppelgänger' Schubert begins with a hypermetric version of the tetrameter schema that Malin refers to as 'two-plus-two'.[20] Normally this means that there are two strong syllables per bar, as in 'Die Wetterfahne', from *Winterreise* (see Example 18.4).

In 'Der Doppelgänger' there is only one strong syllable, but because the four-bar bass pattern that repeats throughout the song is divided into two-bar groupings, there is a clear two-bar hypermetre, and we hear two strong syllables in each hypermeasure. At the beginning of the song, Schubert varies the pattern slightly by delaying the first strong syllable of each pair until the second beat of the bar, so the pattern becomes [- 2 - / 1 - - / - 2 - / 1 - -] (see Example 18.5).[21]

Example 18.4 Schubert, *Winterreise*, D 911/2, 'Die Wetterfahne', bars 6–9: vocal line with declamatory rhythm

Example 18.5 Schubert, *Schwanengesang*, D 957/13, 'Der Doppelgänger', bars 5–12: vocal line with declamatory rhythm

The declamation starts to become irregular in the third strophe, as the narrator describes seeing his doppelgänger. The first couplet (bars 25–28) retains the schema, but in the second couplet the climactic f♯, which sets the third strong syllable, is suspended into the downbeat of bar 32 and the last strong syllable is delayed until the third beat of that bar (see Example 18.6).

The vocal phrase is thus expanded to five bars, but since Schubert omits the two-bar echo in the accompaniment that ended each of the first two strophes, the third strophe is actually one bar shorter. The next strong syllable, at the beginning of the fourth strophe, is also delayed, coming on the downbeat of the second bar of the phrase (bar 35). Schubert compensates for this delay by speeding up the rest of the couplet, so that two bars set three strong syllables, which come on three consecutive beats (see Example 18.7). In this case Schubert is responding to a subtle irregularity in the scansion of Heine's poem. Every other line is divided grammatically in the middle, between the two pairs of poetic feet. But in this line Heine places a caesura after the first strong syllable, so that in reading the poem one would naturally adopt a rhythm that is similar to Schubert's. In both poem and song this has the effect of emphasising both the narrator's first direct reference to himself and his feeling of horror as he realises that he is seeing his own figure.

The most extreme and dramatic irregularity comes in the fifth strophe, as the narrative perspective shifts to second-person address (see Example 18.8).

Example 18.6 Schubert, *Schwanengesang*, D 957/13, 'Der Doppelgänger', bars 25–33: vocal line with declamatory rhythm

Example 18.7 Schubert, *Schwanengesang*, D 957/13, 'Der Doppelgänger', bars 34–37: vocal line with declamatory rhythm

Example 18.8 Schubert, *Schwanengesang*, D 957/13, 'Der Doppelgänger', bars 43–56: vocal and bass lines with declamatory rhythm and harmony

Again, the first couplet retains the original declamatory schema, but in the fifth bar of the strophe (bar 47) the rate of declamation suddenly doubles, so that four bars set two lines of text, and the entire eight-bar vocal phrase sets the first three lines of the stanza. To a large extent, the striking effect that Schubert creates at this moment in the song results from the simultaneous speeding up of the declamatory rhythm and slowing down of the harmonic and phrase rhythms. The harmony is essentially suspended on a D♯ minor chromatic passing chord in bars 47–50, as I have noted, at the exact moment where the vocal melody declaims more quickly. And the phrase rhythm of the voice and piano are also out of sync, since the vocal melody cadences in bar 50, while the accompaniment creates a continuous fourteen-bar phrase that goes all the way to the perfect cadence in bar 56.

There are six bars of music after the vocal cadence in bar 50, but only one more line of text, so the surface rhythm slows down and the rate of declamation decreases. With the arrival of the dominant in bar 52, the harmonic progression comes to a complete standstill as the $^6_4$ appoggiatura resolves to a V^7 over the course of four bars. Now melody and accompaniment are once more in sync, rhythmically speaking, and together they create a painfully slow composed-out ritardando that exaggerates the ironically melodramatic tone of Heine's final lines.

Declamation and Phrase Rhythm in 'Der Atlas'

Despite the irregularities in its declamatory rhythm, 'Der Doppelgänger' retains the stanzaic structure and poetic metre of Heine's poem. In 'Der Atlas,' on the other hand, Schubert repeats text, omits words and rearranges line breaks to such an extent that he leaves virtually no trace of the poem's original form. Heine's poetic text has numerous enjambments and internal caesuras, but it still maintains a strict metrical regularity, which results in frequent conflicts between grammatical syntax and poetic metre. Schubert resolves almost every one of these conflicts in favor of the syntax, essentially turning the poem into free verse (see Table 18.1).[22]

Rufus Hallmark and Ann Fehn have observed that pentameter lines pose 'a special problem' for the lied composer, both because they tend to be 'metrically and syntactically more complex' than trimeter and tetrameter lines, and also because they are less compatible with duple or triple metre and phrase rhythm. Hallmark and Fehn identify two conventional strategies that Schubert uses to fit pentameter lines to either duple or triple metre, respectively. One possibility is to compress two feet, so that five poetic feet occupy 'four units of musical time'. The other is either to extend one foot or to place a rest at the end of the line, so that five feet occupy six units.[23]

Table 18.1 Heine and Schubert's texts of 'Der Atlas' "Der Atlas"

Heine	feet	Schubert	feet
Ich únglücksel'ger Átlas! éine Wélt,	5	Ich únglücksel'ger Átlas,	3
		Ich únglücksel'ger Átlas! éine Wélt,	5
Die gánze Wélt der Schmérzen, múß ich trágen,	5	Die gánze Wélt der Schmérzen, múß ich trágen,	5
		Die gánze Wélt múß ich trágen,	4
Ich tráge Únertráglichés, und bréchen	5	Ich tráge Únertráglichés,	4
Will mír das Hérz im Léibe.	3	Und bréchen will mír das Hérz im Léibe.	4
Du stólzes Hérz! du hást es já gewóllt!	5	Du stólzes Hérz, du hást es já gewóllt,	5
Du wólltest glücklich séin, unéndlich glücklich	5	Du wólltest glücklich séin, unéndlich glücklich	5
Óder unéndlich élend, stólzes Hérz,	5	Óder unéndlich élend, unéndlich élend,	5
Und jétzo bíst du élend.	3	Stólzes Hérz, und jétzo bíst du élend.	5
		Ich únglücksel'ger Átlas,	3
		Ich únglücksel'ger Átlas,	3
		Die gánze Wélt der Schmérzen, múß ich trágen,	5
		Die gánze Wélt múß ich trágen,	4
		Die gánze Wélt der Schmérzen, múß ich trágen.	5

In 'Der Atlas,' which is in triple metre but has a strongly duple hypermetre, Schubert uses neither of these conventions. Instead, he takes advantage of the caesura that follows the third foot of the first line and repeats the first three feet, so that the song actually begins with a trimeter line—'Ich unglücksel'ger Atlas'—which Schubert sets with the triple-metre version of the conventional schema: [1 - 3 / 1 - -] (see Example 18.9). When, on the repetition, he adds the two remaining feet, and thus sets the entire pentameter line—'Ich unglücksel'ger Atlas, eine Welt'—he simply extends the schema: [1 - 3 / 1 - 3 / 1 - -]. Schubert sets the second line of the poem—'Die ganze Welt der Schmerzen muß ich tragen'—using the same extended schema and then extends it further as he repeats the line in a compressed version that omits the third foot—'Die

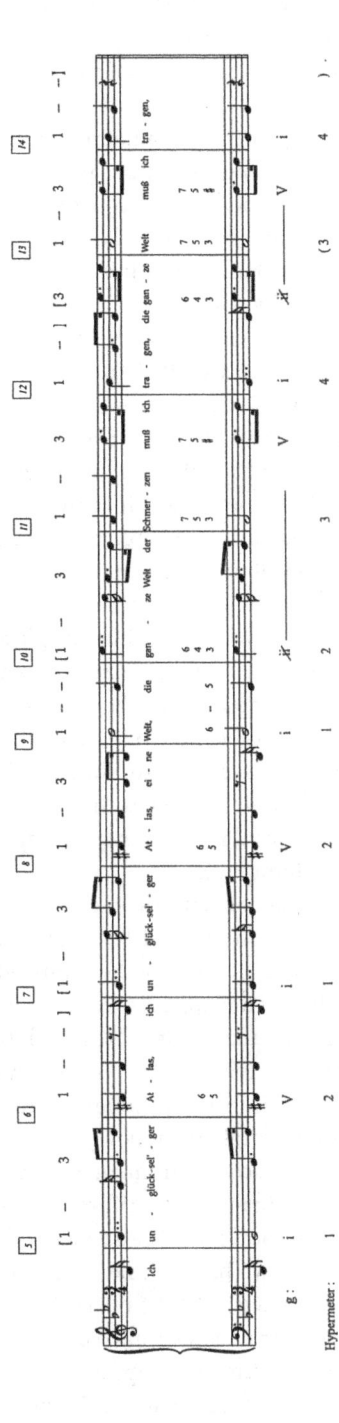

Example 18.9 Schubert, 'Der Atlas', bars 5–14: vocal and bass lines with declamatory rhythm, harmony and hypermetre

ganze Welt muß ich tragen'. Schubert thus transforms two lines of pentameter verse into four irregular lines—trimeter, pentameter, pentameter, tetrameter—and sets them with four irregular units of musical time—two bars, three bars, three bars, two bars.

Given the irregularity of the declamatory rhythm, it is curious that these lines of text are set with a single eight-bar phrase, in strict duple hypermetre, which is grouped 2 + 2 + 4 and followed by a two-bar suffix. The moment when the declamatory and phrase rhythms fall out of sync comes, logically enough, with the last two feet of Heine's first line—'eine Welt'—an interjection that stands alone grammatically. The first strong syllable of the foot comes on the third beat of bar 8 and thus continues the declamatory schema that begins in the previous bar. This creates a subtle but significant break between the vocal melody and the bass line, which otherwise move in virtually the same rhythm (and virtually in unison) throughout the first twenty bars of the song. The bass line has a rest on the third beat of bar 8, following the pattern set up in bars 5–6, and this creates the second of a pair of two-bar groupings. The downbeat of bar 9, which is the last strong syllable of the schema in the vocal melody, is the beginning of a new four-bar grouping in the accompaniment. Because the following pentameter line occupies three bars, the declamatory and phrase rhythms are once again in sync by the time the phrase cadences in bar 12.

This subtle and momentary disjunction between the rhythms of the vocal line and those of the accompaniment foreshadows a far more dramatic rupture in bar 22, at the beginning of the B section. This is the moment in the text when the narrative perspective abruptly shifts, and the protagonist's memory of his past feelings and desires becomes dissociated from his present state of consciousness. Here the vocal melody and accompaniment fall out of sync on several metric and rhythmic levels.

In the first section of the song, the slow tempo, heavy texture, double-dotted rhythms and emphasis on the second beat allude to a stately Baroque sarabande. The vocal line continues to sing the sarabande in the B section, but the piano suddenly switches to the opposite extreme and plays an impossibly fast and somewhat hysterical waltz rhythm. Although the notated tempo remains the same, the continuous triplet rhythm essentially turns each bar of 3/4 into three bars of 3/8, so that we feel as though there is a three-bar hypermetre moving at three times the original tempo.

At the same time, the accompaniment retains the duple and quadruple groupings of the notated bars, so we still feel the slower hypermetre as well (see Example 18.10). The vocal melody also has a quadruple hypermetre as the B section begins, but it is two bars behind. In the accompaniment, the abrupt shift from tremolos to triplets, and the resolution to the first B major triad in the song, lead us to hear bar 22 as a strong bar, which begins a four-bar pattern, grouped 1 + 1 + 2. This pattern then repeats, creating a second hypermeasure in bars 26–29. The voice is silent in bars 22–23, beginning its phrase only with

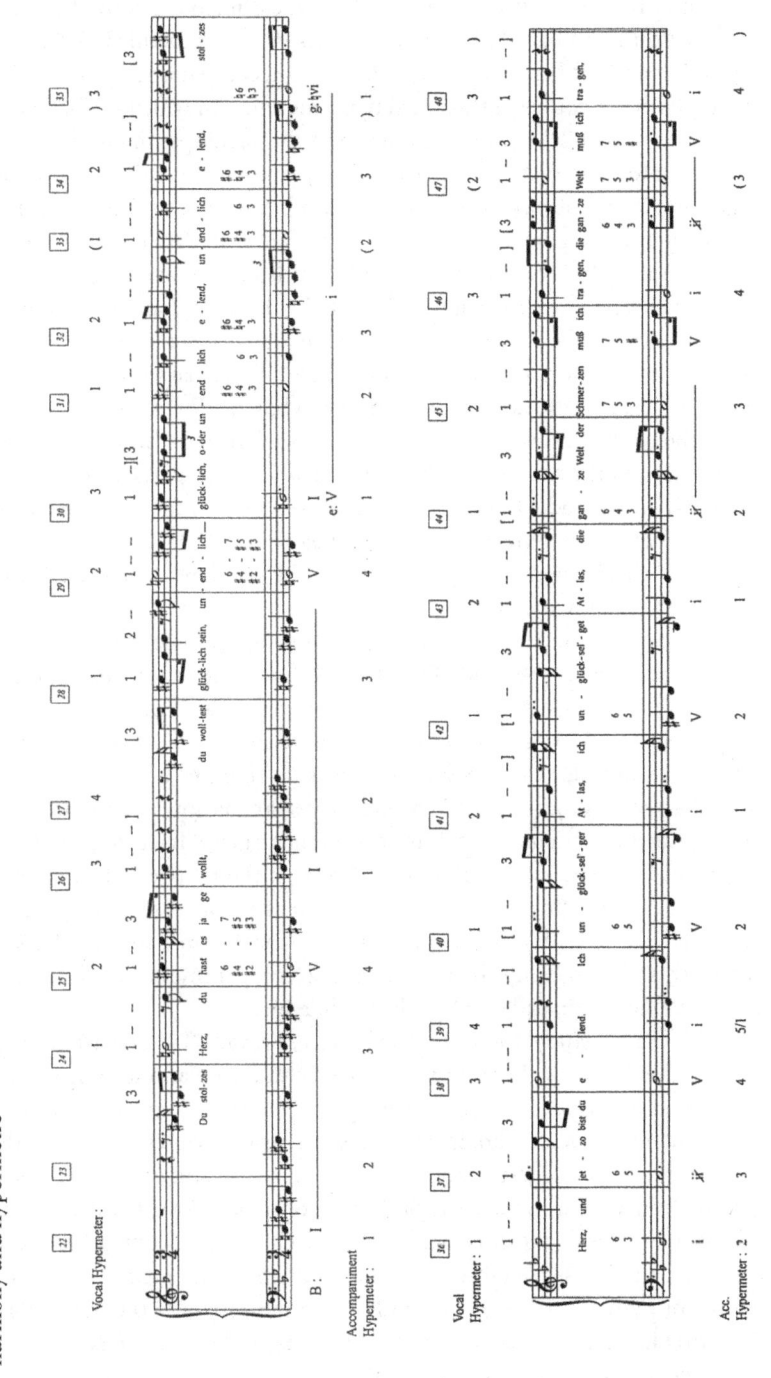

Example 18.10 Schubert, *Schwanengesang*, D 957/8, 'Der Atlas', bars 22–48: vocal and bass lines with declamatory rhythm, harmony and hypermetre

the pickup to bar 24, so the third bar of the accompaniment's hypermeasure is the first bar of the vocal melody's. The vocal melody's second hypermeasure, beginning in bar 28, is only three bars, so when its third hypermeasure begins in bar 31, it is only one bar behind the accompaniment's, which begins in bar 30. In the course of this third hypermeasure, in which melody and bass line move in parallel tenths, the voice and the accompaniment momentarily fall back into hypermetric sync. The accompaniment has a three-bar grouping beginning in bar 30, which is followed by a two-bar echo. The vocal line has a two-bar grouping beginning in bar 31 which is also followed by a two-bar echo, and it is this echo, in bars 33–34, that is coordinated between the two parts. The rising bass line that begins with the pickup to bar 35 begins a fourth hypermeasure in the accompaniment, which takes us from E minor to the final cadence in G minor, and which is expanded to five bars through a written-out ritardando on the dominant harmony in bar 38. The vocal melody is once again one bar behind as it begins this hypermeasure, with the pickup to bar 36, in imitation of the bass line at the fifth above. The two parts cadence together in bar 39, but the cadential bar is elided in the accompaniment—it is the initial bar of the eight-bar phrase that we first heard in bars 5–12, and thus the beginning of the thematic reprise—but not in the vocal melody, which begins its phrase in the following bar.

Voice and accompaniment are thus again out of sync when the opening phrase comes back at the end of the song. When we first hear the opening line of the poem, in bar 5, the vocal melody doubles the bass line and the harmonic progression is i–V. When the same text returns in bar 40, it is set to an independent vocal melody that begins one bar later than the accompaniment, and so the harmonic progression has been reversed and is now V–i. In the A section of the song it is the 'eine Welt' interjection that causes the melody and accompaniment to momentarily fall out of phase. In the reprise, it is only by leaving out the interjection altogether—which turns Schubert's second pentameter line into a trimeter line, and compresses the vocal phrase to seven bars—that Schubert is able to bring the melody and accompaniment back into sync, so that they once again cadence together in bar 46.

In his classic study *The Composer's Voice*, Edward T. Cone argues that, in accompanied song, we hear the vocal melody and the piano accompaniment as two separate voices, or personae. He equates the vocal persona with the voice of the poetic character who, in a first-person lyric, narrates the poem. The accompaniment, he suggests, can play a variety of different dramatic roles. It indirectly 'conveys certain aspects of the subconscious of the vocal persona', but it 'may also refer to the environment of the character'. Moving beyond these two roles, and in a sense subsuming both of them, Cone argues that the accompaniment 'symbolically suggests both the impingement of the outer world on the individual represented by the vocal persona, and the subconscious reaction of the individual to this impingement'.[24]

As Cone acknowledges, there is no direct analogue between the narrative conventions of literature and the dramatic and narrative aspects of song, and so his analogy is necessarily imprecise and incomplete.[25] One limitation is that it accounts adequately neither for the variety of narrative models in the poetry that a composer such as Schubert sets, nor for the range of musical responses to those models. In poems Nos. 20 and 24 from Heine's *Heimkehr*, the narrator suddenly experiences a psychological rupture within his own consciousness, which results in the splitting of his narrative voice. In the final stanzas of these poems, the narrator becomes both the *ich* who is speaking and the *du* who is being addressed. The striking and unusual relationships that Schubert creates between the vocal and instrumental personae as he turns these poems into songs are musical responses to the unusual narrative model that Heine offers him.

Notes

1. Jean-Paul Richter, *Werke*, ed. Norbert Miller, vol. 2 (Munich: Carl Hanser Verlag, 1959), p. 66. Jean Paul and Heine both write the word as 'Doppeltgänger'. When Schubert set Heine's poem No. 20 from *Die Heimkehr*, he changed the spelling to the form that has become more familiar in both German and English, and it is this form that I use throughout the chapter.

2. Otto Rank, *The Double: a Psychoanalytic Study*, trans. Harry Tucker (Chapel Hill: University of North Carolina Press, 1971), pp. 49–68.

3. Robert Graves, *The Greek Myths*, ed. Michel W. Pharand (Manchester: Carcanet Press, 2001), p. 287.

4. Rank, *The Double*, pp. 69–74.

5. Sigmund Freud, *The Uncanny*, trans. David McClintock (New York: Penguin Books, 2003), pp. 147–8.

6. They appeared in *Der Gesellschafter oder Blätter für Geist und Herz* on 26 March 1824, together with what eventually became poems Nos. 2, 4, 21 and 22. Heinrich Heine, *Historisch-Kritische Gesamtausgabe der Werke*, ed. Manfred Windfuhr, vol. 1/2, *Buch der Lieder: Apparat*, ed. Pierre Grappin (Hamburg: Hoffmann & Campe, 1973).

7. Michael Perraudin, *Heinrich Heine: Poetry in Context* (Oxford: Berg, 1989), pp. 72–3.

8. Heinrich Heine, *Sämtliche Schriften*, ed. Klaus Briegleb, vol. 1, *Buch der Lieder* (Munich: DtV, 1997), pp. 116–20.

9. S. S. Prawer, *Heine: Buch der Lieder* (Great Neck, NY: Barron's Educational Series, 1960), p. 37.

10. Susan Youens, *Heinrich Heine and the Lied* (Cambridge: Cambridge University Press, 2007), pp. 11–12.

11. David Tom Bretherton, 'The Poetics of Schubert's Song-Forms' (PhD diss., Oxford University, 2007), pp. 83 and 86. My Example 1 is very similar to

Bretherton's analysis of the song, except that he analyses the i⁶ chord in bar 36 as a return of $\hat{3}$ in the minor mode. See his Examples 2.15b and 2.16. According to Timothy Jackson, Carl Schachter proposed another analysis, which differs somewhat from both mine and Bretherton's. He argues that the initial $\hat{3}$, B♭, actually functions as an enharmonically spelled leading note to the 'real' $\hat{3}$, B♮. Timothy Jackson, 'Hinauf strebt's: Song Study with Carl Schachter', in L. Poundie Burstein and David Gagné (eds), *Structure and Meaning in Tonal Music* (Hillsdale, NY: Pendragon Press, 2006), p. 193 and Plate 2.

12. Lawrence Kramer, 'The Schubert Lied: Romantic Form and Romantic Consciousness', in Walther Frisch (ed.), *Schubert: Critical and Analytical Studies* (Lincoln: University of Nebraska Press, 1986), p. 220. See also Lawrence Kramer, *Franz Schubert: Sexuality, Subjectivity, Song* (Cambridge: Cambridge University Press, 1998), p. 55. David Loberg Code also argues that the progression 'can be clearly heard as a half cadence'. Code, 'Listening for Schubert's Doppelgängers', *Music Theory Online* 1/4 (1995), [p. 6].

13. Richard Kurth, 'Music and Poetry, a Wilderness of Doubles: Heine—Nietzsche—Schubert—Derrida', *19th-Century Music* 21/1 (1997), p. 21.

14. David Schwarz, *Listening Subjects: Music, Psychoanalysis, Culture* (Durham, NC: Duke University Press, 1997), p. 71, Example 30. Lawrence Kramer and Code analyse just the second of the two chords, in bar 41, as an augmented sixth in E minor. See Kramer, 'The Schubert Lied', p. 222, and *Franz Schubert*, p. 58; and Code, 'Listening for Schubert's Doppelgängers', [p. 15].

15. Kramer, 'The Schubert Lied', p. 221; and Code, 'Listening for Schubert's Doppelgängers', [p. 18].

16. Kramer, 'The Schubert Lied', p. 221; and Kurth, 'Music and Poetry', p. 23.

17. Robert Samuels makes the same point the other way around. He describes the voice-leading analysis of D♯ minor as a 'betrayal' both of Schubert's 'performance instructions' and of 'the passage as a whole'. Richard Kramer describes the tonicisation of D♯ minor as an 'ironic tonic-dominant dance', a 'false cadencing around the mediant' that is subsequently contradicted by 'the true augmented sixth and the true cadence' in B minor to which the tonicisation leads. Robert Samuels, 'The Double Articulation of Schubert: Reflections on "Der Doppelgänger"', *Musical Quarterly* 93 (2010), p. 214; and Richard Kramer, *Distant Cycles: Schubert and the Conceiving of Song* (Chicago: University of Chicago Press, 1994), pp. 131–2.

18. Schwarz and Samuels both analyse D♯ minor as a divider harmony itself, despite the prominence throughout the song of the more prototypical III. Schwarz, *Listening Subjects*, p. 71, Example 30; and Samuels, 'The Double Articulation of Schubert', p. 210, Example 3.

19. Yonatan Malin, *Songs in Motion: Rhythm and Meter in the German Lied* (New York: Oxford University Press, 2010), pp. 15–25. In Malin's notation, which I adopt in the rest of this chapter, brackets set off each line of poetry, diagonal slash marks indicate bar lines, arabic numbers refer to the beats in the bar that have strong syllables, and dashes refer to the beats that do not.

20. Malin, *Songs in Motion*, p. 20.

21. There is a slight irregularity in bar 11, where Schubert places the syllable 'wohn-' on beat 1 instead of beat 2, but this does not disrupt the pattern in any meaningful way.

22. Heine's text is from Heine, *Sämtliche Schriften*, p. 120; and Schubert's is from *Franz Schubert: Neue Ausgabe sämtlicher Werke*, ser. IV, vol. 14a, ed. Walther Dürr (Kassel: Bärenreiter, 1964–), pp. 142–5.

23. Rufus Hallmark and Ann C. Fehn, 'Text and Music in Schubert's Settings of Pentameter Poetry,' in Jürgen Thym (ed.), *Of Poetry and Song: Approaches to the Nineteenth-Century Lied* (Rochester, NY: University of Rochester Press, 2010), pp. 156–7.

24. Edward T. Cone, *The Composer's Voice* (Berkeley and Los Angeles: University of California Press, 1974), pp. 35–6.

25. Ibid., p. 15.

19

'The Messenger of a Faithful Heart'
Reassessing the Role of 'Die Taubenpost'
in Schubert's *Schwanengesang*

Richard Giarusso

The contentious history of *Schwanengesang* (considered as a group of fourteen songs) began in December 1828, when Schubert's brother Ferdinand presented a manuscript of thirteen poems on texts of Ludwig Rellstab and Heinrich Heine to the Viennese music publisher Tobias Haslinger. With the addition of 'Die Taubenpost', Schubert's last completed lied, the fourteen songs were published in a handsome two-volume edition in May 1829. Haslinger himself added the romantic title of *Schwanengesang*.[1]

To this day, many unresolved and ultimately unanswerable questions surround *Schwanengesang*, but perhaps none is more persistent than the conundrum of 'Die Taubenpost'. The song was not in the manuscript with the Rellstab and Heine settings, and, if the songs are performed consecutively, it presents a drastic change of mood from 'Der Doppelgänger', which, in Haslinger's publication, precedes it. Many observers consider 'Die Taubenpost' to be a trifling successor to the weightiness of the Heine settings, casually appended to the collection at the time of publication. John Reed describes the song as 'a comparatively lightweight piece thrown in by the publisher for good measure'.[2] Alfred Einstein dismisses it as 'not much more than a charming song'.[3] A more recent commentator has suggested that '["Die Taubenpost"] has nothing to do with the remainder of the collection and its place, if it has one, in performances of *Schwanengesang*, is as an encore.'[4] Others, dubious of the possibility that Schubert ever intended even the Rellstab and Heine settings to be grouped together, dismiss the inclusion of 'Die Taubenpost' as the most egregious of the alleged 'sales gimmicks' in Haslinger's 1829 edition.[5] Similar opinions are in ready supply; these are but a representative sampling of the condescending attitudes that have often surrounded discussions of this song.

While no concrete evidence exists to prove that Haslinger's edition does reflect the composer's intentions, there is likewise little evidence to support the contrary viewpoint. To that end, although no one can argue conclusively that 'Die Taubenpost' does have a place in *Schwanengesang*, there are flaws in the reasoning of those who would categorically dismiss 'Die Taubenpost' from the set. In this essay, I wish to suggest ways in which, far from being a sales gimmick, Haslinger's decision to place the song at the end of *Schwanengesang* might be viewed instead as an entirely appropriate and fitting conclusion to this last published collection of Schubert's lieder. While I will admit that I, like others who have trodden this path before, am incapable of offering conclusive proof to support this claim, I hope at least to open some questions that will help us to re-evaluate not only this issue but other commonly held conceptions about Schubert's late style.[6]

We might begin by considering the generic classification of *Schwanengesang* and what we can intuit about Schubert's intentions in this regard and also Haslinger's assumptions in publishing the work. At the risk of stating the obvious, *Schwanengesang* is patently not a song cycle, at least not one that resembles Schubert's earlier work in the genre. Haslinger himself does not call the set a 'song cycle'. But he does number the songs consecutively throughout the two volumes, and he includes the singular moniker 'Letztes Werk' (last work) on the title pages of both volumes of his 1829 publication, suggesting, perhaps, that he viewed the individual songs as part of a larger sequential whole.

With regard to Schubert's intentions, we know only that the thirteen Rellstab and Heine settings were compiled in the same manuscript, a fair copy dated August 1828. Although the songs are collected in a single manuscript, the Heine songs were likely written in early 1828, and the Rellstab songs followed in the spring and early summer. Schubert himself gave no title to this gathering of songs, nor did he number the songs, as he had done in Die schöne Müllerin and *Winterreise*. In a letter dated October 1828, Schubert offered the Leipzig pubisher H. A. Probst 'several songs by Heine of Hamburg'.[7] On the basis of this evidence, some have suggested that Schubert viewed at least the Heine settings, if not the entire set, as an integrated collection. In a similar vein, many observers have been prompted to read a narrative coherence into the Heine songs in an attempt to validate them as a 'sub-cycle' within the set. An April 1829 essay by Joseph von Spaun and Anton Ottenwalt offered the following insight into Haslinger's publication: '[Schubert] wrote ... about 400 songs, [and] shortly before his death another fourteen completely new ones, which, dedicated to his friends, are being published by Haslinger in Vienna, and among which "Die Taubenpost" was the last'.[8] Although the dedication didn't appear in Haslinger's edition, Spaun's comments imply a relationship between the songs on the basis of their 'novelty' and the fact that the fourteen songs, grouped together, would carry a single dedication. These are still, however, fairly shaky assumptions, and we come back to the fact that it is difficult to say much of certainty with regard to either Schubert's or Haslinger's understanding of the relationship between the fourteen songs of *Schwanengesang*.

In the absence of any solid evidence that either Schubert or Haslinger ever intended or even imagined a strong sense of song-to-song coherence in *Schwanengesang*, why should Haslinger's decision to publish the isolated Seidl lied prove so controversial? Consider, for instance, the assessment of Reed, who states that the addition of 'Die Taubenpost' to the Rellstab and Heine settings was 'not in accordance with Schubert's intentions or wishes', adding that 'there is no stylistic or other good reason for associating it with the two groups'.[9] Reed surely goes too far in this regard. The fact remains that we simply do not know what 'Schubert's intentions or wishes' were with regard to the song, and to claim that Haslinger's decision was a deliberate contradiction of Schubert's vision is spurious. Furthermore, Reed's 'stylistic' argument seems to be founded only on the observation that the song 'dances along' in a 'simple and conventional' manner. Surely this is too quickly and casually dismissive. Indeed, as I will attempt to show below, style, considered somewhat more broadly, can also be used to argue for the appropriateness of the song's inclusion in the published collection.

Dietrich Fischer-Dieskau accuses Haslinger of cobbling together the songs without sufficiently 'examining' them. In nearly the same breath, he acknowledges matter-of-factly that *Schwanengesang* is a 'collection of disparate elements'.[10] Is it not possible that Haslinger did 'examine' the Rellstab and Heine settings, identify the lack of song-to-song coherence, and choose to build upon the already un-unified manuscript by contributing a final song that would provide the greatest contrast yet? In a 'collection of disparate elements' that was nonetheless gathered together by the composer into a single manuscript, heterogeneity and disorder may themselves serve as an unlikely means of organisation. The shock of 'Die Taubenpost,' while not explicitly sanctioned by the composer, would seem, from this perspective, to be in keeping with the dis-organisational norms established in the Rellstab and Heine settings.

Arguments challenging the association of 'Die Taubenpost' with the Heine and Rellstab songs are often strongly articulated, but ultimately they rest on rather flimsy evidence. Opinions such as those quoted above are really just that—opinions, and rather speculative ones at that. Overwhelmingly, their justification stems from certain assumptions about what is or is not appropriate or consistent about 'Die Taubenpost' (both Seidl's text and Schubert's setting) when considered in comparison with the Heine and Rellstab songs. But is this question even valid? As Graham Johnson has observed, one could even reasonably argue that, regardless of Haslinger's role in the publication of the final version, Schubert himself might have planned to write a collection of lieder lacking in unity.[11] In a review published in the summer of 1828, a Munich writer criticised Part 1 of *Winterreise* as suffering from 'a certain monotony'. As an alternative, the writer recommends the 'unfolding' of songs in 'single flowers' such that each may 'live its own life'.[12] If Schubert saw this report, or if the report itself was representative of a certain critical attitude towards the song cycle, is it not possible that Schubert might have sought to follow this advice in planning a cycle of sharply differentiated lieder?

This hypothesis is bolstered when one considers the varying treatments of cyclic form already present in the two earlier cycles. While *Die schöne Müllerin* follows a clear narrative trajectory from beginning to end, with *Winterreise* Schubert strays from this model. In Theodor Adorno's memorable assessment, each song in *Winterreise* is 'equally close to the centre', and the protagonist hovers around this point, making 'no actual progress'.[13] Rather than a tightly conceived narrative like that of *Die schöne Müllerin*, *Winterreise* is, more accurately, a series of kaleidoscopic vignettes on related themes of regret, isolation, despair and loss, and *Schwanengesang* may well be seen as an extension of this model.

Moreover, in *Winterreise* Schubert had already displayed an apparent lack of regard for the narrative coherence of Müller's original set of twenty-four poems. As is well-known, Schubert's delayed discovery of Müller's final collection of twenty-four poems led to an arrangement of the song texts in Schubert's finished cycle that differed significantly from Müller's intended order. Elsewhere I have argued that this was not merely a quick fix that spared Schubert the trouble of reordering his original set of twelve songs, but a conscious choice that enabled a calculated and essential degree of disorder in the completed cycle.[14] In 1828, when the song cycle was still in its adolescence, when structural norms for the genre were not yet codified, and when Schubert himself had already displayed a willingness to embrace a striking element of textual disorder in *Winterreise*, there is no reason to believe that he would have hesitated to exploring new and more radical concepts of cyclical form in the collection of songs eventually published as *Schwanengesang*.[15]

It has long been fashionable to question the place of 'Die Taubenpost' in *Schwanengesang* by casting aspersions on the motivations of Haslinger himself, portraying him as a profit-minded businessman whose 1829 pastiche betrays the 'true' intentions of the composer—whatever those might be. The sternest critics denounce both the format of the fourteen songs as a consecutively numbered set and the use of a 'catchy' title as little more than cheap sales tactics.[16] Granted, Haslinger's prepublication announcement in the *Wiener Zeitung* does employ some rather inflated language. It is, after all, an advertisement, fighting to be noticed on the crowded page of a general newspaper, and, then as now, a bit of excess is to be expected. In spite of the occasionally overwrought style, the announcement is, at its core, sincere and poignant in its praise of Schubert's talents. Indeed, the advertisement bespeaks an intimate, personal acquaintance with a wide range of Schubert's lieder:

> Under the above title [of *Schwanengesang*] are offered to the numerous friends of [Schubert's] classical muse, the last blossoms of his noble spirit. They are those musical compositions which he wrote in August 1828, shortly before his departure from this world. Works, which proclaim in the most verifiable manner the professionalism of his richly endowed mastery.[17]

Others assert that Haslinger included 'Die Taubenpost' at the end of *Schwanengesang* 'only to make good on [his] claim that his publication included the "last blossomings of Schubert's art"'.[18]

Like so much of the *Schwanengesang* mythology, this kind of sanctimonious cant rests upon a very unstable foundation, and stronger evidence suggests that Haslinger, far from being an unscrupulous profiteer with little regard for the integrity of the composer's work, was perhaps the most astute and conscientious of Schubert's publishers and one of the most widely respected music publishers of his time. He cultivated a close personal relationship with Beethoven, and letters suggest that the composer maintained an unusually high degree of admiration for Haslinger, who, like Schubert, also served as a torch-bearer at Beethoven's funeral in 1827. Having issued a range of Schubert's vocal and instrumental works in the years before the composer's death, he probably possessed a knowledge of Schubert's music that was equaled by few if any of his peers. Haslinger's working relationship with Schubert persisted until the very last days of the composer's life, as the two collaborated on the corrections for the proofs of Part 2 of *Winterreise*, and he was the first publisher to acquire items from the composer's musical estate.[19] His earlier publications of Schubert's music were frequently singled out for praise by contemporary reviewers. For example, Haslinger's edition of the Piano Sonata in G Major, D 894, was 'commended' in the *Wiener Zeitschrift für Kunst*. The writer went on to add that its high quality was 'like that of all the publications issued by the firm in question'.[20] Similarly, an overwhelmingly positive review of the first twelve songs of *Winterreise* notes that Haslinger's presentation is 'worthy' of the set.[21]

Haslinger was a composer in his own right and also skilled as an arranger of other composers' works, among which were a set of piano transcriptions (one each for two and four hands) of Beethoven's Symphony No. 8.[22] He was therefore naturally attuned to subtle details of literary and musical nuance, and his edition of *Schwanengesang* bears evidence of the most scrupulous attention to notational details of Schubert's autograph. Having labored painstakingly to reproduce Schubert's crescendo-decrescendo hairpins exactly as they appear in the autograph (a detail absent from many modern editions, including Bärenreiter's definitive *Neue Schubert-Ausgabe*), is it reasonable to assume that Haslinger would have made the cavalier decision to throw together a collection of songs that had not been in some way sanctioned by the composer? On the contrary, Haslinger's record of professionalism in dealing with Schubert, especially when set against the composer's frustrating interactions with Probst and Schott in the summer and fall of 1828, should bolster his credibility.[23] If Haslinger were motivated by base commercial interests, as indeed seems to have been the case with Probst and Schott in 1828,[24] wouldn't he have been more likely to suppress some or all of the Heine settings—songs which, with their dark, brooding character, were hardly in keeping with the prevailing aesthetic of the lied as a light and entertaining genre?[25]

The critical reception of the Heine songs has often pointed to a singular quality in the songs that overshadows not only the rest of *Schwanengesang* but much of Schubert's output in the final year of his life. The radical novelty of the Heine songs has coloured a view of 'lateness' in Schubert that has had especially unfortunate consequences for 'Die Taubenpost'. Echoing Walther Benjamin in her essay 'Under the Sign of Saturn', Susan Sontag cautions that 'one cannot use the life to interpret the work'.²⁶ This is advice that should be taken to heart in evaluating *Schwanengesang*, for biographical considerations have figured perhaps too prominently in shaping opinions of this work, especially with regard to the Heine settings and their role in setting the tone for both *Schwanengesang* and the late works in general.²⁷

As is well-known, the death of Beethoven in March 1827 was a defining moment in Schubert's career, and for the remaining year and a half of his own life, Schubert felt keenly the weight of the mantle that he had inherited. Schubert's self-conscious engagement with the Beethovenian legacy manifested itself in numerous ways, not least with regard to the Rellstab settings in *Schwanengesang*, which, according to Anton Schindler and the poet himself, were initially given to Beethoven but later passed on to Schubert following the elder composer's death.²⁸ According to a popular anecdote, the aura of Beethoven lingered until the very end: Schubert supposedly requested a private performance of the String Quartet Op. 131 in the days before he died. Ludwig Nohl reports on Schubert's reaction to Beethoven's music:

> Schubert was sent into such transports of delight and enthusiasm and was so overcome that they all feared for him. A slight indisposition, from which he had been suffering and from which he had not completely recovered, grew enormously worse, developed into typhoid fever and in five days Schubert was dead. The C-sharp Minor Quartet was the last music that he heard! The King of Harmony had sent the King of Song a friendly blessing to the crossing! They both reached the kingdom of the Blessed penniless!²⁹

In Nohl's account, Schubert's last days are underscored by the visionary grandeur of Beethoven's late style, and his death itself is interpreted as a reaction to the overwhelming emotional impact of the music. John Reed comments that the story 'cannot fail to stir the imagination', as one is led to think of Schubert's personal connection with 'those intimations of immortality that seem to be embodied in the most mystical of Beethoven's compositions'.³⁰ Indeed, Reed's imagination, along with that of countless others, was stirred, and the mythology of late Beethoven, rich with metaphors of introversion, alienation, austerity and unprecedented innovation, inevitably shades our understanding of Schubert's life in his last months.³¹

Reading Schubert's last months through the lens of late Beethoven, it is unsurprising that critics invoke *Winterreise* and the Heine songs as the works most characteristic of Schubert's late style. Reed sets the stage:

> Two works set the tone for the final creative phase of Schubert's life, *Winterreise* and the Heine songs. The continuity of the theme is plain. Heine himself acknowledged his debt to Müller, sharpening the cutting edge of Müller's irony as the alienated Wanderer becomes the embittered artist at war with a philistine society. The emotional intensity of the Heine songs prove[s] that for Schubert too this theme struck home.[32]

The theme of alienation, among others, is a key element of the imagery in Beethoven's late works; one is reminded of Wendell Kretzschmar's description of Beethoven, in Thomas Mann's *Doctor Faustus*, as 'an ego painfully isolated in its own absoluteness'.[33] In this attempt to 'use the life to interpret the work', the introverted, transgressive rhetoric of *Winterreise* and the Heine songs is understood as the 'essence of Schubert's imaginative vision'.[34]

As the musical manifestation of Schubert's alleged absorption in the 'inner life,' *Winterreise* and the Heine songs are seen as a clear point of culmination in Schubert's development as a composer of lieder, and the Heine songs live up to their role as valedictory works. As Paul Stefan sees it, they are 'the real swan song' in *Schwanengesang*.[35] Fischer-Dieskau says that 'one must have mixed feelings of astonishment and regret at the artistic breakthrough which they represent,' adding that 'no other prematurely deceased artist ever produced such startling innovations in the last months of his life'.[36] Similarly, Einstein looks on the Heine songs (specifically 'Der Doppelgänger' and 'Die Stadt') as the 'threshold of a new development'.[37] The Rellstab songs, while generally acknowledged to be less exceptional as a whole than the Heine set, are also accepted as works that, in content and tone, are at least congruent with this particular view of late Schubert. The heightened expressivity and stentorian quality of such songs as 'Kriegers Ahnung', 'Aufenthalt' and 'In der Ferne' certainly resonate with the sense of radical innovation that so often characterises the Heine set.

In comparison, 'Die Taubenpost' is judged to be a regression to a past style of 'pleasantness' that is strikingly at odds with the bold novelty of the Heine and Rellstab settings. Stefan assesses it as an example of the 'old lied style', which is comparatively 'impersonal' when compared with the 'revelation' of the Heine settings.[38] Traditional narratives of great creative lives do not suddenly retreat into convention. Reed goes so far as to say that the song 'turns its back on adventures of the soul'.[39] Maurice Brown contends that the song 'belongs neither in body nor in spirit to either the Rellstab group or to the Heine group of songs; for all that it can inspire an affectionate response in the Schubertian'.[40] 'Die Taubenpost' therefore somehow rings false, and, like 'Der Hirt auf dem Felsen',[41] another seemingly aberrant work of the fall of 1828, must be explained away as a trifle or a concession to public taste.[42]

I cannot accept this. Are we not short-sighted in evaluating Schubert's late style in the long shadow of Beethoven and in terms of the darker imagery of Romantic 'genius'? True, there are works of 1827 and 1828, *Winterreise* and the Heine songs foremost among them, which echo the disintegration, alienation and irascible subjectivity of late Beethoven. But for each of these moments, are there not many others that adopt a completely contrary viewpoint, turning the intensity of the inward gaze gently outward? Even *Winterreise*, for all of its bleakness, ends with a turning outward and a question.

Rather than relying upon the Beethovenian model, would it not be more accurate to characterise the style of the late Schubert as one predicated upon radical heterogeneity?[43] Having transformed the very identity of the lied in the Heine settings and engaged yet again with the legacy of Beethoven in the Rellstab songs, Schubert returns in 'Die Taubenpost' to the context that he knew best—a seemingly effortless, tuneful treatment of a poem of no particular consequence by a local writer. Reworking this humble text, Schubert creates an outwardly 'pleasant' song that is in no way simple or conventional. Both the text and Schubert's setting belie the casualness that the song seems to project. Yes, the song may appear to '[dance] along, all sweetness and good humor', but beneath this surface lies a deeper and more subtle character that argues against the outwardly present trappings.[44] Schubert's contemporaries seem to have recognised the stylistic and expressive paradoxes—the successive or even simultaneous juxtapositions of conflicting character—inherent in these works of the mid- to late 1820s. A March 1828 review of the first part of *Winterreise* suggests as much:

> Schubert's mind shows a bold sweep everywhere, whereby he carries everyone away with him who approaches him, and he takes them through the immeasurable depth of the human heart into the far distance, where premonitions of the infinite dawn upon them longingly in a rosy radiance, but where at the same time the shuddering bliss of an inexpressible presentiment is companioned by the gentle pain of the constraining present which hems in the boundaries of human existence.[45]

This description of the 'shuddering bliss of an inexpressible presentiment ... companioned by the gentle pain of the constraining present' seems an ideal assessment of 'Die Taubenpost', with its persistent and heartfelt questioning ('Sie heißt!—die Sehnsucht. / Kennt ihr sie?') and its resigned melancholy in the absence of an answer.

Furthermore, while the song is sometimes dismissed as just another in a long series of Schubert's explorations in modified strophic form, the structure of the song is also more subtle than it first appears. In entertaining his intriguing theory that *Schwanengesang* stands as a kind of *Kunst des Liedes*, Edward T. Cone highlights the exceptional structural complexity of 'Die Taubenpost'—an amalgam of ternary, strophic, and through-composed forms.[46] As such, even within the framework of the familiar 'pleasing' style,

Schubert is offering something new in 'Die Taubenpost,' and the song reveals but another facet of Schubert's unprecedented and varied exploration of form, content and style in the lieder of *Schwanengesang*.[47]

Beyond *Schwanengesang*, other lieder of 1828 suggest a similar juxtaposition of an outwardly pleasing style, an apparently lightweight, unassuming text, and a blurring of boundaries between conventional lied forms. Consider, for instance, the two great Karl Gottfried von Leitner settings of January 1828, 'Die Sterne' and 'Der Winterabend.' As in 'Die Taubenpost', Schubert alludes in these songs to elements of a more conventional lied aesthetic while at the same time suggesting bold new directions in his conception of the genre. In the case of these two late Leitner settings, the most immediately novel aspects are their extreme length, their peculiar tendency towards repetition, and the extended introductions and interludes for piano. Set in comparison with the naive optimism of 'Die Sterne' and the cosy domesticity of 'Der Winterabend', these features (and the formal complexity that stems from them) find points of connection with 'Die Taubenpost' and suggest that, far from being aberrations, such juxtapositions are in fact central to Schubert's late song style.

In attempting to draw some conclusions, it is perhaps useful to return to the simple question, entertained at the outset of this essay, of what exactly *Schwanengesang* is and, by extension, what it may mean to say that 'Die Taubenpost' does or does not have a place within this particular collection of songs. Essential to this discussion is the context in which Haslinger and his contemporaries might have understood the generic identity of his publication. As Martin Chusid points out, Haslinger's 1829 publication was printed in such a way as to enable individual songs to be sold separately.[48] In this regard, it is worth pointing out that many of the opinions that challenge the place of 'Die Taubenpost' in *Schwanengesang* proceed from the notion that it is some kind of a cycle, or, at the very least, that Haslinger intended for it to be perceived as such. Apart from the fact that Haslinger introduced consecutive numbering in the 1829 publication, there is nothing to suggest that he ever viewed *Schwanengesang* as anything more than a collection of Schubert's last songs.

The status of *Schwanengesang* as a compendium, if not an integrated cycle, of late songs gains greater significance when compared with Haslinger's efforts, between 1817 and 1823, to attempt a collected edition of Beethoven's works, the result of which was a deluxe edition of handwritten copies in sixty-two volumes.[49] While Haslinger's Beethoven edition was obviously of much vaster scope than his collection of fourteen late Schubert songs, the project reveals an anthologising sensibility that might well resurface, albeit in more modest form, in *Schwanengesang*.

As stated at the outset of this chapter, the most persistent questions about *Schwanenegesang* will, in the absence of any new evidence, remain unanswerable. Inasmuch as *Schwanengesang* lives up to its name, 'Die Taubenpost' is, of course, the only song in the cycle that truly represents the 'last blossom' of Schubert's talent.[50] It is his true swan song, and, indeed, something akin to the 'fairest prize' promised in the final stanza of Seidl's poem.[51] Whether or not Schubert ever intended for the fourteen songs of *Schwanengesang* to be heard together, Haslinger's edition is a prescient commentary on the essential lack of unity in Schubert's late style. 'Die Taubenpost' is a brilliant and even necessary aberration, and its position at the end of *Schwanengesang* is utterly appropriate.[52]

Notes

1. For more on the composition and publication history of *Schwanengesang*, see Walburga Litschauer, 'The Origin and Early Reception of *Schwanengesang*,' in Martin Chusid (ed.), *A Companion to Schubert's 'Schwanengesang': History, Poets, Analysis, Performance* (New Haven, CT: Yale University Press, 2000), pp. 5–13.

2. John Reed, *Schubert: the Final Years* (New York: St. Martin's Press, 1972), p. 223.

3. Alfred Einstein, *Schubert*, trans. David Ascoli (London: Cassell, 1951), p. 354.

4. This statement, by Misha Donat, is found in the notes accompanying the 2005 recording of *Schwanengesang* by Matthias Goerne (baritone) and Alfred Brendel (piano) Decca CD 475 6011, p. 4.

5. Julian Armitage Smith, 'Schubertian Legacy', *The Musical Times* (June 1975), p. 541.

6. Among other attempts to justify the inclusion of 'Die Taubenpost' in *Schwanengesang*, that of Edward T. Cone is perhaps most noteworthy. See Cone, 'Repetition and Correspondence in *Schwanengesang*', in Martin Chusid (ed.), *A Companion to Schubert's 'Schwanengesang': History, Poets, Analysis, Performance* (New Haven, CT: Yale University Press, 2000), pp. 85–9.

7. Otto Erich Deutsch, *The Schubert Reader*, trans. Eric Blom (New York: W. W. Norton, 1947), p. 811.

8. Spaun's essay originally appeared in issues of the *Österreichisches Bürgerblatt für Verstand, Herz, und gute Laune* (Linz). The essay is reprinted and translated in Deutsch, *The Schubert Reader*, pp. 865–82. Spaun's comment on *Schwanengesang* is found on p. 875.

9. John Reed, *The Schubert Song Companion* (Manchester: Mandolin, 1997), p. 200.

10. Dietrich Fischer-Dieskau, *Schubert's Songs: a Biographical Study*, trans. Kenneth A. Whitton (New York: Alfred A. Knopf, 1977), p. 277.

11. Graham Johnson, notes to vol. 37 of the Hyperion Schubert Edition (CDJ33036), p. 22.

12. Review from *Allgemeine Musikzeitung* (Munich), 28 July 1828; reprinted in Deutsch, *The Schubert Reader*, p. 795.

13. Theodor W. Adorno, 'Schubert' (1928), trans. Jonathan Dunsby and Beate Perrey, *19th-Century Music* 29/1 (2005), p. 10.

14. Richard Giarusso, 'Beyond the 'Leiermann': Disorder, Reality, and the Power of Imagination in the Final Songs of Schubert's *Winterreise*,' in Barbara

Reul and Lorraine Byrne Bodley (eds), *The Unknown Schubert* (Aldershot: Ashgate, 2008), pp. 25–42.

15. Among others, Elmar Budde has acknowledged the challenges involved in considering the cyclic identity of the *Schwanengesang* lieder and the ultimate futility of speculating upon Schubert's intentions for the songs. While accepting that these questions can never be answered definitively, Budde does observe that Schubert might, at the very least, have planned the Rellstab and Heine songs as two separate *Liederhefte*. He points out that, if this had indeed been Schubert's plan, it would have been in keeping with the composer's practice of issuing sets of songs with texts by the same poet but without a cyclical plan under a single opus number. See Budde, *Schuberts Liederzyklen: Ein musikalischer Werkführer* (Munich: C. H. Beck, 2003), p. 97. In another study, Richard Kramer offers a provocative reading of Schubert's ordering of the Heine lieder that suggests a further ambivalence on the composer's part about the cyclic identity of the *Schwanengesang* lieder. See Kramer, *Distant Cycles: Schubert and the Conceiving of Song* (Chicago: University of Chicago Press, 1994), pp. 125–47.

16. Julian Armitage-Smith, response to Joshua Rifkin, *The Musical Times* (October 1975), p. 878.

17. The excerpt quoted here is taken from Litschauer, 'The Origin and Early Reception of *Schwanengesang*', p. 7. The announcement, which appeared in the *Wiener Zeitung* on 31 January 1829, added that the printing of the songs was to be 'dedicated to Schubert's patrons and friends', though, as mentioned earlier, the dedication never appeared in Haslinger's 1829 publication. Elsewhere Haslinger underscores the personal resonance of *Schwanengesang* for the members of Schubert's circle, stating that the list of subscribers to the first edition would 'appear as a survey of Schubert's admirers and friends, indeed in a way represent a list of the mourners' names'. See Deutsch, *The Schubert Reader*, p. 884.

18. Reed, *The Schubert Song Companion*, p. 259.

19. Haslinger purchased the autograph scores of the fourteen songs that would later be published as *Schwanengesang*, along with the last three piano sonatas, from Schubert's brother Ferdinand on 17 December 1828—less than a month after Schubert's death. For more on Haslinger, his working relationship with Schubert and his distinguished career, see Peter Clive, *Schubert and his World: a Biographical Dictionary* (Oxford: Oxford University Press, 1997), pp. 70–2.

20. Deutsch, *The Schubert Reader*, p. 675.

21. Ibid., p. 759.

22. Peter Clive, *Beethoven and his World: a Biographical Dictionary* (Oxford: Oxford University Press, 2001), p. 152.

23. In supporting the view that Haslinger was not motivated simply by commercial interests, Martin Chusid invokes Walther Dürr's assessment of Haslinger's professionalism and integrity as a publisher. Dürr writes: 'Among Schubert's publishers of the time [the composer's last years] Tobias Haslinger stands out; in addition to *Winterreise* . . . he published Opp. 80–83 (as he had published Op. 79 previously). On principle, his prints are distinguished by special care, a care not only for the pitches, but also for the dynamic and articulation markings and

even for the punctuation of the [poetic] text.' Franz Schubert, *Neue Ausgabe sämtlicher Werke*, ser. IV, vol. 14a, *Lieder 14*, ed. Walther Dürr (Kassel: Bärenreiter, 1988), p. xv. Quoted in Martin Chusid, 'The Sequence of the Heine Songs and Cyclicism in *Schwanengesang*', in Chusid (ed.), *A Companion to Schubert's 'Schwanengesang': History, Poets, Analysis, Performance* (New Haven, CT: Yale University Press, 2000), p. 173.

24. In the correspondence from the summer and fall of 1828, Probst and Schott appear consistently evasive and dismissive in their communications with Schubert. While Schubert's letters requesting updates on works currently under contract become increasingly desperate in the fall of 1828, Probst maintains an almost cavalier tone with regard to the extraordinary delays of the Trio in E♭ major and asks only for more material that will be commercially viable. See Deutsch, *The Schubert Reader*, pp. 811–12.

25. Though initial reception of the songs was largely favourable, contemporary reports do highlight both the songs' technical difficulty (for both singer and pianist) and their predominantly dark character. In his October 1829 article in the *Allgemeine Musikalische Zeitung*, G. F. Fink points out that, owing to the challenges of certain songs, 'singer and pianist should rehearse well together if they do not want to ruin thoughtlessly the pleasure in these gifts for themselves and others'. He goes on to add that the songs are recommended to 'more serious amateurs' and ends the article by reminding his readers that the music is 'not always light and entertaining'. It is especially noteworthy that, while acknowledging that 'Die Taubenpost' is 'very pleasing melodically', Fink still underscores an element of difficulty with regard to its execution, adding that it 'demands an assured performance and lasting strength'. See Litschauer, 'The Origin and Early Reception of *Schwanengesang*', pp. 8–9.

26. Susan Sontag, *Under the Sign of Saturn* (New York: Picador, 1972), p. 111.

27. Consider, for instance, the assessment of Brian Newbould, who stresses the qualities of 'alienation', 'introversion' and 'unendurable Angst' in the Heine songs. See Newbould, *Schubert: the Music and the Man* (London: Victor Gollancz, 1997), pp. 311–14. As early as 1829,'Mayrhofer invoked explicit parallels between events in the composer's life and the dark tone of the late works, in this case *Winterreise*: '[*Winterreise*] shows how much more serious the composer became. He had been long and seriously ill, had gone through disheartening experiences, and life for him had shed its rosy colour; winter had come for him'. From Mayrhofer, *Recollections of Franz Schubert* (Vienna, 1829). Quoted in Otto Erich Deutsch, *Schubert: Memoirs by his Friends*, trans. Rosamond Ley and John Nowell (New York: Macmillan, 1958), p. 15. Christopher Gibbs also offers an enlightening summary of past attempts at reading biography into Schubert's music, especially as a means of illuminating some of the more unusual features of the composer's work in the last six years of his life. See Gibbs, *The Life of Schubert* (Cambridge: Cambridge University Press, 2000), pp. 91–114.

28. Deutsch, *Schubert: Memoirs by his Friends*, p. 319.

29. Ludwig Nohl, 'Beethoven, Liszt, Wagner' (Vienna: Wilhelm Braumüller, 1874), pp. 11ff. Quoted and translated in Deutsch, *Schubert: Memoirs by his Friends*, p. 299. According to Nohl, his account is based upon a report by the violinist Karl Holz (1798–1858), who arranged the performance of the Beethoven Quartet.

30. Reed, *Schubert: the Final Years*, p. 253.

31. More recently, Gibbs has compared the 'psychological innovations' in the Heine lieder to those of the late Beethoven quartets. See Gibbs, *The Life of Schubert*, p. 165.

32. Reed, *The Schubert Song Companion*, p. 260.

33. Thomas Mann, *Doctor Faustus*, trans. John E. Woods (New York: Knopf, 1997), p. 57.

34. Reed, *Schubert: the Final Years*, p. 265.

35. Paul Stefan, *Franz Schubert* (Berlin: Volksverband der Bücherfreunde, Wegweiser-Verlag, 1928), p. 224.

36. Fischer-Dieskau, *Schubert's Songs*, p. 280.

37. Einstein, *Schubert*, p. 356.

38. Stefan, *Franz Schubert*, p. 225.

39. Reed, *The Schubert Song Companion*, p. 200.

40. Maurice Brown, *Schubert: a Critical Biography* (London: Macmillan, 1958), p. 306.

41. It is worth pointing out here that it was Haslinger who brought out the first edition of 'Der Hirt auf dem Felsen' in June 1830.

42. Reed, *Schubert: the Final Years*, p. 250.

43. Others, of course, have made similar arguments in attempts to define Schubert's 'late' style. With reference to *Schwanengesang* in particular, Steven Lubin acknowledges the seminal importance of stylistic heterogeneity in the music of Schubert's last year. He likewise asserts that the reluctance to accept this view of Schubert's 'late' style is likely indebted to the influence of the Beethovenian paradigm. See Lubin, 'The Three Styles of *Schwanengesang*: a Pianist's Perspective', in Martin Chusid (ed.), *A Companion to Schubert's 'Schwanengesang': History, Poets, Analysis, Performance* (New Haven, CT: Yale University Press, 2000), pp. 191–204.

44. The quotation is from Reed, *The Schubert Song Companion*, p. 200.

45. Review from the *Wiener Theaterzeitung*, 29 March 1828. Quoted and translated in Deutsch, *The Schubert Reader*, p. 758.

46. Cone, 'Repetition and Correspondence in Schwanengesang,' in Chusid, *A Companion to Schubert's 'Schwanengesang'*, pp. 87–8.

47. Susan Youens offers a characteristically nuanced reading of the many textual, structural, harmonic and melodic intricacies of 'Die Taubenpost' in *Schubert's Late Lieder: Beyond the Song Cycles* (Cambridge: Cambridge University Press, 2002), pp. 404–14.

48. Martin Chusid, 'Introductory Remarks on the Autograph, the Sketches and the First Edition', in Franz Schubert, *'Schwanengesang': Facsimiles of the Autograph Score and Sketches, and Reprint of the First Edition* (New Haven, CT: Yale University Press, 2000), p. xxiii. In Haslinger's 1829 edition, each song has its own title page, and each of the songs has its own plate number. The pagination of the edition is likewise arranged so as to allow any song to be excerpted as an individual fascicle from the collection.

49. For more on Haslinger's Beethoven project, see Elliot Forbes (ed. and rev.), *Thayer's Life of Beethoven*, vol. 2 (Princeton, NJ: Princeton University Press, 1967), p. 692.

50. The term was used by Haslinger in his initial advertisement of the songs; see n. 15.

51. 'Drum heg' ich sie auch so treu an der Brust / Versichert des schönsten Gewinns; / Sie heißt—die Sehnsucht! / Kennt ihr sie? Die Botin treuen Sinns' (I cherish her as truly in my heart, / Certain of the fairest prize; / Her name is— Longing! Do you know her? / The messenger of a faithful heart'). Translation adapted from Richard Wigmore in *Schubert: the Complete Song Texts* (London: Victor Gollancz, 1988), p. 317.

52. As a final note, I offer here, for what it's worth, my own perspective on this issue as a performer. Having sung *Schwanengesang* on a number of occasions, I can only say that the transition from 'Der Doppelgänger' to 'Die Taubenpost' always feels indescribably and improbably right. The opening measures of 'Die Taubenpost', with the right-hand syncopations gradually reconstituting a comparative sense of rhythmic, harmonic and melodic ease in the wake of 'Der Doppelgänger', signal a return of sorts—bringing us back, as Martin Chusid points out, to the mood, the imagery and even the key of 'Liebesbotschaft' and inverting the intense introspection of the preceding songs. See Chusid, 'The Sequence of Heine Songs', in *A Companion to Schubert's 'Schwanengesang'*, p. 171. As Youens puts it, 'We dance onward and outward into life, with sheer happiness the impelling force'; *Schubert's Late Lieder*, p. 406. While it is, of course, purely subjective, the sense of profound and unlikely closure offered by 'Die Taubenpost' in performance is, I think, a factor that cannot be ignored.

20

Disability, Self-Critique and Failure in Schubert's 'Der Doppelgänger'

Benjamin Binder

Schubert's 'Der Doppelgänger' has become a critique of its own reception. The protagonist of the song feels compelled to revisit the deserted city street where his beloved once lived, only to encounter to his horror a ghostly incarnation of his past self aping his lovelorn anguish from years ago (Heinrich Heine's poem is given in Table 20.1). Likewise, musicologists and theorists continue to be drawn to 'Der Doppelgänger' more than any other song in the Schubert canon, only to risk the awful discovery that anything they might say about it has already been said before by one of their many scholarly antecedents. In this essay, I succumb to the temptation once again, but in recognition of the dangers I face, let me be clear: if there is anything new in what I hope to accomplish here, it will be to use the interpretative prism(s) of 'late style' in order to reveal a layer of personal significance that is potentially embedded in this song, which may thus far have escaped our attention.

We know that the idiosyncrasies found in Schubert's very particular musical readings of poetry were sometimes intended to communicate specific meanings within the context of his social circle, meanings that would not necessarily be comprehended or even detected by a general public more inclined to interpret the poem and its musical setting at face value alone. The prime example of a critical approach to Schubert's songs attuned to such meanings remains Kristina Muxfeldt's investigation of the August von Platen settings 'Die Liebe hat gelogen' and 'Du liebst mich nicht'.[1] Muxfeldt argues that Platen's poetic encoding of frustrated same-sex desire and Schubert's empathetic support of his friend Johann Senn, who had recently been banished from Vienna (probably for political and sexual improprieties), explicate certain striking moments of heightened expressivity in the scores that would otherwise seem puzzling and unmotivated. Muxfeldt's seminal study is just one reminder that Schubert's songs were, among other things, personal documents—they were shared among friends and sometimes said things that only friends would fully understand. Moreover, in the police state of Metternich's Vienna, where censorship and surveillance were woven into the fabric of everyday life, the encryption of private meaning into intentionally multivalent public expressions was a familiar habit, even if the more exclusive content was not especially incendiary or politically charged.[2]

Table 20.1 Heinrich Heine, *Die Heimkehr* no. 20

Still ist die Nacht, es ruhen die Gassen,	The night is silent, the streets rest,
In diesem Hause wohnte mein Schatz;	in this house my sweetheart lived;
Sie hat schon längst die Stadt verlassen,	she has long since left the town,
Doch steht noch das Haus auf demselben Platz.	but the house still stands in the same place.
Da steht auch ein Mensch und starrt in die Höhe,	There too a man stands and stares upwards,
Und ringt die Hände, vor Schmerzensgewalt;	and wrings his hands, because pain overpowers him;
Mir graust es, wenn ich sein Antlitz sehe,—	I become filled with dread, when I see his face—
Der Mond zeigt mir meine eigne Gestalt.	the moon shows me my own form.
Du Doppeltgänger! du bleicher Geselle!	You ghostly double! you pale fellow!
Was äffst du nach mein Liebesleid,	Why do you ape the pain of love
Das mich gequält auf dieser Stelle,	that tormented me on this spot,
So manche Nacht, in alter Zeit?[1]	so many a night, in times gone by?

[1] Text taken from *Buch der Lieder* (Hamburg: Hoffmann & Campe, 1827), p. 198.

Leaving aside some vague but suggestive evidence furnished by the early publication and performance histories of 'Der Doppelgänger',[3] my argument about its personal significance will rest primarily on features of the score situated in the context of certain aspects of Schubert's biography and compositional oeuvre. In short, Schubert's distinctive musical interpretation of Heine's 'Der Doppelgänger' leads me to hear in this song a self-portrait of the composer in his final years, physically, psychologically and creatively crippled by the effects of the syphilis he had contracted in November 1822.[4] Put another way, in my reading the song will become a self-critique of Schubert's compositional persona and physical being in what would turn out to be the last year of his life. Critics have often observed how Heine's poem and Schubert's setting critique the very idea of a coherent, authentic self, reflecting the alienation, fragmentation and disillusionment of post-Romantic Biedermeier subjectivity in general.[5] Here, however, I want to focus more on the ways in which Schubert may be heard to critique and reflect upon his own specific self, upon a particular identity formed both from his life experiences and from his body of work as a composer.

The notion of a composer's engaging in 'self-critique' immediately calls to mind one of the two interrelated forms of 'lateness' that I believe may be helpful in this regard. According to this first and most familiar understanding of late style, a composer at the end of a long career will subject his or her musical language to a rigorous deconstructive analysis, exposing its fundamental premises in order to reassess its expressive validity. The *locus classicus* of this mode of criticism is Theodor Adorno's account of late Beethoven, the gist of which is succinctly adumbrated in this passage from Adorno's *Aesthetic Theory*: 'Beethoven's late works mark the revolt of one of the most powerful classicistic artists against the deception implicit in the principle of his own work.'[6] Aside from studies by Daniel Chua and Michael Spitzer that have amplified and enriched Adorno's interpretation of Beethoven,[7] other recent examples of the self-critique approach to late style include Margaret Notley's assessment of Brahms and Marianne Wheeldon's analogous treatment of Debussy.[8]

In the company of Beethoven, Brahms and Debussy, Schubert is perhaps an unlikely candidate for late-style analysis of this sort. His compositional career was relatively short—he died at the age of thirty-one, still a young man—and most modern biographies suggest that he didn't quite know he was at the end of that career as he was writing the Heine songs sometime between the spring and early autumn of 1828.[9] Nonetheless, Schubert had understood himself to be in a precarious state of health for some time; as Christopher H. Gibbs remarks, 'one can [therefore] reasonably speculate that Schubert consciously embarked on his final creative stage, a period customarily associated with the autumnal glow of later years, when he was only in his mid-twenties'.[10] Moreover, as Richard Kramer has suggested, in the Heine songs (and especially 'Der Doppelgänger') we see Schubert's tendencies as a composer pushed to the extreme in an effort to find a musical mode of expression that would match the poet's ironic despair. 'Der Doppelgänger,' Kramer writes, 'follows Heine's neurotic lover to the void'.[11] As Schubert responds to Heine, then, we might not be surprised to find him taking an obsessive, self-critical look at his own compositional style in the process. In the reading of 'Der Doppelgänger' that I shall advance here, we will observe Schubert not only negating or ossifying the basic elements of the style with which he had become identified, but also unsuccessfully resisting the temptation to attempt a return to that earlier style. Using the protagonist of the song as an alter ego, Schubert portrays himself as knowing the tragic impossibility of going back to the way things were in the past, but in the end he cannot help himself from trying to do just that, and the results are painfully flawed.

This brings us to the other, more recent concept of lateness that seems applicable here: what Joseph N. Straus calls 'disability style'. Straus has proposed that so-called late-style musical features might be more fruitfully interpreted as representations of the 'non-normative mental and bodily states' experienced by the aged or infirm composer.[12] Again, in 1828 Schubert was not late in life, but he certainly lived in the shadow of grave infirmity and knew that he might have to return to his sickbed at any time. Elsewhere Straus cites Edward T. Cone's analysis of the sixth *Moment musical* in A♭ major, D 780, and offers his own reading of the first movement of the Piano Sonata in B♭ major, D 960, as examples of this kind of critical approach to Schubert's music. Both authors hear a particular chromatic note as a toxic foreign element, analogous to the contagion of syphilis, which enters and infects the healthy diatonic body of the piece. In Straus's reading of the Sonata, the dissonance of its famous G♭ trill is ultimately 'accommodated', whereas in Cone's analysis of the *Moment musical* a strikingly unresolved leading note (the E♮ of bar 12) gradually wreaks disastrous havoc on the piece's tonal integrity.[13]

David Løberg Code hears a variant of Cone's tragic-illness narrative enacted in 'Der Doppelgänger'. He tells a story of a latent subdominant (E minor) which gradually emerges to overtake the dominant and problematises the tonic status of B minor by the end of the song, all of which represents the 'gradual affliction of the disease within Schubert himself'.[14] Lawrence Kramer interprets the persistent appearance of C♮ in the bass line that effects this turn to the subdominant as a force that 'degrades' the dominant, creating a 'musical image of a literally underlying reality that breaks into the familiar world and insists there on incommensurable truths'.[15] This process leads ultimately to the song's conclusion on a functionally ambiguous B major triad, the tonal uncertainty of which epitomises 'the musical space where the double goes to perform his nightly ritual, beyond the reach of recuperation either from his erotic wound or by any norm of mental health or social propriety. And where the double goes, the subject follows.'[16]

I also hear in this song something repressed that eventually manifests itself and wounds the subject in some way—not, however, an illness working its way to the surface, the biological workings-out of a disease with its graphic effects, nor the unleashing of disruptive sociopathic energies. Instead, my reading runs in nearly the opposite direction: I hear a subject who is already incapacitated slowly yielding to the urge to behave as though he weren't ill, as though he were normal, as though it were a time before November 1822 and the onset of a debilitating, incurable disease. In this, my interpretation of 'Der Doppelgänger' forms a productive counterpoint to Blake Howe's discussion of Schubert's Mayrhofer settings from 1824. Howe understands Schubert's music in these songs to depict the subject's transcendence of the limitations of corporeal disability; the songs repeatedly feature a spiritual force breaking free from the confinement and limitations of an ailing body.[17] In 'Der Doppelgänger', on the other hand, I hear a threadbare subject chastened by illness whose survival seems to depend precisely on staying within overly circumscribed limits. The catastrophes of the song occur when he violates those limits—that is, when he fails to maintain them. In my reading, failure is what will unite self-critique and disability as two overlapping dimensions of the same 'late' phenomenon. In this song, I hear Schubert's personal identity as a composer and as a physical human being who is living under the constant threat of failure. Eventually this identity is pushed to fail, spectacularly and heartbreakingly, in three domains for which Schubert was (and is) justifiably celebrated: repetition, dance, and song. I will address each of these in turn, since they are dealt with in this order in the song itself.

Repetition

I begin as the song does, with the music of the first four bars (see Example 20.1). In the musicological literature, the sombre, desolate figure traced by the outer octaves in the piano has been linked to the B–A–C–H motive[18] and to Baroque cruciform figures such as the subject of the C♯ minor fugue from the first book of Bach's *Well-Tempered Clavier*[19] and the principal motive of the Agnus Dei of Schubert's own Mass in E♭, D 950.[20] In the next four bars, as the voice enters with the first words of the poem, the piano repeats its earlier figure verbatim, clarifying

Example 20.1 Schubert, *Schwanengesang*, D 957/13, 'Der Doppelgänger'

Example 20.1 Continued

the figure's meaning: it is the ground bass of an unfolding passacaglia. Why would Schubert resort to this antiquated Baroque procedure, and in such starkly drawn terms? Some critics see the use of the archaic passacaglia as an emblem of a historically remote age that corresponds in some way to the 'alte Zeit' mentioned at the end of Heine's poem.[21] Even before the protagonist spots his doppelgänger at the start of the second stanza of the poem, Schubert may have already led us to sense his presence through the haunting otherness of this desiccated old motive.[22]

We might remind ourselves, however, that in the most straightforward reading of Heine's poem, the 'alte Zeit' from which the protagonist's doppelgänger hails is simply an earlier period in the protagonist's own life. From this literalist perspective, it would be rather odd for Schubert to choose the passacaglia in order to evoke the protagonist's past, especially if we consider that the protagonist is speaking in the mid-to-late 1820s and that the passacaglia would have been a contemporary feature of musical style only as recently as the early eighteenth century. Moreover, the words 'alte Zeit' are not actually heard until the very end of the song, and in a much different musical context, as I will consider later.

For now, I want to suggest that the passacaglia is not so much a token of the protagonist's past as it is an indication of his defective present. What matters most to me about the ground bass is that it is a markedly alien device within the range of possibilities found in Schubert's usual compositional language, and yet it foregrounds one of Schubert's trademark techniques: repetition.[23] Under normal circumstances, Schubert should need no help from a musty old passacaglia in order to build up a musical texture from repetition. In fact, when Schubert does employ ostinato-like repetition in his music, it is usually much more flexible and quivering with life, creating a charmed island of stasis amid the flow of musical business-as-usual. For instance, in the final movement of the Piano Trio in B♭ major, D 898 (see Example 20.2), the development section of the sonata form begins characteristically enough with a motive from the exposition. But from this motive (played first by the cello in bar 250), Schubert creates a stable two-bar unit of music, underpinned by a tonic pedal, that is subsequently repeated and then kaleidoscopically altered for eleven bars without ever disturbing the pattern's mesmerising regularity and periodicity. The overriding sense of secure expansiveness and the total cessation of forward momentum in the music even permit an extra bar to grow out of the pattern in bars 258–260 without breaking the spell.[24] In other places in Schubert's music, rhythmic groove sessions like this may sometimes lead to an explosion of 'volcanic temper', as Hugh Macdonald once described it;[25] but regardless of whether they heighten or suspend the tension, they are fundamental to Schubert's identity as a composer.

Within this broader Schubertian context, what is the effect of the passacaglia in 'Der Doppelgänger', with its forbidding and unfamiliar stiffness? To my ear, this ground bass serves to create an ersatz identity for a compositionally disabled Schubert. The composer shows himself pointedly resorting to the ground bass as a rickety old crutch, hauled up from the dusty basement of history, which will help him hobble through this song and cobble together a rigid sense of identity from its foreordained pattern of exact repetition. The unyielding ground bass thus parodies or critiques Schubert's customary mastery of pliable repetition and is in that sense a deformed double of what the composer's style used to be and no longer is. In order to establish identity in this song, both in the sense of the protagonist's identity and his own compositional identity, a Schubert who has lost the suppleness of his repetition technique must find help where he can—hence the passacaglia.

But as anyone familiar with the song is well aware, the ground bass ultimately does yield, and after only two four-bar iterations—in fact, in all its mechanical strictness, it is set up to fail, to reveal its brittleness. Even with the

Example 20.2 Schubert, Piano Trio in B♭ Major, D 898, iv, bars 242–65

help of the crutch, Schubert's repetitive powers are here portrayed as faulty. I side with those critics who hear in the changes to the ostinato pattern a gradual progression or distortion,[26] rather than an alternation of variants,[27] and I would characterise that progression as a dissolution of present identity, which the subject unsuccessfully resists.

First, in bars 5–8, the protagonist enters the song vocally with speech-like declamation centred on an F♯. As Susan Youens aptly describes it, the vocal line here is 'an idiosyncratic species of a distorted litany or chant in which the singer is fixated on a reciting tone'. This sort of vocal delivery, she rightfully maintains, 'is like nothing else in Schubert'—again Schubert negates his past compositional identity.[28] The vocal F♯ doubles the inactive tone F♯ in the piano, imbuing this tone with melodic agency even as the protagonist maintains an aloof, narrational perspective by not budging much from this noncommittal fifth scale degree. The vocal subject thus passively identifies with the ground bass as he begins to talk about what he observes in the nocturnal streetscape.

Now, beneath the voice's fixed F♯, the piano part of the song's composite persona begins slouching towards some other identity. As the musical setting of the first poetic stanza unfolds, the passacaglia convulses with distortion at precisely those moments when the vocal subject's narration of the present moment brushes up against his past experience. This happens twice: first in bars 9–14, when he spots a house and first mentions the beloved who once lived there, and then again in bars 19–24, when he notices that her house is still there in the same place. The warping of the three-octave ostinato occurs when its second pitch, A♯, instead slips down to A♮ in bars 10 and 20. This sets in motion a textural thickening in the piano from two to three to four real voices across bars 10–12 and 20–22. As the ostinato continues to unfold, now with only the lower two of its three octaves intact, the expanding voice-leading strands freeze into an accented dominant seventh chord on F♯ in second inversion, held for three bars in bars 12–14 and 22–24. In these two passages, it is as though the inner workings of the creaky passacaglia machine get gummed up after one of its gears wears loose, and only an awful chromatic tightening of screws can stop it from breaking down further, as A is wrenched back up to the leading note, A♯, in bars 11–12 and 21–22. In the glacial unfolding of this calamity and the deliberate effort to contain it, we hear the subject struggling to keep from coming undone, resisting the collapse of his fragile four-note identity.

This explains why the two-bar piano interludes of bars 13–14 and 23–24 are so horribly uncanny. According to the logic of a normal passacaglia, there should be no room for interpolations like these, especially after only three cycles through the ground-bass pattern. In each of the two interludes, the piano echoes the last two bars of the vocal melody in a gesture that is usually quite characteristic of Schubert's song-writing style. Here, however,

Self-Critique in 'Der Doppelgänger'

in another moment of compositional self-critique, the interludes seem to be hollow echoes of that style. As a point of comparison, we can consider the first few vocal phrases of 'Liebesbotschaft', the first song in the *Schwanengesang* collection, published in 1829, which also contained 'Der Doppelgänger' (see Example 20.3). Here the protagonist sings to a babbling brook, urging it to hurry towards his distant beloved as his representative. As the vocal protagonist addresses the piano's brook, the two musical personae happily and freely allow their identities to interpenetrate as the tenor line in the piano repeats the end of each vocal phrase (bars 7 and 10) with slight variations, first inverting the melody's earlier figure (bar 8), then altering its initial note (bar 11). In 'Der Doppelgänger', on the other hand, the echoes arise in a knee-jerk reaction that fills the awkward silence left in the wake of the ostinato's failure. It is as though the piano misreads the temporary breakdown of the passacaglia machine as the proper ending of a phrase and therefore steps forward to fulfil its customary duty, but with the tentative, sheepish character of someone who has stumbled into a place where they do not actually belong and into a situation they do not truly understand. These pared-down piano interludes are pale shadows, not only of the somewhat more elaborate vocal phrases that they echo, but also of the very gesture of echo-interlude as we have come to know it in other Schubert songs.

In Schubert's setting of the second stanza of the poem (bars 25–42), as the subject gradually recognises his former self standing in the darkness, he cannot stop the ostinato from further degradation and eventually loses the battle to maintain his present identity, so tenuously established at the beginning of the song. As he first notices the man in bars 25–26 ('Da steht auch ein Mensch'),

Example 20.3 Schubert, 'Liebesbotschaft', D 957, bars 6–11

the vocal protagonist retakes his original F♯ from below on the word 'Mensch', at the precise moment when the man's presence is revealed in the poem. This causes an aura of otherness to infiltrate the subject's melodic identity tone of F♯ and undermines his narrative detachment, sending him slowly up the octave on a jag of empathy with the man's anguished staring into the heights in bars 27–32. In his vocal ascent to the high F♯ of bar 32, the subject is also bracing himself for the jarring eighth bar of the malfunctioning ostinato sequence, in anticipation of yet another mechanical failure, when the pattern's C♯ will slip to C♮ in bar 32. The gathering of vocal intensity as a means of generating strength for an act of resistance is necessary because, as Lawrence Kramer points out, the piano is wearing away at the subject here with enormous manual force.[29] It abandons its former legato contouring in favour of accents in almost every bar and pounds its way forward into the next fracture of the ostinato with a crescendo that culminates in brutal *fortissimi* and *fortississimi*. In this first round of mortal combat with the piano, the vocal subject manages to attain enough potential energy on his high F♯ to withstand the impact of the unsettling C♮ in bar 32 and then discharges this energy on the second beat, hurtling back down the octave. For now, his F♯ is still secure and unchanged, over and against the clangourous failure of the ostinato, which continues to deform from its original shape.

However, in the first of the song's three most stunning moments of rupture, the protagonist will lose the second round of this battle. In bar 34, the ostinato machine gone haywire lumbers back into motion after only one extra bar. The inexorable progress of the warping passacaglia now permits no time for self-conscious reflection in the piano, such that the protagonist has only this one bar in which to recover from the exertions of bars 31–32. (Even this is not much of a rest, as Schubert insists that the protagonist sing all the way up until the third beat of bar 33.) Textually, the protagonist's anguish in bars 25–33 was the product of empathy for the man in the shadows, but in bars 34–42, as the protagonist ascends again to the high F♯, anguish seizes him directly: '*mir* graust es, wenn ich sein Antlitz sehe'. This blurring of identities in the dramaturgy of the poem paves the way for the disintegration of identity in the melodic line: at the moment when the moon finally reveals the man's face, on the words 'meine eig'ne Gestalt' in bars 40–41, F♯ gives way to G. As the protagonist is forced to confront his own past identity, the disruptive power of the buckling ostinato loosens the protagonist's white-knuckled grip on F♯, resulting in the turbulent resonance of a heady, ringing G that dissolves the sense of unified identity so firmly lodged in the F♯ from the very beginning of the song. In the end, the protagonist—a stand-in for Schubert himself—is shown to be unable to resist the impulses that compel his inflexible and enfeebled ostinato towards changes and alterations that he can ill afford in his compromised condition. It is the protagonist's conspicuous failure at repetition that ultimately undermines his precarious present identity and puts him back in touch with a painfully irretrievable past. In the wider context of Schubert's life and works, such failure cuts close to the bone.

Dance

We may now ask: what does it mean for the protagonist of Schubert's song (as opposed to that of Heine's poem) to be forced to revisit his past identity as a result of the breakdown of a present identity that was frail to begin with? To answer this question, we might first observe how Schubert divides up the rest of the poem in his setting. Heine's last stanza begins with two indexical thrusts that together comprise the longest line of the poem at eleven syllables—'Du Doppeltgänger! du bleicher Geselle!'—but the final three lines are the poem's shortest and bleed into one another, forming a single question, the energy of which trails off into two fragmentary clauses that seem to fade out into the distant past towards which they gesture. But as we shall see, Schubert's music separates the last line of the stanza from the middle two lines and uses the first line as a kind of transition. If, as Joseph von Spaun and Anton Ottenwalt observed in their 1829 obituary of Schubert, the composer always 'knew how to find the most characteristic moment' of the poems he interpreted in song,[30] then why in this song did Schubert seize upon these particular moments with this sort of music? Here is where I think Schubert's self-critical appropriation of Heine's poem takes an especially personal turn, which would have resonated with his friends and patrons: we hear Schubert's powers fail in the arenas of dance and song.

In bar 42 G slumps back down to F♯, and in bar 43 we again find ourselves at the four-bar ostinato's ground zero. Now, however, that identity-defining pattern is completely taken over by the rising semitone that had flared up earlier as a painful symptom of the ostinato's failure: first in bars 11–12 and 21–22, when A was pushed back up to A♯, and then again in bars 40–41, when F♯ escaped to G. The energy of these semitones presses upwards in bars 43–46 from B through D until it reaches D♯ in bar 47, bursting the ostinato's upper boundary for the first time. Against his will, the subject is pushed out of the fragile comfort zone traced by the ostinato into a sharp-filled chromatic mediant, D♯ minor, which registers as an aggressive alternative to the tonic, all of its teeth showing. The common note between B minor and D♯ minor is F♯, the subject's identity pitch and still very much the focus of the melodic line in bars 43–46. But in the new harmonic context of bar 47, F♯ loses its passive, observational stance. It is now an expressive, mode-defining $\hat{3}$ in D♯ minor, rather than a purely structural $\hat{5}$. In the passage that follows this rupture into the new key (bars 47–50), the protagonist directly addresses his suffering doppelgänger, but it is really he himself who suffers. He no longer narrates the present—instead, he is being made to relive his past, and against his will.

Of what does this past consist? Although D♯ minor is vividly, agonisingly present here, more so than B minor ever was, there is also something false and flawed about it. For Richard Kurth, the passage in D♯ minor, with its standard-issue tonic and dominant chords, is only 'aping the gestures of tonality', conjuring some Schenkerian *Scheintonalität*,[31] while for Susan Youens it is a 'truncated intruder that cannot really set down roots and remain'.[32] D♯ minor creates an air of gruesome mockery, but what exactly is Schubert mocking? What is really being 'aped' here? The object of self-critical scorn, I would suggest, is Schubert's present ability to do something he used to do in the past: dance, or at least make dance music at the piano.[33] If we maintain the faster tempo achieved by the accelerando that starts in bar 43 until the end of the D♯ minor passage in bar 50, then the beginnings of a fitful, arthritic mazurka, or perhaps a rather starchy German dance, emerge from the complementary two-bar phrases of the melody in bars 47–50. The piano supports the vocal line with tonic and dominant harmonies that have the voicing of an oom-pah-pah left-hand accompaniment but not the actual rhythmic motion; both hands are required here, and they can only stammer out single accented chords. Example 20.4 shows what this dance might sound like if normalised and completed.

Schubert's friends repeatedly confirmed that the composer did not dance.[34] Nonetheless, Schubert was by no means a stranger to the physicality of dance. He played his dance music at Schubertiades and at house parties with gusto, even if it sometimes taxed the limits of his body. Eduard Bauernfeld recalled that at these parties Schubert 'had to play his latest waltzes over and over

Example 20.4 *Schwanengesang*, D 957/13, 'Der Doppelgänger': normalisation and completion of dance music in bars 47–50

again, until the whole thing had turned itself into an endless Cotillion, so that the small, corpulent little fellow, dripping with perspiration, was only able to regain his ease over the modest supper'.[35] In the D♯ minor passage of 'Der Doppelgänger', Schubert's past identity as a sweaty, delirious, dance-playing machine floods into the present; but in his current state, compromised by illness, the results of pushing his physical limits again are tragically uncomfortable. The defective dance music that explodes into the song in bar 47 creates an impression that Schubert is giving in to an unwelcome compulsion to rise from his sickbed and take his place at the piano for a vigorous dance session, only to find himself capable of nothing more than awkward, spasmodic bursts that make him palpably aware of the failure of his own body and of the enormous gulf that separates his disabled present from his healthy past. In Heine's poem, it is the wringing of hands that embodies the protagonist's tortured relationship with his past; but in Schubert's song, it is the gestures of dance.

Song

Although Schubert's friends rarely saw him dance, they did hear him sing his songs while accompanying himself at the piano on many occasions, from spontaneous get-togethers to more formal gatherings.[36] It was largely the strength and beauty of Schubert's voice as a boy soprano that earned him his place in the Imperial Court Chapel choir at the age of eleven;[37] but even after his voice changed and lost its professional viability, Schubert still felt confident enough about it to sing his songs without hesitation when he wished.[38] While he often accompanied others in the performance of his songs (most notably the professional tenor Johann Michael Vogl and the amateur baritone Karl Freiherr von Schönstein), singing seems to have been a normal, routine part of Schubert's self-expression within his social circle.

In bars 51–56 of 'Der Doppelgänger', the surge of energy that brought Schubert to his feet in bars 43–50 is now gathered up for one last effort—the effort to sing. This final vocal phrase is the only passage in the song that might qualify as a bona fide lyrical melody. Schubert's ability to write captivating melodies was regularly acknowledged as one of his greatest compositional gifts, yet this hallmark feature of Schubert's songs is withheld entirely from this piece until now. It is perhaps not surprising, then, that some critics are divided about the authenticity, or lack thereof, of this final melody. For example, Lawrence Kramer suggests that with this eruption of 'florid song', the protagonist 'sings in the double's missing voice, masking his own lack by confessing it in a mode that proclaims, "Listen! I can still sing!"'[39] This 'trope of revocalization seeks to rehumanize the revenant: to piece together a whole from this fragmentary relic of personhood'.⁴⁰ Yet Kramer thus admits that this act of 'revocalization' is indeed a 'trope', a mere 'figure', even a 'readymade'.⁴¹ My reading of the melody is sympathetic to the tension within Kramer's provocative interpretation. The vocal subject tries to reclaim a voice—his own voice—but eventually he falls back on stereotype. In this melody I believe we hear Schubert portraying the failure of his voice, physically and compositionally, with unflinching directness. In the end, despite his evident desire to do so, he can't sing after all.

In bar 51, a German augmented sixth chord violently tears us away from the D♯ minor dance scene and back to B minor with a disjunct leap of an augmented second in the bass.⁴² I hear this as a savage gathering of strength, the weakened subject bracing himself for one final push. The impact of the chord seems to compel the singer to take a giant breath on the downbeat, so that he can rear back, reset his technique, and launch into the tessitura of the high F♯ one last time. What follows in bars 52–53 is an oceanic wailing on the first syllable of the word 'manche', not really a melody at all but more of a primal scream, *fortissisimo*, a release of vocal sound that overflows the bounds of supple Schubertian lyricism. There is something of the melodramatic torch song here, something put on and play-acted, which continues as the melody subsides into a teary, overdetermined turn-like cadential figure, and at a suddenly withdrawn dynamic level. Susan Youens hears this figure as a sign of the Baroque, 'advertising its antiquity', that depicts the 'alte Zeit' now mentioned in the text.⁴³ To my ear, however, the figure alludes to nothing quite so distant. It reminds me instead of the oboe cadenza in the middle of the first movement of Beethoven's Fifth Symphony, which is to say that it is simply an expressive, sentimental turn shape familiar in music of the early nineteenth century. Schubert gives this icon of Romantic yearning a mournful, overburdened farewell, much as Mahler would later bid farewell to the very same figure in the final movement of his Ninth Symphony.⁴⁴ In the course of bars 51–56, the lineaments of Schubertian melody first disintegrate and then congeal from too much expressive pressure. Schubert has yet to give us anything that even approaches one of his quintessential melodies in this song, and now we know why—he no longer can. Every last drop of expression is wrung from a tune which cannot possibly bear all that is asked of it, either physically or stylistically.⁴⁵ In this last vocal heave of a disabled subject, we hear a fragment of a song that can never be sung again, and in the very intensity of its singing we feel the loss of what it used to provide. In that sense, this passage in 'Der Doppelgänger' is a kind of swan song. The final melody may humanise the subject, but it does not affirm him. It reveals his very human failure.

After this terminal effort, nothing is left except the resumption of the ostinato in bars 56–59, as though all this time it had been quietly continuing to unfold beneath the clamour of Schubert's botched attempts at dance and song. The unsettling clarity of the root-position C major chord in bar 59 that now occupies the ostinato's fourth bar has been a lightning rod for critical reflection, and rightly so. In light of the reading of the song I have been pursuing here, its greatest significance is that it is the direct result of the ostinato's earlier deformations: recalling bar 32, C♯ is again replaced by C, and at the same moment, recalling bar 41, F♯ again moves to G.[46] This profoundly dysfunctional chord, suffused with arcane otherness in the tonal context of B minor, bears witness to the ongoing breakdown of the ostinato's original identity. There is no longer even any resistance to this breakdown; we hear no wilful attempt at harmonic recalibration as in bars 9–12 and 19–22. Instead, the ostinato drifts with an empty, eerie stillness towards some other pitch configuration, some other key centre, some other unforeseen iteration of the pattern. Simply put, the protagonist's attempt to preserve his identity has failed. In the last four bars of the song, the piano crumples into a churchly cadence, once again resorting to an outmoded Baroque stereotype in order to execute a basic musical function—not repetition, as with the passacaglia, but closure.[47] The tonal ambivalence of the final B major triad is yet another poignant testament to the protagonist's diminished capacities.

Ultimately, in the reading of 'Der Doppelgänger' I have proposed here, the 'alte Zeit' in Schubert's personal remaking of Heine's poem turns out not to be a time before 1815 and the miseries of the Restoration, nor the early eighteenth century, nor some ancient, primeval past beyond all imagining. Instead, the gesture towards an 'alte Zeit' recalls something even closer to home for the composer: 'so many a night in times gone by' when Schubert sang and played his lieder for his friends and patrons. In this song Schubert laments a time when lyricism and dance were natural, unencumbered, effortless components of his identity as a physical human being and as a composer. He does so not by conjuring up that time in a nostalgic, idealised memory, but rather by brutally confronting the limitations of his present self in a fearless self-critique. John Gingerich has characterised the Heine songs, along with the String Quintet in C major, D 956, as 'music of tremendous courage in its refusal to shrink from the remembrance of loss or from the self-dividing consequences of introspection'.[48] In this reading of 'Der Doppelgänger,' I hope to have revealed yet another perspective on just what it was that Schubert felt he had lost.

Notes

1. Kristina Muxfeldt, 'Schubert, Platen, and the Myth of Narcissus', *Journal of the American Musicological Society* 49/3 (1996), pp. 480–527. Muxfeldt updated and expanded this essay in *Vanishing Sensibilities: Schubert, Beethoven, Schumann* (Oxford: Oxford University Press, 2012), pp. 160–209.

2. For a thorough account of censorship and police surveillance in early nineteenth-century Vienna and their effects on the cultural and artistic life of the city, see Alice M. Hanson, *Musical Life in Biedermeier Vienna*

(Cambridge: Cambridge University Press, 1985), pp. 34–60. See also Muxfeldt, *Vanishing Sensibilities*, p. xx.

3. Walburga Litschauer summarises this history in 'The Origin and Early Reception of *Schwanengesang*', in Martin Chusid (ed.), *A Companion to Schubert's 'Schwanengesang': History, Poets, Analysis, Performance* (New Haven, CT: Yale University Press, 2000), pp. 5–13.

4. For a summary of the particulars of the first few years of Schubert's illness, see Elizabeth Norman McKay, *Franz Schubert: a Biography* (Oxford: Clarendon Press, 1996), pp. 164–8.

5. For the most recent assertions of this claim, see David Bretherton, 'In Search of Schubert's Doppelgänger', *The Musical Times* 184/1884 (2003), p. 48; and Susan Youens, *Heinrich Heine and the Lied* (Cambridge: Cambridge University Press, 2007), p. 77. For literary critical commentary on Heine's poem along these lines, see S. S. Prawer, *Heine: the Tragic Satirist* (Cambridge: Cambridge University Press, 1961), pp. 4–5; and Andrew J. Webber, *The Doppelgänger: Double Visions in German Literature* (Oxford: Clarendon Press, 1996), p. 11.

6. As quoted by Richard Leppert in Theodor W. Adorno, *Essays on Music*, ed. Richard Leppert, trans. Susan H. Gillespie (Berkeley and Los Angeles: University of California Press, 2002), p. 520. The two essays by Adorno which deal with Beethoven's late style most directly are 'Late Style in Beethoven' (1937) and 'Alienated Masterpiece: the *Missa Solemnis*' (1959), in Adorno, *Essays*, pp. 564–83.

7. Daniel K. L. Chua, *The 'Galitzin' Quartets of Beethoven: Opp. 127, 132, 130* (Princeton, NJ: Princeton University Press, 1995); and Michael Spitzer, *Music as Philosophy: Adorno and Beethoven's Late Style* (Bloomington: Indiana University Press, 2006).

8. Margaret Notley, *Lateness and Brahms: Music and Culture in the Twilight of Viennese Liberalism* (Oxford: Oxford University Press, 2007); and Marianne Wheeldon, *Debussy's Late Style* (Bloomington: Indiana University Press, 2009).

9. See Christopher H. Gibbs, *The Life of Schubert* (Cambridge: Cambridge University Press, 2000), pp. 159–61; and McKay, *Franz Schubert*, pp. 318–20. For the basic facts pertaining to the question of when the songs in the *Schwanengesang* collection were composed, see Litschauer, 'The Origin and Early Reception of *Schwanengesang*', pp. 5–6.

10. Gibbs, *The Life of Schubert*, 109.

11. Richard Kramer, *Distant Cycles: Schubert and the Conceiving of Song* (Chicago: University of Chicago Press, 1994), p. 102. For more on this point, see Youens, *Heinrich Heine*, pp. 10–11; and Brian Newbould, *Schubert: the Music and the Man* (Berkeley and Los Angeles: University of California Press, 1997), p. 314.

12. Joseph N. Straus, *Extraordinary Measures: Disability in Music* (Oxford: Oxford University Press, 2012), p. 85. Chapter 5 (pp. 82–102) applies Straus's view of 'late style' as 'disability style' to works by Stravinsky, Bartók and Copland.

13. See ibid., pp. 63–6. Cone's original essay ('Schubert's Promissory Note: an Exercise in Musical Hermeneutics') can be found in Walther Frisch (ed.), *Schubert: Critical and Analytical Studies* (Lincoln: University of Nebraska Press, 1986), pp. 13–30.

14. David Løberg Code, 'Listening for Schubert's Doppelgängers', *Music Theory Online* 1/4 (1995).

15. Lawrence Kramer, *Franz Schubert: Sexuality, Subjectivity, Song* (Cambridge: Cambridge University Press, 1998), p. 57.

16. Ibid., p. 59.

17. Blake Howe, 'The Allure of Dissolution: Bodies, Forces, and Cyclicity in Schubert's Final Mayrhofer Settings', *Journal of the American Musicological Society* 62/2 (2009), pp. 271–322.

18. For one of the earliest suggestions of this idea, see Werner Thomas, '"Der Doppelgänger" von Franz Schubert', in Gerhard Schumacher (ed.), *Zur musikalischen Analyse* (Darmstadt: Wissenschaftliche Buchgesellschaft, 1974), p. 365.

19. Youens explores this possibility in *Heinrich Heine*, pp. 78–9.

20. Leo Black reflects on the potential meaning of this allusion in *Franz Schubert: Music and Belief* (Woodbridge: Boydell Press, 2003), pp. 164–5 and 167–8.

21. Chusid briefly considers some theories as to which period of music history Schubert might have been attempting to conjure here in 'Texts and Commentary', in *A Companion to Schubert's 'Schwanengesang'*, pp. 142–3. For a suggestion of what Schubert's use of historically distant compositional materials might mean from an Adornian perspective, see Bretherton, 'In Search of Schubert's Doppelgänger', p. 48.

22. For more on the figure's 'alterity', see Richard Kurth, 'Music and Poetry, a Wilderness of Doubles: Heine—Nietzsche—Schubert—Derrida', *19th-Century Music* 21/1 (1997), p. 24.

23. For a searching critical investigation of Schubertian repetition inspired by Adorno's essay on the composer from 1928, see Scott Burnham, 'Landscape and Music, Landscape as Truth: Schubert and the Burden of Repetition', *19th-Century Music* 29/1 (2005), pp. 31–41. Yonatan Malin explores the representational and psychological effects of repetition in Schubert's songwriting practice in *Songs in Motion: Rhythm and Meter in the German Lied* (Oxford: Oxford University Press, 2010), pp. 95–122.

24. For more on the role of this passage within the form of the movement as a whole, see Thomas Denny, 'Articulation, Elision, and Ambiguity in Schubert's Mature Sonata Forms: the Op. 99 Trio Finale in its Context', *Journal of Musicology* 6/3 (1988), pp. 350–2.

25. Hugh Macdonald, 'Schubert's Pendulum', in *Beethoven's Century: Essays on Composers and Themes* (Rochester, NY: University of Rochester Press, 2008), pp. 16–27.

26. Youens, *Heinrich Heine*, pp. 80–2; and Bretherton, 'In Search of Schubert's Doppelgänger', pp. 46–8.

27. Code, 'Listening for Schubert's Doppelgängers'; and Kurth, 'Music and Poetry', pp. 21–6.

28. Youens, *Heinrich Heine*, p. 75.

29. Kramer, *Franz Schubert*, p. 167.

30. 'Wußte er den eigensten Augenblick zu finden'. Till Gerrit Waidelich (ed.), *Franz Schubert: Dokumente 1817–1830*, vol. 1, *Texte: Programme, Rezensionen,*

Anzeigen, Nekrologe, Musikbeilagen und andere gedruckte Quellen (Tutzing: Hans Schneider, 1993), p. 517.

31. Kurth, 'Music and Poetry', p. 25.

32. Youens, *Heinrich Heine*, p. 82.

33. The only suggestion I have found in the literature that hints at the dance music latent in this passage is Kramer's reference to the 'ironic tonic-dominant dance around D sharp minor at "Was äffst du nach mein Liebesleid"' (*Distant Cycles*, 131).

34. See the reminiscences of Joseph von Spaun, Anton Ottenwalt and Leopold Sonnleithner in Otto Erich Deutsch (ed.), *Schubert: Memoirs by his Friends*, trans. R. Ley and J. Nowell (London: Adam & Charles Black, 1958), pp. 25, 121 and 133.

35. Ibid., p. 229.

36. For various accounts of Schubert singing his own songs in different contexts, see ibid., pp. 137–8, 182, 242 and 298.

37. McKay, *Franz Schubert*, pp. 12–13.

38. Schubert's singing voice at various points in his career is characterised by his contemporaries in Deutsch, *Schubert: Memoirs by his Friends*, pp. 76, 144–5, 179, 209–10, 227 and 336–7.

39. Kramer, *Franz Schubert*, p. 169.

40. Ibid., p. 170.

41. Ibid., p. 169.

42. Kramer, *Distant Cycles*, pp. 131–2.

43. Youens, *Heinrich Heine*, 83.

44. For some reflections on the finale of Mahler's Ninth Symphony and its treatment of the turn figure which resonate well with what I am arguing here, see Julian Johnson, *Mahler's Voices: Expression and Irony in the Songs and Symphonies* (Oxford and New York: Oxford University Press, 2009), pp. 277–82.

45. Here I have echoed Theodor Adorno's comment on Mahler's harmony: '[Mahler] charges tonality with an expression that it is no longer constituted to bear. Overstretched, its voice cracks'. See Adorno, *Mahler: a Musical Physiognomy*, trans. Edmund Jephcott (Chicago: University of Chicago Press, 1992), p. 20. Johnson relates this comment to the finale of Mahler's Ninth in *Mahler's Voices*, p. 281.

46. In choosing the word 'deformation' here, I do not mean to invoke the somewhat different and much more elaborate use of the term in James Hepokoski's and Warren Darcy's Sonata Theory, nor do I wish to step into the debate about the historical and cultural implications of the term vis-à-vis the concept of disability that arose as a result of Joseph Straus's critique of Hepokoski and Darcy. See Hepokoski and Darcy, *Elements of Sonata Theory* (New York: Oxford University Press, 2006), especially pp. 614–21; and Straus, *Extraordinary Measures*, pp. 110–16. Regarding the negative connotations of 'deformation', I believe they are appropriate here, but only because of the 'disabled' compositional persona that Schubert has intentionally created in this song.

47. My thanks to Scott Messing for prompting this observation.

48. John M. Gingerich, 'Remembrance and Consciousness in Schubert's C major String Quintet, D 956', *Musical Quarterly* 84/4 (2000), p. 631.

21

Challenging the Context

Reception and Transformation in Schubert's
'Der Musensohn', D 764, Op. 92 No. 1

Lorraine Byrne Bodley

A Brief Reception History of the Relationship between Goethe and Schubert

The impression of an unhappy relationship between Schubert and Goethe has without question been the most influential factor in perpetuating the myth of Goethe's lack of musical discernment. From the earliest days of Goethean reception, nineteenth-century literature bore the imprint of the Goethe cult, vaunting the master's merits in poetic and nationalistic terms, assessing the compositions of Goethe's works and taking a stance for or against the controversial direction of music. Schubert's lieder were seen as being at variance with Goethe's aesthetic theories of song, which scholars maintained demanded a strict adherence to principles of strophic song and the musical metrics of his poetry. Goethe, the canonical artist with the titanic personality, was thus set in antithesis with the image of 'poor Schubert', partly born of the Romantic idea of the 'unrecognised artistic genius, the artist who valiantly struggles for acceptance and yet is inexplicitly ignored by the world until after his death',[1] and this opposition has contributed to misconceptions about the poet's response to Schubert.[2] Goethe's rejection of Schubert's first book of songs was claimed to have been influenced by Carl Friedrich Zelter, to whom Goethe supposedly sent the songs for advice. Such arguments are clearly unfounded: in the 891 letters exchanged between these artists there is no mention of Schubert lieder; on the contrary, the letters prove the dispatch was never sent to Zelter, nor was he in Weimar during the period in which Schubert's first songbook arrived. In their portrayal of a 'neglected Schubert',[3] scholars have overlooked the significance of Goethe's acknowledgement of Schubert's second dedication in his diary as early as 1825:[4] Johann Nepomuk Hummel, Weimar's most eminent musician at the time, and Felix Mendelssohn, friend and musical advisor to Goethe, did not discover Schubert until 1827.[5] Whether Goethe's failure to respond to Schubert in a personal letter of thanks was linked to his reluctance to encourage the younger generation of Romantic literary artists[6] or coloured by the sad fact that Goethe and Schubert never met, we will never know. Yet what

Table 21.1 The wanderer motive in Schubert's Goethe settings

Lied	Date of composition
'Rastlose Liebe' (D 138), Op. 5 No. 1	19 May 1815
'Wandrers Nachtlied I' (D 224), Op. 4 No. 3	5 July 1815
'An die Türen' (D 478), Op. 12 No. 3	1816 & 1822
'Der Musensohn' (D 764), Op. 92 No.1	Beginning of December 1822
'Wandrers Nachtlied II' (D 768), Op. 96 No. 3	Before 24 July 1824

is clear from Metternich's new censorship laws, which were tightened up as a result of the Congress of Vienna, is that without the poet's written permission Schubert could not have published his Op. 19 lieder in Vienna with the dedication to Goethe on the title page.[7] At some point—perhaps on the same day that Goethe acknowledged receipt of these songs in his diary—a written missive *must* have been sent to Vienna to allow these songs to be published with this dedication. The loss of this letter,[8] coupled with the legend of Schubert's neglect and Goethe's 'Olympian aloofness [and] "blindness" to new writers of talent',[9] has fuelled misconceptions surrounding Goethe's neglect of Schubert.

The deep affinity between these artists, which until very recently has been overshadowed by the reception history, is continually unveiled in Schubert's Goethe settings. That Goethe was more important to Schubert that any other poet is affirmed not only by Spaun but by the eighty-two settings inspired by sixty-one of Goethe's poems, and by his intermittent return to a poet who had dominated his 1815 *Liederjahr*. Within these eighty-two Goethe settings are five *Wanderlieder*, two of which were composed between 1822 and 1824, when Schubert's preoccupation with a dispossessed, alienated wanderer figure was particularly intense (see Table 21.1). Goethe's identification with the wanderer theme is well-known. From an examination of his *Wanderlieder* by Goethe—in particular 'Der Musensohn' and 'An die Türen' (sung by Goethe's Harper), as well as the second setting of Goethe's *Wandrers Nachtlieder* poems—it is clear that Schubert is writing music that is defiantly in tune with the laws of his own artistic nature.

The Emergence of the *Wandererlied* in the *Goethezeit*

In order to understand the uniqueness of Schubert's settings of Goethe's *Wanderlieder*, it is important to understand the cultural context into which they were born. The *Wanderlied*, which emerged as a new discourse in the *Goethezeit*, was, of course, unique neither to Goethe nor to Schubert, but it marked the transformation of poetry and society at this time. With the decline around the turn of the nineteenth century of a society based on privilege, mobility became a key concept of modern life, above all through educational reform. Contemporary poetry associated this mobility with the figure of a wandering minstrel, and a sanguine and melancholic variant of being on one's way developed in contemporary literature that culminated in an image of the wanderer travelling through a season hostile to wandering, namely winter, Müller's *Winterreise* being a key example. Whereas seventeenth- and eighteenth-century folk poetry had abounded with *Reise-* and *Abschiedslieder*, such songs were sung by craftsmen whose departure at the door (usually accompanied by drink) symbolised social independence and freedom from the confines of work. By 1800 the wanderer was no longer a craftsman but a young man whose journey was in rapport with nature. Travelling became his home until, after a period of wandering and self-development, he encountered the beloved and recognised once again trusted signs that stemmed from the premise that love is home.

This new portrayal of the wanderer mirrored social developments at a time when knowledge of different cultures was closely connected to place. Whereas in the past those who wandered—for instance, gypsies and travelling musicians—were socially stigmatised, in the early nineteenth century academics and educated businessmen were for the first time encouraged to travel. Four reasons can be traced for this reform: sociological reform, Rousseau, the Alps and German educational reform. Even before the French Revolution, voices had been raised against craftsmen's travelling apprenticeships in favour of formal education. The *Assemblée nationale* implemented what enlightened absolutism had only dreamt of: the *Loi d'Allarde* of 2 March 1791 abolished collective industrial privileges and guilds, restructuring the work market before industrialisation and forcing neighbouring states to follow suit.

As wandering became less strongly associated with trades, it began to be recommended to readers, one of the most influential texts being Jean-Jacques Rousseau's *Émile, ou de l'éducation* (*Émile, or, On Education* [1762]), where the young adolescent is advised to stay close to nature (*status naturalis*) for as long as possible and to enter society (*status civilis*) as late as possible. In his novel Rousseau recommends the true philosophical art of travelling, because enjoyment of nature leads to the study of nature and vice versa; wandering enables one 'körperliche und geistige Bewegungen in eins zu verbinden' (to combine physical and psychological impetus);[10] it determines the natural rhythm of rest and departure. Most significant, at the end of Rousseau's travels there is a veiled reward: wandering leads to the ideal woman, to Sophia—wisdom.[11]

This association of wandering with self-education is evident in the emergence of the nineteenth-century *Bildungsreise*, travel guides and literature in the late eighteenth and early nineteenth centuries. J. R. Schinz's 1773 journey through Switzerland, J. G. Ebel's travel handbook for exploring Switzerland, Horace-Bénédict de Saussure's expeditions in the Alps and K. F. Burdach's *Bemerkungen und Gefühle auf einer Reise durch den Harz* are key examples.[12] In literary circles, Laurence Sterne's *Sentimental Journey through France and Italy* (1768) was particularly influential and was swiftly followed in Germany by J. G. Jacobi's *Winterreise* (1769) and *Sommerreise* (1770).[13] A lesser-known source and example of the type of enlightened absolutism prevalent at the turn of the nineteenth century are Ludwig Achim von Arnim's essay 'Von Volksliedern'—published in his and Clemens Brentano's collection *Des Knaben Wunderhorn* (1805) and dedicated to the composer Johann Friedrich Reichardt—in which society is held up as an *Arbeitshaus* and in which he advocated the need for wanderers and outsiders, without whom society would ossify.[14] That this imperative was directed at students is evident in Achim von Arnim's *Armut, Reichtum, Schuld und Buße der Gräfin Dolores*.[15]

Arnim's student wanderer mirrored the German educational reform known as the Humboldt Reform, in which the imperative of perpetual departure, 'die Wissenschaft als etwas noch nicht ganz Gefundenes und nie ganz Aufzufindendes zu betrachten und unablässig sie also solche suchen' (of knowledge as something not yet quite found, and never to be found once and for all and yet to be sought continuously) was directed at academics.[16] Various writings on the improvement of the educational system programmed the mobility of young men. For Fichte, youth is hostile to lethargy: 'der Jugend eigentlicher Charakter ist rastlose, nie unterbrochene Thätigkeit: natürlich und sich selbst überlassen kann sie nie ohne Beschäftigung seyn. Sie träge zu erblicken ist der Anblick des Winters mitten im Frühling' (the real character of youth is restless, uninterrupted activity: naturally and left to its own devices, it cannot exist without activity. To observe it being lazy is to catch sight of winter in the middle of spring).[17] The philosopher also distinguished between two types of citizens: the urban dweller und the academic, the *Philister* and the *Musensohn*, the former connected with the *artes mechanicae*, the latter with the *artes liberales*. Nineteenth-century literature abounded with both figures: J. M. R. Lenz's *Hochzeitscarmen für einen abtrünnigen Musensohn* (Wedding Song for an Unfaithful *Musensohn*) is an early and humorous example of the *Musenzögling* (*alumnus musarum*);[18] Goethe and Friedrich Schiller openly rebuked philistines in their *Musenalmanach für das Jahr 1797*,[19] and in educational writings J. G. Fichte and Friedrich Schleiermacher followed suit.[20] Whereas philistines were identified with habitual cycles, the connection of the *Musensohn* with movement is perpetually present, a key example of which is found in W. H. Wackenroder's *Herzensergießungen eines kunsliebenden Klosterbruders* (Confessions from the Heart of an Art-Loving Monk),[21] published in the year of Schubert's birth, in which the protagonist, Joseph Berglinger, sets out on a journey not in search of love but to become a musician.

Goethe's Identification with the Wanderer Figure

Just as wandering is a constant motive in Schubert's lieder, in Goethe poetry and wandering are frequently bound. As early as 1771 the poet refers to Shakespeare as the 'größte Wandrer' (greatest wanderer);[22] a late example is found in Wilhelm's reply in the *Wanderjarhre* (1821), where he is asked 'ob ihm nicht auch manchmal ein Lied bei seinen Fußwanderungen einfalle und das er so vor sich hin singe?' (whether sometimes a song also occurred to him on his hikes and which he then sings to himself).[23] In the third part of *Dichtung und Wahrheit* (1814) Goethe recounts how, when he finished his studies, he wandered between Darmstadt, Frankfurt and Bad Homburg and became accustomed 'auf der Straße zu leben' (to living on the street), thus earning him the name 'den Wanderer': 'Mehr als jemals war ich gegen offene Welt und freie Natur gerichtet. Unterwegs sang ich mir nur seltsame Hymne und Dithyramben, wovon noch eine, under dem Titel "Wandrers Sturmlied" übrig ist' (I felt more than ever orientated toward the open world and untamed nature. While walking I would intone strange hymns and dithyrambs, one of which survives under the title 'Wanderer's Storm Song').[24] In book 16 of *Dichtung und Wahrheit*, which was published posthumously, Goethe cites 'Der Musensohn'[25] as an example of the famous 'nachwandlerischen Dichten' (somnambulant inspiration), the *locus classicus* whereby a poet creates with an instrument of which he knows nothing, namely his subconscious:

Ich war dazu gelangt, das mir inwohnende dichterische Talent ganz als Natur zu betrachten, um so mehr als ich darauf angewiesen war, die äußere Natur als den Gegenstand desselben anzusehen. Die Ausübung dieser Dichtergabe konnte zwar durch Veranlassung erregt und bestimmt werden; aber am freudigsten und reichlichsten trat sie unwillkürlich, ja wider Willen hervor.

    Durch Feld und Wald zu schweifen,
    Mein Liedchen wegzupfeifen,
    So ging's den ganzen Tag.

Auch bei'm nächtlichen Erwachen trat derselbe Fall ein, und ich hatte oft Lust, wie einer meiner Vorgänger, mir ein ledernes Wamms machen zu lassen, und mich zu gewöhnen im Finstern, durch's Gefühl, das, was unvermuthet hervorbrach zu fixieren. Ich war so gewohnt mir ein Liedchen vorzusagen, ohne es wieder zusammenfinden zu können, daß ich einigemal an den Pult rannte und mir nicht die Zeit nahm einen quer liegenden Bogen zurecht zu rücken, sondern das Gedicht von Anfang bis zu Ende, ohne mich von der Stelle zu rühren, in der Diagonale herunterschrieb.[26]

[I had come to look upon my innate talent as natural; the more so as I had always been inclined to consider external nature as its proper object. The application of this poetic gift could indeed be inspired and determined by circumstances, but its most joyful, its richest action was spontaneous –even involuntary:

> Roaming through field and forest
> Whistling out my song
> I go from place to place

Awakening at night the same thing happened. I often wanted, like one of my predecessors, to get a leather jacket made for myself and to get used to writing in the dark so as to be able to fix down immediately all such unpremeditated (poems). It happened so often after composing a little piece in my head, that I could not remember it, so that I would hurry to the desk and at one standing write out the poem from beginning to end and, as I could not spare time to fix my paper, whatever way it lay, the [poetic] lines often crossed it diagonally.]

Whereas Goethe cites the first three lines of this lyric as the kind of poetic inspiration that he experienced in youth, when one examines the language and syntax of 'Der Musensohn', it becomes evident that its rhythm and form relate to the *Frühlingsgedichte* of the Classical years. The poem first appeared in a collection of lieder sent to the Berlin publisher Friedrich Gottlieb Unger on 4 November 1799[27] and was published in *Goethes Neue Schriften*, volume 7, the following year.[28]

The Uniqueness of Goethe's 'Der Musensohn' in the Nineteenth-Century *Wanderlied* Tradition

In contrast to nineteenth-century *Wanderlieder*, Goethe's *Wanderlieder* transform winter into spring. Such celebration of winter was evident in contemporary literature—in James Thomson's *Winter* (1726) and in Johann Friedrich Reichardt's *100 Lieder geselliger Freude* (1796–7), the first volume of which contained *Frühlings- und Sommerlieder*, the second volume, *Herbst- und Winterlieder*[29]—yet in contrast to these sources, Goethe's *Musensohn* greets the exchange of opposites in song. Two precursors for this are found in Goethe's *Wanderlieder*: 'Wandrers Sturmlied' (1772), where the poet, battling against winter's elements, is capable of transforming winter into spring:

Wen du nicht verlässest Genius,	Him whom you do not forsake, Genius,
Wirst im Schneegestöber Wärm umhüllen,	You will warp up warmly in the snowdrift;
Nach der Wärme ziehn sich Musen,	Toward the warmth approach the Muses,
Nach der Wärme Charitinnen,	Toward the warmth approach the Graces,
Wen du nicht verlässest Genius.[30]	Him whom you do not forsake, Genius.

and 'Harzreise im Winter' (1777):

Aber den Einsamen hüll'	But eclipse the solitary
In deine Goldwolken,	In your clouds of gold!
Umgib mit Wintergrün,	With winter green
Bis die Rose wieder heranreift,	Till the rose ripens again, encirle,
Die feuchten Haare,	O Love, the drenched locks
O Liebe, deines Dichters! [31]	Of your poet.

in which the designation 'Wintergrün' allows the winter metaphorically to become a spring, making it easier to bear, and love appears as an energy *sui generis* which protects the wanderer and guides him through the travails of winter:

Mit der dämmernden Fackel	With your dim-brimming torch
Leuchtest du ihm	you light his feet,
Durch die Furten bei Nacht,	across fords in the darkness
Über grundlose Wege	along precipitous paths
Auf öden Gefilden,	over desolate wastes;
Mit dem tausendfarbigen Morgen	you gladden his heart with
Lachst du ins Herz ihm;	The laughter of myriad-hued morning;
Mit dem beizenden Sturm	You raise him aloft
Trägst du ihn hoch empor. [32]	On the tingling storm.

It is interesting to see how in both poems the travails of winter are increasingly pushed into the background until in 'Der Musensohn' (1799) they disappear altogether. Whereas in 'Harzreise im Winter' the apostrophe to love is directed towards the 'Vater der Liebe', in 'Der Musensohn', the 'Musen' and the 'Busen' (lines 28 and 29) are two burning points of an ellipse, an antithesis Goethe highlights through the shared end rhyme. By counterpointing the release of the spirit with a desire for repose, Goethe suggests how the ego, in striving for free self-determination, everywhere encounters an objective, resistant element, ironically insinuating how delusive human freedom is. Unlike in Rousseau's *Émile*, there is no *causa finalis*. The Muses—the storm of creativity which flows in winter as in spring (or day and night, as Goethe reports in *Dichtung und Wahrheit*)—are the *causa efficiens*, the necessary and sufficient cause of this movement. Whereas Tieck's *Wanderlied* 'In der Ferne geht die Liebe' (Love Traverses into the Distance) identifies this unity between love and art, in 'Der Musensohn' love is one of the conditions of art.

Goethe's *Musensohn* is, of course, a play upon the legend of Orpheus—son of Apollo and the wisest of the Muses, Calliope, the Muse of epic poetry—and

Mercury (Hermes), whose winged heels signify his status as the god of travel—yet it also bears the imprint of the contemporary revival of interest in Homer, whose *Odyssey* and *Illiad* Calliope is believed to have inspired. In 1735 Thomas Blackwell published his *Enquiry into the Life and Writings of Homer*, which was translated into German by Johann Heinrich Voß (1776).[33] The poet was not portrayed as an outsider, exactly, but as a restless guest in society whose song is improvised—a representation directly mirrored in Goethe's 'Der Sänger' in *Wilhelm Meisters Lehrjahre*, and in the surrounding passages to the Harper's songs in that collection. In the image of Homer 'der Sänger' is 'ein Alter,' whereas Goethe's 'Liebling der Musen' is the nineteenth-century student wanderer. With simple ambiguity, Goethe here negates the Romantic dilemma: on the one hand, creativity is aligned with youth and presented as a phase of life, as endorsed by Goethe's citation of the poem in *Dichtung und Wahrheit*; on the other hand, it is perceived as lifelong.

Whether or not one accepts Goethe's citation of 'Der Musensohn' as an example of the creative powers of his youth, the lyric is clearly related to the *Rollengedichte* he wrote during his *Sturm und Drang* years. From Greek mythology, literature and art, Goethe saw that Greece's artists and thinkers had been racked by the daemon and brought by it near to destruction, but they had been strong enough to master it and turn its dreadful power to peaceful uses. Goethe discovered that although he could project this daemonic struggle outside himself into art, he needed symbols, images drawn from life, which by their very richness in association could be made to convey these manifold meanings, deep or subtle as the case might require. Searching through Classical art, Goethe found figures who seemed to have encountered what he had experienced and what he was seeking to express. In adopting these figures for his poetry, Goethe chose characters which were known to him and to the public and whose experience mirrored his own. 'Der Musensohn' is one such example.

In 'Der Musensohn' Goethe presents a symbol of an instinctive life urge that operates constantly as a necessity of nature. This insatiable drive is an abiding force of the *Musensohn*'s personality, and his relentless movement symbolises the force of existence, the movement of life. In striving with such fervent desire, the *Musensohn* illustrates the will to productive existence and never-ceasing development. This longing for ever-higher achievement suggests how constant and progressive striving gives permanent substance to human beings' existence. In 'Der Musensohn' Goethe suggests how in people, as in nature, there is no rest, no pause, only eternal activity and creation. The questing mind of the *Musensohn* is involved in never-ceasing formation and transformation; yet, paradoxically, in the midst of such variation, a constant is revealed. The unlimited striving that we see in 'Der Musensohn' is operative in nature: just as nature produces new life, new existence, our lives are presented as a process of gradual, constant becoming.

This concept of *Steigerung*, an upward intensification and constant striving for perfection, mirrors the eighteenth-century belief that humans' capacity for perfecting themselves and their will to do so were an expression of a universal tendency. In 'Der Musensohn' Goethe reveals how this principle of 'perfectibility' is immanent in the world: in its life processes and in all living things, the spiritual potency of an 'ever-striving ascent' is at work. Whereas 'Meeresstille' and its companion poem, 'Glückliche Fahrt', portray the polarity by which the movement of life is produced, in 'Der Musensohn' Goethe suggests the need of another basic force to give this movement an inner dynamic that drives it forwards and gives it direction.[34] By juxtaposing the protagonist's continuous endeavour with a desire for rest, the poet propounds an ever-striving polarity and progress through intensification.

Goethe's perception of music is personified in 'Der Musensohn'. In his appraisal of this lyric, Trunz argues that Goethe's identification with the figure of the artist (an *Augenmensch*) is more characteristic of the poet.[35] However, although Goethe related to the artist during his early period, his identification with the musician continued throughout his life.[36] The poet's continual involvement with music manifests itself not only in the *Sprachmusik* or euphony of his verse, but also in the figures he portrays, Goethe's *Musensohn* and Harper being key examples.[37] When one considers the theme of the daemon, it is characteristic that Goethe should choose a musician,[38] rather than an artist, as his protagonist, for he considered the daemon to be 'present in music to the highest degree'[39] and maintained that 'it manifests itself more in musicians than in painters'.[40] Throughout the poem the *Musensohn* is defined in terms of his musical attributes (see Table 21.2);[41] all of these properties are introduced and accompanied by the strong rhythms of the piece, and there is so much emphasis laid on the aspects of language which share a common ground with music that it is difficult to imagine the piece as not being sung.

Whereas Plato and Aristotle depict the musician as a sinister figure who has the power to subvert his audience,[42] Goethe's *Musensohn* is, characteristically, a benevolent figure through whom the poet explores the relationship between the musician and his language, and between his language and the world.[43] This perception of music as a highly refined and subtle means of exchange and interfusion pervades Goethe's correspondence and literary works. In a letter to Zelter dated 28 June 1831, he speaks of music as a 'symbolische Sprache die jeder verstehn muß' (symbolic language which everyone must understand),[44] while in the *Wanderjahre* we are told that music's very vagueness, its freedom from semantic convention, means that the composer 'speaks' to his listeners directly and immediately through musical form.[45] So too the Pythagorean concept of a harmonious universe, found in Leibnizian thought[46] and supported by the pansophists, is explored in Goethe's literary works in various ways.[47] In 'Der Musensohn' the idea of music and concordant social relations is portrayed in various kinds of kinship: the relationship between the sexes, the individual with the group,

Table 21.2 Goethe, 'Der Musensohn': text and translation

'Der Musensohn'[a]		'The Son of the Muses'
Durch Feld und Wald zu schweifen,	a	Roaming through fields and woods
Mein Liedchen wegzupfeifen,	a	Whistling out my song
So gehts von Ort zu Ort!	b	I go from place to place!
[*So gehts von Ort zu Ort!*]		[*I go from place to place!*]
Und nach dem Takte reget,	c	And they all stir,
Und nach dem Maß beweget	c	They all move on in measure with me,
6 Sich alles an mir fort.	b	Keeping time with me.
[*Und nach dem Maß beweget*		[*They all move on in measure with me,*
Sich alles an mir fort.]		*Keeping time with me.*]
Ich kann sie kaum erwarten		I can scarcely wait for them to appear
Die erste Blum' im Garten,		The first flower in the garden
Die erste Blüt' am Baum.		The first blossom on the tree.
Sie grüßen meine Lieder,		They greet my songs,
Und kommt der Winter wieder,		And when the winter comes again
12 Sing' ich noch jenen Traum.		I am still singing my dream of them
[*Sing' ich noch jenen Traum.*]		[*I am still singing my dream of them.*]
Ich sing' ihn in der Weite,		I sing it far and wide,
Auf Eises Läng' und Breite,		Up and down and across the ice,
Da blüht der Winter schön!		And the winter blossoms in beauty!
[*Da blüht der Winter schön!*]		[*And the winter blossoms in beauty!*]
Auch diese Blüte schwindet,		This blossom also vanishes,
Und neue Freude findet		And new pleasures are to be found
18 Sich auf bebauten Höhn.		On the fertile hills
[*Und neue Freude findet*		[*And new pleasures are to be found*
Sich auf bebauten Höhn.]		*On the fertile hills.*]
Denn wie ich bei der Linde		For when, under the linden tree,
Das junge Völkchen finde,		I find a crowd of young people,
Sogleich erreg' ich sie.		I at once stir them to excitement.
Der stumpfe Bursche bläht sich,		Dull lads puff themselves up
Das steife Mädchen dreht sich		And prim girls pirouette
24 Nach meiner Melodie.		To my melody.
[*Nach meiner Melodie.*]		[*To my melody.*]

'Der Musensohn'[a]	'The Son of the Muses'
Ihr gebt den Sohlen Flügel	You who give my feet wings,
Und treibt, durch Tal und Hügel,	And drive, over hill and dale,
Den Liebling weit von Haus.	your favourite far from home
[*Den Liebling weit von Haus.*]	[*your favourite far from home*]
Ihr lieben holden Musen,	You dear sweet Muses,
Wann ruh' ich ihr am Busen	When shall I at last find rest again
30 Auch endlich wieder aus?	On her bosom?
[*Wann ruh' ich ihr am Busen*	[*When shall I at last find rest again*
Auch endlich wieder aus?]	*On her bosom?*]

[a] Goethe, 'Der Musensohn', in Karl Richter, Herbert G. Gopfert, Norbert Miller, Gerhard Sauder and Edith Zehm (eds), *Werke*, 23 vols (Munich: Carl Hanser Verlag, 2002), vol. 6, no. 1, pp. 43–4.

the individual and group with the world. Through this idea of *Harmonie* as a coordinated whole,[48] an interaction of opposites, Goethe alludes to a more comprehensive harmony via the principle of *Steigerung*.[49] These Pythagorean rhythms of systole and diastole, of arsis and thesis, are explored in the *Tonlehre*, where Goethe connects musical rhythm directly and explicitly with physical movement.[50] Although this association is evident from the opening lines of 'Der Musensohn', Goethe crystallises the image in stanza 5. The linden tree is renowned for its soporific qualities, yet the stolid youth, who is transmuted to one teeming with a sense of pride, or the demure girl, who pirouettes to the piper's song, suggest how the *Musensohn* dissolves resistance.[51] As August Wilhelm Schlegel remarked, 'In ihrem Ursprunge macht Poesie mit Musik und Tanz ein unteilbares Ganzes aus' (in their origins poetry, music and dance constitute an indivisible unity), here too— as in Ludwig Tieck's *Franz Sternbalds Wanderungen* and Goethe's portrayal of Mignon—boundaries between music, poetry and dance dissolve.[52]

Schubert's setting of 'Der Musensohn', D 764, Op. 92 No. 1 (Early December 1822)

Schubert's setting is the best-known of the four Goethe settings he composed in December 1822.[53] Although the direction, *ziemlich lebhaft*, is almost always interpreted in relation to speed, Schubert used this term to indicate vivacity: it denotes the mood of the poem, not the tempo. The piano prelude, which opens with a waltz-like figuration in 6/8 time alternating between the upper and lower voices, immediately apprehends the iambic tetrameter patterns of

Goethe's six-line stanzas: *aabccb*, a Rococo lyrical form popular in the eighteenth century (see Example 21.1).[54]

In verses 1, 3 and 5 Schubert elongates these six-line stanzas by repeating the third line, thereby imparting a quadratic construction to the first half of the strophe and extending the second half to five lines. Through this extension, each section is granted a codetta: as the first section cadences twice on the tonic, the sixth line passes through the dominant before returning to the tonic on the repeat of the fifth and sixth lines. Schubert thus alters Goethe's stanzaic structure, but his melodic structure accentuates the metrical patterns of Goethe's verse, in which the main stress of lines 1 and 2, and lines 4 and 5 ('schweifen', 'wegfeifen', 'reget' and 'beweget', 'findet' and 'schwindet' in the third stanza) falls on the penultimate syllable, thereby mirroring Goethe's feminine end rhymes, all of which endorse the piper's movement. For the second and fourth stanzas, Schubert changes the key signature to B major and modulates to the new key via a pivot note, B♮, which is common to both tonic chords. Schubert's tonality changes without the connecting modulation, as the vocal line moves from the upbeat in one key to the downbeat in another. While this fluent though sudden change from the tonic to the mediant major is characteristic of Schubert's style, the musical consequences of the pairing of G major and B (or A♭ and C in the first variant[55]) runs deep. It mirrors the emergence of the lyrical 'ich' in stanza 2 and observes the structure of Goethe's strophes, where verses 1, 3 and 5 portray the reality of the *Musensohn*'s wandering, while in verses 2 and 4 the piper-poet's feelings are expressed. Schubert underscores this change by altering the wandering motive in the accompaniment without slowing the rhythm (see Example 21.2).

He also breaks the iambic rhythm of Goethe's verse for the first time in favour of stressing a central development in Goethe's *Wanderlied*—'die erste Blüt' (bars

Example 21.1 Schubert, 'Der Musensohn', D 764, bars 1–4

Example 21.2 Schubert, 'Der Musensohn', D 764, bars 30–32

34–35), where winter finally yields to spring. Schubert stresses the *Musensohn*'s ability to turn winter to spring by composing the final line of Goethe's poem with a simple melody punctuated by quaver accompaniment. Its restatement is then rhythmically and musically embellished, signalling a return to frivolity of section 1, where the *Musensohn* recognises winter as 'schön blühend'.

Although 'Der Musensohn' is much acclaimed, it is generally held that Schubert misinterprets the poet's 'Ariel-like longing for release' in the final stanza.[56] This desire for repose does not signal a change of tone, but is a rhetorical question affirming how the *Musensohn* can never rest, never fulfil himself, except at the cost of renouncing all action.[57] When one peruses Goethe's final strophe, this movement is continued through the active verbs 'geben' and 'treiben' as the poet is driven far from home. Schubert's setting does not misinterpret or consciously ignore the poet's call for rest, but follows the movement inherent in this strophe, from which the poet seeks repose. Schubert's *piano* dynamic and ritardando on the first syllable of 'Busen' also highlights Goethe's polarisation of 'Busen' and 'Musen' and accentuates the two poles of human existence.[58] Just as the cyclical alteration of Schubert's setting is an image of unlimited becoming, the incessant movement of his conclusion endorses the myth of eternal homecoming; symbol, idea and phenomenon coincide and are grasped as one.

As with all of Schubert's *Wanderlieder*, the wandering rhythms of 'Der Musensohn', with their regular beat, not only express physical motion but also indicate a path through life in the sense of a personal destiny. Goethe's mysterious Mignon walks a solitary path through life: several of her songs put one in mind of the pavane or *Totentanz*, which in Schubert's hands gently points towards an inexorable fate. In 'An die Türen' the descending bass line intimates the dragging footsteps of the Harper, who predicts the onset of madness. Only in 'Wandrers Nachtlied'[59] is rest granted (see Table 21.3). Whereas Goethe recognised the inevitability of his own eventual death when he wrote this lyric on the wall of a wooden hunting cabin on the Gickelhahn on the evening of 6

Table 21.3 Goethe, 'Wandrers Nachtlied II': text and translation

'Wandrers Nachtlied II'	'The Wayfarer's Night Song II'
Über allen Gipfeln	Over all the hilltops
Ist Ruh,	It is still,
In allen Wipfeln	In all the treetops
Spürest du	You can hardly feel
Kaum einen Hauch;	A breath stirring.
Die Vöglein schweigen im Walde.	The little birds are silent in the forest.
Warte nur, balde	Wait! Soon
Ruhest du auch.	You too will be still

September 1780, when he returned to Illmenau, on the eve of his eighty-third birthday, he was moved to tears as he reread his own verse. Impending death was a reality just as it was for Schubert when he set this poem. Although poetically and musically 'Wandrers Nachtlied' seems to be the polar opposite of 'Der Musensohn', the same principle is at work in both poems. Both wanderers are embraced by nature and reveal an extraordinary permeation of self and world; both portray natural scenes which record the poet's intuitive comprehension of a specific reality; both invite us to ponder the meaning of 'ruhen' in their closing lines, where the lyrical 'ich' is now exchanged for 'du'.[60] In conversation with Chancellor Friedrich von Müller on 6 June 1830, Goethe used the term in relation to his own death, claiming, 'I am old enough to desire repose'. In 'Der Musensohn', as in 'Wandrers Nachtlied', rest is linked with labour, with life, and it alludes to the concept of circularity as it effects regeneration: death is presented and accepted as a phenomenon of life. In 'Wandrers Nachtlied', Goethe captures the tension between these countervailing forces in line 5, where he writes 'hardly a breath'. The image implies death, and yet, by introducing the word 'kaum' (hardly), Goethe suggests signs of life. Goethe's notion of nothingness in 'Wandrers Nachtlied' is not the absolute negation experienced in 'Meeresstille' but indifferentiation or, in other words, the absence of conflicts and contrasts in 'Der Musensohn'.

It would be easy to read each of these settings as a confessional identification with Goethe's wanderer. Yet Schubert, like Goethe, understood that personality is an invention as much as a discovery—that a personal voice is only achieved self-consciously, over the long haul. In other words, art takes one beyond self-expression and moves towards the realisation of new selves. For Schubert there is never a single 'self'; his music reflects the reality of multiple, even antithetical selves. So while his settings of Goethe's *Wanderlieder* are clearly rooted in 'significant soil', a place that possessed autobiographical resonance for Schubert, the notion that art directly mirrors reality is rather callow. In his earlier writings Wittgenstein tended to see language as a mirror of reality.[61] Richard Rorty, in *Philosophy and the Mirror of Nature* (1982), argues that language does not hold a mirror up to nature but offers tools for dislodging shards of meaning from reality.[62] Applying this to music: although Schubert's and Goethe's *Wanderlieder* are artefacts standing apart from reality, reality nonetheless inheres in their particulars.

In 'Wanderers Nachtlied II' as in 'Der Musensohn', Goethe's wanderer is not merely the poet, but a finite being whose existence is endeavour, whose striving never slackens—however he may try to suppress it—until death. This philosophical principle found expression in Schubert's life and lieder. We only have to glance at Schubert's compositional output to be reminded of how rigorously and extensively and in what singular solitude he entered upon a way to art and followed it to the end. Despite the personal tragedy in his life, there is a wonderful steadiness of endeavour in the works of Schubert, and it is this pilgrim tenacity that gives the music its staying power. Although Schubert clearly identified with Goethe's *Wanderlieder*, it is not hindsight which makes these songs sound like a gauntlet thrown down before history. Schubert's early death may have reinforced a tragic association with Goethe's Harper, but in his music he is a constant reminder of the daemonic strength of his art, its covenant with the singing voice of Orpheus, the sheer spellbinding power of song.

Notes

1. Christopher Gibbs, '"Poor Schubert": Images and Legends of the Composer', in Gibbs (ed.), *The Cambridge Companion to Schubert* (Cambridge: Cambridge University Press, 1997), pp. 36–55.

2. See, for example, R. Boehmer-Aachen, 'Goethe und Schubert', *Rheinische Musik- und Theaterzeitung* 14 (1913), pp. 486–9; Konrad Volker, 'Schubert und Goethe', *Die Musik* 14 (1915), p. 129; M. Zeiner, 'Goethe und Schubert', *Die Quelle* 79 (1929), p. 105; Paul Riesenfeld, 'Goethe und Schubert', *Signale für die musikalische Welt* 90 (1932), p. 267; Konrad Huschke, 'Schubert und Goethe', *Musica* 7 (1953), pp. 580–1; Alexander Witeschnik, 'Goethe und Schubert: Die Geschichte einer einseitigen Liebe', *Jahrbuch des Wiener-Goethe Vereins* 67 (1963), pp. 78–85; Joseph Müller-Blattau, 'Franz Schubert, der Sänger Goethes', in Müller-Blattau (ed.), *Goethe und die Meister der Musik* (Stuttgart: Klett, 1969), pp. 62–80; David Dalton, 'Goethe and the Composers of his Time', *The Music Review* 34 (1973), pp. 157–74; Ronald Taylor, 'Goethe, Schubert and the Art of Song', in Volker Dürr and Géza v. Molnár (eds), *Versuche zu Goethe: Festschrift für Erich Heller* (Heidelberg: Lothar Stiehm Verlag, 1976), pp. 141–9; and Frederick W. Sternfeld, *Goethe and Music: a List of Parodies and Goethe's Relationship to Music: a List of References* (New York: New York Public Library, 1954), pp. v–ix and 7–22.

3. Gibbs, 'Poor Schubert', pp. 46–8. See also the review of Newman Flower, *Franz Schubert: the Man and his Circle*, in the *New York Times*, 25 November 1928, cited in Robert Winter, *Whose Schubert?*, 19th-Century Music 17/1 (1993), p. 97.

4. 'Sendung von Schubert aus Wien, von meinen Liedern Kompositionen' (Package of My Song Compositions from Franz Schubert of Vienna), in Gustav von Loeper, Erich Schmidt, Hermann Friedrich Grimm, Wilhelm Scherer, Bernhard Seuffert and Ludwig Suphan (eds), *Goethes Werke* (Weimar: Hermann Bohlaus Nachfolger, 1887–1912); hereafter cited as Goethe, *WA (Weimarer Ausgabe)*; WA, ser. III, vol. 10, 16 June 1825, pp. 68–9.

5. R. Larry Todd, *Mendelssohn: a Life in Music* (Oxford: Oxford University Press, 2003), p. 72.

6. Johann Peter Eckermann, *Gespräche mit Goethe*, 2 vols (Leipzig: F. A. Brockhaus, 1836; reprint, Stuttgart: Reclam, 1998), p. 343.

7. Otto Biba, 'Goethe in the Vienna Music Scene of his Era', in, Lorraine Byrne Bodley (ed.), *Goethe: Musical Poet, Musical Catalyst* (Dublin: Carysfort Press, 2004), p. 27.

8. Ibid.

9. Lesley Sharpe, introduction to Lesley Sharpe (ed.), *The Cambridge Companion to Goethe* (Cambridge: Cambridge University Press, 2002), p. 2.

10. Jean-Jacques Rousseau, *Emil, oder Über die Erziehung*, trans. Ludwig Schmidts, 4th edn (Paderborn: Ferdinand Schöningh, 1978), p. 127.

11. 'Wenn Sophie, ehe wir fünfzig Meilen [lieue à 4 km = ca. 200 km] auf diese Weise gewandert sind, nicht vergessen ist, muss ich wenig geschickt oder Emil wenig neugierig gewesen sein' (If Sophie has not been forgotten before we've gone fifty miles, I must be unskilful or Emil not curious). Rousseau, *Emil*, pp. 450f.

12. Johann Rudolf Schinz, *Beyträge zur nähern Kenntniß des Schweizerlandes*, 2 vols (Zurich, 1783), Vorerinnerung, vol. 1, p. iv, and *Die vergnügte Schweizerreise anno 1773*, ed. James Schwarzenbach (Zurich: Thomas Verlag o. J., 1773 [1952]). Johann Gottfried Ebel, *Anleitung auf die nützlichste und genussvollste Art in der Schweiz zu reisen*, 2 vols (Leipzig: Breitkopf, 1798; rev. 1802), vol. 1, p. 3. Horace-Bénédict de Saussure, *Voyages dans les Alpes, precédés d'un essai sur l'histoire naturelle des environs de Genève*, 2 vols (Genève, 1779), vol. 1, 'Discurs préliminaire', p. xix. Karl Friedrich Burdach, *Bemerkungen und Gefühle auf einer Reise durch den Harz* (Leipzig, 1798 [r.1800]).

13. Laurence Sterne, *Sentimental Journey through France and Italy* (London: T. Becket & P. A. de Hondt, 1768). Johann Georg Jacobi, *Winterreise* (Düsseldorf, 1769). Johann Georg Jacobi, *Die Sommerreise* (Halle im Magdeburgischen: C. H. Hemmerde, 1770).

14. Ludwig Achim von Arnim, 'Von Volksliedern', in *Des Knaben Wunderhorn*, ed. Achim von Arnim and Clemens Brentano (Berlin: Riemer, 1805–8).

15. Ludwig Achim von Arnim, *Armut, Reichtum, Schuld und Buße der Gräfin Dolores* (Berlin: Riemer, 1810), in Achim von Arnim, *Sämtliche Romane und Erzählungen*, ed. Walther Migge (Munich: Carl Hanser Verlag, 1962–5), vol. 1.

16. See, for example, Wilhelm von Humboldt, 'Über die innere und äußere Organization der höheren wissenschaftlichen Anstalten in Berlin' (1810), in Ernst Anrich (ed.), *Die Idee der deutschen Universität: Die fünf Grundschriften aus der Zeit ihrer Neubegründung durch klassischen Idealismus und romantischen Realismus* (Darmstadt: Wissenschaftliche Buchgesellschaft,1964), p. 376; Heinrich Steffans, 'Vorlesungen über die Idee der Universitäten' (1808–9), in Anrich, *Die Idee der deutschen Universität*, pp. 352–3; Friedrich Schleiermacher, *Gelegentliche Gedanken über Universitäten in deutschen Sinn: Nebst einem Anhang über eine neu zu errichtende*, in Anrich, *Die Idee der deutschen Universität*, p. 283; and Johann Gottlieb Fichte, 'Einige Vorlesungen über die Bestimmung des Gelehrten' (1794), in Fichte, *Werke*, ed. I. H. Fichte (Bonn: Adolphus-Marcus, 1834–5; reprint, Berlin: Walther de Gruyter, 1971), vol. 6, p. 328.

17. Johann Gottlieb Fichte, *Über das Wesen des Gelehrten und seine Erscheinungen im Gebiete der Freiheit* (1805), in Fichte, *Werke*, ed. I. H. Fichte (Berlin: Walther de Gruyter, 1971), vol. 6, p. 398.

18. Jakob Michael Reinhold Lenz, *Hochzeitscarmen für einen abtrünnigen Musensohn*, in Lenz, *Werke und Briefe*, ed. Sigrid Damm, 3 vols (Leipzig: Insel Verlag, 1987).

19. See, for example, Johann Wolfgang von Goethe, *Xenien*, No. 43: 'Fort ins Land der Philister, ihr Füchse mit brennenden Schwänzen / Und verderbet der Herrn reife papierene Saat' (Off to the land of the Philistines, you foxes with burning tails / And destroy man's intellectual harvest).

20. Fichte, 'Über das Wesen des Gelehrten', p. 395; and Friedrich Schleiermacher, 'Gelegentliche Gedanken über Üniversitäten in deutschem Sinn: Nebst einem Anhang über eine neu zu errichtende', in Ernst Anrich (ed.), *Die Idee der deutschen Universität: Die fünf Grundschriften aus der Zeit ihrer Neubegründung durch klassischen Idealismus und romantischen Realismus* (Darmstadt: Wissenschaftliche Buchgesellschaft, 1964), 229.

21. Wilhelm Heinrich Wackenroder, *Herzensergießungen eines kunsliebenden Klosterbruders* (Berlin: Ungeer, 1797), in Wilhelm Heinrich Wackenroder, *Sämtliche Werke und Briefe: Historisch-kritische Ausgabe*, ed. Silvio Vietta and Richard Littlejohns (Heidelberg: Winter, 1991).

22. Johann Wolfgang von Goethe, *Werke*, ed. Erich Trunz (Hamburg: Deutscher Taschenbuch Verlag, 2008); hereafter cited as *HA* (*Hamburger Ausgabe*); *HA* 12, p. 224.

23. *HA* 8, p. 312.

24. *HA* 9, p. 521.

25. The date of 'Der Musensohn' is uncertain. The *Berliner Ausgabe* dates it to 1775, establishing it in the early Frankfurt years, whereas Trunz places it in the years leading up to 1799. See Goethe, *Werke*, ed. Karl Richter, Herbert G. Gopfert, Norbert Miller, Gerhard Sauder and Edith Zehm, 23 vols (Munich: Carl Hanser Verlag, 2002); hereafter cited as *MA* (*Münchner Ausgabe*); *MA* 6.1, p. 43; *MA* 16, p. 716.

26. *Dichtung und Wahrheit*, book 4, chapter 16; *HA* 10, pp. 80f.

27. Goethe to Unger, 4 November 1799; *WA* IV, 4, pp. 212–14.

28. The edition of the text which Schubert used was *Gedichte von Goethe: Erster Theil; Lyrische Gedichte* (Vienna, 1810), pp. 9–10.

29. Johann Friedrich Reichardt, *100 Lieder geselliger Freude* (1796–7), in Johann Friedrich Reichardt, *Lieder für die Jugend* (Leipzig: G. Fleischer der Jüngern, 1799).

30. Goethe, 'Wandrers Sturmlied'; *MA* 1.1, p. 197.

31. Goethe, 'Harzreise im Winter', lines 60–6; *MA* 2.1, p. 41.

32. Ibid. (lines 67–74).

33. Thomas Blackwell, *Enquiry into the Life and Writings of Homer* (London: J. Oswald, 1775); trans. Johann Heinrich Voß as *Untersuchung über Homers Leben und Schriften* (Leipzig, 1776).

34. Stephen Jackson's reading of 'Der Musensohn' (D 764), who 'dances off through clear air to a land of immortal youth', is an example of the misunderstanding of Goethe's verse in musicology; see Jackson, *Franz Schubert: an Essential Guide to his Life and Works* (London: Pavillion Books, 1996), p. 44.

35. *HA* 1, p. 643. Trunz's opinion is shared by many musicologists; see Romain Rolland, 'Goethe's Interest in Music', *Musical Quarterly* 17 (1931), p. 158.

36. See Goethe, *Farbenlehre; HA* 13, p. 493.

37. See Johann Wolfgang von Goethe, 'Der Musiker', *Aus einem Maskenzug*, in Goethe, *Werke*, 22 vols (Berlin: Aufbau, 1965-78); hereafter cited as *BA* (*Berliner Ausgabe*); *BA* 4, pp. 608-42.

38. For a contrary opinion, see Trunz, who considers that 'Der Musensohn' is 'ohne dämonische Tiefe und ohne innere Gefahr'; *HA* 1, p. 643.

39. Eckermann, *Gespräche mit Goethe*, 8 March 1831, pp. 358-9; 7 April 1829, pp. 263-6; 6 December 1829, pp. 283-5; 14 February 1831, pp. 341-2; and 2 March 1831, pp. 356-7. Goethe's letters to Zelter also develop this theme: see, for example, 24 August 1823, *MA* 20.1, pp. 745-8; and 9 November 1829, *MA* 20.2, pp. 1274-6.

40. Eckermann, *Gespräche mit Goethe*, 2 March 1831, p. 356; see also Goethe to Zelter, 19 October 1829, *MA* 20.2, pp. 1265-7; *Schriften zur Natur- und Wissenschaftslehre, WA* II, 11, pp. 174; and *Wilhelm Meisters Wanderjahre*, book 1, chapter 6, *HA* 8, p. 69.

41. The image of wings that Goethe employs in 'Der Musensohn' is one which he often uses in relation to music; see, for example, his reference to Hummel's musical genius in Eckermann, *Gespräche mit Goethe*, 7 April 1829, p. 1264.

42. See, for example, Plato, *Politics*, book VIII, p. vi, and the *Republic*, book III, p. 373.

43. See, for example, 'Der Rattenfänger'; *Novella*; 'Kunstgeschichte', hereafter cited *MuR (Maximen und Reflexionen); HA* 12, p. 474.

44. Goethe to Zelter, 28 June 1831, *MA* 20.2, pp. 1495-7; and Goethe to Zelter, 9 November 1829, *MA* 20.2, pp. 1274-6.

45. *Wanderjahre*, 'Betrachtungen im Sinne der Wanderer', *HA* 8, p. 290; *Schriften zur Natur- und Wissenschaftslehre: Physikalische Wirkungen, WA* II, 11, p. 174.

46. Gottfried Wilhelm Leibniz, *Monadologie* (1714; reprint, Dordrecht: Kluwer Academic, 1996).

47. *Wilhelm Tischbeins Idyllen* 14, *WA* I, 49, p. 329; *MuR, HA* 12, p. 474.

48. *Wanderjahre* II, 1, *HA* 8, p. 152 and II, 8, p. 244; *MuR*, 'Nachlaß', *HA* 12, p. 474. *Goethe Briefe*, Goethe to Christiane, 12 September 1815, *HA* 3, pp. 319-20.

49. *MuR, HA* 12, p. 473; *Farbenlehre, WA* II, 1, p. 305.

50. *Tonlehre*, 'Rhythmik', *WA* II, 11, p. 290. See also *MuR, BA* 18, p. 248.

51. Goethe's scene of youthful pleasure, which is reminiscent of 'Branders Lied', *Faust I*, 'Vor dem Tor', 'Bauern unter der Linde', line 949, *HA* 3, pp. 36-7.

52. See, for example, Goethe's *Lehrjahre, HA* 7, p. 131; *Werther* I, 16 July, *HA* 6, pp. 38-9; *Novelle, BA* 12, p. 429; and *Wanderjahre* III, 1, *HA* 8, p. 312.

53. See Otto Erich Deutsch, *Schubert: Die Dokumente seines Lebens und Schaffens*, 3rd edn, (Leipzig: Breitkopf & Härtel, 1996), hereafter cited as *Dok.*; *Dok*, pp. 173 and 526; and *Schubert: Die Erinnerungen seiner Freunde*, 2nd edn (Leipzig: Breitkopf & Härtel, 1996), hereafter cited as *Erinn.; Erinn.*, p. 26.

54. Bernd Witte, Theo Buck, Hans-Dietrich Dahnke, Regina Otto and Peter Schmidt (eds), *Goethe-Handbuch*, 4 vols. (Stuttgart: J. B. Metzler, 1996–9), vol. 1, p. 269.

55. I am referring here to Maurice Brown's categorisation, where 'variant' is intended as a revision of a song as opposed to a different version (a re-setting); see 'The Posthumous Publication of the Songs', in *Essays on Schubert* (London: Macmillan, 1966), p. 268. In Susan Youens's article 'Schubert and his Poets: Issues and Conundrums', in Gibbs, *The Cambridge Companion to Schubert*, she uses the term 'version' in her discussion of Schubert's resettings. See Sterling Lambert's insightful discussion of this issue in his introduction to *Re-Reading Poetry: Schubert's Multiple Settings of Goethe* (Suffolk: Boydell & Brewer, 2009), pp. 1–15, especially pp. 5–7.

56. John Reed, *The Schubert Song Companion* (Manchester: Manchester University Press, 1985), p. 120; and Richard Capell, *Schubert's Songs*, ed. M. Cooper (New York: Da Capo Press, 1977), p. 181. For an alternative reading, see Richard Kramer's reading of the autograph manuscript of 'Der Musensohn', 'An die Entfernte', 'Am Flusse' and 'Wilkommen und Abschied' in his chapter, 'A Poetics of the Remote: Goethe's Entfernte' in Richard Kramer, Distant Cycles. Schubert and the Conceiving of Song (Chicago and London: The University of Chicago Press, 1994), pp. 85–101.

57. Brian Newbould interprets this in relation to Schubert's infection with syphilis; Newbould, *Schubert: the Music and the Man* (Berkeley and Los Angeles: University of California Press, 1999), 184.

58. For an alternative interpretation see Dietrich Fischer-Dieskau, *Schubert und seine Lieder* (Stuttgart: Deutsche Verlags-Anstalt, 1996), p. 218, and Kramer's discussion of this concept in the set of Goethe songs of 1822, pp. 96–97.

59. *MA* 2.1, p. 53.

60. The anonymous 'es' of 'Der Musensohn' appears and is exchanged for 'du' in the closing lines of 'Wilhelm's Lied' in the *Wanderjahre:* 'Und dein Streben seis in Liebe / Und dein Leben sei die Tat'; Johann Wolfgang von Goethe, *Wilhelm Meisters Wanderjahre*, in Goethe, *Sämtliche Werke*, ed. Gerhardt Neumann and Hans-Georg Dewitz, 40 vols (Frankfurt am Main: Deutscher Klassik Verlag ,1989), vol. 10, p. 166. Compare *HA* 8, p. 132.

61. Ludwig Wittgenstein, *Tractatus Logico-Philosophicus* (1921), trans. David Pears and Brian McGuinness (London: Routledge & Kegan Paul, 1961).

62. Richard Rorty, *Philosophy and the Mirror of Nature* (Minneapolis: University of Minnesota Press, 1982).

22

A Gauntlet Thrown

Schubert's 'Einsamkeit,' D 620, and Beethoven's *An die ferne Geliebte*

Susan Youens

> Once more
> Uncontradicting solitude
> Supports me on its giant palm;
> And like a sea-anemone
> Or simple snail, there cautiously
> Unfolds, emerges, what I am.
>
> (Philip Larkin, 'Best Society')

It is inconceivable that Schubert would not have responded to Beethoven's *An die ferne Geliebte*, Op. 98, first published by Sigmund Anton Steiner in 1816, within his own music, given his massive investment in reshaping the song composition of his day and his minute attention to his great contemporary's works.[1] One imagines Schubert searching for an appropriate text to which he could fit his own *Liederkreis*-under-one-roof, or at least being alive to the possibility of the right words, should they come along. And so they did, in his friend Johann Mayrhofer's lengthy poem 'Einsamkeit' (Solitude), which Schubert set to music at Zseliz during his residence there in 1818 as tutor to the Esterházy family. Did Mayrhofer write the poem to order? Was it intended from inception to be a challenge to Beethoven? In a letter of 3 August 1818 to Spaun, Schober, Mayrhofer, and Johann Senn, Schubert wrote that he was 'composing like a god ... Mayrhofer's *Einsamkeit* is finished, and I believe it to be the best thing I have done [*mein Bestes, was ich gemacht habe*], for I was without a care.'[2] The early days in Hungary were marked by a certain sense of relief at escape from the conflicts with his father over his future; 'solitude' might have been a word with a special subtext that summer.

The 1818 autograph manuscript of 'Einsamkeit' is, sadly, lost. Four years later, in June 1822, he would revisit the work; the manuscript of that endeavour is preserved in the Library of Congress.[3] Why Schubert returned to a four-year-old song in order to revise it is anyone's guess: was he prepping it for possible publication? But he did not publish this work, despite its evident importance to him, and one must wonder why.[4] Not until volume 32 of the

Nachgelassene Lieder appeared in 1840 did the world have a chance to know this singularity in Schubert's oeuvre. Speculating about why he did not seek to bring it to the public gaze over the span of a decade between its inception and his death has been my parlour game of late. After all, many issues converge at the vanishing point of this work, first and foremost, Schubert's conflicted response to Beethoven. In addition, there is Schubert's full-throttle harmonic, tonal, and formal experimentation in early adulthood as a matter of marvel. Because poet and composer knew one another, we might speculate how such personal knowledge could affect the joint work of art, and at the intersection of life, art, and culture, we find philosophies of modern thought turned into music. This is a thought-provoking work.

While I am not the first to notice the challenge to Beethoven's *An die ferne Geliebte* in 'Einsamkeit,' both the work itself and the Beethovenian reminiscences have received relatively little attention.[5] In his poems for Beethoven's cycle, Alois Isidor Jeitteles adopted the feint of Goethean *Erlebnislyrik* (the poetry of personal experience) and merged it with an artistic credo. At the heart of it all is an artist's existential dilemma vis-à-vis the world of other people, a question asked and triumphantly answered in six stages stitched together by instrumental corridors, conducting us to the next thought, realisation, memory. In Mayrhofer's ode, a very different persona recounts his quest for what to be and do in the world, and he too invokes memory, desire, and Nature. Schubert acknowledges the Beethovenian model overtly when he sets his friend's lengthy poem in six 'chapters' or sections, each one multi-partite, and ties them together in non-stop fashion, but where Beethoven sought a new merger of folk-song simplicity and art-song nuance in his cycle, Schubert is all about maximal complexity in a work that blends cantata, cycle, and song. Where Beethoven pares things down for the sake of immediacy and maintains stylistic and generic consistency throughout, Schubert showcases a variety of distinctive musical types meant to provide stark contrast as we go from one to the next. Quasi-antique sacred strains are made modern by harmonic means and followed in turn by dramatic recitative (called upon in each episode), by dance- and social music of several varieties, Italianate operatic lyricism to tell of love in cantabile manner, funereal military and battle strains, and a concluding three-part song. Far from Beethoven's quasi-*volkstümlich* directness, Schubert pulls out all the stops of harmonic and tonal ingenuity to portray a complex, restless persona. There is a distinct element of 'one-upping' Beethoven in the unfurling panoply of *echt* Schubertian procedures throughout 'Einsamkeit,' and yet, the beating heart of the song for me is one particular moment of nearness-to-Beethoven, a reminiscence of a passage from his great contemporary's cycle but engineered to be different as well: 'inspired by,' not 'quoted from.' Like Russian nesting dolls, memories lie within memories that contain still more memories, the protagonist remembering his youth and Schubert remembering Beethoven—and not at a distance. The speed with which he found a way to respond to Op. 98 is remarkable: 'Einsamkeit' dogs a living composer's heels.

Given the length of this work (410 bars, with sixteen changes of tempo after the initial *langsam* section) and its extraordinary tonal richness, I will restrict myself to just a few of the topics one could cull from it, some drawn from the surrounding cultural context (the external realm of this inquiry) and some from the musical workings of the song (the internal realm). Mayrhofer's ode must be the starting point, with particular emphasis on the poet's evident awareness of debates in late eighteenth-century popular philosophy about solitude and its relationship to 'Geselligkeit,' the social world; these are themes central to Enlightenment concerns. Mayrhofer's laconic title tells us that the solitary state is of paramount importance—it frames the tale told here –, and defining 'Einsamkeit' entails consideration of its peopled opposites. Seguing to Schubert's setting, I will outline the entire ode but will confine discussion to the first three episodes, in which one kind of solitude is contrasted with 'Tätigkeit' and 'Geselligkeit.' The 'Tätigkeit' episode in particular calls up two distant but still recognisable reminiscences of *An die ferne Geliebte*, and the where, when, why, and how of the second brief recollection is among my chief concerns here. Finally, I will return to the issue of solitude in order to speculate about why Schubert's musical extravagance in an extraordinary and experimental work has not followed Beethoven's footsteps into the canon, now that the risk of political disapprobation from Mayrhofer's own censorship bureau (Clio has a penchant for bitter irony) has long since vanished.[6]

Observations on Mayrhofer's Ode

Reading through Mayrhofer's poetry, one encounters certain themes repeatedly, including the making of poetry and the passage of time. He compared the effort of crafting poetic forms to labour in a smithy, and his poems are often vehicles by which he could simultaneously define his aesthetic, enact it, and engage in muscular self-exhortation.[7] This preoccupation with *poiesis* is frequently yoked to the venerable theme of 'the Ages of Man' or the journey through life; over and over, he imagines old age and surveys in retrospect the road that brought the poetic 'I' to fruition, Nature's embrace, peaceful death, or all of the above. For example, in the dialogue-poem 'Gewährung' (Grant), the first speaker is shocked to behold the ravages of time on a boyhood friend's face. The friend reassures him, saying that he has come through the turmoil of youth to ripe contentment: 'Ich gewann' (I won), he declares.[8] Similarly, one finds in the last stanza of 'Trost' (Consolation) an encapsulation of the Three Ages of Man in the wake of stanzas that almost, but not quite, cohere.

Was den Jüngling angewidert,	What the Youth found repellent,
Prüft des Mannes heller Auge,	Is examined by the Man with a clear eye,
Und dem reifen Greise wird es,	And will, one day, we hope
Hoffen wir, einst Freude geben![9]	Give pleasure to the Old Man in his maturity.

One might summarise this enigmatic poem as follows: 'You,' having equilibrium, do not feel envy (stanza 1); each individual has his own relationship to the Creator (stanza 2—although who 'you' and 'she' might be is a mystery); what Youth despises, Man considers, and Age enjoys (stanza 3). In the cycle 'Der Karthäuser' (The Carthusian), Mayrhofer's dying persona recounts his life's course, his restless youth, his exploits as a soldier, his sense of peacefulness in nature, his ten years in a Carthusian monastery, his passionate love for someone unnamed, and a fervent patriotism that turns to disdain for the worldly exercise of power. Almost all of those elements are present and accounted for in 'Einsamkeit.' 'Nachtstück' (Night Piece), set to music by Schubert (D 672), is a truncated instance of Mayrhofer's paired 'Ages of Man' and 'the making of poetry' obsessions in which an elderly minstrel goes into the forest still singing, to be welcomed by Nature as he dies. This is the best of good deaths for a singer of songs in the wake of a long life. There are other examples as well, but this will suffice to demonstrate that 'Einsamkeit' belongs to a subset of Mayrhofer's works having to do with the search for a productive life. In almost all of these poems, the ending is optimistic, with fruitful, contented old age following in the wake of youthful striving. He himself would not be so fortunate.

Mayrhofer organises his long ode to solitude as a modern adaptation of an ancient poetic form. Of the six episodes into which the poem is divided, each of the first five is structured as a paired strophe and antistrophe, two octave stanzas made up of rhyming couplets in mostly iambic tetrameters. The strophe always begins with a demand for the 'fullness' of some state or other, demands addressed to—Fate? his inmost self? the world? all of the above? One notes that these peremptory statements, part-plea, part-command in the imperative, are placed in quotation marks to set them apart from lines 2–8 and that their dactyls and trochees are rhythmically distinct from the lines in iambs that follow. That this persona does not do things by halves is soon evident; he submerges himself utterly in each attempt to discover what he should be and do. Embarking on a quest for a human framework to which he might belong, he engages in role-playing in one context after another; restless, easily disillusioned and dissatisfied, he casts off identities—monk, man of business, social being, lover, warrior—like a snake sloughing off a series of skins. Only when he rejects human company altogether for solitude in Nature is he at peace, and there is something both compelling and disquieting about the relief he so obviously finds in the absence of humanity.[10]

'Give me my fill of solitude!', he demands at the start—the solitude of religious withdrawal from the world. Mayrhofer paints a Romantic canvas for the reader in the first strophe.[11]

'Gib mir die Fülle der Einsamkeit!'	'Give me my fill of solitude!'
Im Tal, von Blüten überschneit,	In the valley, bedecked with snowy flowers, there
Da ragt ein Dom, und nebenbei	a cathedral soars up, and nearby the abbey in
In hohem Stile die Abtei.	Gothic style,
Wie ihr Begründer, fromm und still,	Like its founder, devout and quiet,
Der Müden Hafen und Asyl,	haven and refuge of the weary.
Hier kühlt mit heiliger Betauung,	Here never-ending contemplation
Die nie versiegenden Beschauung.	cools the spirit with holy refreshment.
Doch den frischen Jüngling quälen	But the young man is tormented,
Selbst in gottgeweihten Zellen	even in his consecrated cell,
Bilder, feuriger verjüngt;	by fiery images ever renewed;
Und ein wilder Strom entspringt	and a wild torrent pours
Aus der Brust, die er umdämmt	from his breast that he seeks to
Und in einem Augenblick	repress, but in a single moment,
Ist der Ruhe zartes Glück	the sweet happiness of tranquility
Von den Wellen weggeschwemmt.	is swept away by the flood.

Four of the five antistrophes begin with the hinge word 'Doch' that signals the rejection of each mode of life in its turn. 'Fiery images,' we are told, torment the youth in his monastic cell, accumulating in a 'wild torrent' of feeling. The refusal to be specific, the adjectives 'fiery' and 'wild,' hint at sexual desires that prayer cannot repress.

Bright lights and the big city beckon as the persona forsakes monastic solitude for urban bustle in the second strophe-antistrophe pair.

'Gib mir die Fülle der Tätigkeit!'	Give me my fill of activity!'
Menschen wimmeln weit und breit,	'Everywhere there are throngs of people;
Wagen kreuzen sich und stäuben,	Coaches pass each other, throwing up dust;
Käufer sich um Läden treiben,	customers crowd around shops;
Rotes Gold und heller Stein	Red gold and bright gems
Lockt die Zögernden hinein,	tempt the hesitant inside.
Und Ersatz für Landesgrüne	Masked balls and plays
Bieten Maskenball und Bühne.[12]	substitute for the green countryside.
Doch in prangenden Palästen,	But in splendid palaces,
Bei der Freude lauten Festen,	amid noisy, joyful feasts,

Spriesst empor der Schwermut Blume	the flower of melancholy springs up,
Senkt ihr Haupt zum Heiligtume	and bows her head toward the sanctuary
Seiner Jugend Unschuldslust,	of his youthful, happy innocence,
Zu dem blauen Hirtenland	to the blue land of shepherds
Und der lichten Quelle Rand.	and the edge of the sparkling stream.
Ach, dass er hinweg gemusst![13]	Alas, that he had to leave!

Friendship (a crucial thematic obsession of Mayrhofer's),[14] love, and the bloody alliance of patriotism and war[15] follow in swift succession.

'Gib mir das Glück der Geselligkeit!'	'Give me the pleasure of good company!'
Genossen, freundlich angereiht	Friends, cheerfully seated
Der Tafel, stimmen Chorus an	at table, strike up a song
Und ebenen die Felsenbahn!	to smooth life's rocky path.
So geht's zum schönen Hügelkranz	So we go up to the fair hills
Und abwärts zu des Stromes Tanz,	and down to the dancing river,
Und immer mehr befestiget sich Neigung	and our affection grows ever stronger
Mit treuer, kräftiger Verzweigung.	with other true, devoted attachments.
Doch, wenn die Genossen schieden,	But when friends depart,
Ist's getan um seinen Frieden.[16]	his peace is gone.
Ihn bewegt der Sehnsucht Schmerz,	Pierced by the pain of longing,
Und er schauet himmelwärts:	he gazes heavenwards;
Das Gestirn der Liebe strahlt.	there, the star of love shines.
Liebe, Liebe ruft die laue Luft.	Love calls in the balmy air,
Liebe, Liebe atmet Blumenduft	love wafts from the fragrant flowers,
Und sein Inn'res Liebe hallt.	and his inmost being resounds with love.
'Gib mir die Fülle der Seligkeit!'	'Give me my fill of bliss!'
Nun wandelt er in Trunkenheit	Now he walks enraptured,
An ihrer Hand in schweigenden Gesprächen,[17]	holding her hand in silent communion,
Im Buchengang, an weissen Bächen	along the beech tree avenue, beside the clear brook,
Und muss er auch durch Wüsteneien,	and even if he has to walk through deserts,
Ihm leuchtet süsser Augenschein;	her sweet eyes will shine for him.
Und in der feindlichsten Verwirrung	And amid the most hostile turmoil,
Vertrauet er der Holden Führung.	he trusts his gentle guide.

Doch die Särge grosser Ahnen,	But the tombs of his great forebears,
Siegerkronen, Sturmesfahnen	The conquerors' crowns, the war banners,
Lassen ihn nicht fürder ruh'n:	Allow him no more peace.
Und er muss ein Gleiches tun,	He must do as they did,
Und wie sie unsterblich sein.	And like them, become immortal.
Sieh, er steigt aufs hohe Pferd,	See, he mounts his noble steed,
Schwingt und prüft das blanke Schwert,	Tests his shining sword with a flourish,
Reitet in die Schlacht hinein.	And rides into battle.
'Gib mir die Fülle der Düsterkeit!'	'Give me my fill of gloom!'
Da liegen sie im Blute hingestreut,	There they lie in their own blood,
Die Lippe starr, das Auge wild gebrochen,	They who at first defied terror,
Die erst dem Schrecken Trotz gesprochen.	Their lips rigid, their eyes wild in death.
Kein Vater kehr den Seinen mehr,	No father returns to his family;
Und heimwärts kehrt ein ander Heer,	A different army returns home,
Und denen Krieg das Teuerste genommen,	And those who have lost their dearest in the war now
Begrüssen nun mit schmerzlichem Willkommen.[18]	bid that army a sorrowful welcome.
So däucht ihm des Vaterlandes Wächter	His fatherland's guardians
Ein ergrimmter Bruderschlächter,	now appear to him as enraged murderers,
Der der Freiheit edel Gut	nurturing noble freedom
Düngt mit rotem Menschenblut.	with red human blood.
Mit dem Forste, grün und kühl,	And he curses giddy fame
Und erflucht dem tollen Ruhm	and exchanges the noisy tumult
Und tauschet lärmendes Gewühl	for the forest, green and cool,
Mit dem Siedlerleben um.[19]	for a hermit's life.

It is impossible not to read this ode with Mayrhofer *in propria persona* in mind, given his penchant for autobiographical matter woven into the other stuff of his verse. After all, Mayrhofer's stay in St. Florian's was followed by a stint of law studies in Vienna ('Tätigkeit' of a sort) and by 'Geselligkeit' with the Schubert circle, its dances and *Tafelmusik* memorialised here, while his own tendencies to 'Düsterkeit' make that plea perhaps the most characteristic of all. Melancholic from the start, he seems to have regarded his existence as 'harsh and difficult' from an early age, and his poems tell us that Nature's beauty was among the few consolations for unremitting psychological pain. If he never engaged in actual battle, he was obsessed with freedom, democracy, and their classical models, with those who fought for their ideals, and his intense patriotism was at odds with official policy and his official employment. Given his gloomy temperament and his need for creative solitude on the one hand and his loyalty to close friends on the other, he had ample reason to ponder the balance between seclusion and social engagement. There is, one feels, much of the man himself on display here, however abstracted for poetic purposes.

Finally, at the end comes the classical epode, the completion of what is usually a three-part structure (strophe-antistrophe-epode). For this final section, Mayrhofer retains the pairing of two octave stanzas, but this time, the second stanza acts to amplify, rather than negate, the first stanza. In the first stanza, we are in the persona's fictive present as he describes a beautiful, wild forest scene, complete with bird song and a waterfall (Nature's music), while the second stanza tells us that this is the site where memory transfigures past experience. In this differently consecrated solitude, devoid of any trace of religion, Mayrhofer's alter ego celebrates release from every sort of passion in old age.

'Gib mir die Weihe der Einsamkeit!'	'Give me the blessing of solitude!'
Durch dichte Tannendunkelheit	Through the darkness of dense pines,
Dringt Sonnenblick nur halb und halb,	the sun only half penetrates
Und färbet Nadelschichten falb.	and colours the beds of needles with a dusky tint.
Der Kuckuck ruft aus Zweiggeflecht,	The cuckoo calls from the thicket,
An grauer Rinde pickt der Specht,	the woodpecker pecks at the gray bark,
Und donnernd über Klippenhemmung	and the bold torrent thunders
Ergeht des Giessbachs kühne Strömung.	over the rocky barrier.
Was er wünschte, was er liebte,	Whatever he desired, whatever he loved,
Ihn erfreute, ihn betrübte,	whatever made him rejoice, made him sad, floats by with gentle rapture,
Schwebt mit sanfter Schwärmerei	
Wie im Abendrot vorbei.	as if in evening's glow.
Jünglings Sehnsucht—Einsamkeit,	Solitude, the young man's longing,
Wird dem Greisen nun zu teil,	is now the old man's lot,
Und ein Leben rauh und steil	and a harsh, difficult life
Führte doch zur Seligkeit.[20]	leads at last to happiness.

The solace to be gained from the solitary contemplation of Nature and the past—this is a hymn to the healing power of memory—is among the most prized species of 'Einsamkeit' discussed in popular philosophy as part of the so-called 'problem of solitude,' and it is the capstone and culmination of Mayrhofer's ode.

The 'Problem of Solitude'

Mayrhofer had numerous predecessors who contemplated notions of the solitary state and social life before he came along and whose ideas about 'the problem of solitude' he critiques here. Many of the treatises, poems, novels, etc. on solitude earlier in the eighteenth century were responses to Daniel Defoe's *Robinson Crusoe* (1719), which is all about how to create a world entirely by oneself, isolated from other people. When Defoe produced a sequel the following year (1720) entitled *Serious Reflections during the Life and Surprising Adventures of Robinson Crusoe*, his first chapter was a meditation entitled 'Of Solitude,'[21] and the so-called 'Robinsonades' that followed spun variations on Defoe's island isolation. Some sixty years later, it was Jean-Jacques Rousseau who impelled another round of meditations on the matter with his *Rêveries du promeneur solitaire* (Reveries of a solitary walker) of 1782, ten essays recounting the struggle between his yearning for solitude and his need for society. His hours of solitude, Rousseau declared, are the only ones 'during which I am fully myself and for myself, without diversion, without obstacle, and during which I can truly claim to be what nature willed,'[22] and he had plenty of company in saying so. In fact, 'company' was usually debated as the Janus-face of the solitary state. Given the Enlightenment's concern with the nature of a well-constituted society, the relationship of 'Einsamkeit' to 'Geselligkeit' (sociability) furrowed many a brow, with meditations on the nature and requirements of genius increasingly woven into the discussions as the century wore on.

All those who contemplated 'Einsamkeit' and its evil twin 'Alleinsein' (alone-ness, which is nearly always depicted as sad, even pathological) soon arrived at those ultimate issues yoked to any serious consideration of solitude. What is the proper balance between our need for other people and our need for solitude? What is 'healthy' and 'necessary' solitude? What solitary states are morbid and unhealthy? What is the nature of human happiness? What are the conditions of creativity? How are solitude and coming to grips with death linked? The way was paved for Mayrhofer's ode by poetic works such as Johann Friedrich von Cronegk's *Einsamkeiten* (Solitudes—plural, one notes),[23] Christoph August Tiedge's Epicurean-philosophical poem *Die Einsamkeit*,[24] and—most important for Schubert—Goethe's Harper in

Wilhelm Meisters Lehrjahre, to name only a few. But the most voluminous work on solitude in the immediate aftermath of Rousseau was the Swiss physician and popular philosopher Johann Georg Zimmerman's four-volume treatise *Ueber die Einsamkeit* of 1784–1785, translated into many languages and reprinted many times.[25] Like Mount Everest, this tome, weighing in at 1,648 pages in my second edition copy, was unavoidably *there*, and Zimmermann's combative style guaranteed that still more works condemning or supporting his views would follow.[26] He was a cranky, eccentric, paradoxical creature whose views on the relationship between asceticism and sexual neurosis anticipate Freud, and who hated Catholicism with a passion, a conservative, misogynistic, pro-aristocratic/anti-republican character whose opinions are never mild.[27] The most outraged respondents to bad reviews in the *TLS* are nothing compared to his ire when contradicted. If he ever pulled a punch, I do not know about it.

In his analysis, striking a balance between the *right* kind of social life and the *right* kind of solitude constitutes the systolic and diastolic heartbeats of a properly ordered existence. While he saw in society little more than snobbery conjoined with erotic wheeling-and-dealing, he warns that creative solitude must be balanced with social dealings of a fruitful sort. One should be 'like a gentle river that flows not only through lonely valleys but also through peopled cities,'[28] he writes—he had a picturesque way with words. The inner drive to seek solitude can be either condemnable (arising from misanthropy, laziness, shame, guilt, hypochondria, and religious fanaticism) or good (stemming from the desire for true peace, freedom,[29] self-knowledge, and creative or scholarly endeavours). True solitude is a moral state of being, a condition of the soul that one consciously fashions, and it is necessary for any therapeutic examination of the self: this is what Zimmermann and others in his day called 'productive solitude' or 'active solitude,' in which being by oneself is a means to an end, not an end unto itself.[30] Goethe in *Dichtung und Wahrheit* calls his creations 'the children of solitude' and insists that only when the artist is alone can significant works come into being.[31] But he also understood the dangers of solitude and created a diagnostic picture of the diseased solitary state in the figure of the Harper from *Wilhelm Meisters Lehrjahre*, a tormented figure who believes that 'Einsamkeit' leads inevitably to 'Alleinsein,' merging with it in a pathological condition from which suicide is the sole escape.[32] 'Wer sich der Einsamkeit ergibt,' he sings, 'Ach, der ist bald allein.' Bettine von Arnim subsequently wrote a parody of this poem (in the sense of a model, not a caricature) in order to elucidate the contrast between the sort of frivolous 'Geselligkeit' that Zimmermann condemns many times over ('Germany has never been as 'clubby' and 'social' as it is now,' he sniffed[33]) and productive solitude. Stanzas 2–4 of her poem are particularly apropos:

(stanzas 2–4 of 5)

Wer sich dem Weltgewühl ergibt,	He who surrenders to the social whirl
Der ist zwar nie allein.	Is in truth never alone,
Doch was er lebt und was er liebt,	But what he experiences and what he loves
Es wird wohl nimmer sein.	Is never truly his own.
Nur wer der Muse hin sich gibt,	Only he who gives himself to the Muse
Der weilet gern allein,	Gladly lingers alone;
Er ahnt, daß sie ihn wieder liebt,	He knows that She returns his love,
Von ihm geliebt will sein.	Will be beloved by him.
Sie kränzt den Becher und Altar,	She crowns the chalice and the altar,
Vergöttlicht Lust und Pein,	Makes divine both joy and sorrow,
Was sie ihm gibt, es ist so wahr,	What she gives him is true,
Gewährt ein ewig Sein.[34]	Ensured of immortality.
	(trans. Uri Liebrecht)

Almost every aspect of 'Einsamkeit' and 'Geselligkeit' that Mayrhofer presents in his ode, with the exception of war and soldiering, is subjected to lengthy discussion in Zimmermann's tome. He recognises the urge to seek religious solitude out of genuine piety and the desire to flee the world and its dangers (Mayrhofer's Episode 1, strophe), although the mostly anti-Catholic physician-philosopher is more inclined to find superstition, ignorance, and misplaced pride at the root of decisions to enter cloisters and convents (a spasm or two of tolerance is evident on occasion).[35] Zimmermann is at great pains to assert that all of our passions accompany us when we withdraw from the world into religious havens and there bedevil us more intensely than before, combining and multiplying until they become Mayrhofer's 'raging torrent' (Episode 1, antistrophe).[36] While he recognises that it is natural and beneficial to seek company when the working day is over ('A completely solitary creature is a miserable creature'[37]), he inveighs against 'assemblies, balls, Redouten' for the empty coquetry and sensuality on display at such gatherings (Episode 2, strophe and antistrophe).[38] Even the company of good friends leaves emptiness in its wake when the gathering disperses. 'People gladly throw themselves into whatever promises the most activity and want to be where they can expect cheerfulness, renewed vitality, and happiness,'[39] he writes, but 'sweet rest and quiet happiness are not to be found in the noisiness of the world'[40] (episode 3, antistrophe). Love, which Zimmermann calls 'häuslicher oder vertrauter Geselligkeit' (domestic or intimate companionship),[41] is a magnetic force, a burning desire on the part of all who live; it can make one forget 'envy with all its spite, the lack of mercy and kindness from those in authority, failed projects, every misfortune of every kind,' especially when it seeks Nature as its setting (episode 4, strophe).[42] It is easier to renounce the world, Zimmermann declares, than it is to forgo love or to escape from thoughts of it when it is no more. But best of all is solitude in nature: this is the proper context for the retrospective gaze of age, the proper site for self-knowledge, contemplation, and peace (both stanzas of episode 6, the epode).[43] It is this species of the solitary state that elicits Zimmermann's most lyrical prose and his highest praise.

We have no record of either Schubert or Mayrhofer reading Zimmermann, but scrolling through Mayrhofer's ode is evidence of the poet's awareness of the lively eighteenth-century literature on the subject of 'the solitary life' and society, a literature in which many others echo Zimmermann's categories and themes. Songs are social documents, after all, commentaries on, reflections of, participants in the issues of their day, and the quest for individual identity in the midst of surrounding social structures was a subject of paramount importance in the Enlightenment. Two-hundred years and more later, in another place and a different culture, we tend to focus more on the workings of Schubert's complex music than the residue of those long-ago debates, but I think that enlarging the frame around Schubert's challenge to Beethoven to include the philosophical context not only augments our understanding of a radical work but makes the necessary point yet again that Schubert was keenly aware of all the cultural issues of the day.

Schubert and Songs of Solitude

If Zimmermann's tome never came to Schubert's attention, life itself impelled him, as it does most of us, to contemplate the essential isolation of human existence.[44] In a lost notebook for 27 March 1824, Schubert wrote, 'There is no one who understands the pain or the joy of others! We always imagine we are coming together, and we always merely go side by side. Oh, what torture for those who recognise this!'—a statement possibly impelled by the recent publication of the single poetic anthology by Mayrhofer to appear in his lifetime.[45] Six years earlier, however, the two were in joyous collaboration on the creation of a work Schubert deemed important, and he lavished extensive musical pains on the work, evident in the form and features of the first two strophe-antistrophe pairs. Here, the composer establishes the larger architectural patterns that will prevail throughout 'Einsamkeit,' reveals the ambitious nature of the work, contrasts solitude with worldly activity, and twice refers obliquely to Beethoven. We can tell who and what was on his mind as he wrote.

For the strophe of Episode 1 about religious solitude (bars 1–49), Schubert took on a dual and paradoxical task: evoking both a mystical, hushed, unchanging ecclesiastical world and the discontented mind housed within it. There is not a single rest for the piano; the heavy tread of these organ chords grinds on nonstop, and yet there is no harmonic peace here. The section begins and ends in a closed B♭ major, but the short-lived internal emphases on D minor, F major, G minor, D♭ major, G♭ major/F♯ major and D major are a foreshadowing *in nuce* of the harmonic and tonal relationships in the B♭ major Sonata to follow ten years later. 'Song enables Schubert to transform Classical structures,' Susan Wollenberg writes, and one could cite the distant but still palpable relationship between this passage and the grand sonata as another example of that truth.[46] 'How many different mediant relationships can I pack into this section?' Schubert might have asked himself as he was getting underway (see Table 22.1 for a summary of the song's tonal plan).

It is a notable feature of the introduction's heavy harmonies, with a pseudo-ecclesiastical whole-note chord filling each bar, that we begin with misdirection. The repeated B♭ chords in bars 1–2, their pitches bunched tightly together, might seem to be an announcement of the tonic key, but the phrase veers towards D minor almost immediately, such that the singer's elided entrance over a return of the B♭ chord in bar 8 is deceptive in its effect (Ex. 22.1).

We turn away from D minor thoughts (of death, borrowed from Mozart's Requiem?) at the last minute. Everything about this beginning bespeaks a persona already unsure of being in the right place and straying towards another, darker realm; this is harmonic progression as psychological portraiture. When the persona demands solitude in bars 8–12 over the initial progression in the piano, its topmost voice foreshadowing and then doubling the singer's imperative, he steers it this time to safer harbour on the dominant of B♭, averting (temporarily) the danger of D minor. But peace is not to be had here, whatever the slow harmonic rhythm and mimicry of tolling bells in the piano, as Schubert tells us in bars 22–23 when a common-tone related diminished seventh chord moves us briefly by side-slipping motion—a musical pun on Mayrhofer's 'nebenbei'—to ♭III, D♭ major. Thereafter, the section is shot through with unstable tonicisations crowding on each other's heels. None of them last; it is as if the persona is constantly asking whether this tonal cell or that one or perhaps this one will provide peace, 'der Müden Hafen und Asyl' (Ex. 22.2).

It is only at the end that the harmonic to-ing and fro-ing comes to a dully conventional conclusion, sinking as if in exhaustion to tonic closure prolonged by a fermata. The persona has had to repeat the words 'Hier kühlt mit heiliger Betauung / die nie versiegende Beschauung' in order to make them lead back to B♭ and confirm that key, but because so much harmonic shiftiness is on display throughout the strophe, we hear the cadence and its confirmation in the piano postlude as something that cannot last. Anything that follows in the wake of such harmonic restlessness cannot really be stable; something else is surely in the offing.

The repudiations of a prior way of life in the musical antistrophes of this ode always begin with modulatory restlessness and usually entail several changes of key, altered textures in the piano, different accompanimental patterns, and the incorporation of dramatic recitative. Here in bars 55–60, the corridor away from St Florian's and out into the world begins with the previous B♭ triad moving softly

Table 22.1 Summary of the tonal plan of 'Einsamkeit'

Strophe 1, 'Gib mir die Fülle der Einsamkeit', bars 1–54	B♭ major, with brief tonicisations of G minor, D♭ major, G♭ major, D major, C minor
Antistrophe 1, 'Doch den frischen Jüngling', bars 55–96	Unstable F♯ major/B minor, tonicisations of D major, B minor, C minor leading to piano postlude in more stable F minor, but heading to an unrealised A♭ major
Strophe 2, 'Gib mir die Fülle der Tätigkeit', bars 97–155	E major, ending E minor
Antistrophe 2, 'Doch in prangenden Palästen', bars 156–179	Chromatic modulatory corridor leading to D major, ending D minor
Strophe 3, 'Gib mir das Glück der Geselligkeit', bars 180–231	F major
Antistrophe 3, 'Doch, wenn die Genossen schieden', bars 232–256	Chromatic corridor leading to E♭ minor, G♭ major, short-lived and unstable D major
Strophe 4, 'Gib mir die Fülle der Seligkeit', bars 257–284	B major, with internal emphases on G♯ minor
Antistrophe 4, 'Doch die Särge großer Ahnen', bars 285–320	Chromatic corridor leading to G♭ major, brief emphasis on C major, ending on F♯ major
Strophe 5, 'Gib mir die Fülle der Düsterheit', bars 321–339	F♯ minor, unstable chromaticism with emphases on G minor, B♭ major, E♭ minor, and back to cadence on B minor
Antistrophe 5, 'So däucht ihn des Vaterlandes Wächter', bars 340–366	Chromatic instability leading to arrival at B major
Epode, stanza 1, 'Gib mir die Weihe der Einsamkeit', bars 367–390	G major/B♭ major
Epode, stanza 2, 'Was er wünschte', bars 391–410	G major, with brief internal emphases on E minor

Example 22.1 Schubert, 'Einsamkeit' D 620, bars 1-12

Example 22.2 Schubert, 'Einsamkeit' D 620, bars 26-43

to a diminished seventh chord whose C♭ and A♭ pitches already act to contradict B♭ major's semblance of certitude. There the music sits for almost two bars, as if the persona's soul was momentarily frozen in place on an unstable chord that could either retreat back into the monk's cell in B♭ or go elsewhere. But return is not possible, not for *this* persona, and the diminished seventh chord morphs violently into its enharmonic equivalent before moving to a sudden thunderous cadence on F♯ major—which immediately becomes the dominant of B minor (Ex. 22.3).

And there we sit on F♯ in the bass for six bars (bars. 61–66), a remarkably tense refusal to go fully into the key of deepest misery according to eighteenth-century *Affektenlehre*. A 'wild torrent' of chromatic motivic development takes us to a battering ram of multiple diminished seventh harmonies (bars 80–86), followed by a melancholy cadence on F minor that confirms the loss of 'sweet

Example 22.3 Schubert, 'Einsamkeit' D 620, bars 55-63

peace.' As if repeating the grim fact to himself silently, the piano postlude to the antistrophe twice repeats that cadence and then, in mid-bar (bar 93) comes to a decision to do something positive, to make A♭ major lemonade out of F minor lemons—but at bar 97, instead of that tonicised harmony we expect, we hear a G♯ minor chord en route to E major for the strophe of episode 2 ('Tätigkeit'). Where to go, what to be, what to do: this music could hardly be more unsettled than it is.

After such immersion in harmonic restlessness, 'Tätigkeit' by contrast stays in E major (bars 97–155), with spirituality and the social whirl thus amusingly set at the distance of a tritone from one another, as far apart as possible. Schubert construes 'busyness-business' as considerable chromatic scurrying about, but without any tonal change of place. All this mercantile activity and prancing about to balls and plays is much ado about nothing and does not really go anywhere, this music says, and it is here that Schubert 'channels' the triplet-rhythm vivacity of the beginning of 'Leichte Segler in den Höhen,' the third song of *An die ferne Geliebte*, with its puffs of cloud that the persona would have bear messages to the beloved. The lightness of Nature's joyous scudding motion through the air in Beethoven becomes the sounding depiction of frivolous babble in Schubert, of gossip and tattle and rushing about to no purpose in an urban environment that is the opposite of Beethoven's clouds and streams; Graham Johnson points out that this is the sole mention of shops in all of Schubert's songs.[47] In the *geschwinder* piano corridor in bars 133–155 that leads to the antistrophe, we hear, in place of the triplet scurrying, music that evokes the grand processionals at the start of a ball (bars 130–154); one can imagine richly clad revelers making their grand entrance. From the resounding peak of this passage in bars 139f, we descend lower and lower, grow ever softer, and finally turn, first to parallel minor and then to silence: the famous Schubertian hallmark of a fermata-sustained bar or two of silence to mark crucial moments in the architecture of a work.[48] The grandiloquence drains out of the ceremonial strains before the emptiness of despair takes its place. Silence, as in another and even greater Mayrhofer song, 'Auf der Donau,' represents the passage of time, an unknown interval before the persona can marshall words and tones to tell of yet another failure in his quest for belonging (Ex. 22.4).

For the second antistrophe (bars 156–179), Schubert takes Mayrhofer's single 'sentence' and divides it musically into two zones, each with its own rhythmic and tonal identity. The first half (bars 156–166) recounts the intrusion of melancholy in the midst of 'splendid palaces and joyous festivities,' leading to thoughts of the 'holiness' of innocent, youthful happiness;' adulthood and melancholy are twinned in Mayrhofer's world. Beginning from the deceptive, empty clarity of C major chords in bars 156–157, Schubert's harmonies then tell us that melancholy renders

Example 22.4 Schubert, 'Einsamkeit' D 620, bars 139-155

everything unstable, unmoored, shifting. A remarkable chromatic corridor ensues; first, the bright E major of 'Maskenball und Bühne' just preceding is emptied out and then darkened by a flat-side sequence as the register of evolving, blossoming melancholy ('Schwermut Blume'—a vivid image) in bars 159–163, followed by enharmonic transformation to impel the return to lighter, brighter climes. The whole process culminates in a cadence on D major (bars 166–167); we heard a shorter-lived tonicisation of D for the 'Müden Hafen und Asyl' in Episode 1, Strophe 1, bars. 33–35, and this memory too is a tragically brief harbour for someone weary in heart and soul.

'O wüßt ich doch den Weg zurück zum Kinderland:' Schubert recalls Beethoven

When Mayrhofer's persona remembers the land of his youth, Schubert remembers the second song, 'Wo die Berge so blau,' from Beethoven's cycle, and no wonder: the memories are structurally similar, but with Mayrhofer's version tragically abbreviated by comparison. In Jeitteles, a series of parallel 'Wo'-clauses (where the blue mountains look down from the misty gray, where the sun ceases to shine, where the clouds cover the sky) lead to the proclamation 'möchte ich sein' (that is where I would like to be). This same structure is repeated and varied slightly in the second stanza before evocations of remembered place give way to a focus on personal pain in the third stanza.

(stanzas 1 and 2)	
Wo die Berge so blau	Where the mountains so blue
Aus dem nebligen Grau	look down
Schauen herein,	from the gray mists,
Wo die Sonne verglüht,	where the sun vanishes,
Wo die Wolke umzieht,	where the cloud envelops,
Möchte ich sein!	there I should like to be!
Dort im ruhigen Thal	There in the peaceful valley
Schweigen Schmerzen und Qual.	sorrows and torment are stilled.
Wo im Gestein	Where in the rock
Still die Primel dort sinnt,	the primrose muses,
Weht so leise der Wind,	where the wind blows so softly,
Möchte ich sein!	there I should like to be!

Mayrhofer too creates successive 'zum' and 'zu-' clauses, the first two explicit and the second implicit (to the holiness of his innocent happiness in youth, to the blue land of shepherds and [to] the edge of the bright stream), followed not by the

Beethovenian persona's expression of desire to be there but by its opposite: the more hopeless recognition that departure from this pastoral bliss had to be, that one cannot stay either young or at home. What is perhaps most remarkable is that Schubert brings the music to a point of arrival at 'Jugend Unschuldslust' in mid-poetic sentence, in the middle of a string of dependent clauses; to have a perfect authentic cadence occur in conjunction with a comma articulation in the text rather than a period, a semi-colon, or a colon is an unusual interpretive decision, and a brilliant one. The effect is to set the remembered landscape apart in a room of its own and to underscore the homage to Beethoven when it appears—suddenly. With a wave of a modulatory wand, we are transported elsewhere.

Jeitteles's and Beethoven's persona lingers in the remembered realm of Nature and love, but Mayrhofer's tormented, restless protagonist can only remain in the 'blue land of shepherds' for a brief passage, not an entire song-within-a-song (Examples 22.5a and b).

Example 22.5(a) Schubert, 'Einsamkeit' D 620, bars 166–179

*) Bars 178-179, *ossia*, cf. *Quellen und Lesarten*.

Example 22.5(b) Ludwig van Beethoven, 'Wo die Berge so blau' from *An die ferne Geliebte*, Op. 98, bars 1-10

Schubert repeats these words ('zu dem blauen Hirtenland und der lichten Quelle Rand') in order to make their wistfulness register properly, and the piano accompaniment for the repetition is an exact duplicate of what came before, an attempt to stay in this beautiful place-in-the-mind by dint of sheer longing. The passage is almost completely pure in its diatonicism, with only the slight, telling emphases on the subdominant to reinforce the utter peacefulness of the remembered scene. In the piano, we hear the horn-call figures so often emblematic of memory in Schubert's songs (we hear them at the end of the piano introduction to 'Der Lindenbaum'), stitched together by repeated pitches that also recall 'Wo die Berge so blau' and have a similar incantatory effect. By this means, we understand that both personae are fixed in place, their gaze focused on the beloved inward vista. But the vocal line is not repeated exactly: the repetition entails enlargement and elevation, with ascending jumps of a major sixth and a minor seventh, gestures that go beyond the perfect fourths and stepwise motion of the phrase on its first incarnation. Longing intensifies with repetition, and the persona tries to leap via melody into mountains of memory.[49]

Among the 'red threads' throughout the six songs of *An die ferne Geliebte* are the touches of parallel minor mode, this in a cycle in which every principal key and most of the subsidiary keys are major mode. The lapses into minor are righted each time by a return to major mode; this is music's corollary to the effort of will required to overcome stabs of mental pain. Even when the cycle veers into a relatively lengthy stretch of parallel minor in the third song (beginning at the words 'Wird sie an den Büschen stehen'), the key signature remains in major mode, and the entirety of the fourth song, 'Diese Wolken in den Höhen,' then must correct that indulgence in grief by thoroughly reestablishing A♭ major. The determination to be of right mind and stout heart, to turn grief into good, straw into gold, is evident throughout and culminates in the triumph of 'a loving heart.' Schubert too resorts to his signature modal contrasts at the ends both of the 'Tätigkeit' strophe and its antistrophe for a different purpose: this is how he tells of something slipping away, first darkening and then vanishing into the shadows. In the piano postlude (bars 176–177) to this brief moment in the land of memory, the D major that seems more like something hovering in mid-air, a reiterated cadential phrase rather than a more rooted, developed passage in Beethovenian manner, darkens to D minor before ceding with characteristic abruptness to another, very different state of being ('Geselligkeit,' beginning with a C major cadential statement and proceeding in F major). Schubert's dreamlike D major with slight but telling emphases on the subdominant harmony of G major is—surely not coincidentally—the twinned obverse of Beethoven's G major key and its dominant harmony of D

Example 22.6 Schubert, 'Einsamkeit' D 620, bars 367-375

major. Schubert even treats the 3/4 meter of the 'blue land of shepherds' in a manner deliberately close to, but still distinct from, the 6/8 meter of 'Wo die Berge so blau.' That he is courting comparisons to Beethoven is obvious.

Nor does it seem coincidental that the final, blissful state of solitude in Mayrhofer's epode ('Gib mir die Weihe der Einsamkeit / Durch dichte Tannendunkelheit') is set in G major, with an inner passage of cuckoo song in B♭—a reminiscence of the monk's cell in Episode 1, but this time stable, more diatonic and peaceful by far. The turning figure in the piano throughout this last section—the wheel of Fate coming full circle?—is a variant of the turning figure in the reminiscence of 'Wo die Berge so blau' (for example, D–E–F♯–D–D–F♯–G–F♯ in bars 171–173) to underscore in subtle fashion the relationship between peacefulness remembered from the past and peacefulness achieved in the present. That these figures turn within the circumference of a third recalls Beethoven's more straightforward traversals of a third in the melody for 'Wo die Berge so blau,' while their conjunction with chiming repeated pitches also recalls the beautiful Beethovenian predecessor (Ex. 22.6).

To remember with right mind and heart, to do so surrounded by Nature's loveliness: this is bliss, and both Schubert and Beethoven knew how to make music from it.

In Conclusion

The few who have written about 'Einsamkeit' uniformly assert that it deserves to be better known than it is, but where *An die ferne Geliebte* is ensconced in the canon, Schubert's challenge to it is a marginalized creation. He never published it, and any careful acquaintance with the work makes that decision seem multiply determined, perhaps even *over*-determined. The 'Düsterkeit' episode made the censors' wrath likely (and Schubert's boldness in composing it therefore notable); after the composer's brush with the police in 1820, some degree of caution was surely on his mind. In addition, one wonders whether Schubert decided against making public the gauntlet thrown down to Beethoven because the relationship was too obvious, both in the structure and in the wisps of reminiscence. Even the drastic divergences seem to have Beethoven in mind, the pendulum of creation swinging to the other side. 'Secretly, in my heart of hearts, I still hope to be able to make something out of myself, but who can do anything after Beethoven?', Joseph Spaun remembers Schubert saying,[50] and the dilemma resounds in 'Einsamkeit.' Later, he could devise his own idiosyncratic conception of the song cycle in *Die schöne Müllerin* and *Winterreise*; those he was happy to display to the world.

But I also wonder whether Schubert's withholding this work from public view and its subsequent neglect has to do in some measure with the persona we meet here. I thought irresistibly of 'Einsamkeit' a few months ago when I was reading Jacques Derrida's *The Beast and the Sovereign*, with its meditations on solitude as a fundamental subjective orientation of literary and philosophical modernity. In meditations juxtaposing *Robinson Crusoe* and Heidegger's essay on the concepts of world, finitude, and solitude, Derrida locates the attraction of Defoe's island in fantasies of a self uncontaminated by dependencies, impregnable against the intrusions and demands of others, free from the enslavements of sexual desire, sovereign and omnipotent in a kingdom of one's own. To say 'I am alone,' Derrida writes, is to announce both deprivation and exception, that is, helpless abandonment on the one hand and irreplaceability, election, and unicity (the quality or state of being unique of its kind) on the other.[51] Such fantasies of solitude secretly feed on the bestial other its creators want so desperately to banish; the animal and the sovereign are always in danger of merging.

But Robinson Crusoe is a beloved literary character, and Mayrhofer's persona in 'Einsamkeit' is not, whatever their occasional philosophical similarities. Where then is the difference? Perhaps it is because Crusoe is deposited by chance into a solitary state he did not choose and must thereafter respond to fate by meditating long and hard on those moral gains he is determined to garner from his time in exile. When he is brought back into society, his experience of the company of others is sharpened by his knowledge that 'Mitsein,' sharing a world in common with others, is also the very condition of solitude. Mayrhofer's 'Ich,' on the other hand, elects entry into one social context after another in a search for the 'right' one, only to depart disillusioned each time, nor is his final solitude motivated by the desire to reach out through artistic creation to a loved other, both singular and en masse. One might argue that the creation of Mayrhofer's ode constitutes reaching out so that people might better understand the genesis of his poetic project, and certainly most of us can understand from within our own bones the 'discontents of civilization' and the fantasy of sovereign solitude. But as Mayrhofer's persona ticks off all of the major forms of human dependency and allegiance and rejects each one in turn, we shudder, and the cumulative weight of those rejections compromises the seeming idyll at the end.

It is in retrospect no wonder that Beethoven chose a transformed *Volkston* idiom for *his* music while Schubert, with the exception of his chosen echoes from *An die ferne Geliebte*, steered clear of anything folk-like in 'Einsamkeit.' It is perhaps the uneasy awareness of a psychological wound too deep for any human balm that drives people away from 'Einsamkeit,' despite the richness of Schubert's music. Even when Schubert's other personae endure misery on the scale of his miller lad and winter wanderer, we feel empathy born of our own experience of love lost, our own quests for self-understanding, and the tragedies in our own lives, especially when emblazoned in transcendent music. Not so here. The 'völlig einsame Mensch' was, most philosophers agreed, a sad phenomenon, and very distant from the 'loving heart' whose joy at the end of Beethoven's quest is so moving. In the final analysis, I wonder whether

Schubert's sequestration of this experimental work might have stemmed in some measure from a desire to shield his erstwhile friend from exposure of a pathology whose nature he could recognise more keenly than the poet.

Notes

1. The scholarly literature on Beethoven's cycle includes: Joseph Kerman, 'An die ferne Geliebte' in *Beethoven Studies 1*, ed. Alan Tyson (New York, 1973), pp. 123–57, reprinted in *Write All These Down: Essays on Music* (Berkeley, California: University of California Press, 1994), pp. 173–206; Raymond Knapp, 'Reading Gender in Late Beethoven: 'An die Freude' and *An die ferne Geliebte*' in *Acta Musicologica*, vol. 75, no. 1 (2003), pp. 45–63; Nicholas Marston, 'Voicing Beethoven's Distant Beloved' in *Beethoven and his World*, ed. Scott Burnham and Michael P. Steinberg (Princeton: Princeton University Press, 2000), pp. 124–47; Nicolas Marston, '"Wie aus der Ferne": Pastness and Presentness in the Lieder of Beethoven, Schubert, and Schumann' in *Schubert durch die Brille*, vol. 21 (1998), pp. 126–2; Christopher Reynolds, 'The Representational Impulse in Late Beethoven, I: *An die ferne Geliebte*' in *Acta Musicologica*, vol. 60 (1988), pp. 3–61; Charles Rosen, 'Mountains and Song Cycles' in *The Romantic Generation* (Cambridge, Massachusetts: Harvard University Press, 1995), pp. 166–74.

2. Otto Erich Deutsch, *Schubert: Die Dokumente seines Lebens* (Kassel & Basel: Bärenreiter, 1964), p. 232.

3. See Franz Schubert, *Neue Ausgabe sämtlicher Werke*, Series IV: *Lieder*, vol. 12 (Kassel and Basel: Bärenreiter, 1996), pp. 232–3, for the critical commentary on the sources, and the 'Vorwort,' pp. xvii–xviii, for notes on the genesis of the work. Dürr points out that the manuscript now in the Library of Congress (ML 30.8b. S35E4) shows signs of care at the beginning and greater haste thereafter, that the many corrections visible in the manuscript hint at revisions to the original version from four years earlier.

4. The song's genesis and revision span almost the entirety of the so-called years of crisis in Schubert's life (1818–23) but precede the catastrophe of his syphilitic infection.

5. Richard Capell missed the Beethovenian background entirely and calls the piece 'impossible' as well as 'enormous and unpractical,' and refers to its hero as 'an abstraction,' but he praises the 'self-contained song' at the end. See Capell, *Schubert's Songs* (London: Pan Books, 1973), p. 140. John Reed, *The Schubert Song Companion* (Manchester: Manchester University Press, 1985), p. 214, also praises the final section and attributes the oblivion into which the work has fallen to 'Mayrhofer at his most mediocre,' his ideas being 'too grand and impersonal for the particularity and sensuousness of Schubert's genius.' See also Walther Dürr, Michael Kube, Uwe Schweikert, Stefanie Steiner and Michael Kohlhäufl (eds), *Schubert Liedlexikon* (Kassel: Bärenreiter, 2012), pp. 491–3. The latest and by far the most comprehensive evaluation comes from Graham Johnson, *Franz Schubert: the Complete Songs*, vol. 1,

A–I (New Haven and London: Yale University Press, 2013), pp. 479–8; Johnson discusses the challenge to *An die ferne Geliebte* and points to the links between the 'Tätigkeit' strophe and the third song in Beethoven's cycle. My own remarks are hugely indebted to his astute observations.

6. Johnson, *Franz Schubert: the Complete Songs*, vol. 1, p. 483, points out that the tenth octave stanza—what I am calling the antistrophe of the fifth episode—would not have passed muster with the censors in 1822; 'So he sees that the Fatherland's guardian / Is but the raging murderer of his own brother, / Nurturing noble freedom / With the red blood of mankind' are sentiments to which Metternich's police would surely have objected. They are, however, typical of Mayrhofer, who wrote, in his 'Gesang der Promethiden', 'Wann wird der Retter uns erstehen / Und enden unverdiente Noth? / Wann werden wir es wiedersehen / Der Freiheit schönes Morgenroth? / Einst glüht' es auf Olympos Zinnen— / Doch nur zu bald schwand es von hinnen.'

7. Johann Mayrhofer, *Gedichte von Johann Mayrhofer: Neue Sammlung*, ed. Ernst Freiherr von Feuchtersleben (Vienna: Ignaz Klang, 1843), 'In der Schmiede,' pp. 182–3. Only work in the smithy brings peace, he declares, and he exhorts himself not to gild *his* images, hewn from ore.

8. Ibid., p. 165.

9. Ibid., p. 164.

10. Might 'Einsamkeit' perhaps be a covert specimen of Mayrhofer's fascination with Ulrich von Hutten (1488–1523)? Its persona seems like a conflation of the humanist-reformer and the poet himself, his works often at least partially autobiographical, along with various literary prototypes and abstractions. Both Hutten and Mayrhofer began their adult lives in the cloister, Mayrhofer with the Augustinians in Linz, Hutten with the Benedictines. Both men studied law, and both men fought (Hutten) or believed in fighting (Mayrhofer) for their ideals. Both engaged in satirical and passionate invective, Hutten more so than Mayrhofer, and Hutten's writings on illness (he suffered from syphilis and wrote about it) might have been another attraction for the hypochondriac poet. Furthermore, Hutten's choice of seclusion in his last years on the island of Ufenau and his death there gripped the Romantic imagination, as in Caspar David Friedrich's painting of *Hutten's Tomb* (1823–4). Mayrhofer wrote a verse drama on Hutten that was subsequently lost.

11. See Johann Mayrhofer, *Gedichte* (Vienna: F. Volke, 1824), pp. 135–9; and Maximilian Schochow and Lily Schochow, *Franz Schubert: Die Texte seiner einstimmig komponierten Lieder und ihre Dichter* (Hildesheim: Olm, 1974), p. 347. The Schochows list almost forty variants between Schubert's song text and the published poem; the trend is towards greater emphasis in the *Gedichte*.

12. The third stanza in the 1824 anthology reads, "Gib mir die Fülle der Tätigkeit!' / *Sieh*, Menschen wimmeln weit und breit, / *Gewühl der Wagen braust und stäubt*, / Käufer sich um Läden treiben, / *Es locket* Gold und heller Stein / Lockt *den Unentscheidenen* hinein,— / Und *Entschädigung* für Landesgrüne / *Verheissen* Maskenball und Bühne.'

13. In the 1824 *Gedichte*, the fourth stanza is as follows: 'Doch in prangenden Palästen, / Bei der Freude lauten Festen, / *Wird er ernst und trüb und stumm*, /

Sehnt sich nach dem Heiligtum / Seiner Jugend Unschuldslust,— / *Wünscht zurück sein* Hirtenland / *Mit der Quelle Silberband.* / Ach, dass er hinweg gemusst.'

14. See Ilija Dürhammer, "Du liebst mich! tief hab ich's empfunden'. Freundschaft bei Johann Mayrhofer', in Dürhammer, *Schuberts literarische Heimat: Dichtung und Literaturrezeption der Schubert-Freunde* (Vienna: Böhlau, 1999), pp. 221–34.

15. See Ilija Dürhammer, "Deutsche Jünglinge, O liebt euer Vaterland': Vaterlandsliebe und Freiheitssinn', in ibid., pp. 273–81, for a discussion of Mayrhofer's earlier patriotic ideals.

16. The only change to the sixth stanza in the 1824 *Gedichte* is the verb in the third line: 'Ihn *ergreift* der Sehnsucht Schmerz.'

17. Mayrhofer changed only one word in the third line: 'In ihrer Hand, in *Lust*gesprächen.'

18. The seventh line in the 1824 *Gedichte* reads, '*Das Liebste hat der Krieg genommen!*'

19. Mayrhofer reverses the original ordering of 'Menschen' and 'Brüder' in 1824. The emended second line evokes 'Ein ergimmter *Menschenschlächter*,' while the emended fourth line reads, 'Düngt mit *seiner Brüder* Blut.'

20. In the 1824 *Gedichte*, lines 2 and 3 are as follows: 'Ihn *entzückte*, ihn betrübte,— / Schwebt *gelinder* Schwärmerei.'

21. Daniel Defoe, *Robinson Crusoe: an Authoritative Text, Contexts, Criticism*, ed. Michael Shinagel, 2nd ed. (New York and London: W. W. Norton, 1994). See also Daniel Defoe, *Serious Reflections during the Life and Surprising Adventures of Robinson Crusoe* (London: W. Taylor, 1720), and its first German translation, *Ernstliche und wichtige Betrachtungen des Robinson Crusoe welche er bey den erstaunnungsvollen Begebenheiten seines Lebens gemacht hat benebst seines Gesicht von der Welt der Engel* (Amsterdam, 1721).

22. Jean-Jacques Rousseau, *Les Rêveries du promeneur solitaire*, ed. Marcel Raymond (Geneva: Librairie Droz, 1967), p. 18. See also Bronislaw Baczko, *Rousseau: Einsamkeit und Gemeinschaft* (Vienna: Europa Verlag, 1970).

23. Johann Friedrich Cronegk, 'Einsamkeiten: Ein Gedicht in zween Gesängen' and 'Einsamkeiten in sechs Gesängen' in *Des Freyherrn Johann Friedrich von Cronegk Schriften*, ed. Johann Peter Uz, newly ed. Werner Gundel, 2 vols., 7th edn (Ansbach: Verlage Alte Post, 2003), pp. 294–325. Cronegk is a transitional figure between rationalist Enlightenment views of solitude and the forthcoming theme of the irrational solitary. Other contemporary sources include Adolph Freiherr von Knigge's chapter 'Umgang mit sich selber' in his treatise *Über den Umgang mit Menschen*, ed. Karl-Heinz Göttert (5th edn, 1796; reprint, Stuttgart: Philipp Reclam jun., 1991), and Nicolas Chamfort's chapters 'On Society, the High-Born, the Rich, the Worldly' and 'On the Taste for Solitude and on Dignity of Character', in Chamfort, *Maximes et pensées*, vol. 1 of *Oeuvres complètes de Chamfort*, ed. P. T. Auguis (Geneva: Slatkine, 1968), pp. 373–401.

24. Christoph August Tiedge, *Die Einsamkeit* (Leipzig: Sommer, 1792). Musicians know Tiedge primarily from Beethoven's 'An die Hoffnung,' a setting

of an extract from Tiedge's *Urania: Über Gott, Unsterblichkeit und Freiheit; Ein lyrisch-didaktisches Gedicht in sechs Gesängen* (Halle: Renger, 1801).

25. Johann Georg Zimmermann, *Ueber die Einsamkeit*, 4 vols (Leipzig: Weidmanns Erden und Reich, 1784–5). Most of the subsequent English-language copies were based on the first French version, *La Solitude considérée relativement à l'esprit et au coeur*, trans. Jean-Baptiste Mercier (Paris: Leroy, 1788).

26. In a response to Zimmermann, Christian Garve observed in his *Ueber Gesellschaft und Einsamkeit*, vol. 1 (Breslau: Wilhelm Gottlieb Korn, 1797), that 'nowadays, we reserve earnest pursuits for solitude and are frivolous in company,' an observation applicable in some measure to Schubert's life.

27. Zimmermann studied medicine in Göttingen, went to Hannover in 1768 as physician to George III and served for a time in London before returning to Switzerland. See Rudolf Ischer, *Johann Georg Zimmermann's Leben und Werke: Litterarhistorische Studie* (Bern: K. J. Wyss, 1893); Eduard Bodemann, *Johann Georg Zimmermann: Sein Leben und bisher ungedruckte Briefe an denselben von Bodmer, Breitinger, Geßner, Sulzer, Moses Mendelssohn, Nicolai, der Karschin, Herder und G. Forster* (Hannover: Hahn, 1878); August Bouvier, *J. G. Zimmermann: Un Représentant suisse du cosmopolitisme littéraire au XVIIIe siècle* (Geneva: Georg, 1925); Markus Zenker, *Therapie im literarischen Text: Johann Georg Zimmermanns Werk 'Über die Einsamkeit in seiner Zeit'* (Tübingen: Max Niemeyer Verlag, 2007); and Christoph Weiss, 'Royaliste, Antirépublicain, Antijacobin et Antiilluminé: Johann Georg Zimmermann und die "politische Mordbrennerey in Europe"', in Christoph Weiss and Wolfgang Albrecht (eds), *Von 'Obscuranten' und 'Eudämonisten': Gegenaufklärerische, konservative und antirevolutionäre Publizisten im späten 18. Jahrhundert* (St. Ingbert: Röhrig, 1997), pp. 367–401.

28. Zimmermann, *Ueber die Einsamkeit*, vol. 4, p. 289.

29. 'It is precisely this love of liberty which leads men into Solitude, that they may throw off the chains by which they are confined in the world: it is from this disposition to be free, that he who thinks in Solitude boldly speaks a language which perhaps in society he would not have dared to hazard.' See Zimmermann, *Solitude Considered, with respect to its influence upon the mind and the heart* (London: C. Dilly, 1791), p. 171.

30. See Georg Dehrmann, *Produktive Einsamkeit: Studien zu Gottfried Arnold, Shaftesbury, Johann Georg Zimmermann, Jacob Hermann Obereit und Christoph Martin Wieland* (Hannover: Wehrhahn Verlag, 2002).

31. See Johann Wolfgang von Goethe, *Goethe: the Collected Works*, vol. 4: *From My Life: Poetry and Truth*, ed. Thomas P. Saine and Jeffrey L. Sammons (Princeton, NJ: Princeton University Press, 1987), p. 469.

32. The distinction is still of concern to poets and philosophers. Richard Jones's poem 'White Towels' begins, 'I have been studying the difference / between solitude and loneliness, / telling the story of my life/to the clean white towels taken warm from the dryer.' See Carmela Ciuraru (ed.), *Solitude: Poems* (New York: Alfred A. Knopf, 2005), p. 146. The epigraph to this chapter (ibid.,

p. 77) is another reflection of this attitude. Larkin visited the theme of solitude versus the social life in another poem, with its lines: 'Funny how hard it is to be alone. / I could spend half my evenings, if I wanted, / Holding a glass of washing sherry, canted / Over to catch the drivel of some bitch / Who's read nothing but *Which*, / Just think of all the spare time that has flown // Straight into nothingness by being filled / With forks and faces, rather than repaid / Under a lamp, hearing the noise of wind, / And looking out to see the moon thinned / To an air-sharpened blade. / A life, and yet how sternly it's instilled // *All solitude is selfish.*' Larkin, 'Vers de société', in Peter Washington (ed.), *Comic Poems* (New York and London: Alfred Knopf, 2001), pp. 136-7.

33. Zimmermann, *Ueber die Einsamkeit*, vol. 1, pp. 26-7.

34. Bettina von Arnim, *Werke und Briefe*, vol. 4 (Frechen: Bartmann, 1963), p. 125.

35. Zimmermann, *Ueber die Einsamkeit*, vol. 1, chap. 3, 'Trieb zur Einsamkeit,' pp. 100-1, and vol. 4, chap. 12, 'Uebersicht des Ganzen,' pp. 345-6.

36. Ibid., vol. 2, chap. 7, 'Nachtheilige Einwirkung der Einsamkeit auf die Leidenschaft, zumal bey Einsiedlern und Mönchen,' pp. 212-464.

37. Ibid., vol. 4, chap. 12, 'Uebersicht des Ganzen,' p. 264.

38. Ibid., vol. 1, chap. 2, 'Trieb zur Gesellichkeit,' p. 35. See also ibid., vol. 3, chap. 9, 'Allgemeine Vortheile der Einsamkeit,' in which he discusses such topics as 'Skizze einer Assemblee' (p. 97), 'Schilderung eines Gastmahls' (p. 100) and 'Wahres gesellschaftliches Vergnügen' (p. 100).

39. Ibid., p. 34.

40. Ibid., p. xxvi.

41. Ibid., p. 25.

42. Ibid., vol. 2, chap. 7, 'Nachtheilige Einwirkung der Einsamkeit auf die Leidenschaften, zumal bey Einsiedlern und Mönchen,' pp. 223, and ibid., vol. 4, chap.11, 'Vortheile der Einsamkeit für das Herz,' p. 153 ('Liebe gesellet sich gerne zu allen Blicken in die schöne Natur').

43. Ibid., vol. 4, chap. 11, 'Vortheile der Einsamkeit für das Herz,' with such topics as 'Ruhe kommt in das Herz, wenn man Freude hat an erhabener Natur, und an jedem Blümchen der Thäler' (p. 2f.), 'Alle Traurigkeit über verlohrene Freuden der Liebe, wird am Ende doch durch wohlbenutzte Einsamkeit ersetzet' (p. 185) and 'Und dann macht Einsamkeit, die man mit einem liebenden Wesen theilt, jede Hütte zum Sitze des Vergnügens, dann erleichtert sie alle Leiden des Lebens, dann streut sie Blumen auf alle unsere Wege' (p. 191). See also ibid., vol. 3, chap. 9, 'Allgemeine Vortheile der Einsamkeit,' with such topics as 'Wie Einsamkeit auch in mancherley Fällen von Widerwärtigkeiten des Lebens nützlich wird' (p. 136).

44. Thanks to the ubiquity of the solitude-versus-society themes in the culture of the day, many of Schubert's songwriting predecessors wrote entire collections devoted to one or the other state. For example, Johann Friedrich Reichardt's *Lieder der Liebe und der Einsamkeit zur Harfe und zum Clavier zu singen* (Leipzig: Gerhard Fleischer, 1798) is one of the Janus-face sides of his *Lieder geselliger Freude* (Leipzig: G. Fleischer, 1796-7) and *Neue Lieder geselliger Freude*

(Leipzig: Fleischer, 1799–1800). Schubert's songs of solitude and *Geselligkeit* include 'Die Einsiedelei,' D 393 and D 563 (Johann Gaudenz von Salis-Seewis); the SATB quartet 'Die Geselligkeit (Lebenslust),' D 609 (Johann Karl Unger), with its proclamation 'Allein sein ist öde' (Being alone is odious); 'Der Einsame,' D 800 (Karl Lappe); and—greatest of all—'Wer sich der Einsamkeit ergibt,' D 325 and 478 and 'An die Türen will ich schleichen,' D 479 (Goethe).

45. 'Keiner, der den Schmerz des Andern, und Keiner, der die Freude des Andern versteht! Man glaubt immer, zu einander zu gehen, und man geht immer nur neben einander. O Qual für den, der dieß erkennt!' See Otto Erich Deutsch, *Schubert: Die Dokumente seines Lebens* (Kassel: Bärenreiter, 1964), p. 232.

46. Susan Wollenberg, *Schubert's Fingerprints: Studies in the Instrumental Works* (Surrey: Ashgate, 2011), p. 289.

47. Johnson, *Franz Schubert: the Complete Songs*, vol. 1, p. 484. A passing reference in 'Der Goldschmiedgesell,' D 560, is the only other instance of shops in Schubert, without being the point and purpose of the passage, as it is here.

48. What precedes the moment of silence is noteworthy. The last repetition of the 'processional figure'—a scalewise descending pattern on the scale degrees $\hat{5}-\hat{4}-\hat{3}-\hat{2}$, doubled in thirds in the right hand—stops short on the last beat of bar 154 with a typically Schubertian disposition of chord tones: over a hollow open fifth E–B in the bass, the right hand juxtaposes the leading note and supertonic pitch, an amalgam of tonic and dominant tones that do not resolve. But after the moment of silence, the right hand *does* resolve as expected to E and G—but with C in the bass. Deceptive motion is everywhere in this song cycle–cantata.

49. Six years after beginning work on 'Einsamkeit,' Schubert would do something similar in the final section of another Mayrhofer song, 'Auflösung,' D 807, whose persona attempts repeatedly to vault into the empyrean by means of intervallic leaps.

50. 'Heimlich im Stillen hoffe ich wohl selbst etwas aus mir machen zu können, aber wer vermag nach Beethoven noch etwas zu machen?', in Otto Erich Deutsch, *Schubert: Die Erinnerungen seiner Freunde* (Leipzig, 1966), p. 150; translated into English by Rosamund Ley and John Nowell as *Schubert: Memoirs by his Friends* (London: Adam & Charles Black, 1958), p. 128. See also Walther Dürr, 'Wer vermag nach Beethoven noch etwas zu machen? Gedanken über die Beziehungen Schuberts zu Beethoven', *Beethoven-Jahrbuch* vol.9 (1973–7), pp. 47–67, reprinted in Heinz-Klaus Metzger and Rainer Riehn (eds), *Musik-Konzepte Sonderband Franz Schubert* (Munich, 1979), pp. 10–25.

51. Jacques Derrida, *The Beast and the Sovereign*, vol. 2, trans. Geoffrey Bennington (Chicago: University of Chicago Press, 2012).

23

'Die Wegweiser'—Signposts on an Accompanist's Journey to Scholarship

Homage to Walther Dürr

Graham Johnson

The coming together of the worlds of performance and musicology is not something that happens easily, or even every day; when it does so, it can be an uncomfortable collision, and it can also be life-changing. I was a young pianist who was raised to be a performer and who learned, over many years, to become something of a scholar. It was also my good fortune to encounter, towards the end of this journey, one or two of the greatest living musicologists.

As a student pianist in the erstwhile Rhodesia (now Zimbabwe), I grew up on a diet of editions published by the Associated Board of the Royal Schools of Music, those of Bach and Beethoven in particular. In this way the name Donald Francis Tovey entered my life, alongside those of performing scholars such as Harold Samuel and Harold Craxton. I would be less than honest if I claimed that the Tovey commentaries, considered models of their kind, interested me half as much as the music itself, if at all; knowing nothing of editors, I erroneously figured Harold Samuel's fingering to be Bach's own. I was only nine years old but I was already capable of making the music for myself at the keyboard, if only after a fashion. I instinctively regarded all written introductions as a waste of time and space, a block against the immediately sensual gratification of euphony. I was of course aware that there should be an intermediary between the great composers and a sprat like me, but this oracle was a good deal nearer home than Professor Tovey. The middleman (or woman, in this case) was my piano teacher, Nora, my on-the-spot guide and keyboard goddess. While I was studying with her, the garnering of information from written sources, so that I might form my own rebellious concepts, simply did not occur to me. The idea of having a relationship of my very own with the printed music, based on my own reading and deciphering of it, was a Lutheran audacity, and I was innocent of any such heresy. At that age of hammering pianos (to the sound of slammed doors) I had no theses to nail, only ten unruly fingers.

On the other hand, there was already something in me that was not immune to writings about music, especially if more attractively packaged than the severe Associate Board volumes. In 1959, in Bulawayo's largest department store, I saw for sale a book that took my breath away with its handsome sequence of colour plates and illustrations. I ached to possess this *Concise Encyclopaedia of Music and Musicians*, edited by one Martin Cooper (how could I ever guess that one day I would become good friends with his brilliant pianist daughter, Imogen?). The publisher was Hutchinson (I remember this because it was also the name of my piano teacher), but the price tag—59s/6d[1]—put it firmly out of my family's reach. That was, after all, what we paid for a month of piano lessons.

From within the colonially restricted boundaries of my own musical horizons, I gradually became aware of a phalanx of people, like the enigmatic Martin Cooper, who were essential to the world of music but were neither composers nor performers. (I had no idea that Tovey had been a composer, that Samuel was a famous pianist or that Cooper was a feared critic). The music critic of the *Bulawayo Chronicle* worked under the psudonym of 'Thespian'; he was massively opinionated (the Municipal Orchestra was regularly lambasted), but people said that he himself could play no instrument. This anonymous panjandrum never had to suffer the nerves, by which I was tortured, of having to play in public. I realised that the kind of person who busied himself around music, rather than in it, could easily appear to be more important than instrumentalists, and that such people had always played a part in music history. As a child in Africa I knew the name Köchel almost as a soon as I could play a seemingly easy piece by Mozart (although the same did not apply to Hoboken and my early attempts at Haydn). What a happy fate it was for this unknown Köchel (often shortened to 'K') always to be mentioned in the same breath as one of the greatest men who ever lived!

Most composers had opus numbers, and I relished being able to memorise those that were attached to the Beethoven piano sonatas and concertos, and later the chamber music. (It was in attempting to decipher Beethoven's rather long-winded dedications and tempo directions that I first fell in love with the German language and felt an overwhelming desire to learn it.). Of course I had no idea of the Kinsky-Halm catalogue of Beethoven's works, much less those of Hess and Biamonti. A gift of the *Oxford Companion to Music*, circa 1960, introduced me to the world of Percy Scholes; at the time I was unaware that this heavy book, dazzlingly magical for the younger reader in its chaotic profusion of information, was a feat brought off, against the odds, by a great all-rounder and eccentric. (If I had been a young American presented with *Baker's Biographical Dictionary of Musicians*, I would similarly have taken Nicholas Slominsky's opinions as gospel; today it would be Taruskin.) It would take me some time to learn that it was far more usual for scholars to concentrate on writing about a much smaller field, and that there were some musicologists (a new word for me, this) whose lives were dedicated to the works of a single composer. In that respect, the acquisition by my school library in 1966 of the fifth edition of *Grove's Dictionary of Music and Musicians* (with its enormous number of contributors) was a revelation.

I had no real record library at home, and it was easier to borrow books about music than records; it was not unusual for me to have read about a work (such as Debussy's *Pelléas et Mélisande*) some years before I actually heard it. When I arrived in London in 1967 there was a lot of catching up to do, with the help of the Porchester Road Music Library (an Aladdin's cave in London W2, one of many at that happy time, of scores and LPs) and a portable gramophone in my student digs. I knew a great deal about many pieces from reading about them, and now they came blazingly to life as I listened and followed the scores. I had known nothing of Benjamin Britten in Africa, but suddenly he became a star in my firmament. Wanting to read something about his works, I discovered the book about him edited by Donald Mitchell and Hans Keller. Having acquired the habit in Rhodesia of reading about music (because I had no means there of hearing it), it was now natural for me to seek out words that could complement, validate and enrich my aural experiences.

The music of Schubert was part of this, my recently acquired cultural palimpsest, where word meets tone—the definition of song itself, perhaps, but so much more. In the 1950s, editions of his piano music available to me in Africa were printed with opus numbers (only where applicable). I had at first classed Schubert as an 'opus-number person', but only more or less—numbers like Op. 90 and Op. 140 (post.) were part of the mental picture I attached to him, and other pieces were numberless. In an adolescent phase of useless comparisons I remember thinking, 'Well, at least you know were you are with Beethoven', but that was years before I encountered WoO numbers. I was given a heavy set of 78s of the B♭ major Piano Trio (Cortot, Thibaud and Casals), shellac stored in book-like leaves gathered together in a handsomely embossed sleeve with 'Op. 99' emblazoned in gold on the cover. (At this stage of my life I was not yet a song accompanist, so I knew nothing of this composer's Opp. 1 and 2 and so on). I came to London to study at the Royal Academy of Music in the late 1960s and attempted to play the last of Schubert's piano sonatas. By that time the number D 960 was attached to that masterpiece in my newly purchased Henle edition; the name 'Deutsch' was at last for me becoming, as the Germans put it, a *Begriff*. Deutsch, like Köchel, was a name that had stuck unequivocally to a composer—here there were no Longo-Kirkpatrick Scarlatti rivalries, no Raab-Searle Liszt dislocations, just the supremely authoritative Otto Erich Deutsch himself, with his surname attached to every Schubert work that was ever written.

It was not very long before I became obsessed with Schubert, not on account of his piano sonatas, but because of his lieder. I longed to know how many there were. In a library I encountered Deutsch's *Thematic Catalogue of All his Works in Chronological Order*, printed in 1951, the year after I was born. The modest proportions of the book and its no-nonsense blue cloth covers (I only realised much later that the original dust jacket had been bright red) belied its importance to me as the document that was to define for me the boundaries of a new-found musical world. Untold riches were nestling in those matter-of-fact pages that somehow told the tale of a book produced in wartime austerity. Hearing *Winterreise* in the flesh at Aldeburgh in 1971 (Pears and Britten) was a pivotal experience, a revelation. I simply had to have the music of *all* the Schubert songs. Without being able to afford it, I splurged out on a set of the Peters edition, seven volumes in red cloth bindings. At almost the same time, two massive box sets of records with Dietrich Fischer-Dieskau and Gerald Moore appeared, the first in light blue, the second in darker blue—twenty-five LPs in all, with a third box of four as a follow-up.

It was soon obvious (and I recall feeling cheated) that the famous duo had not recorded all of the Schubert songs (the women's songs and many others were missing) and that those seven Peters volumes contained only 446 songs. Whatever my great joy in first making the acquaintance of so many lieder hitherto unknown to me, the gaps in the catalogue were a devastating disappointment. I count it as one of the happiest days in my life that a fellow record collector (for I was by now a passionate enthusiast of song performances on 78 records) informed me that Constables in Orange Street was selling off remaindered copies of the Dover hardback reprint of the Bretikopf und Härtel Schubert *Gesamtausgabe* for £3.75—each Dover volume encompassing, in slightly smaller size, two of the Breitkopf folio song volumes (not that I knew anything about these originals until much later). For £18 I acquired the five volumes that were devoted to Schubert's lieder—the bargain of the century! Having these at my disposal from 1973 on (during many years when copies of that edition, both the original and the reprint, were truly a rarity) was an incomparable boon. Countless singers, never the most assiduous visitors to libraries, asked me for copies of Schubert songs that they could find in no music shop or antiquarian dealer's (the Internet has changed everything of course, and now such availability is taken for granted), and I was happy to oblige. I was able to programme some of these rarities for recitals in London and elsewhere. There are some 158 songs in 'Mandyczewski' that are not to be found in Peters.

The very name 'Mandyczewski' reminds me of the tone of voice of my beloved mentor Gerald Moore; he always referred to the Breitkopf und Härtel Edition by the name of its famous editor. Eusebius Mandyczewski (1857–1929) is one of the great heroes of Schubert scholarship. Thanks to him and the 'park-like pages' of his edition (as Richard Capell described them in 1928), we are able to follow Schubert's progress as a song composer from the beginning to his life to the end—even though we now know that 'Hagars Klage', D 5, is not quite the beginning. Despite some inevitable mistakes and misapprehensions (this was 1894, remember, and the solutions to many of the editorial problems have taken decades to emerge), the work is astonishingly valid and interesting to this day, beautiful to handle, and a sumptuous feast for the eye on the library shelf. (I still use my Dover reprints, now falling to bits, but pride of place on my shelves goes to Moore's pristine ten-volume set in brown and gold, come down to me with the markings he made for his recordings with Fischer-Dieskau). One of Mandyczewski's greatest achievements (apart from the gathering and studying of manuscripts from all over the world at a time when communications were far slower) was in overruling the advice of Johannes Brahms, who had wanted a more selective (and less complete) publication of the songs' various versions. In insisting on the publication of all available autographs, it was Mandyczewski who proved himself not only a true lover of Schubert, but a truly modern musicologist. It is a measure of this great man's relative obscurity today that a distinguished reference book erroneously published a picture of Max Friedlaender (an important man in the history of Schubert songs to be sure, but less of a heavyweight) in its Mandyczewski article.[2] Friedlaender is here shown as a dapper youngster, but the real Mandyczewski was a bearded prophet in a skullcap, an old man even in his youth. Hans Gál's memories of him (published in an essay by Maurice Brown)[3] give us some indication of the veneration in which he was held by younger scholars.

Long before discovering anything about Mandyczewski, I realised that Deutsch's contributions to Schubert studies were far more substantial than his modest 1951 catalogue (in any case replaced, in 1978, by a much larger one). The English edition of the *Documentary Biography*, the fruit of Deutsch's enforced exile in England during the war years, empowered every Schubert enthusiast to become his own scholar and theoretician; this truly was a Gutenberg Bible for Schubertians, who were free to read the facts and interpret matters for themselves. The effect on me of this substantial (and sometimes dangerous) book with its pale green cover, as well as the wonderful iconographical volume acquired some years later (the luxurious fruit of Deutsch's acumen as an art historian), was to turn me into a card-carrying Schubertian, a member of that worldwide society of those who love this composer more than any other, and who regard this devotion as something given unconditionally and for life. It was not only hearing or playing the music that had turned me into this kind of fanatical admirer, but also reading about it and around it. In one way or another this music had been presented to me, made available to me, by those who had gone before me—and a list of those names would include not only a number of great singers and pianists from the past, as well as my own past, but a number of great musicologists as well, and equally indispensable.

Having related my Schubertian progress from childhood to the earlier years of my playing career, I suppose this is where this chapter might easily have ended. I had spent a great deal more money than I could ever afford on buying music and books and records. I thought myself as well and truly 'set'; now I had everything I needed to deepen my Schubertian knowledge, and it was my enormous, and unaccountable, good fortune to be invited to record the complete Schubert songs. I must acknowledge here, as I always do when given the chance, my enormous debt to Eric Sams, who was my mentor as a writer about lieder. Without him I would never have had the confidence to invent something as unusual as the Songmakers' Almanac, and then regularly to put pen to paper as part of bringing that idea to fruition. Some years later, when I began to record Schubert, I was grateful for the help of such famous Schubertians as John Reed and Reinhard Van Hoorickx.

At this stage of my life, the discovery of the lieder series of the *Neue Schubert-Ausgabe* in about 1975 (the first volume of songs had been published in 1968) came as something of an unsettling surprise in a rather Schubertian way. It was as if I had already composed twelve songs of a cycle—believing it to be complete and a done deal—only to discover another set of twelve poems from the same cycle that I had somehow overlooked. (It is far from unusual for even distinguished musicians to be routinely out of the loop regarding the latest scholarly publications.) At first I was perplexed. The available (and extremely expensive) volumes at that point were 7 (1968), 6 (1969) and 1 (1972). This was far from the calmly logical appearance of the songs in Mandyczewski, where the subscribers of the time were led through the lieder, from first to last, in a grand sequence. Volume 6 of this new edition was where the song sequence *began*, with 'Hagars Klage', and it took me quite some time to cotton on to the logic of the first five volumes (four of which had not appeared by that time). These were devoted to the opus numbers as they were published in Schubert's lifetime, beginning only in 1821. Thus volume 1 began with 'Erlkönig', Op. 1 (D 328).

I remember reading a disclaimer, at the beginning of Fischer-Dieskau's recording of the Schubert songs for Deutsche Grammophon (circa 1971), that his recordings would not be able to take into account the latest scholarship of the *Neue Schubert-Ausgabe*, then in its initial stages. I began my own complete recording of Schubert songs for Hyperion sixteen years later, in 1987, finishing in 2001, and the lieder series of the *Neue Schubert-Ausgabe* was still more than a decade away from completion. It was like watching a vast jigsaw puzzle gradually assuming its final shape with the passing of the years. As a latecoming subscriber, I did not realise at first that the editor of the series, Walther Dürr, was thoroughly and methodically revolutionising Schubert song scholarship; although he himself was modest and unruffled in editorial manner, his changes were groundbreaking in effect. This was really 'rethinking Schubert'. Mandyczewski had decided that he needed to establish a song chronology (Deutsch-like, *avant la lettre*) and had paid no attention to the opus numbers that had hitherto been used as a framework for Schubert chronology (as, for example, in the Nottebohm catalogue of 1874). Nevertheless, these groupings are not simply a set of numbers with a flawed chronology; in fact, they show Schubert's hand as an inventor of his own garlands of songs (although to a lesser extent than claimed by some enthusiasts who these days strain to gather everything the composer wrote into bundles of cycles), revealing the composer in a state of continuing and ongoing growth as reviser, perfectionist and proud parent of his own creations. Although 'Erlkönig' came into being in 1815 (and

Mandyczewski correctly places it in chronological order as one of the songs of that year), it achieved its final form only upon its publication in 1821.

From Dürr's novel point of view, 'Erlkönig' had been composed *between* 1815 and 1821, a time scale that applied to all the songs from Schubert's earlier years that were later published. (Of course, for those songs composed after 1821, there were a number whose progress into print was considerably quicker and, in a few cases, almost immediate). The changes Schubert made between autograph and printed artefact (the proofs would have minutely traced this progress, but they were always destroyed by the publishers) were sometimes only tiny and sometimes very significant, but it is these metamorphoses of phrasing, articulation and dynamics (much more than these things) that Dürr revealed as carefully as if he were involved on an archaeological dig in Luxor. (We must immediately recognise that Deutsch did little along these trench-digging lines as far as the music itself was concerned).

By separating out, in the first five volumes of the edition, the songs that Schubert himself had carefully prepared for public consumption, we learn that W. H. Auden's adage about a poem's never really being finished, only abandoned, applied equally to those hundreds of songs that Schubert had left unpublished. Of course many of these works (appearing in volumes 6 to 14 of the *Neue Schubert-Ausgabe*) are masterpieces just as they are—it would appear to Schubert's admirers around the world that most of them need no revision at all. Nevertheless, this composer was not only a creature of the heat of the moment (though he could also create in that mode); his artistic conscience and his attention to detail, not to mention his endless and unflagging invention, permitted him constantly to renew and vary and improve. We know beyond doubt that if Schubert had had time to bring all of his songs to publication (instead of leaving the task, posthumously, to the likes of Anton Diabelli), then the richness of his musical legacy would have been greater still.

Virginia Woolf once described George Eliot's *Middlemarch* as 'one of the few English novels written for grown-up people'.[4] The life's of Walther Dürr is one of the few examples of Schubert scholarship for grown-up people, and certainly grown-up performers. I confess to growing *into* it over the years (I was certainly not ready for it in my twenties), little realising, at first, the monumental task that Dürr had set himself and the single-minded manner in which he aimed to reach his goal. For all his wonderful abilities, this is the kind of work that Deutsch, not a musicologist by training, could never have undertaken. In fact Dürr's is a continuation of Mandyczewski's work, carried to unprecedented levels of detail. The *Neue Schubert-Ausgabe* volumes are far smaller in format than the old *Gesamtausgabe*, a tiny bit bigger than the Peters edition but containing far fewer songs in each volume (until, that is, the later volumes of the series). The grey binding, apart from the red of the composer's imprinted signature, reinforces the idea of no-nonsense efficiency. But what lies within these somewhat minimalist exteriors represents a level of intellectual exertion that would have made even Mandyczewski blanch. The word 'meticulous' is completely insufficient to describe Dürr's attention to detail—'terrifying' would be a better choice. The written material at the front of each volume of the *Neue Schubert-Ausgabe*, as well as the 'Quellen und Lesarten' sections at the back, are essential reading for any scholar—often containing completely new insights—but it is within the bright-blue paperback volumes of the *Kritischer Bericht* (one volume for each volume of the *Neue Schubert-Ausgabe*, and with volume 9 still to emerge as I write) that Dürr shows us his credentials. There is no man alive who has spent more time with each page, each bar, *each note*, of Schubert's song autographs—and not only the autographs but also the contemporary copies, some of which are just as important as the autographs.

How many of us realise, for example, that there is a veritable genealogy of how one copy derives from another, and how these may or may not go back to different autographs? Dürr's diagrams of these relationships are detective work of a thrilling kind, as is his study of the watermarks of the paper the composer used. The amount of time that all this forensic investigation has taken—many decades—is, to my mind, completely justified and entirely understandable. There are certain songs that must have taken weeks of concentrated study, a bar at a time—and the same applies to the literary sources and variations (one can never forget that, among his many achievements, Dürr studied singing and *Germanistik*).

On a personal note: I remember Dürr visiting my home in London in 2010, at the time he came to inspect a hitherto unknown autograph copy of 'Blondel zu Marien', D 626, for sale at Sotheby's. On that occasion I was able to give him a copy of an old Viennese school textbook, *Sammlung Deutscher Beyspiele für Bildung des Styls* (1808), a possible early source of song texts. It was little enough to thank him for years of inspiration. Long after the publication of volume 10 of the *Neue Schubert-Ausgabe* (2002), but before the appearance of the *Kritischer Bericht* for that volume (2009), I discovered in an almanac published in Berlin in 1805 that the unknown Ernestine von Krosigk was the poet of 'Aus Diego Manazares: Ilmerine,' D 458, a song that had been attributed to Franz von Schlechta for over 150 years. A strong argument for the authenticity of Schlechta's authorship had been made in the *Neue Schubert-Ausgabe* in the prefatory material for volume 10. The joy with which Dürr received the information I was able to send him, and the grace with which the matter was subsequently corrected in the *Kritischer Bericht* were ample evidence of someone who cared only for the truth, no matter how inconvenient.

A little while after Dürr's visit to London, I visited him in Tübingen. In 2011 I had been invited to Stuttgart as a judge of the Hugo Wolf lieder-singing competition, and there was a day off in which I could travel. The welcome I received at the station, in excellent English, was unforgettably hospitable. It was a short walk to 'the office' and I was privileged to see the room in which all this work had been done, as well as the library that this great scholar uses for his day-to-day investigations. Some of these volumes had belonged to Deutsch; I remember envying a wonderfully annotated and indexed copy of the biography of Johann Herbeck. On the same visit I met Dürr's colleague Christine Martin. In due course the conversation moved from his office to hers, and the language shifted (gratifyingly for me) from English to German. Formalities were dissolved, and the theme was our shared Schubertian passion. How is it that a boy from the English-speaking colonies felt so at home in this company, where every song raised for discussion, however obscure in the opinion of the outside world, was something mutually shared and ineffably dear? It was a convivial visit in every sense of the word, with Schubert somehow smiling down on us. I felt enormously privileged to be received as a fellow Schubertian within these hallowed walls (hallowed at least for me) in the middle of that beautiful university town, Germany's Cambridge, within walking distance of the first premises of Cotta, Goethe's great publisher, and countless echoes in the streets and buildings of the lives of Hölderlin, Uhland and Mörike. It also seemed to me (however heretical it may be to say so) that the kind of quiet, methodical work that was taking place in Tübingen might have been less comfortably accomplished in Vienna, Schubert's own town certainly, but also famous for its disruptive musical politics. Of course we should gratefully record here that the level of intense scholarship typified by the *Neue Schubert-Ausgabe* requires the support of a major publisher, self-evidently a German publisher, so it's hats off to Bärenreiter Verlag, the Internationale Schubert-Gesellschaft and the various German and Austrian state and city institutions whose subventions make such ongoing work possible.

There are certain people who have worked with Schubert for all their lives in such an open-hearted way that they become, in a sense, Schubert himself in this age of the world. I do not really think this metamorphosis was something that happened to Deutsch (he strikes me as someone whose imposing theme was the dazzling totality of Schubert's Vienna, rather than simply the composer himself). On the other hand, I think that Schubert's modesty and kindness, his affability and his disinterested approach to music, without political overtones (see, for example, the composer's own uncomplicated admiration for Rossini or Conradin Kreutzer), is something that has penetrated the very fabric of Dürr's scholarship. The same could be said of the work of John Reed and Susan Youens. It took me rather a long time to appreciate what Dürr was doing (his fabulously detailed work is not for the Schubertian neophyte), but when I was writing my book *Franz Schubert: the Complete Songs*, his sagacious advice—not personally, I hasten to add, simply in terms of his writings—was the most valuable of all guides available to me. Imagine my joy in opening the last volume of his life's work, volume 9 of the *Neue Schubert-Ausgabe*, and finding a bombshell that was bound to take the breath away of any Schubert scholar: he had come to the conclusion, after decades of reflection, that the Goethe settings 'An den Mond', D 296 (the second setting), and 'Hoffnung',

D 295, were both written *after February 1820*. For the casual reader, or even the dedicated music lover, such an announcement may seem to be small beer, but this shifts Deutsch's original date for these songs forward by five years at the least. From the point of view of Schubert scholarship, this is important news.

When I can claim to have such information at my fingertips, I speak of myself not only as a writer, but as a pianist: for me, the two modes of performance have become interchangeable. It is a mystery to me how musicology actually changes the performing style and sound of those whose primary profession is on stage or in the recording studio. I have lived for the last four decades with Dürr's work and paid closer and closer attention to it as the years have gone by. There are many instances where I wish I had been more assiduous in my studies before performing this or that song. I suspect that much of Dürr's work, laid down for the ages, will long await the kind of discovery that leads to a practical application of its wisdom. But with such an enduring figure as Schubert, we can afford that kind of patience.

Knowledge is a kind a power, and when a performer approaches a piece he or she has really examined—and taken to heart in every way—there is no doubt that a there is a process of empowerment, a feeling of ownership, not in any bombastic sense, but in knowing about it in one's bones, much as one's own family history is automatically part and parcel of who one is. Those who spend their lives with Schubert somehow become part of his extended family. In my own case, there were no sudden decisions to play his music in a different way: the process has been a long and indefinable one, but the respectful care with which Dürr annotates the composer's wishes, every marking and every articulation, has thrown the spotlight of the best kind of science on some of the murkier mysteries of interpretation. This has undoubtedly changed both how I see, and then how I play, Franz Schubert's heavenly music.

I come from a profession where even the most distinguished practitioners are in danger of being underestimated and underappreciated. For this reason, I feel that accompanists and naturally modest and self-effacing musicologists like Walther Dürr (and my kindest colleague in recent years, Susan Youens) are comrade soldiers in the trenches. In some ways we come from opposite ends of the Earth, both personally and musically, but what we have in common in that it is in our DNA (D NSA, perhaps) to fight for our chosen composer without question. That I have Franz Schubert in common with such great scholars as Youens and Dürr is an abiding joy and privilege. I would advise all singers and accompanists of the future to adopt them, and scholars like them, as indispensable guides. As for Dürr's unique contribution to our understanding of this composer, we can be sure that for very many years to come no one else will engage with Schubert's handwritten legacy with greater application, greater thoroughness and greater love.

Notes

1. In present-day British money, £2.98.
2. Ernst Hilmar and Margret Jestremski, *Schubert-Enzyklopädie*, 2 vols (Tutzing: Hans Schneider, 2004), vol. 2, p. 464.
3. Maurice J. E. Brown, *Essays on Schubert* (London: Macmillan, and New York: St Martin's Press, 1966), pp. 187–93.
4. Virginia Woolf, 'George Eliot', *The Times Literary Supplement*, 20 November 1919.

Bibliography

Achim von Arnim, Ludwig. 'Von Volksliedern'. In *Des Knaben Wunderhorn*. Berlin: Riemer, 1805–8.
———. *Armut, Reichtum, Schuld und Buße der Gräfin Dolores*. Berlin: Riemer, 1810.
Adler, Guido. *Der Stil in der Musik*. Leipzig: Breitkopf & Härtel, 1911.
Adorno, Theodor W. 'Spätstil Beethovens'. *Der Auftakt* 17, 5/6 (1937), pp. 65–7. Translated into English as 'Late Style in Beethoven', in Adorno, *Essays on Music*, ed. Richard Leppert. Berkeley and Los Angeles: University of California Press, 2002. Pp. 564–6.
Adorno, Theodor W. 'Spätstil Beethovens [1937]'. In *Gesammelte Schriften*, ed. Rolf Tiedemann. 20 vols. Frankfurt am Main: Suhrkamp, 1993. Vol. 17, pp. 13–17.
———. *Beethoven: Philosophie der Musik: Fragmente und Texte*. Ed. Rolf Tiedemann. Frankfurt am Main: Suhrkamp, 1993.
———. 'Schubert' (1928). Trans. Jonathan Dunsby and Beate Perrey. *19th-Century Music* 29/1 (2005), pp. 3–14.
Agawu, V. Kofi. 'On Schubert's "Der greise Kopf"'. *In Theory Only* 8/1 (1984), pp. 3–22.
Aldrich, Richard. 'The Heavenly Lengths in Schubert'. *The New York Times*, 9 November 1919. Section 8, p. 3.
Arnim, Bettina von. *Werke und Briefe*. Vol. 4. Frechen: Bartmann, 1963.
Aschauer, Michael. 'Drei Stationen einer Auseinandersetzung mit dem System Metternichs: Franz Schuberts politische und weltanschauliche Haltung, dargelegt anhand seiner Schriften, ausgewählter Liedtexte und dreier Freundesgestalten'. *Studien zur Musikwissenschaft* 48 (2002), pp. 373–88.
Baczko, Bronislaw. *Rousseau: Einsamkeit und Gemeinschaft*. Vienna: Europa Verlag, 1970.
Badura-Skoda, Paul. 'Possibilities and Limitations of Stylistic Criticism in the Cating of Schubert's "Great" C major Symphony'. In Eva Badura-Skoda and Peter Branscombe (eds), *Schubert Studies: Problems of Style and Chronology*. Cambridge: Cambridge University Press, 1982. Pp. 187–208.
Bailey, Robert (ed.). *Wagner, Prelude and Transfiguration from 'Tristan und Isolde'*. New York: Norton, 1985.
Barry, Barbara. '"Sehnsucht" and Melancholy: Explorations of Time and Structure in Schubert's *Winterreise*'. In *The Philosopher's Stone: Essays in the Transformation of Musical Structure*. Hillsdale, NY: Pendragon Press, 2000. Pp. 181–202.

Bartsch, Rudolf Hans. *Schwammerl: Ein Schubert-Roman.* Leipzig: L. Staackmann, 1912.
Bauernfeld, Eduard von. *Bilder und Persönlichkeiten aus Alt-Wien.* Ed. Wilhelm Zentner. Altötting: Verlag 'Bücher der Heimat', 1948.
Bekker, Paul. *Beethoven.* Berlin: Schuster & Loeffler, 1912.
Boehmer-Aachen, R. 'Goethe und Schubert'. *Rheinische Musik- und Theaterzeitung* 14 (1913), pp. 486–9.
Biba, Otto. 'Goethe in the Vienna Music Scene of his Era'. In Lorraine Byrne Bodley (ed.), *Goethe: Musical Poet, Musical Catalyst.* Dublin: Carysfort Press, 2004. Pp. 7–40.
Black, Brian. 'Remembering a Dream: the Tragedy of Romantic Memory in the Transitional Process of Schubert's Sonata Forms'. *Intersections* 25/1–2 (2005), pp. 202–28.
Black, Leo. *Franz Schubert: Music and Belief.* Woodbridge: Boydell & Brewer, 2003.
Blackwell, Thomas. *Enquiry into the Life and Writings of Homer.* London: J. Oswald, 1775.
Blanken, Christine. *Franz Schuberts 'Lazarus' und das Wiener Oratorium zu Beginn des 19. Jahrhunderts. Schubert: Perspektiven—Studien 1.* Stuttgart: Steiner, 2002.
Bodemann, Eduard. *Johann Georg Zimmermann: Sein Leben und bisher ungedruckte Briefe an denselben von Bodmer, Breitinger, Geßner, Sulzer, Moses Mendelssohn, Nicolai, der Karschin, Herder und G. Forster.* Hannover: Hahn, 1878.
Böttcher, Helmuth M. *Der Unvollendete: Franz Schubert und sein Kreis.* Rudolstadt: Greifenverlag, 1954.
Bostridge, Ian. *Schubert's Winter Journey: Anatomy of an Obsession.* London: Faber & Faber.
Botstein, Leon. 'Realism Transformed: Franz Schubert and Vienna'. In Christopher H. Gibbs (ed.), *The Cambridge Companion to Schubert.* Cambridge: Cambridge University Press, 1997. Pp. 15–17.
Bouvier, August. *J. G. Zimmermann: un représentant suisse du cosmopolitisme littéraire au XVIIIe siècle.* Geneva: Georg, 1925.
Branscombe, Peter. 'Schubert and the Ungers: a Preliminary Study'. In Brian Newbould (ed.), *Schubert Studies*, 2006. Pp. 209–19.
Brett, Philip. 'Piano Four-Hands: Schubert and the Performance of Gay Male Desire'. *19th-Century Music* 21/2 (1997), pp. 49–76.
Brendel, Alfred. 'Form and Psychology in Beethoven's Piano Sonatas'. In Brendel, *Alfred Brendel on Music: Collected Essays.* Chicago: A Cappella, 2001. Pp. 42–57.
Bretherton, David. 'In Search of Schubert's Doppelgänger'. *The Musical Times* 184/1884 (2003), p. 48.
——. 'The Poetics of Schubert's Song-Forms'. PhD diss., Oxford University, 2007.
Bribitzer-Stull, Matthew. 'The A♭–C–E Complex: the Origin and Function of Chromatic Major Third Collections in Nineteenth-Century Music'. *Music Theory Spectrum* 28 (2006), pp. 167–90.
Brown, Clive. *Classical and Romantic Performing Practice, 1750–1900.* New York and Oxford: Oxford University Press, 1999.

Brown, Maurice J. *Schubert: a Critical Biography*. London: Macmillan, 1966.
——. 'The Posthumous Publication of the Songs'. In *Essays on Schubert*. London: Macmillan, 1966. Pp. 267–90.
Brusatti, Otto. *Schubert im Wiener Vormärz: Dokumente 1829–1848*. Graz: Adeva, 1978.
Burdach, Karl Friedrich. *Bemerkungen und Gefühle auf einer Reise durch den Harz*. Leipzig, 1798.
Budde, Elmar. 'Franz Schubert—Caspar David Friedrich: Eine Studie'. In *Von Dichtung und Musik 1797–1997 'Der Flug der Zeit': Franz Schubert: Ein Lesebuch*. Tutzing: H. Schneider, 1997. Pp. 127–62.
——. *Modulationsmanie und Perspektivenwechsel: Über Franz Schubert und Caspar David Friedrich*. In Otto Kolleritsch (ed.), *'Dialekt ohne Erde . .'..Franz Schubert und das 20. Jahrhundert*. Graz: Universal Edition, 1998. Pp. 121–38.
——. 'Tonalität und Perspektive: Anmerkungen zu Franz Schubert und Caspar David Friedrich'. In Thomas Ertelt (ed.), *Werk und Geschichte: Musikalische Analyse und historischer Entwurf*. Mainz: Schott, 2005. Pp. 115–24.
Burnham, Scott. *Beethoven Hero*. Princeton, NJ: Princeton University Press, 1995.
——. 'Landscape as Music, Landscape as Truth: Schubert and the Burden of Repetition'. *19th-Century Music* 29/1 (2005), pp. 31–41.
Burstein, L. Poundie. 'Devil's Castles and Schubert's Strange Tonic Allusions'. *Theory and Practice* 27 (2002), pp. 69–84.
——. 'Lyricism, Structure and Gender in Schubert's G major String Quartet'. *Musical Quarterly* 81/1 (1997), pp. 51–63.
Byrne Bodley, Lorraine. *Schubert's Goethe Settings*. Farnham: Ashgate, 2003.
——. *Goethe and Zelter: Musical Dialogues*, Farnham Ashgate, 2009.
Byrne Bodley, Lorraine, and Barbara Reul (eds). *The Unknown Schubert*. Farnham: Ashgate, 2008.
Capell, Richard. *Schubert's Songs*. 3rd edn. London: Duckworth, 1973.
Caplin, William E. *Classical Form: a Theory of Formal Functions for the Music of Haydn, Mozart, and Beethoven*. New York and Oxford: Oxford University Press, 1998.
Carner, Mosco. 'Ländler'. In Stanley Sadie and John Tyrrell (eds), *The New Grove Dictionary of Music and Musicians*, 2nd edn. London: Macmillan, 2001. Vol. 14, p. 223.
Celestini, Federico. *Die Unordnung der Dinge: Das musikalische Groteske in der Wiener Moderne (1885–1914)*. Stuttgart: Steiner, 2006.
Chamfort, Nicolas. *Maximes et pensées*. In *Oeuvres complètes de Chamfort*, ed. P. T. Auguis, vol. 1. Geneva: Slatkine, 1968.
Chua, Daniel K. L. *The 'Galitzin' Quartets of Beethoven: Opp. 127, 132, 130*. Princeton, NJ: Princeton University Press, 1995.
Chusid, Martin. 'The Chamber Music of Schubert'. PhD diss., University of California, 1961.
—— (ed). *A Companion to Schubert's 'Schwanengesang': History, Poets, Analysis, Performance*. New Haven, CT: Yale University Press, 2002.

Clark, Suzannah. *Analyzing Schubert*. Cambridge: Cambridge University Press, 2012.

———. 'On the Imagination of Tone in Schubert's *Liedesend* (D 473), *Trost* (D 523), and *Gretchens Bitte* (D 564)'. In Edward Gollin and Alexander Rehding (eds), *The Oxford Handbook of Neo-Riemannian Theories*. New York: Oxford University Press, 2011. Pp. 294–321.

———. 'Schubert, Theory and Analysis'. *Music Analysis* 21/2 (2002), pp. 209–43.

Clive, Peter. *Schubert and his World: a Biographical Dictionary*. Oxford: Clarendon Press, 1997.

Clough, John. 'Flip-Flop Circles and their Groups'. In Jack Douthett, Martha M. Hyde and Charles J. Smith (eds), *Chords, Collections, and Transformations: Music Theory and Mathematics*. Rochester, NY: University of Rochester Press, 2008. Pp. 23–48.

Cobley, Paul. *Narrative*. London: Routledge, 2001.

Code, David Løberg. 'Listening for Schubert's Doppelgängers'. *Music Theory Online* 1/4 (1995).

Cohn, Richard. '"As Wonderful as Star Clusters": Instruments for Gazing at Tonality in Schubert'. *19th-Century Music* 22/3 (1998), pp. 9–40.

———. *Audacious Euphony: Chromaticism and the Triad's Second Nature*. New York and Oxford: Oxford University Press, 2012.

Cone, Edward T. 'Schubert's Beethoven'. *The Musical Quarterly* 56 (1970), pp. 779–93.

———. 'Schubert's Unfinished Business'. *19th-Century Music* 7/3 (1984), pp. 222–32.

Cooper, Martin. *Beethoven: the Last Decade, 1817–1827*. Oxford: Oxford University Press, 1985.

Croll, Gerhard. 'Kanons von Michael Haydn'. In Heinrich Hüschen (ed.), *Musicae Scientiae Collectanea: Festschrift Karl Gustav Fellerer*. Cologne: Arno Volk, 1973. Pp. 64–9.

Cronegk, Johann Friedrich. 'Einsamkeiten: Ein Gedicht in zween Gesängen' and 'Einsamkeiten in sechs Gesängen'. In Werner Gundel (ed.), *Des Freyherrn Johann Friedrich von Cronegk Schriften*, 7th edn. 2 vols. Ansbach: Verlage Alte Post, 2003. Pp. 294–325.

Dalton, David. 'Goethe and the Composers of his Time'. *The Music Review* 34(1973), pp. 157–74.

Dahlhaus, Carl. 'Franz Schubert und das "Zeitalter Beethovens und Rossinis"'. In *Franz Schubert: Jahre der Krise 1818–1823*. Kassel: Bärenreiter, 1985. Pp. 22–8.

———. *Ludwig van Beethoven und seine Zeit*. Laaber: Laaber-Verlag, 1987.

———. *Die Musik des 19. Jahrhunderts*. Wiesbaden: Akademische Verlagsgesellschaft Athenaion, 1980.

———. 'Sonata Form in Schubert: the First Movement of the G major String Quartet, Op. 161 (D. 877)'. Trans. Thilo Reinhard in Walther Frisch (ed.), *Schubert: Critical and Analytical Studies*. Lincoln: University of Nebraska Press, 1986. Pp. 13–30.

Damschroder, David. *Harmony in Haydn and Mozart*. Cambridge: Cambridge University Press, 2012.

———. *Harmony in Schubert*. Cambridge: Cambridge University Press, 2010.

———. *Thinking about Harmony: Historical Perspectives on Analysis*. Cambridge: Cambridge University Press, 2008.

Daverio, John. *Crossing Paths: Schubert, Schumann, and Brahms*. New York and Oxford: Oxford University Press, 2002.

———. *Nineteenth-Century Music and German Romantic Ideology*. New York: Schirmer, 1993.

———. 'Schumann's "Im Legendenton" and Friedrich Schlegel's *Arabeske*'. *19th Century Music* 11/2 (1987), pp. 150–63.

———. 1996. 'The Song Cycle: Journeys through a Romantic Landscape'. In Rufus Hallmark (ed.), *German Lieder in the Nineteenth Century*. New York: Schirmer, 1996. Pp. 279–312.

Daviau, Gertraud Steiner. 'Opposing Views: Franz Schubert in the Films of Willi Forst (1933) and Fritz Lehner (1986)'. In Robert Pichl and Clifford A. Bernd(eds), *The Other Vienna: The Culture of Biedermeier Austria: Österreichisches Biedermeier in Literatur, Musik, Kunst und Kulturgeschichte*. Vienna: Lehner, 2002. Pp. 315–22.

Defoe, Daniel. *Robinson Crusoe: an Authoritative Text, Contexts, Criticism*, ed. Michael Shinagel. 2nd edn. New York and London: W. W. Norton, 1994.

Dehrmann, Georg. *Produktive Einsamkeit: Studien zu Gottfried Arnold, Shaftesbury, Johann Georg Zimmermann, Jacob Hermann Obereit und Christoph Martin Wieland*. Hannover: Wehrhahn Verlag, 2002.

Denny, Thomas A. 'Articulation, Elision, and Ambiguity in Schubert's Mature Sonata Forms: The Op. 99 Trio Finale in its Context.' *Journal of Musicology* 6/3 (1988), pp. 340–66.

———. 'Schubert's "Fierrabras" and Barbaja's Opera Business'. In *Schubert: Perspektiven* 5 (2005), pp. 19–45.

Deutsch, Otto Erich. *Franz Schubert: Die Dokumente seines Lebens*. Kassel: Bärenreiter-Verlag, 1964, rev. edn. Wiesbaden: Breikopf & Hartel, 1996.

———. *Schubert: A Documentary Biography*, trans. Eric Blom, London: J. M. Dent & Sons, 1946.

———. *The Schubert Reader: A Life of Franz Schubert in Letters and Documents*. New York: W. W. Norton & Co., 1949.

——— (ed.). *Schubert: Die Erinnerungen seiner Freunde*. Leipzig: Breitkopf & Härtel, 1957.

———. *Schubert: Memoirs by His Friends*, trans. Rosamond Ley and John Nowell, London: Adam and Charles Black, 1958.

de Saussure, Horace-Bénédict. 'Discurs préliminaire'. In *Voyage dans les Alps, précédé d'un essai sur l'histoire naturelle des environs de Genève*, vol. 1. 2 vols. Genève, 1779.

De Voto, Mark. *Schubert's Great C Major: Biography of a Symphony*. Hillsdale, NY: Pendragon Press, 2011.

Dineen, Murray. 'Tonal Problem, Carpenter Narrative, and Carpenter Motive in Schubert's Impromptu, Op. 90, No. 3'. *Theory and Practice* 30 (2005), pp. 97–120.

Dittrich, Marie-Agnes. 'The Lieder of Schubert'. In James Parsons (ed.), *The Cambridge Companion to the Lied*. Cambridge: Cambridge University Press, 2004. Pp. 85–100.

Douthett, Jack, and Peter Steinbach. 'Parsimonious Graphs: a Study in Parsimony, Contextual Transformations, and Modes of Limited Transposition'. *Journal of Music Theory* 42 (1998), pp. 241–63.

Dürr, Walther. 'Schuberts romantisch-heroische Oper Alfonso und Estrella im Kontext französischer und italienischer Tradition'. In Erich Wolfgang Partsch and Oskar Pausch (eds.), *Der vergessene Schubert: Franz Schubert auf der Bühne* [exhibition catalogue]. Vienna: , 1997. Pp. 79–105.

———.'Über Schuberts Verhältnis zu Bach'. In Ingrid Fuchs (ed.), *Johann Sebastian Bach: Beiträge zur Wirkungsgeschichte*. Vienna: Kongressbericht Wien, 1992. Pp. 69–79.

———. 'Wer vermag nach Beethoven noch etwas zu machen? Gedanken über die Beziehungen Schuberts zu Beethoven', *Beethoven-Jahrbuch* 9 (1973-7), pp. 47–68.

Dürr, Walther, Michael Kube, Uwe Schweikert and Stefanie Steiner (eds). *Schubert-Liedlexikon*. Kassel: Bärenreiter Verlag, 2012.

Dürhammer, Ilija. 'Homoerotische Chiffren im Schubert-Kreis'. *Kunstpunkt* 24 (2002), pp. 19–20.

Ebel, Johann Gottfried. *Anleitung auf die nützlichste und genussvollste Art in der Schweiz zu reisen* 2 vols. Leipzig: Breitkopf, 1798.

Einstein, Alfred. *Schubert: Ein musikalisches Porträt*. Zurich: Pan-Verlag, 1952.

Entwistle, Erik. 'Dussek's "*L'Invocation*" Sonata and the Mystique of the Last Work'. In Roberto Illiano and Rohan H. Stewart-MacDonald(eds), *Jan Ladislav Dussek (1760-1812): a Bohemian Composer 'en Voyage' through Europe*. Quaderni Clementiani 4. Bologna: Ut Orpheus, 2012. Pp. 347–73.

Everett, Walther. 'Grief in *Winterreise*: a Schenkerian Perspective'. *Music Analysis* 9/2 (1990), pp. 157–75.

Feil, Arnold. *Franz Schubert: Die schöne Müllerin; Die Wintrerreise*. Stuttgart: Reclam, 1975.

Ferris, David. *Schumann's Eichendorff 'Liederkreis' and the Genre of the Romantic Cycle*. New York: Oxford University Press, 2000.

Fertonani, Cesare. *La memoria del canto: rielaborazioni liederistiche nella musica strumentale di Schubert*. Milan: LED, 2005.

Fichte, Johann Gottlieb. *Über das Wesen des Gelehrten und seine Erscheinungen im Gebiete der Freiheit*. In Fichte, *Werke*. Berlin: Walther de Gruyter, 1971.

Fischer-Dieskau, Dietrich. *Schubert's Songs: a Biographical Study*. Trans. Kenneth A. Whitton. New York: Alfred A. Knopf, 1977.

Fisk, Charles. 'Edward T. Cone's "The Composer's Voice": Questions about the Persona of Schubert's "Wanderer" Fantasy'. *College Music Symposium* 29 (1989), pp. 19–30.

———. *Returning Cycles: Contexts for the Interpretation of Schubert's Impromptus and Last Sonatas*. Berkeley and Los Angeles: University of California Press, 2001.

———. 'Schubert's Last Finales'. The TASI Journal: a Publication of the American Schubert Institute 1 (1997), pp. 3–17.

Flothius, Marius. 'Schubert Revises Schubert'. In Eva Badura-Skoda and Peter Branscombe(eds), *Schubert Studies: Problems of Style and Chronology*. Cambridge: Cambridge University Press, 1982. Pp. 61–84.

Fowler, Alastair. *A History of English Literature: Forms and Kinds from the Middle Ages to the Present*. Oxford: Basil Blackwell, 1987.

Frisch, Walther. 'Schubert's "Nähe des Geliebten" (D 162): Transformation of the Volkston'. In Frisch (ed.), *Schubert: Critical and Analytical Studies*. Lincoln: University of Nebraska Press, 1986. Pp. 175–99.

———. '"You Must Remember This": Memory and Structure in Schubert's String Quartet in G Major, D 887'. *Musical Quarterly*, 84/4 (2000), pp. 582–603.

Giarusso, Richard. 'Beyond the Leiermann: Disorder, Reality, and the Power of Imagination in the Final Songs of Schubert's *Winterreise*'. In Lorraine Byrne Bodley and Barbara Reul(eds), *The Unknown Schubert*. Farnham: Ashgate, 2008. Pp. 25–42.

Gibbs, Christopher H. German Reception: Schubert's "Journey to Immortality"'. In Gibbs (ed.), *The Cambridge Companion to Schubert*. Cambridge: Cambridge University Press, 1997. Pp. 241–53.

———. *The Life of Schubert*. Cambridge: Cambridge University Press, 2000.

Gingerich, John. 'Remembrance and Consciousness in Schubert's C-Major String Quintet, D956'. *Musical Quarterly* 84/4 (2000), pp. 619–34.

———.*Schubert's Beethoven Project*. Cambridge: Cambridge University Press, 2004.

———. 'Unfinished Considerations: Schubert's "Unfinished" Symphony in Context of His Beethoven Project'. *19th-Century Music* 31/2 (2007), pp. 99–112.

———. '"To How Many Shameful Deeds Must You Lend Your Image": Schubert's Pattern of Telescoping and Excision in the Texts of his Latin Masses'. *Current Musicology* 70 (2000), pp. 61–99.

Godel, Arthur. *Schuberts letzte drei Klaviersonaten (D 958-960): Entstehungs- geschichte, Entwurf und Reinschrift, Werkanalyse*. Baden-Baden: Koerner, 1985.

Goethe, Johann Wolfgang von. *Goethe: the Collected Works*. Vol. 4, *From My Life: Poetry and Truth*. Ed. Thomas P. Saine and Jeffrey L. Sammons. Princeton, NJ: Princeton University Press, 1987.

Gottdang, Andrea. '"Ich bin unsern Ideen nicht untreu geworden": Moritz von Schwind und der Schubert-Freundeskreis'. *Schubert: Perspektiven* 4 (2004), pp. 1–48.

Gramit, David. *Cultivating Music: the Aspirations, Interests, and Musical Limits of German Musical Cuture, 1770–1848*. Berkeley and Los Angeles: University of California Press, 2002.

Griffel, L. Michael. 'Reappraisal of Schubert's Methods of Composition'. *The Musical Quarterly* 63/2 (1977), pp. 186–210.

Grimm, Herman. *Das Leben Raphael's*. Berlin: W. Hertz, 1896.

Gülke, Peter. *Franz Schubert und seine Zeit*. Laaber: Laaber-Verlag, 1991.

———. 'Neue Beiträge zur Kenntnis des Sinfonikers Schubert...'. In Heinz-Klaus Metzger and Rainer Riehm (eds), *Musik-Konzepte Sonderband Franz Schubert*. Munich: text+kritik, 1979. Pp. 187–220.

Hafer, Edward Michael. 'The Wanderer Archetype in the Music of Franz Schubert and the Paintings of Caspar David Friedrich.' PhD diss., University of Illinois at Urbana-Champaign, 2006.

Hallmark, Rufus.'The Literary and Musical Rhetoric of Apostrophe in *Winterreise*'. *19th-Century Music* 35/1 (2011), pp. 3–33.

Hallmark, Rufus and Ann C. Fehn. 'Text and Music in Schubert's Settings of Pentameter Poetry'. In Jürgen Thym (ed.), *Of Poetry and Song: Approaches to the Nineteenth-Century Lied*. Rochester, NY: University of Rochester Press, 2010. Pp. 156–7.

Hanslick, Eduard. *Concerte, Componisten und Virtuosen der letzten fünfzehn Jahre, 1870–1885: Kritiken*. 2nd edn. Berlin: Allgemeiner Verein für Deutsche Literatur, 1886.

──.*Aus dem Concert-Saal: Kritiken und Schilderungen aus 20 Jahren des Wiener Musiklebens, 1848–1868*. Vienna and Leipzig: W. Braumüller, 1897.

Hanson, Alice. 'The Significance of the *Ludlamshöhle* for Franz Schubert'. In Barbara Haggh (ed.), *Essays on Music and Culture in Honor of Herbert Kellman*. Paris and Tours: Minerve, 2001. Pp. 496–502.

Harrison, Daniel. *Harmonic Function in Chromatic Music*. Chicago: University of Chicago Press, 1994.

Hascher, Xavier. *Cahiers Franz Schubert: Revue de musique classique et romantique* 1–17 (1992–2009).

──. *Schubert, la forme sonate et son evolution*. Bern: Peter Lang, 1996.

──. *Le Style instrumental de Schubert: sources, analyse, évolution*. Paris: Publications de la Sorbonne, 2007.

Hatten, Robert S. 'Schubert the Progressive: the Role of Resonance and Gesture in the Piano Sonata in A, D 959', *Integral* 7 (1993), pp. 38–81.

──. *Interpreting Musical Gestures, Topics, and Tropes: Mozart, Beethoven, Schubert*. Bloomington: Indiana University Press, 2004.

Hepokoski, James, and Warren Darcy. *Elements of Sonata Theory: Norms, Types, and Deformations in the Late-Eighteenth-Century Sonata*. New York and Oxford: Oxford University Press, 2006.

Herbeck, Ludwig. *Johann Herbeck: Ein Lebensbild*. Vienna: Albert J. Gutmann, 1885.

Hilmar, Ernst. *Franz Schubert: Drei große Sonaten für das Pianoforte, D 958, D 959 und D 960 (frühe Fassungen): Faksimile nach den Autographen in der Wiener Stadt- und Landesbibliothek*. Tutzing: Hans Schneider, 1987.

──. *Verzeichnis der Schubert-Handschfriten in der Musiksammlung der Wiener Stadt- und Landesbibliothek*. Catalogus Musicus 8. Kassel: Metzler Verlag, 1978.

────── (ed.). *Schubert durch die Brille*. Vols 1–3. Vienna: Mitteilungen des Internationalen Franz Schubert Instituts, 1988–9.

────── (ed.). *Schubert durch die Brille*. Vols 4–30. Tutzing: Hans Schneider, 1990–2003.

Hilmar, Ernst, and Margret Jestremski (eds). *Schubert-Enzyklopädie*. 2 vols. Tützing: Schneider, 2004.

Hinrichsen, Hans-Joachim. '"Bergendes Gehäuse" und "Hang ins Unbegrenzte": Die Kammermusik'. In Walther Dürr and Andreas Krause (eds), *Schubert-Handbuch*. Kassel and Stuttgart: Bärenreiter-Verlag, 1997. Pp. 451–511.

———. 'Modellfall der Philosophie der Musik: Beethoven', in Richard Klein, Johann Kreuzer and Stefan Müller-Doohm(eds), *Adorno-Handbuch*. Stuttgart, Weimar: Metzler-Verlag, 2011. Pp. 85–96.

———. '"Rendering per orchestra". Luciano Berios komponierter Essay über Schuberts Spätwerk'. *Schubert: Perspektiven* 2 (2002), pp. 135–66.

———. 'Die Sonatenform im Spätwerk Franz Schuberts'. *Archiv für Musikwissenschaft* 45 (1988), pp. 16–49.

———. *Untersuchungen zur Entwicklung der Sonatenform in der Instrumentalmusik Franz Schubert*. Tutzing: Schneider, 1994.

Hinrichsen, Hans-Joachim, and Till Gerrit Waidelich (eds). *Schubert: Perspektiven*. Stuttgart: Franz Steiner Verlag, 2001–.

Hirsch, Marjorie Wing. *Schubert's Dramatic Lieder*. Cambridge: Cambridge University Press, 1993.

Hoeckner, Berthold. 'Paths through *Dichterliebe*'. *19th-Century Music* 30/1 (2006), pp. 65–80.

Hook, Julian. 'Signature Transformations'. In Jack Douthett, Martha M. Hyde and Charles J. Smith (eds), *Music Theory and Mathematics: Chords, Collections, and Transformations*. Rochester: University of Rochester Press, 2008. Pp. 137–60.

Horak, Karl. 'Ländler'. In Walther Deutsch, Harald Dreo, Gerlinde Haid and Karl Horak (eds), *Volksmusik in Österreich*. Vienna: Oesterreichischer Bundesverlag Gesellschaft, 1984. Pp. 55–70.

Howe, Blake. 'The Allure of Dissolution: Bodies, Forces, and Cyclicity in Schubert's Final Mayrhofer Settings'. *Journal of the American Musicological Society* 62/2 (2009), pp. 271–322.

Hug, Fritz. *Franz Schubert: Tragik eines Begnadeten*. Munich: Wilhelm Heyne Verlag, 1976.

Hüttenbrenner, Anselm. *Lieder für eine Singstimme mit Klavierbegleitung*, ed. Ulf Bästlein, Alice Aschauer and Michael Aschauer. 3 vols. Warngau: Accolade, 2008–10.

Huron, David. *Sweet Anticipation: Music and the Psychology of Expectation*. Cambridge, MA: MIT Press, 2006.

Hyer, Brian. 'Reimag(in)ing Riemann'. *Journal of Music Theory* 39 (1995), pp. 101–38.

Hyland, Anne M. 'The "Tightened Bow": Analysing the Juxtaposition of Drama and Lyricism in Schubert's Paratactic Sonata-form Movements'. In Gareth Cox and Julian Horton (eds), *Irish Musical Studies*, vol. 11, *Irish Musical Analysis*. Dublin: Four Courts Press, 2014. Pp. 17–40.

Humboldt, Wilhelm von. 'Über die innere und äußere Organization der höheren wissenschaftlichen Anstalten in Berlin' (1810). In Ernst Anrich (ed.), *Die Idee der deutschen Universität: Die fünf Grundschriften aus der Zeit ihrer Neubegründung durch klassischen Idealismus und romantischen Realismus*. Darmstadt: Wissenschaftliche Buchgesellschaft, 1964. Pp. 375ff.

Ischer, Rudolf. *Johann Georg Zimmermann's Leben und Werke: Litterarhistorische Studie*. Bern: K. J. Wyss, 1893.

Jacobi, Johann Georg. *Die Sommerreise*. Halle im Magdeburgischen: C. H. Hemmerde, 1770.
——. *Winterreise*. Düsseldorf, 1796.
Jackson, Timothy L. '*Hinauf strebt's*: Song Study with Carl Schachter'. In L. Poundie Burstein and David Gagné(eds), *Structure and Meaning in Tonal Music*. Hillsdale, NY: Pendragon Press, 2006. Pp. 192–4.
Jary-Janecka, Friederike. *Franz Schubert am Theater und im Film*. Anif and Salzburg: Müller-Speiser, 2000.
Johnson, Graham. *Franz Schubert: the Complete Songs*. London and New Haven, CT: Yale University Press, 2014.
Johnson, Julian. *Mahler's Voices: Expression and Irony in the Songs and Symphonies*. Oxford and New York: Oxford University Press, 2009.
Jurgenmeiser, Charles. 'Salomon Sulzer and Franz Schubert: a Musical Collaboration'. In Leonard J. Greenspoon (ed.), *I Will Sing and Make Music: Jewish Music and Musicians throughout the Ages: Proceedings of the Nineteenth Annual Symposium of the Klutznik Chair in Jewish Civilisation— Harris Centre for Judaic Studies, 29–30 October 2006*. Omaha, NB: Creighton University Press, 2008.
Kaminsky, Peter. 'Principles of Formal Structure in Schumann's Early Piano Cycles'. *Music Theory Spectrum* 11/2 (1989), pp. 207–25.
Kerman, Joseph. '*An die ferne Geliebte*'. In Alan Tyson (ed.), *Beethoven Studies 1*. New York: Norton, 1973. Pp. 123–57.
——. 'A Romantic Detail in Schubert's "Schwanengesang"'. In Walther Frisch (ed.), *Schubert: Critical and Analytical Studies*. Lincoln: University of Nebraska Press, 1986. Pp. 48–64.
Kier, Herfried. *Raphael Georg Kiesewetter (1773–1850): Wegbereiter des musikalischen Historismus*. Regensburg: Gustav Bosse Verlag. 1968.
Kiesewetter, R. G. *Geschichte der Euopaisch-Abendländischen oder unser heutigen Musik*. Leipzig: Breitkopf & Härtel, 1846.
Kinderman, William. 'Schubert's Tragic Perspective'. In Walther Frisch (ed.), *Schubert: Critical and Analytical Studies*. Lincoln: University of Nebraska Press, 1986. Pp. 65–83.
——. 'Wandering Archetypes in Schubert's Instrumental Music'. *19th-Century Music* 21/2 (1997), pp. 219–222.
——. 'Das Werturteil in der Kunst und die Ästhetik Hermann Brochs: Beispiele aus der Musik Beethovens'. In Michael Benedikt, Reinhold Knoll and Cornelius Zehetner (eds), *Philosophie in Österreich*. Vol. 6. Vienna: Facultas, 2010. Pp. 750–64.
Knapp, Raymond. 'Reading Gender in Late Beethoven: "An die Freude" and *An die ferne Geliebte*'. *Acta Musicologica*, 75/1 (2003), pp. 45–63.
Költzsch, Hans. *Franz Schubert in seinen Klaviersonaten*. Leipzig: Breitkopf & Härtel, 1927.
Kopp, David. *Chromatic Transformations in Nineteenth-Century Music*. Cambridge: Cambridge University Press, 2002.

Kos, Wolfgang, and Christian Rapp (eds). *Alt-Wien: Die Stadt, die niemals war: Sonderausstellung des Wien Museums im Künstlerhaus, 25. November bis 28. März 2005*. Wien: Czernin Verlag, 2004.
Kraemer, Florian. *Entzauberung der Musik: Beethoven, Schumann und die romantische Ironie*. Paderborn: Fink, 2014.
Kramer, Lawrence. *Franz Schubert: Sexuality, Subjectivity, Song*. Cambridge: Cambridge University Press, 1998.
———. 'Performance and Social Meaning in the Lied: Schubert's "Erster Verlust"'. *Current Musicology* 45 (1994), pp. 5–23.
Kramer, Richard. *Distant Cycles: Schubert and the Conceiving of Song*. Chicago: University of Chicago Press, 1994.
———. 'Gradus ad Parnassum: Beethoven, Schubert, and the Romance of Counterpoint'. *19th-Century Music* 11/2 (1987), pp. 107–20.
———. 'The Hedgehog: of Fragments Finished and Unfinished'. *19th-Century Music* 21/2 (1997), p. 140.
Krause, Andreas. *Die Klaviersonaten Franz Schuberts: Form, Gattung, Ästhetik*. Kassel: Bärenreiter, 1991.
Kube, Manfred. '"... dass alle Spieler hinlänglich beschäftigt sind": Schuberts Klaviertrio Es-dur (D 929) aus satztechnischer Perspektive'. *Schubert-Jahrbuch* (1998), pp. 125–32.
Kube, Michael. '"Nährstoff" nationaler Identifikation: Zur Bedeutung der Volksmusik in nordeuropäischer Kunstmusik'. In Walther Salmen and Giselher Schubert(eds), *Verflechtungen im 20. Jahrhundert: Komponisten im Spannungsfeld elitär—popular*. Frankfurter Studien 10. Mainz: Schott, 2005. Pp. 88–130.
Kurth, Richard. 'Music and Poetry, a Wilderness of Doubles: Heine—Nietzsche—Schubert—Derrida'. *19th-Century Music* 21/1 (1997), pp. 3–37.
———. 'On the Subject of Schubert's "Unfinished" Symphony: *Was bedeutet die Bewegung?*', *19th-Century Music* 23/1 (1999), pp. 3–32.
Kreißle von Hellborn, Heinrich. *Franz Schubert*. Vienna: Carl Gerold, 1865.
Lambert, Sterling. *Re-Reading Poetry: Schubert's Multiple Settings of Goethe*. Suffolk and Rochester: Boydell & Brewer, 2009.
Lange, Fritz. 'Schuberts letzte Pläne: Bisher unbekannte Reminiszenzen von Schubert'. *Neues Wiener Journal*, 22 May 1910, p. 6.
Latham, Edward D. '*Drei Nebensonnen*: Forte's Linear-Motivic Analysis, Korngold's *Die tote Stadt*, and Schubert's *Winterreise* as Visions of Closure'. *Gamut* 2/1 (2009), pp. 299–346.
Lenz, Jakob Michael Reinhold. *Hochzeitscarmen für einen abtrünnigen Musensohn*. In Jakob Michael Reinhold Lenz, *Werke und Briefe*, ed. Sigrid Damm. 3 vols. Leipzig: Insel Verlag, 1987.
Lerdahl, Fred. *Tonal Pitch Space*. New York and Oxford: Oxford University Press, 2004.
Lichtenstein, Sabine. 'Franz Schubert en Salomon Sulzer: Een joods-christelijke samenwerking in romantisch Wenen'. In *Nieuwsbrief Schubert Stichting* 13/1 (2008–9), pp. 3–12.

Lewin, David. 'Auf dem Flusse: Image and Background in a Schubert Song'. *19th-Century Music* 6/1 (1982–3), pp. 47–59.

——. *Generalized Musical Intervals and Transformations*. New Haven, CT: Yale University Press, 1987.

——. *Studies in Music with Text*. New York: Oxford University Press, 2006.

Lidov, David. *Is Language a Music? Writings on Musical Form and Signification*. Bloomington: Indiana University Press, 2005.

Lindmayr-Brandl, Andrea. *Franz Schubert: Das fragmentarische Werk*. Schubert: Perspektiven—Studien 2. Stuttgart: Steiner, 2003.

Litschauer, Walburga. 'The Origin and Early Reception of Schwanengesang'. In Martin Chusid (ed.), *A Companion to Schubert's 'Schwanengesang': History, Poets, Analysis, Performance*. New Haven, CT: Yale University Press, 2000. Pp. 5–13.

Lubin, Steven. 'The Three Styles of *Schwanengesang*: a Pianist's Perspective'. In Martin Chusid (ed.), *A Companion to Schubert's 'Schwanengesang': History, Poets, Analysis, Performance*. New Haven, CT: Yale University Press, 2002. Pp. 191–204.

Lux, Joseph August. *Franz Schubert: Ein Lebensbild aus deutscher Vergangenheit*. Berlin: Fleming & Wiskot, 1922.

Macdonald, Hugh. 'Schubert's Pendulum'. In *Beethoven's Century: Essays on Composers and Themes*. Rochester, NY: University of Rochester Press, 2008. Pp. 16–27.

——. 'Schubert's Volcanic Temper'. *The Musical Times* 119 (1978), pp. 949–52.

Marston, Nicholas. ' "Wie aus der Ferne": Pastness and Presentness in the Lieder of Beethoven, Schubert, and Schumann'. In Ernst Hilmar (ed.), *Schubert durch die Brille*, vol. 21. Tutzing: Hans Schneider, 1998. Pp. 126–2.

——. 'Voicing Beethoven's Distant Beloved'. In Scott Burnham and Michael P. Steinberg (eds), *Beethoven and his World*. Princeton, NJ: Princeton University Press, 2000. Pp. 124–47.

——. 'Schubert's Homecoming'. *Journal of the Royal Musical Association* 125/2 (2000), p. 248.

Mak, Su-Yin. *Schubert's Lyricism Reconsidered: Structure, Design and Rhetoric*. Saarbrücken: Lambert, 2010.

——. 'Schubert's Sonata Forms and the Poetics of the Lyric'. *Journal of Musicology* 23/2 (2006), pp. 263–306.

Malin, Yonatan. *Songs in Motion: Rhythm and Meter in the German Lied*. New York: Oxford University Press, 2010.

Mann, Alfred. 'Schubert's Lesson with Sechter'. *19th-Century Music* 6/2 (1982), pp. 159–65.

——. *Schuberts Studien*. Vol. 2 of Franz Schubert, *Neue Ausgabe sämtlicher Werke*, ser. 8. Kassel: Bärenreiter, 1986.

Martin, Nathan, and Steven Vande Moortele. 'Formal Functions and Retrospective Reinterpretation in the First Movement of Schubert's String Quintet'. *Music Analysis* 33/2 (2014), pp. 130–55.

Marx, A. B. *Die Lehre von der musikalischen Komposition*. 4 vols. Leipzig: Breitkopf & Härtel, 1837–47.

Mayrhofer, Johann. *Gedichte von Johann Mayrhofer: Neue Sammlung*, ed. Ernst Freiherr von Feuchtersleben. Vienna: Ignaz Klang, 1843.
McClary, Susan. 'Constructions of Subjectivity in Schubert's Music'. In Philip Brett, Elizabeth Wood and Gary C. Thomas(eds), *Queering the Pitch*. New York: Routledge, 1994. Pp. 205–33.
McKay, Elizabeth Norman. *Franz Schubert: a Biography*. Oxford: Oxford University Press, 1996.
Messing, Scott. *Schubert in the European Imagination* 2 vols. Rochester, NY: University of Rochester Press, 2006–7.
Metzger, Karl-Heinz, and R. Riehn (eds). *Musik-Konzepte: Sonderband Franz Schubert*. Munich: Text + Kritik, 1979.
Meyer, Leonard B. *Music, the Arts, and Ideas: Patterns and Predictions in Twentieth-Century Culture*. Chicago: University of Chicago Press, 1994.
Michaelsen, René. *Der komponierte Zweifel: Robert Schumann und die Selbstreflexion in der Musik*. Paderborn: Fink, 2013.
Mühlhäuser, Siegfried. *Die Handschriften und Varia der Schubertiana-Sammlung Taussig in der Universitaetsbibliothek Lund*. Quellenkataloge zur Musikgeschichte 17. Wilhelmshaven: Nötzel, 1981.
Müller-Blattau, Joseph. 'Franz Schubert, der Sänger Goethes'. In Joseph Müller-Blattau (ed.), *Goethe und die Meister der Musik*. Stuttgart: Klett, 1969. Pp. 62–80.
Muxfeldt, Kristina. 'Schubert, Platen, and the Myth of Narcissus'. *Journal of the American Musicological Society* 49/3 (1996), pp. 480–527.
——. *Vanishing Sensibilities: Schubert, Beethoven, Schumann*. New York: Oxford University Press, 2012.
Newbould, Brian. 'Schubert's Last Symphony'. *The Musical Times* 126/1707 (1985), pp. 272–5.
——. *Schubert: the Music and the Man*. Berkeley and Los Angeles: University of California Press, 1997.
—— (ed.). *Schubert the Progressive: History, Performance Practice, Analysis*. Aldershot: Ashgate, 2003.
Noeske, Nina. 'Schubert, das Erhabene und die letzte Sonate D 960—oder: Die Frage nach dem Subjekt'. *Schubert: Perspektiven* 7 (2007), pp. 22–36.
Nohl, Ludwig. *Beethoven, Liszt, Wagner*. Vienna: Wilhelm Braumüller, 1874.
Notley, Margaret. 'Schubert's Social Music: the "Forgotten Genres"'. In Christopher Gibbs (ed.), *The Cambridge Companion to Schubert*. Cambridge: Cambridge University Press, 1997. Pp. 138–54.
Perraudin, Michael. *Heinrich Heine: Poetry in Context*. Oxford: Berg, 1989.
Perrey, Beate Julia. *Schumann's Dichterliebe and Early Romantic Poetics: Fragmentation of Desire*. Cambridge: Cambridge University Press, 2002.
Porter, Ernest G. *Schubert's Song Technique*. London: Dennis Dobson, 1961.
Prawer, S. S. *Heine: Buch der Lieder*. Great Neck, NY: Barron's Educational Series, 1960.
Pritchard. T. C. L. 'The Unfinished Symphony'. *The Music Review* 3 (1942), pp. 10–32.

———. 'The Schubert Idiom'. In Gerald Abraham (ed.), *The Music of Schubert*. New York: W. W. Norton, 1947. Pp. 234–53.

Rank, Otto. *The Double: a Psychoanalytic Study*. Trans. Harry Tucker. Chapel Hill: University of North Carolina Press, 1971.

Rast, Nicholas. 'Une déclaration d'amour en code? La Fantaisie en *fa* mineur D 940 de Schubert et la comtesse Caroline Esterházy'. *Cahiers Franz Schubert*, 13 (1998), pp. 5–16.

———. '"Schöne Welt wo bist du?" Motive and Form in Schubert's A Minor String Quartet'. In Brian Newbould (ed.), *Schubert the Progressive: History, Performance Practice, Analysis*. Aldershot: Ashgate, 2003. Pp. 81–8.

Reddy, William. *The Navigation of Feeling: a Framework for the History of Emotions*. Cambridge: Cambridge University Press, 2001.

Reed, John. *Schubert: the Final Years*. London: Faber, 1972.

———. *The Schubert Song Companion*. Manchester: Manchester University Press, 1997.

———. 'How the Great C Major was Written'. *Music and Letters*, 56/1 (1975), pp. 18–25.

Rentsch, Ivana, and Klaus Pietschmann. *Schubert: Interpretationen* (= *Schubert: Perspektiven—Studien 3*). Stuttgart: Franz Steiner Verlag, 2014.

Roček, Roman. *Dämonie des Biedermeier: Nikolaus Lenaus Lebenstragödie*. Vienna: Böhlau, 2005.

Reiser, Salome. *Franz Schuberts frühe Streichquartette: Eine klassische Gattung am Beginn einer nachklassischen Zeit*. Kassel: Bärenreiter, 1999.

Reynolds, Christopher. 'The Representational Impulse in Late Beethoven, I: *An die ferne Geliebte*'. *Acta Musicologica*, 60 (1988), pp. 3–61.

Reichardt, Johann Friedrich. *Lieder der Liebe und der Einsamkeit zur Harfe und zum Clavier zu singen*. Leipzig: Gerhard Fleischer, 1804.

———. *100 Lieder geselliger Freude*. Leipzig: G. Fleischer, 1796–7.

———. *Neue Lieder geselliger Freude*. Leipzig: Fleischer, 1799–1800.

Riemann, Hugo. 'Ideen zu einer "Lehre von den Tonvorstellungen"'. Trans. Robert W. Wason and Elizabeth West Marvin. *Journal of Music Theory* 36, (1992), pp. 81–117.

Riezler, Walther. *Beethoven*. Berlin: Atlantis-Verlag, 1936.

Riesenfeld, Paul. 'Goethe und Schubert'. *Signale für die musikalische Welt* 90 (1932), p. 267.

Rings, Steven. *Tonality and Transformation*. New York and Oxford: Oxford University Press, 2011.

Rolland, Romain. 'Goethe's Interest in Music'. *Music Quarterly* 17 (1931), pp. 157–94.

Rorty, Richard. *Philosophy and the Mirror of Nature*. Minneapolis: University of Minnesota Press, 1982.

Rosen, Charles. *The Classical Style*. New York: W. W. Norton, 1972.

———. 'Influence: Plagiarism and Inspiration'. *19th-Century Music* 4/2 (1980), pp. 87–100.

———. *The Romantic Generation*. Cambridge and London: Harper Collins, 1996.
———. 'Schubert's Inflections of Classical Form'. In Christopher Gibbs (ed.), *The Cambridge Companion to Schubert*. Cambridge: Cambridge University Press, 1997. Pp. 72–98.
———. *Sonata Forms*. New York: W. W. Norton, 1980.
Rothstein, William. 'Common-Tone Tonality in Italian Opera: an Introduction'. *Music Theory Online* 14 (2008).
Rousseau, Jean-Jacques. *Emil, oder Über die Erziehung*. Trans. Ludwig Schmidts. 4th edn. Paderborn: Ferdinand Schöningh, 1978.
———. *Les rêveries du promeneur solitaire*. Ed. Marcel Raymond. Geneva: Librairie Droz, 1967.
Said, Edward W. *On Late Style: Music and Literature against the Grain*. New York: Pantheon, 2006.
Salzer, Felix. 'Die Sonatenform bei Franz Schubert'. *Studien zur Musikwissenschaft* 15 (1928), pp. 86–125.
Samuels, Robert. 'The Double Articulation of Schubert: Reflections on *Der Doppelgänger*'. *The Musical Quarterly* 93 (2010), pp. 192–233.
Schinz, Johann Rudolf. *Beyträge zur nähern Kenntniß des Schweizerlandes*. 2 vols. Zurich, 1783.
———. *Die vergnügte Schweizerreise anno 1773*. Ed. James Schwarzenbach. Zurich: Thomas Verlag o.J., 1952.
Schochow, Maximilian, and Lily Schochow. *Franz Schubert, die Texte seiner einstimmig komponierten Lieder und ihre Dichter*. Hildesheim: Olms, 1974.
Schmalfeldt, Janet. *In the Process of Becoming: Analytic and Philosophical Perspectives on Form in Early Nineteenth-Century Music*. New York and Oxford: Oxford University Press, 2011.
Schneider, Otto. 'Vor 100 Jahren: Eine Schubert-Uraufführung im Jahre 1865'. *Österreichische Musizeitschrift* 20 (1965), p. 608.
Schoenberg, Arnold. *Fundamentals of Musical Composition*. London: Faber & Faber, 1967.
Schorske, Carl. *Fin-de-siècle Vienna*. New York: Alfred A. Knopf, 1980.
Schumann, Christiane et al (eds). *Schubert–Jahrbuch*. Kassel: Bärenreiter Verlag, 1996–2013.
Seidel, Wilhelm. 'Die Kadenz als Figur ihrer selbst'. In Bert Siegmund (ed.), *Gestik und Affekt in der Musik des 17. und 18. Jahrhunderts*. Dößel: Stekoics, 2003. Pp. 169–84.
Sharpe, Lesley. 'Introduction'. In Sharpe (ed.), *The Cambridge Companion to Goethe*. Cambridge: Cambridge University Press, 2002. Pp. 1–5.
Siciliano, Michael. 'Two Neo-Riemannian Analyses'. *College Music Symposium* 45 (2005). Pp. 81–107.
Sly, Gordon. 'Innovations in Sonata Form: Compositional Logic and Structural Interpretation,' *Journal of Music Theory* 45/1 (2001), pp. 130–4.
Spitzer, Michael. *Metaphor and Musical Thought*. Chicago: University of Chicago Press, 2004.

———. *Music as Philosophy: Adorno and Beethoven's Late Style*. Bloomington and Indianapolis: Indiana University Press, 2006.

———. 'Sad Flowers: Affective Trajectories in Schubert's "Trockne Blumen"'. In T. Cochrane, B. Fantini and K. R. Scherer (eds), *The Emotional Power of Music: Multidisciplinary Perspectives on Musical Arousal, Expression, and Social Control*. Oxford: Oxford University Press. Pp. 7–22.

Steblin, Rita. *A History of Key Characteristics in the 18th and Early 19th Centuries*. 2nd edn. Rochester, NY: University of Rochester Press, 2002.

———. 'Schubert's Love Affair with Marie von Spaun and the Role Played by Helene Schmith, the Wife of Mozart's First Violinist'. *Schubert: Perspektiven* 8 (2008), pp. 49–87.

———. 'Schubert's Pepi: his Love Affair with the Chamber Maid Josepha Pöcklhofer and her Surprising Fate'. *The Musical Times* 149 (2008), pp. 47–69.

———. 'Who Commissioned Schubert's Oratorio *Lazarus*? A Solution to the Mystery: Salieri and the Tonkünstler-Societät'. *Schubert-Perspektiven* 9/2 (2009), pp. 145–81.

Steblin, Rita, and Frederick Stocken. 'Studying with Sechter: Newly Recovered Reminiscences about Schubert by his Forgotten Friend, the Composer Joseph Lanz'. *Music and Letters* 88 (2007), pp. 226–65.

Stefan, Paul. *Franz Schubert*. Berlin: Volksverband der Bücherfreunde, Wegweiser-Verlag, 1928.

Sterne, Laurence. *Sentimental Journey through France and Italy*. London: T. Becket & P. A. de Hondt, 1768.

Stillmark, Alexander. '"Es war alles gut und erfüllt": Rudolf Hans Bartsch's "Schwammerl" and the Making of the Schubert Myth'. In Ian F. Roe and John Warren(eds), *The Biedermeier and Beyond*. Bern: Peter Lang, 1999. Pp. 225–34.

Sobaskie, James William. 'A Balance Struck: Gesture, Form, and Drama in Schubert's E flat Major Piano Trio'. In Xavier Hascher (ed.), *Le Style instrumental de Schubert: sources, analyse, contexte, évolution*. Paris: Publications de la Sorbonne, 2007. Pp. 115–46.

———. 'The "Problem" of Schubert's String Quintet'. *Nineteenth-Century Music Review* 2/1 (2005), pp. 57–92.

———. 'Schubert's Self-Elegies'. *Schubert Familiar and Unfamiliar: New Perspectives*, special issue, *Nineteenth-Century Music Review* 5/2 (2008), pp. 71–105.

———. 'Tonal Implication and the Gestural Dialectic in Schubert's A Minor Quartet'. In Brian Newbould (ed.), *Schubert the Progressive: History, Performance Practice, Analysis*. Aldershot: Ashgate, 2003. Pp. 53–80.

Solomon, Maynard. 'Franz Schubert and the Peacocks of Benvenuto Cellini'. *19th-Century Music* 12/3 (1988–9), pp. 14–25.

Sontag, Susan. *Under the Sign of Saturn*. New York: Picador, 1972.

Staiger, Emil. *Grundbegriffe der Poetik* [1946]. Trans J. C. Hudson and L. T. Frank as *Basic Concepts of Poetics*, ed. M. Burkhard and L. T. Frank. Philadelphia: Pennsylvania State University Press, 1991.

Steinbeck, Wolfram. 'Lied und Sonatensatzform bei Schubert: Zum Kopfsatz der Klaviersonate A-Dur D 644'. In Wolfgang Horschmann (ed.), *Aria: Eine Festschrift für Wolfgang Ruf*. Hildesheim: Olms, 2011. Pp. 590–602.

Sternfeld, Frederick W. *Goethe and Music: a List of Parodies and Goethe's Relationship to Music: a List of References*. New York: New York Public Library, 1954.

Szabó-Knotik, Cornelia. 'Franz Schubert und die österreichische Identität im Tonfilm der 1930er Jahre'. In Michael Kube, Walburga Litschauer and Gernot Gruber(eds), *Schubert und die Nachwelt: I. Internationale Arbeitstagung zur Schubert-Rezeption Wien 2003: Kongreßbericht*. München-Salzburg: Katzbichler, 2007. Pp. 309–19.

Talbot, Michael. *The Finale in Western Instrumental Music*. Oxford: Oxford University Press, 2001.

Taylor, Benedict. 'Schubert and the Construction of Memory: the String Quartet in A minor, D. 804 ("Rosamunde")'. *Journal of the Royal Musical Association* 139/1 (2014), pp. 41–88.

Taylor, Ronald. 'Goethe, Schubert and the Art of Song'. In Volker Dürr and Géza v. Molnăr(eds), *Versuche zu Goethe: Festschrift für Erich Heller*. Heidelberg: Lothar Stiehm Verlag, 1976. Pp. 141–9.

Tiedge, Christoph August. *Die Einsamkeit*. Leipzig: Sommer, 1792.

———. *Urania: Über Gott, Unsterblichkeit und Freiheit: Ein lyrisch-didaktisches Gedicht in sechs Gesängen*. Halle: Renger, 1801.

Todd, R. Larry. *Mendelssohn: a Life in Music*. New York and Oxford: Oxford University Press, 2003.

Tovey, Donald Francis. 'Tonality'. *Music and Letters* 9 (1928), pp. 341–63.

Thomas, Werner. 'Die fast verlorene Zeit: Zum Adagio in Schuberts Streichquintett in C'. In Thomas (ed.), *Schubert-Studien*. Frankfurt am Main: Peter Lang, 1990. Pp. 137–58.

Tyson, Alan. *Mozart: Studies of the Autograph Scores*. Cambridge, MA, and London: Harvard University Press, 1987.

Urbanek, Nikolaus. *Auf der Suche nach einer zeitgemäßen Musikästhetik: Adornos 'Philosophie der Musik' und die Beethoven-Fragmente*. Bielefeld: Transcript, 2010.

van Hoorickx, Reinhard. 'The Chronology of Schubert's Fragments and Sketches' [1953]. In Eva Badura-Skoda and Peter Branscombe(eds), *Schubert Studies: Problems of Style and Chronology*. Cambridge: Cambridge University Press, 1982. Pp. 297–326.

Vetter, Walther. *Der Klassiker Schubert*. Leipzig: Deutscher Verlag für Musik, 1953.

Vogler, Abbé Georg Joseph. *Handbuch zur Harmonielehre und für den Generalbaß*. Prague: K. Brath, 1802.

Volker, Konrad. 'Schubert und Goethe'. *Die Musik* 14 (1915), pp. 129.

Wackenroder, Wilhelm Heinrich. *Herzensergießungen eines kunsliebenden Klosterbruders*. Berlin: Ungeer, 1797.

Waidelich, Till Gerrit, Renate Hilmar-Voit and Andreas Mayer. *Franz Schubert: Dokumente 1817–1830*, vol. 1, *Texte: Programme, Rezensionen, Anzeigen,*

Nekrologe, Musikbeilagen und andere gedruckte Quellen. Tutzing: Hans Schneider Verlag, 1993.

———. 'Zur Überlieferung des Textes "Mein Traum"'. *Schubert: Perspektiven* 5 (2005), pp. 138–61.

———. '"Torpson" und Franz von Schobert: Leben und Wirken des von Frauen, Freunden und Biographen umworbenen Schubert- und Schwind-Freundes'. *Schubert: Perspektiven* 6 (2006), pp. 1–237, and 7 (2007), pp. 107–20.

———. 'Unbekannte Schubert-Dokument aus Breslau'. *Schubert-Perspektiven* 8 (2008), pp. 17–48.

Waldbauer, Ivan. 'Recurrent Harmonic Patterns in the First Movement of Schubert's Piano Sonata in A major, D 959'. *19th-Century Music* 12/1 (1989), pp. 64–73.

Webber, Andrew J. *The Doppelgänger: Double Visions in German Literature*. Oxford: Clarendon Press, 1996.

Weber, Gottfried. *Versuch einer geordneten Theorie der Tonsetzkunst*. 3 vols. Mainz: B. Schott, 1817–21.

Weber, Rudolf. 'Mythen und Legenden um die Entstehung von Schubert Unvollendeter'. In Claudia Bullerjahn and Wolfgang Löffler(eds), *Musikermythen: Alltagstheorien, Legenden und Medieninszenierungen*. Hildesheim: Georg Olms Verlag, 2004. Pp. 191–221.

Webster, James. 'Schubert's Sonata Form and Brahms' First Maturity'. *19th-Century Music* 2 (1978), pp. 18–35, and 3 (1979), pp. 52–71.

Weiss, Christoph. 'Royaliste, Antirépublicain, Antijacobin et Antiilluminé: Johann Georg Zimmermann und die "politische Mordbrennerey in Europa"'. In Christoph Weiss and Wolfgang Albrecht(eds), *Von 'Obscuranten' und 'Eudämonisten': Gegenaufklärerische, konservative und antirevolutionäre Publizisten im späten 18. Jahrhundert*. St. Ingbert: Röhrig, 1997. Pp. 367–401.

Whittall, Arnold. 'The Sonata Crisis: Schubert in 1828'. *The Music Review* 30 (1969), pp. 124–129.

Willfort, Manfred. 'Das Urbild des Andante aus Schuberts Klaviertrio Es-dur, D 929'. *Österreichische Musikzeitschrift* 33 (1978), pp. 277–83.

Winter, Robert. 'Paper Studies and the Future of Schubert Research'. In Eva Badura-Skoda and Peter Branscombe(eds), *Schubert Studies: Problems of Style and Chronology*. Cambridge: Cambridge University Press, 1982. Pp. 209–76.

———. 'Whose Schubert?' *19th-Century Music* 17/1 (1993), pp. 94–101.

Wirth, Franz. 'Zur Diskussion Gestellt: Anklänge an Beethovens 9. Symphonie in Schuberts C-Dur Symphonie D 944'. *Bonner Beethoven-Studien* 5 (2006), pp. 183–96.

Witeschnik, Alexander. 'Goethe und Schubert: Die Geschichte einer einseitigen Liebe'. *Jahrbuch des Wiener-Goethe Vereins* 6 (1963), pp. 78–85.

Wittgenstein, Ludwig. *Tractatus Logico-Philosophicus*. Trans. David Pears and Brian McGuinness. London: Routledge & Kegan Paul, 1961.

Wollenberg, Susan. 'The C Major String Quintet D 956: Schubert's "Dissonance Quartet"'. In Ernst Hilmar (ed.), *Schubert durch die Brille*, vol. 28. Tutzing: Hans Schneider, 2002. Pp. 45–54.

——. 'Schubert and the Dream'. *Studi musicali* 9 (1980), pp. 135–50.

——. *Schubert's Fingerprints: Studies in the Instrumental Works*. Farnham: Ashgate, 2011.

Wolf, Werner. 'Metareference across Media: the Concept, its Transmedial Potentials and Problems, Main Forms and Functions'. In Werner Wolf (ed.), *Metareference across Media: Theory and Case Studies*. Amsterdam: Rodopi, 2009. Pp. 1–85.

Youens, Susan. *Heinrich Heine and the Lied*. Cambridge: Cambridge University Press, 2007.

——. *Retracing a Winter's Journey: Schubert's 'Winterreise'*. Ithaca, NY: Cornell University Press, 1991.

——. *Schubert's Late Lieder: Beyond the Song Cycles*. Cambridge: Cambridge University Press, 2002.

——. 'Wegweiser in Winterreise'. *Journal of Musicology* 5/3 (1987), pp. 357–79.

Zeiner, M. 'Goethe und Schubert'. *Die Quelle* 79 (1929), p. 105.

Zimmermann, Johann Georg. *Ueber die Einsamkeit*. 4 vols. Leipzig: Weidmanns Erden & Reich, 1784–5.

Index

Adler, Guido, 19
Adrich, Richard, 174, 176, n302
Adorno, Theodor, W., 2
   on characteristics of Schubert
      works, 41
   on late work of Beethoven, 18–19, 420
   on late work of Beethoven and
      Schubert, 23–25
   on *Winterreise*, 407
Aldrich, Richard, 174
alienation, in Beethoven's late works, 410
Almén, Byron, 12n48, 158
Antcliff, Herbert, 173
*Armut, Reichtum, Schuld und
   Buße der Gräfin Dolores*
   (Arnim), 440
Arnim, Achim von, 440
Arnim, Bettine von, 465–66
Atlas motive, 50
Auden, W.H., 491

Bach, Johann Sebastian, 30
Bachmann, Ingeborg, 116
Badura-Skoda, Paul, 209
Bartsch, Rudolf 117 n124, n125
Bauernfeld, Eduard von, 333, 334,
   341, 348, 350, 430–31
Beethoven, Ludwig van
   death of, 409
   developing variation, 5
   An die ferne Geliebte, Op. 98, 456,
      457–58, 473–77

   late works of, 17–19, 23–25,
      409–10, 420
   Piano Sonata Op. 31 No. 2,
      Tempest, 218–19
   Piano Sonata in C minor,
      Op.111, 42
   reception of works of, 56–57
   Schubert's artistic interpretation
      of, 30, 43–44, 47, 48, 53–55
   and Schubert's final sonata
      trilogy, 52
   Schubert's study of, 30
   and Schubert's Symphony
      no. 7 in B minor, D 759
      (*Unfinished*), 116–20
   Schubert's turn towards, 30,
      43–44, 48
   Schubert versus, 41–43,
      48–49, 106n29
   songfulness in instrumental music
      of, 218, 220
   comparison between Schubert
      and, 3, 77–78
   Symphony no. 3, Op. 55,
      Eroica, 149
   Symphony no. 5, Op. 67, 42
   Symphony no. 9, Op. 125, 47
   use of recitative, 218
Bekker, Paul, 17
Berg, Isak Albert, 33–36
Berio, Luciano
   Rendering, 25–26

Biedermeier, 25
Bildung, 283, 289, 439–40
Black, Leo, 65
Blackwell, Thomas, 444
Byrne Bodley, Lorraine, 331n24
Brahms, Johannes, 26, 489
Brendel, Alfred
   on final sonata trilogy, D 958,
      D 959, D 960, 202
   on Piano Sonata in B♭ Major, D 960,
      60n37, 196–97, 199–200
   on Piano Sonata in C minor,
      D 958, 29, 52, 59n23
   on Schubert as wanderer, 58n14
   on Schubert compared to
      Beethoven, 41–42
Bretherton, David, 388, 401–2n11
Britten, Benjamin, 487
Brown, Clive, 244
Brown, Maurice J. E., 241,
      330n11, 410
Bruchmann, Franz von, 275
Bruckner, Anton, 23, 131
Budde, Elmar, 52–53, 414n15
Burnham, Scott, 2

canons, in Schubert's late composi-
      tions, 30, 31–32, 39n18
Capell, Richard, 479n5
Caplin, William E., 160
Chusid, Martin, 23, 24, 26, 129, 412
Clark, Susannah, 105n16, 163–64,
      165, 172n41, 253–54
Code, David Løberg, 390, 421
Cohn, Richard L., 80
Cone, Edward T., 53, 255, 295, 397,
      411, 420–21
contextual processes in Schubert's
   late sacred music,
   295–96, 327–28
   Deutsche Messe, D 872, 297–303

Hymnus an den heiligen Geist,
      D 948, 303–9
Mass in E♭ major, D 950, 309–18
Tantum ergo, D 962, 318–24
Cook, Nicholas, 348
Cooper, Martin, 61, 63–64
counterpoint
   in Schubert's late compositions,
      30–33, 39n7, 62
   Schubert's study of, 73n8
Craxton, Harold, 485
Cronegk, Johann Friedrich, 481n23
cycles
   in Fantasy for Violin and Piano in
      C Major, D 934, 19–20
   in 'Schwanengesang,' D 957, 287–88

Dahlhaus, Carl, 17, 33
Damschroder, David, 148, 155
Darcy, Warren, 160, 164, 166,
      172n41, 225–26
Das Dreimäderlhaus, 112, 117-121
Daverio, John, 368
death, in 'Der Wegweiser,'
      D 911, no. 20, 356
declamation
   in 'Der Atlas,' D 957, no. 8,
      397–401
   in 'Der Doppelgänger,' D 957,
      no. 13, 391–97
Defoe, Daniel
   Robinson Crusoe, 464, 478
Denny, Thomas, 148, 165, 168n5
Derrida, Jacques
   The Beast and the Sovereign, 478
Deutsch, Otto Erich, 493
   *Schubert: Die Dokumente seines
      Lebens*, 489
   *Schubert: Die Erinnerungen seiner
      Freunde*, 487–88
Diabelli, Anton, 202

Dibben, Nicola, 348
disability style, 420
Dittrich, Marie-Agnes, 276
Das Dreimäderlhaus, 117–21
Dürr, Walther, 177, 414–15n23, 490, 491–94
Dussek, Jan Ladislav
  Sonata Op. 77, 'L'Invocation,' 62
Dvořák, Antonin, 23,

Einstein, Alfred, 20, 404, 410
Eliot, George, 491
Émile, ou de l'éducation (Rousseau), 439
emotion, attitudes toward, in eighteenth and nineteenth centuries, 338–39, 348
Entwistle, Erik, 62–63

Fehn, Ann, 397
Ferris, David, 378
Fichte, J. G., 440
fifths, circle of, in 'Great' Symphony versus 'Reliquie,' 156–57
Fink, Gottfried Wilhelm, 275–76, 289
Fischer-Dieskau, Dietrich, 406, 410
Fisk, Charles, 60n37, 86, 175, 198, 215–16, 235–36n2, 355
Flothius, Marius, 204n10
Fowler, Alastair, 339
Franz Schubert—Ein Leben in zwei Sätzen, 116
Freud, Sigmund, 137, 383–84
Friedlaender, Max, 489
Frisch, Walter, 197

Gál, Hans, 489
Garve, Christian, 482n26
German sixth, 214, 217, 324, 390–91, 432
Gesang, versus *Lied*, 276
Gesellschaft für Musikfreunde 38
Gibbs, Christopher H., 420

Gingerich, John, 170nn23, 24, 433
Godel, Arthur, 50, 175, 177, 178, 181, 190
Goethe, Johann Wolfgang von
  'An den Mond', 493
  cultural context of
    Wanderlieder, 438–40
  'Der Musensohn' text and translation, 446–47t
  Dichtung und Wahrheit, 441 443, 444,
  'Harzreise im Winter 443,
  'Hoffnung',
  identification with wanderer figure, 440–41
  relationship with Schubert, 437–38
  on solitude, 465
  uniqueness of 'Der Musensohn' in *Wanderlied* tradition, 442–47
  'Wandrers Nachtlied II,' 449–50
  'Wandrers Sturmlied', 441–442
Graf von Gleichen, 333
Graves, Robert, 383
Grob,Theresa 116, n.329
grief, in 'Der Wegweiser,' D 911, no. 20, 356
Griffel, L. Michael, 174
Grillparzer, Franz, 26, 29, 38, 334
Grimm, Herman, 17
Gülke, Peter, 26, 29, 33, 47

Hallmark, Rufus, 397
Handel, George Frideric, 30
Hanslick, Eduard, 111, 113–15, 117, 131, 132
harmonic prolongations
  in 'Great' Symphony versus 'Reliquie,' 154–55, 157–58
  in *Tantum ergo*, D 962, 322–24
harmonic theory, Schubert and recent evolution of, 2
Harrison, Daniel, 274n17

Hascher, Xavier, 2
Haslinger, Tobias, 202, 404–6, 407–8, 412, 414–15n23, 414nn17, 19
Hatten, Robert S., 54, 60n32
Haydn, Josef, 486
Haydn, Michael, 30
Heidegger, Martin, 158–59
Heine, Heinrich
   Die Heimkehr, 49, 384–86, 401, 419t
   'Ihr Bild,' D 957, no. 9, 80–81, 105n19
Heine Lieder, 405, 406, 409–11
Hepokoski, James, 160, 164, 166, 172n41, 225–26
Herbeck, Johann Ritter von, 112–13
Herder, Johann Gottfried, 289
Hilmar, Ernst, 1, 59–60n28, 175, 177, 291n5
Hinrichsen, Hans-Joachim, 2, 50
Hook, Julian, 281
Hoorickx, Reinhard Van, 174, 490
Howe, Blake, 421
Hug, Fritz, 115
Humboldt Reform, 440
Hummel, Johann Nepomuk, 437
Hutten, Ulrich von, 480n10
Hüttenbrenner, Anselm, 112, 113
Hüttenbrenner, Josef, 112, 117
Hyer, Bryan, 285
Hyland, Anne, 2

identity
   repetition in 'Der Doppelgänger,' D 957, no. 13, 422–29
   Schubert and self-concept in 'Der Doppelgänger,' D 957, no. 13, 429–31
instrumental works
   shift towards, 21
   style of Schubert's late, 61–72
isomorphism, 148

Jacobi, Friedrich Heinrich, 440, n452
Jeitteles, Alois Isidor, 457
Johnson, Graham, 406, 471, 479–80nn5, 6
Jones, Richard, 482n32

Kärntnertortheater, 20–21
Kerman, Joseph, 479,
Kiesewetter, Raphael, 239
Kinderman, William, 81
Klimt, Gustav, 238
Koch, Heinrich Christoph, 130
Kontarsky, Alfons, 120
Kopp, David, 285
Kotzebue, August, 237
Kramer, Lawrence, 388, 390
Kramer, Richard
   on 'Der Doppelgänger,' D 957, no. 13, 402n17, 420, 421, 428, 431–32
   on 'Der Wegweiser,' D 911, no. 20, 209–10, 355, 377
   on Piano Sonata in C major, D 840, 'Reliquie,' 166
Krause, Andreas, 168n4, 177
Kreißle von Hellborn, Heinrich, 112
Kreutzer, Conradin, 493
Krosigk, Ernestine von, 492
Kube, Manfred, 40n27
Kube, Michael, 40n22
Kupelwieser, Leopold, 20–21, 22, 74n30, 118, 125n34
Kurth, Richard, 388, 430

Ländler, 240–41
Lanz, Joseph, 31, 38–39n7
Larkin, Philip, 456, 483n32
last works
   as expressing 'lateness,' 61–62
   of Schubert, 19–26
lateness, 61–62, 419–21

late sacred music, contextual processes in, 295–96, 327–28
Deutsche Messe, D 872, 297–303
Hymnus an den heiligen Geist, D 948, 303–9
Mass in E♭ major, D 950, 309–18
Tantum ergo, D 962, 318–24
late style, 220, 419–21
late works. *See also* late sacred music, contextual processes in
of Beethoven and Schubert, 17–19, 23–25, 409–10
compositional strategies in Schubert's, 29–30
counterpoint in Schubert's, 30–33
and last works, 19–25
Lubin on Schubert's, 416n43
motivation behind Schubert's, 239–40
motivic and sub-motivic connections in, 33–36
sonority in Schubert's, 36–38
stylistic traits of Schubert's, 25–26, 61–72
tonal structure in Schubert's, 103
Leitner, Karl Gottfried von, 264, 412
Lewin, David, 285
Lied, versus *Gesang*, 276
Liszt, Franz, 23, 111
Litschauer, Walburga, 175
Loi d'Allarde (1791), 439
Luib, Ferdinand, 103
Lubin, Steven, 416n43
Lux, Joseph August, 115, 117
lyricism, in sonata form, 90
lyric poetry, 158–59, 160, 166, 167

Macdonald, Hugh, 424
Mahler, Gustav, 29, 72n6, 432, 436n45
Mak, Su Yin, 171n36
Malin, Yonatan, 391, 392

Mandyczewski, Eusebius, 488–89, 490–91
Mann, Alfred, 73n8
Mann, Thomas, 24, 57
Märchen genre, 334–35
Marischka, Ernst, 118
Marston, Nicholas, 175
Martin, Christine, 493
Marx, A. B., 285
Mayrhofer, Johann, 415n27, 456, 458–64, 472, 478, 480n10
McClary, Susan, 79, 105n16
McKay, Elizabeth Norman, 75n35, 147, 167, 167n4, 170n22
Mendelssohn, Felix, 437
Mendelssohn Hensel, Fanny, 63
Messing, Scott, 1
Metternich, Prince Klemmens von, 237
Meyer, Leonard, 254
moments of crisis, in Symphony No. 7 in B minor, D 759 (*Unfinished*), 137–40
Moore, Gerald, 488
Mozart, Wolfgang Amadeus
Piano Sonata in A minor, K 310/300d, 58n12
Müller, Wilhelm, 356–59
Musäus, Johann Karl August
Melechsala, 333–40
musical causality, 207–8
cadential formula in Piano Sonata in A major, D 959, 208–14
post-cadential space in Piano Sonata in A major, D 959, 214–18
Muxfeldt, Kristina, 418

narcissism, 383–84
Narcissus, 383
narrative
in Piano Sonata in C major, 'Reliquie,' D 840, 158–63
of poetic genres, 148

narrative programme
 primary, 127–28
 secondary, 128
nature, as vehicle for poetic
 expressivity, 356–58
Neapolitan key, 166, 214, 217
neighbour-note motive, 64, 65, 94–95
neo-Riemannian theory, 253, 264, 275,
 280, 281, 283–90, 293–94n22, 26
Neue Schubert-Ausgabe, 2, 490–93
 Kritischer Bericht, 492
Neumann, Johann Philipp, 297, 299,
 302*ex.*, 329–30n11
Newbould, Brian, 163, 174, 330n17, 331n22
Nohl, Ludwig, 409
Notley, Margaret, 240, 420, n434
novella, characteristics of, 335, 338

opera, generic characteristics of, 335
Ottenwalt, Anton, 405, 429

Perraudin, Michael, 384
plagal harmony, in Symphony
 No. 7 in B minor, D 759
 (*Unfinished*), 140–42
Platen, August von, 418
Plato, 445, n454
Porter, Ernest G., 293n22
Prawer, S. S., 385
Preyer, Gottfried von, 31
Pritchard, T.C.L., 174
Probst, Heinrich Albert, 63, 201, 405,
 408, 415n24

Rank, Otto, 383
Ratner, Leonard, 128
recapitulations, in Piano Sonata
 in C major, 'Reliquie,'
 D 840, 163–64, 166–67,
 169n18, 171n30
Reddy, William M., 338

Reed, John, 174, 404, 405–6, 409,
 410, 479n5
Reichardt, Johann Friedrich, 289–90
Rellstab songs, 405, 406, 410
Rembrandt, Harmenszoon van
 Rijn, 273
repetition
 in 'Der Doppelgänger,'
 D 957, no. 13, 422–29
 at octave's displacement, in final
 sonata trilogy, 181
 in Piano Sonata in B♭ Major,
 D 960, 193–200
 in String Quartet in D minor,
 D 810, 94
Ricoeur, Paul, 148
Riemann, Hugo, 2, 283–84
Riezler, Walter, 18
Rings, Steven, 285
Rorty, Richard, 450
Rosen, Charles, 4, 49–50, 53, 58n17,
 107n35, 171n32, 254, 368, 376
Rossini, Gioachino
 Guillaume Tell, 347
Rousseau, Jean-Jacques, 464
 Émile, ou de l'éducation, 439

Salieri, Antonio, 30, 329n7
Salzer, Felix, 79, 90, 94, 107n32
Sams, Eric, 489–90
Samuel, Harold, 485
Samuels, Robert, 402n17
Santi, Raffaelo, 17
Schachter, Carl, 402n11
Schenker, Heinrich, 145n22, 258, 282
Schering, Arnold, 115
Schiller, Friedrich, 42, 65
Schindler, Anton, 409
Schlechta, Franz von, 492
Schlegel, August Wilhelm, 368,
 378, 447

Index

Schlegel, Friedrich, 368
Schmidl, Anton 304,
Schober, Franz von, 177
Schoenberg, Arnold, 77, 285
Scholes, Percy, 486
Schorske, Carl, 238
Schott, B., 408, 415n24
Schubert, Ferdinand, 404
Schubert, Franz
   'An den Mond,' D 296, 493–94
   'Der Atlas,' D 957, no. 8, 51*ex.*, 52–53, 385, 386–88, 391–92, 397–401
   'Auf dem Wasser zu singen,' D 774, 67
   'Auf der Donau,' D 553, 289
   'Auflösung,' D 807, 484n49
   competing portrayals of, 238
   compositional methods of, 173–76
   counterpoint in late compositions, 30–33, 39n7, 62
   dances for piano, 240–41, 429–31
   'Der Winterabend,' D 938
      axial lyrical space in, 264–72
      axial progression in, 254–55, 264–72
   Deutsche Messe, D 872, 329–30n11
      'Das Gebet des Herrn,' 299–303
      'Schlussgesang,' 297–99
   developmental processes, 77–78
   'Der Doppelgänger,' D 957, no. 13, 383, 384–86, 388–97, 404, 418–33
   dichotomy of joy and sorrow in, 238–39
   Die Zauberharfe D 644, 36, 163, n171
   'Einsamkeit,' D 620
      and Beethoven's *An die ferne Geliebte*, 457–58, 473–77
      composition of, 467–73
      observations on Mayrhofer's 'Einsamkeit,' 458–64
      publication of, 456–57, 477–78
      summary of tonal plan, 469*t*
   'Erlkönig,' 43, 490–91
   Fantasy for Violin and Piano in C Major, D 934, 19–20
   Fantasy in F Minor for Piano Duet, D 940, 61, 66, 68*ex.*, 69–72
   Fierrabras, D 796, 21, 22
   final months of, 296
   final sonata trilogy. *See also* Piano Sonata in A major, D 959; Piano Sonata in B♭ Major, D 960; Piano Sonata in C minor, D 958
      compositional genesis of, 52–56, 176–77
      continuity drafts, 178–90, 203
      publication of, 202
      and Schubert's compositional methods, 173–76
      and Schubert's 'new style,' 47–48
      as self-contained cycle, 200–202
   'Das Fischermädchen,' D 957, no. 10, 52–53
   four-hand piano music, 63, 240
   friends of, 203n2
   'Der Goldschmiedgesell,' D 560, 484n47
   Der Graf von Gleichen, D 918, 333–34
      design of Act II, 341–43, 353nn22, 23
      emotional responses of characters in, 339
      flower symbolism in, 337–38
      musical tension and resolution among characters in, 343–45

Schubert, Franz (*Cont.*)
   public and private spheres in consideration of genre, 348–50
   quintet as symbol of multivalent love, 345–48
   Grand Duo, D 812, 63, n169, n294
   'Gretchen am Spinnrade,' D 118, 43
   'Hagars Klage,' D 5, 488
   handling of Classical style, 78, 79, 105n16, 142
   heavenly length, 2, 5, 23, 27n20, 61, 67–68
   'Der Hirt auf dem Felsen,' D 965, 20
   'Hoffnung,' D 296, 493–94
   Hymnus an den heiligen Geist, D 948, 303–9, 330n13
   'Ihr Bild,' D 957, no. 9, 80–84, 105n19
   illness of, 238
   'Im Freien,' D 880
      analytical and critical neglect of, 253
      asymmetrical axial progressions in, 254–55
      axial lyrical space in, 255–64
      axial progression in, 254–55, 256–58
   importance of, for present condition of musical scholarship, 2
   Impromptu in A♭, D 899, No. 4, 67
   Impromptu in G♭ Major, D 899, Op. 90, No. 3, 84–89, 295–96
   large-scale works of, 239–40
   Lazarus D 689, n12, 29, n292,
   Mass in E♭ major, D 950, 309–10
      Agnus Dei, 313–18, 331nn22, 24
      performance of, 330n16
      Sanctus, 310–13, 314*ex*.
   Mass in F major, D 105, 329n7
   'Mein Traum,' 43
   melancholy, 237–48, 371
   Miriams Siegesgesang D 942, 30,
   Moments musicaux in A♭, D 780, 67, 295, 420–21
   'Der Musensohn,' D 764, Op. 92 No. 1, 447–51. *See also* Goethe, Johann Wolfgang von
   'Mut,' D 911/ 22, from *Winterreise*, 67
   neglect of music of, 41
   Offertorium: Intende voci, D 963, 324–27
   Piano Sonata in A major, D 959, 183*ex*. *See also* final sonata trilogy
      Andantino movement, 243
      and Beethoven's Sonata Op. 31 No. 2, 218–19
      coda of the coda in, 207, 213, 215, 217, 219–20
      continuity drafts of, 178–81
      expression of melancholy in, 245–48
      and musical causality, 207–8
      Rondo finale of, 250n23
      and Schubert's 'new style,' 53–55
      tempi of select recordings, 244*t*
   Piano Sonata in A minor, D 845, 176
   Piano Sonata in B♭ Major, D 960, 54*ex*., 185*ex*, 186*ex*, 187–88*ex*, 189*ex*. *See also* final sonata trilogy
      comparison of continuity draft and final versions, 190–95
      conspicuous six-phrase chords in closing movement, 225–26, 234–35
      contextual processes in, 295–96
      Edward T. Cone's reading of, 420–21

Index

expositional repeats in, 195–200
first movement, 66, 184
first-time bars and expositional repeat, 195–200
and Schubert's 'new style,' 55–56
tempo, 244–45
tragedy in the midst of celebration in, 243
Piano Sonata in C major, 'Reliquie,' D 840, 147–49
correlation with 'Great' Symphony, 152–58, 167n3, 169n18
5– 6 shift in, 166
narrative and temporality, 158–63
precedents, 149–52
rotation, 158–63, 166
scholarship and reception, 164–67
significance of recapitulation in tonal schemes of first movement and Minuet, 163–64
Piano Sonata in C minor, D 958, 49–52, 53, 59n18, 178, 179*ex*, 182*ex*, 183*ex*, 184*ex*, 186*ex*, 187*ex*. See also final sonata trilogy
Piano Sonata in D major, D 850, 176
Piano Sonata in E♭ major, D 568, 176
Piano Sonata in G major, D 894, Op. 78, 36, 40n27, 64, 176, 243, 408
Piano Trio in B♭ major, D 898, Op. posth. 99, 67, 424, 425*ex*.
Piano Trio in E♭ major, D 929, 240, 241*ex*.
Piano Trio in E♭ major, D 929, Op. 100, 29, 30–38, 63, 67, 68–69, 295
Quartettsatz in C minor, D 703, 44–46, 62, 64, 66, 127, 142
Quintet in A major, D 667, Op. 114,'Trout, ' 253–54
reception of works of, 56–57
relationship with Goethe, 437–38
religious convictions of, 331n28
revision of work, 173–76, 178–90
scholarship on, 1–3
Die schöne Müllerin, D 795, Op. 25, 56–57, 407
'Schöne Welt, wo bist du?' ('Die Götter Griechenlands,' D 677), 65, 67
'Schwanengesang,' D 957. See also 'Der Doppelgänger,' D 957, no.13
classification of, 405
composition of, 278–83
'Liebesbotschaft,' D 957, no. 1, 427
neo-Riemannian interpretation of, 283–90
'Die Taubenpost,' D 965A, 404–13
text of, 275–78, 291–92n11
Sechzehn Ländler und zwei Ecossaisen, D 734, 241, 242*ex*.
'Sei mir gegrüßt,' D 741, 20
'Selig Welt,' D 743, 275–76, 288–89
sexual orientation of, 249n4
Sonata for Piano Four Hands in C major, D 812,'Grand Duo, ' 169n17
and Stadtkonvikt choir, 329n7
Stabat Mater D383, 30,
String Quartet in C major, D 46, 169n17

Schubert, Franz (*Cont.*)
   String Quartet in A minor, D 804, 65, 67, 295
   String Quartet no.14 in D minor, D 810, *Death and the Maiden*, 22, 62, 91–96, 241, 329n10
   String Quartet no. 15 in G major, D 887, 67
   String Quintet in C major, D 956, 47–48, 49*ex*., 62, 74n23, 96–103, 130, 295, 433
   Symphony No. 4 in C minor, D 417, 146n28
   Symphony No. 7 in B minor, D 759 (*Unfinished*), 45–46
      as 'death fragment,' 120–21
      genesis and first performance of, 111–12
      moments of crisis, 137–40
      narrative dislocations in, 127
      narrative trajectory, 127–32
      plagal harmony, 140–42
      programme note of premiere, 114*fig.*
      rediscovery of, 112–15
      relation to Beethoven, 116–20
      relation to Schubert's biography, 115–16
      revisions to, 174
      Scherzo, 145n18
      scholarship on, 174
   Symphony no. 8 in C major, D 944, *Great*, 47, 21–23, 152–58, 167n3, 169n18, 174
   Symphony in D major, D 936A, 25–26
   Tantum ergo, D 962, 318–24
   'Trost,' D 523, 254
   Twelve Deutsche for Piano, D 790, 241, 242*ex*., 245, 246*ex*.
   'Wanderer' Fantasy, D 760, 61, 66, 75n35, 143
   Wanderlieder, 438–40
   'Der Winterabend,' D 938, 253, 254–55, 264–72
   Winterreise, D 911
      'Auf dem Fluße,' D 911, no. 7, 356, 358
      'Der greise Kopf,' D 911, no. 14, 217, 358
      'Der Leiermann,' D 911, no. 24, 355, 359
      'Der Lindenbaum,' D 911, no. 5, 356, 358, 365–66*ex*.
      'Der stürmische Morgen,' D 911, no. 18, 358
      'Der Wegweiser,' D 911, no. 20, 355–68
      'Die Krähe,' D 911, no. 15, 358
      'Die Nebensonnen,' D 911, no. 23, 359
      'Die Post,' D 911, no. 13, 358
      'Die Wetterfahne,' D 911, no. 2, 393*ex*.
      'Gute Nacht,' D 911, no. 1, 363*ex*.
      'Im Dorfe,' D 911, no. 14, 358
      'Irrlicht,' D 911, no. 9, 356, 358
      'Letzte Hoffnung,' D 911, no. 16, 358, 359
      'Mut,' D 911, no. 22, 67, 359
      'Rast,' D 911, no. 10, 367*ex*.
      as Romantic fragment, 368–70, 376
      'Rückblick,' D 911, no. 8, 359, 364*ex*.
      structure of, 407
      'Täuschung,' D 911, no. 19, 358
      tonal design of, 371–77
      tragic aspects of wanderer motive in, 46–47
      wanderer's destiny in, 377–78
Schubertiades, 238
Schumann, Robert, 23, 26, 67, 176, 202
Schuppanzigh, Ignaz, 22
Schütz, Heinrich, 62

Schwarz, David, 390
Schwind, Moritz von, 125n31, 238, 334, 350n4
Sechter, Simon, 26, 39n7, 73n8, 328, 331–32n29
Seidel, Johann Gabriel, 255
self-critique, 419–20
Senn, Johann Chrysostomus, 238, 275–77, 290, 291–92nn5, 11, 418
sensuous
   as constructive force in Schubert's late works, 77–78
   definition, 104n8
   in Impromptu in G♭ Major, D 800, No. 3, Op. 90, 84–89
   and projection of 'Ihr Bild''s cycle of loss, 80–84
   and projection of tonal structure in Schubert's late music, 103
   in reception history of Schubert's music, 79–80
   in Schubert's sonata forms, 90–91
   in String Quartet in D minor, D 810, *Death and the Maiden*, 91–96
   in String Quintet in C major, D 956, 96–103
Serkin, Rudolf, 244
Siboni, Josef, 33
silent bars, addition of, in final sonata trilogy, 185
Sly, Gordon, 155
Smallman, Basil, 67–68
'social' music, 237–48
solitude, problem of, 464–67
sonata form(s)
   Adorno on Schubert's handling of, 23–24
   criticism of Schubert's approach to, 79, 94
   in Fantasy for Violin and Piano in C Major, D 934, 20
   Hepokoski and Darcy's conception of, 225–26
   Schubert's constructive and innovative handling of, 23
   Schubert's innovations in, 49–50
   in Schubert's late compositions, 65
   String Quartet in G major, D 887, Op. posth. 161, 65
sonata-rondo, 225–26
song
   informing Schubert's late instrumental writing, 67
   Schubert as composer of, 431–33
songfulness, in Schubert's late instrumental music, 218, 220
Sonnleithner, Leopold von, 33, 203n2, 240, 250n11
sonority, in Schubert's late compositions, 36–38
Sontag, Susan, 409
Spaun, Joseph von, 103, 173, 405, 429
Staiger, Emil, 148, 158, 159, 166, 167
Stefan, Paul, 115, 410
Steigerung, 255, 258–59, 260, 263, 273n10, 445, 447
Stifter, Adalbert, 24
Straus, Joseph N., 420–21
study of counterpoint, 73n8
Sturm und Drang, 149, 338
style
   of Beethoven and Schubert, 3, 77–78
   last works and suspicion of late style, 19
   Schubert's instrumental, 61–72
   seeds of late style in early works, 62
sub-motivic connections, in Schubert's late compositions, 33–36
Suurpää, Lauri, 371
symbolism, in Beethoven versus Schubert, 42–43

temporality, in Piano Sonata in C
　　major, 'Reliquie,' D 840, 158–63
thematic progression, in *Offertorium:*
　　Intende voci, D 963, 326–27
thematic relations, in String Quartet
　　in D minor, D 810, 91–96
theory of poetics, 148
third relations, 6, 78, 79, 90, 230
thirds, circle of, in 'Great' Symphony
　　versus 'Reliquie,' 155–56,
　　170nn22-24
Thomas, Werner, 48
three-key exposition, 90–91
Tiedge, Christoph August, 481–82n24
tonal relationships
　　in *Hymnus an den heiligen*
　　　Geist, 303–5
　　in Impromptu in G♭ Major, D 800,
　　　Op. 90, No. 3, 84–89
　　in Piano Sonata in C major,
　　　'Reliquie,' D 840, 165
　　in String Quartet in D minor,
　　　D 810, 91–96
　　in *Winterreise*, D 911, 371–77
Tovey, Donald Francis, 2, 55, 79, 190,
　　285, 485, 486
tragedy
　　in Beethoven works, 42
　　in Schubert works, 42–43, 46–47
Trunz, Erich, 445
Tyson, Alan, 61

Uncanny, the, 383–84
Unterhaltungsmusik, 249n5

variation, developing variation in
　　Schubert's late compositions,
　　5, 65, 77–78
Vetter, Walther, 29
violent outbursts, in Schubert's late
　　compositions, 66–67
Vogl, Johann Michael, 173, 431

Vogler, Abbé, 285
Volkert, Franz, 334

Wackenroder, Wilhelm
　　Heinrich, 440
Wagner, Richard
　　Lohengrin, 348–50
Waidelich, Till Gerrit, 1, 57n5
wanderer figure, Goethe's
　　identification with, 440–41
wanderer motif in Schubert's music,
　　46–47, 438
wandering, cultural and social
　　contexts, 439–40
Weber, Carl Maria von
　　Der Freischütz, 211–12
Weber, Gottfried, 285
Webster, James, 79, 90, 198
Weigel, Hans, 116
Werlé, Heinrich, 115
Wheeldon, Marianne
Whittall, Arnold, 41, 50,
　　59nn18, 22
Wilford, Manfred, 33–34
Winter, Robert, 72n6, 177
Wittgenstein, Ludwig, 450
Wolf, Hugo, 116
Woolf, Virginia 491
Wollenberg, Susan, 3, 129, 132,
　　144n9, 468

Youens, Susan
　　on 'Der Doppelgänger,' D 957,
　　　no. 13, 426, 430, 432
　　on *Die Heimkehr* No. 20, 385
　　on 'Einsamkeit,' D 620, 10
　　on *Winterreise*, 355, 377

Zelter, Carl Friedrich, 437
Zimmerman, Johann Georg,
　　482nn27, 29
　　Ueber die Einsamkeit, 465–67